INSTRUCTOR'S EDITION

INTERACTING
WITH ESSAYS

CHARLES E. MAY
California State University–Long Beach

D. C. Heath and Company
Lexington, Massachusetts   Toronto

Address editorial correspondence to:
D. C. Heath and Company
125 Spring Street
Lexington, MA 02173

Acquisitions Editor: Paul A. Smith
Development Editor: Linda M. Bieze
Production Editor: Carolyn Ingalls
Designer: Judith Miller
Production Coordinator: Charles Dutton
Permissions Editor: Margaret Roll

International Standard Book Number: 0-669-35524-0 (Student Edition)
                                                 0-669-35525-9 (Instructor's Edition)

Library of Congress Catalog Number: 95-68935

10 9 8 7 6 5 4 3 2 1

PREFACE

The reasons that students who read a great deal write better than those who do not are obvious: Those who read encounter a wide range of ideas, pick up a great deal of specific knowledge, and unconsciously internalize a variety of strategies and tactics specific to the writing process. Sometimes I would like to tell students to delay taking my composition class and to spend the next several years reading anything and everything they can get their hands on. Then they can come back to learn about writing in my class. However, since I cannot demand that students compensate quantitatively for lost reading time, the only choice left is to help them make up for it qualitatively. The structure of *Interacting with Essays* and the selections and apparatus that comprise it are designed to do just that: to provide students with a number of opportunities for careful, self-conscious, analytical interactions with good writing.

About the Book

After reading hundreds of essays, I have chosen the sixty in this book because they focus on subjects with which most students should be able to interact without special knowledge: growing up, understanding the natural world, living in a multicultural society, getting along with friends, understanding gender, dealing with media, coping with family, and living in the world of work—to name a few. I have chosen essays by such well-known and respected contemporary writers as Edward Hoagland, Eudora Welty, Maxine Hong Kingston, Tobias Wolff, Raymond Carver, John Updike, Annie Dillard, Leslie Marmon Silko, Alice Walker, Ishmael Reed, and Gloria Steinem because I think students should be aware of the contributions these writers have made to modern thought and letters and because their writing models what good writing can be and do. I have chosen essays primarily written within the last two decades because they seem the most likely to engage the interests of students today and are thus the most likely to stimulate active interaction rather than passive skimming. Although some of the selections are excerpts from longer works, all of them stand alone as essays; that is, they have a point of view, a purpose, and a unified structure. Most of the essays are relatively short and therefore not only serve as models for student essays but also sustain close analysis of ideas and techniques without being overwhelming.

The structure of the book follows a natural progression from essays dealing with the personal past, to essays focusing on everyday experiences in the physical world, to essays centering on living in an increasingly non-sexist and multicultural society, to essays that reflect analysis and argument, and finally to essays that compel the use of multiple perspectives and sources. Parts One, Two, and Three present essays in pairs that invite comparison and contrast. For example, in "Exploring the Personal Past," John Tarkov and Gay Talese relate, in quite different ways, the experience of being U.S.-born sons of European immigrants, while Raymond Carver, a white male, and Le Ly Hayslip, a Vietnamese female, explore their relationships to their fathers.

Part Four, "Analyzing and Arguing a Case," offers sets of three essays on similar subjects to provide more depth and to permit comparison of different perspectives. Part Five, "Using Sources," presents five essays each on two familiar subjects—families and work—to provide even more depth of information and analysis and to encourage further research. These essays can serve as the stimulus for a research paper, if your course calls for one, or as the basis for an exploration of how to synthesize information and write critically about a variety of perspectives. At the end of "Using Sources" I have included a large number of possible topics derived from the essays that will lead students to further research, reading, analysis, and synthesis.

The "Exploring Ideas" and "Exploring Rhetoric" sections at the end of each essay in Parts One through Four are designed to help students get in the habit of interacting with the ideas developed in the essays, as well as with the writing techniques and strategies on which those ideas depend. The prompts—which include reading questions, analysis questions, brainstorming suggestions, and essay topics—are not simple content questions for which there are routine answers but rather are provocative suggestions meant to involve the students in the complexity of the issues and the subtleties of the rhetorical technique embodied in the essays. The table of contents features a key quotation from each essay to suggest its central purpose or style, and each essay is preceded by a biographical headnote about the writer, as well as a brief introductory statement about the essay to provide an opening perspective. I have purposely kept the general introduction and the part introductions to short and simple descriptions of the rationale of the book and its sections; the introductions are meant to be orientations to the essays, rather than my own pedagogical substitutions for them. In the Instructor's Manual I include some suggestions about how I have used the essays.

About the Software

A software package of my own design, called **Interactive Essay**, is available with this book. I developed this program because a program I created a few years ago, called *HyperStory*, has been successful in my own classroom in helping students learn to read short stories in self-paced, reader-centered ways. Preliminary versions of **Interactive Essay** that I have used have also been successful in helping students develop skill in reading and responding to nonfiction essays.

Interactive Essay is not intended to take the place of classroom instruction. I created it as a supplement to the book *Interacting with Essays*, to be used in group sessions in computer writing labs or by students working alone with a computer. A simple point-and-click application, it does not assume that students have any prior computer knowledge, and it can be used alone or with any word processing program. Available for both Macintosh machines and IBM compatibles running Windows, the program provides twenty essays from *Interacting with Essays* in a hypertext format that allows students to interact with the essays in a more direct way than they can with the printed versions. In the book's table of contents, each of the twenty essays included in the **Interactive Essay** software is identified by ⊟.

Although some may think that there is something cold and mechanical about reading essays on a computer screen, my own experience and research with hundreds of students using hypertext reading applications indicates that students do not share that feeling. There is nothing intrinsically interactive about the page of a book, nor is there anything sacrosanct about book technology as the only way that the language of texts can be communicated. In fact, if the purpose of teaching reading is to get students in the habit of reading interactively rather than passively, then hypertext versions of texts may be more effective than book pages. When students use a mouse to click an icon on the computer screen and "make things happen" to which they can immediately respond—such as a suggestion, a query, a cross reference, or a relevant task—they experience a powerful sense of interaction. I describe **Interactive Essay**'s features and discuss some of the ways it may be used in the User's Guide that accompanies the software.

Acknowledgments

I owe a debt of thanks to the many students who have used my computer applications for reading short stories and essays over the past few years. They have continually kept me on my technological toes, suggesting features to make the applications as useful and friendly as possible. I also thank the members of the W.R.I.T.E. project (Writing, Research, and Instruction Team Effort) at California State University–Long Beach, who, during the

1994–1995 academic year, were willing to try out rough draft versions of *Interacting with Essays* and **Interactive Essay** in their classes: Mark Wiley, Eileen Klink, Steve Whilhite, Dean Franco, Donna Stewart, Kevin Kolkmeyer, Justin Hill, and Sean Donnell. I send a special note of appreciation to my colleague and friend, Cynthia Hallett, who offered gracious encouragement and intelligent advice on the book via e-mail across the Internet from Nova Scotia. I also thank all those who read the manuscript at various stages in its development and offered valuable advice: Sarah L. Bane, Murray State University; John Boe, University of California, Davis; Daun Daemon, North Carolina State University; Dorothy M. Guinn, Florida Atlantic University; Michelle LeBeau, University of New Mexico–Valencia Campus; James C. McDonald, University of Southwestern Louisiana; James Strickland, Slippery Rock University; Paul Taylor, Texas A & M University; Gretchen Van Galder-Janis, Johnson County Community College; and Linda Woodson, University of Texas, San Antonio. Thanks also to the wonderful professionals—Paul Smith, Linda Bieze, Carolyn Ingalls, Margaret Roll, Ronna Weaver, and Terry McCollum—at D. C. Heath who have seen this book through the publishing process.

I dedicate this book to Dad, Jimmy, Uncle Jim, and Charlie—men who have meant much to me.

Charles E. May

CONTENTS

INTRODUCTION: Reading and Writing Essays   1

PROLOGUE ❧ Writing   5

EDWARD HOAGLAND, *What I Think, What I Am*   6   •

"An essayist soon discovers that he doesn't have to tell the whole truth and nothing but the truth; he can shape or shave his memories, as long as the purpose is served of elucidating a truthful point."

GILBERT HIGHET, *How to Write an Essay*   9

"It is not hard to write an essay, if you can write decently and think a little."

PART ONE ❧ Exploring the Personal Past   17

EUDORA WELTY, *Learning to Listen*   19

"Long before I wrote stories, I listened for stories. Listening children know stories are *there*. When their elders sit and begin, children are just waiting and hoping for one to come out, like a mouse from its hole."

MAXINE HONG KINGSTON, *Finding a Voice*   25

"It was when I found out that I had to talk that school became a misery, that the silence became a misery. I did not speak and felt bad each time that I did not speak."

JOHN TARKOV, *Fitting In* 🖫   30

"This Melting Pot of ours absorbs the second generation over a flame so high that the first is left encrusted on the rim."

🖫 Essays followed by this disk icon are available in hypertext **Interactive Essay** format.

GAY TALESE, *Playing Catch* 🖫 34

"He seemed to be very embarrassed. He who cared so much about appearances had tried his best, and yet the results were pitiful. It was a sorrowful moment for both of us."

TOBIAS WOLFF, *Going West*   40

"It was 1955 and we were driving from Florida to Utah, to get away from a man my mother was afraid of and to get rich on uranium. We were going to change our luck."

JEANNE WAKATSUKI HOUSTON AND JAMES D. HOUSTON, *Manzanar*   44

"As the months at Manzanar turned to years, it became a world unto itself, with its own logic and familiar ways."

RICHARD RODRIGUEZ, *Complexion*   50

"Throughout adolescence, I felt myself mysteriously marked. Nothing else about my appearance would concern me so much as the fact that my complexion was dark."

JOHN UPDIKE, *At War with My Skin*   53

"Psoriasis keeps you thinking. Strategies of concealment ramify, and self-examination is endless. You are forced to the mirror, again and again; psoriasis compels narcissism, if you can suppose a Narcissus who did not like what he saw."

MAYA ANGELOU, *Getting a Job* 🖫 60

"To be left alone on the tightrope of youthful unknowing is to experience the excruciating beauty of full freedom and the threat of eternal indecision."

AUDRE LORDE, *The Fourth of July* 🖫 67

"The . . . white heat and the white pavement and the white stone monuments of my first Washington summer made me sick to my stomach for the whole rest of that trip and it wasn't much of a graduation present after all."

RAYMOND CARVER, *My Father's Life*   71

"I put it up on my wall, and each time we moved, I took the picture along and put it up on another wall. I looked at it carefully from time to time, trying to figure out some things about my dad, and maybe about myself in the process."

LE LY HAYSLIP, *My Father's Death*   80

"Once my father was properly buried and his soul dwelled comfortably in our spirit house, I discovered that a good many things had been buried with him."

PART TWO ❧ Exploring the Everyday World 89

ANNIE DILLARD, *Untying the Knot* 🖫 91

"Time is the continuous loop, the snakeskin with scales endlessly overlapping without beginning or end, or time is an ascending spiral if you will, like a child's toy Slinky."

LEWIS THOMAS, *The Tucson Zoo* 🖫 95

"Maybe altruism is our most primitive attribute, out of reach, beyond our control. Or perhaps it is immediately at hand, waiting to be released, disguised now, in our kind of civilization, as affection or friendship or attachment."

EDWARD ABBEY, *Come On In* 99

"The Colorado Plateau can best be understood and given human significance by poets who have their feet planted in concrete—concrete data—and by scientists whose heads and hearts have not lost the capacity for wonder."

BILL MCKIBBEN, *The End of Nature* 103

"An idea, a relationship, can go extinct, just like an animal or a plant. The idea in this case is 'nature,' the separate and wild province, the world apart from man to which he adapted, under whose rules he was born and died."

LARRY WOIWODE, *Wanting an Orange* 106

"Each orange, stripped of its protective wrapping, as vivid in your vision as a pebbled sun, encouraged you to picture a whole pyramid like this in a bowl on our dining room table."

PETER SCHJELDAHL, *Cyclone!* 110

"The coaster is actually an ornate means of falling and a poem about physics in parts or stanzas, with jokes."

PHYLLIS ROSE, *Of Shopping* 🖫 115

"It is a misunderstanding of the American retail store to think we go there necessarily to buy. Some of us shop. There's a difference. Shopping has many purposes, the least interesting of which is to acquire new articles."

WILLIAM SEVERINI KOWINSKI, *Mallaise: How to Know If You Have It* 🖫 119

"Malls . . . do things to people that people are unaware of or don't understand, but if they knew or understood, they probably wouldn't like it."

KENNETH GOINGS, *Memorabilia That Have Perpetuated Stereotypes About African Americans* 124

"These items of material culture gave a physical reality to ideas of racial inferiority. They were the props that helped reinforce the racist ideology that emerged after Reconstruction."

NANCY MASTERSON SAKAMOTO, *Conversational Ballgames* 128

"But if you have been trained all your life to play one game, it is no simple matter to switch to another, even if you know the rules. Knowing the rules is not at all the same thing as playing the game."

JUDITH VIORST, *Friends, Good Friends—and Such Good Friends* 132

"The friendships I have and the friendships I see are conducted at many levels of intensity, serve many different functions, meet different needs."

MARGARET MEAD AND RHODA METRAUX, *On Friendship* 137

"A friend is someone who chooses and is chosen. Related to this is the sense each friend gives the other of being a special individual, on whatever grounds this recognition is based."

PART THREE ✳ Dealing with Differences 143

ROBERT L. HEILBRONER, *Don't Let Stereotypes Warp Your Judgments* 145

"Stereotypes are a kind of gossip about the world, a gossip that makes us prejudge people before we ever lay eyes on them. Hence it is not surprising that stereotypes have something to do with the dark world of prejudice."

GLORIA YAMATO, *Something About the Subject Makes It Hard to Name* 150

"Like a virus, it's hard to beat racism, because by the time you come up with a cure, it's mutated to a 'new cure-resistant' form. One shot just won't get it."

NOEL PERRIN, *The Androgynous Man* 🖻 155

"What it does mean to be spiritually androgynous is a kind of freedom. . . . The sad part is that many of us never discover that."

AMY GROSS, *The Appeal of the Androgynous Man* 🖻 159

"Male chauvinism is an irritation, but the real problem I have with the all-man man is that it's hard for me to talk to him. He's alien to me, and for this I'm at least half to blame."

Susan Brownmiller, *Femininity* 🖫 164

"It does not require a great leap of imagination for a woman to understand the feminine principle as a grand collection of compromises, large and small, that she simply must make in order to render herself a successful woman."

Paul Theroux, *Being a Man* 🖫 169

"I have always disliked being a man. The whole idea of manhood in America is pitiful, in my opinion. This version of masculinity is a little like having to wear an ill-fitting coat for one's entire life."

Brent Staples, *Just Walk On By* 🖫 174

"It was in the echo of that terrified woman's footfalls that I first began to know the unwieldy inheritance I'd come into—the ability to alter public space in ugly ways."

Judith Ortiz Cofer, *The Myth of the Latin Woman: I Just Met a Girl Named María* 🖫 179

"Mixed cultural signals have perpetuated certain stereotypes—for example, that of the Hispanic woman as the 'Hot Tamale' or sexual firebrand. It is a one-dimensional view that the media have found easy to promote."

Leslie Marmon Silko, *Yellow Woman and a Beauty of the Spirit* 186

"In the old time Pueblo world, beauty was manifested in behavior and in one's relationship with other living beings. Beauty was as much a feeling of harmony as it was a visual, aural or sensual effect."

Alice Walker, *The Black Writer and the Southern Experience* 195

"What the black Southern writer inherits as a natural right is a sense of *community*. Something simple but surprisingly hard, especially these days, to come by."

Arthur L. Campa, *Anglo vs. Chicano: Why?* 202

"A century of association has inevitably acculturated both Hispanos and Anglo-Americans to some extent, but there still persist a number of culture traits that neither group has relinquished altogether."

Ishmael Reed, *America: The Multinational Society* 208

"Such blurring of cultural styles occurs in everyday life in the United States to a greater extent than anyone can imagine and is probably more prevalent than the sensational conflict between people of different backgrounds that is played up and often encouraged by the media."

PART FOUR ❧ Analyzing and Arguing a Case   213

STEPHEN KING, *Why We Crave Horror Movies* 🖫 *215*

"The mythic horror movie, like the sick joke, has a dirty job to do. It deliberately appeals to all that is worse in us."

ROBERT BRUSTEIN, *Reflections on Horror Movies*   *219*

"Aside from modest shock motives, horror films always try to involve us in certain underground assumptions. They have been serving up a mess of cultural pottage whose seasoning gives science (and sometimes all knowledge) a bad taste."

MICHAEL VENTURA, *On Kids and Slasher Movies* 🖫 *229*

"In order to live, in order not to go mad, this boy is acclimating himself to the idea of the killer-maniac, because killer-maniac energy is so present in his world."

ROBERT MACNEIL, *The Trouble with Television* 🖫 *232*

"The trouble with television is that it discourages concentration. . . . It sells us instant gratification. It diverts us only to divert, to make the time pass without pain."

MARIE WINN, *Television Addiction* 🖫 *236*

"The television habit distorts the sense of time. It renders other experiences vague and curiously unreal while taking on a greater reality for itself."

TONY SCHWARTZ, *Communication in the Year 2000*   *241*

"The problem with all of this new technology is not the equipment, which exists and works, but what to do with it now that we have it."

WILLIAM F. BUCKLEY, JR., *Why Don't We Complain?* 🖫 *249*

"I think the observable reluctance of the majority of Americans to assert themselves in minor matters is related to our increased sense of helplessness in an age of technology and centralized political and economic power."

VICTORIA A. SACKETT, *Discriminating Tastes: The Prejudice of Personal Preferences* 🖫 *255*

"The irony is that, as the nation has grown more tolerant and welcoming of all kinds of ethnic and other diversity, individuals succumbing to their petty prejudices now comprise veritable lynch mobs."

JULIANNE MALVEAUX, *Angry*   260

"Anger is a sign of something gone wrong. Every hell-raiser knows that. What alert Black woman in this racist society doesn't have a right to be angry?"

JAMES BALDWIN, *If Black English Isn't a Language, Then Tell Me, What Is?*   266

"A people at the center of the western world, and in the midst of so hostile a population, has not endured and transcended by means of what is patronizingly called a 'dialect.'"

RACHEL L. JONES, *What's Wrong with Black English?*   270

"It hurts me to hear black children use black English, knowing that they will be at yet another disadvantage in an educational system already full of stumbling blocks."

GLORIA NAYLOR, *"Mommy, What Does* Nigger *Mean?" A Question of Language*   274

"The people in my grandmother's living room took a word that whites used to signify worthlessness or degradation and rendered it impotent. . . . They transformed *nigger* to signify the varied and complex human beings they knew themselves to be."

PART FIVE ❧ Using Sources   279

Families

JANE HOWARD, *Families*   282

"As a member in reasonable standing of six or seven tribes in addition to the one I was born to, I have been trying to figure which earmarks are common to both kinds of families."

MICHAEL NOVAK, *The Family Out of Favor*   286

"Choosing to have a family used to be uninteresting. It is, today, an act of intelligence and courage."

JERROLD FOOTLICK, WITH ELIZABETH LEONARD, *What Happened to the Family?*   291

"We enter the 21st century with a heightened sensitivity to family issues. Helping parents and children is a bottom-line concern, no longer a matter of debate."

GEORGE GALLUP, JR., *The Faltering Family*   297

"Most people know instinctively, without having to read a poll or a book, that happiness and satisfaction in life are rooted largely in the quality of our personal relationships."

ARLENE SKOLNICK, *The Paradox of Perfection*   305

"Can the family be at once a cherished 'value' and a troubled institution? I am inclined to think, in fact, that they go hand in hand."

Work

BERTRAND RUSSELL, *Work*   315

"There is certainly much work which is exceedingly irksome, and an excess of work is always very painful. I think, however, that, provided work is not excessive in amount, even the dullest work is to most people less painful than idleness."

ERICH FROMM, *Work in an Alienated Society*   320

"Modern man does not know what to do with himself, how to spend his lifetime meaningfully, and he is driven to work in order to avoid an unbearable boredom."

LANCE MORROW, *What Is the Point of Working?*   325

"Work is still the complicated and crucial core of most lives, the occupation melded inseparably to identity. . . . Work is the most thorough and profound organizing principle in American life."

ROBERT COLES, *On the Meaning of Work*   330

"As never before, our industrial societies are now being forced to look inward, so to speak, to become aware of the implications of our policies, among them those followed by the thousands of businesses that employ millions of workers."

GLORIA STEINEM, *The Importance of Work*   334

"Under attack, we still tend to present ourselves as creatures of economic necessity and familial devotion. 'Womenworkbecausewehaveto' has become the easiest thing to say."

ACKNOWLEDGMENTS   343

INDEX OF AUTHORS AND TITLES   347

READING AND WRITING ESSAYS

T his anthology is named *Interacting with Essays* because it is based on the assumption that to read essays in such a way as to improve your own writing you must do more than just skim over the pages, scoop out the major point, and finish as soon as possible. Instead, you must interact with the essay's ideas and methods of communicating those ideas, using them as springboards for your own ideas and as models of methods that other writers have used successfully. Reading interactively means responding aggressively to ideas: exploring them, posing questions about them, and arguing with them. Reading interactively also means understanding the techniques writers use: considering why they used an anecdote, an example, a comparison, a definition, this word instead of that word, a particular sentence structure instead of one of the many other possibilities.

People who do not have much experience writing are often puzzled at their own inability to write well and think that writing must be a natural gift. However, people who write frequently—for example, politicians, lawyers, authors, and teachers—know that there is no such thing as a natural gift for writing well. Rather, good writing results from wide reading and paying careful attention to the techniques of writing that we call rhetoric—all the methods writers use to communicate, affect, influence, or persuade their readers. The ability to use rhetoric is not something we are born with but rather something we can learn from studying the work of writers who use it effectively. Over the centuries writers have developed a multitude of rhetorical techniques for communicating and persuading. To improve your own writing, you should learn some of these techniques by studying how effective writers use them.

People who write a great deal know that to write well, you must be honest and clear, and you must have a cold-blooded sense of intention. Unless you are writing in a diary or journal, most writing you will do is meant to communicate something to someone else. And the problem with using writing to communicate to someone else is that once you write something, you physically disappear from the scene. You are no longer there to watch people's faces as you talk; you cannot rephrase as you go along, trying different approaches when you see that one is not working; you cannot respond to questions, argue against objections, talk louder, wave your arms, point your finger, wink, or use any of the other devices available to you when dealing with people directly. Consequently, you must form a mental picture of your intended reader and then figure out ways to embed in your writing all those rhetorical devices, word choices, sentence rhythms, and methods of development best suited to communicate your ideas to that person. Only through reading will you discover what these rhetorical techniques are.

The essays in this book are organized in categories that correspond to some of the most common subjects that people write about. In Part One, writers explore personal experiences from their own past and try to discover some meaning in those experiences. In Part Two, writers examine the physical and human world around them and seek to derive some meaning from their observation. Part Three focuses on experiencing the diversity of human society and culture. In Part Four, writers analyze social experiences and create arguments based on their analyses. Finally, because creating arguments often requires finding out what others have said about a subject, Part Five focuses on using sources to discover more about two very common human contexts: families and work.

The essays in this book were chosen because they focus on feelings, perceptions, and ideas with which you, as a student in a college-level writing class, will probably be relatively familiar. Each essay in Parts One through Four is followed by two sets of questions, comments, brainstorming ideas, and writing suggestions. One set, called "Exploring Ideas," is designed to help you interact with the feelings, perceptions, and ideas that the writer is trying to communicate; the other, called "Exploring Rhetoric," is designed to assist you in exploring the rhetorical conventions, devices, and techniques that the writer uses. In the first three parts, the essays are presented in pairs based on their similarity of subject. In Part Four, three essays on the same subject are grouped together to provide a deeper look at the issue. Part Five contains five essays on families and five essays on work (followed by a number of topics for further research) to illustrate the importance of using various sources in formulating ideas.

The two essays that form the Prologue to this book are about writing essays. Edward Hoagland, a well-known essayist, reminds us in "What I Think, What I Am" that although a personal essay is like a human voice, it usually makes a point. In his essay, we can indeed hear his voice as he tries to make his point about the essay's hanging on a line between the two poles of "this is what I think, and this is what I am." Although we can also hear the voice of Gilbert Highet relating personal experiences about his own efforts in trying to learn "How to Write an Essay," he may sound more like a formal academic speaker than the more casual Edward Hoagland does.

Highet emphasizes a number of points about writing successful essays. One of the most important is the writer's own engagement in the subject at hand. The first law of an essayist, says Highet, is "Be interested and you will be interesting." Equally important to the success of an essay, he continues, is its form—the sense of shape that holds it together. The sixty essays in this book are by writers who seem interested in what they are writing about and who have learned to master the techniques of form. If you read the essays interactively, not only will you be interested in what they say, but also you will learn some of the techniques that make them effective. Reading interactively is the way professional writers improve their writing; it is the way you can improve your writing also.

PROLOGUE

WRITING

What I Think, What I Am

EDWARD HOAGLAND

Edward Hoagland was born in 1932 in New York City. He graduated from Harvard University in 1954 and served in the army for two years. He is best known for his essay collections, which include *The Courage of Turtles,* 1970; *Walking the Dead Diamond River,* 1973; *Red Wolves and Black Bears,* 1976; *Seven Rivers West,* 1986; and *Heart's Desire: The Best of Edward Hoagland,* 1988.

In "What I Think, What I Am," Hoagland sets out his personal description of a very personal form of writing—the essay—thus illustrating that which he describes. Essays combine two kinds of expression, Hoagland suggests: what the writer thinks about something and who the writer is as a person in the world. He defines the form by comparing and contrasting it to the nonfiction article and the short story.

1   Our loneliness makes us avoid column readers these days. The personalities in the San Francisco *Chronicle,* Chicago *Daily News,* New York *Post* constitute our neighbors now, some of them local characters but also the opinionated national stars. And movie reviewers thrive on our yearning for somebody emotional who is willing to pay attention to us and return week after week, year after year, through all the to-and-fro of other friends, to flatter us by pouring out his/her heart. They are essayists of a type, as Elizabeth Hardwick is, James Baldwin was.

2   We sometimes hear that essays are an old-fashioned form, that so-and-so is the "last essayist," but the facts of the marketplace argue quite otherwise. Essays of nearly any kind are so much easier than short stories for a writer to sell, so many more see print, it's strange that though two fine anthologies remain that publish the year's best stories, no comparable collection exists for essays. Such changes in the reading public's taste aren't always to the good, needless to say. The art of telling stories predated even cave painting, surely; and if we ever find ourselves living in caves again, it (with painting and drumming) will be the only art left, after movies, novels, photography, essays, biography, and all the rest have gone down the drain—the art to build from.

3   One has the sense with the short story as a form that while everything may have been done, nothing has been overdone; it has a permanence. Essays, if a comparison is to be made, although they go back four hundred years to Montaigne, seem a mercurial, newfangled, sometimes hokey affair that has lent itself to many of the excesses of the age, from spurious autobiography to spurious hallucination, as well as to the

shabby careerism of traditional journalism. It's a greased pig. Essays are associated with the way young writers fashion a name—on plain, crowded newsprint in hybrid vehicles like the *Village Voice, Rolling Stone,* the *New York Review of Books,* instead of the thick paper stock and thin readership of *Partisan Review.*

Essays, however, hang somewhere on a line between two sturdy 4 poles: this is what I think, and this is what I am. Autobiographies which aren't novels are generally extended essays, indeed. A personal essay is like the human voice talking, its order the mind's natural flow, instead of a systematized outline of ideas. Though more wayward or informal than an article or treatise, somewhere it contains a point which is its real center, even if the point couldn't be uttered in fewer words than the essayist has used. Essays don't usually boil down to a summary, as articles do, and the style of the writer has a "nap" to it, a combination of personality and originality and energetic loose ends that stand up like the nap on a piece of wool and can't be brushed flat. Essays belong to the animal kingdom, with a surface that generates sparks, like a coat of fur, compared with the flat, conventional cotton of the magazine article writer, who works in the vegetable kingdom, instead. But essays, on the other hand, may have fewer "levels" than fiction, because we are not supposed to argue much about their meaning. In the old distinction between teaching and storytelling, the essayist, however cleverly he camouflages his intentions, is a bit of a teacher or reformer, and an essay is intended to convey the same point to each of us.

This emphasis upon mind speaking to mind is what makes essays 5 less universal in their appeal than stories. They are addressed to an educated, perhaps a middle-class, reader, with certain presuppositions, a frame of reference, even a commitment to civility that is shared—not the grand and golden empathy inherent in every man or woman that a storyteller has a chance to tap.

Nevertheless, the artful "I" of an essay can be as chameleon as any 6 narrator in fiction; and essays do tell a story quite as often as a short story stakes a claim to a particular viewpoint. Mark Twain's piece called "Corn-pone Opinions," for example, which is about public opinion, begins with a vignette as vivid as any in *Huckleberry Finn.* Twain says that when he was a boy of fifteen, he used to hang out a back window and listen to the sermons preached by a neighbor's slave standing on top of a woodpile: "He imitated the pulpit style of the several clergymen of the village, and did it well and with fine passion and energy. To me he was a wonder. I believed he was the greatest orator in the United States and would some day be heard from. But it did not happen; in the distribution of rewards he was overlooked. . . . He interrupted his preaching now and then to saw a stick of wood, but the sawing was a pretense—he did it with his mouth, exactly imitating the sound the bucksaw makes in shrieking its way through the wood. But it served its purpose, it kept his master from coming out to see how the work was getting along."

7   A novel would go on and tell us what happened next in the life of the slave—and we miss that. But the extraordinary flexibility of essays is what has enabled them to ride out rough weather and hybridize into forms that suit the times. And just as one of the first things a fiction writer learns is that he needn't actually be writing fiction to write a short story—that he can tell his own history or anybody else's as exactly as he remembers it and it will be "fiction" if it remains primarily a story—an essayist soon discovers that he doesn't have to tell the whole truth and nothing but the truth; he can shape or shave his memories, as long as the purpose is served of elucidating a truthful point. A personal essay frequently is not autobiographical at all, but what it does keep in common with autobiography is that, through its tone and tumbling progression, it conveys the quality of the author's mind. Nothing gets in the way. Because essays are directly concerned with the mind and the mind's idiosyncrasy, the very freedom the mind possesses is bestowed on this branch of literature that does honor to it, and the fascination of the mind is the fascination of the essay.

EXPLORING IDEAS

1. Hoagland says that newspaper columnists are our neighbors and that newspaper movie reviewers are personalities who week after week pour their hearts out to us. Are television talk show personalities also essayists of a type? Brainstorm for an essay about TV talk show personalities, comparing and contrasting their different styles.

2. Brainstorm for an essay in which you explain why you do or do not read essays in newspapers, magazines, and books.

3. Hoagland says telling stories is the oldest art form. Brainstorm some reasons that stories developed before explanations, analyses, and arguments did. What makes storytelling "the art to build from"?

4. What does Hoagland mean by the phrases "spurious autobiography," "spurious hallucination," and "shabby careerism"? Try to recall an example of one of these forms that you have either read or read about. Discuss what makes it spurious or shabby.

5. Hoagland says that personal essays are like a human voice following the mind's natural flow instead of a systematized outline of ideas, but that essays must have a point. How can an essay follow the mind's natural flow and still have a point? Doesn't the mind just wander most of the time? Brainstorm some ideas for an essay in which you discuss the problems you have in writing essays with a point.

6. Hoagland says the essayist is a bit of a teacher and that the essay should convey the same point to each of us. Does he mean there is no room for interpretation in an essay, whereas there should be room for interpretation in a story? Write a comparison between essays and stories explaining why there might be this difference between the two forms.

7. Why does Hoagland say that essays are less universal than stories? Does he mean that whereas anyone can read a story, not everyone can read an essay? Does this suggest that essayists are somewhat elitist?

8. Hoagland says an essayist does not have to tell the whole truth; the author can shape or alter personal memories as long as the essay explains a truthful point. Explain how an author who alters the truth or invents falsehoods can yet be telling the truth.

EXPLORING RHETORIC

1. Why does Hoagland say, "If we ever find ourselves living in caves again . . ."? What kind of tone does this phrase suggest? What kind of attitude does it suggest?

2. Comment on the effectiveness of the language in the following statement: "Essays . . . seem a mercurial, newfangled, sometimes hokey affair. . . . It's a greased pig."

3. Comment on the effectiveness of the following metaphors:
"Essays . . . hang somewhere on a line between two sturdy poles."
"The style of the writer has a 'nap' to it."
"Essays belong to the animal kingdom . . . [but articles belong to] the vegetable kingdom."

4. What does Hoagland mean by the phrase the "artful 'I' "? If you write an essay in which you use the pronoun "I," how does the "natural I" become an "artful I"? What is the difference between the "natural I" and the "artful I"?

5. Discuss the relevance of Hoagland's example from Mark Twain. How is it related to his central focus?

6. Explain the metaphors in the following statement: "But the extraordinary flexibility of essays is what has enabled them to ride out rough weather and hybridize into forms that suit the times."

How to Write an Essay

GILBERT HIGHET

Gilbert Highet was born in 1906 in Glasgow, Scotland. He was educated at the University of Glasgow and Oxford University and taught classical literature for most of his career at Columbia University. Among his many books are *The Classical Tradition,* 1949; *The Art of Teaching,* 1950; *The Anatomy of Satire,* 1962; and *Talents and Geniuses,* 1957. He died in 1978.

Whereas Edward Hoagland uses an informal comparison-contrast method to define the essay, Highet depends on a more formal method of recounting the history of the form, referring to a number of examples, and describing the essay's basic structural characteristics. Hoagland and Highet agree on a number of attributes of the essay, such as the importance of the writer's personal voice, but Hoagland suggests that the essay has little structure except that of the writer's mind, whereas Highet says that every essay must have a definite shape.

1   At school they tried to teach me how to write an essay, and how to draw a large brass pot full of zinnias. I grieve to say that they failed in both these laudable aims. I am not sure why I could never draw a brass pot full of zinnias, but I know why my schoolmasters could not teach me to write an essay. The first reason was that they gave us rather unattractive models to study and emulate: Charles Lamb, who is a great deal too quaint and old-fashioned for modern youngsters; Robert Louis Stevenson, whose style is often affected and artificial*; and E. F. Benson, whose essays *From a College Window* are mild and flaccid and middle-aged and uninspiring. The other reason was that they never explained to us what an essay was, and what purpose we were attempting to achieve when we wrote one.

2   But there are other ways of learning how to write an essay—by trial and error, observation and meditation. There are plenty of good stimulating contemporary models. A newspaper editorial is only a short essay; so is a review of a new book, a play, or a concert; so are the articles of newspaper columnists. Some of the columnists write well, some of them atrociously, but they all try to obey the first law of the essayist: *Be interested and you will be interesting.*

3   Also, I now know what an essay is. One good way to get a clear idea of any literary form is to look at its origins, and see what the men who first practiced it thought they were doing. The first man in modern times to write essays was the eccentric and charming Montaigne, who apparently invented the name as well as the pattern: essay = attempt, that is, an exploration, something tentative and incomplete, but suggestive and stimulating. He was quickly followed by the English statesman and philosopher Francis Bacon. These men both thought in print: they mused on subjects they considered to be important, and they allowed the public to share their thoughts by overhearing. They were not trying

---

* In a memorable but unfortunate phrase, Stevenson said he had formed his own style by imitating many earlier writers, and making himself a "sedulous ape."

to teach systematically and completely, but rather to stir and interest their readers' minds and to give some instruction while doing so. In shape and method many of these early essays derive from the letters written on philosophical subjects in ancient Greece and Rome. The letters of Epicurus to his pupils and of Seneca to his friend Lucilius are really philosophical essays; some of the letters of St. Paul are religious essays; and Montaigne's essay on the education of children is set out as a letter to a lady.

An essay is a fairly short and fairly informal discussion—of what? 4 Of any subject in the world, any topic whatever which can be discussed in public. It has two purposes—to interest its readers, and to inform them; but it is far more important that it should interest them. One of William Hazlitt's finest essays is about a champion player of handball, or fives. There are few subjects nowadays about which I care less than handball; I gave the game up when I got a heart warning thirty years ago; and I should not normally turn a single page of print in order to get information about the game and its champions. But Hazlitt writes so warmly and with such conviction that I have read his essay ("The Death of John Cavanagh") thirty or forty times, always with delight. One of G. K. Chesterton's wittiest essays is simply "On Running after One's Hat": now, there is a topic on which most people would not even waste a couple of sentences, and on which nobody (except perhaps a heart specialist) could give us any useful data; but in less than four pages Chesterton takes this piece of trivia and builds it into a fanciful little philosophical system. Essays are intended not to exhaust the subject— which usually means exhausting the reader—but rather to say a few good things about it, and to give readers the pleasure of continuing the author's thought along their own channels.

It is not hard to write an essay, if you can write decently and think a lit- 5 tle. The first essential is to choose a subject which is clear and precise in your mind and which interests you personally—so that you really enjoy thinking and talking and writing about it. Now that it comes to mind, that was a third reason why I never learned to write essays in school: the master was inclined to choose vague and tepid subjects. For instance, "Scenery." Very few boys and girls can really appreciate scenery; and only an aesthetically trained mind can have anything rich and challenging to say about scenery in general. *Scenery:* the word fell on our minds like a thick coating of mud, chill and stifling. I remember that I once escaped from it, and infuriated my unfortunate preceptor, by writing about the unique scenic qualities of the industrial city of Glasgow, with ironically rhapsodical paragraphs about the view of the gasworks from the slag heaps, and the superb assemblage of factory chimneys, some of which (Dixon's Blazes) resembled the divine guardian of the Children of

Israel in the Exodus, a pillar of smoke by day and a pillar of fire by night. At least I felt that aspect of the subject, and I knew it precisely.

6 The next thing is to devise a form for your essay. This, which ought to be obvious, is not. I learned it for the first time from an experienced newspaperman. When I was at college I earned extra pocket- and book-money by writing several weekly columns for a newspaper. They were usually topical, they were always carefully varied, they tried hard to be witty, and (an essential) they never missed a deadline. But once, when I brought in the product, a copy editor stopped me. He said, "Our readers seem to like your stuff all right; but we think it's a bit amateurish." With due humility I replied, "Well, I am an amateur. What should I do with it?" He said, "Your pieces are not coherent; they are only sentences and epigrams strung together; they look like a heap of clothespins in a basket. Every article ought to have a shape. Like this" (and he drew a big letter S on his pad) "or this" (he drew a descending line which turned abruptly upward again) "or this" (and he sketched a solid central core with five or six lines pushing outward from it) "or even this" (and he outlined two big arrows coming into collision). I never saw the man again, but I have never ceased to be grateful to him for his wisdom and for his kindness. Every essay must have a shape. You can ask a question in the first paragraph, discussing several different answers to it till you reach one you think is convincing. You can give a curious fact and offer an explanation of it. You can take a topic that interests you and do a descriptive analysis of it: a man's character (as Hazlitt did with his fives champion), a building, a book, a striking adventure, a peculiar custom. There are many other shapes which essays can take; but the principle laid down by the copy editor was right. Before you start you must have a form in your mind; and it ought to be a form felt in paragraphs or sections, not in words or sentences—so that, if necessary, you could summarize each paragraph in a single line and put the entire essay on a postcard.

7 No. Perhaps that is going too far. Reading through some of the most brilliant essays of Virginia Woolf and E. M. Forster, we realize that they have no obvious form: they often try to break away from patterns and abstract outlines. But they are held together by two factors which not all of us can use. Neither Virginia Woolf nor E. M. Forster was capable of writing a dull commonplace obvious sentence; and both of them—in spite of, and indeed because of, their eccentricities—had minds which were organic wholes, so that whatever they wrote, although sometimes apparently discontinuous, reflected the activity of a single imagination, as the same light is caught in many broken reflections from the surface of a pool. Virginia Woolf's talk and some of her novels were slightly incoherent in rather the same way; but they formed spiritual unities. However, others who cannot claim to possess minds so intense and so

deeply penetrated with harmonious impulses might find it dangerous to write without a preconceived form; and their readers might find the result tedious. Never forget the immortal remark of Richard Brinsley Sheridan:

Easy writing's vile hard reading.

When you plan the shape of your essay, should you also plan its 8 length? Yes, and no. You should always realize that whatever you write as an essay is going to be incomplete: a Sunday afternoon drive is not the Mille Miglia race. You will therefore say to yourself, thinking over the topic, that this particular subject demands forty pages or so—because you have not only to discuss the character of the man but to describe his friends and enemies and lovers; while this one—for instance, the new pleasure of aqualung diving—can have enough said about it in ten pages. But when writing (as in conversation, and even, if you are smart, in making a speech) you will always leave room for new ideas, fresh insights, "ad libs": you can cut them out later if they seem forced or extraneous. But think often of conversation and of letter writing. No one says to himself, "I am now going to talk to this attractive woman for exactly twelve minutes"; no one thinks, "I want to tell my sister about our trip to Japan: I shall take exactly four pages." An essay is a conversation between oneself and an unseen friend.

One more hint from the newspaper and magazine world. Find a good 9 lead sentence. The opening words are important. They are far too often bungled. If they are effective, they will catch the reader's interest and start to mold his feelings. They should therefore be rather vivid, even dramatic, and contain a certain emotional charge; or else be hard and bright and factual, so that the reader knows at once what is to be discussed. There are a large number of critics writing on political and social problems, literature, music, and art, who habitually begin their essays with a sentence so long, so precious, so involved, so obscure, so filled with scholastic allusions and in-jokes and ripostes to unknown opponents that they repel every reader who is not already initiated into the clique and prepared to be impressed. Turn to the good essayists: what do you find? Bacon opens his essay on "Gardens" with the remarkable but true statement:

God Almighty first planted a garden.

George Orwell begins a touching essay on the Moroccan city of Marrakesh with a drastic but significant sentence: "As the corpse went past the flies left the restaurant table in a cloud and rushed after it, but they came back a few minutes later." Another of Orwell's essays, written during the second world war, starts even more dramatically: "As I write, highly civilized human beings are flying overhead, trying to kill me." Once you have read such an opening, hard must be your heart and busy (or empty) your brain if you do not wish to read on. But here is the opening of an essay which, like bad antipasto, kills the appetite for anything else:

> The imbecility with which Verecundulus complains that the presence of a numerous assembly freezes his faculties, is particularly incident to the studious part of mankind, whose education necessarily secludes them in their earlier years from mingled converse, till, at their dismission from schools and academies [= universities], they plunge at once into the tumult of the world, and, coming forth from the gloom of solitude, are overpowered by the blaze of public life.

The subject of this essay is "Bashfulness." The author is Samuel Johnson. The idea is good. Intellectuals are often uncomfortable in large groups of people. They have spent most of their time thinking, reading, and talking with other specialists—or making scientific experiments which cannot be discussed in general language; and they have few subjects of social conversation. (In a way, this essay is a remote precursor of C. P. Snow's *Two Cultures*.) But what a way to start discussing the idea! The first sentence contains seventy-one words and is made up of one principal clause with at least six subordinate clauses and phrases hanging onto it like lampreys on a lake trout. And apart from that, who is Verecundulus? Who has heard his complaints? Not I. Not you. Only Samuel Johnson. His essay is in fact a reply to an imaginary letter asking for sympathy and perhaps advice; but he might have invented a few sentences of the letter itself, to lead into the essay. As for the name Verecundulus, that is really pedantic. No one who does not know a reasonable amount of Latin will understand the word; and in Latin the word does not exist in this form: Johnson invented it. It means only "Shy little man." Addison or Steele would have produced a delightful essay on the same subject, built around a character called "Mr. Modest," or "Dr. Diffident"; but Johnson had to take the Latin *uerecundus* [= shy] and build a diminutive out of it, Verecundulus, which sounds not like a shy man but like a new kind of orchid.

10 I hope this does not make you feel that it is necessarily hard work to write, or even to read, an essay. If I have, then either I have mistaken the technique of writing this pleasant form of literature, or I have failed to show you how delightful it is to read a good essay. Would you like to receive an interesting letter from someone who once met you and who wants to tell you something you did not know and would like to learn? If so, you can either read or write an essay, or both.

EXPLORING IDEAS

1. Highet lists three reasons he did not learn how to write essays from his teachers: old-fashioned models, weak subjects, and lack of definition and purpose of essays. Brainstorm for an essay in which you explain why you have either failed or succeeded in learning how to write essays.

2. Highet says the first law of an essayist is to "be interested and you will be interesting." What if you have to write an essay on a topic in which you are not interested? Can you find a way to become interested? Can you fake being interested? Brainstorm for an essay on this first law, using examples from your own experience.

3. Highet says that examining the origins of something is a good way of finding out what it is. How can knowing the origins of something help us define it? Try to define a familiar activity—such as a sport, a game, a hobby, or a job—by examining its origin.

4. Highet says that early essayists "thought in print" and "allowed the public to share their thoughts by overhearing." But if you write an essay in which you just loosely think about something, won't the essay just seem like ramblings? Discuss your answer.

5. Highet says that letters once were a form of essay. If people do not write letters as much as they once did, how do they communicate? Explain how phone voice mail or computer electronic mail differs from letter writing.

6. Highet says you must have a form in mind before you start writing an essay. Is it possible to develop the form as you write rather than before? When do you typically discover form in your writing: during prewriting and outlining, during drafting, or during postwriting and revision?

7. Brainstorm the difference between people who you think can write without difficulty and people who have a great deal of trouble writing.

EXPLORING RHETORIC

1. Why does Highet begin his essay by comparing learning how to write an essay with learning how to draw a brass pot full of zinnias? What tone does this comparison establish? How does it make the reader feel about Highet?

2. Highet suggests that an essayist can write on any subject, no matter how trivial, if he or she makes it interesting. Does he seem to contradict his earlier statement that he did not learn to write essays in school because his teachers suggested weak subjects?

3. Does Highet's suggestion that to write an essay you must first choose a subject that is clear and precise in your mind contradict his earlier statement that the essays of Montaigne and Bacon were "musings" or "thinking in print"? If you have no subjects that are clear and precise in your mind, how can you make them so?

4. Comment on the effectiveness of the metaphor in the following sentence: "*Scenery:* the word fell on our minds like a thick coating of mud, chill and stifling." What is the relevance of Highet's anecdote about writing about the scenery of slag heaps and factory chimneys?

5. Discuss the relevance of Highet's anecdote about the newspaperman's advice to him concerning the form of an essay. Is it true that essays have shapes that you can draw? Try drawing the shape of an essay you have already written. How would you draw the form of Highet's essay?

6. Why does Highet quote the long passage from Samuel Johnson's essay on bashfulness? Is a quotation the only way to illustrate the difference between bad opening sentences and good opening sentences? Is it ever possible to start an essay with a long sentence? Are short sentences always better opening sentences than long ones?

7. Highet says he hopes that he has not made you think writing an essay is hard work. Write an essay explaining why you think it is hard work to write an essay—or an essay explaining why you think this sort of writing is pleasant and easy.

PART ONE

EXPLORING THE PERSONAL PAST

In "How to Write an Essay," Gilbert Highet says it is most important to choose a subject that is clear and precise in your mind and that interests you personally. The first subject that may come to mind as being interesting, at least to yourself, is, of course, yourself. The initial problem here, as in all other human relationships, is figuring out how to make yourself interesting to others. Moreover, it is not as easy to write about personal experiences as you might at first think. Although you may feel that certain past experiences are important, when you try to think clearly and precisely about them, you may not be quite sure why they were significant.

In the following twelve essays, people describe and explore past personal experiences to discover what they mean and to communicate that discovery to others. You may think that this is a simple, straightforward task; all you have to do is narrate the events, one after another, as they occurred. However, narrative appears simple only when it is done well, and to do it well requires more than just relating events one after another. You will notice that the writers in this part do not merely relate incidents one after another randomly. They all have a point to make about their experiences—a point with which they hope their readers will be able to identify.

Eudora Welty describes how she learned to recognize a voice in what she read and thus to develop her own voice, while Maxine Hong Kingston describes how, as a stranger in a strange land, she had difficulty learning how to find a voice of her own. John Tarkov and Gay Talese use baseball as a metaphor to explore the difference between their own experience as Americans and the experience of their immigrant fathers. Tobias Wolff and Jeanne Wakatsuki Houston describe the experience of being transported to a new home—one with hope for the future and the other with longing for the past. Richard Rodriguez and John Updike, although for quite different reasons, recall their struggle with adolescent appearance. Maya Angelou and Audre Lorde recount an important transition in their lives when they made a discovery about entering the adult world. Finally, Raymond Carver and Le Ly Hayslip, from two different cultural backgrounds, write about their relationship to their fathers.

As these writers show, exploring your personal past can be a rewarding experience but also a painful one. To make such an exploration interesting to someone else, you must be honest, but at the same time, as Edward Hoagland reminds us, you must make, not truth, but a truthful point the controlling purpose of the essay. If getting at a truthful point means taking some liberties with the precise details of the experience, then most writers are willing to do so. Although writing from personal experience begins with open exploration, as the writing continues, you must gradually discover a truthful point in the experience. Once you make that discovery, you can return to the writing, shaving away details, no matter how interesting in themselves, that are not relevant to that point and embellishing or even inventing details that best contribute to clarifying it. It is this dedication to the truthful point, not merely truthful details, that gives a personal essay its sense of form and relevance.

Learning to Listen

EUDORA WELTY

Eudora Welty was born in Jackson, Mississippi, in 1909. She attended Jackson State College for Women and the University of Wisconsin, where she received her B.A. in 1929. After a year at the Columbia University School of Advertising, she returned to Jackson and worked for several newspapers and radio stations, as well as the Works Projects Administration (WPA) as a publicity agent. Her first collection of stories, *A Curtain of Green,* was published in 1941, followed by *The Wide Net* in 1943, *The Golden Apples* in 1949, and *The Bride of Innesfallen* in 1955. *The Collected Stories of Eudora Welty* was published in 1980. Her novels include *The Robber Bridegroom,* 1942; *Delta Wedding,* 1947; *The Ponder Heart,* 1954; *Losing Battles,* 1970; and *The Optimist's Daughter,* 1972, for which she won the Pulitzer Prize. Her memoir, *One Writer's Beginning,* from which the following selection is taken, stayed on the best-seller list for several months when it was published in 1984.

Eudora Welty is one of the most respected American writers. Her short stories, for which she is best known, are characterized by a magical quality in which ordinary characters are transformed into mythical figures. In the selection here, Welty attempts to explain how she learned to listen for stories, to know what stories were, and to hear the voice with which they are told. For Welty, learning to listen is the first step toward learning to develop one's own voice.

Learning stamps you with its moments. Childhood's learning is made 1 up of moments. It isn't steady. It's a pulse.

In a children's art class, we sat in a ring on kindergarten chairs and 2 drew three daffodils that had just been picked out of the yard; and while I was drawing, my sharpened yellow pencil and the cup of the yellow daffodils gave off whiffs just alike. That the pencil doing the drawing should give off the same smell as the flower it drew seemed part of the art lesson—as shouldn't it be? Children, like animals, use all their senses to discover the world. Then artists come along and discover it the same way, all over again. Here and there, it's the same world. Or now and then we'll hear from an artist who's never lost it.

In my sensory education I include my physical awareness of the 3 *word.* Of a certain word, that is; the connection it has with what it stands for. At around age six, perhaps, I was standing by myself in our front yard waiting for supper, just at that hour in a late summer day when the sun is already below the horizon and the risen full moon in the visible sky stops being chalky and begins to take on light. There comes the moment, and I saw it then, when the moon goes from flat to round. For the first time it met my eyes as a globe. The word "moon" came into my mouth as though fed to me out of a silver spoon. Held in my mouth the moon became a word. It had the roundness of a Concord grape Grandpa took off his vine and gave me to suck out of its skin and swallow whole, in Ohio.

4   This love did not prevent me from living for years in foolish error about the moon. The new moon just appearing in the west was the rising moon to me. The new should be rising. And in early childhood the sun and moon, those opposite reigning powers, I just as easily assumed rose in east and west respectively in their opposite sides of the sky, and like partners in a reel they advanced, sun from the east, moon from the west, crossed over (when I wasn't looking) and went down on the other side. My father couldn't have known I believed that when, bending behind me and guiding my shoulder, he positioned me at our telescope in the front yard and, with careful adjustment of the focus, brought the moon close to me.

5   The night sky over my childhood Jackson was velvety black. I could see the full constellations in it and call their names; when I could read, I knew their myths. Though I was always waked for eclipses, and indeed carried to the window as an infant in arms and shown Halley's Comet in my sleep, and though I'd been taught at our diningroom table about the solar system and knew the earth revolved around the sun, and our moon around us, I never found out the moon didn't come up in the west until I was a writer and Herschel Brickell, the literary critic, told me after I misplaced it in a story. He said valuable words to me about my new profession: "Always be sure you get your moon in the right part of the sky."

6 My mother always sang to her children. Her voice came out just a little bit in the minor key. "Wee Willie Winkie's" song was wonderfully sad when she sang the lullabies.

7   "Oh, but now there's a record. She could have her own record to listen to," my father would have said. For there came a Victrola record of "Bobby Shafftoe" and "Rock-a-Bye Baby," all of Mother's lullabies, which could be played to take her place. Soon I was able to play her my own lullabies all day long.

8   Our Victrola stood in the diningroom. I was allowed to climb onto the seat of a diningroom chair to wind it, start the record turning, and set the needle playing. In a second I'd jumped to the floor, to spin or march around the table as the music called for—now there were all the other records I could play too. I skinned back onto the chair just in time to lift the needle at the end, stop the record and turn it over, then change the needle. That brass receptacle with a hole in the lid gave off a metallic smell like human sweat, from all the hot needles that were fed it. Winding up, dancing, being cocked to start and stop the record, was of course all in one the act of *listening*—to "Overture to *Daughter of the Regiment*,"

"Selections from *The Fortune Teller*," "Kiss Me Again," "Gypsy Dance from *Carmen*," "Stars and Stripes Forever," "When the Midnight Choo-Choo Leaves for Alabam," or whatever came next. Movement must be at the very heart of listening.

Ever since I was first read to, then started reading to myself, there has never been a line read that I didn't *hear*. As my eyes followed the 9 sentence, a voice was saying it silently to me. It isn't my mother's voice, or the voice of any person I can identify, certainly not my own. It is human, but inward, and it is inwardly that I listen to it. It is to me the voice of the story or the poem itself. The cadence, whatever it is that asks you to believe, the feeling that resides in the printed word, reaches me through the reader-voice. I have supposed, but never found out, that this is the case with all readers—to read as listeners—and with all writers, to write as listeners. It may be part of the desire to write. The sound of what falls on the page begins the process of testing it for truth, for me. Whether I am right to trust so far I don't know. By now I don't know whether I could do either one, reading or writing, without the other.

My own words, when I am at work on a story, I hear too as they go, 10 in the same voice that I hear when I read in books. When I write and the sound of it comes back to my ears, then I act to make my changes. I have always trusted this voice.

In that vanished time in small-town Jackson, most of the ladies I was fa- 11 miliar with, the mothers of my friends in the neighborhood, were busiest when they were sociable. In the afternoons there was regular visiting up and down the little grid of residential streets. Everybody had calling cards, even certain children; and newborn babies themselves were properly announced by sending out their tiny engraved calling cards attached with a pink or blue bow to those of their parents. Graduation presents to high-school pupils were often "card cases." On the hall table in every house the first thing you saw was a silver tray waiting to receive more calling cards on top of the stack already piled up like jackstraws; they were never thrown away.

My mother let none of this idling, as she saw it, pertain to her; she 12 went her own way with or without her calling cards, and though she was fond of her friends and they were fond of her, she had little time for small talk. At first, I hadn't known what I'd missed.

When we at length bought our first automobile, one of our neigh- 13 bors was often invited to go with us on the family Sunday afternoon ride. In Jackson it was counted an affront to the neighbors to start out for anywhere with an empty seat in the car. My mother sat in the back with her friend, and I'm told that as a small child I would ask to sit in the middle, and say as we started off, "Now *talk*."

14   There was dialogue throughout the lady's accounts to my mother. "I said" . . . "He said" . . . "And I'm told she very plainly said" . . . "It was midnight before they finally heard, and what do you think it *was?*"

15   What I loved about her stories was that everything happened in *scenes.* I might not catch on to what the root of the trouble was in all that happened, but my ear told me it was dramatic. Often she said, "The crisis had come!"

16   This same lady was one of Mother's callers on the telephone who always talked a long time. I knew who it was when my mother would only reply, now and then, "Well, I declare," or "You don't say so," or "Surely not." She'd be standing at the wall telephone, listening against her will, and I'd sit on the stairs close by her. Our telephone had a little bar set into the handle which had to be pressed and held down to keep the connection open, and when her friend had said goodbye, my mother needed me to prize her fingers loose from the little bar; her grip had become paralyzed. "What did she say?" I asked.

17   "She wasn't *saying* a thing in this world," sighed my mother. "She was just ready to talk, that's all."

18   My mother was right. Years later, beginning with my story "Why I Live at the P.O.," I wrote reasonably often in the form of a monologue that takes possession of the speaker. How much more gets told besides!

19   This lady told everything in her sweet, marveling voice, and meant every word of it kindly. She enjoyed my company perhaps even more than my mother's. She invited me to catch her doodlebugs; under the trees in her backyard were dozens of their holes. When you stuck a broom straw down one and called, "Doodlebug, doodlebug, your house is on fire and all your children are burning up," she believed this is why the doodlebug came running out of the hole. This was why I loved to call up her doodlebugs instead of ours.

20   My mother could never have told me her stories, and I think I knew why even then: my mother didn't believe them. But I could listen to this murmuring lady all day. She believed everything she heard, like the doodlebug. And so did I.

21   This was a day when ladies' and children's clothes were very often made at home. My mother cut out all the dresses and her little boys' rompers, and a sewing woman would come and spend the day upstairs in the sewing room fitting and stitching them all. This was Fannie. This old black sewing woman, along with her speed and dexterity, brought along a great provision of up-to-the-minute news. She spent her life going from family to family in town and worked right in its bosom, and nothing could stop her. My mother would try, while I stood being pinned up. "Fannie, I'd rather Eudora didn't hear that." "That" would

be just what I was longing to hear, whatever it was. "I don't want her exposed to gossip"—as if gossip were measles and I could catch it. I did catch some of it but not enough. "Mrs. O'Neil's oldest daughter she had her wedding dress *tried on,* and all her fine underclothes feather-stitched and ribbon run in and then—" "I think that will do, Fannie," said my mother. It was tantalizing never to be exposed long enough to hear the end.

Fannie was the worldliest old woman to be imagined. She could do 22 whatever her hands were doing without having to stop talking; and she could speak in a wonderfully derogatory way with any number of pins stuck in her mouth. Her hands steadied me like claws as she stumped on her knees around me, tacking me together. The gist of her tale would be lost on me, but Fannie didn't bother about the ear she was telling it to; she just liked telling. She was like an author. In fact, for a good deal of what she said, I daresay she *was* the author.

Long before I wrote stories, I listened for stories. Listening *for* them 23 is something more acute than listening *to* them. I suppose it's an early form of participation in what goes on. Listening children know stories are *there.* When their elders sit and begin, children are just waiting and hoping for one to come out, like a mouse from its hole.

It was taken entirely for granted that there wasn't any lying in our 24 family, and I was advanced in adolescence before I realized that in plenty of homes where I played with schoolmates and went to their parties, children lied to their parents and parents lied to their children and to each other. It took me a long time to realize that these very same every-day lies, and the stratagems and jokes and tricks and dares that went with them, were in fact the basis of the *scenes* I so well loved to hear about and hoped for and treasured in the conversation of adults.

My instinct—the dramatic instinct—was to lead me, eventually, on 25 the right track for a storyteller: the *scene* was full of hints, pointers, suggestions, and promises of things to find out and know about human beings. I had to grow up and learn to listen for the unspoken as well as the spoken—and to know a truth, I also had to recognize a lie.

EXPLORING IDEAS

1. Welty says that during childhood we learn in separate moments rather than over time. Try to recall one or more moments in your past when "learning stamped you." Describe the moment, and explain what you learned.

2. In paragraph 3, Welty describes a moment when she made a connection between the word "moon" and the roundness of the moon itself, when, as she says, "the moon became a word." Many authors say that to be a good writer, one must love language as if it were a physical reality. Why do you think such a love of language is important for a writer?

3. Welty describes how her mother's singing to her was replaced by a phonograph. Brainstorm some differences between hearing songs and stories from a person and hearing them from records, tapes, radio, television, or some other machine. Is something lost as a result of this shift from people to machines, or is something gained?

4. Welty says that when she reads, she hears a voice. When you read silently, do you hear a voice? Do you see pictures? What is the difference between hearing words and seeing pictures when reading or hearing a story? What does hearing the voice have to do with learning to write?

5. Welty says she often writes in the form of a monologue in which much gets told beyond the speaker's words. Try creating a monologue in which the speaker unintentionally reveals his or her character or personality by what he or she says.

6. Welty describes being exposed to gossip. Discuss how gossip is related to storytelling.

7. Welty says she had to learn to listen for the unspoken as well as the spoken. Why do writers have to learn to listen for the unspoken? How can you listen for the unspoken? What does Welty mean that to know a truth, she had to recognize a lie? How can storytellers tell the truth by making up stories that never happened?

EXPLORING RHETORIC

1. Why does Welty devote two paragraphs to her misunderstanding about where the moon rises? How is this misunderstanding related to her central ideas about learning?

2. Why does Welty say, "Movement must be at the very heart of listening"? How is this particularly true of listening to music? Brainstorm some more connections between listening and movement.

3. Why does Welty devote a paragraph to describing how people in Jackson, Mississippi, always had calling cards? What does this description have to do with her central focus on listening?

4. Why does Welty describe a woman who believes everything she hears? Why does she like to call up that lady's doodlebugs better than her own? What does this lady have to do with Welty's central focus on listening?

5. Note the description of the sewing woman in paragraph 22: "Her hands steadied me like claws as she stumped on her knees around me, tacking me together." How is this more vivid than this: "She held on to me as she kneeled down and moved around putting pins in my dress?"

6. What kind of image does this essay create of Welty as she was when the events took place? What kind of image does it create of her as she is when she writes the essay?

Finding a Voice

MAXINE HONG KINGSTON

Maxine Hong Kingston was born in Stockton, California, in 1940. She received her degree from the University of California at Berkeley and has taught high school in California and Hawaii. She has also held teaching positions at the University of Hawaii, Eastern Michigan University, and the University of California at Berkeley. Her autobiographical books include *The Woman Warrior: Memories of a Girlhood Among Ghosts*, 1976, which won the National Book Critics Circle Award for nonfiction, and *China Men*, 1980, which won the American Book Award. Her novel *Tripmaster Monkey: His Fake Book* was published in 1989.

In this selection from her memoir *The Woman Warrior*, Kingston recalls how miserable she felt when she had to talk in class and how equally miserable she felt when she was silent. Kingston's description of her painful silence should be familiar to all who have struggled to find their own voice and the confidence to use it.

Long ago in China, knot-makers tied string into buttons and frogs, and 1 rope into bell pulls. There was one knot so complicated that it blinded the knot-maker. Finally an emperor outlawed this cruel knot, and the nobles could not order it anymore. If I had lived in China, I would have been an outlaw knot-maker.

Maybe that's why my mother cut my tongue. She pushed my tongue 2 up and sliced the frenum. Or maybe she snipped it with a pair of nail scissors. I don't remember her doing it, only her telling me about it, but all during childhood I felt sorry for the baby whose mother waited with scissors or knife in hand for it to cry—and then, when its mouth was wide open like a baby bird's, cut. The Chinese say "a ready tongue is an evil."

I used to curl up my tongue in front of the mirror and tauten my 3 frenum into a white line, itself as thin as a razor blade. I saw no scars in my mouth. I thought perhaps I had had two frena, and she had cut one. I made other children open their mouths so I could compare theirs to mine. I saw perfect pink membranes stretching into precise edges that looked easy enough to cut. Sometimes I felt very proud that my mother committed such a powerful act upon me. At other times I was terrified—the first thing my mother did when she saw me was to cut my tongue.

"Why did you do that to me, Mother?" 4

"I told you." 5

"Tell me again." 6

7   "I cut it so that you would not be tongue-tied. Your tongue would be able to move in any language. You'll be able to speak languages that are completely different from one another. You'll be able to pronounce anything. Your frenum looked too tight to do those things, so I cut it."

8   "But isn't 'a ready tongue an evil'?"

9   "Things are different in this ghost country."

10   "Did it hurt me? Did I cry and bleed?"

11   "I don't remember. Probably."

12   She didn't cut the other children's. When I asked cousins and other Chinese children whether their mothers had cut their tongues loose, they said, "What?"

13   "Why didn't you cut my brothers' and sisters' tongues?"

14   "They didn't need it."

15   "Why not? Were theirs longer than mine?"

16   "Why don't you quit blabbering and get to work?"

17   If my mother was not lying she should have cut more, scraped away the rest of the frenum skin, because I have a terrible time talking. Or she should not have cut at all, tampering with my speech. When I went to kindergarten and had to speak English for the first time, I became silent. A dumbness—a shame—still cracks my voice in two, even when I want to say "hello" casually, or ask an easy question in front of the check-out counter, or ask directions of a bus driver. I stand frozen, or I hold up the line with the complete, grammatical sentence that comes squeaking out at impossible length. "What did you say?" says the cab driver, or "Speak up," so I have to perform again, only weaker the second time. A telephone call makes my throat bleed and takes up that day's courage. It spoils my day with self-disgust when I hear my broken voice come skittering out into the open. It makes people wince to hear it. I'm getting better, though. Recently I asked the postman for special-issue stamps; I've waited since childhood for postmen to give me some of their own accord. I am making progress, a little every day.

18   My silence was thickest—total—during the three years that I covered my school paintings with black paint. I painted layers of black over houses and flowers and suns, and when I drew on the blackboard, I put a layer of chalk on top. I was making a stage curtain, and it was the moment before the curtain parted or rose. The teachers called my parents to school, and I saw they had been saving my pictures, curling and cracking, all alike and black. The teachers pointed to the pictures and looked serious, talked seriously too, but my parents did not understand English. ("The parents and teachers of criminals were executed," said my father.) My parents took the pictures home. I spread them out (so black and full of possibilities) and pretended the curtains were swinging open, flying up, one after another, sunlight underneath, mighty operas.

During the first silent year I spoke to no one at school, did not ask 19
before going to the lavatory, and flunked kindergarten. My sister also
said nothing for three years, silent in the playground and silent at lunch.
There were other quiet Chinese girls not of our family, but most of them
got over it sooner than we did. I enjoyed the silence. At first it did not
occur to me I was supposed to talk or to pass kindergarten. I talked
at home and to one or two of the Chinese kids in class. I made motions
and even made some jokes. I drank out of a toy saucer when the water
spilled out of the cup, and everybody laughed, pointing at me, so I did it
some more. I didn't know that Americans don't drink out of saucers.

I liked the Negro students (Black Ghosts) best because they laughed 20
the loudest and talked to me as if I were a daring talker too. One of the
Negro girls had her mother coil braids over her ears Shanghai-style like
mine; we were Shanghai twins except that she was covered with black
like my paintings. Two Negro kids enrolled in Chinese school, and the
teachers gave them Chinese names. Some Negro kids walked me to
school and home, protecting me from the Japanese kids, who hit me and
chased me and stuck gum in my ears. The Japanese kids were noisy and
tough. They appeared one day in kindergarten, released from concentration camp, which was a tic-tac-toe mark, like barbed wire, on the map.

It was when I found out I had to talk that school became a misery, 21
that the silence became a misery. I did not speak and felt bad each time
that I did not speak. I read aloud in first grade, though, and heard the
barest whisper with little squeaks come out of my throat. "Louder," said
the teacher, who scared the voice away again. The other Chinese girls
did not talk either, so I knew the silence had to do with being a Chinese
girl.

Reading out loud was easier than speaking because we did not have 22
to make up what to say, but I stopped often, and the teacher would think
I'd gone quiet again. I could not understand "I." The Chinese "I" has
seven strokes, intricacies. How could the American "I," assuredly wearing a hat like the Chinese, have only three strokes, the middle so straight?
Was it out of politeness that this writer left off strokes the way a Chinese
has to write her own name small and crooked? No, it was not politeness;
"I" is a capital and "you" is lower-case. I stared at that middle line and
waited so long for its black center to resolve into tight strokes and dots
that I forgot to pronounce it. The other troublesome word was "here," no
strong consonant to hang on to, and so flat, when "here" is two moun-
tainous ideographs. The teacher, who had already told me every day
how to read "I" and "here," put me in the low corner under the stairs
again, where the noisy boys usually sat.

When my second grade class did a play, the whole class went to the 23
auditorium except the Chinese girls. The teacher, lovely and Hawaiian,

should have understood about us, but instead left us behind in the class-room. Our voices were too soft or nonexistent, and our parents never signed the permission slips anyway. They never signed anything unnec-essary. We opened the door a crack and peeked out, but closed it again quickly. One of us (not me) won every spelling bee, though.

24   I remember telling the Hawaiian teacher, "We Chinese can't sing 'land where our fathers died.' " She argued with me about politics, while I meant because of curses. But how can I have that memory when I couldn't talk? My mother says that we, like the ghosts, have no memories.

25   After American school, we picked up our cigar boxes, in which we had arranged books, brushes, and an inkbox neatly, and went to Chinese school, from 5:00 to 7:30 P.M. There we chanted together, voices rising and falling, loud and soft, some boys shouting, everybody reading to-gether, reciting together and not alone with one voice. When we had a memorization test, the teacher let each of us come to his desk and say the lesson to him privately, while the rest of the class practiced copying or tracing. Most of the teachers were men. The boys who were so well be-haved in the American school played tricks on them and talked back to them. The girls were not mute. They screamed and yelled during recess, when there were no rules; they had fist-fights. Nobody was afraid of children hurting themselves or of children hurting school property. The glass doors to the red and green balconies with the gold joy symbols were left wide open so that we could run out and climb the fire escapes. We played capture-the-flag in the auditorium, where Sun Yat-sen and Chiang Kai-shek's pictures hung at the back of the stage, the Chinese flag on their left and the American flag on their right. We climbed the teak ceremonial chairs and made flying leaps off the stage. One flag headquarters was behind the glass door and the other on stage right. Our feet drummed on the hollow stage. During recess the teachers locked themselves up in their office with the shelves of books, copy-books, inks from China. They drank tea and warmed their hands at a stove. There was no play supervision. At recess we had the school to ourselves, and also we could roam as far as we could go—downtown, Chinatown stores, home—as long as we returned before the bell rang.

26   At exactly 7:30 the teacher again picked up the brass bell that sat on his desk and swung it over our heads, while we charged down the stairs, our cheering magnified in the stairwell. Nobody had to line up.

27   Not all of the children who were silent at American school found voice at Chinese school. One new teacher said each of us had to get up and recite in front of the class, who was to listen. My sister and I had memorized the lesson perfectly. We said it to each other at home, one

chanting, one listening. The teacher called on my sister to recite first. It was the first time a teacher had called on the second-born to go first. My sister was scared. She glanced at me and looked away; I looked down at my desk. I hoped that she could do it because if she could, then I would have to. She opened her mouth and a voice came out that wasn't a whisper, but it wasn't a proper voice either. I hoped that she would not cry, fear breaking up her voice like twigs underfoot. She sounded as if she were trying to sing though weeping and strangling. She did not pause or stop to end the embarrassment. She kept going until she said the last word, and then she sat down. When it was my turn, the same voice came out, a crippled animal running on broken legs. You could hear splinters in my voice, bones rubbing jagged against one another. I was loud, though. I was glad I didn't whisper. There was one little girl who whispered.

EXPLORING IDEAS

1. Knot-making is the art or craft of making things by knotting string, cord, or rope; it is somewhat like macramé. Why does Kingston say she would have been an outlaw knot-maker if she had lived in China long ago? Why would she have wanted to make a knot so complicated that it was cruel?

2. Kingston says she had difficulty as a child speaking to people. Many people are uncomfortable speaking before a group. Try to explain why you have difficulty speaking or why speaking in public is easy for you. Discuss how this difficulty or ease has affected your life.

3. Kingston says she still has trouble speaking to people; only recently was she able to ask the postman for special-issue stamps. Does her reluctance have to do with shyness, insecurity, fear, or something else? Were you shy as a child? Did you know someone who was? Try to define shyness or to characterize a shy person.

4. As an example of her sense of cultural difference, Kingston says she drank out of a saucer, not knowing that Americans do not drink out of saucers. Write a brief account of something you did that transgressed against the customs of the people you were among.

5. Kingston writes about being chased and hit by a group of students. Describe an experience when you were the victim of a bully or bullies, or brainstorm for an essay in which you try to define bullies and explain what motivates them.

6. What are some of the differences between the author's American school and the Chinese school? How do you account for these differences? Brainstorm some memories about your own elementary school experiences. Try to find a topic that will allow you to explore and explain some aspect of your elementary school experience.

EXPLORING RHETORIC

1. The knot is often used as a metaphor. Read the essay "Untying the Knot" by Annie Dillard elsewhere in this book for another example. According to Greek legend, a king tied a knot, called the Gordian knot, so complicated that no one could untie it. It was said that whoever could undo it would rule all of Asia. In the legend, Alexander the Great cut it with his sword. Thus, to "cut the Gordian knot" means to solve complex problems quickly and decisively. Write a paragraph in which you describe some human experiences for which a knot might be a metaphor. Or write about a personal experience when you metaphorically cut the Gordian knot.

2. Why does Kingston refer to herself in third person as a baby whose mother cut her tongue? What effect is gained by her saying she felt sorry for the baby, as if the child were someone else? Describe a memory from your childhood as if the child were not you but someone you observed.

3. Discuss the appropriateness of the following metaphors Kingston uses: "mouth ...wide open like a baby bird's," "as thin as a razor blade."

4. Did Kingston's mother really cut her tongue, or is this just a story the mother told the child? How can you tell from the dialogue between Kingston as a child and her mother whether this episode did or did not happen?

5. What does the mother's reason for cutting Kingston's tongue have to do with the basic focus of Kingston's essay? Why does Kingston say her mother should have cut more?

6. Kingston says that a telephone call makes her throat bleed and takes up that day's courage. Is this an exaggeration? How can you tell? If it is, why does Kingston exaggerate?

7. Discuss the rhetorical effectiveness of the following sentence: "During the first silent year I spoke to no one at school, did not ask before going to the lavatory, and flunked kindergarten."

8. Discuss the effectiveness of the metaphors in the last few sentences of the final paragraph, beginning with "like twigs underfoot." Rewrite the sentences without the metaphors, and compare the two versions.

Fitting In

JOHN TARKOV

John Tarkov is a writer and editor, residing in New York. In this brief remembrance of his father, Tarkov describes the difference between the son who, having been born in the United States, feels comfortably part of U.S. culture and the immigrant father, who never really got "the hang of this country." Like

Gay Talese, in the next essay in this book, Tarkov uses the metaphor of the American sport of baseball to underscore his cultural difference from his father.

Not quite two miles and 30 years from the church where these thoughts 1
came to me, is a small, graveled parking lot cut out of the New Jersey
pines, behind a restaurant and a dance hall. On road signs, the town is
called Cassville. But to the several generations of Russian-Americans
whose center of gravity tipped to the Old World, it was known as Roova
Farms. I think the acronym stands for Russian Orthodox Outing and Vacation Association. In the summers, the place might as well have been on
the Black Sea.

One day during one of those summers, my old man showed up from 2
a job, just off a cargo ship. He made his living that way, in the merchant
marine. With him, he had a brittle new baseball glove and a baseball as
yet unmarked by human error. We went out to that parking lot and
started tossing the ball back and forth; me even at the age of 8 at ease
with the motions of this American game, him grabbing at the ball with
his bare hands then sending it back with an unpolished stiff-armed
heave. It was a very hot day. I remember that clearly. What I can't remember is who put the first scuff mark on the ball. Either I missed it, or
he tossed it out of my reach.

I chased it down, I'm sure with American-kid peevishness. I wonder 3
if I said anything. Probably I mouthed off about it.

Last winter, the phone call comes on a Saturday morning. The old 4
man's heart had stopped. They had started it beating again. When I get
to the hospital, he's not conscious. They let me in to see him briefly. Then
comes an afternoon of drinking coffee and leaning on walls. Around 4
o'clock, two doctors come out of coronary care. One of them puts his
hand on my arm and tells me. A nurse takes me behind the closed door.

Two fragments of thought surface. One is primitive and it resonates 5
from somewhere deep: *This all began in Russia long ago.* The other is sentimental: *He died near the sea.*

I join the tips of the first three fingers of my right hand and touch 6
them to his forehead, then his stomach, then one side of his chest, then
the other. It's what I believe. I pause just briefly, then give him a couple
of quick cuffs on the side of his face, the way men do when they want to
express affection but something stops them from embracing. The nurse
takes me downstairs to sign some forms.

He never did quite get the hang of this country. He never went to the 7
movies. Didn't watch television on his own. Didn't listen to the radio.
Ate a lot of kielbasa. Read a lot. Read the paper almost cover to cover

every day. He read English well, but when he talked about what he'd read, he'd mispronounce some words and put a heavy accent on them all. The paper was the window through which he examined a landscape and a people that were nearly as impenetrable to him as they were known and manageable to me. For a touch of home, he'd pick up *Soviet Life*. "I'm not a Communist," he used to tell me. "I'm a Russian." Then he'd catch me up about some new hydroelectric project on the Dnieper.

8 And so he vaguely embarrassed me. Who knows how many times, over the years, this story has repeated itself: the immigrant father and the uneasy son. This Melting Pot of ours absorbs the second generation over a flame so high that the first is left encrusted on the rim. In college, I read the literature—Lenski on the three-generation hypothesis, stuff like that—but I read it to make my grades, not particularly to understand that I was living it.

9 When he finally retired from the ocean, he took his first real apartment, on the Lower East Side, and we saw each other more regularly. We'd sit there on Saturday or Sunday afternoons, drinking beer and eating Chinese food. He bought a television set for our diversion, and, depending on the season, the voices of Keith Jackson and Ara Parseghian or Ralph Kiner and Lindsey Nelson would overlap with, and sometimes submerge, our own.

10 After the game, he'd get us a couple more beers, and we would become emissaries: from land and sea, America and ports of destination. We were never strangers—never that—but we dealt, for the most part, in small talk. It was a son trying—or maybe trying to try—to share what little he knew with his father, and flinching privately at his father's foreignness. And it was a father outspokenly proud of his son, beyond basis in reason, yet at times openly frustrated that the kid had grown up unlike himself.

11 Every father has a vision of what he'd like his son to be. Every son has a vision in kind of his father. Eventually, one of them goes, and the one remaining has little choice but to extinguish the ideal and confront the man of flesh and blood who was. Time and again it happens: The vision shed, the son, once vaguely embarrassed by the father, begins to wear the old man's name and story with pride.

12 Though he read it daily, the old man hated this newspaper. Sometimes I think he bought it just to make himself angry. He felt the sports editor was trying to suppress the growth of soccer in America. So naturally, I would egg him on. I'd say things like: "Yeah, you're right. It's a conspiracy. The sports editor plus 200 million other Americans." Then we'd start yelling.

13 But when it came time to put the obituary announcements in the press, after I phoned one in to the Russian-language paper, I started

to dial *The Times*. And I remembered. And I put the phone down. And started laughing. "O.K.," I said. "O.K. They won't get any of our business."

So he went out Russian, like he came in. Up on the hill, the church is   14 topped by weathered gold onion domes—sort of like back in the Old Country, but in fact just down the road from his attempt to sneak us both into America through a side door in New Jersey, by tossing a baseball back and forth on a hot, still, bake-in-the-bleachers kind of summer day.

I believe he threw the thing over my head, actually. It *was* a throwing   15 error, the more I think about it. No way I could have caught it. But it was only a baseball, and he was my father, so it's no big deal. I bounced a few off his shins that day myself. Next time, the baseball doesn't touch the ground.

EXPLORING IDEAS

1. Tarkov recalls playing catch with his father in a parking lot. In a paragraph or two, describe a place you remember from your childhood. Try to account for why you thought of this place. What experience do you associate with it?

2. Some sociologists are concerned about men's "bonding" with their male children by engaging in "men-type" activities such as playing ball, for they fear that these activities will encourage male stereotypes and gender bias. Do you agree or disagree with the sociologists' concerns?

3. Tarkov says that the ball is unmarked by human error. Keeping things "just as they were when new" is an obsession with some people. Write a paragraph or two about someone like this, explaining what effect this behavior has on the person's life.

4. Tarkov does not describe his feelings on his father's death. Have you ever had an experience that was too painful to talk about or that left you speechless? Describe that experience, and try to explain why you were not able to talk about it then.

5. When people react in an overly emotional way, we may call them "sentimental." Write a definition of sentimentalism using specific examples. Or write a character sketch of a sentimental person using specific examples.

6. Tarkov says his father never did quite get the hang of this country. Describe an experience in which you tried to learn the customs of another country, another culture, or another generation.

7. Write a paragraph or two about the cultural or generational gap that exists between parents and their children. Is such a gap inevitable? Try to explain why such a gap seems to exist.

8. In one paragraph, discuss some positive aspects of immigrants' and minorities' being absorbed into American culture. In a second paragraph, discuss the positive aspects of holding on to one's cultural identity.

9. Tarkov says every father has a vision of what he wants his son to be, and every son has a vision of his father. Brainstorm a list of visions you think your father had for you. Then brainstorm a second list of visions you had for your father. Try to discover an essay topic from these two lists.

EXPLORING RHETORIC

1. Why does Tarkov open with a reference to "two miles and 30 years"? Is it confusing to combine space and time this way? Why does he introduce the essay by identifying his thoughts with a specific place?

2. What significance is suggested by a father's playing baseball with his son in a parking lot? Why is baseball more effective than football for suggesting this significance? Why is a parking lot more effective than a field?

3. What do such words as "peevishness" and "mouthed off" suggest about the author? How would the effect have been different if he had used the words "irritable" or "talked back" instead?

4. Explain the basis of the metaphor of a newspaper as a "window" on a "landscape." How is a newspaper like a window? How is what we see in a newspaper like a landscape?

5. Explain Tarkov's metaphor that the melting pot "absorbs the second generation over a flame so high that the first is left encrusted on the rim."

6. Write a paragraph or two in which you explain how Tarkov is using the metaphor of his father and himself as emissaries. In what way are they emissaries to each other? How do they follow the rules of emissary behavior?

7. Tarkov tells us about his embarrassment over his father, but he never tells his father about his embarrassment. Why doesn't he?

8. Write a brief analysis of Tarkov's use of the baseball metaphor in this essay. Explain how the metaphor works, and comment on its effectiveness.

9. Write a brief analysis describing how Tarkov mixes humor and sadness in this essay.

Playing Catch

GAY TALESE

Gay Talese was born in Ocean City, New Jersey, in 1932. He was a reporter for the *New York Times* between 1955 and 1965 and contributed numerous articles to magazines during the 1960s, especially *Esquire*. His books include *The Bridge*, 1964; *The Kingdom and the Power*, 1969; *Honor Thy Father*, 1971; *Thy Neighbor's Wife*, 1975; and *Unto the Sons*, 1992, from which the following selection has been taken.

Combining history and autobiography and taking Talese over ten years to research and write, *Unto the Sons* is an epic account of the immigration of Italians
to America at the turn of the century, centering on Talese's father, a tailor, who,
during World War II, felt torn between his allegiance to his brothers who were
fighting against the Americans in Africa and his new country. The following essay
focuses on an event that illustrates the gap between the father, still bound to Old
World ways and attitudes, and the son, who, born in America, yearns to escape
the conflict of the two cultures.

I became hooked on baseball during the summer of 1941, as the New   1
York Yankees' center fielder, Joe DiMaggio, was breaking a major-league
record by hitting in fifty-six successive games. Even on my provincial island, where the fans were partial to the teams from Philadelphia, the
New York slugger was admired by the crowds that gathered on the
boardwalk or under the green-striped awning of a midtown grocery
market, where a radio loudly played a new song recorded by Les
Brown's band:

> *From Coast to Coast, that's all you hear*
> *Of Joe the One-Man Show*
> *He's glorified the horsehide sphere,*
> *Jolting Joe DiMaggio . . .*
> *Joe . . . Joe . . . DiMaggio . . .*
> *We want you on our side . . .*

One day as I strolled into my parents' store whistling that tune, my   2
father, who recognized it immediately, turned away and walked back to
the cutting room, slowly shaking his head. I continued with my
whistling, albeit less forcefully, throughout the day; and I recognize this
as perhaps my first sign of rebellion against my father, a rebellion that
would intensify during the next two years to the point that now, in December 1943, as my agitated mind wandered in the backseat of my father's Buick, I was planning my escape from parochial school when the
Yankees began spring training the following March.

I would not have to go far. It had recently been announced on the lo-   3
cal sports page that, as a result of wartime restrictions on long-distance
travel, the Yankees would forgo Florida to train in Atlantic City. After
reading this, I secretly marked the passage of each grim, cold day, anticipating a glorious spring in which I would travel by trolley across
the marshlands to the rickety little stadium that would be ennobled by
the presence of baseball's World Champions. I revealed none of these
plans to my father, of course, and I vowed that my rendezvous with the

Yankees would be realized no matter what he said or did to justify his abnormal aversion to the national pastime.

4   If truth be told, however, I would one day understand my father's lack of appreciation of sports. When he was a boy growing up in his village during World War I, there were no games to be played, no opportunities for leisure or relaxation—it was a time and place in which child labor was not only accepted but demanded by the destitute conditions of the day; and my father passed through his adolescent years without knowing what it was like to be young.

5   As he was quick to remind me whenever I complained about having to help out in the store, *he* had been forced to hold down two demanding jobs while attending grammar school. He rose at dawn to serve as a tailor's apprentice in his uncle's shop in the village; later, after school, he toiled in the valley on his grandfather's farm, which was short of workers because increased numbers of men had been conscripted by the Italian army.

6   Among those summoned was my father's older brother, Sebastian, who would return from the front in 1917 crippled and mentally disturbed from inhaling poison gas and being bombarded by artillery shells during the trench warfare against the Germans. Since Sebastian never fully recovered, and since my father's father, Gaetano, had died three years earlier of asbestosis soon after returning to Italy from his factory job in America, my father became prematurely responsible for the welfare of his widowed mother and her three younger children.

7   Two of these children (my father's brothers Nicola and Domenico) were Italian infantrymen, united with the Germans against the Allied armies attacking Italy. Almost every night after I went to bed, I could overhear my father's whispered prayers as he knelt before the portrait of Saint Francis, begging the monk to save his brothers from death or the fate that had befallen Sebastian, and pleading also for the protection of his mother and other family members who were now trapped in the war. Sicily had surrendered by this time, but the Allies had not yet conquered all of southern Italy, and throughout 1943, in our apartment and in the store, I was aware of my father's volatile behavior, his moods abruptly shifting between resignation and peevishness, tenderness and aloofness, openness and secrecy. On this flag-waving island where my father wished to be publicly perceived as a patriotic citizen, I instinctively understood and sympathized with his plight as a kind of emotional double agent.

8   After returning from school, I would see his uneasiness when the postman walked into the store to drop a pack of mail on the counter. When the postman had left, my father would approach the mail tentatively and sift through it to see whether it contained any of those flimsy gray envelopes sent from overseas. If he found any, he would place them

unopened next to the cash register in my mother's dress department for her to open later and read.

My mother, who was candid and direct in ways antithetical to my 9 circuitous father, had earlier confided to me that most of these letters were from a prisoner-of-war camp in North Africa where one of my father's relatives was imprisoned. This relative had been captured with several hundred other Italian soldiers after the British victory over the Germans at El Alamein; but this imprisonment did not prevent him from forwarding to my father information that he had somehow learned inside the camp about the welfare of the people in and around my father's village.

After the doors of the store were closed and locked, my mother 10 would open and silently read each overseas letter, while my father watched her face for any sign of shock or sadness. If she showed neither, he would be reassured that there had been no disaster and would quietly take the letter from her and read it himself.

Perhaps what I was witnessing was a superstitious stratagem on his 11 part, an idiosyncrasy that could be traced back to some strange turn of mind that had shaped the occult character of his ancient, isolated village. Or maybe he was simply using my mother as a crutch in this period of uncertainty and anxiety—a guarantee against the possibility that he would be the sole recipient of the news of death.

But whatever the reason, I was disturbed by these scenes and 12 wanted to remain as detached as possible from the complex reality that embraced my life. There were many times when I wished that I had been born into a different family, a plain and simple family of impeccable American credentials—a no-secrets, nonwhispering, no-enemy-soldiers family that never received mail from POW [prisoner-of-war] camps, or prayed to a painting of an ugly monk, or ate Italian bread with pungent cheese.

I would have preferred having a mother who spent less time in the 13 store with the island's leading Protestant ladies, to whom she sold dresses, and more time playing parish politics with the nuns and the mainland Irish women who invaded our school on PTA evenings and Bingo Nights. And I would have welcomed a father who could have become more relaxed and casual, and who on weekends would have removed his vest and tie and played ball with me on the beach or in the small park across from the Methodist Tabernacle church. But this last wish, I knew, was pure fantasy on my part—I had made the discovery the summer before, after I had spent a half-hour bouncing a red rubber ball against a brick wall in the parking lot behind our shop. I was supposed to be working in the store at the time, affixing long thin cardboard guards to the bottom of wire hangers, then lining up these hangers on a pipe rack within reach of two black men who were pressing trousers and

jackets. But after I had hung up about fifty hangers with the guards attached, I disappeared through the clouds of steam rising from the pressing machines and, with the ball in my pocket, slipped out the back door
into the cool breeze of the parking lot. There I began to fling the ball
against the wall and practice fielding it on the short hop in imitation of
the Yankees' star second baseman, the acrobatic, dark-eyed Joe Gordon,
to whom I fancied I bore a resemblance.

14   I assumed that my father was away from the store having lunch, as
he always did in the middle of Saturday afternoons; I was therefore suddenly shaken by the sight of him opening the back door, then walking
toward me with a frown on his face. Not knowing what to do, but
nonetheless compelled by nervous energy to do *something,* I quickly took
the ball in my right hand, cocked my arm, and threw it at him.

15   The ball soared forty feet in a high arc toward his head. He was so
startled to see it coming that he halted his step and stared skittishly up at
the sky through his steel-rimmed glasses. Then—as if not knowing
whether to block the ball or try to catch it—he extended his arms upward
and cupped his soft tailor's hands, and braced himself for the impact.

16   I stood watching anxiously from the far corner of the lot, no less
shocked than he that I had chosen this moment to confront him—perhaps for the first time in his life—with the challenge of catching a ball. I
cringed as I saw the ball hit him solidly on the side of the neck, carom off
a shoulder, rebound against the wall behind him, and come rolling
slowly back to his feet, where it finally stopped.

17   As I waited, holding my breath, he lowered his head and began to
rub his neck. Then, seeing the ball at his feet, he stooped to pick it up.
For a moment he held the rubber ball in his right hand and examined it
as if it were a strange object. He squeezed it. He turned it around in his
fingers. Finally, with a bashful smile, he turned toward me, cocked his
arm awkwardly, and tried to throw the ball in my direction.

18   But it slipped from his grip, skidded weakly at an oblique angle, and
rolled under one of his dry-cleaning trucks parked along the edge of the
lot.

19   As I hastened to retrieve it, I saw him shrug his shoulders. He
seemed to be very embarrassed. He who cared so much about appearances had tried his best, and yet the results were pitiful. It was a sorrowful moment for both of us.

20   But I heard my father make no excuses as I crawled under the truck
to get the ball. And when I got up again, I saw that he was gone.

EXPLORING IDEAS

1. Talese says he became "hooked" on baseball. Although the metaphor comes
from fishing, it is primarily used to refer to drug addiction. Brainstorm for an ac-

tivity you have become "hooked" on. Explain its fascination for you and discuss the results of this fascination.

2. Talese recalls the first sign of rebellion against his father. Try to recall your own first act of rebellion against a parent or guardian. Describe it in such a way that you explain its significance.

3. Talese says that when he became an adult, he understood his father's aversion to baseball—something he did not understand as a child. Write an essay in which you describe how you came to realize something about a parent or guardian that you did not understand as a child.

4. Talese tells how his father reminded him of how hard he had to work as a child. Brainstorm for an essay, serious or humorous, about your own experience with adults who tell you how tough it was when they were young.

5. Talese says his mother is candid and direct and that his father leaves certain duties up to her to perform. Brainstorm for an essay in which you describe basic differences between your parents or guardians. How do the two complement each other or conflict with each other?

6. Try writing an essay, serious or comic, starting with the following sentence: "There were many times when I wished that I had been born into a different family."

7. Talese writes about mysterious secrets in his family from which he wished to remain detached. When you were a child, did you ever feel you were forced to be involved with adult complexities that you wanted no part of? Or did you feel that there were adult secrets from which you were unfairly excluded? Can you find an essay in such memories?

8. Talese describes being caught doing something he was not supposed to: playing ball when he should have been working. Describe a similar incident in your own life; try to explain the significance of the experience.

9. Talese describes a "sorrowful moment" for him and his father. Describe a similar experience with a parent or guardian.

EXPLORING RHETORIC

1. Why does Talese quote from the song about Joe DiMaggio? Is the song relevant only if you have heard it, or does it matter? What effect does the song quotation have on the reader?

2. Talese begins by referring to an incident in 1941, then shifts to two years later in 1943, as he is riding in the back seat of his parents' car. In paragraph 4, he refers to a much later time when he is an adult. What is the purpose of shifting back and forth between two different time periods—both in the past? Is the shift confusing, or does it make sense in the essay?

3. Analyze the tone of the following sentence: "After reading this, I secretly marked the passage of each grim, cold day, anticipating a glorious spring in which I would travel by trolley across the marshlands to the rickety little stadium that would be ennobled by the presence of baseball's World Champions." Whose voice do you hear: the adult's or the child's?

4. Why does Talese go into such detail about his father's family in paragraphs 6 and 7? Is this detail consistent with his purpose in the essay, or is it an irrelevancy that breaks up the unity of the essay? Discuss your answer.

5. Why does Talese call his father an "emotional double agent"? Is this metaphor from international espionage and spy thrillers a bit extreme, or does it seem justified by Talese's description of his father's situation?

6. For the experience that forms the conclusion of this essay, Talese once again shifts in time to "the summer before." Does he mean the summer before 1941, when he became hooked on baseball, or the summer before 1943, when he recalls riding in the back seat of his parents' car? What is the effect of this additional time shift?

7. Analyze Talese's description of his father's failure to catch and throw the ball. Explain what makes the description work and how it affects the reader.

8. Why does Talese use the particular episode of throwing the ball to his father to end the essay? What is the significance of the episode? Why does baseball seem the most appropriate symbolic activity to convey this significance? Compare this use of baseball with John Tarkov's use of baseball as a metaphor in the previous selection.

Going West

TOBIAS WOLFF

Tobias Wolff was born in Birmingham, Alabama, in 1945 and grew up in Washington State, where his mother moved after a divorce. Instead of finishing high school, he joined the army and served four years as a paratrooper. Later he attended Oxford University, from which he received a degree in English literature. He also studied creative writing at Stanford University. He has received several awards, including a Guggenheim Fellowship and the P.E.N./Faulkner Award for Fiction for his novella, *The Barracks Thief,* 1984. His other books include two collections of short stories, *In the Garden of the North American Martyrs,* 1981, and *Back in the World,* 1985. His memoir, *This Boy's Life,* 1989, from which the following selection is taken, was made into a film in 1992. He currently teaches at Syracuse University in New York State.

In "Going West," the first section of Wolff's memoir, we hear the voice of a young boy who, leaving one life and heading toward another, is torn between loss of the past and hope for the future.

1   Our car boiled over again just after my mother and I crossed the Continental Divide. While we were waiting for it to cool we heard, from somewhere above us, the bawling of an airhorn. The sound got louder and

then a big truck came around the corner and shot past us into the next curve, its trailer shimmying wildly. We stared after it. "Oh, Toby," my mother said, "he's lost his brakes."

The sound of the horn grew distant, then faded in the wind that 2 sighed in the trees all around us.

By the time we got there, quite a few people were standing along the 3 cliff where the truck went over. It had smashed through the guardrails and fallen hundreds of feet through empty space to the river below, where it lay on its back among the boulders. It looked pitifully small. A stream of thick black smoke rose from the cab, feathering out in the wind. My mother asked whether anyone had gone to report the accident. Someone had. We stood with the others at the cliff's edge. Nobody spoke. My mother put her arm around my shoulder.

For the rest of the day she kept looking over at me, touching me, 4 brushing back my hair. I saw that the time was right to make a play for souvenirs. I knew she had no money for them, and I had tried not to ask, but now that her guard was down I couldn't help myself. When we pulled out of Grand Junction I owned a beaded Indian belt, beaded moccasins, and a bronze horse with a removable, tooled-leather saddle.

It was 1955 and we were driving from Florida to Utah, to get away from 5 a man my mother was afraid of and to get rich on uranium. We were going to change our luck.

We'd left Sarasota in the dead of summer, right after my tenth birth- 6 day, and headed West under low flickering skies that turned black and exploded and cleared just long enough to leave the air gauzy with steam. We drove through Georgia, Alabama, Tennessee, Kentucky, stopping to cool the engine in towns where people moved with arthritic slowness and spoke in thick, strangled tongues. Idlers with rotten teeth surrounded the car to press peanuts on the pretty Yankee lady and her little boy, arguing among themselves about shortcuts. Women looked up from their flower beds as we drove past, or watched us from their porches, sometimes impassively, sometimes giving us a nod and a flutter of their fans.

Every couple of hours the Nash Rambler boiled over. My mother 7 kept digging into her little grubstake but no mechanic could fix it. All we could do was wait for it to cool, then drive on until it boiled over again. (My mother came to hate this machine so much that not long after we got to Utah she gave it away to a woman she met in a cafeteria.) At night we slept in boggy rooms where headlight beams crawled up and down the walls and mosquitoes sang in our ears, incessant as the tires whining on the highway outside. But none of this bothered me. I was caught up in my mother's freedom, her delight in her freedom, her dream of transformation.

8   Everything was going to change when we got out West. My mother
had been a girl in Beverly Hills, and the life we saw ahead of us was con-
jured from her memories of California in the days before the Crash. Her
father, Daddy as she called him, had been a navy officer and a paper millionaire. They'd lived in a big house with a turret. Just before Daddy lost
all his money and all his shanty-Irish relatives' money and got himself
transferred overseas, my mother was one of four girls chosen to ride on
the Beverly Hills float in the Tournament of Roses. The float's theme was
"The End of the Rainbow" and it won that year's prize by acclamation.
She met Jackie Coogan. She had her picture taken with Harold Lloyd
and Marion Davies, whose movie *The Sailor Man* was filmed on Daddy's
ship. When Daddy was at sea she and her mother lived a dream life in
which, for days at a time, they played the part of sisters.

9   And the *cars* my mother told me about as we waited for the Rambler
to cool—I should have seen the cars! Daddy drove a Franklin touring
car. She'd been courted by a boy who had his own Chrysler convertible
with a musical horn. And of course there was the Hernandez family,
neighbors who'd moved up from Mexico after finding oil under their
cactus ranch. The family was large. When they were expected to appear
somewhere together they drove singly in a caravan of identical Pierce-
Arrows.

10   Something like that was supposed to happen to us. People in Utah
were getting up poor in the morning and going to bed rich at night. You
didn't need to be a mining engineer or a mineralogist. All you needed
was a Geiger counter. We were on our way to the uranium fields, where
my mother would get a job and keep her eyes open. Once she learned
the ropes she'd start prospecting for a claim of her own.

11   And when she found it she planned to do some serious compensat-
ing: for the years of hard work, first as a soda jerk and then as a novice
secretary, that had gotten her no farther than flat broke and sometimes
not that far. For the breakup of our family five years earlier. For the misery of her long affair with a violent man. She was going to make up for
lost time, and I was going to help her.

12 We got to Utah the day after the truck went down. We were too
late—months too late. Moab and the other mining towns had been over-
run. All the motels were full. The locals had rented out their bedrooms
and living rooms and garages and were now offering trailer space in
their front yards for a hundred dollars a week, which was what my
mother could make in a month if she had a job. But there were no jobs,
and people were getting ornery. There'd been murders. Prostitutes
walked the streets in broad daylight, drunk and bellicose. Geiger coun-
ters cost a fortune. Everyone told us to keep going.

13   My mother thought things over. Finally she bought a poor man's
Geiger counter, a black light that was supposed to make uranium trace

glow, and we started for Salt Lake City. She figured there must be ore somewhere around there. The fact that nobody else had found any meant that we would have the place pretty much to ourselves. To tide us over she planned to take a job with the Kennecott Mining Company, whose personnel officer had responded to a letter of inquiry she'd sent from Florida some time back. He had warned her against coming, said there was no work in Salt Lake and that his own company was about to go out on strike. But his letter was so friendly! My mother just knew she'd get a job out of him. It was as good as guaranteed.

So we drove on through the desert. As we drove, we sang—Irish bal-   14 lads, folk songs, big-band blues. I was hooked on "Mood Indigo." Again and again I world-wearily crooned "You ain't been blue, no, no, no" while my mother eyed the temperature gauge and babied the engine. Then my throat dried up on me and left me croaking. I was too excited anyway. Our trail was ending. Burma Shave ads and bullet-riddled mileage signs ticked past. As the numbers on those signs grew smaller we began calling them out at the top of our lungs.

EXPLORING IDEAS

1. What impression do you get of Wolff from the fact that he made a play for souvenirs when his mother let her guard down? What impression do you get of the mother from the fact that she bought him all the souvenirs he requested?

2. Discuss the basic theme of Wolff's essay announced in paragraph 7. Brainstorm ideas about some point in your life when you identified with a parent or guardian or when you felt caught up in a sense of freedom and transformation.

3. Paragraphs 8 and 9 provide background information about Wolff's mother, which she told him. What does this account tell us about the mother and the central theme of the essay? Why does she tell him these details about her past?

4. Discuss the implications of Wolff's saying that his mother was going to make up for lost time, "and I was going to help her"? How could a ten-year-old boy help his mother make up for lost time? Is he deceiving himself? What is the relationship between Wolff and his mother? Brainstorm about a time when you felt a special, even equal, relationship with one of your parents or guardians.

5. Write a character sketch of Wolff's mother, based on what you know of her from this brief essay. What is she like? How do you know?

EXPLORING RHETORIC

1. Note how much information Wolff packs in the first sentence: "Our car boiled over again just after my mother and I crossed the Continental Divide." What do you learn about Wolff and his situation in this sentence?

2. Note the language Wolff uses to describe the incident about the truck. Comment on the effectiveness of the following words and phrases: "bawling," "shot past," "shimmying wildly," "sighed in the trees," "on its back," "pitifully small," "feathering out."

3. Note the details and metaphors in paragraph 3. Comment on the effectiveness of the following phrases in other parts of the selection; "dead of summer," "skies that turned black and exploded," "air gauzy with steam," "arthritic slowness," "strangled tongues," "rotten teeth," "boggy rooms."

4. Note the sentences in paragraph 12. The paragraph begins with short sentences, has one long sentence in the middle, and ends with short ones. Read the paragraph aloud. Why does Wolff use this variety of sentence structure here?

5. How would you characterize the personality of the young boy portrayed in this essay? What kind of words and sentences does Wolff use to communicate this personality?

Manzanar

JEANNE WAKATSUKI HOUSTON AND JAMES D. HOUSTON

Jeanne Wakatsuki Houston was born in 1935 in California. After the Japanese attack on Pearl Harbor when she was seven years old, she was sent with thousands of other Americans of Japanese descent to an internment camp, where she lived from 1942 to 1945. Over 110,000 Americans of Japanese descent lost their civil rights when they were placed in these camps during World War II. Houston once said that writing about the experience helped her come to terms with it. James D. Houston was born in 1933 and was educated at San Jose State University and Stanford University. He is an author and teacher and has taught writing at several universities. He and Jeanne Wakatsuki were married in 1956.

In this selection from the highly respected memoir, *Farewell to Manzanar,* Jeanne Wakatsuki Houston describes how she and her family adapted to their forced confinement in the internment camp, surviving in their closed-in world by repressing their rage and despair and trying to recreate a sense of a normal life.

1   In Spanish, Manzanar means "apple orchard." Great stretches of Owens Valley were once green with orchards and alfalfa fields. It has been a desert ever since its water started flowing south into Los Angeles, sometime during the twenties. But a few rows of untended pear and apple trees were still growing there when the camp opened, where a shallow water table had kept them alive. In the spring of 1943 we moved to Block 28, right up next to one of the old pear orchards. That's where we stayed until the end of the war, and those trees stand in my memory for the turning of our life in camp, from the outrageous to the tolerable.

Papa pruned and cared for the nearest trees. Late that summer we 2
picked the fruit green and stored it in a root cellar he had dug under our
new barracks. At night the wind through the leaves would sound like
the surf had sounded in Ocean Park, and while drifting off to sleep I
could almost imagine we were still living by the beach.

Mama had set up this move. Block 28 was also close to the camp hos- 3
pital. For the most part, people lived there who had to have easy access
to it. Mama's connection was her job as dietician. A whole half of one
barracks had fallen empty when another family relocated. Mama hustled us in there almost before they'd snapped their suitcases shut.

For all the pain it caused, the loyalty oath finally did speed up the re- 4
location program. One result was a gradual easing of the congestion in
the barracks. A shrewd house-hunter like Mama could set things up
fairly comfortably—by Manzanar standards—if she kept her eyes open.
But you had to move fast. As soon as the word got around that so-and-so
had been cleared to leave, there would be a kind of tribal restlessness, a
nervous rise in the level of neighborhood gossip as wives jockeyed for
position to see who would get the empty cubicles.

In Block 28 we doubled our living space—four rooms for the twelve 5
of us. Ray and Woody walled them with sheetrock. We had ceilings this
time, and linoleum floors of solid maroon. You had three colors to
choose from—maroon, black, and forest green—and there was plenty of
it around by this time. Some families would vie with one another for the
most elegant floor designs, obtaining a roll of each color from the supply
shed, cutting it into diamonds, squares, or triangles, shining it with heat-
ing oil, then leaving their doors open so that passers-by could admire
the handiwork.

Papa brought his still with him when we moved. He set it up behind 6
the door, where he continued to brew his own sake and brandy. He
wasn't drinking as much now, though. He spent a lot of time outdoors.
Like many of the older Issei* men, he didn't take a regular job in camp.
He puttered. He had been working hard for thirty years and, bad as it
was for him in some ways, camp did allow him time to dabble with hobbies he would never have found time for otherwise.

Once the first year's turmoil cooled down, the authorities started 7
letting us outside the wire for recreation. Papa used to hike along the
creeks that channeled down from the base of the Sierras. He brought
back chunks of driftwood, and he would pass long hours sitting on the
steps carving myrtle limbs into benches, table legs, and lamps, filling
our rooms with bits of gnarled, polished furniture.

---

* A Japanese person who emigrated to the United States after the 1907 exclusion proclamation and
so was unable to become an American citizen.

8   He hauled stones in off the desert and built a small rock garden outside our doorway, with succulents and a patch of moss. Near it he laid flat steppingstones leading to the stairs.

9   He also painted watercolors. Until this time I had not known he could paint. He loved to sketch the mountains. If anything made that country habitable it was the mountains themselves, purple when the sun dropped and so sharply etched in the morning light the granite dazzled almost more than the bright snow lacing it. The nearest peaks rose ten thousand feet higher than the valley floor, with Whitney, the highest, just off to the south. They were important for all of us, but especially for the Issei. Whitney reminded Papa of Fujiyama, that is, it gave him the same kind of spiritual sustenance. The tremendous beauty of those peaks was inspirational, as so many natural forms are to the Japanese (the rocks outside our doorway could be those mountains in miniature). They also represented those forces in nature, those powerful and inevitable forces that cannot be resisted, reminding a man that sometimes he must simply endure that which cannot be changed.

10   Subdued, resigned, Papa's life—all our lives—took on a pattern that would hold for the duration of the war. Public shows of resentment pretty much spent themselves over the loyalty oath crises. *Shikata ga nai** again became the motto, but under altered circumstances. What had to be endured was the climate, the confinement, the steady crumbling away of family life. But the camp itself had been made livable. The government provided for our physical needs. My parents and older brothers and sisters, like most of the internees, accepted their lot and did what they could to make the best of a bad situation. "We're here," Woody would say. "We're here, and there's no use moaning about it forever."

11   Gardens had sprung up everywhere, in the firebreaks, between the rows of barracks—rock gardens, vegetable gardens, cactus and flower gardens. People who lived in Owens Valley during the war still remember the flowers and lush greenery they could see from the highway as they drove past the main gate. The soil around Manzanar is alluvial and very rich. With water siphoned off from the Los Angeles–bound aqueduct, a large farm was under cultivation just outside the camp, providing the mess halls with lettuce, corn, tomatoes, eggplant, string beans, horseradish, and cucumbers. Near Block 28 some of the men who had been professional gardeners built a small park, with mossy nooks, ponds, waterfalls and curved wooden bridges. Sometimes in the evenings we could walk down the raked gravel paths. You could face away from the barracks, look past a tiny rapids toward the darkening mountains, and for a while not be a prisoner at all. You could hang suspended

---

* A Japanese phrase meaning, "It can't be helped."

in some odd, almost lovely land you could not escape from yet almost didn't want to leave.

As the months at Manzanar turned to years, it became a world unto   12 itself, with its own logic and familiar ways. In time, staying there seemed far simpler than moving once again to another, unknown place. It was as if the war were forgotten, our reason for being there forgotten. The present, the little bit of busywork you had right in front of you, became the most urgent thing. In such a narrowed world, in order to survive, you learn to contain your rage and your despair, and you try to re-create, as well as you can, your normality, some sense of things continuing. The fact that America had accused us, or excluded us, or imprisoned us, or whatever it might be called, did not change the kind of world we wanted. Most of us were born in this country; we had no other models. Those parks and gardens lent it an oriental character, but in most ways it was a totally equipped American small town, complete with schools, churches, Boy Scouts, beauty parlors, neighborhood gossip, fire and police departments, glee clubs, softball leagues, Abbott and Costello movies, tennis courts, and traveling shows. (I still remember an Indian who turned up one Saturday billing himself as a Sioux chief, wearing bear claws and head feathers. In the firebreak he sang songs and danced his tribal dances while hundreds of us watched.)

In our family, while Papa puttered, Mama made her daily rounds   13 to the mess halls, helping young mothers with their feeding, planning diets for the various ailments people suffered from. She wore a bright yellow, long-billed sun hat she had made herself and always kept stiffly starched. Afternoons I would see her coming from blocks away, heading home, her tiny figure warped by heat waves and that bonnet a yellow flower wavering in the glare.

In their disagreement over serving the country, Woody and Papa   14 had struck a kind of compromise. Papa talked him out of volunteering; Woody waited for the army to induct him. Meanwhile he clerked in the co-op general store. Kiyo, nearly thirteen by this time, looked forward to the heavy winds. They moved the sand around and uncovered obsidian arrowheads he could sell to old men in camp for fifty cents apiece. Ray, a few years older, played in the six-man touch football league, sometimes against Caucasian teams who would come in from Lone Pine or Independence. My sister Lillian was in high school and singing with a hillbilly band called The Sierra Stars—jeans, cowboy hats, two guitars, and a tub bass. And my oldest brother, Bill, led a dance band called The Jive Bombers—brass and rhythm, with cardboard fold-out music stands lettered J. B. Dances were held every weekend in one of the recreation halls. Bill played trumpet and took vocals on Glenn Miller arrangements of such tunes as *In the Mood, String of Pearls,* and *Don't Fence Me In.* He didn't sing *Don't Fence Me In* out of protest, as if trying quietly to mock the authorities. It just happened to be a hit song one year, and they all wanted to be an up-to-date American swing band. They would blast it out into recreation barracks full of bobby-soxed, jitter-bugging couples:

Oh, give me land, lots of land,
Under starry skies above.
Don't fence me in.
Let me ride through the wide
Open country that I love.

15   Pictures of the band, in their bow ties and jackets, appeared in the high school yearbook for 1943–1944, along with pictures of just about everything else in camp that year. It was called *Our World.* In its pages you see school kids with armloads of books, wearing cardigan sweaters and walking past rows of tarpapered shacks. You see chubby girl yell leaders, pompons flying as they leap with glee. You read about the school play, called *Growing Pains,* ". . . the story of a typical American home, in this case that of the McIntyres. They see their boy and girl tossed into the normal awkward growing up stage, but can offer little assistance or direction in their turbulent course . . ." with Shoji Katayama as George McIntyre, Takudo Ando as Terry McIntyre, and Mrs. McIntyre played by Kazuko Nagai.

16   All the class pictures are in there, from the seventh grade through twelfth, with individual head shots of seniors, their names followed by the names of the high schools they would have graduated from on the outside: Theodore Roosevelt, Thomas Jefferson, Herbert Hoover, Sacred Heart. You see pretty girls on bicycles, chicken yards full of fat pullets, patients back-tilted in dental chairs, lines of laundry, and finally, two large blowups, the first of a high tower with a searchlight, against a Sierra backdrop, the next a two-page endsheet showing a wide path that curves among rows of elm trees. White stones border the path. Two dogs are following an old woman in gardening clothes as she strolls along. She is in the middle distance, small beneath the trees, beneath the snowy peaks. It is winter. All the elms are bare. The scene is both stark and comforting. This path leads toward one edge of camp, but the wire is out of sight, or out of focus. The tiny woman seems very much at ease. She and her tiny dogs seem almost swallowed by the landscape, or floating in it.

EXPLORING IDEAS

1. Houston compares her new residence to her previous one, making a parallel between the sound of the surf and the sound of the wind. Describe an experience in which you, or someone you imagine, is discovering a new place and at the same time missing an old place.

2. Note the description of the social life established in the camp, for example, the "tribal restlessness" and the rise in the level of neighborhood gossip. Describe some of the social rituals that make your neighbors, your classmates, your friends, your family, or your fellow workers into a group.

3. Houston says her father putters. Do you know someone who putters—for example, a family member, a neighbor, a friend? Describe "puttering" activities in such a way as to explain the word to someone who does not know its meaning.

4. How can natural scenery provide spiritual sustenance? Is this a cultural characteristic, or is it common to all people? Brainstorm for an essay about how different kinds of scenery provide different kinds of spiritual feelings—for example, oceans, mountains, deserts, forests; or write a brief description of a natural scene, making clear how it evokes certain feelings.

5. Write an essay in which you describe an experience in which you had to make the best of a bad situation. What alternatives to making the best of it were there? How did you handle the situation? What is the significance of that situation to you now?

6. What is the central point of Houston's description of the yearbook pictures? Pick out a picture in your own high school yearbook and describe it to someone; try to communicate the significance of the picture—for example, how it suggests a cultural value or lifestyle.

EXPLORING RHETORIC

1. Houston says that the pear trees "stand in" her memory for the turning of her life in the camp from "the outrageous to the tolerable." What does it mean for an object to "stand for an experience"? Write a paragraph in which you describe an experience that you associate with a certain object or objects.

2. Note the detail in the following sentence: "Mama hustled us in there almost before they'd snapped their suitcases shut." This is probably an exaggeration, but why is it more effective than had the author written, "Mama moved us in as soon as the previous residents moved out"?

3. What is the point of paragraph 11? What unifies it? Try stating the central point of the paragraph in one sentence. Write a paragraph in which you try to explain Houston's point about hanging suspended in something she could not escape from yet almost didn't want to leave; or write about a similar situation in your own life.

4. Paragraphs 13 and 14 summarize what the rest of the family was doing during this period Houston describes. If this were filmed, it might be a wordless montage with a musical background. Why does Houston spend most of this summary on her oldest brother's dance band? Why is this more effective than describing the activities of the mother or the other children?

5. Why is the final picture in the yearbook given the most attention? Like the pear trees in the first paragraph, does it "stand for" something? Try to explain what it stands for and why.

Complexion

RICHARD RODRIGUEZ

Richard Rodriguez was born in 1944 in San Francisco of Mexican-American parents, and he did not learn English until he went to elementary school in Sacramento. He received a B.A. from Stanford University, an M.A. from Columbia University, and a Ph.D. from the University of California at Berkeley, where he also taught for a time. He is a writer, editor, and lecturer, having published articles in *Saturday Review, American Scholar,* and *Harper's.* His memoir, *Hunger of Memory,* 1982, from which the following selection is taken, deals with growing up in two cultures.

Rodriguez recalls his early adolescence when he felt cut off from others and divorced from his body because of his dark complexion. However, it is not a racial inferiority he feels but rather a sexual inferiority, because he feels ugly. In other essays in this book, John Updike and Leslie Silko also describe their feelings of childhood alienation because of their appearance.

1   My first conscious experience of sexual excitement concerns my complexion. One summer weekend, when I was around seven years old, I was at a public swimming pool with the whole family. I remember sitting on the damp pavement next to the pool and seeing my mother, in the spectators' bleachers, holding my younger sister on her lap. My mother, I noticed, was watching my father as he stood on a diving board, waving to her. I watched her wave back. Then saw her radiant, bashful, astonishing smile. In that second I sensed that my mother and father had a relationship I knew nothing about. A nervous excitement encircled my stomach as I saw my mother's eyes follow my father's figure curving into the water. A second or two later, he emerged. I heard him call out. Smiling, his voice sounded, buoyant, calling me to swim to him. But turning to see him, I caught my mother's eye. I heard her shout over to me. In Spanish she called through the crowd: "Put a towel over your shoulders." In public, she didn't want to say why. I knew.

2   That incident anticipates the shame and sexual inferiority I was to feel in later years because of my dark complexion. I was to grow up an ugly child. Or one who thought himself ugly. (*Feo.*) One night when I was eleven or twelve years old, I locked myself in the bathroom and carefully regarded my reflection in the mirror over the sink. Without any pleasure I studied my skin. I turned on the faucet. (In my mind I heard the swirling voices of aunts, and even my mother's voice, whispering, whispering incessantly about lemon juice solutions and dark, *feo* children.) With a bar of soap, I fashioned a thick ball of lather. I began soaping my arms. I took my father's straight razor out of the medicine

cabinet. Slowly, with steady deliberateness, I put the blade against my flesh, pressed it as close as I could without cutting, and moved it up and down across my skin to see if I could get out, somehow lessen, the dark. All I succeeded in doing, however, was in shaving my arms bare of their hair. For as I noted with disappointment, the dark would not come out. It remained. Trapped. Deep in the cells of my skin.

Throughout adolescence, I felt myself mysteriously marked. Noth- 3 ing else about my appearance would concern me so much as the fact that my complexion was dark. My mother would say how sorry she was that there was not money enough to get braces to straighten my teeth. But I never bothered about my teeth. In three-way mirrors at department stores, I'd see my profile dramatically defined by a long nose, but it was really only the color of my skin that caught my attention.

I wasn't afraid that I would become a menial laborer because of my 4 skin. Nor did my complexion make me feel especially vulnerable to racial abuse. (I didn't really consider my dark skin to be a racial characteristic. I would have been only too happy to look as Mexican as my light-skinned older brother.) Simply, I judged myself ugly. And, since the women in my family had been the ones who discussed it in such worried tones, I felt my dark skin made me unattractive to women.

Thirteen years old. Fourteen. In a grammar school art class, when 5 the assignment was to draw a self-portrait, I tried and I tried but could not bring myself to shade in the face on the paper to anything like my actual tone. With disgust then I would come face to face with myself in mirrors. With disappointment I located myself in class photographs— my dark face undefined by the camera which had clearly described the white faces of classmates. Or I'd see my dark wrist against my long-sleeved white shirt.

I grew divorced from my body. Insecure, overweight, listless. On hot 6 summer days when my rubber-soled shoes soaked up the heat from the sidewalk, I kept my head down. Or walked in the shade. My mother didn't need anymore to tell me to watch out for the sun. I denied myself a sensational life. The normal, extraordinary, animal excitement of feeling my body alive—riding shirtless on a bicycle in the warm wind created by furious self-propelled motion—the sensations that first had excited in me a sense of my maleness, I denied. I was too ashamed of my body. I wanted to forget that I had a body because I had a brown body. I was grateful that none of my classmates ever mentioned the fact.

I continued to see the *braceros*, those men I resembled in one way 7 and, in another way, didn't resemble at all. On the watery horizon of a Valley* afternoon, I'd see them. And though I feared looking like them, it

---

* The valley of the Sacramento River in California.

was with silent envy that I regarded them still. I envied them their physical lives, their freedom to violate the taboo of the sun. Closer to home I would notice the shirtless construction workers, the roofers, the sweating men tarring the street in front of the house. And I'd see the Mexican gardeners. I was unwilling to admit the attraction of their lives. I tried to deny it by looking away. But what was denied became strongly desired.

8   In high school physical education classes, I withdrew, in the regular company of five or six classmates, to a distant corner of a football field where we smoked and talked. Our company was composed of bodies too short or too tall, all graceless and all—except mine—pale. Our conversation was usually witty. (In fact we were intelligent.) If we referred to the athletic contests around us, it was with sarcasm. With savage scorn I'd refer to the "animals" playing football or baseball. It would have been important for me to have joined them. Or for me to have taken off my shirt, to have let the sun burn dark on my skin, and to have run barefoot on the warm wet grass. It would have been very important. Too important. It would have been too telling a gesture—to admit the desire for sensation, the body, my body.

EXPLORING IDEAS

1. Rodriguez says that his first conscious experience of sexual excitement occurred when he was seven years old. Does this seem unusually young, or is it typical for a child of seven to experience sexual excitement? What is the difference between conscious sexual excitement and unconscious sexual excitement?

2. Rodriguez says the incident at the swimming pool was the first time he realized that his parents had a relationship he knew nothing about. Try to recall when you first became aware of such a relationship between your parents, guardians, or other adults. Can you recall how you felt about this realization? Did the discovery affect you in any way?

3. Rodriguez says he felt trapped deep in the cells of his skin because he felt ugly. What does this feeling have to do with the old saying, "Beauty is only skin deep"?

4. Rodriguez says that throughout adolescence he felt "mysteriously marked." Many adolescents go through similar experiences because of their size, their skin, their hair, or some other individual characteristic. Brainstorm for an essay in which you describe how you dealt with a similar feeling of being "mysteriously marked" during adolescence.

5. What is the difference between feeling oneself unattractive and feeling oneself unattractive to the opposite sex? Why would people want to be attractive, if not to the opposite sex?

6. What does it mean to be "divorced" from your body? Discuss means by which many people today try to find ways to become "at one with" their bodies.

7. Rodriguez describes how he denied himself a life of physical sensation. How important are such physical sensations? Is it not possible to live a life without seeking such physical sensations? Why does Rodriguez feel that such a denial of sensations is also a denial of his maleness?

8. How is it possible that Rodriguez fears looking like the Mexican farm laborers yet at the same time envies them? Brainstorm for an essay from your own experience when "what was denied became strongly desired."

EXPLORING RHETORIC

1. Why does Rodriguez use three different adjectives—"radiant, bashful, astonishing"—to describe his mother's smile? What does each adjective suggest? What other adjectives might he have selected?

2. Why does Rodriguez use the example of seeing himself in a three-way mirror at department stores? Do we see ourselves differently in such mirrors?

3. The incident Rodriguez describes of trying to remove his dark skin with a razor has both pathetic and comic elements. Discuss how Rodriguez is able to combine these two opposing aspects in the scene.

4. In paragraph 5, Rodriguez describes four different examples of his awareness of his dark skin. Read the paragraph aloud, and discuss the effectiveness of the rhythm of the sentences.

5. What is the relevance of Rodriguez's description of the group of boys that he kept company with in high school? What is the relevance of his suggestion that these boys who were physical outcasts were intelligent?

6. Rodriguez says he and his friends were sarcastic about and scornful of the athletes. How does this attitude make you react to him? How does his subsequent confession that it would have been important for him to join the athletes make you feel about him?

At War with My Skin

JOHN UPDIKE

John Updike was born in Shillington, Pennsylvania, in 1932. He graduated *summa cum laude* from Harvard University in 1954 and studied art for a year on a fellowship in England. He joined the staff of the *New Yorker* magazine in the mid-1950s and wrote the column "Talk of the Town" for two years, before moving to Massachusetts to begin writing full time in 1957. He has written twelve collections of short stories, fourteen novels, and twelve collections of poetry and essays. His best-known works include the story collections *Pigeon Feathers,* 1962; *The Music School,* 1966, and *The Afterlife,* 1994, and the novels *Rabbit*

Run, 1960, *Couples,* 1968; *Rabbit Redux,* 1971; *The Witches of Eastwick,* 1984, and *Rabbit at Rest,* 1990. His nonfiction essays are included in *Picked-up Pieces,* 1975, and *Self-Consciousness,* 1989.

Updike has often been identified as a *New Yorker* writer, a term suggesting a slick, self-consciously lyrical and stylized style. In this personal essay about his coping with a chronic skin disorder, Updike combines vivid description with analysis in an effort to understand and explain the nature of the disorder and how it affected his life and his relationship with others.

1　My mother tells me that up to the age of six I had no psoriasis; it came on strong after an attack of measles in February of 1938, when I was in kindergarten. The disease—"disease" seems strong, for a condition that is not contagious, painful, or debilitating; yet psoriasis has the volatility of a disease, the sense of another presence coöccupying your body and singling you out from the happy herds of healthy, normal mankind— first attached itself to my memory while I was lying on the upstairs side porch of the Shillington house, amid the sickly, oleaginous smell of Siroil, on fuzzy sun-warmed towels, with my mother, sunbathing. We are both, in my mental picture, not quite naked. She would have been still a youngish woman at the time, and I remember being embarrassed by something, but whether by our being together this way or simply by my skin is not clear in this mottled recollection. She, too, had psoriasis; I had inherited it from her. Siroil and sunshine and not eating chocolate were our only weapons in our war against the red spots, ripening into silvery scabs, that invaded our skins in the winter. Siroil was the fore-most medication available in the Thirties and Forties: a bottled prepara-tion the consistency of pus, tar its effective ingredient and its drippy texture and bilious color and insinuating odor deeply involved with my embarrassment. Yet, as with our own private odors, those of sweat and earwax and even of excrement, there was also something satisfying about this scent, an intimate rankness that told me who I was.

2　One dabbed Siroil on; it softened the silvery scales but otherwise did very little good. Nor did abstaining from chocolate and "greasy" foods like potato chips and French fries do much visible good, though as with many palliations there was no knowing how much worse things would be otherwise. Only the sun, that living god, had real power over psoria-sis; a few weeks of summer erased the spots from all of my responsive young skin that could be exposed—chest, legs, and face. Inspecting the many photographs taken of me as a child, including a set of me cavort-ing in a bathing suit in the back yard, I can see no trace of psoriasis. And I remember, when it rained, going out in a bathing suit with friends to play in the downpour and its warm puddles. Yet I didn't learn to swim, because of my appearance; I stayed away from "the Porgy," the dammed pond beyond the poorhouse, and from the public pool in West Reading, and the indoor pool at the Reading "Y," where my father in winter coached the high-school swimming team. To the travails of my freshman year at Harvard was added the humiliation of learning at last to swim, with my spots and my hydrophobia, in a class of quite naked boys. Recently the chunky, mild-spoken man who taught that class over thirty years ago came up to me at a party and pleasantly identified himself; I could scarcely manage politeness, his face so sharply brought back that old suppressed rich mix of chlorine and fear and brave gasping and naked, naked shame.

Psoriasis is a metabolic disorder that causes the epidermis, which 3 normally replaces itself at a gradual, unnoticeable rate, to speed up the process markedly and to produce excess skin cells. The tiny mechanisms gone awry are beyond the precise reach of internally taken medicine; a derivative of vitamin A, etretinate, and an anti-cancer drug, methotrexate, are effective but at the price of potential side-effects to the kidneys and liver more serious than the disease, which is, after all, superficial—too much, simply, of a good thing (skin). In the 1970s, dermatologists at Massachusetts General Hospital developed PUVA, a controlled light treatment: fluorescent tubes radiate long-wave ultraviolet (UV-A) onto skin sensitized by an internal dose of methoxsalen, a psoralen (the "P" of the acronym) derived from a weed, *Ammi majus*, which grows along the river Nile and whose sun-sensitizing qualities were known to the ancient Egyptians. So a curious primitivity, a savor of folk-medicine, clings to this new cure, a refinement of the old sun-cure. It is pleasant, once or twice a week, to stand nearly naked in a kind of glowing telephone booth. It was pleasant to lie on the upstairs porch, hidden behind the jig-sawed wooden balusters, and to feel the slanting sun warm the fuzzy towel while an occasional car or pack of children crackled by on Shilling Alley. One became conscious, lying there trying to read, of birdsong, of distant shouts, of a whistle calling men back to work at the local textile factory, which was rather enchantingly called the Fairy Silk Mill.

My condition forged a hidden link with things elemental—with the 4 seasons, with the sun, and with my mother. A tendency to psoriasis is in-herited—only through the maternal line, it used to be thought. My mother's mother had had it, I was told, though I never noticed anything wrong with my grandmother's skin—just her false teeth, which slipped down while she was napping in her rocking chair. Far in the future, I would marry a young brunette with calm, smooth, deep-tanning skin and was to imagine that thus I had put an end to at least my particular avenue of genetic error. Alas, our fourth child inherited my complexion and, lightly, in her late teens, psoriasis. The disease favors the fair, the dry-skinned, the pallid progeny of cloud-swaddled Holland and Ireland and Germany. Though my father was not red-haired, his brother Arch was, and when I grew a beard, as my contribution to the revolutionary Sixties, it came in reddish. And when I shaved it off, red spots had thrived underneath.

5   Psoriasis keeps you thinking. Strategies of concealment ramify, and self-examination is endless. You are forced to the mirror, again and again; psoriasis compels narcissism, if we can suppose a Narcissus who did not like what he saw. In certain lights, your face looks passable; in slightly different other lights, not. Shaving mirrors and rearview mirrors in automobiles are merciless, whereas the smoky mirrors in airplane bathrooms are especially flattering and soothing: one's face looks as tawny as a movie star's. Flying back from the Caribbean, I used to admire my improved looks; years went by before I noticed that I looked equally good, in the lavatory glow, on the flight down. I cannot pass a reflecting surface on the street without glancing in, in hopes that I have somehow changed. Nature and the self, the great moieties of earthly existence, are each cloven in two by a fascinated ambivalence. One hates one's abnormal, erupting skin but is led into a brooding, solicitous attention toward it. One hates the Nature that has imposed this affliction, but only this same Nature can be appealed to for erasure, for cure. Only Nature can forgive psoriasis; the sufferer in his self-contempt does not grant to other people this power. Perhaps the unease of my first memory has to do with my mother's presence; I wished to be alone with the sun, the air, the distant noises, the possibility of my hideousness eventually going away.

6   I recall remarkably few occasions when I was challenged, in the brute world of childhood, about my skin. In the second grade, perhaps it was, the teacher, standing above our obedient rows, rummaged in my hair and said aloud, "Good heavens, child, what's this on your head?" I can hear these words breaking into the air above me and see my mother's face when, that afternoon, I recounted them to her, probably with tears; her eyes took on a fanatic glare and the next morning, like an arrow that had fixed her course, she went to the school to "have it out" with the teacher who had heightened her defective cub's embarrassment. Our doctor, Doc Rothermel in his big grit-and-stucco house, also, eerily, had psoriasis; far from offering a cure out of his magical expanding black bag, he offered us the melancholy confession that he had felt prevented, by his scaly wrists, from rolling back his sleeves and becoming—his true ambition—a surgeon. " 'Physician, heal thyself,' they'd say to me," he said. I don't, really, know how bad I looked, or how many conferences among adults secured a tactful silence from above. My peers (again, as I remember, which is a choosing to remember) either didn't notice anything terrible about my skin or else neglected to comment upon it. Children are frank, as we know from the taunts and nicknames they fling at one another; but also they all feel im-

perfect and vulnerable, which works for mutual forbearance. In high school, my gym class knew how I looked in the locker room and shower. Once, a boy from a higher class came up to me with an exclamation of cheerful disgust, touched my arm, and asked if I had syphilis. But my classmates held their tongues, and expressed no fear of contagion.

I participated, in gym shorts and tank top, in the annual gym exhibi- 7 tions. Indeed, as the tallest of the lighter boys, I stood shakily on top of "Fats" Sterner's shoulders to make the apex of our gymnastics pyramid. I braved it through, inwardly cringing, prisoner and victim of my skin. It was not really *me*, was the explanation I could not shout out. Like an obese person (like good-natured Fats so sturdy under me, a human rock, his hands gripping my ankles while I fought the sensation that I was about to lurch forward and fly out over the heads of our assembled audi- ence of admiring parents), and unlike someone with a withered arm, say, or a port-wine stain splashed across his neck and cheek, I could change—every summer I *did* become normal and, as it were, beautiful. An overvaluation of the normal went with my ailment, a certain ideal- ization of everyone who was not, as I felt myself to be, a monster.

Because it came and went, I never settled in with my psoriasis, never 8 adopted it as, inevitably, part of myself. It was temporary and in a way illusionary, like my being poor, and obscure, and (once we moved to the farm) lonely—a spell that had been put upon me, a test, as in a fairy story or one of those divinely imposed ordeals in the Bible. "Where's my public?" I used to ask my mother, coming back from the empty mailbox, by this joke conjuring a public out of the future.

My last public demonstration of my monstrosity, in a formal social 9 setting, occurred the day of my examination for the draft, in the summer of 1955. A year in England, with no sun, had left my skin in bad shape, and the examining doctor took one glance up from his plywood table and wrote on my form, "4-F: Psoriasis." At this point in my young life I had a job offer in New York, a wife, and an infant daughter, and was far from keen to devote two years to the national defense; I had never gone to summer camp, and pictured the Army as a big summer camp, with extra-rough bullies and extra-cold showers in the morning. My trepida- tion should be distinguished from political feelings; I had absolutely no doubts about my country's need, from time to time, to fight, and its right to call me to service. So suddenly and emphatically excused, I felt re- lieved, guilty, and above all ashamed at being singled out; the naked American men around me had looked at my skin with surprise and now were impressed by the exemption it had won me. I had not foreseen this result; psoriasis would handicap no killing skills and, had I reported in another season, might have been nearly invisible. My wife, when I got back to my parents' house with my news, was naturally delighted; but my mother, always independent in her moods, seemed saddened, as if

she had laid an egg which, when candled by the government, had been
pronounced rotten.

10   It pains me to write these pages. They are humiliating—"scab-
picking," to use a term sometimes levelled at modern autobiographical
writers. I have written about psoriasis only twice before: I gave it to
Peter Caldwell in *The Centaur* and to an anonymous, bumptious cerami-
cist in the short story "From the Journal of a Leper." I expose it this third
time only in order to proclaim the consoling possibility that whenever in
my timid life I have shown some courage and originality it has been because of my skin. Because of my skin, I counted myself out of any of
those jobs—salesman, teacher, financier, movie star—that demand being
presentable. What did that leave? Becoming a craftsman of some sort,
closeted and unseen—perhaps a cartoonist or a writer, a worker in ink
who can hide himself and send out a surrogate presence, a signature that
multiplies even while it conceals. Why did I marry so young? Because,
having once found a comely female who forgave me my skin, I dared not
risk losing her and trying to find another. Why did I have children so
young? Because I wanted to surround myself with people who did not
have psoriasis. Why, in 1957, did I leave New York and my nice employment there? Because my skin was bad in the urban shadows, and nothing, not even screwing a sunlamp bulb into the socket above my
bathroom mirror, helped. Why did I move, with my family, all the way
to Ipswich, Massachusetts? Because this ancient Puritan town happened
to have one of the great beaches of the Northeast, in whose dunes I
could, like a sin-soaked anchorite of old repairing to the desert, bake and
cure myself.

EXPLORING IDEAS

1. Updike says that a disease gives you the sense of another presence occupying
your body, "singling you out from the happy herds of healthy, normal
mankind." If you had (or have) an illness or condition that made you feel different from others, try to recall with as much specific detail as possible how you felt
this difference.

2. Updike mentions meeting the man who taught his swimming class thirty
years earlier and feeling the same sense of shame all over again. Have you ever
met someone from your past who brought back a past feeling? Describe the
meeting and the memory in such a way that you account for its importance.

3. Updike says his condition created a hidden link with the seasons, the sun, and
his mother. Brainstorm for an essay about how some of your own physical, mental, or emotional characteristics create a link between you and someone else.

4. Updike says his condition encourages narcissism. Narcissus was a handsome
young Greek who loved his own appearance so much that he wanted to possess

his image in a pond. A narcissist, therefore, is one who exhibits a great deal of admiration for his or her own physical appearance. Brainstorm for an essay about someone you know who is narcissistic; or brainstorm for an essay about the narcissism of people in general who exercise constantly and worry about their appearance.

5. Updike refers to the "brute world" of childhood. Is this characterization of childhood a bit extreme, or is there some truth to it? Brainstorm for an essay in which you either agree or disagree with Updike's view of childhood. Use specific examples to support your argument.

6. Brainstorm for an essay on the following description: "Children are frank, as we know from the taunts and nicknames they fling at one another; but also they all feel imperfect and vulnerable, which works for mutual forbearance."

7. Updike recalls an experience in gym class in a public exhibition when, on top of a human pyramid, he wanted to call out, "It was not really *me*." Have you ever done something or been seen in such a way that you wanted to cry out, "This is not really me"? Describe the experience. Why did you feel that way?

Exploring Rhetoric

1. Updike says his first memory of his psoriasis is "mottled," a word that means spots of shading that contrasts with the rest of the surface on which they are found. Discuss the effectiveness of this metaphor. Is memory like this? Discuss the effectiveness of the phrase "silvery scabs." How is this different from another choice he might have made—say, "white scabs," "dry scabs," or "scaly scabs"?

2. Why does Updike refer to the sun as a "living god"? Is this a bit extreme, or does it seem to fit with the purpose of his essay?

3. In paragraph 3, Updike makes an abrupt shift from personal memories of his psoriasis. Is the shift justified or a break in the unity of the essay?

4. Why does Updike balance the two sentences: "It is pleasant, once or twice a week, to stand nearly naked in a kind of glowing telephone booth. It was pleasant to lie on the upstairs porch . . . and to feel the slanting sun warm the fuzzy towel"? How does this balanced pair of sentences emphasize the focus of paragraph 3?

5. Discuss the effectiveness of the language in the following sentence: "The disease favors the fair, the dry-skinned, the pallid progeny of cloud-swaddled Holland and Ireland and Germany."

6. Notice the language of paragraph 5 in which Updike discusses Nature and the self. Is this language more philosophical than the rest of the essay? Does it seem to break the tone of the personal experience parts of the essay, or does it seem to be consistent with them? Discuss your answer.

7. Comment on the effectiveness of Updike's description of his mother's feeling when he was turned down for military service: "as if she had laid an egg which, when candled by the government, had been pronounced rotten."

8. Updike says it pains him to write these pages, for it is like "scab-picking." How does this confession make you feel about Updike? What kind of autobiographical writing do you think some critics call "scab-picking"? Have you ever read such an autobiography? If so, refer to it to explain what Updike means by this term.

Getting a Job

MAYA ANGELOU

Maya Angelou was born Marguerita Johnson in 1928 in St. Louis, Missouri, and grew up in Stamps, Arkansas. She was northern coordinator for the Southern Christian Leadership Conference and has worked as a journalist in Egypt and Ghana. She wrote the screenplay and musical score for the film *Georgia, Georgia* and also wrote and produced a ten-part series on African traditions in American life for the Public Broadcasting System. Her books include her memoir, *I Know Why the Caged Bird Sings,* 1970; *Gather Together in My Name,* 1974; *Singin' and Swingin' and Getting Merry Like Christmas,* 1976; *The Heart of a Woman,* 1981; *All God's Children Need Traveling Shoes,* 1986; and *I Shall Not Be Moved,* 1990. In 1993, she read the poem "On the Pulse of Morning" at the inauguration of President Clinton. She is now a professor at Wake Forest University.

In this selection from *I Know Why the Caged Bird Sings,* Angelou describes the problems she faced as a young African-American high school student trying to land a job as a streetcar conductor in San Francisco. Her success in triumphing over prejudice and the independence that comes with her new job, however, alienate her from her classmates and make her aware of the burdens of freedom that go with growing up.

1   Once I had settled on getting a job, all that remained was to decide which kind of job I was most fitted for. My intellectual pride had kept me from selecting typing, shorthand or filing as subjects in school, so office work was ruled out. War plants and shipyards demanded birth certificates, and mine would reveal me to be fifteen, and ineligible for work. So the well-paying defense jobs were also out. Women had replaced men on the streetcars as conductors and motormen, and the thought of sailing up and down the hills of San Francisco in a dark-blue uniform, with a money changer at my belt, caught my fancy.

2   Mother was as easy as I had anticipated. The world was moving so fast, so much money was being made, so many people were dying in Guam, and Germany, that hordes of strangers became good friends

overnight. Life was cheap and death entirely free. How could she have the time to think about my academic career?

To her question of what I planned to do, I replied that I would get a 3 job on the streetcars. She rejected the proposal with: "They don't accept colored people on the streetcars."

I would like to claim an immediate fury which was followed by the 4 noble determination to break the restricting tradition. But the truth is, my first reaction was one of disappointment. I'd pictured myself, dressed in a neat blue serge suit, my money changer swinging jauntily at my waist, and a cheery smile for the passengers which would make their own work day brighter.

From disappointment, I gradually ascended the emotional ladder to 5 haughty indignation, and finally to that state of stubbornness where the mind is locked like the jaws of an enraged bulldog.

I would go to work on the streetcars and wear a blue serge suit. 6 Mother gave me her support with one of her usual terse asides, "That's what you want to do? Then nothing beats a trial but a failure. Give it everything you've got. I've told you many times, 'Can't do is like Don't Care.' Neither of them have a home."

Translated, that meant there was nothing a person can't do, and 7 there should be nothing a human being didn't care about. It was the most positive encouragement I could have hoped for.

In the offices of the Market Street Railway Company, the receptionist 8 seemed as surprised to see me there as I was surprised to find the interior dingy and the décor drab. Somehow I had expected waxed surfaces and carpeted floors. If I had met no resistance, I might have decided against working for such a poor-mouth-looking concern. As it was, I explained that I had come to see about a job. She asked, was I sent by an agency, and when I replied that I was not, she told me they were only accepting applicants from agencies.

The classified pages of the morning papers had listed advertise- 9 ments for motorettes and conductorettes and I reminded her of that. She gave me a face full of astonishment that my suspicious nature would not accept.

"I am applying for the job listed in this morning's *Chronicle* and I'd 10 like to be presented to your personnel manager." While I spoke in supercilious accents, and looked at the room as if I had an oil well in my own backyard, my armpits were being pricked by millions of hot pointed needles. She saw her escape and dived into it.

"He's out. He's out for the day. You might call tomorrow and if he's 11 in, I'm sure you can see him." Then she swiveled her chair around on its rusty screws and with that I was supposed to be dismissed.

"May I ask his name?" 12

13   She half turned, acting surprised to find me still there.

14   "His name? Whose name?"

15   "Your personnel manager."

16   We were firmly joined in the hypocrisy to play out the scene.

17   "The personnel manager? Oh, he's Mr. Cooper, but I'm not sure
you'll find him here tomorrow. He's . . . Oh, but you can try."

18   "Thank you."

19   "You're welcome."

20   And I was out of the musty room and into the even mustier lobby. In
the street I saw the receptionist and myself going faithfully through
paces that were stale with familiarity, although I had never encountered
that kind of situation before and, probably, neither had she. We were like
actors who, knowing the play by heart, were still able to cry afresh over
the old tragedies and laugh spontaneously at the comic situations.

21   The miserable little encounter had nothing to do with me, the me of
me, any more than it had to do with that silly clerk. The incident was a
recurring dream, concocted years before by stupid whites and it eter-
nally came back to haunt us all. The secretary and I were like Hamlet
and Laertes in the final scene, where, because of harm done by one an-
cestor to another, we were bound to duel to the death. Also because the
play must end somewhere.

22   I went further than forgiving the clerk, I accepted her as a fellow victim of the same puppeteer.

23   On the streetcar, I put my fare into the box and the conductorette
looked at me with the usual hard eyes of white contempt. "Move into the
car, please move on in the car." She patted her money changer.

24   Her Southern nasal accent sliced my meditation and I looked deep
into my thoughts. All lies, all comfortable lies. The receptionist was not
innocent and neither was I. The whole charade we had played out in that
crummy waiting room had directly to do with me, Black, and her, white.

25   I wouldn't move into the streetcar but stood on the ledge over the
conductor, glaring. My mind shouted so energetically that the announce-
ment made my veins stand out, and my mouth tighten into a prune.

26   I WOULD HAVE THE JOB. I WOULD BE A CONDUCTORETTE
AND SLING A FULL MONEY CHANGER FROM MY BELT. I WOULD.

27   The next three weeks were a honeycomb of determination with apertures for the days to go in and out. The Negro organizations to whom I
appealed for support bounced me back and forth like a shuttlecock on
a badminton court. Why did I insist on that particular job? Openings
were going begging that paid nearly twice the money. The minor officials with whom I was able to win an audience thought me mad. Possibly I was.

28   Downtown San Francisco became alien and cold, and the streets I
had loved in a personal familiarity were unknown lanes that twisted

with malicious intent. Old buildings, whose gray rococo façades housed my memories of the Forty-Niners, and Diamond Lil, Robert Service, Sutter and Jack London, were then imposing structures viciously joined to keep me out. My trips to the streetcar office were of the frequency of a person on salary. The struggle expanded. I was no longer in conflict only with the Market Street Railway but with the marble lobby of the building which housed its offices, and elevators and their operators.

During this period of strain Mother and I began our first steps on the 29 long path toward mutual adult admiration. She never asked for reports and I didn't offer any details. But every morning she made breakfast, gave me carfare and lunch money, as if I were going to work. She comprehended the perversity of life, that in the struggle lies the joy. That I was no glory seeker was obvious to her, and that I had to exhaust every possibility before giving in was also clear.

On my way out of the house one morning she said, "Life is going to 30 give you just what you put in it. Put your whole heart in everything you do, and pray, then you can wait." Another time she reminded me that "God helps those who help themselves." She had a store of aphorisms which she dished out as the occasion demanded. Strangely, as bored as I was with clichés, her inflection gave them something new, and set me thinking for a little while at least. Later when asked how I got my job, I was never able to say exactly. I only knew that one day, which was tiresomely like all the others before it, I sat in the Railway office, ostensibly waiting to be interviewed. The receptionist called me to her desk and shuffled a bunch of papers to me. They were job application forms. She said they had to be filled in triplicate. I had little time to wonder if I had won or not, for the standard questions reminded me of the necessity for dexterous lying. How old was I? List my previous jobs, starting from the last held and go backward to the first. How much money did I earn, and why did I leave the position? Give two references (not relatives).

Sitting at a side table my mind and I wove a cat's ladder of near 31 truths and total lies. I kept my face blank (an old art) and wrote quickly the fable of Marguerite Johnson, aged nineteen, former companion and driver for Mrs. Annie Henderson (a White Lady) in Stamps, Arkansas.

I was given blood tests, aptitude tests, physical coordination tests, 32 and Rorschachs, then on a blissful day I was hired as the first Negro on the San Francisco streetcars.

Mother gave me the money to have my blue serge suit tailored, and I 33 learned to fill out work cards, operate the money changer and punch transfers. The time crowded together and at an End of Days I was swinging on the back of the rackety trolley, smiling sweetly and persuading my charges to "step forward in the car, please."

For one whole semester the street cars and I shimmied up and 34 scooted down the sheer hills of San Francisco. I lost some of my need for the Black ghetto's shielding-sponge quality, as I clanged and cleared my way down Market Street, with its honky-tonk homes for homeless sailors, past the quiet retreat of Golden Gate Park and along closed undwelled-in-looking dwellings of the Sunset District.

35   My work shifts were split so haphazardly that it was easy to believe that my superiors had chosen them maliciously. Upon mentioning my suspicions to Mother, she said, "Don't worry about it. You ask for what you want, and you pay for what you get. And I'm going to show you that it ain't no trouble when you pack double."

36   She stayed awake to drive me out to the car barn at four thirty in the mornings, or to pick me up when I was relieved just before dawn. Her awareness of life's perils convinced her that while I would be safe on the public conveyances, she "wasn't about to trust a taxi driver with her baby."

37   When the spring classes began, I resumed my commitment with formal education. I was so much wiser and older, so much more independent, with a bank account and clothes that I had bought for myself, that I was sure that I had learned and earned the magic formula which would make me a part of the gay life my contemporaries led.

38   Not a bit of it. Within weeks, I realized that my schoolmates and I were on paths moving diametrically away from each other. . . . They concentrated great interest on who was worthy of being student body president, and when the metal bands would be removed from their teeth, while I remembered . . . conducting a streetcar in the uneven hours of the morning.

39   Without willing it, I had gone from being ignorant of being ignorant to being aware of being aware. And the worst part of my awareness was that I didn't know what I was aware of. I knew I knew very little, but I was certain that the things I had yet to learn wouldn't be taught to me at George Washington High School.

40   I began to cut classes, to walk in Golden Gate Park or wander along the shiny counter of the Emporium Department Store. When Mother discovered that I was playing truant, she told me that if I didn't want to go to school one day, if there were no tests being held, and if my school work was up to standard, all I had to do was tell her and I could stay home. She said that she didn't want some white woman calling her up to tell her something about her child that she didn't know. And she didn't want to be put in the position of lying to a white woman because I wasn't woman enough to speak up. That put an end to my truancy, but nothing appeared to lighten the long gloomy day that going to school became.

41   To be left alone on the tightrope of youthful unknowing is to experience the excruciating beauty of full freedom and the threat of eternal in-

decision. Few, if any, survive their teens. Most surrender to the vague but murderous pressure of adult conformity. It becomes easier to die and avoid conflicts than to maintain a constant battle with the superior forces of maturity.

Until recently each generation found it more expedient to plead   42
guilty to the charge of being young and ignorant, easier to take the punishment meted out by the older generation (which had itself confessed to the same crime short years before). The command to grow up at once was more bearable than the faceless horror of wavering purpose, which was youth.

The bright hours when the young rebelled against the descending   43
sun had to give way to twenty-four-hour periods called "days" that were named as well as numbered.

The Black female is assaulted in her tender years by all those com-   44
mon forces of nature at the same time that she is caught in the tripartite crossfire of masculine prejudice, white illogical hate and Black lack of power.

The fact that the adult American Negro female emerges a formidable   45
character is often met with amazement, distaste and even belligerence. It is seldom accepted as an inevitable outcome of the struggle won by survivors and deserves respect if not enthusiastic acceptance.

Exploring Ideas

1. Although you may not have the difficulty Maya Angelou had, getting your first job is often a significant event. Brainstorm for an essay about your first job. How old were you? What was the job? Why did you want it? What was the significance of this first job to you?

2. Angelou talks about trying to decide what kind of job for which she was best suited. Write an essay in which you describe the kind of job for which you are best suited. Why are you most suited for it? If you already have such a job, discuss how you discovered its suitability for you.

3. Angelou says that during World War II, hordes of strangers became friends overnight. Describe a similar experience you have had or have witnessed in which people became friends overnight. What does such an experience mean?

4. Angelou's mother always has an aphorism or saying for her. Brainstorm some sayings that your own parents or guardians have told you. What is the value of such sayings, if any?

5. When Angelou is confronted by the white conductorette with the southern accent, she comes to a sudden realization that she has been lying to herself. Try to think of a similar experience in which you came to a sudden realization that you were wrong about something. What caused the realization? How did the realization affect you?

6. Angelou says that the period when she was trying to get her first job was one in which she and her mother began their "first steps on the long path toward mutual adult admiration." Try to develop an essay in which you describe such a period in your own youth when you and a parent, guardian, or other adult began to develop such a mutual adult admiration.

7. Write an essay on Angelou's following realization: "She comprehended the perversity of life, that in the struggle lies the joy." Do you believe this is true? What is perverse about such a truth?

8. Write an essay on the topic suggested by the following sentence: "Without willing it, I had gone from being ignorant of being ignorant to being aware of being aware."

EXPLORING RHETORIC

1. Discuss the effectiveness of the following sentence: "Life was cheap and death entirely free."

2. Discuss the effectiveness of the following metaphors: "ascended the emotional ladder" and "the mind is locked like the jaws of an enraged bulldog."

3. What is the relevance of the dingy appearance of the Market Street Railway Company and Angelou's disappointment when she first goes to the office?

4. In paragraph 16, Angelou begins a metaphor of "playing out the scene" that she extends through paragraph 24. Identify the elements of the metaphor and comment on their effectiveness.

5. Discuss the effectiveness of the following metaphors: "my mouth tighten into a prune," "the next three weeks were a honeycomb of determination," "bounced me back and forth like a shuttlecock."

6. Paragraph 28 is filled with historical references: John August Sutter, on whose property the Gold Rush of 1849 was started; Robert Service, the author of sentimental poetry and fiction; Jack London, an author who lived in the San Francisco area. Why does Angelou refer to these people?

7. What is the relevance of Angelou's description of the contrast between her classmates and herself to her overall focus?

8. Comment on the effectiveness of the following sentences: "To be left alone on the tightrope of youthful unknowing is to experience the excruciating beauty of full freedom and the threat of eternal indecision. Few, if any, survive their teens."

9. Explain the following sentence: "The bright hours when the young rebelled against the descending sun had to give way to twenty-four-hour periods called 'days' that were named as well as numbered."

10. Does Angelou's general conclusion about the challenges of being a black female follow from her specific descriptions of her efforts to get a job, or is she making an unjustified leap in the conclusion? Comment on the effectiveness of the overall structure of the essay.

The Fourth of July

AUDRE LORDE

Audre Lorde was born in New York City in 1934, of immigrant parents from Grenada in the West Indies. She was educated at Hunter College and Columbia University and taught at City University of New York and Hunter College. Her books include *Between Ourselves,* 1976; *Chosen Poems,* 1982; a collection of essays, *A Burst of Light,* which won the American Book Award in 1989; and an autobiography, *Zami: A New Spelling of My Name,* 1982. She was named poet-laureate of New York in 1991. In an interview she described herself as a "black-lesbian-feminist-warrior-mother." She died in 1992.

Audre Lorde describes her first childhood encounter with race prejudice in an ice cream parlor in Washington, D.C.—a sad irony in the heart of a society dedicated to the proposition that everyone is created equal.

1   The first time I went to Washington, D.C. was on the edge of the summer when I was supposed to stop being a child. At least that's what they said to us all at graduation from the eighth grade. My sister Phyllis graduated at the same time from high school. I don't know what she was supposed to stop being. But as graduation presents for us both, the whole family took a Fourth of July trip to Washington, D.C., the fabled and famous capital of our country.

2   It was the first time I'd ever been on a railroad train during the day. When I was little, and we used to go to the Connecticut shore, we always went at night on the milk train, because it was cheaper.

3   Preparations were in the air around our house before school was even over. We packed for a week. There were two very large suitcases that my father carried, and a box filled with food. In fact, my first trip to Washington was a mobile feast; I started eating as soon as we were comfortably ensconced in our seats, and did not stop until somewhere after Philadelphia. I remember it was Philadelphia because I was disappointed not to have passed by the Liberty Bell.

4   My mother had roasted two chickens and cut them up into dainty bite-size pieces. She packed slices of brown bread and butter and green pepper and carrot sticks. There were little violently yellow iced cakes with scalloped edges called "marigolds," that came from Cushman's Bakery. There was a spice bun and rock-cakes from Newton's, the West Indian bakery across Lenox Avenue from St. Mark's School, and iced tea in a wrapped mayonnaise jar. There were sweet pickles for us and dill pickles for my father, and peaches with the fuzz still on them, individually wrapped to keep them from bruising. And, for neatness, there were

piles of napkins and a little tin box with a washcloth dampened with rosewater and glycerine for wiping sticky mouths.

5   I wanted to eat in the dining car because I had read all about them, but my mother reminded me for the umpteenth time that dining car food always cost too much money and besides, you never could tell whose hands had been playing all over that food, nor where those same hands had been just before. My mother never mentioned that Black people were not allowed into railroad dining cars headed south in 1947. As usual, whatever my mother did not like and could not change, she ignored. Perhaps it would go away, deprived of her attention.

6   I learned later that Phyllis's high school senior class trip had been to Washington, but the nuns had given her back her deposit in private, explaining to her that the class, all of whom were white, except Phyllis, would be staying in a hotel where Phyllis "would not be happy," meaning, Daddy explained to her, also in private, that they did not rent rooms to Negroes. "We will take among-you to Washington, ourselves," my father had avowed, "and not just for an overnight in some measly fleabag hotel."

7   American racism was a new and crushing reality that my parents had to deal with every day of their lives once they came to this country. They handled it as a private woe. My mother and father believed that they could best protect their children from the realities of race in america and the fact of american racism by never giving them name, much less discussing their nature. We were told we must never trust white people, but *why* was never explained, nor the nature of their ill will. Like so many other vital pieces of information in my childhood, I was supposed to know without being told. It always seemed like a very strange injunction coming from my mother, who looked so much like one of those people we were never supposed to trust. But something always warned me not to ask my mother why she wasn't white, and why Auntie Lillah and Auntie Etta weren't, even though they were all that same problematic color so different from my father and me, even from my sisters, who were somewhere in-between.

8   In Washington, D.C., we had one large room with two double beds and an extra cot for me. It was a back-street hotel that belonged to a friend of my father's who was in real estate, and I spent the whole next day after Mass squinting up at the Lincoln Memorial where Marian Anderson had sung after the D.A.R. refused to allow her to sing in their auditorium because she was Black. Or because she was "Colored," my father said as he told us the story. Except that what he probably said was "Negro," because for his times, my father was quite progressive.

9   I was squinting because I was in that silent agony that characterized all of my childhood summers, from the time school let out in June to the

end of July, brought about by my dilated and vulnerable eyes exposed to the summer brightness.

I viewed Julys through an agonizing corolla of dazzling whiteness 10 and I always hated the Fourth of July, even before I came to realize the travesty such a celebration was for Black people in this country.

My parents did not approve of sunglasses, nor of their expense. 11

I spent the afternoon squinting up at monuments to freedom and 12 past presidencies and democracy, and wondering why the light and heat were both so much stronger in Washington, D.C. than back home in New York City. Even the pavement on the streets was a shade lighter in color than back home.

Late that Washington afternoon my family and I walked back down 13 Pennsylvania Avenue. We were a proper caravan, mother bright and father brown, the three of us girls step-standards in-between. Moved by our historical surroundings and the heat of the early evening, my father decreed yet another treat. He had a great sense of history, a flair for the quietly dramatic and the sense of specialness of an occasion and a trip.

"Shall we stop and have a little something to cool off, Lin?" 14

Two blocks away from our hotel, the family stopped for a dish of 15 vanilla ice cream at a Breyer's ice cream and soda fountain. Indoors, the soda fountain was dim and fan-cooled, deliciously relieving to my scorched eyes.

Corded and crisp and pinafored, the five of us seated ourselves one 16 by one at the counter. There was I between my mother and father, and my two sisters on the other side of my mother. We settled ourselves along the white mottled marble counter, and when the waitress spoke at first no one understood what she was saying, and so the five of us just sat there.

The waitress moved along the line of us closer to my father and 17 spoke again. "I said I kin give you to take out, but you can't eat here. Sorry." Then she dropped her eyes looking very embarrassed, and suddenly we heard what it was she was saying all at the same time, loud and clear.

Straight-backed and indignant, one by one, my family and I got 18 down from the counter stools and turned around and marched out of the store, quiet and outraged, as if we had never been Black before. No one would answer my emphatic questions with anything other than a guilty silence. "But we hadn't done anything!" This wasn't right or fair! Hadn't I written poems about Bataan and freedom and democracy for all?

My parents wouldn't speak of this injustice, not because they had 19 contributed to it, but because they felt they should have anticipated it and avoided it. This made me even angrier. My fury was not going to be acknowledged by a like fury. Even my two sisters copied my parents' pretense that nothing unusual and anti-american had occurred. I was left to write my angry letter to the president of the united states all by myself, although my father did promise I could type it out on the office typewriter next week, after I showed it to him in my copybook diary.

20   The waitress was white, and the counter was white, and the ice cream I never ate in Washington, D.C. that summer I left childhood was white, and the white heat and the white pavement and the white stone monuments of my first Washington summer made me sick to my stomach for the whole rest of that trip and it wasn't much of a graduation present after all.

EXPLORING IDEAS

1. Lorde announces the focus of her essay in the first sentence: "The first time I went to Washington, D.C. was on the edge of the summer when I was supposed to stop being a child." Brainstorm for an essay describing an experience when you were supposed to stop being a child.

2. The trip Lorde describes is to the "fabled and famous capital of our country." Write an essay about your first trip to a place that you had read and heard about, a place about which you had certain expectations. In your essay, try to make clear whether the place did or did not live up to your expectations.

3. Lorde says that her mother ignored what she did not like, thinking perhaps it would go away if it were deprived of her attention. Brainstorm for an essay on this idea of "Just ignore it, and it will go away."

4. Lorde says she was told never to trust white people, but she was not told why: "Like so many other vital pieces of information in my childhood, I was supposed to know without being told." Use this sentence as the thesis statement for an essay. Can you recall some vital information you were never told but were just supposed to know?

5. Lorde says her father had a "flair for the quietly dramatic and the sense of specialness of an occasion and a trip." Write an essay about such a flair. What does it mean? Why do some people "dramatize" reality or make an event seem special? What does the specialness of an event have to do with the sense of drama?

6. Lorde says her parents were not angry at the injustice but angry at themselves for not anticipating it; she was angry at the injustice but even angrier because the rest of her family pretended "that nothing unusual and anti-american had occurred." Write about an experience in which you were the victim of, or were witness to, an injustice that others did not recognize as an injustice. Try to explain your feelings about this experience.

EXPLORING RHETORIC

1. List each piece of information you learn from paragraph 1. Discuss the relevance of each of these items to the overall focus of Lorde's essay.

2. What is the relevance of Lorde's saying she was disappointed not to have passed by the Liberty Bell in Philadelphia?

3. What do you know about the family from the list of food they took on the train? What would have been lost if Lorde had not said that the iced tea was in a wrapped mayonnaise jar, or if she had not noted that there were sweet pickles for the children and dill pickles for her father, or if she had not pointed out that the peaches still had the fuzz on them? Discuss the value of such specific details.

4. In paragraph 5, Lorde introduces the subject of racism and then provides another example of it in paragraph 6. How do these paragraphs lead up to the long paragraph 7? What is the function of paragraph 7?

5. Why does Lorde not capitalize "America" or "United States"? Is she justified in her style, or is she showing an unjustified lack of respect? Brainstorm some other examples of showing a lack of respect for American symbols, such as burning the flag or refusing to stand for the playing of the national anthem. How do you feel about these gestures?

6. Why does Lorde mention that in 1941, the D.A.R. (Daughters of the American Revolution) prevented the great opera and gospel singer Marian Anderson from singing in Constitution Hall? Why does she not provide the additional information that the free concert Anderson gave at the Lincoln Memorial (attended by 75,000 people) was supported by President Franklin Roosevelt and his wife, Eleanor?

7. Why does Lorde say that her eyes were very sensitive to the sun? How is this detail relevant to her overall focus in this essay?

8. Comment on the effectiveness of the following sentence: "We were a proper caravan, mother bright and father brown, the three of us girls step-standards in-between."

9. In three short paragraphs, Lorde describes the experience at the soda fountain. Write a brief analysis of the description in which you try to explain the elements that make it effective.

10. Comment on the effectiveness of the final paragraph. Does Lorde overemphasize whiteness, or is the repetition of the word justified by the rest of the essay?

My Father's Life

RAYMOND CARVER

Raymond Carver was born on May 25, 1938, in Clatskanie, Oregon. He went to Chico State College in California, where he studied under the writer John Gardner, and to California's Humboldt State College, where he received his B.A. degree in 1963. He held a number of jobs in the 1960s while he gained a modest reputation for his poetry and short fiction. His early poetry collections include *Near Klamath*, 1968; *Winter Insomnia*, 1970; and *At*

Night the Salmon Move, 1976. His first important book, a collection of short stories entitled *Will You Please Be Quiet, Please?* (1976), was nominated for the National Book Award. He received a Guggenheim Fellowship in 1979. In 1981, he published a highly praised collection of stories, *What We Talk About When We Talk About Love,* and, in 1983 another significant collection of stories, *Cathedral.* His other poetry collections are *Where Water Comes Together with Other Water,* 1985; *Ultramarine,* 1986; and *A New Path to the Waterfall,* 1989. His final collection of short stories, *Where I'm Calling From,* was published in 1988, the year of his death. Two books of his miscellaneous writings, *Fires,* 1983, and *No Heroics, Please,* 1991, have been published.

   Carver has been widely recognized as the master of a prose style that seems simple, yet manages to suggest a great deal of meaning by implication. The following personal essay about his father is a good example of his style, for even as Carver seems merely to describe details without explanation, the reader gradually understands that the essay is as much about Carver's fears about himself as it is about his father.

1 My dad's name was Clevie Raymond Carver. His family called him Raymond and friends called him C. R. I was named Raymond Clevie Carver Jr. I hated the "Junior" part. When I was little my dad called me Frog, which was okay. But later, like everybody else in the family, he began calling me Junior. He went on calling me this until I was thirteen or fourteen and announced that I wouldn't answer to that name any longer. So he began calling me Doc. From then until his death, on June 17, 1967, he called me Doc, or else Son.

2   When he died, my mother telephoned my wife with the news. I was away from my family at the time, between lives, trying to enroll in the School of Library Science at the University of Iowa. When my wife answered the phone, my mother blurted out, "Raymond's dead!" For a moment, my wife thought my mother was telling her that I was dead. Then my mother made it clear *which* Raymond she was talking about and my wife said, "Thank God. I thought you meant *my* Raymond."

3   My dad walked, hitched rides, and rode in empty boxcars when he went from Arkansas to Washington State in 1934, looking for work. I don't know whether he was pursuing a dream when he went out to Washington. I doubt it. I don't think he dreamed much. I believe he was simply looking for steady work at decent pay. Steady work was meaningful work. He picked apples for a time and then landed a construction laborer's job on the Grand Coulee Dam. After he'd put aside a little money, he bought a car and drove back to Arkansas to help his folks, my grandparents, pack up for the move west. He said later that they were about to starve down there, and this wasn't meant as a figure of speech. It was during that short while in Arkansas, in a town called Leola, that my mother met my dad on the sidewalk as he came out of a tavern.

"He was drunk," she said. "I don't know why I let him talk to me. 4
His eyes were glittery. I wish I'd had a crystal ball." They'd met once, a
year or so before, at a dance. He'd had girlfriends before her, my mother
told me. "Your dad always had a girlfriend, even after we married. He
was my first and last. I never had another man. But I didn't miss anything."

They were married by a justice of the peace on the day they left for 5
Washington, this big, tall country girl and a farmhand-turned-construc-
tion worker. My mother spent her wedding night with my dad and his
folks, all of them camped beside the road in Arkansas.

In Omak, Washington, my dad and mother lived in a little place not 6
much bigger than a cabin. My grandparents lived next door. My dad
was still working on the dam, and later, with the huge turbines producing electricity and the water backed up for a hundred miles into Canada,
he stood in the crowd and heard Franklin D. Roosevelt when he spoke at
the construction site. "He never mentioned those guys who died building that dam," my dad said. Some of his friends had died there, men
from Arkansas, Oklahoma, and Missouri.

He then took a job in a sawmill in Clatskanie, Oregon, a little town 7
alongside the Columbia River. I was born there, and my mother has a
picture of my dad standing in front of the gate to the mill, proudly holding me up to face the camera. My bonnet is on crooked and about to
come untied. His hat is pushed back on his forehead, and he's wearing a
big grin. Was he going in to work or just finishing his shift? It doesn't
matter. In either case, he had a job and a family. These were his salad
days.

In 1941 we moved to Yakima, Washington, where my dad went to 8
work as a saw filer, a skilled trade he'd learned in Clatskanie. When war
broke out, he was given a deferment because his work was considered
necessary to the war effort. Finished lumber was in demand by the
armed services, and he kept his saws so sharp they could shave the hair
off your arm.

After my dad had moved us to Yakima, he moved his folks into the 9
same neighborhood. By the mid-1940s the rest of my dad's family—his
brother, his sister, and her husband, as well as uncles, cousins, nephews,
and most of their extended family and friends—had come out from
Arkansas. All because my dad came out first. The men went to work at
Boise Cascade, where my dad worked, and the women packed apples in
the canneries. And in just a little while, it seemed—according to my
mother—everybody was better off than my dad. "Your dad couldn't
keep money," my mother said. "Money burned a hole in his pocket. He
was always doing for others."

The first house I clearly remember living in, at 1515 South Fifteenth 10
Street, in Yakima, had an outdoor toilet. On Halloween night, or just any
night, for the hell of it, neighbor kids, kids in their early teens, would

carry our toilet away and leave it next to the road. My dad would have to get somebody to help him bring it home. Or these kids would take the toilet and stand it in somebody else's backyard. Once they actually set it on fire. But ours wasn't the only house that had an outdoor toilet. When I was old enough to know what I was doing, I threw rocks at the other toilets when I'd see someone go inside. This was called bombing the toilets. After a while, though, everyone went to indoor plumbing until, suddenly, our toilet was the last outdoor one in the neighborhood. I remember the shame I felt when my third-grade teacher, Mr. Wise, drove me home from school one day. I asked him to stop at the house just before ours, claiming I lived there.

11   I can recall what happened one night when my dad came home late to find that my mother had locked all the doors on him from the inside. He was drunk, and we could feel the house shudder as he rattled the door. When he'd managed to force open a window, she hit him between the eyes with a colander and knocked him out. We could see him down there on the grass. For years afterward, I used to pick up this colander—it was as heavy as a rolling pin—and imagine what it would feel like to be hit in the head with something like that.

12   It was during this period that I remember my dad taking me into the bedroom, sitting me down on the bed, and telling me that I might have to go live with my Aunt LaVon for a while. I couldn't understand what I'd done that meant I'd have to go away from home to live. But this, too—whatever prompted it—must have blown over, more or less, anyway, because we stayed together, and I didn't have to go live with her or anyone else.

13   I remember my mother pouring his whiskey down the sink. Sometimes she'd pour it all out and sometimes, if she was afraid of getting caught, she'd only pour half of it out and then add water to the rest. I tasted some of his whiskey once myself. It was terrible stuff, and I don't see how anybody could drink it.

14   After a long time without one, we finally got a car, in 1949 or 1950, a 1938 Ford. But it threw a rod the first week we had it, and my dad had to have the motor rebuilt.

15   "We drove the oldest car in town," my mother said. "We could have had a Cadillac for all he spent on car repairs." One time she found someone else's tube of lipstick on the floorboard, along with a lacy handkerchief. "See this?" she said to me. "Some floozy left this in the car."

16   Once I saw her take a pan of warm water into the bedroom where my dad was sleeping. She took his hand from under the covers and held it in the water. I stood in the doorway and watched. I wanted to know what was going on. This would make him talk in his sleep, she told me. There were things she needed to know, things she was sure he was keeping from her.

Every year or so, when I was little, we would take the North Coast 17
Limited across the Cascade Range from Yakima to Seattle and stay in the
Vance Hotel and eat, I remember, at a place called the Dinner Bell Cafe.
Once we went to Ivar's Acres of Clams and drank glasses of warm clam
broth.

In 1956, the year I was to graduate from high school, my dad quit his 18
job at the mill in Yakima and took a job in Chester, a little sawmill town
in northern California. The reasons given at the time for his taking the
job had to do with a higher hourly wage and the vague promise that he
might, in a few years' time, succeed to the job of head filer in this new
mill. But I think, in the main, that my dad had grown restless and simply
wanted to try his luck elsewhere. Things had gotten a little too predictable for him in Yakima. Also, the year before, there had been the
deaths, within six months of each other, of both his parents.

But just a few days after graduation, when my mother and I were 19
packed to move to Chester, my dad penciled a letter to say he'd been
sick for a while. He didn't want us to worry, he said, but he'd cut himself
on a saw. Maybe he'd got a tiny sliver of steel in his blood. Anyway,
something had happened and he'd had to miss work, he said. In the
same mail was an unsigned postcard from somebody down there telling
my mother that my dad was about to die and that he was drinking "raw
whiskey."

When we arrived in Chester, my dad was living in a trailer that be- 20
longed to the company. I didn't recognize him immediately. I guess for a
moment I didn't want to recognize him. He was skinny and pale and
looked bewildered. His pants wouldn't stay up. He didn't look like my
dad. My mother began to cry. My dad put his arm around her and patted
her shoulder vaguely, like he didn't know what this was all about, either.
The three of us took up life together in the trailer, and we looked after
him as best we could. But my dad was sick, and he couldn't get any better. I worked with him in the mill that summer and part of the fall. We'd
get up in the mornings and eat eggs and toast while we listened to the
radio, and then go out the door with our lunch pails. We'd pass through
the gate together at eight in the morning, and I wouldn't see him again
until quitting time. In November I went back to Yakima to be closer to
my girlfriend, the girl I'd made up my mind I was going to marry.

He worked at the mill in Chester until the following February, when 21
he collapsed on the job and was taken to the hospital. My mother asked
if I would come down there and help. I caught a bus from Yakima to
Chester, intending to drive them back to Yakima. But now, in addition to
being physically sick, my dad was in the midst of a nervous breakdown,
though none of us knew to call it that at the time. During the entire trip
back to Yakima, he didn't speak, not even when asked a direct question.
("How do you feel, Raymond?" "You okay, Dad?") He'd communicate if

he communicated at all, by moving his head or by turning his palms up as if to say he didn't know or care. The only time he said anything on the trip, and for nearly a month afterward, was when I was speeding down a gravel road in Oregon and the car muffler came loose. "You were going too fast," he said.

22   Back in Yakima a doctor saw to it that my dad went to a psychiatrist. My mother and dad had to go on relief, as it was called, and the county paid for the psychiatrist. The psychiatrist asked my dad, "Who is the President?" He'd had a question put to him that he could answer. "Ike," my dad said. Nevertheless, they put him on the fifth floor of Valley Memorial Hospital and began giving him electroshock treatments. I was married by then and about to start my own family. My dad was still locked up when my wife went into this same hospital, just one floor down, to have our first baby. After she had delivered, I went upstairs to give my dad the news. They let me in through a steel door and showed me where I could find him. He was sitting on a couch with a blanket over his lap. *Hey,* I thought. *What in hell is happening to my dad?* I sat down next to him and told him he was a grandfather. He waited a minute and then he said, "I feel like a grandfather." That's all he said. He didn't smile or move. He was in a big room with a lot of other people. Then I hugged him, and he began to cry.

23   Somehow he got out of there. But now came the years when he couldn't work and just sat around the house trying to figure what next and what he'd done wrong in his life that he'd wound up like this. My mother went from job to crummy job. Much later she referred to that time he was in the hospital, and those years just afterward, as "when Raymond was sick." The word *sick* was never the same for me again.

24   In 1964, through the help of a friend, he was lucky enough to be hired on at a mill in Klamath, California. He moved down there by himself to see if he could hack it. He lived not far from the mill, in a one-room cabin not much different from the place he and my mother had started out living in when they went west. He scrawled letters to my mother, and if I called she'd read them aloud to me over the phone. In the letters, he said it was touch and go. Every day that he went to work, he felt like it was the most important day of his life. But every day, he told her, made the next day that much easier. He said for her to tell me he said hello. If he couldn't sleep at night, he said, he thought about me and the good times we used to have. Finally, after a couple of months, he regained some of his confidence. He could do the work and didn't think he had to worry that he'd let anybody down ever again. When he was sure, he sent for my mother.

25   He'd been off from work for six years and had lost everything in that time—home, car, furniture, and appliances, including the big freezer that had been my mother's pride and joy. He'd lost his good name

too—Raymond Carver was someone who couldn't pay his bills—and his self-respect was gone. He'd even lost his virility. My mother told my wife, "All during that time Raymond was sick we slept together in the same bed, but we didn't have relations. He wanted to a few times, but nothing happened. I didn't miss it, but I think he wanted to, you know."

During those years I was trying to raise my own family and earn a 26 living. But, one thing and another, we found ourselves having to move a lot. I couldn't keep track of what was going down in my dad's life. But I did have a chance one Christmas to tell him I wanted to be a writer. I might as well have told him I wanted to become a plastic surgeon. "What are you going to write about?" he wanted to know. Then, as if to help me out, he said, "Write about stuff you know about. Write about some of those fishing trips we took." I said I would, but I knew I wouldn't. "Send me what you write," he said. I said I'd do that, but then I didn't. I wasn't writing anything about fishing, and I didn't think he'd particularly care about, or even necessarily understand, what I was writing in those days. Besides, he wasn't a reader. Not the sort, anyway, I imagined I was writing for.

Then he died. I was a long way off, in Iowa City, with things still to 27 say to him. I didn't have the chance to tell him goodbye, or that I thought he was doing great at his new job. That I was proud of him for making a comeback.

My mother said he came in from work that night and ate a big sup- 28 per. Then he sat at the table by himself and finished what was left of a bottle of whiskey, a bottle she found hidden in the bottom of the garbage under some coffee grounds a day or so later. Then he got up and went to bed, where my mother joined him a little later. But in the night she had to get up and make a bed for herself on the couch. "He was snoring so loud I couldn't sleep," she said. The next morning when she looked in on him, he was on his back with his mouth open, his cheeks caved in. *Graylooking,* she said. She knew he was dead—she didn't need a doctor to tell her that. But she called one anyway, and then she called my wife.

Among the pictures my mother kept of my dad and herself during 29 those early days in Washington was a photograph of him standing in front of a car, holding a beer and a stringer of fish. In the photograph he is wearing his hat back on his forehead and has this awkward grin on his face. I asked her for it and she gave it to me, along with some others. I put it up on my wall, and each time we moved, I took the picture along and put it up on another wall. I looked at it carefully from time to time, trying to figure out some things about my dad, and maybe myself in the process. But I couldn't. My dad just kept moving further and further away from me and back into time. Finally, in the course of another move, I lost the photograph. It was then that I tried to recall it, and at the same time make an attempt to say something about my dad, and how I thought that in some important ways we might be alike. I wrote the poem when I was living in an apartment house in an urban area south of San Francisco, at a time when I found myself, like my dad, having trouble with alcohol. The poem was a way of trying to connect up with him.

Photograph of My Father in His Twenty-Second Year

October. Here in this dank, unfamiliar kitchen
I study my father's embarrassed young man's face.
Sheepish grin, he holds in one hand a string
of spiny yellow perch, in the other
a bottle of Carlsberg beer.

In jeans and flannel shirt, he leans
against the front fender of a 1934 Ford.
He would like to pose brave and hearty for his posterity,
wear his old hat cocked over his ear.
All his life my father wanted to be bold.

But the eyes give him away, and the hands
that limply offer the string of dead perch
and the bottle of beer. Father, I love you,
yet how can I say thank you, I who can't hold my liquor either
and don't even know the places to fish.

30   The poem is true in its particulars, except that my dad died in June and not October, as the first word of the poem says. I wanted a word with more than one syllable to make it linger a little. But more than that, I wanted a month appropriate to what I felt at the time I wrote the poem—a month of short days and failing light, smoke in the air, things perishing. June was summer nights and days, graduations, my wedding anniversary, the birthday of one of my children. June wasn't a month your father died in.

31   After the service at the funeral home, after we had moved outside, a woman I didn't know came over to me and said, "He's happier where he is now." I stared at this woman until she moved away. I still remember the little knob of a hat she was wearing. Then one of my dad's cousins—I didn't know the man's name—reached out and took my hand, "We all miss him," he said, and I knew he wasn't saying it just to be polite.

32   I began to weep for the first time since receiving the news. I hadn't been able to before. I hadn't had the time, for one thing. Now, suddenly, I couldn't stop. I held my wife and wept while she said and did what she could do to comfort me there in the middle of that summer afternoon.

33   I listened to people say consoling things to my mother, and I was glad that my dad's family had turned up, had come to where he was. I

thought I'd remember everything that was said and done that day and maybe find a way to tell it sometime. But I didn't. I forgot it all, or nearly. What I do remember is that I heard our name used a lot that afternoon, my dad's name and mine. But I knew they were talking about my dad. *Raymond,* these people kept saying in their beautiful voices out of my childhood. *Raymond.*

EXPLORING IDEAS

1. Why does Carver say that he does not think his father dreamed much? Write a paragraph in which you discuss whether your father, your mother, or a guardian "dreamed much." Try to think of particular events that support your assumption.

2. Why does Carver say that the whiskey was terrible stuff and he couldn't see how anyone could drink it? Is this comment related to the overall theme or focus of the essay, or is it an unimportant detail?

3. Discuss the thematic relevance of Carver's juxtaposing the events in his father's life with the events in his own.

4. What is the relevance of losing one's "good name" to the overall theme of this essay? What is the significance of Carver's father losing his "virility"? How are these qualities culturally important?

5. Why is Carver's career aim of becoming a writer so alien to his father? Are there cultures in which writing is more respected than in the cultural framework of Carver's life?

6. When someone dies, people often want to know the details of the last day or hours of that life. Try writing a brief analysis of why humans want to know these details.

7. How is paragraph 29 thematically important in the essay? Write a brief analysis in which you explain the thematic relevance of each detail in the paragraph.

8. Many cultures make a distinction between women crying and men crying. Write a paragraph in which you explore the reasons for this distinction. Or write one arguing that there should be no difference between the way in which men are viewed when they cry and the way women are viewed.

EXPLORING RHETORIC

1. What is the relevance of Carver's name and nickname to the total essay? What is the significance of the several short sentences in paragraph 1? What is the purpose of the anecdote about Carver's wife's response to the telephone call about his father's death?

2. Why does Carver quote his mother in paragraph 4? Is this more effective than telling in his own words about his father's being drunk when he met his future wife and about his father's later infidelity to her? Why or why not?

3. Note Carver's description of the photograph in paragraph 7. What is the point of the detail that his bonnet is about to come untied? Why does he wonder whether his father was going to or returning from work? Write a description of a photograph of you when you were a small child; provide a context for it, in both time and space. What does the photograph mean to you?

4. Carver writes that his father kept his saws so sharp they could "shave the hair off your arm." How is this different from simply saying that his father sharpened saws during the war?

5. What is the point of the description of toilets in paragraph 10? Would it not have been simpler for Carver merely to have said that when he was a child he was ashamed because his family had an outdoor toilet?

6. Why does Carver pick up the colander and wonder what it would feel like to be hit by it? Why does he say it is heavy as a rolling pin, rather than any other object he might have compared it to?

7. Read paragraph 20 carefully. Notice that the sentences are short and the language simple. Write a stylistic analysis in which you explain what creates the emotional effect of this paragraph.

8. Is the poem in paragraph 29 a mere description of the photograph, or does it add something not in the photograph? Discuss.

9. It is the writer in Carver, not the son, who speaks in paragraph 30, for he explains why he makes a factual change in the poem for a rhetorical purpose. What other details in the poem may have been for rhetorical purposes?

10. How does the last paragraph relate to the opening paragraph and the central thematic paragraph of the essay? Write a brief analysis in which you state the theme of the essay and explain how Carver develops that theme.

My Father's Death

LE LY HAYSLIP

L e Ly Hayslip was born in 1949 in the small village of Ky La near Danang in central Vietnam. Sympathetic to the Vietcong fighting to free Vietnam from outside invaders, she was captured and tortured by South Vietnamese soldiers; when released, she was suspected of being friendly to the enemy and raped by two Vietcong soldiers. As the war become more severe, she went to Danang and later to Saigon and traded in the black market. Eventually she met and married an American soldier and came to the United States. Her autobiography, *When Heaven and Earth Changed Place: A Vietnamese Woman's Journey from War to Peace,* written with the help of Jay Wurts and published in 1990, has been made into a feature film.

In this selection from her autobiography, Le Ly Hayslip describes the various customs and rituals that had to be performed after her father's suicide. In burying her father properly, she says was able to come to terms with many conflicts in her life, concluding, "From my father's death, I had finally learned how to live."

My father's death caused special problems for me, my mother, and my 1 sisters. In addition to being on our own, with no male head of the house to guide us, we wanted to give my father a traditional funeral—despite great odds against it.

First, we had to gain approval from the Republican district officials 2 who regulated activities in the village. Then, we had to secure permission from the Americans, who oversaw all comings and goings in the local area. Finally, we had to submit our plan through Uncle Luc to the Viet Cong, who viewed themselves as the rightful peasant government and who could easily disrupt any gathering and cause great loss of life. We also needed their permission if my mother and myself were to return to Ky La openly without fear of reprisals.

An hour after Chin arrived with word of my father's death, I went to 3 claim my father's body at the Nha Xac morgue. It was a long, low concrete building of such dispiriting coldness that even trees and grass refused to grow outside. Inside, the unmarked bodies were arrayed on stretchers and covered with sheets and flies, bestowing on the place the hellish perfume of rotting flesh that gagged me as I went in.

Gathering all my strength, I made my way down row after row of 4 the dead, uncovering old women and girls and boys and farmers with their heads and arms blown off and vitals blown out but tossed back in with the body so that the victims, as much as possible, would appear to go whole to their graves. After a survey of twenty such corpses I finally found him.

My father's brown face was unnaturally blanched and his purple 5 lips were drawn back from his toothless gums by muscles contracted in death. His eyes were tear-swollen blue slits—as if his soul was still trapped inside and crying for release. I kissed his waxy, stubbly cheek and repeated his name, telling him, "Don't worry; I'm taking you home."

Because I had seen plenty of death in my time, my father's mortal- 6 ity—his change from man to corpse—did not affect me as much as his new inaccessibility. He was now in a place I could not reach and from which he could not visit, except by the weird and tortuous ways of spirits. I regretted I did not know more about how such connections were made and vowed to make it my job to find out.

Because everybody thought I had a head for business, I was chosen 7 to buy the coffin. However, I was in no mood to bargain and going to the first mortician I found, bought the best casket I could afford without questioning the price. I next had to bribe our local policeman, the one we "tipped" sometimes to get extra protection, to deliver me with the funeral clothes and casket to the morgue after curfew so that my father would not have to lie naked on a stretcher.

8   The next day, Uncle Nhu's son, Nu, the Republican officer who helped me when Hung was born, requisitioned a truck to transport my father and the rest of us from Danang to the village. And so we went: my father's casket on a wooden pallet between us with his wife and daughters and assorted aunts and uncles on troop seats along the sides.

9   Compared with our usual, secretive way of coming and going, the dusty drive on the rutted, shell-pocked dirt road seemed almost like a royal return. The spring air was full of blossoms and a sizable crowd had gathered when we finally parked and transferred the coffin into our house. As it was with so many wartime funerals, we had not had the luxury of consulting a wizard for the correct astrological time for transferring my father's body to the coffin or for putting him into the ground. We only knew that we must not bury him under his own or his eldest son's (Bon Nghe's) astrological sign, which would result in the family's destruction within three years or within three generations. We had come close enough to that without the curse of heaven.

10   The pallbearers conveyed my father's casket, feet first, through our home's middle door (which was used only for festivals and funerals), to his bed, which had been covered with white cloth. Each of its four legs had been placed in china dishes which were filled with water and kerosene to keep crawling bugs away. As many of his worldly goods as we could find were lined up between the bed and the wall. Through my father's clenched teeth my mother put the traditional ball of sweet rice (mixed with three coins and a hard-cooked egg—no one wants his beloved to depart for the spirit world poor and hungry), as well as a little sandalwood to keep the body from smelling. With the assistance of my uncles, she wrapped him in the red and white monk's robe that would be his gown for eternity. They also wrapped his hands and feet with cloth so that his bones would stay together in case his body was moved to another cemetery. In this manner he lay in state for two days and one night, so that relatives and friends could come for his funeral.

11   On April 7, Hai, Ba, Lan, and I, dressed correctly in white clothes and no jewelry, put three sticks on incense and two white candles above his pillowed head, then chanted sutras with the Buddhist priest who had been summoned for the occasion. In strict accordance with custom, my mother and sisters and I sat on the floor while the male relatives stood. First we prayed for the Buddha, and then for my father's departed soul—that it should not grieve for us or for leaving its worldly possessions behind. Because we did not have *Cao Vong* silk to catch his spirit while he was dying, we went straight to the *Cao To* ceremony, which in-

forms the soul that the body will be buried properly and that it should not worry. Part of this meant writing my father's name on a scroll with our other ancestors and departed relatives, which included my brother Sau Ban.

When all this was done, it was time to carry my father's coffin to the graveyard. First went the scroll carriers, the youngest children in the family who were capable of that task, and relatives who threw *giay tien dang bac*—paper money—side to side to pay the old ghosts to look after their newest member. Then came the bearers (in this case, my aunts) of sweet rice and cooked pork and tea. After them came the altar carriers and drum players—village men who gave up a morning's labor to help us out—followed by the catafalque, which bore my father, feet first, in the direction of his grave. At the end of the procession came the women—my mother and sisters and me, bowed in homage, shuffling and crying in the dust of all the rest. 12

At the gravesite, our wailing became more formal. From now on, our mourning was solely to show *song goi thac ve*—that we recognized the new spirit life of Phung Trong, husband and father, as he would come to occupy our home. My sisters and I got down on the ground to bring our mourning closer to the earth which held his bones, for we knew his spirit would be pleased by this sign of love and attention to ceremonial detail. As was the custom, all the guests clasped their hands together like Chinese and gave three bows. 13

For the next hundred days, while my father was being judged in the spirit world for taking his own life, we followed the norms of public mourning. Three days after the funeral, we held the "open grave" ceremony (although the grave is still closed) wherein all the family members who could be reached brought incense and flowers to decorate his grave. For the next forty-nine days, we put an extra serving of food at our table and every seventh night prayed with the Buddhist priests that my father's soul should find the nearest temple. 14

On the hundredth day itself, we held the "stop crying" ceremony, which would be followed, on the first anniversary of my father's death, by a memorial service in which we would burn a paper bed, paper clothing, and special funeral money printed for this purpose. Those in my father's immediate family wore the *ao tang* made of linen: a smock with three fringes in the back and an emblem showing our position in the family—in my case, the device of a sixth child who was an unmarried, natural daughter. My mother continuously wore a linen scarf on her head; and I did, too, until it became too cumbersome for business. Life went on, and I knew my father's spirit would not be pleased if my son and mother went hungry because a customer refused to deal with a mourning daughter. No matter how we mourned, though, we made it 15

clear in our hearts (and to others when we helped them) that each chari-
table act we did was in the name of Phung Trong, so that his passage
from hell to heaven would be hastened.

16   In all of these things, my duty was to lead my mother and sisters.
When my father was alive, my mother and Ba and Hai and Lan were
content (indeed, they were required) to leave such rituals to him. When
Bon Nghe went north, my father's remaining son, Sau Ban, received his
instructions in spiritual matters to ensure that the worship of our ancestors and the proper ceremonies of daily life could continue should something happen to our father. Still, my father worried that without his sons
around, he would lack a proper funeral, so he gave his eldest daughter,
Hai, some training too. When sister Hai went to Saigon and Sau Ban was
killed, these duties naturally fell to me—a puny, sixth-born girl—simply
because I was at hand. As things turned out, I was a better student in
these matters than anyone expected.

17   At the end of the hundred days, five Buddhist monks performed a
three-day mass to celebrate my father's release from fear and want, and
to entice his soul back to our house through continuous chanting. (I
learned from my father that if a person dies away from home, his spirit
will roam the countryside until prayers can guide it back.) We knew
these prayers were working because on the second night, a neighbor
woman (the widow of Manh, my old teacher) reported that my father's
ghost had entered her house to tell her about the money and gold he left
buried around our farm. We chanted louder and on the third morning,
the monks were satisfied that my father's spirit had found its way home.

18   Later that day, a wizard called Thay Dong, a spirit teacher from another village, offered himself as a vessel for my father's spirit. This was
necessary because my father died without leaving a will and only a
stranger could act as a medium for the distribution of his property.

19   To give the wizard privacy while this channeling took place, he was
put into a bamboo cage, which we covered with a blanket. To see if his
trance had been successful, some of us walked by and asked if he could
identify us correctly. When he did, we knew his spirit eyes were working
and the ceremony could go forward. We let the wizard out and followed
him to our rice paddies, and our sweet potato and cinnamon fields. With
a long stick, he marked the ground into segments of nearly equal size for
my father's surviving relatives. He also spoke in spirit language of
places where my father had hidden gold and money, but because nobody could translate this clearly into Vietnamese, most of his savings,
what little of it there had been, were never found.

20   Finally, the wizard led us to my father's gravesite (this was really
spooky, because the stranger had no idea where my father was buried)
and spoke to each relative in turn. Because she was the eldest offspring
present, my father (using the medium's voice) commanded my sister

Hai to occupy the family house and tend his shrine and see to the worship of our ancestors. Although Hai knew she couldn't decline my father's last request, she begged his forgiveness because she could not correctly identify all the family graves or remember all the rituals. My father, through Thay, told her not to worry, and recommended my assistance when it was necessary. "In any case," the wizard said, "those duties will pass to your brother Bon Nghe when he returns from the war. Till then, just do the best you can."

This last seemed to exhaust the medium and we knew the time of   21
my father's possession was near an end. The stranger hugged everyone tearfully while thanking them for coming to his funeral, and then bowed politely to the monks. When the man stood up again, my father's spirit had rejoined his ancestors at our family shrine.

Hai returned to our house at once and continued working the land in   22
our father's place. Within a week, a neighbor asked Hai if he could purchase a fruit tree that was on our land. Hai said yes, and sold him the tree for a small sum of money, which she needed badly to repair the house. The next day, however, the man came back and said he had fallen down every time he tried to pick some fruit. He asked if Hai had *xin keo*—consulted our father on the matter—and she replied that she had not—and could not—because he was deceased. The man laughed and showed her how to make requests of the dead by using two coins painted white on one side. If the coins land with one white side showing, the answer is "yes." If both coins land with the same side up, the answer is "no." When the two coins showed her father was in favor of the sale, the man said that was all the answer she needed. He returned to the tree and filled his basket without incident and Hai went on with her work. After that, Hai consulted our father frequently on matters of our family's welfare, for—dead or alive, and certainly for as long as she lived or until Bon Nghe came back—he would still be head of the house.

Once my father was properly buried and his soul dwelled comfortably   23
in our spirit house, I discovered that a good many things had been buried with him. I was no longer confused about where my duty lay—with the Viet Cong? With the legal government and its allies? With the peasants in the countryside? No—my duty lay with my son, and with nurturing life, period. My father taught me this on our hilltop years before as the night of war was falling, but only now was this duty as clear as the morning sun. I no longer had to struggle with myself to achieve it day by day. I had only to live and love and act in concert with those feelings. My father himself had demonstrated this principle many times in his life, most recently when he forgave me for my sin of *chua hoam*—becoming an unwed mother—and embraced my little child to his heart. He

had not been angry at me for bringing new life into the world—far from it! He was angry that I did it in such a way that my child was denied a father. After all, where would I myself be—how long would I have survived a war that claimed so many others—without Phung Trong to guide me? Through him, I learned that although great love alone cannot remove all obstacles, it certainly puts no new ones in the path toward peace: between soldiers, civilians, and between a woman and herself. I saw that a determination to live, no matter what, was more powerful than a willingness to die. Just as the Christians believed Jesus gave his life so that they might live forever, I believed my father's death was his way of giving me eternal peace—not in the hereafter, but for every instant of every day I was alive. Vietnam already had too many people who were ready to die for their beliefs. What it needed was men and women—brothers and sisters—who refused to accept either death or death-dealing as a solution to their problems. If you keep compassion in your heart, I discovered, you never long for death yourself. Death and suffering, not people, become your enemy; and anything that lives is your ally. It was as if, by realizing this, an enormous burden had been lifted from my young shoulders. From my father's death, I had finally learned how to live.

EXPLORING IDEAS

1. Discuss the assumption that the head of household must be male and that women need a male to "guide" the household. Should this assumption be rejected in all cultures or respected in certain cultures?

2. Hayslip says her father's mortality did not affect her as much as his new inaccessibility. Discuss the difference between mortality as an abstract concept and inaccessibility as a concrete reality.

3. There is something incongruous about the necessity of doing practical things, such as picking out a coffin, when someone close has died. If you have ever had such an experience, write a brief description of the experience, trying to communicate this incongruity.

4. Note the cultural importance here of not burying the father under his own or his eldest son's astrological sign. Would you characterize this as a religious or a superstitious belief? What is the difference between these two beliefs? Can you think of similar religious or superstitious beliefs concerning burial from your own cultural or religious background?

5. A number of things are done to prepare the father for his journey to the spirit world. Discuss the incongruity between putting money in the coffin and putting in sandalwood to keep the body from smelling. Write a brief discussion of your own culture's rituals for funeral preparation in which both spiritual and physical things are prepared. For example, in some cultures, the body is prepared with makeup and dressed in the person's best clothes.

6. Why is it important that rituals are followed so "correctly" in funeral ceremonies? Why do they have to be done in a certain way and no other? Write a brief explanation for the importance of "correctness" and attention to detail during funerals.

7. Hayslip writes that the family followed the "norms of public mourning." Why are there certain expectations in societies about how to behave after a family member or other loved one has died? Write a brief narrative description in which you or someone else violated these norms. Try to direct the narrative/description toward the purpose of questioning or reaffirming the importance of these norms.

Exploring Rhetoric

1. What kind of imaginative justification or rhetorical logic underlies the statement that the morgue was so cold and dispiriting that trees and grass "refused to grow outside"?

2. Why does the writer use the expression "covered with sheets and flies"? What is the rhetorical value of the phrase "hellish perfume"? Why is her description of the bodies so graphic and detailed? Why did she not just say "there were many dead bodies"?

3. Hayslip often uses parentheses to insert information. Look particularly at the two sets of parentheses in paragraph 17 and the two in paragraph 20. What kind of information is being inserted? Could it be included without parentheses? What is the effect of so much use of parentheses in this essay?

4. Discuss the significance of the incident in the essay of flipping coins to determine whether something is right. Brainstorm some examples in your own experience of interpreting a chance even as meaningful. Write a brief discussion of these events, exploring why we want to interpret things that "just happen" as things that "happen meaningfully."

5. How would you characterize the style of the language in this essay: formal, informal, elaborate, straightforward? What impression of the character of the narrator does the style communicate?

6. In the last paragraph, Hayslip follows a common essay convention of explaining the meaning of the experience she has described. Read the paragraph carefully and determine how the experience helped her "discover" that many other things were "buried" with her father.

PART TWO

EXPLORING THE
EVERYDAY WORLD

S econd only to the personal experiences of your past, which,
because they are part of your individual memory are the
most accessible subjects for exploring in writing, are the
everyday experiences we have of the world around us. Such
experiences as walking in the woods, shopping in the mall, or
being with friends are not as easy to write about as experiences
of our personal past because we do not possess them in our
mind as we do memories. Moreover, we usually engage in such
experiences without thinking about them; thus, they don't seem
to have much significance for us.

The twelve writers represented in this part have the writer's
habit of paying careful attention to everyday objects and experiences and then writing about them as a way to discover what
they mean. The essays by Annie Dillard, Lewis Thomas, Edward Abbey, and Bill McKibben explore meaning in the natural
world. These writers do more than describe natural events or
scenes; they perceive something significant at work in those
events or scenes.

Larry Woiwode and Peter Schjeldahl find meaning in simple human activities, such as eating an orange or riding a roller
coaster. Although most people might engage in such experiences for their pure physical pleasure, Woiwode and Schjeldahl,

in the manner of writers, try to find significance in them. Phyllis Rose and William Severini Kowinski, in quite different ways, discuss shopping, a common activity, but they do not see shopping as merely going out to buy something and malls as merely convenient places to make such a purchase; rather, they regard shopping as a meaningful human activity and malls as a complex social phenomenon that fulfills a number of subtle purposes. Kenneth Goings explains how common household objects that many Americans once collected are images of a deep-seated racism, while Nancy Masterson Sakamoto describes some basic differences in conversational styles of Japanese and Americans. Finally, Judith Viorst classifies the many types of friends she has, and Margaret Mead and Rhoda Metraux describe different cultural attitudes toward friends.

The key to writing effective essays on everyday objects and activities is to get in the habit of looking at the world carefully and analytically. Writers are not content merely to observe the activity or simply engage in it; rather, they analyze and explore it for its possible significance. Writers often see everything in their experience as possible subjects for examination, analysis, and discussion, for this is the ultimate human way of making sense out of the world.

Untying the Knot

ANNIE DILLARD

Annie Dillard was born in Pittsburgh, Pennsylvania, in 1945. She received her B.A. and her M.A. from Hollins College in 1967 and 1968, respectively. She has been a contributing editor to *Harper's* magazine and has taught English at Western Washington College and Wesleyan University. Her personal observations about the natural world, *Pilgrim at Tinker Creek*, 1974, won the Pulitzer Prize for general nonfiction. Her other books include a collection of poems, *Tickets for a Prayer Wheel*, 1974; two books of literary criticism, *Living by Fiction*, 1982, and *Conversations with Chinese Writers*, 1984; a prose poem, *Holy the Firm*, 1978; a collection of essays, *Teaching a Stone to Talk*, 1982; a memoir, *An American Childhood*, 1987; a book about the writing process, *The Writing Life*, 1989; and a novel, *The Living*, 1993.

In this meditative essay, Dillard describes finding a snakeskin tied in what seems like an endless knot that defies untying. The skin becomes the stimulus for Dillard's thoughts on the mysterious unending loop of time—that constantly repeating spirit that rolls through life like some divine wheel of fire.

Yesterday I set out to catch the new season, and instead I found an old 1 snakeskin. I was in the sunny February woods by the quarry; the snakeskin was lying in a heap of leaves right next to an aquarium someone had thrown away. I don't know why that someone hauled the aquarium deep into the woods to get rid of it; it had only one broken glass side. The snake found it handy, I imagine; snakes like to rub against something rigid to help them out of their skins, and the broken aquarium looked like the nearest likely object. Together the snakeskin and the aquarium made an interesting scene on the forest floor. It looked like an exhibit at a trial—circumstantial evidence—of a wild scene, as though a snake had burst through the broken side of the aquarium, burst through his ugly old skin, and disappeared, perhaps straight up in the air, in a rush of freedom and beauty.

The snakeskin had unkeeled scales, so it belonged to a nonpoiso- 2 nous snake. It was roughly five feet long by the yardstick, but I'm not sure because it was very wrinkled and dry, and every time I tried to stretch it flat it broke. I ended up with seven or eight pieces of it all over the kitchen table in a fine film of forest dust.

The point I want to make about the snakeskin is that, when I found 3 it, it was whole and tied in a knot. Now there have been stories told, even by reputable scientists, of snakes that have deliberately tied themselves in a knot to prevent larger snakes from trying to swallow them— but I couldn't imagine any way that throwing itself into a half hitch would help a snake trying to escape its skin. Still, ever cautious, I figured that one of the neighborhood boys could possibly have tied it in a knot in the fall, for some whimsical boyish reason, and left it there, where it dried and gathered dust. So I carried the skin along thoughtlessly as I walked, snagging it sure enough on a low branch and ripping it in two for the first of many times. I saw that thick ice still lay on the quarry pond and that the skunk cabbage was already out in the clearings, and then I came home and looked at the skin and its knot.

4   The knot had no beginning. Idly I turned it around in my hand, searching for a place to untie; I came to with a start when I realized I must have turned the thing around fully ten times. Intently, then, I traced the knot's lump around with a finger: it was continuous. I couldn't untie it any more than I could untie a doughnut; it was a loop without beginning or end. These snakes *are* magic, I thought for a second, and then of course I reasoned what must have happened. The skin had been pulled inside-out like a peeled sock for several inches; then an inch or so of the inside-out part—a piece whose length was coincidentally equal to the diameter of the skin—had somehow been turned right-side out again, making a thick lump whose edges were lost in wrinkles, looking exactly like a knot.

5   So. I have been thinking about the change of seasons. I don't want to miss spring this year. I want to distinguish the last winter frost from the out-of-season one, the frost of spring. I want to be there on the spot the moment the grass turns green. I always miss this radical revolution; I see it the next day from a window, the yard so suddenly green and lush I could envy Nebuchadnezzar down on all fours eating grass. This year I want to stick a net into time and say "now," as men plant flags on the ice and snow and say, "here." But it occurred to me that I could no more catch spring by the tip of the tail than I could untie the apparent knot in the snakeskin; there are no edges to grasp. Both are continuous loops.

6   I wonder how long it would take you to notice the regular recurrence of the seasons if you were the first man on earth. What would it be like to live in open-ended time broken only by days and nights? You could say, "it's cold again; it was cold before," but you couldn't make the key connection and say, "it was cold this time last year," because the notion of "year" is precisely the one you lack. Assuming that you hadn't yet noticed any orderly progression of heavenly bodies, how long would you have to live on earth before you could feel with any assurance that any one particular long period of cold would, in fact, end? "While the earth remaineth, seedtime and harvest, and cold and heat, and summer and winter, and day and night shall not cease": God makes this guarantee very early in Genesis to a people whose fears on this point had perhaps not been completely allayed.

It must have been fantastically important, at the real beginnings of 7 human culture, to conserve and relay this vital seasonal information, so that the people could anticipate dry or cold seasons, and not huddle on some November rock hoping pathetically that spring was just around the corner. We still very much stress the simple fact of four seasons to schoolchildren; even the most modern of modern new teachers, who don't seem to care if their charges can read or write or name two products of Peru, will still muster some seasonal chitchat and set the kids to making paper pumpkins, or tulips, for the walls. "The people," wrote Van Gogh in a letter, "are very sensitive to the changing seasons." That we are "very sensitive to the changing seasons" is, incidentally, one of the few good reasons to shun travel. If I stay at home I preserve the illusion that what is happening on Tinker Creek is the very newest thing, that I'm at the very vanguard and cutting edge of each new season. I don't want the same season twice in a row; I don't want to know I'm getting last week's weather, used weather, weather broadcast up and down the coast, old-hat weather.

But there's always unseasonable weather. What we think of the 8 weather and behavior of life on the planet at any given season is really all a matter of statistical probabilities; at any given point, anything might happen. There is a bit of every season in each season. Green plants—deciduous green leaves—grow everywhere, all winter long, and small shoots come up pale and new in every season. Leaves die on the tree in May, turn brown, and fall into the creek. The calendar, the weather, and the behavior of wild creatures have the slimmest of connections. Everything overlaps smoothly for only a few weeks each season, and then it all tangles up again. The temperature, of course, lags far behind the calendar seasons, since the earth absorbs and releases heat slowly, like a leviathan breathing. Migrating birds head south in what appears to be dire panic, leaving mild weather and fields full of insects and seeds; they reappear as if in all eagerness in January, and poke about morosely in the snow. Several years ago our October woods would have made a dismal colored photograph for a sadist's calendar: a killing frost came before the leaves had even begun to brown; they drooped from every tree like crepe, blackened and limp. It's all a chancy, jumbled affair at best, as things seem to be below the stars.

Time is the continuous loop, the snakeskin with scales endlessly 9 overlapping without beginning or end, or time is an ascending spiral if you will, like a child's toy Slinky. Of course we have no idea which arc on the loop is our time, let alone where the loop itself is, so to speak, or down whose lofty flight of stairs the Slinky so uncannily walks.

The power we seek, too, seems to be a continuous loop. I have al- 10 ways been sympathetic with the early notion of a divine power that exists in a particular place, or that travels about over the face of the earth as a man might wander—and when he is "there" he is surely not here. You can shake the hand of a man you meet in the woods; but the spirit seems to roll along like the mythical hoop snake with its tail in its mouth. There are no hands to shake or edges to untie. It rolls along the mountain ridges like a fireball, shooting off a spray of sparks at random, and will not be trapped, slowed, grasped, fetched, peeled, or aimed. "As for the wheels, it was cried unto them in my hearing, O wheel." This is the hoop of flame that shoots the rapids in the creek or spins across the dizzy meadows; this is the arsonist of the sunny woods: catch it if you can.

EXPLORING IDEAS

1. Dillard says the snakeskin and the aquarium make an interesting scene, like circumstantial evidence at a trial. Then she reconstructs what might have happened based on this evidence. Discuss other examples of the human need to determine the circumstances of a past event by looking at the results. Or write about an experience when you had to reconstruct an event by examining the evidence that remained.

2. Dillard says she cannot untie the knot, for it seems to have no beginning or end. Knots are often used as metaphors for complex problems that are hard to solve. Try to recall an experience in your own life that was like a knot. Describe what made the knot so complex and how you managed to unravel it.

3. As Dillard looks at the knot, she thinks, "These snakes *are* magic"; then she "reasons" what must have happened. Try to recall some thing or event you have seen that at first seemed to be magic but for which, on reflection, you developed a natural or logical explanation. Describe the experience, and explain its point.

4. Dillard says we still stress the fact of four seasons to schoolchildren. Try to recall how the seasons were marked in elementary schoolrooms when you were a child. Reveal some point about this practice in your essay.

5. Dillard says there is a bit of every season in each season and that everything overlaps and tangles up again. What point does Dillard make about "unseasonable weather"? Write a brief essay about some "unseasonable" weather you have experienced. How did it affect you?

6. Dillard says time is an ascending spiral, like a child's toy Slinky. Brainstorm some other metaphors for time, and explain how they reflect aspects of time.

7. Explain what Dillard means by the following sentence: "You can shake the hand of a man you meet in the woods; but the spirit seems to roll along like the mythical hoop snake with its tail in its mouth." What spirit is she talking about? Brainstorm some other metaphors for this spirit or power Dillard says we seek.

EXPLORING RHETORIC

1. Gilbert Highet, in his essay in Part One on how to write an essay, says the first sentence of this form of writing is very important. Discuss the effectiveness of

Dillard's first sentence: "Yesterday I set out to catch the new season, and instead I found an old snakeskin."

2. Dillard begins paragraph 3, "The point I want to make about the snakeskin is that, when I found it, it was whole and tied in a knot." Why does she feel she has to make a point? Does the rest of the essay center around this point?

3. Why does Dillard describe the thick ice that still lies on the quarry pond and the skunk cabbage that is already out in the clearings? How are these details relevant to her overall point?

4. Read Dillard's description in paragraph 4 of how the knot came to be. Can you visualize the process? Try to describe it another way. What is the relevance of the fact that it was not a knot at all, only something that looked like a knot?

5. Note the shift in paragraph 5: "So. I have been thinking about the change of seasons." Is this shift abrupt, or does it make sense within the overall purpose of the essay?

6. In the Old Testament Book of Daniel, Nebuchadnezzar is humbled by God for his boasting by being driven mad and made to live in the fields and eat grass. Why does Dillard use this reference? How is it relevant to her overall purpose?

7. Dillard makes the relevance of the snakeskin knot to her main point explicit in paragraph 5 when she says that spring is like the knot: neither has edges, and both are continuous loops. How is this perception related to her metaphor: "This year I want to stick a net into time and say 'now,' as men plant flags on the ice and snow and say, 'here' "?

8. Discuss the effectiveness of the metaphors in the following passages:

> "The earth absorbs and releases heat slowly, like a leviathan breathing."
> "Several years ago our October woods would have made a dismal colored photograph for a sadist's calendar."
> "The leaves drooped from every tree like crepe, blackened and limp."

The Tucson Zoo

LEWIS THOMAS

L ewis Thomas was born in 1913 in Flushing, New York. He received his education at Princeton University and Harvard Medical School. He held many different positions, including dean of the School of Medicine at New York University and Yale University and president of the Sloane-Kettering Cancer Center. He began writing a monthly column about science for the *New England Journal of Medicine* called "Notes of a Biology Watcher" in 1971; when these were collected and published as *Lives of a Cell* in 1974, the book won the National Book Award for Arts and Letters and became a best-seller. Thomas also published three more essay collections: *The Medusa and the Snail: More Notes of a Biology Watcher,* 1979; *Late Night Thoughts on Listening to Mahler's Ninth Symphony,* 1983; and *Etcetera, Etcetera,* 1990. His book *The Youngest Science,*

1983, is an autobiography focusing on medicine and medical research. His last book, *A Long Line of Cells: Collected Essays,* was published in 1990. Thomas died in 1993.

Observing beavers and otters in the Tucson Zoo, Lewis Thomas learns something about himself and perhaps about all animals: that we are genetically coded to respond to each other with a "surprised affection." Altruism, not animosity, may be our most primitive attribute, says Thomas. Left to ourselves, "we hanker for friends."

1   Science gets most of its information by the process of reductionism, exploring the details, then the details of the details, until all the smallest bits of the structure, or the smallest parts of the mechanism, are laid out for counting and scrutiny. Only when this is done can the investigation be extended to encompass the whole organism or the entire system. So we say.

2   Sometimes it seems that we take a loss, working this way. Much of today's public anxiety about science is the apprehension that we may forever be overlooking the whole by an endless, obsessive preoccupation with the parts. I had a brief, personal experience of this misgiving one afternoon in Tucson, where I had time on my hands and visited the zoo, just outside the city. The designers there have cut a deep pathway between two small artificial ponds, walled by clear glass, so when you stand in the center of the path you can look into the depths of each pool, and at the same time you can regard the surface. In one pool, on the right side of the path, is a family of otters; on the other side, a family of beavers. Within just a few feet from your face, on either side, beavers and otters are at play, underwater and on the surface, swimming toward your face and then away, more filled with life than any creatures I have ever seen before, in all my days. Except for the glass, you could reach across and touch them.

3   I was transfixed. As I now recall it, there was only one sensation in my head: pure elation mixed with amazement at such perfection. Swept off my feet, I floated from one side to the other, swiveling my brain, staring astounded at the beavers, then at the otters. I could hear shouts across my corpus callosum, from one hemisphere to the other. I remember thinking, with what was left in charge of my consciousness, that I wanted no part of the science of beavers and otters; I wanted never to know how they performed their marvels; I wished for no news about the physiology of their breathing, the coordination of their muscles, their vision, their endocrine systems, their digestive tracts. I hoped never to have to think of them as collections of cells. All I asked for was the full hairy complexity, then in front of my eyes, of whole, intact beavers and otters in motion.

It lasted, I regret to say, for only a few minutes, and then I was back 4 in the late twentieth century, reductionist as ever, wondering about the details by force of habit, but not, this time, the details of otters and beavers. Instead, me. Something worth remembering had happened in my mind, I was certain of that; I would have put it somewhere in the brain stem; maybe this was my limbic system at work. I became a behavioral scientist, an experimental psychologist, an ethologist, and in the instant I lost all the wonder and the sense of being overwhelmed. I was flattened.

But I came away from the zoo with something, a piece of news about 5 myself: I am coded, somehow, for otters and beavers. I exhibit instinctive behavior in their presence, when they are displayed close at hand behind glass, simultaneously below water and at the surface. I have receptors for this display. Beavers and otters possess a "releaser" for me, in the terminology of ethology, and the releasing was my experience. What was released? Behavior. What behavior? Standing, swiveling flabbergasted, feeling exultation and a rush of friendship. I could not, as the result of the transaction, tell you anything more about beavers and otters than you already know. I learned nothing new about them. Only about me, and I suspect also about you, maybe about human beings at large: we are endowed with genes which code out our reaction to beavers and otters, maybe our reaction to each other as well. We are stamped with stereotyped, unalterable patterns of response, ready to be released. And the behavior released in us, by such confrontations, is, essentially, a surprised affection. It is compulsory behavior and we can avoid it only by straining with the full power of our conscious minds, making up conscious excuses all the way. Left to ourselves, mechanistic and autonomic, we hanker for friends.

Everyone says, stay away from ants. They have no lessons for 6 us; they are crazy little instruments, inhuman, incapable of controlling themselves, lacking manners, lacking souls. When they are massed together, all touching, exchanging bits of information held in their jaws like memoranda, they become a single animal. Look out for that. It is a debasement, a loss of individuality, a violation of human nature, an unnatural act.

Sometimes people argue this point of view seriously and with deep 7 thought. Be individuals, solitary and selfish, is the message. Altruism, a jargon word for what used to be called love, is worse than weakness, it is sin, a violation of nature. Be separate. Do not be a social animal. But this is a hard argument to make convincingly when you have to depend on language to make it. You have to print up leaflets or publish books and get them bought and sent around, you have to turn up on television and catch the attention of millions of other human beings all at once, and then you have to say to all of them, all at once, all collected and paying attention: be solitary; do not depend on each other. You can't do this and keep a straight face.

8   Maybe altruism is our most primitive attribute, out of reach, beyond our control. Or perhaps it is immediately at hand, waiting to be released, disguised now, in our kind of civilization, as affection or friendship or attachment. I don't see why it should be unreasonable for all human beings to have strands of DNA coiled up in chromosomes, coding out instincts for usefulness and helpfulness. Usefulness may turn out to be the hardest test of fitness for survival, more important than aggression, more effective, in the long run, than grabbiness. If this is the sort of information biological science holds for the future, applying to us as well as to ants, then I am all for science.

9   One thing I'd like to know most of all: when those ants have made the Hill, and are all there, touching and exchanging, and the whole mass begins to behave like a single huge creature, and *thinks,* what on earth is that thought? And while you're at it, I'd like to know a second thing: when it happens, does any single ant know about it? Does his hair stand on end?

EXPLORING IDEAS

1. What is the difference between looking at the whole and looking at the parts of something? What difference does it make whether you begin with an overall impression or with a careful analysis of the parts?

2. Write a definition of the word "play." Describe the difference between play for humans and play for other mammals you have observed, such as cats or dogs.

3. What does it mean to be "filled with life"? Write a character sketch about someone you know or have read about who is "filled with life."

4. Brainstorm about an experience that you wanted to "feel" rather than "know about." Explain why you sought a sensation. How can you describe an experience that you feel but can't know about?

5. Is it necessarily true that if you become a behavioral scientist or a psychologist, you lose all the wonder of experience? Read the essay by Bill McKibben elsewhere in Part Two for a different point of view.

6. Brainstorm for an essay on the following topic: "Alone or in a group: When are you most human? When are you most yourself?"

7. Thomas suggests that altruism may be our most primitive attribute. Compare this thought with the assumption that selfishness is our most primitive attribute.

8. Write an essay using the following thesis sentence: "Usefulness may turn out to be the hardest test of fitness for survival, more important than aggression, more effective, in the long run, than grabbiness."

EXPLORING RHETORIC

1. Why does Thomas begin with a statement about how science gets information rather than with the anecdote about the zoo? Why does he end paragraph 1 with the sentence, "So we say"?

2. Very early in the essay, Thomas tells the reader that the personal experience he is going to write about is meant to illustrate a misgiving he has about the way science gets information. Brainstorm for an essay in which you recall (or invent) a personal experience that illustrates the validity of the way science gets information.

3. Why does Thomas say he could hear "shouts across his corpus callosum"? Why does he say he was "transfixed," "swept off his feet," "floating"? Are these exaggerations? Brainstorm for an essay in which you describe an experience of being transfixed.

4. Why does Thomas say he was "coded" for otters, that he has "receptors" for this display, and that beavers and otters possess a "releaser" for him? Why does he use this kind of language?

5. Why does Thomas use ants as an example? Find and read the fable "The Grasshopper and the Ants." Compare it with Thomas's example of the ants.

6. Why does Thomas end paragraph 7 with the sentence, "You can't do this and keep a straight face"?

7. By what rhetorical means does Thomas move from his initial misgivings about the methods of science to a final affirmation of the methods of science?

8. Discuss the effectiveness of Thomas's conclusion. What makes him believe that when the ants begin to behave like a single creature, they will think? Why does he say he wants to know what the thought is? What are the implications of the final question: "Does his hair stand on end?"

Come on In

EDWARD ABBEY

Edward Abbey was born in Pennsylvania in 1926. He worked for the National Park Service and the U.S. Forest Service. His books, primarily collections of his essays, include *Desert Solitaire*, 1968; *Cactus Country*, 1973; *Abbey's Road*, 1979; *Down the River*, 1982; *Slumgullion Stew: An Edward Abbey Reader*, 1984; *The Fool's Progress*, 1988; and *One Life at a Time, Please*, 1988. He also wrote a novel, *The Monkey Wrench Gang*, 1976, about a group of environmentalists who plot to blow up Arizona's Glen Canyon Dam. He died in 1989.

As the title of the following essay suggests, Abbey invites the reader to join him in the awe-inspiring appreciation and understanding of the Colorado

Plateau, a task that he says requires a combination of the close analysis of the scientist and the sense of wonder of the poet.

1   The canyon country of southern Utah and northern Arizona—the Colorado Plateau—is something special. Something strange, marvelous, full of wonders. As far as I know there is no other region on earth much like it, or even remotely like it. Nowhere else have we had this lucky combination of vast sedimentary rock formations exposed to a desert climate, a great plateau carved by major rivers—the Green, the San Juan, the Colorado—into such a surreal land of form and color. Add a few volcanoes, the standing necks of which can still be seen, and cinder cones and lava flows, and at least four separate laccolithic mountain ranges nicely distributed about the region, and more hills, holes, humps and hollows, reefs, folds, salt domes, swells and grabens, buttes, benches and mesas, synclines, monoclines, and anticlines than you can ever hope to see and explore in one lifetime, and you begin to arrive at an approximate picture of the plateau's surface appearance.

2   An approximate beginning. A picture framed by sky and time in the world of natural appearances. Despite the best efforts of a small army of writers, painters, photographers, scientists, explorers, Indians, cowboys, and wilderness guides, the landscape of the Colorado Plateau lies still beyond the reach of reasonable words. Or unreasonable representation. This is a landscape that has to be seen to be believed, and even then, confronted directly by the senses, it strains credulity.

3   Comprehensible, yes. Perhaps nowhere is the basic structure of the earth's surface so clearly, because so nakedly, revealed. And yet—when all we know about it is said and measured and tabulated, there remains something in the soul of the place, the spirit of the whole, that cannot be fully assimilated by the human imagination.

4   My terminology is far from exact; certainly not scientific. Words like "soul" and "spirit" make vague substitutes for a hard effort toward understanding. But I can offer no better. The land here is like a great book or a great symphony; it invites approaches toward comprehension on many levels, from all directions.

5   The geologic approach is certainly primary and fundamental, underlying the attitude and outlook that best support all others, including the insights of poetry and the wisdom of religion. Just as the earth itself forms the indispensable ground for the only kind of life we know, providing the sole sustenance of our minds and bodies, so does empirical truth constitute the foundation of higher truths. (If there is such a thing as higher truth.) It seems to me that Keats was wrong when he asked, rhetorically, "Do not all charms fly . . . at the mere touch of cold philosophy?" The word "philosophy" standing, in his day, for what we now call

"physical science." But Keats was wrong, I say, because there is more charm in one "mere" fact, confirmed by test and observation, linked to other facts through coherent theory into a rational system, than in a whole brainful of fancy and fantasy. I see more poetry in a chunk of quartzite than in a make-believe wood nymph, more beauty in the revelations of a verifiable intellectual construction than in whole misty empires of obsolete mythology.

The moral I labor toward is that a landscape as splendid as that of 6 the Colorado Plateau can best be understood and given human significance by poets who have their feet planted in concrete—concrete data— and by scientists whose heads and hearts have not lost the capacity for wonder. Any good poet, in our age at least, must begin with the scientific view of the world; and any scientist worth listening to must be something of a poet, must possess the ability to communicate to the rest of us his sense of love and wonder at what his work discovers.

The canyon country does not always inspire love. To many it appears barren, hostile, repellent—a fearsome land of rock and heat, sand dunes and quicksand, cactus, thornbush, scorpion, rattlesnake, and agoraphobic distances. To those who see our land in that manner, the best reply is, yes, you are right, it is a dangerous and terrible place. Enter at your own risk. Carry water. Avoid the noonday sun. Try to ignore the vultures. Pray frequently.

For a few others the canyon country is worth only what they can dig 8 out of it and haul away—to the mills, to the power plants, to the bank.

For more and more of those who now live here, however, the great 9 plateau and its canyon wilderness is a treasure best enjoyed through the body and spirit, *in situ* as the archeologists say, not through commercial plunder. It is a regional, national and international treasure too valuable to be sacrificed for temporary gain, too rare to be withheld from our children. For us the wilderness and human emptiness of this land is not a source of fear but the greatest of its attractions. We would guard and defend and save it as a place for all who wish to rediscover the nearly lost pleasures of adventure, adventure not only in the physical sense, but also mental, spiritual, moral, aesthetic and intellectual adventure. A place for the free.

Here you may yet find the elemental freedom to breathe deep of un- 10 poisoned air, to experiment with solitude and stillness, to gaze through a hundred miles of untrammeled atmosphere, across redrock canyons, beyond blue mesas, toward the snow-covered peaks of the most distant mountains—to make the discovery of the self in its proud sufficiency which is not isolation but an irreplaceable part of the mystery of the whole.

Come on in. The earth, like the sun, like the air, belongs to everyone— 11 and to no one.

EXPLORING IDEAS

1. Abbey opens his essay by calling the Colorado Plateau "strange, marvelous, full of wonders"—terms that suggest something supernatural. Brainstorm for an essay about your own sense of something magical or supernatural about a natural scene or a geographic area.

2. Abbey says the Colorado Plateau lies beyond the reach of "reasonable words" and "unreasonable representation"—that it is a landscape that has to be seen to be believed. Is it possible that poets and painters can "capture" that which others cannot? Do poets use "unreasonable" words?

3. Abbey says that even when you see the Colorado Plateau, it strains credulity. Have you ever had the experience in which you felt, "I see it, but I still don't believe it"? Try describing that experience, explaining why it made you feel this way.

4. Abbey suggests that even when everything about the area is measured, tabulated, and analyzed, there remains something that the human imagination cannot assimilate. What does the word "assimilate" mean in this context? Is this the same experience of elation that Lewis Thomas describes in the previous essay on the Tucson Zoo?

5. Writers often talk about the "spirit" or "soul" of a place. What do they mean? Brainstorm for an essay in which you describe a place that seems to have a spirit or soul.

6. Abbey says that to understand the Colorado Plateau and give it human significance requires both science and poetry. What does he mean? Brainstorm the basic differences between science and poetry. Do these differences make them incompatible with each other? Brainstorm basic similarities between science and poetry.

7. How can a mere landscape inspire fear? Brainstorm some natural phenomena that inspire fear. Explain how they do so. Write a personal experience essay about being afraid of a natural phenomenon (e.g., an earthquake, a storm, mountains, the desert, the sea).

EXPLORING RHETORIC

1. What effect does Abbey's use of geologic terms (with which most readers will not be familiar) have? Why does he use such terms?

2. Discuss the effectiveness of Abbey's metaphors of the Colorado Plateau as a "picture framed by sky and time," "a great book," or a "great symphony." Why does he use these comparisons to artworks?

3. Discuss the effectiveness of Abbey's comparison between the earth as the ground for the only life we know and empirical truth as the foundation of higher truth. Does this comparison hold up?

4. Why does Abbey quote the English romantic poet John Keats? Is Abbey using the term "poetry" in the same way that Keats used it? What does Abbey mean by the term "poetry" when he says, "I see more poetry in a chunk of quartzite than in a make-believe wood nymph"?

5. Why does Abbey use the term "moral" instead of "point" or "idea" when he says, "The moral I labor toward . . ."?

6. Why does Abbey use the following language in paragraph 7: "Enter at your own risk. Carry water. Avoid the noonday sun. Try to ignore the vultures. Pray frequently"? What tone does this language suggest? What effect does it have on the reader?

7. Analyze the sentence style of paragraph 9. Point out the examples of parallelism and balance in the paragraph.

8. Explain how the series of parallel phrases in paragraph 10 lead up to the invitation in paragraph 11. Discuss the effectiveness of Abbey's conclusion.

The End of Nature

BILL MCKIBBEN

B ill McKibben was born in Palo Alto, California, in 1960. After receiving his B.A. from Harvard University in 1982, he became a staff writer and later an editor for the *New Yorker* magazine. His book, *The End of Nature*, 1990, for which the following selection is the title essay, laments the loss of nature as an untouched wilderness. McKibben argues that the very idea of nature as a world apart from the world of human beings is in danger of extinction.

Almost every day, I hike up the hill out my back door. Within a hundred yards the woods swallows me up, and there is nothing to remind me of human society—no trash, no stumps, no fence, not even a real path. Looking out from the high places, you can't see road or house; it is a world apart from man. But once in a while someone will be cutting wood farther down the valley, and the snarl of a chain saw will fill the woods. It is harder on those days to get caught up in the timeless meaning of the forest, for man is nearby. The sound of the chain saw doesn't blot out all the noises of the forest or drive the animals away, but it does drive away the feeling that you are in another, separate, timeless, wild sphere.

Now that we have changed the most basic forces around us, the noise of that chain saw will always be in the woods. We have changed the atmosphere, and that will change the weather. The temperature and rainfall are no longer to be entirely the work of some separate, uncivilizable force, but instead in part a product of our habits, our economies, our ways of life. Even in the most remote wilderness, where the strictest laws forbid the felling of a single tree, the sound of that saw will be clear, and a walk in the woods will be changed—tainted—by its whine. The world outdoors will mean much the same thing as the world indoors, the hill the same thing as the house.

3   An idea, a relationship, can go extinct, just like an animal or a plant. The idea in this case is "nature," the separate and wild province, the world apart from man to which he adapted, under whose rules he was born and died. In the past, we spoiled and polluted parts of that nature, inflicted environmental "damage." But that was like stabbing a man with toothpicks: though it hurt, annoyed, degraded, it did not touch vital organs, block the path of the lymph or blood. We never thought that we had wrecked nature. Deep down, we never really thought we could: it was too big and too old; its forces—the wind, the rain, the sun—were too strong, too elemental.

4   But, quite by accident, it turned out that the carbon dioxide and other gases we were producing in our pursuit of a better life—in pursuit of warm houses and eternal economic growth and of agriculture so productive it would free most of us from farming—*could* alter the power of the sun, could increase its heat. And that increase *could* change the patterns of moisture and dryness, breed storms in new places, breed deserts. Those things may or may not have yet begun to happen, but it is too late to altogether prevent them from happening. We have produced the carbon dioxide—we are ending nature.

5   We have not ended rainfall or sunlight; in fact, rainfall and sunlight may become more important forces in our lives. It is too early to tell exactly how much harder the wind will blow, how much hotter the sun will shine. That is for the future. But the *meaning* of the wind, the sun, the rain—of nature—has already changed. Yes, the wind still blows—but no longer from some other sphere, some inhuman place.

6   In the summer, my wife and I bike down to the lake nearly every afternoon for a swim. It is a dogleg Adirondack lake, with three beaver lodges, a blue heron, some otter, a family of mergansers, the occasional loon. A few summer houses cluster at one end, but mostly it is surrounded by wild state land. During the week we swim across and back, a trip of maybe forty minutes—plenty of time to forget everything but the feel of the water around your body and the rippling, muscular joy of a hard kick and the pull of your arms.

7   But on the weekends, more and more often, someone will bring a boat out for waterskiing, and make pass after pass up and down the lake. And then the whole experience changes, changes entirely. Instead of being able to forget everything but yourself, and even yourself except for the muscles and the skin, you must be alert, looking up every dozen strokes to see where the boat is, thinking about what you will do if it comes near. It is not so much the danger—few swimmers, I imagine,

ever die by Evinrude. It's not even so much the blue smoke that hangs low over the water. It's that the motorboat gets in your mind. You're forced to think, not feel—to think of human society and of people. The lake is utterly different on these days, just as the planet is utterly different now.

EXPLORING IDEAS

1. Why is it harder for McKibben to "get caught up in the timeless meaning of the forest" when people are about? Aren't people as mysterious and timeless as the forest? Brainstorm for an essay about the basic difference between humans and nature, as well as the basic similarities between humans and nature. If humans are not a part of nature, then what are they?

2. McKibben says that the sound of the chain saw does not blot out the "noises of the forest"; rather, it drives away the feeling that one is in another, separate, timeless wild sphere. What is important about being in such a sphere? What effect do the "noises of the forest" have? Why do some people buy tapes of natural sounds, such as wind in the trees or water flowing in a mountain stream?

3. What are the implications of McKibben's statement that temperature and rainfall will no longer be the work of some separate, uncivilizable force but rather a product of our way of life? Does he mean that humans should not try to control the weather or that human activity is having a dangerous effect on the weather?

4. McKibben says that nature is an idea that can die. In what way is nature an idea rather than a physical entity? Brainstorm for an essay in which you explain how nature is an idea.

5. McKibben seems to suggest that there is a basic difference between nature and society, between life indoors and life outdoors. Brainstorm for an essay on this topic. Because the topic is so broad and general, be sure to develop some specific details to support your contrast.

6. McKibben complains that the motorboat on the lake spoils his experience because he is unable to forget everything but the muscles and skin of the self. Is this why people like to go on vacations in natural surroundings—to forget that they are human beings in a society and to act as if they are part of their natural surroundings? Brainstorm this idea for an essay.

EXPLORING RHETORIC

1. Discuss the effectiveness of the metaphor in "the woods swallows me up." How is this different from "I go into the woods" or "I disappear into the woods"?

2. What does McKibben mean when he says that even in woods where the strictest laws forbid cutting trees, "the sound of that saw will be clear, and a walk in the woods will be changed—tainted—by its whine"? Is he speaking literally or metaphorically? Is this an exaggeration? Haven't humans in America always been dependent on lumber? What's the difference between hearing a power saw in the woods and hearing an axe in the woods?

3. Discuss the effectiveness of the metaphor in the following sentence: "But that was like stabbing a man with toothpicks." How is this metaphor appropriate for the subject and the tone of McKibben's essay?

4. Is McKibben exaggerating when he says "we are ending nature"? What does he mean by this statement?

5. Explain what McKibben means when he says that although we are not ending rainfall or sunlight, we are ending the meaning of the wind, the sun, the rain? Why is it important that these things come from some "inhuman" place? What is wrong with these phenomena being created or influenced by humans?

6. Why does McKibben end his essay with another anecdote or personal experience? Why does he never provide facts and statistics about how human beings are influencing the atmosphere? Is the fact that there are motorboats on the lake a powerful support for McKibben's central point, or is it a trivial one?

Wanting an Orange

LARRY WOIWODE

L arry Woiwode was born in 1941 in Carrington, North Dakota. A freelance writer, his books include: *What I'm Going to Do, I Think,* 1969; *Beyond the Bedroom Wall: A Family Album,* 1975; and *Poppa John,* 1981. He has also published stories, poems, and essays in the *New Yorker,* the *Atlantic Monthly,* and the *New York Times.* In the brief essay that follows, Woiwode demonstrates that even the simplest and most familiar act—such as eating an orange—can become vivid, fresh, and significant if it is observed carefully, engaged in actively, and described in precise detail.

1 Oh, those oranges arriving in the midst of the North Dakota winters of the forties—the mere color of them, carried through the door in a net bag or a crate from out of the white, winter landscape. Their appearance was enough to set my brother and me to thinking that it might be about time to develop an illness, which was the surest way of receiving a steady supply of them.

2   "Mom, we think we're getting a cold."

3   "*We?* You mean, you two want an orange?"

4   This was difficult for us to answer or dispute; the matter seemed moved beyond our mere wanting.

5   "If you want an orange," she would say, "why don't you ask for one?"

"We want an orange."   6

" 'We' again. *'We want an orange.'* "   7

"May we have an orange, please."   8

"That's the way you know I like you to ask for one. Now, why don't   9
each of you ask for one in that same way, but separately?"

"Mom . . ." And so on. There was no depth of degradation that we   10
wouldn't descend to in order to get one. If the oranges hadn't wended
their way northward by Thanksgiving, they were sure to arrive before
the Christmas season, stacked first in crates at the depot, filling that
musty place, where pews sat back to back, with a springtime acidity, as if
the building had been rinsed with a renewing elixir which set it right for
yet another year. Then the crates would appear at the local grocery store,
often with the top slats pried back on a few of them, so that we were
aware of a resinous smell of fresh wood, in addition to the already
orangy atmosphere that foretold the season more explicitly than any
calendar.

And in the broken-open crates (as if burst by the power of the or-   11
anges themselves), one or two of the lovely spheres would lie free of the
tissue they came wrapped in—always purple tissue, as if that were the
only color that could contain the populations of them in their nestled positions. The crates bore paper labels at one end—of an orange against a
blue background, or of a blue goose against an orange background—
signifying the colorful otherworld (unlike our wintry one) that these
phenomena had arisen from. Each orange, stripped of its protective
wrapping, as vivid in your vision as a pebbled sun, encouraged you to
picture a whole pyramid like this in a bowl on your dining room table,
glowing in the light, as if giving off the warmth that came through the
windows from the real winter sun. And all of them came stamped with a
blue-purple name as foreign as the otherworld that you might imagine
as their place of origin, so that on Christmas day you would find yourself digging past everything else in your Christmas stocking, as if tun-
neling down to the country of China, in order to reach the rounded
bulge at the tip of the toe which meant that you had received a personal
reminder of another state of existence, wholly separate from your own.

The packed heft and texture, finally, of an orange in your hand—this   12
is it!—and the eruption of smell and the watery fireworks as a knife, in
the hand of someone skilled, like our mother, goes slicing through the
skin so perfect for slicing. This gaseous spray can form a mist like
smoke, which can then be lit with a match to create actual fireworks, if
there is a chance to hide alone with a match (matches being forbidden)
and the peel from one. Sputtery ignitions can also be produced by
squeezing a peel near a candle (at least one candle is generally always
going at Christmastime), and the leftover peels are set on the stovetop to
scent the house.

13   And the ingenious way in which oranges come packed into their globes! The green nib at the top, like a detonator, can be bitten off, as if disarming the orange, in order to clear a place for you to sink a tooth under the peel. This is the best way to start. If you bite at the peel too much, your front teeth will feel scraped, like dry bone, and your lips begin to burn from the bitter oil. Better to sink a tooth in this greenish or creamy depression, and then pick at that point with the nail of your thumb, removing a little piece of the peel at a time. Later, you might want to practice to see how large a piece you can remove intact. The peel can also be undone in one continuous ribbon, a feat which maybe your father is able to perform, so that after the orange is freed, looking yellowish, the peel, rewound, will stand in its original shape, although empty.

14   The yellowish whole of the orange can now be divided into sections, usually about a dozen, by beginning with a division down the middle; after this, each section, enclosed in its papery skin, will be able to be lifted and torn loose more easily. There is a stem up the center of the sections like a mushroom stalk, but tougher; this can be eaten. A special variety of orange, without any pits, has an extra growth or nubbin, like one half of a tiny orange, tucked into its bottom. This nubbin is nearly as bitter as the peel but it can be eaten, too; don't worry. Some of the sections will have miniature sections imbedded in them and clinging as if for life, giving the impression that babies are being hatched, and should you happen to find some of these you've found the sweetest morsels of any.

15   If you prefer to have your orange sliced in half, as some people do, the edges of the peel will abrade the corners of your mouth, making them feel raw, as you eat down into the white of the rind (which is the only way to do it) until you can see daylight through the orangy bubbles composing its outside. Your eyes might burn; there is no proper way to eat an orange. If there are pits, they can get in the way, and the slower you eat an orange the more you'll find your fingers sticking together. And no matter how carefully you eat one, or bite into a quarter, juice can always fly or slip from a corner of your mouth; this happens to everyone. Close your eyes to be on the safe side, and for the eruption in your mouth of the slivers of watery meat, which should be broken and rolled fine over your tongue for the essence of orange. And if indeed you have sensed yourself coming down with a cold, there is a chance that you will feel it driven from your head—your nose and sinuses suddenly opening—in the midst of the scent of a peel and eating an orange.

16   And oranges can also be eaten whole—rolled into a spongy mass and punctured with a pencil (if you don't find this offensive) or a knife, and then sucked upon. Then, once the juice is gone, you can disembowel the orange as you wish and eat away its pulpy remains and eat once more into the whitish interior of the peel which scours the coating from off your teeth and makes your numbing lips and the tip of your tongue

start to tingle and swell up from behind, until, in the light from the windows (shining through an empty glass bowl), you see orange again from the inside. Oh, oranges, solid *os*, light from afar in the midst of the freeze, and not unlike that unspherical fruit which first went from Eve to Adam and from there (to abbreviate matters) to my brother and me.

"Mom, we think we're getting a cold."   17

"You mean, you want an orange?"   18

This is difficult to answer or dispute or even to acknowledge, finally, 19 with the fullness that the subject deserves, and that each orange bears, within its own makeup, into this hard-edged yet insubstantial, incomplete, cold, wintry world.

EXPLORING IDEAS

1. Try writing a description of a familiar, natural object or a common, everyday process in such a way that you communicate your attitude toward it.

2. The success of such writing as Woiwode's "Wanting an Orange" depends on making us see something that we have taken for granted in a new way. Such writing defamiliarizes the familiar and makes it new. Try describing something familiar in such a way that you make it seem new.

3. Woiwode's essay has little idea content; it rests on style. Is there really any value in writing about such mundane subjects as oranges?

4. Is there something special about oranges that makes this essay possible, or is it primarily Woiwode's method that makes it work? Could one write a similar essay on apples, bananas, pears, peaches, or some other fruit? Why would anyone want to?

5. Why does Woiwode say that oranges are not unlike the fruit that went from Eve to Adam? What implications for the orange does this analogy carry?

6. What is the meaning of Woiwode's final paragraph? Rewrite it using your own words.

EXPLORING RHETORIC

1. Woiwode begins the essay with a childhood reminiscence. What stylistic elements in the first paragraph suggest that the reminiscence will be nostalgic?

2. Why does Woiwode use dialogue, rather than summary or narrative, to recreate the memory of oranges?

3. What tone is suggested by the phrase "depth of degradation"? Why does Woiwode use the verb "wended" instead of a more familiar verb such as "been transported" or even "traveled"?

4. Point out each time that Woiwode uses the expression "as if" in paragraphs 10 through 14. Does he overdo this phrase? What effect does the repetition of this wording have?

5. Point out the sensory images Woiwode uses in paragraphs 10 and 11. What senses predominate Woiwode's description? Why are these the most important?

6. Point out the language in paragraph 11 that gives the oranges a sense of having a life of their own.

7. Point out the imagery in paragraph 11 that suggests that the oranges come from some magical, supernatural world.

8. Discuss Woiwode's imagery and metaphor in paragraph 12: "eruption," "watery fireworks," "mist like smoke," "sputtery ignitions." Does this language seem appropriate or overdone?

9. Discuss the metaphor of the green nib at the top like a detonator, which can be bitten off as if disarming the orange. Is the metaphor appropriate to the tone and subject of the essay? How does it fit with the teller's point of view?

10. Describe the rhetorical technique Woiwode uses to describe the process of peeling an orange. Is this such a simple and obvious task that it does not require a description?

11. Why does Woiwode go into such detail describing the appearance of an orange? Don't most people know what an orange looks like?

12. What is the rhetorical effect of Woiwode's addressing oranges as if they were sacred objects?

Cyclone

PETER SCHJELDAHL

P eter Schjeldahl was born in North Dakota in 1942 and attended Carleton College in Minnesota. He has been an art critic for *Art News* and has contributed to the *Village Voice*, the *New York Times*, and *Vanity Fair*. He has written many catalogs to accompany exhibits of artists, as well as the following collections of poetry: *White Country*, 1968; *An Adventure of the Thought Police*, 1971; *Dreams*, 1973; and *Since 1964*, 1978.

A ride on a roller coaster may be a short and simple thrill for most people, but by thinking carefully about it and examining its separate parts in this detailed and joyful analysis, Peter Schjeldahl helps us understand why we are willing to pay for the privilege of thinking we are going to be killed.

1 The Cyclone is art, sex, God, the greatest. It is the most fun you can have without risking bad ethics. I rode the Cyclone seven times one afternoon last summer, and I am here to tell everybody that it is fun for fun's sake, the pure abstract heart of the human capacity for getting a kick out of anything. Yes, it may be anguishing initially. (I promise to tell the truth.) Terrifying, even, the first time or two the train is hauled upward with

groans and creaks and with you in it. At the top then—where there is sudden strange quiet but for the fluttering of two tattered flags, and you have a poignantly brief view of Brooklyn, and of ships far out on the Atlantic—you may feel very lonely and that you have made a serious mistake, cursing yourself in the last gleam of the reflective consciousness you are about, abruptly, to leave up there between the flags like an abandoned thought-balloon. To keep yourself company by screaming may help, and no one is noticing: try it. After a couple of rides, panic abates, and after four or five you aren't even frightened, exactly, but *stimulated,* blissed, sent. The squirt of adrenaline you will never cease to have at the top as the train lumbers, wobbling slightly, into the plunge, finally fuels just happy wonderment because you can't, and never will, *believe* what is going to happen.

Every roller coaster has that first, immense drop. In practical terms, 2 it provides the oomph for the entire ride, which is of course impelled by nothing but ecologically sound gravity, momentum, and the odd slingshot of centrifugal force. The coaster is basically an ornate means of falling and a poem about physics in parts or stanzas, with jokes. The special quality of the Cyclone is how different, how *articulated,* all the components of its poem are, the whole of which lasts a minute and thirty-some seconds—exactly the right length, composed of distinct and perfect moments. By my fifth ride, my heart was leaping at the onset of each segment as at the approach of a dear old friend, and melting with instantaneous nostalgia for each at its finish.

I think every part of the Cyclone should have a name, the better to 3 be recalled and accurately esteemed. In my mind, the big drop is Kismet—fate, destiny. I can't think of what to call the second, a mystery drop commenced in a jiffy after we have been whipped around, but good, coming out of Kismet. (Someday soon I will devote particular attention to the huge and violent but elusive second drop.) I do know that the third drop's name can only be Pasha. It is so round and generous, rich and powerful, looking like a killer going in but then actually like a crash landing in feathers that allows, for the first time in the ride, an instant for luxuriating in one's endorphin rush.

This brings me to another important function of the first drop, which 4 (I firmly contend) is to trigger the release of endorphins, natural morphine, into the bloodstream by persuading the organism that it is going to die. I know all about endorphins from reading the *New York Times* science section, and from an accident a few years ago. I broke my elbow, which is something not to do. It hurts. Or let me put it this way: in relation to what I had previously understood of pain, the sensation of breaking an elbow was *a whole new idea,* a new continent suddenly—whole unknown worlds of pain out there over the horizon. I was aghast, when I broke my elbow, at the extent of my naïveté about pain—but only for a second. Then I was somewhere else, pain-free, I think it was a cocktail party, but confusing, I didn't recognize anybody. On some level I knew the party wasn't real, that I was in another, real place which had something unpleasant about it that made me not want to be there, but then I began to be afraid that if I stayed at the party I would be unable ever to be real again, so with an effort of will I returned to my body, which was sitting up with family members leaning over. The pain returned, but muffled and dull, drastically lessened. Endorphins.

5   Other things than breaking an elbow can give you an endorphin high, and one of them is suddenly falling ninety-some feet, seeing the ground charge directly at you. I think the forebrain, loaded with all sorts of chemical gimmicks we don't suspect, just there for special occasions, registers the situation, and, quick, pours a last-minute, bon voyage endorphin highball: "Hey, [*your name here*], this one's for you!" That's why it's important to ride the Cyclone many times, to comb out the distraction of terror—which gradually yields to the accumulating evidence that you are not dead—in order to savor the elixir for its own sake and for the sake of loving God or whatever—Nature—for cunningly secreted kindnesses. But Kismet is such a zonk, and the anonymous second drop is so perplexing and a zonk, too, that it isn't until mid-Pasha, in great fleshy Pasha's lap, that consciousness catches up with physiologic ravishment. Some part of my soul, because of the Cyclone, is still and will remain forever in that state, which I think is a zone of overlap among the heavens of all the world's mystic religions, where transcendent swamis bump around with freaked Spanish women saints. Blitzed in Pasha permanently, I have this lasting glimpse into the beyond that is not beyond, and you know what I'm talking about, or you don't.

6   Rolling up out of Pasha, we enter the part of the Cyclone that won't quit laughing. First there's the whoop of a whipping hairpin curve, which, if someone is sitting with you, Siamese-twins you. (Having tried different cars in different company, I prefer being alone at the very front—call me a classicist.) The ensuing dips, humps, dives, and shimmies that roar, chortle, cackle, and snort continue just long enough to suggest that they may go on forever—as worrisome as the thought, when you're laughing hard, that maybe you can never stop—and then it's hello, Irene. Why do I think Irene is the name of the very sharp drop, not deep but savage, that wipes the grin off the laughing part of the Cyclone? (Special about it is a crosspiece, low over the track at the bottom, that you swear is going to fetch you square in the eyebrows.) Irene is always the name—or kind of name, slightly unusual but banal—of the ordinary-seeming girl whom a young man may pursue idly, in a bored time, and then *wham!* fall horribly in love with, blasted in love with this person he never bothered to even particularly look at and now it's too late, she's his universe, Waterloo, *personal* Kismet. This is one

good reason I can think of for growing older: learning an aversion reflex for girls named something like Irene. In this smallish but vicious, sobering drop, abstract shapes of my own youthful romantic sorrows do not fail to flash before my inner eye . . . but then, with a jarring zoom up and around, I am once more grown-up, wised-up me, and the rest of the ride is rejoicing.

The Cyclone differs from other roller coasters in being (a) a work of 7 art and (b) old, and not only old but old-looking, decrepit, rusting in its metal parts and peeling in its more numerous wooden parts, filthy throughout and jammed into a wire (Cyclone!) fence abutting cracked sidewalks of the Third World sinkhole that Coney Island is, intoxicatingly. Nor is it to be denied or concealed that the Cyclone, unlike newer coasters, tends to run *rough,* though each ride is unique and some are inexplicably velvety. One time the vibration, with the wheels shrieking and the cars threatening to explode with strain, made me think, "This is *no fun at all!"* It was an awful moment, with a sickening sense of betrayal and icy-fingered doubt: was my love malign?

That was my worst ride, which left me with a painfully yanked mus- 8 cle in my shoulder, but I am glad to say it wasn't my last. I got back on like a thrown cowboy and discovered that the secret of handling the rough rides is indeed like riding a horse, at trot or gallop—not tensing against it, as I had, but posting and rolling. It's all in the thighs and rear end, as I especially realized when—what the hell—I joined pimpled teenagers in the arms-raised *no hands!* trick. I should mention that a heavy, cushioned restraining bar locks down snugly into your lap and is very reassuring, although, like everything upholstered in the cars, it may be cracked or slashed and leaking tufts of stuffing from under swatches of gray gaffer's tape. One thing consistently disquieting is how, under stress, a car's wooden sides may *give* a bit. I wish they wouldn't do that, or that my imagination were less vivid. If a side did happen to fail on a curve, one would depart like toothpaste from a stomped-on tube.

I was proud of braving the *no hands!* posture—as trusting in the re- 9 straining bar as a devout child in his heavenly Father—particularly the first time I did it, while emerging from the slinging turn that succeeds Irene into the long, long careen that bottoms out at absolute ground level a few feet from the fence where pedestrians invariably gather to watch, transfixed. I call this swift, showy glide Celebrity: the ride's almost over, and afflatus swells the chest. But going *no hands!* soon feels as cheap and callow as it looks, blocking with vulgar self-centeredness the wahoo-glimmering-away-of-personality-in-convulsive-Nirvana that is the Cyclone's essence. A righteous ride is hands on, though lightly, like grace. The payoff is intimacy in the sweet diminuendo, the jiggling and chuckling smart little bumps and dandling dips that bring us to a quick, pillowy deceleration in the shed, smelling of dirty machine oil, where we began and will begin again. It is a warm debriefing, this last part: "Wasn't that *great?*" it says. "Want to go again?"

10   Of course I do, but first there is the final stage of absorption, when you squeeze out (it's easy to bang a knee then, so watch it) to stand wobbly but weightless, euphoric, and then to enjoy the sensation of walking as if it were a neat thing you had just invented. Out on the sidewalk, the object of curious gazes, you see that they see that you see them, earthlings, in a diminishing perspective, through the wrong end of the telescope of your pleasure, and your heart is pitying. You nod, smiling, to convey that yes, they should ride, and no, they won't regret it.

EXPLORING IDEAS

1. Schjeldahl says that riding the Cyclone is fun for fun's sake. Brainstorm some other activities that people engage in just for kicks. Are such activities a waste of time or a healthy, even essential, outlet?

2. Schjeldahl says that when you make the first descent, you keep yourself company by screaming. Brainstorm for an essay on other ways people keep themselves company when they are alone or when they feel alone.

3. Why do human beings engage in activities that involve or simulate danger or are calculated to scare themselves? Brainstorm other such activities, such as bungee jumping and skydiving. Compare the reasons people ride thrill rides to the reasons people go to horror films; read the essay by Stephen King in Part Four.

4. Schjeldahl says when you make the first plunge, you cannot believe what is going to happen. Edward Abbey, in his essay elsewhere in this part, also describes this phenomenon of experiencing something that you cannot really believe is true. Compare Abbey's experience with Schjeldahl's. Brainstorm a similar experience you have had.

5. Schjeldahl says that by his fifth ride, he approached each segment as he would the appearance of an old friend. Brainstorm for an essay on an activity about which you use the same metaphor of approaching an old friend.

6. Schjeldahl says the function of the first drop is to make the rider believe that he or she is going to die. Why would people want to feel they are going to die?

7. Schjeldahl says that when he broke his elbow, he was aghast at his naïveté about pain. Write an essay about the nature of pain, using your own experience as evidence. Can you reexperience a past pain? Can you really describe pain? Are there different kinds of pain? Different tolerance levels for pain?

EXPLORING RHETORIC

1. Discuss the effectiveness of Schjeldahl's opening two sentences. Does his exaggeration work, or is it so ridiculous that it alienates the reader right away?

2. Discuss the effectiveness of Schjeldahl's metaphor of leaving reflective consciousness at the top like "an abandoned thought-balloon." Why does he use this particular metaphor? Compare the desire to leave reflective consciousness in this essay with a similar desire in Lewis Thomas's essay on the Tucson Zoo elsewhere in this part.

3. Discuss the effectiveness of the metaphor of the Cyclone as a poem with perfectly articulated components.

4. Why does Schjeldahl give names to each part of the ride? What effect does naming have? How would his essay have been different without the names?

5. Schjeldahl spends much of the essay discussing endorphin highs. How does he make this biological subject fit the overall tone of his essay?

6. Discuss the effectiveness of Schjeldahl's referring to part of the ride as being a "ravishment." Discuss the effectiveness of the following analogy: "Some part of my soul, because of the Cyclone, is still and will remain forever in that state, which I think is a zone of overlap among the heavens of all the world's mystic religions, where transcendent swamis bump around with freaked Spanish women saints."

7. Discuss the reasons that Schjeldahl names the last drop Irene. Read the essay by Robert Heilbroner on stereotypes in Part Three for a discussion of the stereotypes we attach to names. Brainstorm for an essay on other stereotypes about names.

8. Why does Schjeldahl spend so much time at the end of the essay describing the best way to ride the Cyclone? Do these instructions make more of a simple thrill ride than it really is? Discuss the overall tone of the essay. Is the essay itself, like the thrill ride, just for fun?

Of Shopping

PHYLLIS ROSE

Phyllis Rose was born in New York City in 1942. She has a B.A. from Radcliffe, an M.A. from Yale, and a Ph.D. from Harvard. An English professor at Wesleyan University, she has written the following books: *Woman of Letters: A Life of Virginia Woolf*, 1978; *Parallel Lives: Five Victorian Marriages*, 1983; and *Jazz Cleopatra: Josephine Baker in Her Time*, 1989.

Shopping is not the same as buying, says Phyllis Rose, in this lightly ironic essay about what motivates people to visit the many retail stores in the United States. We shop to cheer ourselves up, she explains, to practice decision making, and to remind ourselves of how much is available to us.

Last year a new Waldbaum's Food Mart opened in the shopping mall on 1
Route 66. It belongs to a new generation of superdupermarkets that have

computerized checkouts and operate twenty-four hours a day. I went to see the place as soon as it opened and I was impressed. There was trail mix in Lucite bins. There was freshly made pasta. There were coffee beans, four kinds of tahini, ten kinds of herb teas, raw shrimp in shells and cooked shelled shrimp, fresh-squeezed orange juice. Every sophistication known to the big city, even goat's cheese covered with ash, was now available in Middletown, Connecticut. People raced from the warehouse aisle to the bagel bin to the coffee beans to the fresh fish market, exclaiming at all the new things. Many of us felt elevated, graced, complimented by the presence of this food palace in our town.

2   This is the wonderful egalitarianism of American business. Was it Andy Warhol who said that the nice thing about Coke is, no can is any better or worse than any other? Some people may find it dull to cross the country and find the same chain stores with the same merchandise from coast to coast, but it means that my town is as good as yours, my shopping mall as important as yours, equally filled with wonders.

3   Imagine what people ate during the winter as little as seventy-five years ago. They ate food that was local, long-lasting, and dull, like acorn squash, turnips, and cabbage. Walk into an American supermarket in February and the world lies before you: grapes, melons, artichokes, fennel, lettuce, peppers, pistachios, dates, even strawberries, to say nothing of ice cream. Have you ever considered what a triumph of civilization it is to be able to buy a pound of chicken livers? If you lived on a farm and had to kill a chicken when you wanted to eat one, you wouldn't ever accumulate a pound of chicken livers.

4   Another wonder of Middletown is Caldor, the discount department store. Here is man's plenty: tennis racquets, pantyhose, luggage, glassware, records, toothpaste, Timex watches, Cadbury's chocolate, corn poppers, hair dryers, warm-up suits, car wax, light bulbs, television sets. All good quality at low prices with exchanges cheerfully made on defective goods. There are worse rules to live by. I feel good about America whenever I walk into this store, which is almost every midwinter Sunday afternoon, when life elsewhere has closed down. I go to Caldor the way English people go to pubs: out of sociability. To get away from my house. To widen my horizons. For culture's sake. Caldor provides me too with a welcome sense of seasonal change. When the first outdoor grills and lawn furniture appear there, it's as exciting a sign of spring as the first crocus or robin.

5   Someone told me about a Soviet émigré who practices English by declaiming, at random, sentences that catch his fancy. One of his favorites is "Fifty percent off all items today only." Refugees from Communist countries appreciate our supermarkets and discount department stores for the wonders they are. An Eastern European scientist visiting Middletown wept when she first saw the meat counter at Waldbaum's. On the other hand, before her year in America was up, her pleasure

turned sour. She wanted everything she saw. Her approach to consumer goods was insufficiently abstract, too materialistic. We Americans are beyond a simple, possessive materialism. We're used to abundance and the possibility of possessing things. The things, and the possibility of possessing them, will still be there next week, next year. So today we can walk the aisles calmly.

It is a misunderstanding of the American retail store to think we go 6 there necessarily to buy. Some of us shop. There's a difference. Shopping has many purposes, the least interesting of which is to acquire new articles. We shop to cheer ourselves up. We shop to practice decision making. We shop to be useful and productive members of our class and society. We shop to remind ourselves how much is available to us. We shop to remind ourselves how much is to be striven for. We shop to assert our superiority to the material objects that spread themselves before us.

Shopping's function as a form of therapy is widely appreciated. You 7 don't really need, let's say, another sweater. You need the feeling of power that comes with buying it or not buying it. You need the feeling that someone wants something you have—even if it's just your money. To get the benefit of shopping, you needn't actually purchase the sweater, any more than you have to marry every man you flirt with. In fact, window shopping, like flirting, can be more rewarding, the same high without the distressing commitment, the material encumbrance. The purest form of shopping is provided by garage sales. A connoisseur goes out with no goal in mind, open to whatever may come his way, secure that it will cost very little. Minimum expense, maximum experience. Perfect shopping.

I try to think of the opposite, a kind of shopping in which the object 8 is all-important, the pleasure of shopping at a minimum. For example, the purchase of blue jeans. I buy new blue jeans as seldom as possible because the experience is so humiliating. For every pair that looks good on me, fifteen look grotesque. But even shopping for blue jeans at Bob's Surplus on Main Street—no-frills, bare-bones shopping—is an event in the life of the spirit. Once again I have to come to terms with the fact that I will never look good in Levi's. Much as I want to be mainstream, I will never be.

In fact, I'm doubly an oddball, neither Misses nor Junior, but Misses 9 Petite. I look in the mirror, I acknowledge the disparity between myself and the ideal, I resign myself to making the best of it: I will buy the Lee's Misses Petite. Shopping is a time of reflection, assessment, spiritual self-discipline.

It is appropriate, I think, that Bob's has a communal dressing room. 10 I used to shop only in places where I could count on a private dressing room with a mirror inside. My impulse was to hide my weaknesses. Now I believe in sharing them. There are other women in the dressing room at Bob's trying on blue jeans who look as bad as I do. We take comfort in one another. Sometimes a woman will ask me which of two items looks better. I always give a definite answer. It's the least I can do. I figure we are all in this together, and I emerge from the dressing room not only with a new pair of jeans, but with a renewed sense of belonging to a human community.

11   When a Solzhenitsyn rants about American materialism, I have to look at my digital Timex and check what year this is. Materialism? Like conformism, a hot moral issue of the 1950s, but not now. How to spread the goods, maybe. Whether the goods are the Good, no. Solzhenitsyn, like the visiting scientist who wept at the beauty of Waldbaum's meat counter but came to covet everything she saw, takes American materialism too materialistically. He doesn't see its spiritual side. Caldor, Waldbaum's, Bob's—these, perhaps, are our cathedrals.

EXPLORING IDEAS

1. Rose says that Americans have an abstract rather than a materialistic approach to consumer goods. What does she mean? Why does she say that Americans have such an abstract approach while Eastern Europeans do not?

2. Use the following thesis sentence for an essay: "Shopping has many purposes, the least interesting of which is to acquire new articles."

3. Rose says that shopping is a form of therapy. Brainstorm for an essay about some other everyday activities that might serve as a form of therapy. What characteristics must an activity have to be therapy? What attitude must one have toward the activity for it to qualify as therapy?

4. Write a set of instructions for someone who has never attended a garage sale. Explain where to go, when to stop, what to look for, how to behave, and how to bargain.

5. Brainstorm for an essay, serious or comic, in which you describe a shopping trip as an "event in the life of the spirit."

6. Rose says when she looks in the mirror at Bob's Surplus, she acknowledges the disparity between herself and the ideal and resigns herself to making the best of it. Brainstorm for an essay about a time when you had to recognize the difference between an ideal and the reality and made the best of it.

7. Why does Rose say that it is appropriate that the dressing room at Bob's Surplus is communal? Does this have anything to do with her opening statement about "the wonderful egalitarianism of American business"?

EXPLORING RHETORIC

1. Rose opens the essay with a list of items to be found in the new supermarket. What rhetorical effect do such lists have? Why did Rose choose these items rather than any of the many others she might have selected? Write a description of a store with which you are familiar—supermarket, sports store, clothing store, hardware store—in which you include a list. Justify the choices you make for the list.

2. Discuss the effectiveness of the following sentence: "Many of us felt elevated, graced, complimented by the presence of this food palace in our town." Is this an exaggeration? Why does Rose use this particular language?

3. What does Rose mean by "the wonderful egalitarianism of American business"? What tone does she use here? What tone is suggested by the phrases "the world lies before you" and "triumph of civilization"?

4. What tone is suggested by the phrase: "All good quality at low prices with exchanges cheerfully made on defective goods"?

5. What is the tone of Rose's statement that Caldor, the large department store, provides her with a welcome sense of seasonal change? Contrast the signs of seasonal change that Rose finds with the signs of seasonal change that Annie Dillard seeks in her essay in this part?

6. Discuss Rose's comparison of shopping with flirting. Is this an effective comparison, or is it just clever?

7. Discuss the effectiveness of Rose's concluding metaphor: "Caldor, Waldbaum's, Bob's—these, perhaps, are our cathedrals." Is this comparison a bit extreme, or is it consistent with her tone throughout the essay?

Mallaise: How to Know If You Have It

WILLIAM SEVERINI KOWINSKI

William Severini Kowinski was born in Pennsylvania. He studied at Knox College in Illinois and at the University of Iowa. He has published articles in *Esquire*, the *New York Times*, and the *New York Times Magazine*, and he has been an editor for the *Boston Phoenix* and *Washington Newsworks*. His book, *The Malling of America*, from which the following selection has been taken, appeared in 1985.

Although Kowinski did a great deal of research for his book on malls in America, his style here is not academic but light and satiric. Kowinski believes that malls are designed to create an alternate world that encourages mall visitors to turn off their minds.

Malls make some people sick. Literally, sometimes. They feel feverish, 1 their eyes glaze, their stomachs tumble, they fall down, they throw up.

Some people are just annoyed by one or another aspect of a mall, or 2 a nonspecific quality of a particular mall, or malls in general. "That mall makes me *sick*!" they say. Or "I don't like malls—I *hate* them." Malls make people angry. Some of these people are shoppers, but some are people who work in malls or even own mall stores.

3   Malls affect people. They're designed to. But in some ways, either by their nature or by a side effect caused by their main ingredients, they do things to people that people are unaware of or don't understand, but if they knew or understood, they probably wouldn't like it. . . .

4   I had my first attack of *mal de mall* in Columbia, Maryland. I was in a restaurant in the Columbia Mall having coffee. The attack was characterized by feverishness, sudden fatigue, and high anxiety, all recurring whenever I glanced out at the mall itself. The thought of going out there again made me sweat and swoon, and I had to fight the hallucinatory certainty that when I left the restaurant I would be in Greengate mall, or maybe Woodfield, or Tysons Corner. Or *all* of them.

5   *Mal de mall,* or mall sickness, is one of the classifications of mallaise, the general term for physical and psychological disturbances caused by mall contact. I know because I made them all up. Among the symptoms I have personally observed or heard about from their victims are these:

6   *Dismallcumbobulation:* "I don't like to go to malls because I always get lost," a woman told me, "and that's embarrassing. I feel stupid. It makes me mad." The hyped-up overabundance of similar products plus the bland sameness of many mall environments make people feel lost even when they aren't. Even familiar malls relocate stores and reconfigure themselves, which adds to the feeling of a continuous featureless space. And the similarity of one mall to another is disorienting. You walk out of the Stuft Potato and you not only don't remember which way your car is, you might not remember what mall this is. There are other kinds of dismallcumbobulation: the loss of a sense of time as well as place, and forgetting one's purpose in coming to the mall—all of which can lead to apathy and hopelessness, loss of consciousness, or fainting. Some victims recommend deep-breathing exercises every fifteen minutes while at the mall.

7   *Inability to Relate to Others:* "It's impossible to talk to someone when you're shopping at the mall," a friend told me, explaining why she prefers to shop alone. "I notice it at the mall all the time—you see two people together but they aren't really talking to each other. They're talking, but they're staring off in different directions, and pretty soon they just wander away from each other." Among the possible effects of this symptom are disenchantment and divorce.

8   *Plastiphobia,* or the fear of being enclosed in a cocoon of blandness. "Suddenly I just stood still and looked around," a young man said. "I saw all the people and what we were all doing there, what we were spending our day doing, and I suddenly just couldn't wait to get out. I

was in a plastic place with plastic people buying plastic products with plastic charge cards. I had to escape." Sometimes this reaction is accompanied by severe anxiety, alienation from the human race, and in at least one very severe case I know of, by all the usual manifestations of a drug overdose.

All of these, and their variations, are unfortunate side effects (or per- 9 haps just extreme cases) of the main psychological effects that the mall intends. Excitement may become overstimulation; relaxation may drift into confusion and torpor. The combination is what I call the Zombie Effect.

There is, in fact, a fine line between the ideal mall shopper and the dis- 10 mayed mall shopper, between mall bliss and mallaise, between the captivated shopper and the Zombie Effect. The best description of the Zombie Effect I've heard was Barbara Lambert's, which she imparted while we toured the malls of Chicagoland.

It hits you, Barbara said, when you're standing there naked, looking 11 in the mirror of the dressing room. Your clothes are in a pile on the floor or draped over a chair. Maybe it's just a little cubicle with a curtain, and you can still hear the hum and buzz of the mall and the tiny timbres of Muzak. You're about to try something on, in an effortless repetition of what you've been doing since you came to the mall. And suddenly you realize *you've been here all day.* Time has in fact been passing while you've been gliding through store after store in a tender fuzz of soft lights and soft music. The plash of fountains, the glow of people, but almost no intrusive sound has broken your floating—no telephone, no demands, nothing to dodge or particularly watch out for. Just a gentle visual parade of clothes, fabric tags, and washing instructions. Racks, displays, cosmetics, brisk signs, flowing greenery, and spasms of color in the dream light. An ice-cream cone, a cup of coffee. Other figures have glided by: walking models of the mall's products, or walking models of the weird. An old man who reminds you of your grandfather, sitting on a blond-wood bench under a potted palm. A woman who may or may not have been your best friend's other best friend in high school, striding by on strange shoes—or maybe that's a new style and yours are strange? You're looking at your naked image in a bare little room, and a little breeze touches you. Whatever you actually came here for is in the distant past. You've been floating here . . . for hours.

But that's the whole idea of this psychological structure: to turn off 12 your mind and let you float; to create a direct and unfettered connection between eyeing and buying; and the more you do, the easier it becomes. Malls make for great eye/hand-on-credit-card coordination.

The way it's done is with a combination of peacefulness and stimu- 13 lation. The environment bathes you in sweet neutrality with soft light, candied music, and all the amenities that reassure and please without grabbing too much individual attention. At the same time, the stores and products dance for you with friendly smiles and colorful costumes. The sheer number of products and experiences you pay for and their apparent variety are in themselves factors that excite and focus.

14   Once again, it's all a lot like television. TV lulls and stimulates simultaneously. The medium itself is familiar and comfortable and friendly; the programs can be interesting but it is not really by accident that they are not as compact, colorful, dramatic, or insistent as the commercials. Watching television we are everywhere and nowhere in particular, just as at the mall. Suddenly you might realize that you've been watching it all day, just floating for hours. And if you look at people watching television—especially their eyes—they look pretty much like mall shoppers: the Zombie Effect.

15   But these effects are all supposed to be pleasant and unconscious. When either the lulling or stimulating quality—or especially the combination and conflict between them—is strongly felt, then it's no longer pleasant. Overstimulation causes anxiety, and sometimes an intense focus on heavy-duty, no-nonsense, get-out-of-my-way shopping, or else a frenzied need to get out of there, fast and forever. The lulling and sense deprivation cause listlessness and confusion, and occasionally rebellion at being Muzaked into implacable mushy madness. The conflict of both going on at the same time can cause the sense of dislocation and exhaustion that is the clearest indicator of the Zombie Effect. The victim shuffles and mumbles, is distant or unduly preoccupied, doesn't listen, acts automatically, and not only can't remember where the car is parked but often doesn't care.

16   There are ancillary symptoms and causes as well: headaches caused by guilt at buying too much; depression at not being able to buy everything; the walking emptiness caused by consistently emphasized, endless greed.

17   The cure for all forms of mallaise is theoretically simple: The victim leaves the mall. There are no laws requiring people to stay in the mall, or even to go there in the first place. It isn't anyone's civic, moral, spiritual, or intellectual duty. The mall may be the best place—or even the only place—to shop for certain products, but that doesn't mean the shopper has to stay there for hours. Nevertheless, it isn't always easy to leave.

18   For that is another aspect of the Zombie Effect: Victims stay for no good or apparent reason, and even beyond their conscious desire to be there. Shoppers mallinger partly because of the mall's psychological apparatus, its implicit promise of safety, sanctuary, and salvation. Of Nirvana! The Crystal City! A New Heaven on a New Earth! The mall hasn't become the most successful artificial environment in America for nothing.

With its real walls and psychological illusions, the mall protects 19
against so many hazards and uncertainties that the mallaise sufferer
may well mallinger a little longer to ponder the consequences of walking out. Such a person may fear trading the malladies of the Zombie Effect for the perils of mall withdrawal, which is characterized by shaking
in downtown areas, fear of crossing streets, inordinate terror in the presence of rain or sunshine, confusion when actual travel is required between purchases, and the feeling of estrangement when wearing a coat.

I wish I could say that medical science is on top of this new set of 20
malladies, but the truth is that it is scandalously behind the times. Right
now, there may be many thousands of Zombie Effect sufferers, untreated
and undiagnosed. If you find this hard to believe—well, have you been
to the mall lately?

EXPLORING IDEAS

1. Some people believe that malls have taken the place of small towns or communities. Brainstorm for an essay comparing and contrasting malls with small
towns or communities. Are small towns or communities likely to make people
sick the way Kowinski says that malls do? Why or why not?

2. Kowinski says that people are not aware that malls affect them. Brainstorm
other activities that have a similar sort of subliminal effect. Try to find an essay
topic in your brainstorming.

3. Kowinski says that malls make people feel lost even when they are not. What
does he mean? Can you think of other situations that might have this effect? Discuss reasons that such situations have been established to create a sense of being
lost.

4. Kowinski says that malls lead to apathy and hopelessness. Isn't this conclusion a bit extreme? Has anyone's life been ruined by malls the way lives have
been ruined by alcoholism, drug addiction, or gambling?

5. Brainstorm the notion of blandness. Using your brainstorming, write a definition of blandness, focusing on any context you wish: personal, social, artistic,
cultural, or something else.

6. Kowinski says that shopping in malls is a lot like television. Compare Kowinski's argument with that of Marie Winn in "Television Addiction" in Part Four.

7. Write an essay using the following sentence as the thesis statement: "Overstimulation causes anxiety."

8. Compare Kowinski's argument about malls with the previous selection, Phyllis Rose's essay, "Of Shopping."

9. Note Kowinski's comic contrast between the "dangers" of shopping in malls
and the "dangers" of shopping in downtown areas. Are there serious reasons,
however, that cause people to shop in malls rather than in downtown areas?
Brainstorm for an essay in which you defend malls against Kowinski's attack.

EXPLORING RHETORIC

1. Kowinski begins his essay with three short paragraphs made up largely of short sentences and phrases followed by one long sentence. Discuss the rhetorical effect of this technique. What tone is established by these opening paragraphs?

2. Examine Kowinski's description of his first attack of "mal de mall." What is the tone of this description? Are we supposed to take it seriously, or is it satiric? Explain and support your response.

3. What is the effect of Kowinski's creating such terms as "mal de mall," "dismallcumbobulation," and "mallaise"? Do these terms suggest that his analysis of and argument about malls is not a serious one?

4. Discuss the effect of the following sentence: "Among the possible effects of this symptom are disenchantment and divorce." Why does Kowinski link such a minor effect as disenchantment to such a major effect as divorce? Does this linkage weaken the effect of his argument?

5. Analyze the long description of the Zombie Effect by Barbara Lambert. How effective is it? What creates its effect?

6. Discuss the tone of the following sentence: "Malls make for great eye/hand-on-credit-card coordination." Find other sentences in Kowinski's essay that have this same tone. What is the effect of these sentences?

7. Discuss the technique Kowinski uses to describe the symptoms of the Zombie Effect in paragraph 15. Focus on individual words as well as sentence structure.

8. Discuss Kowinski's use of exclamations in paragraph 18. What effect do these exclamations have? Isn't this technique a bit overly dramatic?

9. Discuss the effectiveness of Kowinski's concluding sentence. Is this conclusion effective or lazy, clever or corny? Discuss your answer. Try writing an alternative ending sentence.

Memorabilia That Have Perpetuated Stereotypes About African Americans

KENNETH GOINGS

Kenneth Goings is the chair of the history department at Rhodes College in Memphis, Tennessee. The following essay, which appeared in the journal *The Chronicle of Higher Education,* is based in part on Goings's own collection of over 200 pieces of African-American memorabilia. In a clear example of good academic style, Kenneth Goings describes how black memorabilia or collectibles—such as Aunt Jemima and Uncle Mose salt and pepper shakers—have perpetuated gender stereotypes about African Americans from the late seventeenth century to the present day.

In Ralph Ellison's great novel *Invisible Man*, the main character, a black 1 person known as Invisible Man, comes across a piece of "early Americana," a "jolly nigger bank," and sees this gross caricature with its black skin, red lips, and white eyes staring up at him from the floor. Enraged at the object and at the insensitivity of his landlady for keeping such an image around, the Invisible Man inadvertently breaks the bank and tries to sneak the pieces into a neighbor's trash can, but the neighbor stops him. Then he casually tries to leave the bundled pieces along the street, but a good samaritan returns the package to him. Finally, he ends up carrying the pieces with him into his hiding place, underground.

The Invisible Man's attempt to dispose of the broken pieces of the 2 bank is indicative of African America's attempt to throw off racial and gender stereotypes. Every time the stereotypes seem to disappear someone or something brings them back. The something in this case is black memorabilia—often known as black collectibles—which have reflected and perpetuated racial and gender stereotypes about African Americans for years. These objects, produced from the late 17th century to the present, have been almost universally derogatory, with exaggerated racial features that helped "prove" that African Americans were "different" and inferior.

They also have been commonplace, items one might find in any 3 home or yard: housewares (such as Aunt Jemima and Uncle Mose salt and pepper shakers), postcards, advertising cards, toys, lawn ornaments, etc. The everyday nature of these items meant that they were heavily used (the wear and tear on the surviving collectibles attests to this) and that frequency of use reinforced the owners' conscious and unconscious acceptance of the stereotypes. These items of material culture gave a physical reality to ideas of racial inferiority. They were the props that helped reinforce the racist ideology that emerged after Reconstruction.

While collectibles were produced from the late 17th century on, their 4 real significance as icons of racial and gender stereotyping dates back only to the decades immediately after the Civil War, when slavery was no longer a status determiner for African Americans. This was the period from 1880 to 1930, arguably the worst time for black people and race relations in the United States, a time that encompassed the retreat from Reconstruction, the rise of the second Klan, hundreds of lynchings, the Great Migration north, and the race riots during and after World War I. It is during this period that new structures and new routines had to be developed and practiced to create and sustain a "new" or different racial ideology based not on slavery, but on concepts of racial inferiority. Folk-art pieces, sheet music, tourist items, and some housewares dominated this period. Black people, male and female, were portrayed as very dark, generally bug-eyed, nappy headed, childlike, stupid, lazy, deferential but happy. Black women were portrayed in the Jemima/mammy motif: fat, silent, nurturing and taking care of the "massas."

5   From the 1930's to the early 1960's in the United States, racial attitudes began to relax, to soften. Americans, including African Americans, had fought Nazis and Fascists overseas. It became more difficult, consequently, for whites to hold to the hard racist views of the past. Black collectibles reflect this changed perspective. Items, particularly housewares, became more functional and decorative. The skin tones on the collectibles were brighter, and some of the images of black women were slimmed down. Still, African-American women were generally portrayed as mammies and domestic workers and, increasingly, as the harlot. African-American males were represented as harmless, sexless clowns, not as mature workers, except for the image of the old family retainer, Uncle Mose. Their images emerged on salt and pepper shakers, cookie jars, stringholders, utility brushes, games, toys, and cooking utensils.

6   The final period, from the 1960's to the present, is somewhat peripheral to the main body of collectibles, much like the late 17th century to the 1880's. The last three decades have seen the most radical changes in race relations and attitudes. African Americans began calling themselves "black." The activism of the civil-rights movement, the resistance to police brutality linked with the assertiveness of the Black Power movement made it almost impossible to portray African Americans as loyal, servile, but happy Aunt Jemimas and Uncle Moses. Americans had only to turn to their television sets: It was obvious that Aunt Jemima and Uncle Mose were out marching, battling police dogs, and burning down Watts. The exaggerated characteristics of collectibles began to disappear as it became clearly illiberal, if not downright racist, to possess these items. Collectibles became more political: buttons, posters, and bumper stickers abounded. Also, black artists began creating new, more realistic images to replace the distorted images of the past.

7   To some extent, however, new—albeit more positive—stereotypes simply replaced the old. The militant Angela Davis traded places with Aunt Jemima and Malcolm X attempted to put Uncle Mose to rest.

8   Black collectibles are a window into American history. As the nation and ideology changed, the image created of black people by white people changed. Black collectibles were props in the slave/racial ideology that has engulfed America from the 17th century to the present. They were the physical manifestation of a culture that continually negated

and demeaned African Americans and their achievements. Manufacturers produced the props that gave physical reality to the racist ideology that had emerged, and they did so at a profit. Literally, images of black people were being bought, sold, and used much like the slaves of antebellum America.

Perhaps one day, unlike the Invisible Man, African Americans will 9 be able to leave these images in a trash can for keeps.

EXPLORING IDEAS

1. Brainstorm caricatures of various races that have been used in film, television, and advertising. How have these caricatures influenced attitudes toward these groups?

2. Identify other collectibles from a previous era, and discuss how these collectibles reflect the values of that time.

3. Are caricatures always, by their very nature, derogatory? Is it possible for a caricature not to be derogatory? Explain why or why not.

4. Goings argues that memorabilia such as Aunt Jemima and Uncle Mose salt and pepper shakers gave "physical reality to ideas of racial inferiority." Discuss other examples of giving physical reality to ideas of racial inferiority in American culture, for example, images from film or television.

5. Goings says that more positive images such as Angela Davis and Malcolm X replaced the negative Aunt Jemima and Uncle Mose image. Although these newer images may be positive from the point of view of African Americans, what kind of image did many conservative white people have of Angela Davis and Malcolm X?

EXPLORING RHETORIC

1. Discuss the effectiveness of the rhetorical technique Goings uses to open his essay. Why does he use an example from a novel rather than from real life?

2. Discuss the relevance of Goings's describing the three different historical periods of racism in the United States in paragraphs 4 through 6.

3. Why does Goings not describe the images of African Americans created during the militant 1960s? He says that the Aunt Jemima and Uncle Mose image disappeared but does not specify the new images that took their place, such as Afro haircuts and African clothing.

4. Outline the basic structure of Goings's essay. Write a brief one-sentence description of the function of each of the nine paragraphs.

5. Discuss the effectiveness of Goings's final comparison of the trade in black collectibles and the trade in black people.

Conversational Ballgames

NANCY MASTERSON SAKAMOTO

Although Nancy Masterson Sakamoto was born in the United States, she has lived and taught English as a second language in Osaka, Japan. She has also taught at the University of Hawaii and has published a textbook, *Polite Fictions*, 1982, for Japanese students for whom English is a second language. By describing Japanese and Western conversational styles as being like different kinds of ballgames, Sakamoto explains why Japanese speakers of English have trouble conversing with native speakers of English even though both speak the same language.

1   After I was married and had lived in Japan for a while, my Japanese gradually improved to the point where I could take part in simple conversations with my husband and his friends and family. And I began to notice that often, when I joined in, the others would look startled, and the conversational topic would come to a halt. After this happened several times, it became clear to me that I was doing something wrong. But for a long time, I didn't know what it was.

2   Finally, after listening carefully to many Japanese conversations, I discovered what my problem was. Even though I was speaking Japanese, I was handling the conversation in a western way.

3   Japanese-style conversations develop quite differently from western-style conversations. And the difference isn't only in the languages. I realized that just as I kept trying to hold western-style conversations even when I was speaking Japanese, so my English students kept trying to hold Japanese-style conversations even when they were speaking English. We were unconsciously playing entirely different conversational ballgames.

4   A western-style conversation between two people is like a game of tennis. If I introduce a topic, a conversational ball, I expect you to hit it back. If you agree with me, I don't expect you simply to agree and do nothing more. I expect you to add something—a reason for agreeing, another example, or an elaboration to carry the idea further. But I don't expect you always to agree. I am just as happy if you question me, or challenge me, or completely disagree with me. Whether you agree or disagree, your response will return the ball to me.

5   And then it is my turn again. I don't serve a new ball from my original starting line. I hit your ball back again from where it has bounced. I carry your idea further, or answer your questions or objections, or challenge or question you. And so the ball goes back and forth, with each of us doing our best to give it a new twist, an original spin, or a powerful smash.

And the more vigorous the action, the more interesting and exciting 6 the game. Of course, if one of us gets angry, it spoils the conversation, just as it spoils a tennis game. But getting excited is not at all the same as getting angry. After all, we are not trying to hit each other. We are trying to hit the ball. So long as we attack only each other's opinions, and do not attack each other personally, we don't expect anyone to get hurt. A good conversation is supposed to be interesting and exciting.

If there are more than two people in the conversation, then it is like 7 doubles in tennis, or like volleyball. There's no waiting in line. Whoever is nearest and quickest hits the ball, and if you step back, someone else will hit it. No one stops the game to give you a turn. You're responsible for taking your own turn.

But whether it's two players or a group, everyone does his best to 8 keep the ball going, and no one person has the ball for very long.

A Japanese-style conversation, however, is not at all like tennis or 9 volleyball. It's like bowling. You wait for your turn. And you always know your place in line. It depends on such things as whether you are older or younger, a close friend or a relative stranger to the previous speaker, in a senior or junior position, and so on.

When your turn comes, you step up to the starting line with your 10 bowling ball, and carefully bowl it. Everyone else stands back and watches politely, murmuring encouragement. Everyone waits until the ball has reached the end of the alley, and watches to see if it knocks down all the pins, or only some of them, or none of them. There is a pause, while everyone registers your score.

Then, after everyone is sure that you have completely finished your 11 turn, the next person in line steps up to the same starting line, with a different ball. He doesn't return your ball, and he does not begin from where your ball stopped. There is no back and forth at all. All the balls run parallel. And there is always a suitable pause between turns. There is no rush, no excitement, no scramble for the ball.

No wonder everyone looked startled when I took part in Japanese 12 conversations. I paid no attention to whose turn it was, and kept snatching the ball halfway down the alley and throwing it back at the bowler. Of course the conversation died. I was playing the wrong game.

This explains why it is almost impossible to get a western-style con- 13 versation or discussion going with English students in Japan. I used to think that the problem was their lack of English language ability. But I finally came to realize that the biggest problem is that they, too, are playing the wrong game.

Whenever I serve a volleyball, everyone just stands back and 14 watches it fall, with occasional murmurs of encouragement. No one hits it back. Everyone waits until I call on someone to take a turn. And when that person speaks, he doesn't hit my ball back. He serves a new ball. Again, everyone just watches it fall.

15 So I call on someone else. This person does not refer to what the previous speaker has said. He also serves a new ball. Nobody seems to have paid any attention to what anyone else has said. Everyone begins again from the same starting line, and all the balls run parallel. There is never any back and forth. Everyone is trying to bowl with a volleyball.

16 And if I try a simpler conversation, with only two of us, then the other person tries to bowl with my tennis ball. No wonder foreign English teachers in Japan get discouraged.

17 Now that you know about the difference in the conversational ball-games, you may think that all your troubles are over. But if you have been trained all your life to play one game, it is no simple matter to switch to another, even if you know the rules. Knowing the rules is not at all the same thing as playing the game.

18 Even now, during a conversation in Japanese I will notice a startled reaction, and belatedly realize that once again I have rudely interrupted by instinctively trying to hit back the other person's bowling ball. It is no easier for me to "just listen" during a conversation, than it is for my Japanese students to "just relax" when speaking with foreigners. Now I can truly sympathize with how hard they must find it to try to carry on a western-style conversation.

19 If I have not yet learned to do conversational bowling in Japanese, at least I have figured out one thing that puzzled me for a long time. After his first trip to America, my husband complained that Americans asked him so many questions and made him talk so much at the dinner table that he never had a chance to eat. When I asked him why he couldn't talk and eat at the same time, he said that Japanese do not customarily think that dinner, especially on fairly formal occasions, is a suitable time for extended conversation.

20 Since westerners think that conversation is an indispensable part of dining, and indeed would consider it impolite not to converse with one's dinner partner, I found this Japanese custom rather strange. Still, I could accept it as a cultural difference even though I didn't really understand it. But when my husband added, in explanation, that Japanese consider it extremely rude to talk with one's mouth full, I got confused. Talking with one's mouth full is certainly not an American custom. We think it very rude, too. Yet we still manage to talk a lot and eat at the same time. How do we do it?

21 For a long time, I couldn't explain it, and it bothered me. But after I discovered the conversational ballgames, I finally found the answer. Of course! In a western-style conversation, you hit the ball, and while someone else is hitting it back, you take a bite, chew, and swallow. Then

you hit the ball again, and then eat some more. The more people there are in the conversation, the more chances you have to eat. But even with only two of you talking, you still have plenty of chances to eat.

Maybe that's why polite conversation at the dinner table has never 22 been a traditional part of Japanese etiquette. Your turn to talk would last so long without interruption that you'd never get a chance to eat.

EXPLORING IDEAS

1. Sakamoto says that getting excited is not the same as getting angry. What is the difference?

2. Sakamoto says that a good conversation is supposed to be interesting and exciting. When does an exciting conversation become an argument?

3. If a Japanese conversation is like a game of bowling in which all the balls run parallel instead of being sent back and forth between the players, can there be an exchange of ideas? Explain the difference between the two kinds of exchanges of ideas suggested by these two ballgame metaphors.

4. Are there differences between the way other cultures carry on a conversation—for example, African American, Native American, Hispanic? Brainstorm this idea as a topic for an essay.

5. What are the cultural assumptions underlying the differences between the way Japanese and Americans carry on a conversation? Compare these differences with those Arthur L. Campa discusses in his essay, "Anglo vs. Chicano," in Part Three.

6. Some people have suggested that since the beginning of television, conversation has been a lost art. Brainstorm for an essay on this topic.

EXPLORING RHETORIC

1. Discuss the rhetorical method Sakamoto uses to introduce her topic. Explore how she moves from personal anecdote to generalization in paragraphs 1 through 3.

2. Why does Sakamoto use ballgames as her central metaphor for different kinds of conversation? Can you think of another metaphor she might have used to develop her points?

3. Does Sakamoto's tennis metaphor really work if in American conversations the one spoken to "adds something to the ball" before returning it? What do tennis players "add" to the ball when they return it?

4. Explain what Sakamoto means when she says that people try to bowl with a volleyball or bowl with a tennis ball.

5. Why does Sakamoto shift to second person in paragraph 17? Is this shift to "you" distracting or justified?

6. Point out the places in Sakamoto's essay where she shifts from one part of her topic to another.

Friends, Good Friends—and Such Good Friends

JUDITH VIORST

J udith Viorst was born in 1936 in Newark, New Jersey. She has been a contributing editor at *Redbook* magazine and is the author of the well-known children's book, *Alexander and the Terrible, Horrible, No Good, Very Bad Day*, 1982; several collections of light verse, such as *It's Hard to Be Hip over Thirty and Other Tragedies of Modern Life*, 1970, and *How Did I Get to Be Forty and Other Atrocities*, 1984; and *Necessary Losses*, 1986, a study of how people deal with change.

In this humorous personal essay, which first appeared in *Redbook*, Viorst describes the many different kinds of friends that women have.

1   Women are friends, I once would have said, when they totally love and support and trust each other, and bare to each other the secrets of their souls, and run—no questions asked—to help each other, and tell harsh truths to each other (no, you can't wear that dress unless you lose ten pounds first) when harsh truths must be told.

2   Women are friends, I once would have said, when they share the same affection for Ingmar Bergman, plus train rides, cats, warm rain, charades, Camus, and hate with equal ardor Newark and Brussels sprouts and Lawrence Welk and camping.

3   In other words, I once would have said that a friend is a friend all the way, but now I believe that's a narrow point of view. For the friendships I have and the friendships I see are conducted at many levels of intensity, serve many different functions, meet different needs and range from those as all-the-way as the friendship of the soul sisters mentioned above to that of the most nonchalant and casual playmates.

4   Consider these varieties of friendship:

5   1. Convenience friends. These are women with whom, if our paths weren't crossing all the time, we'd have no particular reason to be friends: a next-door neighbor, a woman in our car pool, the mother of one of our children's closest friends or maybe some mommy with whom we serve juice and cookies each week at the Glenwood Co-op Nursery.

6   Convenience friends are convenient indeed. They'll lend us their cups and silverware for a party. They'll drive our kids to soccer when

we're sick. They'll take us to pick up our car when we need a lift to the garage. They'll even take our cats when we go on vacation. As we will for them.

But we don't, with convenience friends, ever come too close or tell   7
too much; we maintain our public face and emotional distance. "Which means," says Elaine, "that I'll talk about being overweight but not about being depressed. Which means I'll admit being mad but not blind with rage. Which means that I might say that we're pinched this month but never that I'm worried sick over money."

But which doesn't mean that there isn't sufficient value to be found   8
in these friendships of mutual aid, in convenience friends.

2. Special-interest friends. These friendships aren't intimate, and   9
they needn't involve kids or silverware or cats. Their value lies in some interest jointly shared. And so we may have an office friend or a yoga friend or a tennis friend or a friend from the Women's Democratic Club.

"I've got one woman friend," says Joyce, "who likes, as I do, to take   10
psychology courses. Which makes it nice for me—and nice for her. It's fun to go with someone you know and it's fun to discuss what you've learned, driving back from the classes." And for the most part, she says, that's all they discuss.

"I'd say that what we're doing is *doing* together, not being together,"   11
Suzanne says of her Tuesday-doubles friends. "It's mainly a tennis relationship, but we play together well. And I guess we all need to have a couple of playmates."

I agree.   12

My playmate is a shopping friend, a woman of marvelous taste, a   13
woman who knows exactly *where* to buy *what*, and furthermore is a woman who always knows beyond a doubt what one ought to be buying. I don't have the time to keep up with what's new in eyeshadow, hemlines and shoes and whether the smock look is in or finished already. But since (oh, shame!) I care a lot about eyeshadow, hemlines and shoes, and since I don't *want* to wear smocks if the smock look is finished, I'm very glad to have a shopping friend.

3. Historical friends. We all have a friend who knew us when . . .   14
maybe way back in Miss Meltzer's second grade, when our family lived in that three-room flat in Brooklyn, when our dad was out of work for seven months, when our brother Allie got in that fight where they had to call the police, when our sister married the endodontist from Yonkers and when, the morning after we lost our virginity, she was the first, the only, friend we told.

The years have gone by and we've gone separate ways and we've   15
little in common now, but we're still an intimate part of each other's past. And so whenever we go to Detroit we always go to visit this friend of our girlhood. Who knows how we looked before our teeth were

straightened. Who knows how we talked before our voice got un-Brook-lyned. Who knows what we ate before we learned about artichokes. And who, by her presence, puts us in touch with an earlier part of ourself, a part of ourself it's important never to lose.

16 "What this friend means to me and what I mean to her," says Grace, "is having a sister without sibling rivalry. We know the texture of each other's lives. She remembers my grandmother's cabbage soup. I remem-ber the way her uncle played the piano. There's simply no other friend who remembers those things."

17 4. Crossroads friends. Like historical friends, our crossroads friends are important for *what was*—for the friendship we shared at a crucial, now past, time of life. A time, perhaps, when we roomed in college to-gether; or worked as eager young singles in the Big City together; or went together, as my friend Elizabeth and I did, through pregnancy, birth and that scary first year of new motherhood.

18 Crossroads friends forge powerful links, links strong enough to en-dure with not much more contact than once-a-year letters at Christmas. And out of respect for those crossroads years, for those dramas and dreams we once shared, we will always be friends.

19 5. Cross-generational friends. Historical friends and crossroads friends seem to maintain a special kind of intimacy—dormant but al-ways ready to be revived—and though we may rarely meet, whenever we do connect, it's personal and intense. Another kind of intimacy exists in the friendships that form across generations in what one woman calls her daughter-mother and her mother-daughter relationships.

20 Evelyn's friend is her mother's age—"but I share so much more than I ever could with my mother"—a woman she talks to of music, of books and of life. "What I get from her is the benefit of her experience. What she gets—and enjoys—from me is a youthful perspective. It's a pleasure for both of us."

21 I have in my own life a precious friend, a woman of 65 who has lived very hard, who is wise, who listens well; who has been where I am and can help me understand it; and who represents not only an ultimate ideal mother to me but also the person I'd like to be when I grow up.

22 In our daughter role we tend to do more than our share of self-revelation; in our mother role we tend to receive what's revealed. It's another kind of pleasure—playing wise mother to a questing younger person. It's another very lovely kind of friendship.

23 6. Part-of-a-couple friends. Some of the women we call our friends we never see alone—we see them as part of a couple at couples' parties. And though we share interests in many things and respect each other's views, we aren't moved to deepen the relationship. Whatever the reason, a lack of time or—and this is more likely—a lack of chemistry, our friendship remains in the context of a group. But the fact that our feeling

on seeing each other is always, "I'm *so* glad she's here" and the fact that we spend half the evening talking together says that this too, in its own way, counts as a friendship.

(Other part-of-a-couple friends are the friends that came with the 24 marriage, and some of these are friends we could live without. But sometimes, alas, she married our husband's best friend; and sometimes, alas, she *is* our husband's best friend. And so we find ourself dealing with her, somewhat against our will, in a spirit of what I'll call *reluctant* friendship.)

7. Men who are friends. I wanted to write just of women friends, but 25 the women I've talked to won't let me—they say I must mention man-woman friendships too. For these friendships can be just as close and as dear as those that we form with women. Listen to Lucy's description of one such friendship:

"We've found we have things to talk about that are different from 26 what he talks about with my husband and different from what I talk about with his wife. So sometimes we call on the phone or meet for lunch. There are similar intellectual interests—we always pass on to each other the books that we love—but there's also something tender and caring too."

In a couple of crises, Lucy says, "he offered himself for talking and 27 for helping. And when someone died in his family he wanted me there. The sexual, flirty part of our friendship is very small, but *some*—just enough to make it fun and different." She thinks—and I agree—that the sexual part, though small, is always *some*, is always there when a man and a woman are friends.

It's only in the past few years that I've made friends with men, in the 28 sense of a friendship that's *mine*, not just part of two couples. And achieving with them the ease and trust I've found with women friends has value indeed. Under the dryer at home last week, putting on mascara and rouge, I comfortably sat and talked with a fellow named Peter. Peter, I finally decided, could handle the shock of me minus mascara under the dryer. Because we care for each other. Because we're friends.

8. There are medium friends, and pretty good friends, and very 29 good friends indeed, and these friendships are defined by their level of intimacy. And what we'll reveal at each of these levels of intimacy is calibrated with care. We might tell a medium friend, for example, that yesterday we had a fight with our husband. And we might tell a pretty good friend that this fight with our husband made us so mad that we slept on the couch. And we might tell a very good friend that the reason we got so mad in that fight that we slept on the couch had something to do with that girl who works in his office. But it's only to our very best friends that we're willing to tell all, to tell what's going on with that girl in his office.

30   The best of friends, I still believe, totally love and support and trust
each other, and bare to each other the secrets of their souls, and run—no
questions asked—to help each other, and tell harsh truths to each other
when they must be told.

31   But we needn't agree about everything (only 12-year-old girl friends
agree about *everything*) to tolerate each other's point of view. To accept
without judgment. To give and to take without ever keeping score. And
to *be* there, as I am for them and as they are for me, to comfort our sorrows, to celebrate our joys.

EXPLORING IDEAS

1. What is the difference between "soul sisters" and "casual playmates" suggested by Viorst? Use examples from your own experience to clarify this difference.

2. Many people make friends as a result of activities connected to their children—for example, soccer, PTA, scouts, and school. Write a humorous essay
about your social life being dependent on your children, or your parents, or
guardians' social life once being dependent on you.

3. Viorst says that with "convenience friends," we maintain our "public face."
What does it mean to maintain a "public face"? Brainstorm for an essay about
the difference between your public face and your private face.

4. Discuss the difference between "doing together" and "being together." Or
write a nostalgic essay about a playmate you had as a child.

5. Write an essay about someone who puts you in "touch with an earlier part"
of yourself that it is important not to lose.

6. Discuss a cross-generational relationship you have had or observed—perhaps a mentor-student position or a parent-child relationship. What are the characteristics of such a relationship?

7. Often when couples divorce, friends are divided up between the former
partners. Write an essay about a situation with which you are familiar when this
happened. Why does this happen? What effects does it have?

8. Write an essay about members of the opposite sex who become close friends.
Discuss the sexual, flirty part of such a friendship and explore whether this facet
is a problem.

9. Friendships that encompass flirting sometimes involve what has been defined as sexual harassment. Write an essay in which you try to make clear the distinction between innocent and not-so-innocent flirting. Or is there a distinction?

10. Write an essay in which you make your own distinctions between medium
friends, pretty good friends, very good friends, and best friends.

EXPLORING RHETORIC

1. Discuss the effectiveness of the technique Viorst uses in the first three paragraphs of her essay. Note particularly her use of parallelism.

2. What do the references to Ingmar Bergman (a foreign film director), Camus (a French existentialist philosopher), and Lawrence Welk (a band leader) tell us about Viorst? Write a brief character sketch of her based on these references.

3. Note the technique of parallelism Viorst uses in discussing "convenience friends." Is this a favored technique of hers? Does it seem particularly appropriate for the subject of this essay? What makes the technique effective?

4. Discuss the effectiveness of Viorst's using dialogue or quotations from a friend in her discussion of "special-interest friends." When is quoting dialogue most valuable? Is it permissible to invent or change dialogue to make a point in an essay such as this one?

5. What kind of tone or attitude is suggested by Viorst's aside "Oh, shame!" in paragraph 13? What image of her does the aside suggest? What tone is suggested by the italicized words in this paragraph?

6. Note the technique Viorst uses in her discussion of "historical friends." Discuss the effectiveness of her examples. Are these true or invented? What difference does that make? Invent a similar list of true or fictional events.

7. Why are there so many short paragraphs in this essay? Do short paragraphs seem appropriate for the essay's subject, structure, or tone?

8. Does Viorst's discussion of men friends break up the unity of the essay? What is your reaction to her explanation of why she discusses men friends? Are there differences between the way she discusses women friends and the way she discusses men friends?

9. Discuss the effectiveness of the technique Viorst uses in paragraph 29 to define the differences among medium friends, pretty good friends, very good friends, and the best of friends.

On Friendship

MARGARET MEAD AND RHODA METRAUX

Margaret Mead, perhaps the most distinguished anthropologist in the world, was born in Philadelphia in 1901 and received her education as an anthropologist at Barnard College and Columbia University. A professor for many years at Columbia University, she was the author of more than twenty books, including *Coming of Age in Samoa,* 1928, one of the most famous books in the history of anthropology; *Growing Up in New Guinea,* 1930; *Male and Female,* 1949; *Culture and Commitment,* 1970, and *Blackberry Winter: A Memoir,* 1972. She died in 1978.

Rhoda Metraux is an anthropologist and was a frequent collaborator with Margaret Mead.

In this essay Mead and Metraux discuss different concepts of friendship in England, France, Germany, and America.

1 Few Americans stay put for a lifetime. We move from town to city to suburb, from high school to college in a different state, from a job in one region to a better job elsewhere, from the home where we raise our children to the home where we plan to live in retirement. With each move we are forever making new friends, who become part of our new life at that time.

2 For many of us the summer is a special time for forming new friendships. Today millions of Americans vacation abroad, and they go not only to see new sights but also—in those places where they do not feel too strange—with the hope of meeting new people. No one really expects a vacation trip to produce a close friend. But surely the beginning of a friendship is possible? Surely in every country people value friendship?

3 They do. The difficulty when strangers from two countries meet is not a lack of appreciation of friendship, but different expectations about what constitutes friendship and how it comes into being. In those European countries that Americans are most likely to visit, friendship is quite sharply distinguished from other, more casual relations, and is differently related to family life. For a Frenchman, a German or an Englishman friendship is usually more particularized and carriers a heavier burden of commitment.

4 But as we use the word, "friend" can be applied to a wide range of relationships—to someone one has known for a few weeks in a new place, to a close business associate, to a childhood playmate, to a man or woman, to a trusted confidant. There are real differences among these relations for Americans—a friendship may be superficial, casual, situational or deep and enduring. But to a European, who sees only our surface behavior, the differences are not clear.

5 As they see it, people known and accepted temporarily, casually, flow in and out of Americans' homes with little ceremony and often with little personal commitment. They may be parents of the children's friends, house guests of neighbors, members of a committee, business associates from another town or even another country. Coming as a guest into an American home, the European visitor finds no visible landmarks. The atmosphere is relaxed. Most people, old and young, are called by first names.

6 Who, then, is a friend?

7 Even simple translation from one language to another is difficult. "You see," a Frenchman explains, "if I were to say to you in France, 'This is my good friend,' that person would not be as close to me as someone about whom I said only, 'This is my friend.' Anyone about whom I have to say *more* is really less."

8 In France, as in many European countries, friends generally are of the same sex, and friendship is seen as basically a relationship between men. Frenchwomen laugh at the idea that "women can't be friends," but

they also admit sometimes that for women "it's a different thing." And many French people doubt the possibility of a friendship between a man and a woman. There is also the kind of relationship within a group—men and women who have worked together for a long time, who may be very close, sharing great loyalty and warmth of feeling. They may call one another *copains*—a word that in English becomes "friends" but has more the feeling of "pals" or "buddies." In French eyes this is not friendship, although two members of such a group may well be friends.

For the French, friendship is a one-to-one relationship that demands 9 a keen awareness of the other person's intellect, temperament and particular interests. A friend is someone who draws out your own best qualities, with whom you sparkle and become more of whatever the friendship draws upon. Your political philosophy assumes more depth, appreciation of a play becomes sharper, taste in food or wine is accentuated, enjoyment of a sport is intensified.

And French friendships are compartmentalized. A man may play 10 chess with a friend for thirty years without knowing his political opinions, or he may talk politics with him for as long a time without knowing about his personal life. Different friends fill different niches in each person's life. These friendships are not made part of family life. A friend is not expected to spend evenings being nice to children or courteous to a deaf grandmother. These duties, also serious and enjoined, are primarily for relatives. Men who are friends may meet in a café. Intellectual friends may meet in larger groups for evenings of conversation. Working people may meet at the little *bistro* where they drink and talk, far from the family. Marriage does not affect such friendships; wives do not have to be taken into account.

In the past in France, friendships of this kind seldom were open to 11 any but intellectual women. Since most women's lives centered on their homes, their warmest relations with other women often went back to their girlhood. The special relationship of friendship is based on what the French value most—on the mind, on compatibility of outlook, on vivid awareness of some chosen area of life.

Friendship heightens the sense of each person's individuality. Other 12 relationships commanding as great loyalty and devotion have a different meaning. In World War II the first resistance groups formed in Paris were built on the foundation of *les copains*. But significantly, as time went on these little groups, whose lives rested in one another's hands, called themselves "families." Where each had a total responsibility for all, it was kinship ties that provided the model. And even today such ties, crossing every line of class and personal interest, remain binding on the survivors of these small, secret bands.

In Germany, in contrast with France, friendship is much more articu- 13 lately a matter of feeling. Adolescents, boys and girls, form deeply sentimental attachments, walk and talk together—not so much to polish their wits as to share their hopes and fears and dreams, to form a common front against the world of school and family and to join in a kind of mutual discovery of each other's and their own inner life. Within the family, the closest relationship over a lifetime is between brothers and sisters. Outside the family, men and women find in their closest friends of the same sex the devotion of a sister, the loyalty of a brother. Appropriately, in Germany friends usually are brought into the family. Children call their father's and their mother's friends "uncle" and "aunt." Between French friends, who have chosen each other for the congeniality of their point of view, lively disagreement and sharpness of argument are the breath of life. But for Germans, whose friendships are based on mutuality of feeling, deep disagreement on any subject that matters to both is regarded as a tragedy. Like ties of kinship, ties of friendship are meant to be irrevocably binding. Young Germans who come to the United States have great difficulty in establishing such friendships with Americans. We view friendship more tentatively, subject to changes in intensity as people move, change their jobs, marry, or discover new interests.

14   English friendships follow still a different pattern. Their basis is shared activity. Activities at different stages of life may be of very different kinds—discovering a common interest in school, serving together in the armed forces, taking part in a foreign mission, staying in the same country house during a crisis. In the midst of the activity, whatever it may be, people fall into step—sometimes two men or two women, sometimes two couples, sometimes three people—and find that they walk or play a game or tell stories or serve on a tiresome and exacting committee with the same easy anticipation of what each will do day by day or in some critical situation. Americans who have made English friends comment that, even years later, "you can take up just where you left off." Meeting after a long interval, friends are like a couple who begin to dance again when the orchestra strikes up after a pause. English friendships are formed outside the family circle, but they are not, as in Germany, contrapuntal to the family nor are they, as in France, separated from the family. And a break in an English friendship comes not necessarily as a result of some irreconcilable difference of viewpoint or feeling but instead as a result of misjudgment, where one friend seriously misjudges how the other will think or feel or act, so that suddenly they are out of step.

15   What, then, is friendship? Looking at these different styles, including our own, each of which is related to a whole way of life, are there common elements? There is the recognition that friendship, in contrast with kinship, invokes freedom of choice. A friend is someone who chooses and is chosen. Related to this is the sense each friend gives the other of being a special individual, on whatever grounds this recognition is based. And between friends there is inevitably a kind of equality of give-

and-take. These similarities make the bridge between societies possible, and the American's characteristic openness to different styles of relationship makes it possible for him to find new friends abroad with whom he feels at home.

EXPLORING IDEAS

1. Write an essay in which you describe the implications of moving from one area of the country to another. What does such a move mean in terms of losing and making friends?

2. Mead and Metraux say that summer is a special time for making new friends. Write a personal experience essay in which you describe a summer friendship.

3. Mead and Metraux suggest that different countries have different expectations about what constitutes friendship. Is this also true of different races, cultures, ethnic groups, and genders? Brainstorm for an essay on this topic.

4. Do Mead and Metraux suggest that Europeans think Americans are basically very friendly people or that Americans have a very loose definition of friendship? Brainstorm for an essay on one of these suggestions.

5. Write an essay with the following thesis sentence: "Anyone about whom I have to say *more* is really less."

6. Write a comparison essay exploring the differences between the way men are friends and the way women are friends.

7. Do you think it is difficult for men and women to be friends? Write an essay on this topic.

8. Write a definition of "pals" in which you make clear the particular kind of friends suggested by this term.

9. Are women more likely to maintain friends from childhood than men? Brainstorm for an essay in which you agree or disagree.

10. Do you have friends who are like relatives to you? Describe these relationships, and explain how they developed. Write an essay about the "extended family" based on your brainstorming.

11. Mead and Metraux say that in Germany, the closest relationship within a family is between brothers and sisters. Write a humorous essay about the usual relationship between brothers and sisters in the United States.

12. Using observations from your own experience, agree or disagree with Mead and Metraux's suggestion that Americans view friendship as tentative and subject to changes in intensity.

EXPLORING RHETORIC

1. Why do Mead and Metraux begin an essay on friendship with a paragraph about how mobile Americans are?

2. Why do Mead and Metraux end paragraph 2 with questions? Why do they pose the question, "Who, then, is a friend?" as an entire paragraph? Are these real or rhetorical questions? What is the difference between these types of questions? Discuss the effectiveness of this technique.

3. Note that Mead and Metraux explicitly state their overall thesis in paragraph 3. Why did they not do so in the first paragraph? How accurately does their thesis statement reflect the overall purpose and structure of their essay?

4. Note how Mead and Metraux organize paragraphs around a topic sentence. Find the topic sentences in paragraphs 9 and 10, for example, and point out how the details in these two paragraphs support their topic sentences.

5. Identify the transitional phrases that Mead and Metraux use to move from French to German friendships. What other techniques do they use to suggest the idea of contrast between the French and the Germans?

6. Discuss how Mead and Metraux use American ideas of friendship as the unifying basis for their discussion of French, German, and English ideas of friendship.

7. Write a single sentence in which you summarize the basic differences Mead and Metraux point out between American ideas of friendship and ideas of friendship in France, Germany, and England.

8. Outline the structure of this essay, using complete sentences to summarize each part. Discuss the effectiveness of the tightly organized structure of the essay. Is the essay overly structured, or is the formal structure necessary here?

PART THREE

DEALING WITH DIFFERENCES

T he time when U.S. society is dominated by one culture and one gender is rapidly drawing to a close. Learning to live with a variety of cultures and an equality of genders is becoming one of the most important responsibilities that people must confront. Because of the relative suddenness with which these cultural changes have taken place, however, many people's experience of our transformed society is still somewhat new and unfamiliar.

In the interests of promoting an understanding and acceptance of gender equality and cultural difference, the twelve writers in this section explore these social changes from their own personal experience and their observation of the world around them. The first two essays, by Robert L. Heilbroner and Gloria Yamato, focus on the most basic barriers to this understanding: stereotyping and racism. The essays by Noel Perrin, Amy Gross, Susan Brownmiller, and Paul Theroux explore the changing meaning of such cultural terms as "femininity" and "masculinity."

Brent Staples uses his personal experience to explain what it means to be an African-American male in a white society that distrusts and fears him for no reason other than his color, while Judith Ortiz Cofer describes her personal experience of being trapped by common stereotypes of Latinas. Leslie Marmon Silko discusses the cultural background of her Native American heritage in the Southwest, and Alice Walker examines the cultural context of the black writer in the American South. Finally, Arthur L. Campa discusses some differences between the attitudes and styles of Anglo and Chicano culture, and Ishmael Reed suggests that these differences are becoming the basis for a multicultural society.

Few concerns in U.S. society today are as pressing as the rapid changes that have occurred in the past two decades as women and minority cultures have rightfully insisted on being freed from damaging stereotypes. These are issues that no one can ignore and that everyone should be able to write about with some experience and engagement. The questions at the end of each essay will guide your thinking and writing about differences of gender and culture. Writing about such issues honestly is not always easy, but it is one of the most effective means we have for honest self-examination and unbiased observation.

Don't Let Stereotypes Warp Your Judgments

ROBERT L. HEILBRONER

> obert Heilbroner, a professor of economics, received his education from
> Harvard University and the New School for Social Research in New York
> City, where he currently teaches. His books include *The Future as History,* 1960; *A Primer of Government Spending: Between Capitalism and Socialism,* 1970; and *An Inquiry into the Human Prospect,* 1974.
>
> Heilbroner wrote the following essay, which appeared in the *Reader's Digest,* for a popular audience. Although, like most other academic writing, it is based on research studies and cites the opinions of experts, the essay explains in a clear and straightforward way why we use stereotypes and how they affect our judgment.

Is a girl called Gloria apt to be better-looking than one called Bertha? Are 1 criminals more likely to be dark than blond? Can you tell a good deal about someone's personality from hearing his voice briefly over the phone? Can a person's nationality be pretty accurately guessed from his photograph? Does the fact that someone wears glasses imply that he is intelligent?

The answer to all these questions is obviously, "No." 2

Yet, from all the evidence at hand, most of us believe these things. 3 Ask any college boy if he'd rather take his chances with a Gloria or a Bertha, or ask a college girl if she'd rather blind-date a Richard or a Cuthbert. In fact, you don't have to ask: college students in questionnaires have revealed that names conjure up the same images in their minds as they do in yours—and for as little reason.

Look into the favorite suspects of persons who report "suspicious 4 characters" and you will find a large percentage of them to be "swarthy" or "dark and foreign-looking"—despite the testimony of criminologists that criminals do *not* tend to be dark, foreign or "wild-eyed." Delve into the main asset of a telephone stock swindler and you will find it to be a marvelously confidence-inspiring telephone "personality." And whereas we all think we know what an Italian or a Swede looks like, it is the sad fact that when a group of Nebraska students sought to match faces and nationalities of 15 European countries, they were scored wrong in 93 percent of their identifications. Finally, for all the fact that horn-rimmed glasses have now become the standard television sign of an "intellectual," optometrists know that the main thing that distinguishes people with glasses is just bad eyes.

5   Stereotypes are a kind of gossip about the world, a gossip that makes us prejudge people before we ever lay eyes on them. Hence it is not surprising that stereotypes have something to do with the dark world of prejudice. Explore most prejudices (note that the word means prejudgment) and you will find a cruel stereotype at the core of each one.

6   For it is the extraordinary fact that once we have typecast the world, we tend to see people in terms of our standardized pictures. In another demonstration of the power of stereotypes to affect our vision, a number of Columbia and Barnard students were shown 30 photographs of pretty but unidentified girls, and asked to rate each in terms of "general liking," "intelligence," "beauty" and so on. Two months later, the same groups were shown the same photographs, this time with fictitious Irish, Italian, Jewish and "American" names attached to the pictures. Right away the ratings changed. Faces which were now seen as representing a national group went down in looks and still farther down in likability, while the "American" girls suddenly looked decidedly prettier and nicer.

7   Why is it that we stereotype the world in such irrational and harmful fashion? In part, we begin to type-cast people in our childhood years. Early in life, as every parent whose child has watched a TV Western knows, we learn to spot the Good Guys from the Bad Guys. Some years ago, a social psychologist showed very clearly how powerful these stereotypes of childhood vision are. He secretly asked the most popular youngsters in an elementary school to make errors in their morning gym exercises. Afterwards, he asked the class if anyone had noticed any mistakes during gym period. Oh, yes, said the children. But it was the *unpopular* members of the class—the "bad guys"—they remembered as being out of step.

8   We not only grow up with standardized pictures forming inside of us, but as grown-ups we are constantly having them thrust upon us. Some of them, like the half-joking, half-serious stereotypes of mothers-in-law, or country yokels, or psychiatrists, are dinned into us by the stock jokes we hear and repeat. In fact, without such stereotypes, there would be a lot fewer jokes. Still other stereotypes are perpetuated by the advertisements we read, the movies we see, the books we read.

9   And finally, we tend to stereotype because it helps us make sense out of a highly confusing world, a world which William James once described as "one great, blooming, buzzing confusion." It is a curious fact that if we don't *know* what we're looking at, we are often quite literally unable to *see* what we're looking at. People who recover their sight after a lifetime of blindness actually cannot at first tell a triangle from a square. A visitor to a factory sees only noisy chaos where the superinten-

dent sees a perfectly synchronized flow of work. As Walter Lippmann has said, "For the most part we do not first see, and then define; we define first, and then we see."

Stereotypes are one way in which we "define" the world in order to 10 see it. They classify the infinite variety of human beings into a convenient handful of "types" towards whom we learn to act in stereotyped fashion. Life would be a wearing process if we had to start from scratch with each and every human contact. Stereotypes economize on our mental effort by covering up the blooming, buzzing confusion with big recognizable cut-outs. They save us the "trouble" of finding out what the world is like—they give it its accustomed look.

Thus the trouble is that stereotypes make us mentally lazy. As S. I. 11 Hayakawa, the authority on semantics, has written: "The danger of stereotypes lies not in their existence, but in the fact that they become for all people some of the time, and for some people all the time, *substitutes for observation*." Worse yet, stereotypes get in the way of our judgment, even when we do observe the world. Someone who has formed rigid preconceptions of all Latins as "excitable," or all teenagers as "wild," doesn't alter his point of view when he meets a calm and deliberate Genoese, or a serious-minded high school student. He brushes them aside as "exceptions that prove the rule." And, of course, if he meets someone true to type, he stands triumphantly vindicated. "They're all like that," he proclaims, having encountered an excited Latin, an ill-behaved adolescent.

Hence, quite aside from the injustice which stereotypes do to others, 12 they impoverish ourselves. A person who lumps the world into simple categories, who type-casts all labor leaders as "racketeers," all businessmen as "reactionaries," all Harvard men as "snobs," and all Frenchmen as "sexy," is in danger of becoming a stereotype himself. He loses his capacity to be himself—which is to say, to see the world in his own absolutely unique, inimitable and independent fashion.

Instead, he votes for the man who fits his standardized picture of 13 what a candidate "should" look like or sound like, buys the goods that someone in his "situation" in life "should" own, lives the life that others define for him. The mark of the stereotype person is that he never surprises us, that we do indeed have him "typed." And no one fits this strait-jacket so perfectly as someone whose opinions about *other people* are fixed and inflexible.

Impoverishing as they are, stereotypes are not easy to get rid of. The 14 world we type-cast may be no better than a Grade B movie, but at least we know what to expect of our stock characters. When we let them act for themselves in the strangely unpredictable way that people do act, who knows but that many of our fondest convictions will be proved wrong?

15   Nor do we suddenly drop our standardized pictures for a blinding vision of the Truth. Sharp swings of ideas about people often just substitute one stereotype for another. The true process of change is a slow one that adds bits and pieces of reality to the pictures in our heads, until gradually they take on some of the blurriness of life itself. Little by little, we learn not that Jews and Negroes and Catholics and Puerto Ricans are "just like everybody else"—for that, too, is a stereotype—but that each and every one of them is unique, special, different and individual. Often we do not even know that we have let a stereotype lapse until we hear someone saying, "all so-and-so's are like such-and-such," and we hear ourselves saying, "Well—maybe."

16   Can we speed the process along? Of course we can.

17   First, we can become *aware* of the standardized pictures in our heads, in other people's heads, in the world around us.

18   Second, we can become suspicious of all judgments that we allow exceptions to "prove." There is no more chastening thought than that in the vast intellectual adventure of science, it takes but one tiny exception to topple a whole edifice of ideas.

19   Third, we can learn to be chary of generalizations about people. As F. Scott Fitzgerald once wrote: "Begin with an individual, and before you know it you have created a type; begin with a type, and you find you have created—nothing."

20   Most of the time, when we type-cast the world, we are not in fact generalizing about people at all. We are only revealing the embarrassing facts about the pictures that hang in the gallery of stereotypes in our own heads.

EXPLORING IDEAS

1. If it is not true that women named Bertha are less attractive than women named Gloria or that men named Cuthbert are less attractive than men named Richard, then where did such beliefs come from?

2. Heilbroner says the "standard television sign" of an intellectual is glasses. Brainstorm some other human stereotypes created by television, and list their characteristics. Write a classification essay in which you discuss these types and develop a thesis about American culture or television stereotyping.

3. Heilbroner says that stereotypes constitute a kind of "gossip about the world." Brainstorm for an essay in which you compare stereotyping with gossiping.

4. Does the example Heilbroner cites—in which students were asked to rate photographs of young women as to "beauty," "intelligence," or "general liking"—suggest that people seem physically different to us once we know their cultural background? How is this possible?

5. Brainstorm Heilbroner's statement that there would be fewer jokes if we did not hold the stereotypes we do. Analyze some jokes you have heard that depend on stereotypes. On what characteristics does their humor depend? How should you react to such jokes in social encounters?

6. Contrast Heilbroner's statement that stereotypes help us "make sense out of a highly confusing world" with S. I. Hayakawa's statement that stereotypes are often "substitutes for observation."

7. How is the world of a person who stereotypes like that of a Grade B movie? Write a humorous essay in which you describe someone who lives in a world that is like a Grade B movie.

8. If a person sees the world in terms of stereotypes, how can he or she ever become aware that the images carried in his or her head are standardized stereotypes rather than reality?

EXPLORING RHETORIC

1. If the answers to the questions Heilbroner poses in the first paragraph are all "obviously, 'No,' " then why does he pose them in the first place? Is this rhetorical tactic effective?

2. Discuss the tone of Heilbroner's statement about people who wear glasses.

3. Note how many times Heilbroner uses the imperative in paragraphs 4 and 5. Is this technique effective?

4. Why doesn't Heilbroner quote any of the jokes about stereotypes he mentions? Would an example have made his argument more convincing?

5. Discuss the effectiveness of Heilbroner's argument that stereotypes are not only an injustice to others but are harmful to the person harboring the stereotypes.

6. Heilbroner's essay is carefully structured in the following parts:

   I.   What stereotypes are
   II. Why we stereotype
   III. How stereotyping affects those who stereotype
   IV. Why stereotypes are not easy to get rid of
   V.   What we can do to get rid of stereotypes

Mark those places where each of these sections begins and ends; discuss the methods Heilbroner uses to support each section.

7. Heilbroner makes use of transitions between paragraphs by repeating key words, referring to previous statements, and using transitional words. Identify these transitional devices.

8. Comment on the effectiveness of Heilbroner's method of concluding the essay. Is the essay too structured? Is it possible for an essay to be too structured?

Something About the Subject
Makes It Hard to Name

GLORIA YAMATO

Gloria Yamato, community relations associate for the Pacific Northwest Regional Office of the American Friends Service Committee, has contributed essays to several books, including *Changing Our Power: An Introduction to Women's Studies,* 1988, where the following essay first appeared. Yamato argues that we must acknowledge the fact that racism—the systematic mistreatment of one group of people by another based on racial heritage—pervades our lives. After describing four different forms of racism, she suggests how whites and people of color can combat it.

1   Racism—simple enough in structure, yet difficult to eliminate. Racism—pervasive in the U.S. culture to the point that it deeply affects all the local town folk and spills over, negatively influencing the fortunes of folk around the world. Racism is pervasive to the point that we take many of its manifestations for granted, believing "that's life." Many believe that racism can be dealt with effectively in one hellifying workshop, or one hour-long heated discussion. Many actually believe this monster, racism, that has had at least a few hundred years to take root, grow, invade our space and develop subtle variations . . . this mind-funk that distorts thought and action, can be merely wished away. I've run into folks who really think that we can beat this devil, kick this habit, be healed of this disease in a snap. In a sincere blink of a well-intentioned eye, presto—poof—racism disappears. "I've dealt with my racism . . . (envision a laying on of hands) . . . Hallelujah! Now I can go to the beach." Well, fine. Go to the beach. In fact, why don't we all go to the beach and continue to work on the sucker over there? Cuz you can't even shave a little piece off this thing called racism in a day, or a weekend, or a workshop.

2   When I speak of *oppression,* I'm talking about the systematic, institutionalized mistreatment of one group of people by another for whatever reason. The oppressors are purported to have an innate ability to access economic resources, information, respect, etc., while the oppressed are believed to have a corresponding negative innate ability. The flip side of oppression is *internalized oppression.* Members of the target group are emotionally, physically, and spiritually battered to the point that they begin to actually believe that their oppression is deserved, is their lot in life, is natural and right, and that it doesn't even exist. The oppression begins to feel comfortable, familiar enough that when mean ol' Massa lay down de whip, we got's to pick up and whack ourselves and each

other. Like a virus, it's hard to beat racism, because by the time you come up with a cure, it's mutated to a "new cure-resistant" form. One shot just won't get it. Racism must be attacked from many angles.

The forms of racism that I pick up on these days are 1) aware/blatant 3 racism, 2) aware/covert racism, 3) unaware/unintentional racism, and 4) unaware/self-righteous racism. I can't say that I prefer any one form of racism over the others, because they all look like an itch needing a scratch. I've heard it said (and understandably so) that the aware/blatant form of racism is preferable if one must suffer it. Outright racists will, without apology or confusion, tell us that because of our color we don't appeal to them. If we so choose, we can attempt to get the hell out of their way before we get the sweat knocked out of us. Growing up, aware/covert racism is what I heard many of my elders bemoaning "up north," after having escaped the overt racism "down south." Apartments were suddenly no longer vacant or rents were outrageously high, when black, brown, red, or yellow persons went to inquire about them. Job vacancies were suddenly filled, or we were fired for very vague reasons. It still happens, though the perpetrators really take care to cover their tracks these days. They don't want to get gummed to death or slobbered on by the toothless laws that supposedly protect us from such inequities.

Unaware/unintentional racism drives usually tranquil white liber- 4 als wild when they get called on it, and confirms the suspicions of many people of color who feel that white folks are just plain crazy. It has led white people to believe that it's just fine to ask if they can touch my hair (while reaching). They then exclaim over how soft it is, how it does not scratch their hand. It has led whites to assume that bending over backwards and speaking to me in high-pitched (terrified), condescending tones would make up for all the racist wrongs that distort our lives. This type of racism has led whites right to my doorstep, talking 'bout, "We're sorry/we love you and want to make things right," which is fine, and further, "We're gonna give you the opportunity to fix it while we sleep. Just tell us what you need. 'Bye!!"—which *ain't* fine. With the best of intentions, the best of educations, and the greatest generosity of heart, whites, operating on the misinformation fed to them from day one, will behave in ways that are racist, will perpetuate racism by being "nice" the way we're taught to be nice. You can just "nice" somebody to death with naïveté and lack of awareness of privilege. Then there's guilt and the desire to end racism and how the two get all tangled up to the point that people, morbidly fascinated with their guilt, are immobilized. Rather than deal with ending racism, they sit and ponder their guilt and hope nobody notices how awful they are. Meanwhile, racism picks up momentum and keeps on keepin' on.

Now, the newest form of racism that I'm hip to is unaware/self- 5 righteous racism. The "good white" racist attempts to shame Blacks into being blacker, scorns Japanese-Americans who don't speak Japanese, and knows more about the Chicano/a community than the folks who make up the community. They assign themselves as the "good whites," as opposed to the "bad whites," and are often so busy telling people of color what the issues in the Black, Asian, Indian, Latino/a communities should be that they don't have time to deal with their errant sisters and brothers in the white community. Which means that people of color are still left to deal with what the "good whites" don't want to . . . racism.

6   Internalized racism is what really gets in my way as a Black woman. It influences the way I see or don't see myself, limits what I expect of myself or others like me. It results in my acceptance of mistreatment, leads me to believe that being treated with less than absolute respect, at least this once, is to be expected because I am Black, because I am not white. "Because I am (*you fill in the color*)," you think, "Life is going to be hard." The fact is life may be hard, but the color of your skin is not the cause of the hardship. The color of your skin may be used as an excuse to mistreat you, but there is no reason or logic involved in the mistreatment. If it seems that your color is the reason; if it seems that your ethnic heritage is the cause of the woe, it's because you've been deliberately beaten down by agents of a greedy system until you swallowed the garbage. That is the internalization of racism.

7   Racism is the systematic, institutionalized mistreatment of one group of people by another based on racial heritage. Like every other oppression, racism can be internalized. People of color come to believe misinformation about their particular ethnic group and thus believe that their mistreatment is justified. With that basic vocabulary, let's take a look at how the whole thing works together. Meet "the Ism Family," racism, classism, ageism, adultism, elitism, sexism, heterosexism, physicalism, etc. All these ism's are systematic, that is, not only are these parasites feeding off our lives, they are also dependent on one another for foundation. Racism is supported and reinforced by classism, which is given a foothold and a boost by adultism, which also feeds sexism, which is validated by heterosexism, and so it goes on. You cannot have the "ism" functioning without first effectively installing its flip-side, the internalized version of the ism. Like twins, as one particular form of the ism grows in potency, there is a corresponding increase in its internalized form within the population. Before oppression becomes a specific ism like racism, usually all hell breaks loose. War. People fight attempts to enslave them, or to subvert their will, or to take what they consider theirs, whether that is territory or dignity. It's true that the various elements of racism, while repugnant, would not be able to do very much damage, but for one generally overlooked key piece: power/privilege.

8   While in one sense we all have power we have to look at the fact that, in our society, people are stratified into various classes and some of

these classes have more privilege than others. The owning class has enough power and privilege to not have to give a good whinney what the rest of the folks have on their minds. The power and privilege of the owning class provides the ability to pay off enough of the working class and offer that paid-off group, the middle class, just enough privilege to make it agreeable to do various and sundry oppressive things to other working-class and outright disenfranchised folk, keeping the lid on explosive inequities, at least for a minute. If you're at the bottom of this heap, and you believe the line that says you're there because that's all you're worth, it is at least some small solace to believe that there are others more worthless than you, because of their gender, race, sexual preference . . . whatever. The specific form of power that runs the show here is the power to intimidate. The power to take away the most lives the quickest, and back it up with legal and "divine" sanction, is the very bottom line. It makes the difference between who's holding the racism end of the stick and who's getting beat with it (or beating others as vulnerable as they are) on the internalized racism end of the stick. What I am saying is, while people of color are welcome to tear up their own neighborhoods and each other, everybody knows that you cannot do that to white folks without hell to pay. People of color can be prejudiced against one another and whites, but do not have an ice-cube's chance in hell of passing laws that will get whites sent to relocation camps "for their own protection and the security of the nation." People who have not thought about or refuse to acknowledge this imbalance of power/privilege often want to talk about the racism of people of color. But then that is one of the ways racism is able to continue to function. You look for someone to blame and you blame the victim, who will nine times out of ten accept the blame out of habit.

So, what can we do? Acknowledge racism for a start, even though and especially when we've struggled to be kind and fair, or struggled to rise above it all. It is hard to acknowledge the fact that racism circumscribes and pervades our lives. Racism must be dealt with on two levels, personal and societal, emotional and institutional. It is possible—and most effective—to do both at the same time. We must reclaim whatever delight we have lost in our own ethnic heritage or heritages. This so-called melting pot has only succeeded in turning us into fast food-gobbling "generics" (as in generic "white folks" who were once Irish, Polish, Russian, English, etc. and "black folks," who were once Ashanti, Bambara, Baule, Yoruba, etc.) Find or create safe places to actually *feel* what we've been forced to repress each time we were a victim of, witness to or perpetrator of racism, so that we do not continue, like puppets, to act out the past in the present and future. Challenge oppression. Take a stand against it. When you are aware of something oppressive going down, stop the show. At least call it. We become so numbed to racism that we don't even think twice about it, unless it is immediately life-threatening.

10   *Whites who want to be allies to people of color:* You can educate yourselves via research and observation rather than rigidly, arrogantly relying solely on interrogating people of color. Do not expect that people of color should teach you how to behave non-oppressively. Do not give into the pull to be lazy. Think, hard. Do not blame people of color for your frustration about racism, but do appreciate the fact that people of color will often help you get in touch with that frustration. Assume that your effort to be a good friend is appreciated, but don't expect or accept gratitude from people of color. Work on racism for your sake, not "their" sake. Assume that you are needed and capable of being a good ally. Know that you'll make mistakes and commit yourself to correcting them and continuing on as an ally, no matter what. Don't give up.

11   *People of color, working through internalized racism:* Remember always that you and others like you are completely worthy of respect, completely capable of achieving whatever you take a notion to do. Remember that the term "people of color" refers to a variety of ethnic and cultural backgrounds. These various groups have been oppressed in a variety of ways. Educate yourself about the ways different peoples have been oppressed and how they've resisted that oppression. Expect and insist that whites are capable of being good allies against racism. Don't give up. Resist the pull to give out the "people of color seal of approval" to aspiring white allies. A moment of appreciation is fine, but more than that tends to be less than helpful. Celebrate yourself. Celebrate yourself. Celebrate the inevitable end of racism.

EXPLORING IDEAS

1. What is the relationship between racism, as Gloria Yamato describes it, and stereotyping, as Robert L. Heilbroner defines that term in his essay elsewhere in this part? Is there any relationship between the inevitability of stereotyping and the pervasiveness of racism?

2. Discuss the relationship between racism and internalized racism as Yamato describes them.

3. What is the difference between aware/blatant racism and aware/covert racism? Brainstorm examples of each, and argue that one is more harmful than the other.

4. Brainstorm how someone can "'nice' somebody to death," as Yamato describes this tactic.

5. What is wrong with whites' learning more about other races and cultures and urging members of those races to be true to their cultures? Why is Yamato so critical of what she calls "unaware/self-righteous racism"?

6. Why does Yamato devote most of her essay to internalized racism?

7. Discuss the basic content of paragraph 7. Try summarizing what Yamato says in this paragraph. Provide an example to support her arguments about the interdependence of the various "isms" she describes.

8. What objection does Yamato have to the melting pot theory of U.S. society?

9. Why does Yamato advise whites who want to be allies of people of color not to ask people of color how they can be of help?

10. Is the issue of racism as Yamato sees it a question only of whites' having racial attitudes toward people of color? Does she believe that whites have also made some people of color prejudiced against other people of color? What evidence does she provide for this stance?

EXPLORING RHETORIC

1. Identify and discuss the technique Yamato uses in paragraph 1. What effect does she achieve by suggesting that racism is so deeply ingrained in human life that it cannot be easily eliminated?

2. Discuss the tone Yamato uses in the last part of paragraph 1.

3. Discuss the appropriateness of Yamato's analogy of racism as being like a virus.

4. Discuss the tone with which Yamato describes unaware / unintentional racism in paragraph 4. Given her description, is there any way for whites not to be racist?

5. Discuss the various examples of informal or slang language Yamato uses in paragraph 8. How effective are they?

6. In the middle of paragraph 8, Yamato says, "What I am saying is . . ." Since this suggests that she is going to repeat what she has already said in a different way, discuss how the second part of the paragraph clarifies the first part.

7. Discuss the tone Yamato uses in paragraphs 9 through 11. What authority does she have for giving such advice to both whites and people of color?

The Androgynous Man

NOEL PERRIN

Noel Perrin, born in 1927, attended Williams College, Duke University, and Cambridge University. A professor of English at Dartmouth College, New Hampshire, his books include *Dr. Bowdler's Legacy,* 1971; *First Person Plural,* 1978; *Second Person Plural,* 1980; and *Third Person Plural,* 1982. Although Perrin claims that he is androgynous and is not trapped in masculine stereotypes, a careful reading of this essay may reveal that old assumptions about what it means to be masculine are hard to overcome.

1   The summer I was 16, I took a train from New York to Steamboat Springs, Colo., where I was going to be assistant horse wrangler at a camp. The trip took three days, and since I was much too shy to talk to strangers, I had quite a lot of time for reading. I read all of "Gone With the Wind." I read all the interesting articles in a couple of magazines I had, and then I went back and read all the dull stuff. I also took all the quizzes, a thing of which magazines were even fuller then than now.

2   The one that held my undivided attention was called "How Masculine/Feminine Are You?" It consisted of a large number of inkblots. The reader was supposed to decide which of four objects each blot most resembled. The choices might be a cloud, a steam engine, a caterpillar and a sofa.

3   When I finished the test, I was shocked to find that I was barely masculine at all. On a scale of 1 to 10, I was about 1.2. Me, the horse wrangler? (And not just wrangler, either. That summer, I had to skin a couple of horses that died—the camp owner wanted the hides.)

4   The results of that test were so terrifying to me that for the first time in my life I did a piece of original analysis. Having unlimited time on the train, I looked at the "masculine" answers over and over, trying to find what it was that distinguished real men from people like me—and eventually I discovered two very simple patterns. It was "masculine" to think the blots looked like man-made objects, and "feminine" to think they looked like natural objects. It was masculine to think they looked like things capable of causing harm, and feminine to think of innocent things.

5   Even at 16, I had the sense to see that the compilers of the test were using rather limited criteria—maleness and femaleness are both more complicated than *that*—and I breathed a huge sigh of relief. I wasn't necessarily a wimp, after all.

6   That the test did reveal something other than the superficiality of its makers I realized only many years later. What it revealed was that there is a large class of men and women both, to which I belong, who are essentially androgynous. That doesn't mean we're gay, or low in the appropriate hormones, or uncomfortable performing the jobs traditionally assigned to our sexes. (A few years after that summer, I was leading troops in combat and, unfashionable as it now is to admit this, having a very good time. War is exciting. What a pity the 20th century went and spoiled it with high-tech weapons.)

7   What it does mean to be spiritually androgynous is a kind of freedom. Men who are all-male, or he-man, or 100 percent red-blooded Americans, have a little biological set that causes them to be attracted to physical power, and probably also to dominance. Maybe even to watching football. I don't say this to criticize them. Completely masculine men are quite often wonderful people: good husbands, good (though sometimes overwhelming) fathers, good members of society. Furthermore,

they are often so unself-consciously at ease in the world that other men seek to imitate them. They just aren't as free as us androgynes. They pretty nearly have to be what they are; we have a range of choices open.

The sad part is that many of us never discover that. Men who are not 8 100 percent red-blooded Americans—say, those who are only 75 percent red-blooded—often fail to notice their freedom. They are too busy trying to copy the he-men ever to realize that men, like women, come in a wide variety of acceptable types. Why this frantic imitation? My answer is mere speculation, but not casual. I have speculated on this for a long time.

Partly they're just envious of the he-man's unconscious ease. Mostly 9 they're terrified of finding that there may be something wrong with them deep down, some weakness at the heart. To avoid discovering that, they spend their lives acting out the role that the he-man naturally lives. Sad.

One thing that men owe to the women's movement is that this kind 10 of failure is less common than it used to be. In releasing themselves from the single ideal of the dependent woman, women have more or less incidentally released a lot of men from the single ideal of the dominant male. The one mistake the feminists have made, I think, is in supposing that *all* men need this release, or that the world would be a better place if all men achieved it. It wouldn't. It would just be duller.

So far I have been pretty vague about just what the freedom of the 11 androgynous man is. Obviously it varies with the case. In the case I know best, my own, I can be quite specific. It has freed me most as a parent. I am, among other things, a fairly good natural mother. I like the nurturing role. It makes me feel good to see a child eat—and it turns me to mush to see a 4-year-old holding a glass with both small hands, in order to drink. I even enjoyed sewing patches on the knees of my daughter Amy's Dr. Dentons when she was at the crawling stage. All that pleasure I would have lost if I had made myself stick to the notion of the paternal role that I started with.

Or take a smaller and rather ridiculous example. I feel free to kiss 12 cats. Until recently it never occurred to me that I would want to, though my daughters have been doing it all their lives. But my elder daughter is now 22, and in London. Of course, I get to look after her cat while she is gone. He's a big, handsome farm cat named Petrushka, very unsentimental, though used from kittenhood to being kissed on the top of the head by Elizabeth. I've gotten very fond of him (he's the adventurous kind of cat who likes to climb hills with you), and one night I simply felt like kissing him on the top of the head, and did. Why did no one tell me sooner how silky cat fur is?

Then there's my relation to cars. I am completely unembarrassed 13 by my inability to diagnose even minor problems in whatever object I happen to be driving, and don't have to make some insider's remark to mechanics to try to establish that I, too, am a "Man With His Machine."

14　　The same ease extends to household maintenance. I do it, of course. Service people are expensive. But for the last decade my house has functioned better than it used to because I've had the aid of a volume called "Home Repairs Any Woman Can Do," which is pitched just right for people at my technical level. As a youth, I'd as soon have touched such a book as I would have become a transvestite. Even though common sense says there is really nothing sexual whatsoever about fixing sinks.

15　　Or take public emotion. All my life I have easily been moved by certain kinds of voices. The actress Siobhan McKenna's, to take a notable case. Give her an emotional scene in a play, and within 10 words my eyes are full of tears. In boyhood, my great dread was that someone might notice. I struggled manfully, you might say, to suppress this weakness. Now, of course, I don't see it as a weakness at all, but as a kind of fulfillment. I even suspect that the true he-men feel the same way, or one kind of them does, at least, and it's only the poor imitators who have to struggle to repress themselves.

16　　Let me come back to the inkblots, with their assumption that masculine equates with machinery and science, and feminine with art and nature. I have no idea whether the right pronoun for God is He, She or It. But this I'm pretty sure of. If God could somehow be induced to take that test, God would not come out macho, and not feminismo, either, but right in the middle. Fellow androgynes, it's a nice thought.

EXPLORING IDEAS

1. Brainstorm the criteria for distinguishing between maleness and femaleness that Perrin discovered in the test he took. Write a serious essay in which you refute the criteria or a satiric essay in which you defend them.

2. Brainstorm for an essay in which you argue that male stereotypes are more harmful to men than they are to women. How do these stereotypes take away freedom?

3. Brainstorm for an essay in which you characterize three types of men: those who are 100 percent masculine, those who are 75 percent masculine, and those androgynous men who are 50 percent masculine.

4. If it is true that "he-men" are drawn to power and dominance, is it likely that men who abuse their wives and children usually identify themselves as "he-men"? Why? Are women who abuse their husbands and children also drawn to power and dominance?

5. Perrin says that men are often likely to imitate "he-man" characteristics. Are there any other male types that men try to imitate? Identify those other male types for a possible topic for an essay.

6. Is it possible for a man to be a "natural mother," as Perrin suggests? Write an essay in which you list and discuss those aspects of masculinity that make it difficult for men to be "natural mothers."

7. Discuss the stereotype that men are supposed to know all about machines and household maintenance. Write a humorous essay in which you expose this belief as a stereotype.

8. Brainstorm for an essay about the difficulty that men have expressing emotion. Discuss both causes and effects.

9. Try writing a speculative essay about a future society in which everyone is androgynous. How would such a society differ from ours today?

Exploring Rhetoric

1. Why does Perrin devote the entire first paragraph to a train trip? Isn't this story likely to lead the reader away from his central point?

2. Why does Perrin tell us that he had to skin a couple of horses that summer and that he had a good time leading troops in combat?

3. Discuss the effectiveness of Perrin's anecdote about the psychological test he took. Is this sort of test so outdated that it can no longer be viewed seriously?

4. Write a brief analysis of Perrin based on your reading of this essay. Do you like him or not? Use specific details in the essay to support your response.

5. What methods does Perrin use to make us trust his authority or believe his discussion? How would a sociological analysis differ from this personal account?

6. Write an analysis of this essay in which you show that Perrin is still caught in the masculine-feminine stereotypes that he claims to have escaped.

7. Discuss the overall tone of this essay. How can you determine Perrin's attitude toward his subject or his purpose in writing about it? Identify the language, examples, logic, and details that communicate this tone.

8. Discuss the effectiveness of the concluding paragraph of the essay.

The Appeal of the Androgynous Man

Amy Gross

Amy Gross, born in 1942, has been a feature editor for *Vogue* magazine. She has also written articles and essays on women's issues for a number of magazines and newspapers, including *Redbook* and the *New York Times*. In the following essay, published in the popular women's magazine

Mademoiselle, Gross lists several negative characteristics of the "all-man man" and explains to women why the androgynous man makes a better "teammate."

1   James Dean was my first androgynous man. I figured I could talk to him. He was anguished and I was 12, so we had a lot in common. With only a few exceptions, all the men I have liked or loved have been a certain kind of man: a kind who doesn't play football or watch the games on Sunday, who doesn't tell dirty jokes featuring broads or chicks, who is not contemptuous of conversations that are philosophically speculative, introspective, or otherwise foolish according to the other kind of man. He is more self-amused, less inflated, more quirky, vulnerable and responsive than the other sort (the other sort, I'm visualizing as the guys on TV who advertise deodorant in the locker room). He is more like me than the other sort. He is what social scientists and feminists would call androgynous: having the characteristics of both male and female.

2   Now the first thing I want you to know about the androgynous man is that he is neither effeminate nor hermaphroditic. All his primary and secondary sexual characteristics are in order and I would say he's all-man, but that is just what he is not. He is more than all-man.

3   The merely all-man man, for one thing, never walks to the grocery store unless the little woman is away visiting her mother with the kids, or is in the hospital having a kid, or there is no little woman. All-men men don't know how to shop in a grocery store unless it is to buy a 6-pack and some pretzels. Their ideas of nutrition expand beyond a 6-pack and pretzels only to take in steak, potatoes, scotch or rye whiskey, and maybe a wad of cake or apple pie. All-men men have absolutely no taste in food, art, books, movies, theatre, dance, how to live, what are good questions, what is funny, or anything else I care about. It's not exactly that the all-man's man is an uncouth illiterate. He may be educated, well-mannered, and on a first-name basis with fine wines. One all-man man I knew was a handsome individual who gave the impression of being gentle, affectionate, and sensitive. He sat and ate dinner one night while I was doing something endearingly feminine at the sink. At one point, he mutely held up his glass to indicate in a primitive, even ape-like way, his need for a refill. This was in 1967, before Women's Liberation. Even so, I was disturbed. Not enough to break the glass over his handsome head, not even enough to mutely indicate the whereabouts of the refrigerator, but enough to remember that moment in all its revelatory clarity. No androgynous man would ever brutishly expect to be waited on without even a "please." (With a "please," maybe.)

4   The brute happened to be a doctor—not a hard hat—and, to all appearances, couth. But he had bought the whole superman package, complete with that fragile beast, the male ego. The androgynous man arrives

with a male ego too, but his is not as imperialistic. It doesn't invade every area of his life and person. Most activities and thoughts have nothing to do with masculinity or femininity. The androgynous man knows this. The all-man man doesn't. He must keep a constant guard against anything even vaguely feminine (*i.e.*, "sissy") rising up in him. It must be a terrible strain.

Male chauvinism is an irritation, but the real problem I have with the all-man man is that it's hard for me to talk to him. He's alien to me, and for this I'm at least half to blame. As his interests have not carried him into the sissy, mine have never taken me very far into the typically masculine terrains of sports, business and finance, politics, cars, boats and machines. But blame or no blame, the reality is that it is almost as difficult for me to connect with him as it would be to link up with an Arab shepherd or Bolivian sandalmaker. There's a similar culture gap. 5

It seems to me that the most masculine men usually end up with the most feminine women. Maybe they like extreme polarity. I like polarity myself, but the poles have to be within earshot. As I've implied, I'm very big on talking. I fall in love for at least three hours with anyone who engages me in a real conversation. I'd rather a man point out a paragraph in a book—wanting to share it with me—than bring me flowers. I'd rather a man ask what I think than tell me I look pretty. (Women who are very pretty and accustomed to hearing that they are pretty may feel differently.) My experience is that all-men men read books I don't want to see paragraphs of, and don't really give a damn what I or any woman would think about most issues so long as she looks pretty. They have a very limited use for women. I suspect they don't really like us. The androgynous man likes women as much or as little as he likes anyone. 6

Another difference between the all-man man and the androgynous man is that the first is not a star in the creativity department. If your image of the creative male accessorizes him with a beret, smock and artist's palette, you will not believe the all-man man has been seriously shortchanged. But if you allow as how creativity is a talent for freedom, associated with imagination, wit, empathy, unpredictability, and receptivity to new impressions and connections, then you will certainly pity the dull, thick-skinned, rigid fellow in whom creativity sets no fires. 7

Nor is the all-man man so hot when it comes to sensitivity. He may be true-blue in the trenches, but if you are troubled, you'd be wasting your time trying to milk comfort from the all-man man. 8

This is not blind prejudice. It is enlightened prejudice. My biases were confirmed recently by a psychologist named Sandra Lipsetz Bem, a professor at Stanford University. She brought to attention the fact that high masculinity in males (and high femininity in females) has been "consistently correlated with lower overall intelligence and lower creativity." Another psychologist, Donald W. MacKinnon, director of the 9

Institute of Personality Assessment and Research at the University of California in Berkeley, found that "creative males give more expression to the feminine side of their nature than do less creative men. . . . [They] score relatively high on femininity, and this despite the fact that, as a group, they do not present an effeminate appearance or give evidence of increased homosexual interests or experiences. Their elevated scores on femininity indicate rather an openness to their feelings and emotions, a sensitive intellect and understanding self-awareness and wide-ranging interests including many which in the American culture are thought of as more feminine. . . ."

10   Dr. Bem ran a series of experiments on college students who had been categorized as masculine, feminine, or androgynous. In three tests of the degree of nurturance—warmth and caring—the masculine men scored painfully low (painfully for anyone stuck with a masculine man, that is). In one of those experiments, all the students were asked to listen to a "troubled talker"—a person who was not neurotic but simply lonely, supposedly new in town and feeling like an outsider. The masculine men were the least supportive, responsive or humane. "They lacked the ability to express warmth, playfulness and concern," Bem concluded. (She's giving them the benefit of the doubt. It's possible the masculine men didn't express those qualities because they didn't possess them.)

11   The androgynous man, on the other hand, having been run through the same carnival of tests, "performs spectacularly. He shuns no behavior just because our culture happens to label it as female and his competence crosses both the instrumental [getting the job done, the problem solved] and the expressive [showing a concern for the welfare of others, the harmony of the group] domains. Thus, he stands firm in his opinion, he cuddles kittens and bounces babies and he has a sympathetic ear for someone in distress."

12   Well, a great mind, a sensitive and warm personality are fine in their place, but you are perhaps skeptical of the gut appeal of the androgynous man. As a friend, maybe, you'd like an adrogynous man. For a sexual partner, though, you'd prefer a jock. There's no arguing chemistry, but consider the jock for a moment. He competes on the field, whatever his field is, and bed is just one more field to him: another opportunity to perform, another fray. Sensuality is for him candy to be doled out as lure. It is a ration whose flow is cut off at the exact point when it has served its purpose—namely, to elicit your willingness to work out on the field with him.

13   Highly masculine men need to believe their sexual appetite is far greater than a woman's (than a nice woman's). To them, females must be seduced. Seduction is a euphemism for a power play, a con job. It pits man against woman (or woman against man). The jock believes he must win you over, incite your body to rebel against your better judgment: in other words—conquer you.

The androgynous man is not your opponent but your teammate. He 14
does not seduce: he invites. Sensuality is a pleasure for him. He's not
quite so goal-oriented. And to conclude, I think I need only remind you
here of his greater imagination, his wit and empathy, his unpredictability, and his receptivity to new impressions and connections.

EXPLORING IDEAS

1. In the first paragraph, Gross contrasts androgynous men with nonandrogy-
nous men. Does this contrast suggest that the only acceptable men are those who
are most like women? What are the characteristics of androgynous women?

2. Is the description Gross provides of "all-men men" a stereotype? If so, then
how valid is her criticism of this type? See Robert Heilbroner's essay elsewhere
in this part for a definition of stereotypes.

3. Do you agree with Gross that most activities and thoughts have nothing to
do with masculinity and femininity? Brainstorm this idea, listing activities that
are masculine or feminine and comparable activities that are not gender specific.

4. Gross says that the most masculine men end up with the most feminine
women. Is this a stereotype, or is there some basis of truth in her conclusion? Explain your answer.

5. Do you agree with Gross that "all-men men" do not really like women? Using specific examples, argue for or against this idea.

6. Gross believes that high masculinity in men and high femininity in women
are correlated with lower intelligence. She calls this "enlightened prejudice." Is
there such a thing as "enlightened prejudice"?

7. Gross's overall argument seems to suggest that women are more caring,
more open, more intelligent, and more creative than men. Do you agree or disagree? Discuss.

8. What do you think about Gross's argument that athletes make poor lovers?
How does one go about proving or disproving such a statement?

9. Gross says that highly masculine men need to believe that their sexual ap-
petites are greater than those of a "nice woman." Do you agree or disagree? Discuss. What does Gross mean by the phrase "nice woman"?

10. Gross says that "seduction" is a euphemism for a power play, a con job. Is
this always true? Is there no place in modern male-female relationships for seduction? What is the difference between flirtation and seduction?

EXPLORING RHETORIC

1. Discuss the tone of Gross's opening sentence about James Dean, an actor who
died in an auto accident in 1955 at the age of twenty-four. What movie star of today might be characterized as an image of the androgynous man?

2. Discuss Gross's use of parallelism and balanced sentences in paragraphs 1
through 3.

3. Discuss the tone of the phrase "doing something endearingly feminine at the sink." Find other examples of this same tone in the essay.

4. Gross extends her argument that the "all-man man" is alien to her by comparing him to men of other cultures, such as an Arab shepherd or a Bolivian sandal-maker. Does she mean that a person of one culture can never have anything in common with someone of another culture? Is this a good analogy?

5. Discuss the tone Gross uses in her list of preferences in a man. Are these meant to be taken seriously, or are they merely meant to be clever? How do you know?

6. Is Gross being a bit extreme when she suggests that the "all-man man" can never be creative or imaginative? What is it about such a man that makes creativity impossible?

7. Discuss the metaphors Gross uses in her discussion of athletes in paragraphs 12 and 13. How effective are the metaphors?

8. Discuss the overall tone of this essay. Compare it with the tone of Noel Perrin's essay on the androgynous man (the previous selection in this book). Create an imaginative dialogue between Perrin and Gross. Do you think they would basically agree or disagree? Would they like each other? Explain why or why not.

Femininity

SUSAN BROWNMILLER

Susan Brownmiller, born in 1935, has worked as an actress in New York and as an editor for various magazines. She helped organize such groups as Women Against Pornography and New York Radical Feminists. Her book *Against Our Will: Women and Rape*, 1975, focuses on how rape is a process of intimidation by which men keep women in fear. Her other books include *Femininity*, 1984, and a novel, *Waverly Place*, 1989.

In the opening to *Femininity*, Brownmiller argues that being "feminine" involves a series of compromises women are compelled to make to succeed in the world. Whereas the feminine woman is given certain privileges and courtesies in society, she enjoys these at the cost of many restrictions on her behavior.

1   We had a game in our house called "setting the table" and I was Mother's helper. Forks to the left of the plate, knives and spoons to the right. Placing the cutlery neatly, as I recall, was one of my first duties, and the event was alive with meaning. When a knife or fork dropped to the floor, that meant a man was unexpectedly coming to dinner. A falling spoon announced the surprise arrival of a female guest. No matter that these visitors never arrived on cue, I had learned a rule of gender identifi-

cation. Men were straight-edged, sharply pronged and formidable, women were softly curved and held the food in a rounded well. It made perfect sense, like the division of pink and blue that I saw in babies, an orderly way of viewing the world. Daddy, who was gone all day at work and who loved to putter at home with his pipe, tobacco and tool chest, was knife and fork. Mommy and Grandma, with their ample proportions and pots and pans, were grownup soup spoons, large and capacious. And I was a teaspoon, small and slender, easy to hold and just right for pudding, my favorite dessert.

Being good at what was expected of me was one of my earliest proj- 2 ects, for not only was I rewarded, as most children are, for doing things right, but excellence gave pride and stability to my childhood existence. Girls were different from boys, and the expression of that difference seemed mine to make clear. Did my loving, anxious mother, who dressed me in white organdy pinafores and Mary Janes and who cried hot tears when I got them dirty, give me my first instruction? Of course. Did my doting aunts and uncles with their gifts of pretty dolls and miniature tea sets add to my education? Of course. But even without the appropriate toys and clothes, lessons in the art of being feminine lay all around me and I absorbed them all: the fairy tales that were read to me at night, the brightly colored advertisements I pored over in magazines before I learned to decipher the words, the movies I saw, the comic books I hoarded, the radio soap operas I happily followed whenever I had to stay in bed with a cold. I loved being a little girl, or rather I loved being a fairy princess, for that was who I thought I was.

As I passed through a stormy adolescence to a stormy maturity, fem- 3 ininity increasingly became an exasperation, a brilliant, subtle esthetic that was bafflingly inconsistent at the same time that it was minutely, demandingly concrete, a rigid code of appearance and behavior defined by do's and don't-do's that went against my rebellious grain. Femininity was a challenge thrown down to the female sex, a challenge no proud, self-respecting young woman could afford to ignore, particularly one with enormous ambition that she nursed in secret, alternately feeding or starving its inchoate life in tremendous confusion.

"Don't lose your femininity" and "Isn't it remarkable how she man- 4 ages to retain her femininity?" had terrifying implications. They spoke of a bottom-line failure so irreversible that nothing else mattered. The pinball machine had registered "tilt," the game had been called. Disqualification was marked on the forehead of a woman whose femininity was lost. No records would be entered in her name, for she had destroyed her birthright in her wretched, ungainly effort to imitate a man. She walked in limbo, this hapless creature, and it occurred to me that one day I might see her when I looked in the mirror. If the danger was so palpable that warning notices were freely posted, wasn't it possible that the small bundle of resentments I carried around in secret might spill out and place the mark on my own forehead? Whatever quarrels with femininity I had I kept to myself; whatever handicaps femininity imposed, they were mine to deal with alone, for there was no women's movement to ask the tough questions, or to brazenly disregard the rules.

5   Femininity, in essence, is a romantic sentiment, a nostalgic tradition of imposed limitations. Even as it hurries forward in the 1980s, putting on lipstick and high heels to appear well dressed, it trips on the ruffled petticoats and hoopskirts of an era gone by. Invariably and necessarily, femininity is something that women had more of in the past, not only in the historic past of prior generations, but in each woman's personal past as well—in the virginal innocence that is replaced by knowledge, in the dewy cheek that is coarsened by age, in the "inherent nature" that a woman seems to misplace so forgetfully whenever she steps out of bounds. Why should this be so? The XX chromosomal message has not been scrambled, the estrogen-dominated hormonal balance is generally as biology intended, the reproductive organs, whatever use one has made of them, are usually in place, the breasts of whatever size are most often where they should be. But clearly, biological femaleness is not enough.

6   Femininity always demands more. It must constantly reassure its audience by a willing demonstration of difference, even when one does not exist in nature, or it must seize and embrace a natural variation and compose a rhapsodic symphony upon the notes. Suppose one doesn't care to, has other things on her mind, is clumsy or tone-deaf despite the best instruction and training? To fail at the feminine difference is to appear not to care about men, and to risk the loss of their attention and approval. To be insufficiently feminine is viewed as a failure in core sexual identity, or as a failure to care sufficiently about oneself, for a woman found wanting will be appraised (and will appraise herself) as mannish or neutered or simply unattractive, as men have defined these terms.

7   We are talking, admittedly, about an exquisite esthetic. Enormous pleasure can be extracted from feminine pursuits as a creative outlet or purely as relaxation; indeed, indulgence for the sake of fun, or art, or attention, is among femininity's great joys. But the chief attraction (and the central paradox, as well) is the competitive edge that femininity seems to promise in the unending struggle to survive, and perhaps to triumph. The world smiles favorably on the feminine woman: it extends little courtesies and minor privilege. Yet the nature of this competitive edge is ironic, at best, for one works at femininity by accepting restrictions, by limiting one's sights, by choosing an indirect route, by scattering concentration and not giving one's all as a man would to his own, certifiably masculine, interests. It does not require a great leap of imagination for a woman to understand the feminine principle as a grand collection of compromises, large and small, that she simply must make in

order to render herself a successful woman. If she has difficulty in satisfying femininity's demands, if its illusions go against her grain, or if she is criticized for her shortcomings and imperfections, the more she will see femininity as a desperate strategy of appeasement, a strategy she may not have the wish or the courage to abandon, for failure looms in either direction.

It is fashionable in some quarters to describe the feminine and masculine principles as polar ends of the human continuum, and to sagely profess that both polarities exist in all people. Sun and moon, yin and yang, soft and hard, active and passive, etcetera, may indeed be opposites, but a linear continuum does not illuminate the problem. (Femininity, in all its contrivances, is a very active endeavor.) What, then, is the basic distinction? The masculine principle is better understood as a driving ethos of superiority designed to inspire straightforward, confident success, while the feminine principle is composed of vulnerability, the need for protection, the formalities of compliance and the avoidance of conflict—in short, an appeal of dependence and good will that gives the masculine principle its romantic validity and its admiring applause. 8

Femininity pleases men because it makes them appear more masculine by contrast; and, in truth, conferring an extra portion of unearned gender distinction on men, an unchallenged space in which to breathe freely and feel stronger, wiser, more competent, is femininity's special gift. One could say that masculinity is often an effort to please women, but masculinity is known to please by displays of mastery and competence while femininity pleases by suggesting that these concerns, except in small matters, are beyond its intent. Whimsy, unpredictability and patterns of thinking and behavior that are dominated by emotion, such as tearful expressions of sentiment and fear, are thought to be feminine precisely because they lie outside the established route to success. 9

If in the beginnings of history the feminine woman was defined by her physical dependency, her inability for reasons of reproductive biology to triumph over the forces of nature that were the tests of masculine strength and power, today she reflects both an economic and emotional dependency that is still considered "natural," romantic and attractive. After an unsettling fifteen years in which many basic assumptions about the sexes were challenged, the economic disparity did not disappear. Large numbers of women—those with small children, those left high and dry after a mid-life divorce—need financial support. But even those who earn their own living share a universal need for connectedness (call it love, if you wish). As unprecedented numbers of men abandon their sexual interest in women, others, sensing opportunity, choose to demonstrate their interest through variety and a change in partners. A sociological fact of the 1980s is that female competition for two scarce resources—men and jobs—is especially fierce. 10

11   So it is not surprising that we are currently witnessing a renewed interest in femininity and an unabashed indulgence in feminine pursuits. Femininity serves to reassure men that women need them and care about them enormously. By incorporating the decorative and the frivolous into its definition of style, femininity functions as an effective antidote to the unrelieved seriousness, the pressure of making one's way in a harsh, difficult world. In its mandate to avoid direct confrontation and to smooth over the fissures of conflict, femininity operates as a value system of niceness, a code of thoughtfulness and sensitivity that in modern society is sadly in short supply.

EXPLORING IDEAS

1. Brownmiller says the little game of "setting the table" was "alive with meaning." Try to think of a ritual in your own family that was, or is, "alive with meaning." Describe it in such a way that you clarify that meaning.

2. Brownmiller identifies the knife and fork with men and the spoon with women. Think of some other common objects that might be used to distinguish men and women. Write a comic (or serious) comparison-contrast essay in which you clarify this difference.

3. Brownmiller says that lessons in the art of being feminine surrounded her. Brainstorm for an essay in which you discuss the books, games, television shows, and so forth that defined the difference between masculine and feminine for you when you were a child.

4. Why does Brownmiller call femininity an "esthetic"? How is femininity like that branch of philosophy that is concerned with what art is and how it is judged?

5. Brainstorm for an essay in which you discuss the basic irony of what Brownmiller calls femininity's competitive edge.

6. Brainstorm for an essay in which you agree or disagree with the following statement: ". . . conferring an extra portion of unearned gender distinction on men, an unchallenged space in which to breathe freely and feel stronger, wiser, more competent, is femininity's special gift."

7. Brownmiller says that unprecedented numbers of men are abandoning their sexual interest in women. Why does she say this? What support does she give for the statement? If this is true, what might be the cause?

8. Why does Brownmiller say there is "a renewed interest in femininity and an unabashed indulgence in feminine pursuits"?

EXPLORING RHETORIC

1. Discuss the effectiveness of Brownmiller's use of each of the following metaphors: "a challenge thrown down to the female sex"; "alternately feeding or starving its inchoate life"; "the pinball machine had registered 'tilt' "; "she walked in limbo"; "small bundle of resentments I carried around"; "place the mark on my own forehead."

2. Write a brief essay in which you develop Brownmiller's metaphor that although femininity hurries forward, it "trips on the ruffled petticoats and hoopskirts of an era gone by."

3. Discuss Brownmiller's metaphor of the "rhapsodic symphony" and being "tone-deaf." Is this an effective metaphor or too self-conscious? What is the difference between effective and forced metaphors?

4. Analyze the style in paragraph 7. How would you characterize Brownmiller's style: concrete, detailed, abstract, general, easy, hard? Refer to the diction and sentence structure in this paragraph to support your analysis.

5. Discuss the logic of Brownmiller's argument about the difference between how masculinity and femininity please in paragraph 9.

6. How does Brownmiller know that a sociological fact of the 1980s is that female competition for men and jobs is especially fierce? How can you argue against this statement?

7. What is Brownmiller's point in the following sentence: "In its mandate to avoid direct confrontation and to smooth over the fissures of conflict, femininity operates as a value system of niceness, a code of thoughtfulness and sensitivity that in modern society is sadly in short supply"? Is she arguing for the values of femininity or against them?

Being a Man

PAUL THEROUX

Paul Theroux, born in 1941 in Medford, Massachusetts, was educated at the University of Maine, the University of Massachusetts, and Syracuse University. He spent ten years in the Peace Corps in Asia and Africa. A novelist, travel writer, poet, and essayist, his books include *The Great Railway Bazaar,* 1975; *The Old Patagonian Express,* 1979; *The Mosquito Coast,* 1982; *Riding the Iron Rooster,* 1988; and *Sunrise with Seamonsters: Travels and Discoveries, 1964–1984,* 1985, from which the following essay is taken.

In this blunt and unrelenting exposition on what it means to be masculine, Paul Theroux has nothing good to say about "manliness," the pursuit of which he calls "right-wing, puritanical, cowardly, neurotic and fueled largely by fear of women."

There is a pathetic sentence in the chapter "Fetishism" in Dr. Norman   1
Cameron's book *Personality Development and Psychopathology.* It goes, "Fettishists are nearly always men; and their commonest fetish is a woman's shoe." I cannot read that sentence without thinking that it is

just one more awful thing about being a man—and perhaps it is an important thing to know about us.

2   I have always disliked being a man. The whole idea of manhood in America is pitiful, in my opinion. This version of masculinity is a little like having to wear an ill-fitting coat for one's entire life (by contrast, I imagine femininity to be an oppressive sense of nakedness). Even the expression "Be a man!" strikes me as insulting and abusive. It means: Be stupid, be unfeeling, obedient, soldierly and stop thinking. Man means "manly"—how can one think about men without considering the terrible ambition of manliness? And yet it is part of every man's life. It is a hideous and crippling lie; it not only insists on difference and connives at superiority, it is also by its very nature destructive—emotionally damaging and socially harmful.

3   The youth who is subverted, as most are, into believing in the masculine ideal is effectively separated from women and he spends the rest of his life finding women a riddle and a nuisance. Of course, there is a female version of this male affliction. It begins with mothers encouraging little girls to say (to other adults) "Do you like my new dress?" In a sense, little girls are traditionally urged to please adults with a kind of coquettishness, while boys are enjoined to behave like monkeys towards each other. The nine-year-old coquette proceeds to become womanish in a subtle power game in which she learns to be sexually indispensable, socially decorative and always alert to a man's sense of inadequacy.

4   Femininity—being lady-like—implies needing a man as witness and seducer; but masculinity celebrates the exclusive company of men. That is why it is so grotesque; and that is also why there is no manliness without inadequacy—because it denies men the natural friendship of women.

5   It is very hard to imagine any concept of manliness that does not belittle women, and it begins very early. At an age when I wanted to meet girls—let's say the treacherous years of thirteen to sixteen—I was told to take up a sport, get more fresh air, join the Boy Scouts, and I was urged not to read so much. It was the 1950s and if you asked too many questions about sex you were sent to camp—boy's camp, of course: the nightmare. Nothing is more unnatural or prison-like than a boy's camp, but if it were not for them we would have no Elks' Lodges, no pool rooms, no boxing matches, no Marines.

6   And perhaps no sports as we know them. Everyone is aware of how few in number are the athletes who behave like gentlemen. Just as high school basketball teaches you how to be a poor loser, the manly attitude towards sports seems to be little more than a recipe for creating bad marriages, social misfits, moral degenerates, sadists, latent rapists and just plain louts. I regard high school sports as a drug far worse than marijuana, and it is the reason that the average tennis champion, say, is a pathetic oaf.

Any objective study would find the quest for manliness essentially 7
right-wing, puritanical, cowardly, neurotic and fueled largely by a fear
of women. It is also certainly philistine. There is no book-hater like a Little League coach. But indeed all the creative arts are obnoxious to the
manly ideal, because at their best the arts are pursued by uncompetitive
and essentially solitary people. It makes it very hard for a creative
youngster, for any boy who expresses the desire to be alone seems to be
saying that there is something wrong with him.

It ought to be clear by now that I have something of an objection to 8
the way we turn boys into men. It does not surprise me that when the
President of the United States [Ronald Reagan] has his customary weekend off he dresses like a cowboy—it is both a measure of his insecurity
and his willingness to please. In many ways, American culture does little more for a man than prepare him for modeling clothes in the L. L.
Bean catalogue. I take this as a personal insult because for many years I
found it impossible to admit to myself that I wanted to be a writer. It was
my guilty secret, because being a writer was incompatible with being
a man.

There are people who might deny this, but that is because the Amer- 9
ican writer, typically, has been so at pains to prove his manliness that we
have come to see literariness and manliness as mingled qualities. But
first there was a fear that writing was not a manly profession—indeed,
not a profession at all. (The paradox in American letters is that it has always been easier for a woman to write and for a man to be published.)
Growing up, I had thought of sports as wasteful and humiliating, and
the idea of manliness was a bore. My wanting to become a writer was
not a flight from that oppressive role-playing, but I quickly saw that it
was at odds with it. Everything in stereotyped manliness goes against
the life of the mind. The Hemingway personality is too tedious to go into
here, and in any case his exertions are well-known, but certainly it was
not until this aberrant behavior was examined by feminists in the 1960s
that any male writer dared question the pugnacity in Hemingway's fiction. All the bullfighting and arm wrestling and elephant shooting di-
minished Hemingway as a writer, but it is consistent with a prevailing
attitude in American writing: one cannot be a male writer without first
proving that one is a man.

It is normal in America for a man to be dismissive or even somewhat 10
apologetic about being a writer. Various factors make it easier. There is a
heartiness about journalism that makes it acceptable—journalism is the
manliest form of American writing and, therefore, the profession the
most independent-minded women seek (yes, it is an illusion, but that is
my point). Fiction-writing is equated with a kind of dispirited failure
and is only manly when it produces wealth—money is masculinity. So is
drinking. Being a drunkard is another assertion, if misplaced, of manliness. The American male writer is traditionally proud of his heavy

drinking. But we are also a very literal-minded people. A man proves his manhood in America in old-fashioned ways. He kills lions, like Hemingway; or he hunts ducks, like Nathanael West; or he makes pronouncements like, "A man should carry enough knife to defend himself with," as James Jones once said to a *Life* interviewer. Or he says he can drink you under the table. But even tiny drunken William Faulkner loved to mount a horse and go fox hunting, and Jack Kerouac roistered up and down Manhattan in a lumberjack shirt (and spent every night of *The Subterraneans* with his mother in Queens). And we are familiar with the lengths to which Norman Mailer is prepared, in his endearing way, to prove that he is just as much a monster as the next man.

11   When the novelist John Irving was revealed as a wrestler, people took him to be a very serious writer; and even a bubble reputation like Eric (*Love Story*) Segal's was enhanced by the news that he ran the marathon in a respectable time. How surprised we would be if Joyce Carol Oates were revealed as a sumo wrestler or Joan Didion active in pumping iron. "Lives in New York City with her three children" is the typical woman writer's biographical note, for just as the male writer must prove he has achieved a sort of muscular manhood, the woman writer—or rather her publicists—must prove her motherhood.

12   There would be no point in saying any of this if it were not generally accepted that to be a man is somehow—even now in feminist-influenced America—a privilege. It is on the contrary an unmerciful and punishing burden. Being a man is bad enough; being manly is appalling (in this sense, women's lib has done much more for men than for women). It is the sinister silliness of men's fashions, and a clubby attitude in the arts. It is the subversion of good students. It is the so-called "Dress Code" of the Ritz-Carlton Hotel in Boston, and it is the institutionalized cheating in college sports. It is the most primitive insecurity.

13   And this is also why men often object to feminism but are afraid to explain why: of course women have a justified grievance, but most men believe—and with reason—that their lives are just as bad.

EXPLORING IDEAS

1. Write an essay in which you refute Theroux's claim that the expression "Be a man" means: "Be stupid, be unfeeling, obedient, soldierly and stop thinking."

2. Why does Theroux call "manliness" a "terrible ambition" and a "hideous and crippling lie"? Is this language a bit extreme, or is Theroux justified? Discuss your answer.

3. Do men generally think that women are a "riddle" and a "nuisance"? Brainstorm the causes and manifestations of such an attitude. Brainstorm examples from your own experience, as well as from books, films, television, and other examples of popular culture.

4. Write an essay in which you explain why it is difficult for men and women to be friends with each other. Is this difficulty all the fault of men, or are women partly to blame?

5. Use the following sentence as the thesis statement of an essay: "Nothing is more unnatural or prison-like than a boy's camp, but if it were not for them we would have no Elks' Lodges, no pool rooms, no boxing matches, no Marines."

6. Theroux says it is hard to imagine any concept of manliness that does not belittle women. This statement sounds extreme. Can you argue against it?

7. Brainstorm for an essay in which you disagree with Theroux's assessment of high school sports as a drug worse than marijuana. Is it possible to write an essay that supports sports without sounding corny and using clichés?

8. Write an essay in which you agree or disagree with Theroux's statement that the creative arts are "obnoxious to the manly ideal." Read Amy Gross's essay on the appeal of the androgynous man (the previous selection in this book) for a discussion of this issue.

9. Why is writing not considered a masculine activity in America?

10. Brainstorm why being a man in America is a burden or a privilege. Write an essay in which you suggest that it is both.

EXPLORING RHETORIC

1. Discuss the example Theroux uses to open his essay. Do you think he is serious when he says that the shoe fetishist adds to his list of how awful it is to be a man, or do you think he chose the example for its rhetorical effect? How can you determine which reason is true?

2. Discuss the effectiveness of Theroux's metaphor of masculinity as being like wearing an ill-fitting coat and of femininity as an oppressive sense of nakedness. Write an essay contrasting the implications of the two metaphors.

3. Why does Theroux say he was urged not to read so much during the "treacherous years" of thirteen to sixteen? Why are these years called "dangerous"?

4. Is Theroux engaging in extreme shock statements when he says that athletes are not gentlemen, basketball teaches how to be a poor loser, and the average tennis champion is a pathetic oaf? Is he stereotyping, or is there enough truth in these statements to make them believable?

5. Comment on the following statement: "Any objective study would find the quest for manliness essentially right-wing, puritanical, cowardly, neurotic and fueled largely by a fear of women." Can this opinion be supported? How does Theroux know that any objective study would find this to be true?

6. How do you respond to Theroux's statement that when he was growing up, he found sports wasteful and humiliating and the idea of manliness a bore? What image of his childhood does he create? How does this image affect his argument or the reader's response to it?

7. What does Theroux mean by the parenthetical statement ("yes, it is an illusion, but that is my point")?

8. Why does Theroux end his essay with references to American authors James Jones, William Faulkner, Jack Kerouac, Norman Mailer, and John Irving? Is he narrowing the relevance of his argument to writers? Does his conclusion suggest that this essay is Theroux's personal complaint against American attitudes toward male writers like himself?

Just Walk On By

BRENT STAPLES

Brent Staples was born in Chester, Pennsylvania, in 1951. He received his B.A. in 1973 from Widener University in Chester, Pennsylvania, and his Ph.D. in psychology in 1982 from the University of Chicago. After working as a reporter for the *Chicago Sun-Times*, he began writing for the *New York Times* in 1985, for which he became assistant metropolitan editor in 1990. He has written for *Down Beat, Harpers, Ms.*, and other magazines.

In this frequently reprinted essay, Staples writes a firsthand account of what it feels like to be feared for no other reason than the color of one's skin. He describes the alienation that results from forever being a suspect and concludes with his own simple device for reducing tension in those he passes.

1   My first victim was a woman—white, well dressed, probably in her early twenties. I came upon her late one evening on a deserted street in Hyde Park, a relatively affluent neighborhood in an otherwise mean, impoverished section of Chicago. As I swung onto the avenue behind her, there seemed to be a discreet, uninflammatory distance between us. Not so. She cast back a worried glance. To her, the youngish black man—a broad six feet two inches with a beard and billowing hair, both hands shoved into the pockets of a bulky military jacket—seemed menacingly close. After a few more quick glimpses, she picked up her pace and was soon running in earnest. Within seconds she disappeared into a cross street.

2   That was more than a decade ago. I was 22 years old, a graduate student newly arrived at the University of Chicago. It was in the echo of that terrified woman's footfalls that I first began to know the unwieldly inheritance I'd come into—the ability to alter public space in ugly ways. It was clear that she thought herself the quarry of a mugger, a rapist, or worse. Suffering a bout of insomnia, however, I was stalking sleep, not defenseless wayfarers. As a softy who is scarcely able to take a knife to a raw chicken—let alone hold it to a person's throat—I was surprised, embarrassed, and dismayed all at once. Her flight made me feel like an ac-

complice in tyranny. It also made it clear that I was indistinguishable from the muggers who occasionally seeped into the area from the surrounding ghetto. That first encounter, and those that followed, signified that a vast, unnerving gulf lay between nighttime pedestrians—particularly women—and me. And I soon gathered that being perceived as dangerous is a hazard in itself. I only needed to turn a corner into a dicey situation, or crowd some frightened, armed person in a foyer somewhere, or make an errant move after being pulled over by a policeman. Where fear and weapons meet—and they often do in urban America—there is always the possibility of death.

In that first year, my first away from my hometown, I was to become 3 thoroughly familiar with the language of fear. At dark, shadowy intersections in Chicago, I could cross in front of a car stopped at a traffic light and elicit the *thunk, thunk, thunk, thunk* of the driver—black, white, male, or female—hammering down the door locks. On less traveled streets after dark, I grew accustomed to but never comfortable with people who crossed to the other side of the street rather than pass me. Then there were the standard unpleasantries with police, doormen, bouncers, cab drivers, and others whose business it is to screen out troublesome individuals *before* there is any nastiness.

I moved to New York nearly two years ago and I have remained an 4 avid night walker. In central Manhattan, the near-constant crowd cover minimizes tense one-on-one street encounters. Elsewhere—visiting friends in SoHo, where sidewalks are narrow and tightly spaced buildings shut out the sky—things can get very taut indeed.

Black men have a firm place in New York mugging literature. Norman Podhoretz in his famed (or infamous) 1963 essay, "My Negro Problem—And Ours," recalls growing up in terror of black males; they "were tougher than we were, more ruthless," he writes—and as an adult on the Upper West Side of Manhattan, he continues, he cannot constrain his nervousness when he meets black men on certain streets. Similarly, a decade later, the essayist and novelist Edward Hoagland extols a New York where once "Negro bitterness bore down mainly on other Negroes." Where some see mere panhandlers, Hoagland sees "a mugger who is clearly screwing up his nerve to do more than just *ask* for money." But Hoagland has "the New Yorker's quick-hunch posture for broken-field maneuvering," and the bad guy swerves away.

I often witness that "hunch posture," from women after dark on the 6 warrenlike streets of Brooklyn where I live. They seem to set their faces on neutral and, with their purse straps strung across their chests bandolier style, they forge ahead as though bracing themselves against being tackled. I understand, of course, that the danger they perceive is not a hallucination. Women are particularly vulnerable to street violence, and young black males are drastically overrepresented among the perpetrators of that violence. Yet these truths are no solace against the kind of alienation that comes of being ever the suspect, against being set apart, a fearsome entity with whom pedestrians avoid making eye contact.

7   It is not altogether clear to me how I reached the ripe old age of 22 without being conscious of the lethality nighttime pedestrians attributed to me. Perhaps it was because in Chester, Pennsylvania, the small, angry industrial town where I came of age in the 1960s, I was scarcely noticeable against a backdrop of gang warfare, street knifings, and murders. I grew up one of the good boys, had perhaps a half-dozen fist fights. In retrospect, my shyness of combat has clear sources.

8   Many things go into the making of a young thug. One of those things is the consummation of the male romance with the power to intimidate. An infant discovers that random flailings send the baby bottle flying out of the crib and crashing to the floor. Delighted, the joyful babe repeats those motions again and again, seeking to duplicate the feat. Just so, I recall the points at which some of my boyhood friends were finally seduced by the perception of themselves as tough guys. When a mark cowered and surrendered his money without resistance, myth and reality merged—and paid off. It is, after all, only manly to embrace the power to frighten and intimidate. We, as men, are not supposed to give an inch of our lane on the highway; we are to seize the fighter's edge in work and in play and even in love; we are to be valiant in the face of hostile forces.

9   Unfortunately, poor and powerless young men seem to take all this nonsense literally. As a boy, I saw countless tough guys locked away; I have since buried several, too. They were babies, really—a teenage cousin, a brother of 22, a childhood friend in his mid-twenties—all gone down in episodes of bravado played out in the streets. I came to doubt the virtues of intimidation early on. I chose, perhaps even unconsciously, to remain a shadow—timid, but a survivor.

10   The fearsomeness mistakenly attributed to me in public places often has a perilous flavor. The most frightening of these confusions occurred in the late 1970s and early 1980s when I worked as a journalist in Chicago. One day, rushing into the office of a magazine I was writing for with a deadline story in hand, I was mistaken for a burglar. The office manager called security and, with an ad hoc posse, pursued me through the labyrinthine halls, nearly to my editor's door. I had no way of proving who I was. I could only move briskly toward the company of someone who knew me.

11   Another time I was on assignment for a local paper and killing time before an interview. I entered a jewelry store on the city's affluent Near North Side. The proprietor excused herself and returned with an enormous red Doberman pinscher straining at the end of a leash. She stood,

the dog extended toward me, silent to my questions, her eyes bulging nearly out of her head. I took a cursory look around, nodded, and bade her good night. Relatively speaking, however, I never fared as badly as another black male journalist. He went to nearby Waukegan, Illinois, a couple of summers ago to work on a story about a murderer who was born there. Mistaking the reporter for the killer, police hauled him from his car at gunpoint and but for his press credentials would probably have tried to book him. Such episodes are not uncommon. Black men trade tales like this all the time.

In "My Negro Problem—And Ours," Podhoretz writes that the hatred he feels for blacks makes itself known to him through a variety of avenues—one being his discomfort with that "special brand of paranoid touchiness" to which he says blacks are prone. No doubt he is speaking here of black men. In time, I learned to smother the rage I felt at so often being taken for a criminal. Not to do so would surely have led to madness—via that special "paranoid touchiness" that so annoyed Podhoretz at the time he wrote the essay. 12

I began to take precautions to make myself less threatening. I move about with care, particularly late in the evening. I give a wide berth to nervous people on subway platforms during the wee hours, particularly when I have exchanged business clothes for jeans. If I happen to be entering a building behind some people who appear skittish, I may walk by, letting them clear the lobby before I return, so as not to seem to be following them. I have been calm and extremely congenial on those rare occasions when I've been pulled over by the police. 13

And on late-evening constitutionals along streets less traveled by, I employ what has proved to be an excellent tension-reducing measure: I whistle melodies from Beethoven and Vivaldi and the more popular classical composers. Even steely New Yorkers hunching toward nighttime destinations seem to relax, and occasionally they even join in the tune. Virtually everybody seems to sense that a mugger wouldn't be warbling bright, sunny selections from Vivaldi's *Four Seasons*. It is my equivalent of the cowbell that hikers wear when they know they are in bear country. 14

EXPLORING IDEAS

1. In paragraph 1, Staples describes his first encounter with someone afraid of him because of his appearance. Was the young woman wrong to be afraid? Are we never justified in making a judgment on people based on their appearance? Argue for or against this question, providing examples to support your point.

2. Staples says he was not what the young woman thought he was. Rather than a mugger, rapist, or worse, he was just a softy suffering from insomnia. Try to recall an incident in which you made an initial judgment about someone based on appearance that you later found out to be incorrect. Does the experience prove anything?

3. Staples says he does not like the sense of alienation he feels by being set apart as some "fearsome entity." Try to think of someone you have known or have read about who desires this sense of being a "fearsome entity." Are soldiers and athletes taught to be "fearsome entities"?

4. Brainstorm Staples's comments about the male romance with the power to intimidate. Write an essay in which you support and explain this aspect of male behavior.

5. Staples says that the basic stereotype for men is that they are not supposed to give an inch on the highway, are supposed to assume the fighter's edge in work, play, and love, and are supposed to be valiant in the face of hostile forces. Is all of this nonsense, as Staples suggests, or is there some value in such an image? Discuss both the positive and the negative aspects of this image of men.

6. Staples provides several anecdotes about how black men are mistaken for dangerous criminals, noting that "Such episodes are not uncommon. Black men trade tales like this all the time." Regardless of your race, has such an error ever been made about you? Describe the event, and discuss what it meant to you.

7. What basic stereotype is suggested by Staples's whistling melodies from classical music when he walks along at night?

EXPLORING RHETORIC

1. Why does Staples begin his essay with the sentence, "My first victim was a woman . . ."? What effect does the word "victim" have on the reader?

2. Note the rhetorical techniques Staples uses. First, he opens with an anecdote that illustrates the point he wants to make; second, he provides the background for the anecdote and states what it means; and third, he provides some additional examples of the point. Using the same tactics, write an essay about an experience in which someone reacted to you in a way that surprised you.

3. Discuss the effectiveness of Staples's use of the following metaphors in paragraphs 2 and 3: "the unwieldy inheritance I'd come into"; "she thought herself the quarry of a mugger, a rapist, or worse"; "I was stalking sleep"; "muggers who occasionally seeped into the area from the surrounding ghetto"; "a vast, unnerving gulf lay between"; "the language of fear"; "hammering down the door locks"; "whose business it is to screen out troublesome individuals." Explain the basis of each one of these metaphors.

4. Comment on Staples's use of the following metaphoric language: "I often witness that 'hunch posture,' from women after dark on the warrenlike streets of Brooklyn where I live. They seem to set their faces on neutral and, with their purse straps strung across their chests bandolier style, they forge ahead as though bracing themselves against being tackled." Rewrite the sentence without metaphors, and then comment on the difference between the two sentences.

5. Discuss the effectiveness of Staples's analogy of the baby's throwing its bottle out of the crib. How does the analogy illustrate the concept of the merging of myth and reality?

6. Although beginning a number of sentences in the same way is not usually effective, Staples uses this rhetorical technique in paragraph 13. How is this technique effective here? How does he vary the sentences so they do not seem simplistic and repetitive?

7. Discuss the effectiveness of Staples's final metaphor: "the cowbell that hikers wear when they know they are in bear country." Is this a trivial conclusion or a relevant one?

8. Discuss the overall tone of Staples's essay. Is it angry, amused, puzzled, hurt, indifferent? Point out specific details to support your analysis.

The Myth of the Latin Woman: I Just Met a Girl Named María

JUDITH ORTIZ COFER

Judith Ortiz Cofer was born in 1952 in Puerto Rico and moved to New Jersey with her family when she was a small child. She was educated at the University of Georgia, Florida Atlantic University, and Oxford University and has taught English at the University of Georgia. Her books include a novel, *The Line of the Sun,* 1985; a collection of essays and stories, *Silent Dancing,* 1990; a collection of poetry, *Terms of Survival, Reaching for the Mainland,* 1987.

Using her own experience as an example of the stereotypes that follow Latinas, Cofer explains how Anglos misinterpret Hispanic cultural signals and argues that the media perpetuate these misinterpretations by presenting Latin women as either whores or domestic servants.

On a bus trip to London from Oxford University where I was earning 1 some graduate credits one summer, a young man, obviously fresh from a pub, spotted me and as if struck by inspiration went down on his knees in the aisle. With both hands over his heart he broke into an Irish tenor's rendition of "María" from *West Side Story.* My politely amused fellow passengers gave his lovely voice the round of gentle applause it deserved. Though I was not quite as amused, I managed my version of an English smile: no show of teeth, no extreme contortions of the facial muscles—I was at this time of my life practicing reserve and cool. Oh, that British control, how I coveted it. But María had followed me to London, reminding me of a prime fact of my life: you can leave the Island, master the English language, and travel as far as you can, but if you are a Latina, especially one like me who so obviously belongs to Rita Moreno's gene pool, the Island travels with you.

2   This is sometimes a very good thing—it may win you that extra minute of someone's attention. But with some people, the same things can make *you* an island—not so much a tropical paradise as an Alcatraz, a place nobody wants to visit. As a Puerto Rican girl growing up in the United States and wanting like most children to "belong," I resented the stereotype that my Hispanic appearance called forth from many people I met.

3   Our family lived in a large urban center in New Jersey during the sixties, where life was designed as a microcosm of my parents' casas on the island. We spoke in Spanish, we ate Puerto Rican food bought at the bodega, and we practiced strict Catholicism complete with Saturday confession and Sunday mass at a church where our parents were accommodated into a one-hour Spanish mass slot, performed by a Chinese priest trained as a missionary for Latin America.

4   As a girl I was kept under strict surveillance, since virtue and modesty were, by cultural equation, the same as family honor. As a teenager I was instructed on how to behave as a proper señorita. But it was a conflicting message girls got, since the Puerto Rican mothers also encouraged their daughters to look and act like women and to dress in clothes our Anglo friends and their mothers found too "mature" for our age. It was, and is, cultural, yet I often felt humiliated when I appeared at an American friend's party wearing a dress more suitable to a semiformal than to a playroom birthday celebration. At Puerto Rican festivities, neither the music nor the colors we wore could be too loud. I still experience a vague sense of letdown when I'm invited to a "party" and it turns out to be a marathon conversation in hushed tones rather than a fiesta with salsa, laughter, and dancing—the kind of celebration I remember from my childhood.

5   I remember Career Day in our high school, when teachers told us to come dressed as if for a job interview. It quickly became obvious that to the barrio girls, "dressing up" sometimes meant wearing ornate jewelry and clothing that would be more appropriate (by mainstream standards) for the company Christmas party than as daily office attire. That morning I had agonized in front of my closet, trying to figure out what a "career girl" would wear because, essentially, except for Marlo Thomas on TV, I had no models on which to base my decision. I knew how to dress for school: at the Catholic school I attended we all wore uniforms; I knew how to dress for Sunday mass, and I knew what dresses to wear for parties at my relatives' homes. Though I do not recall the precise details of my Career Day outfit, it must have been a composite of the above choices. But I remember a comment my friend (an Italian-American) made in later years that coalesced my impressions of that day. She said

that at the business school she was attending the Puerto Rican girls always stood out for wearing "everything at once." She meant, of course, too much jewelry, too many accessories. On that day at school, we were simply made the negative models by the nuns who were themselves not credible fashion experts to any of us. But it was painfully obvious to me that to the others, in their tailored skirts and silk blouses, we must have seemed "hopeless" and "vulgar." Though I now know that most adolescents feel out of step much of the time, I also know that for the Puerto Rican girls of my generation that sense was intensified. The way our teachers and classmates looked at us that day in school was just a taste of the culture clash that awaited us in the real world, where prospective employers and men on the street would often misinterpret our tight skirts and jingling bracelets as a come-on.

Mixed cultural signals have perpetuated certain stereotypes—for 6 example, that of the Hispanic woman as the "Hot Tamale" or sexual firebrand. It is a one-dimensional view that the media have found easy to promote. In their special vocabulary, advertisers have designated "sizzling" and "smoldering" as the adjectives of choice for describing not only the foods but also the women of Latin America. From conversations in my house I recall hearing about the harassment that Puerto Rican women endured in factories where the "boss men" talked to them as if sexual innuendo was all they understood and, worse, often gave them the choice of submitting to advances or being fired.

It is custom, however, not chromosomes, that leads us to choose 7 scarlet over pale pink. As young girls, we were influenced in our decisions about clothes and colors by the women—older sisters and mothers who had grown up on a tropical island where the natural environment was a riot of primary colors, where showing your skin was one way to keep cool as well as to look sexy. Most important of all, on the island, women perhaps felt freer to dress and move more provocatively, since, in most cases, they were protected by the traditions, mores, and laws of a Spanish/Catholic system of morality and machismo whose main rule was: *You may look at my sister, but if you touch her I will kill you.* The extended family and church structure could provide a young woman with a circle of safety in her small pueblo on the island; if a man "wronged" a girl, everyone would close in to save her family honor.

This is what I have gleaned from my discussions as an adult with 8 older Puerto Rican women. They have told me about dressing in their best party clothes on Saturday nights and going to the town's plaza to promenade with their girlfriends in front of the boys they liked. The males were thus given an opportunity to admire the women and to express their admiration in the form of *piropos:* erotically charged street poems they composed on the spot. I have been subjected to a few piropos while visiting the Island, and they can be outrageous, although custom dictates that they must never cross into obscenity. This ritual, as I understand it, also entails a show of studied indifference on the woman's part; if she is "decent," she must not acknowledge the man's impassioned words. So I do understand how things can be lost in translation. When a Puerto Rican girl dressed in her idea of what is attractive meets a man from the mainstream culture who has been trained to react to certain types of clothing as a sexual signal, a clash is likely to take place. The line I first heard based on this aspect of the myth happened when the boy who took me to my first formal dance leaned over to plant a sloppy overeager kiss painfully on my mouth, and when I didn't respond with sufficient passion said in a resentful tone: "I thought you Latin girls were supposed to mature early"—my first instance of being thought of as a fruit or vegetable—I was supposed to *ripen,* not just grow into womanhood like other girls.

9   It is surprising to some of my professional friends that some people, including those who should know better, still put others "in their place." Though rarer, these incidents are still commonplace in my life. It happened to me most recently during a stay at a very classy metropolitan hotel favored by young professional couples for their weddings. Late one evening after the theater, as I walked toward my room with my new colleague (a woman with whom I was coordinating an arts program), a middle-aged man in a tuxedo, a young girl in satin and lace on his arm, stepped directly into our path. With his champagne glass extended toward me, he exclaimed, "Evita!"

10   Our way blocked, my companion and I listened as the man half-recited, half-bellowed "Don't Cry for Me, Argentina." When he finished, the young girl said: "How about a round of applause for my daddy?" We complied, hoping this would bring the silly spectacle to a close. I was becoming aware that our little group was attracting the attention of the other guests. "Daddy" must have perceived this too, and he once more barred the way as we tried to walk past him. He began to shout-sing a ditty to the tune of "La Bamba"—except the lyrics were about a girl named María whose exploits all rhymed with her name and gonorrhea. The girl kept saying, "Oh, Daddy" and looking at me with pleading eyes. She wanted me to laugh along with the others. My companion and I stood silently waiting for the man to end his offensive song. When he finished, I looked not at him but at his daughter. I advised her calmly never to ask her father what he had done in the army. Then I walked between them and to my room. My friend complimented me on my cool handling of the situation. I confessed to her that I really had wanted to push the jerk into the swimming pool. I knew that this same man—probably a corporate executive, well educated, even worldly by most standards—would not have been likely to regale a white woman with a dirty song in public. He would perhaps have checked his impulse by assum-

ing that she could be somebody's wife or mother, or at least *somebody* who might take offense. But to him, I was just an Evita or a María: merely a character in his cartoon-populated universe.

Because of my education and my proficiency with the English lan- 11 guage, I have acquired many mechanisms for dealing with the anger I experience. This was not true for my parents, nor is it true for the many Latin women working at menial jobs who must put up with stereotypes about our ethnic group such as: "They make good domestics." This is another facet of the myth of the Latin woman in the United States. Its origin is simple to deduce. Work as domestics, waitressing, and factory jobs are all that's available to women with little English and few skills. The myth of the Hispanic menial has been sustained by the same media phenomenon that made "Mammy" from *Gone with the Wind* America's idea of the black woman for generations; María, the housemaid or counter girl, is now indelibly etched into the national psyche. The big and the little screens have presented us with the picture of the funny Hispanic maid, mispronouncing words and cooking up a spicy storm in a shiny California kitchen.

This media-engendered image of the Latina in the United States has 12 been documented by feminist Hispanic scholars, who claim that such portrayals are partially responsible for the denial of opportunities for upward mobility among Latinas in the professions. I have a Chicana friend working on a Ph.D. in philosophy at a major university. She says her doctor still shakes his head in puzzled amazement at all the "big words" she uses. Since I do not wear my diplomas around my neck for all to see, I too have on occasion been sent to that "kitchen," where some think I obviously belong.

One such incident that has stayed with me, though I recognize it as a 13 minor offense, happened on the day of my first public poetry reading. It took place in Miami in a boat-restaurant where we were having lunch before the event. I was nervous and excited as I walked in with my note-book in my hand. An older woman motioned me to her table. Thinking (foolish me) that she wanted me to autograph a copy of my brand new slender volume of verse, I went over. She ordered a cup of coffee from me, assuming that I was the waitress. Easy enough to mistake my poems for menus, I suppose. I know that it wasn't an intentional act of cruelty, yet of all the good things that happened that day, I remember that scene most clearly, because it reminded me of what I had to overcome before anyone would take me seriously. In retrospect I understand that my anger gave my reading fire, that I have almost always taken doubts in my abilities as a challenge—and that the result is, most times, a feeling of satisfaction at having won a convert when I see the cold, apprais-ing eyes warm to my words, the body language change, the smile that indicates that I have opened some avenue for communication. That day

I read to that woman and her lowered eyes told me that she was embarrassed at her little faux pas, and when I willed her to look up at me, it was my victory, and she graciously allowed me to punish her with my full attention. We shook hands at the end of the reading, and I never saw her again. She has probably forgotten the whole thing but maybe not.

14   Yet I am one of the lucky ones. My parents made it possible for me to acquire a stronger footing in the mainstream culture by giving me the chance at an education. And books and art have saved me from the harsher forms of ethnic and racial prejudice that many of my Hispanic *compañeras* have had to endure. I travel a lot around the United States, reading from my books of poetry and my novel, and the reception I most often receive is one of positive interest by people who want to know more about my culture. There are, however, thousands of Latinas without the privilege of an education or the entrée into society that I have. For them life is a struggle against the misconceptions perpetuated by the myth of the Latina as whore, domestic or criminal. We cannot change this by legislating the way people look at us. The transformation, as I see it, has to occur at a much more individual level. My personal goal in my public life is to try to replace the old pervasive stereotypes and myths about Latinas with a much more interesting set of realities. Every time I give a reading, I hope the stories I tell, the dreams and fears I examine in my work, can achieve some universal truth which will get my audience past the particulars of my skin color, my accent, or my clothes.

15   I once wrote a poem in which I called us Latinas "God's brown daughters." This poem is really a prayer of sorts, offered upward, but also, through the human-to-human channel of art, outward. It is a prayer for communication, and for respect. In it, Latin women pray "in Spanish to an Anglo God / with a Jewish heritage," and they are "fervently hoping / that if not omnipotent, / at least He be bilingual."

EXPLORING IDEAS

1. Discuss the assumptions underlying the idea that a girl's modesty and virtue are the same as family honor.

2. Why are the dress traditions of Latin women interpreted as a "come-on" by men? Brainstorm the issue of women's clothing being misinterpreted as a sexual signal.

3. Write an essay with the following thesis statement: "Most adolescents feel out of step much of the time."

4. Brainstorm why a woman's "honor" is usually interpreted as sexual, while a man's honor usually has nothing to do with sexuality. Write an essay defining "honor" in male terms and then in female terms.

5. Discuss the metaphor of "Hot Tamale" for the Latin female. Why have such words as "sizzling" and "smoldering" become associated with Latin women? Is this a stereotype created by the media, or are there other sources?

6. Cofer describes a male-female "ritual" in which young males and females play a courting or flirting game. Brainstorm a similar courting ritual in your own culture or, if you are Hispanic, a different courting ritual. Describe the ritual.

7. Are Latin women more likely to be the victims of sexual harassment on the job than others? Without statistical data, how could you support such an argument?

8. Cofer says that instead of being perceived as someone's wife or mother, as a white woman would have been, she was seen by the man who sang the obscene song as "merely a character in his cartoon-populated universe." Brainstorm this concept of being taken for a character in a cartoon-populated universe. Describe the characteristics of cartoon characters. What does it mean to perceive human beings in such a manner?

9. Cofer talks about the image of the Latina in the United States as being "media-engendered." Brainstorm another media-engendered image you are familiar with. Use specific details to describe the image. Discuss what damage this image causes.

10. Cofer says she wants people to get past the "particulars" of her skin color, accent, and clothes. Is that ever possible? If one's skin color, accent, and clothes are particular to a person, is it ever possible to ignore it?

EXPLORING RHETORIC

1. What is the value of opening this essay with an incident or anecdote? How would the essay have been different if Cofer had begun with paragraph 6, where she begins to generalize about her subject?

2. Why does Cofer say she belongs to Rita Moreno's gene pool? Rita Moreno, who is Latina, played a role in *West Side Story* (not María), and has occasionally played roles in which she exaggerates the stereotypes of Latinas. She also has complained that because of these portrayals, she has been typecast unfairly. Discuss other sources of the stereotypes of the Latina from popular culture images.

3. María, a character from the musical *West Side Story*, is a modern version of Juliet from Shakespeare's *Romeo and Juliet*. Why would Cofer resent being referred to as María? Read the essay by Robert Heilbroner on stereotypes elsewhere in this part.

4. Discuss the effectiveness of Cofer's metaphor about being on an island like Alcatraz rather than a tropical island. Is the metaphor appropriate to the subject matter and tone of the essay?

5. If Cofer's purpose is to dispel the myth of the Latin woman, why does she emphasize the cultural traditions of growing up Latina that give rise to those stereotypes? Does her emphasis weaken her argument or strengthen it?

6. Discuss the anecdote Cofer tells of the man who sings "Don't Cry for Me, Argentina" and the obscene song to the tune of "La Bamba" to her. Is this an extreme case that weakens Cofer's argument, or is it a representative incident that strengthens her argument?

7. Why does Cofer tell the anecdote of the woman at the poetry reading who thought she was the waitress, though she admits it was a minor offense and that the woman probably mistook her sheaf of poems for menus?

8. Why does Cofer end her essay by focusing on education? Compare Cofer's argument about education with Rachel Jones's argument about black English in Part Four.

Yellow Woman and a Beauty of the Spirit

LESLIE MARMON SILKO

Leslie Marmon Silko was born in 1948 in Albuquerque, New Mexico, of Mexican, white, and Pueblo Native American descent. She attended the University of New Mexico, where she received her B.A. degree in 1969. She has taught at Navajo Community College in Arizona, at the University of New Mexico, and at the University of Arizona. She has published two collections of fiction, poetry, and memoirs, *Laguna Woman,* 1974, and *Storyteller,* 1981, as well as two novels, *Ceremony,* 1974, and *Almanac of the Dead,* 1990.

The following essay, which appeared in the *Los Angeles Times Magazine* in December 1993, begins with Silko's personal awareness of being different, which she uses as a basis for discussing her central concern: basic differences between the values and view of reality of modern people and the "old-time people" of the Pueblo Native Americans in the Southwest.

1   From the time I was a small child, I was aware that I was different. I looked different from my playmates. My two sisters looked different too. We didn't look quite like the other Laguna Pueblo children, but we didn't look quite white either. In the 1880s, my great grandfather had followed his older brother west from Ohio to the New Mexico territory to survey the land for the U.S. government. The two Marmon brothers came to the Laguna Pueblo Reservation because they had an Ohio cousin who already lived there. The Ohio cousin was involved in sending Indian children thousands of miles away from their families to the War Department's big Indian boarding school in Carlisle, Pa. Both brothers married "full blood" Laguna Pueblo women. My great-grandfather had first married my great-grandmother's older sister, but she died in

childbirth and left two small children. My great-grandmother was 15 or 20 years younger than my great-grandfather. She had attended Carlisle Indian School and spoke and wrote English beautifully.

I called her Grandma A'mooh because that's what I heard her 2 say whenever she saw me. "A'mooh" means "granddaughter" in the Laguna language. I remember this word because her love and her acceptance of me as a small child were so important. I had sensed immediately that something about my appearance was not acceptable to some people, white and Indian. But I did not see any signs of that strain or anxiety in the face of my beloved Grandma A'mooh.

Younger people, people my parents' age, seemed to look at the 3 world in a more "modern" way. The "modern" way included racism. My physical appearance seemed not to matter to the old-time people. They looked at the world very differently; a person's appearance and possessions did not matter nearly as much as a person's behavior. For them, a person's value lies in how that person interacts with other people, how that person behaves toward the animals and the Earth. That is what matters most to the old-time people. The Pueblo people believed this long before the Puritans arrived with their notions of sin and damnation, and racism. The old-time beliefs persist today; thus I will refer to the old-time people in the present tense as well as the past. Many worlds may coexist here.

I spent a great deal of time with my great-grandmother. Her house was 4 next to our house, and I used to wake up at dawn, hours before my parents or younger sisters, and I'd go wait on the porch swing or on the back steps by her kitchen door. She got up at dawn, but she was more than 80 years old so she needed a little while to get dressed and to get the fire going in the cookstove. I had been carefully instructed by my parents not to bother her and to behave, and to try to help her any way I could. I always loved the early mornings when the air was so cool with a hint of rain smell in the breeze. In the dry New Mexico air, the least hint of dampness smells sweet.

My great-grandmother's yard was planted with lilac bushes and 5 iris; there were four o'clocks, cosmos, morning glories and hollyhocks and old-fashioned rose bushes that I helped her water. If the garden hose got stuck on one of the big rocks that lined the path in the yard, I ran and pulled it free. That's what I came to do early every morning: to help Grandma water the plants before the heat of the day arrived.

Grandma A'mooh would tell about the old days, family stories 6 about relatives who had been killed by Apache raiders who stole the sheep our relatives had been herding near Swahnee. Sometimes she read Bible stories that we kids liked because of the illustrations of Jonah in the mouth of a whale and Daniel surrounded by lions. Grandma A'mooh would send me home when she took her nap, but when the sun got low and the afternoon began to cool off, I would be back on the porch swing, waiting for her to come out to water the plants and to haul in firewood for the evening. When Grandma was 85, she still chopped her own kindling. She used to let me carry in the coal bucket for her, but she would not allow me to use the ax. I carried armloads of kindling too, and I learned to be proud of my strength.

7   I was allowed to listen quietly when Aunt Susie or Aunt Alice came to visit Grandma. When I got old enough to cross the road alone, I went and visited them almost daily. They were vigorous women who valued books and writing. They were usually busy chopping wood or cooking but never hesitated to take time to answer my questions. Best of all they told me the "hummah-hah" stories, about an earlier time when animals and humans shared a common language. In the old days, the Pueblo people had educated their children in this manner; adults took time out to talk to and teach young people. Everyone was a teacher, and every activity had the potential to teach the child.

8   But as soon as I started kindergarten at the Bureau of Indian Affairs day school, I began to learn more about the differences between the Laguna Pueblo world and the outside world. It was at school that I learned just how different I looked from my classmates. Sometimes tourists driving past on Route 66 would stop by Laguna Day School at recess time to take photographs of us kids. One day, when I was in the first grade, we all crowded around the smiling white tourists who peered at our faces. We all wanted to be in the picture because afterward the tourists sometimes gave us each a penny. Just as we were all posed and ready to have our picture taken, the tourist man looked at me. "Not you," he said and motioned for me to step away from my classmates. I felt so embarrassed that I wanted to disappear. My classmates were puzzled by the tourists' behavior, but I knew the tourists didn't want me in their snapshot because I looked different, because I was part white.

9 In the view of the old-time people, we are all sisters and brothers because the Mother Creator made all of us—all colors and all sizes. We are sisters and brothers, clanspeople of all the living beings around us. The plants, the birds, fish, clouds, water, even the clay—they all are related to us. The old-time people believe that all things, even rocks and water, have spirit and being. They understood that all things only want to continue being as they are; they need only to be left as they are. Thus the old folks used to tell us kids not to disturb the earth unnecessarily. All things as they were created exist already in harmony with one another as long as we do not disturb them.

10   As the old story tells us, Tse'its'i'nako, Thought Woman, the Spider, thought of her three sisters, and as she thought of them, they came into

being. Together with Thought Woman, they thought of the sun and the stars and the moon. The Mother Creators imagined the earth and the oceans, the animals and the people, and the kat'sina spirits that reside in the mountains. The Mother Creators imagined all the plants that flower and the trees that bear fruit. As Thought Woman and her sisters thought of it, the whole universe came into being. In this universe, there is no absolute good or absolute bad; there are only balances and harmonies that ebb and flow. Some years the desert receives abundant rain, other years there is too little rain, and sometimes there is so much rain that floods cause destruction. But rain itself is neither innocent or guilty. The rain is simply itself.

My great-grandmother was dark and handsome. Her expression in 11 photographs is one of confidence and strength. I do not know if white people then or now would consider her beautiful. I do not know if the old-time Laguna Pueblo people considered her beautiful or if the old-time people even thought in those terms. To the Pueblo way of thinking, the act of comparing one living being with another was silly, because each being or thing is unique and therefore incomparably valuable because it is the only one of its kind. The old-time people thought it was crazy to attach such importance to a person's appearance. I understood very early that there were two distinct ways of interpreting the world. There was the white people's way, and there was the Laguna way. In the Laguna way, it was bad manners to make comparisons that might hurt another person's feelings.

In everyday Pueblo life, not much attention was paid to one's physi- 12 cal appearance or clothing. Ceremonial clothing was quite elaborate but was used only for the sacred dances. The traditional Pueblo societies were communal and strictly egalitarian, which means that no matter how well or how poorly one might have dressed, there was no "social ladder" to fall from. All food and other resources were strictly shared so that no one person or group had more than another. I mention social status because it seems to me that most of the definitions of beauty in contemporary Western culture are really codes for determining social status. People no longer hide their face-lifts, and they discuss their liposuctions because the point of the procedures isn't just cosmetic, it is social. It says to the world, "I have enough spare cash that I can afford surgery for cosmetic purposes."

In the old-time Pueblo world, beauty was manifested in behavior 13 and in one's relationships with other living beings. Beauty was as much a feeling of harmony as it was a visual, aural or sensual effect. The whole person had to be beautiful, not just the face or the body; faces and bodies could not be separated from hearts and souls. Health was foremost in achieving this sense of well-being and harmony; in the old-time Pueblo world, a person who did not look healthy inspired feelings of worry and anxiety, not feelings of well-being. A healthy person, of course, is in harmony with the world around her; she is at peace with herself too. Thus an unhappy person or spiteful person would not be considered beautiful.

14   In the old days, strong, sturdy women were most admired. One of my most vivid preschool memories is of the crew of Laguna women, in their 40s and 50s, who came to cover our house with adobe plaster. They handled the ladders with great ease, and while two women ground the adobe mud on stones and added straw, another woman loaded the hod with mud and passed it up to the two women on ladders, who were smoothing the plaster on the wall with their hands. Since women owned the houses, they did the plastering. At Laguna, men did the basket-making and the weaving of fine textiles; men helped a great deal with the child-care too. Because the Creator is female, there is no stigma on being female; gender is not used to control behavior. No job was a "man's job" or a "woman's job"; the most able person did the work.

15   My Grandma Lily had been a Ford Model A mechanic when she was a teen-ager. I remember when I was young, she was always fixing broken lamps and appliances. She was small and wiry, but she could lift her weight in rolled roofing or boxes of nails. When she was 75, she was still repairing washing machines in my uncle's coin-operated laundry.

16   The old-time people paid no attention to birthdays. When a person was ready to do something, she did it. When she no longer was able, she stopped. Thus the traditional Pueblo people did not worry about aging or about looking old because there were no social boundaries drawn by the passage of years. It was not remarkable for young men to marry women as old as their mothers. I never heard anyone talk about "women's work" until after I left Laguna for college. Work was there to be done by any able-bodied person who wanted to do it. At the same time, in the old-time Pueblo world, identity was acknowledged to be always in a flux; in the old stories, one minute Spider Woman is a little spider under a yucca plant, and the next instant she is a spritely grandmother walking down the road.

17   When I was growing up, there was a young man from a nearby village who wore nail polish and women's blouses and permed his hair. People paid little attention to his appearance; he was always part of a group of other young men from his village. No one ever made fun of him. Pueblo communities were, and still are, very interdependent, but they also have to be tolerant of individual eccentricities because survival of the group means everyone has to cooperate.

18   In the old Pueblo world, differences were celebrated as signs of the Mother Creators' grace. Persons born with exceptional physical or sexual differences were highly respected and honored because their physical differences gave them special positions as mediators between this

world and the spirit world. The great Navajo medicine man of the 1920s, the Crawler, had a hunchback and could not walk upright, but he was able to heal even the most difficult cases.

Before the arrival of Christian missionaries, a man could dress as a woman and work with the women and even marry a man without any fanfare. Likewise, a woman was free to dress like a man, to hunt and go to war with the men and to marry a woman. In the old Pueblo world view, we are all a mixture of male and female, and this sexual identity is changing constantly. Sexual inhibition did not begin until the Christian missionaries arrived. For the old-time people, marriage was about teamwork and social relationships, not about sexual excitement. In the days before the Puritans came, marriage did not mean an end to sex with people other than your spouse. Women were just as likely as men to have a "si'ash," or lover. 19

New life was so precious that pregnancy was always appropriate, and pregnancy before marriage was celebrated as a good sign. Since the children belonged to the mother and her clan, and women owned and bequeathed the houses and farmland, the exact determination of paternity wasn't critical. Although fertility was prized, infertility was no problem because mothers with unplanned pregnancies gave their babies to childless couples within the clan in open adoption arrangements. Children called their mother's sisters "mother" as well, and a child became attached to a number of parent figures. 20

In the sacred kiva ceremonies, men mask and dress as women to pay homage and to be possessed by the female energies of the spirit beings. Because differences in physical appearance were so highly valued, surgery to change one's face and body to resemble a model's face and body would be unimaginable. To be different, to be unique was blessed and was best of all. 21

The traditional clothing of Pueblo women emphasized a woman's sturdiness. Buckskin leggings wrapped around the legs protected her from scratches and injuries while she worked. The more layers of buckskin, the better. All those layers gave her legs the appearance of strength, like sturdy tree trunks. To demonstrate sisterhood and brotherhood with the plants and animals, the old-time people make masks and costumes that transform the human figures of the dancers into the animal beings they portray. Dancers paint their exposed skin; their postures and motions are adapted from their observations. But the motions are stylized. The observer sees not an actual eagle or actual deer dancing, but witnesses a human being, a dancer, gradually changing into a woman/buffalo or a man/deer. Every impulse is to reaffirm the urgent relationships that human beings have with the plant and animal world. 22

23   In the high desert plateau country, all vegetation, even weeds and thorns, becomes special, and all life is precious and beautiful because without the plants, the insects and the animals, human beings living here cannot survive. Perhaps human beings long ago noticed the devastating impact human activity can have on the plants and animals; maybe this is why tribal cultures devised the stories about humans and animals intermarrying, and the clans that bind humans to animals and plants through a whole complex of duties.

24   We children were always warned not to harm frogs or toads, the beloved children of the rain clouds, because terrible floods would occur. I remember in the summer the old folks used to stick big bolls of cotton on the outside of their screen doors as bait to keep the flies from going in the house when the door was opened. The old folks staunchly resisted the killing of flies because once, long, long ago, when human beings were in a great deal of trouble, green bottle fly carried the desperate messages of human beings to the Mother Creator in the Fourth World below this one. Human beings had outraged the Mother Creator by neglecting the Mother Corn altar while they dabbled with sorcery and magic. The Mother Creator disappeared, and with her disappeared the rain clouds, and the plants and the animals too. The people began to starve, and they had no way of reaching the Mother Creator down below. The green bottle fly took the message to the Mother Creator, and the people were saved. To show their gratitude, the old folks refused to kill any flies.

25   The old stories demonstrate the interrelationships that the Pueblo people have maintained with their plant and animal clanspeople. Kochininako, Yellow Woman, represents all women in the old stories. Her deeds span the spectrum of human behavior and are mostly heroic acts, though in at least one story, she chooses to join the secret Destroyer Clan, which worships destruction and death. Because Laguna Pueblo cosmology features a female creator, the status of women is equal with the status of men, and women appear as often as men in the old stories as hero figures. Yellow Woman is my favorite because she dares to cross traditional boundaries of ordinary behavior during times of crisis in order to save the Pueblo; her power lies in her courage and in her uninhibited sexuality, which the old-time Pueblo stories celebrate again and again because fertility was so highly valued.

26   The old stories always say that Yellow Woman was beautiful, but remember that the old-time people were not so much thinking about physical appearances. In each story, the beauty that Yellow Woman possesses is the beauty of her passion, her daring and her sheer strength to act when catastrophe is imminent.

In one story, the people are suffering during a great drought and ac- 27
companying famine. Each day, Kochininako has to walk farther and farther from the village to find fresh water for her husband and children.
One day she travels far, far to the east, to the plains, and she finally lo-
cates a freshwater spring. But when she reaches the pool, the water is
churning violently as if something large had just gotten out of the pool.
Kochininako does not want to see what huge creature had been at the
pool, but just as she fills her water jar and turns to hurry away, a strong,
sexy man in buffalo skin leggings appears by the pool. Little drops of
water glisten on his chest. She cannot help but look at him because he is
so strong and so good to look at. Able to transform himself from human
to buffalo in the wink of an eye, Buffalo Man gallops away with her on
his back. Kochininako falls in love with Buffalo Man, and because of this
liaison, the Buffalo People agree to give their bodies to the hunters to
feed the starving Pueblo. Thus Kochininako's fearless sensuality results
in the salvation of the people of her village, who are saved by the meat
the Buffalo people "give" to them.

My father taught me and my sisters to shoot .22 rifles when we were 28
7; I went hunting with my father when I was 8, and I killed my first mule
deer buck when I was 13. The Kochininako stories were always my favorite because Yellow Woman had so many adventures. In one story, as
she hunts rabbits to feed her family, a giant monster pursues her, but she
has the courage and presence of mind to outwit it.

In another story, Kochininako has a fling with Whirlwind Man and 29
returns to her husband 10 months later with twin baby boys. The twin
boys grow up to be great heroes of the people. Once again, Kochininako's vibrant sexuality benefits her people.

The stories about Kochininako made me aware that sometimes an 30
individual must act despite disapproval, or concern for "appearances"
or "what others may say." From Yellow Woman's adventures, I learned
to be comfortable with my differences. I even imagined that Yellow
Woman had yellow skin, brown hair and green eyes like mine, although
her name does not refer to her color, but rather to the ritual color of the
East.

There have been many other moments like the one with the camera- 31
toting tourist in the schoolyard. But the old-time people always say, remember the stories, the stories will help you be strong. So all these years
I have depended on Kochininako and the stories of her adventures.

Kochininako is beautiful because she has the courage to act in times 32
of great peril, and her triumph is achieved by her sensuality, not through
violence and destruction. For these qualities of the spirit, Yellow Woman
and all women are beautiful.

EXPLORING IDEAS

1. Silko begins by focusing on her awareness that something about her appearance was not acceptable to some people. Read the essays by Richard Rodriguez and John Updike in Part One about their awareness of being different. Brainstorm for an essay about the implications of looking different from others.

2. According to Silko, what is the difference between "modern" people and the "old-time" people? Does Silko suggest that there were no notions of "sin, damnation, and racism" on this continent until they were brought by the white Puritans? Is this possible? Is there any way to argue against this suggestion?

3. Note the anecdote Silko uses to illustrate the first time she realized she looked different from her classmates. Write a one-paragraph anecdote in which you recall an experience when you realized you were different in some way.

4. What implications for the ecology movement might there be if we adopted the beliefs of the "old-time" people that all things have spirit and being?

5. What implications are there for human progress and individuality in the old-time Pueblo belief that making comparisons between people is bad because it might hurt their feelings? Write an essay about a society in which everyone is equal to everyone else and there is no way for anyone to excel. What are the pros and cons of such a state of affairs?

6. Do you agree or disagree with Silko's view that most of the definitions of beauty in contemporary Western culture are really codes for determining social status?

7. Silko notes that health was an important element of harmony and beauty in the old-time Pueblo world. Discuss the relationship between the health movement today and the desire to be beautiful. Do people engage in exercise for health reasons or for beauty reasons?

8. Silko says there were no social boundaries based on age in the old-time world of the Pueblo—that a young man might marry an older woman with no stigma. Brainstorm the implications of age differences for marriages today. What is the perceived difference between a younger woman's marrying an older man and a younger man's marrying an older woman?

9. Are all the values Silko attributes to the old-time world a result of the matriarchal nature of the society? Discuss.

EXPLORING RHETORIC

1. Silko sets up a narrative, descriptive background in paragraphs 4 through 7 to her central point about the differences between the modern and the old-time people. Notice the details about her pulling the garden hose loose if it got stuck on a rock, about her grandmother's not allowing her to use the axe, and about being old enough to cross the road alone. What makes these details effective? Try writing a description of an experience you recall from your own childhood, particularizing it in a meaningful way.

2. What is the relevance of the old stories to Silko's point about modern society? For example, what relevance to modern life is the Pueblo belief that identity is always in flux?

3. How can Silko reconcile her assertion that the Pueblos felt that comparing people was silly with her assertion that people with exceptional physical or sexual differences were highly respected and honored? Is there a contradiction in these two statements?

4. What purpose does Silko have in describing the old Pueblo notion that marriage did not mean an end to sex with other people? What comment on modern society do these old beliefs make?

5. Why does Silko focus on the Yellow Woman figure? Discuss the relationship between sexuality and heroic status in the mythic figure Yellow Woman. Is this related only to the valuing of fertility or to what Silko calls Yellow Woman's "fearless sensuality" and "vibrant sexuality"? How would Yellow Woman's sexuality be viewed in today's world?

6. What is the relationship between the Yellow Woman stories and the fact that Silko was taught to shoot when she was only seven?

7. Silko believes in the power of stories—that stories will help one to be strong. Recall a story from your childhood that has helped you be strong. Narrate it in such a way that you make this point.

8. Silko says that Yellow Woman's strength comes from her sensuality. Is this an image of woman that modern feminists are trying to eradicate? Read Susan Brownmiller's essay on femininity elsewhere in this part. Create an imaginary dialogue between Leslie Silko and Susan Brownmiller. Would they agree or disagree on the power of women?

The Black Writer and the Southern Experience

ALICE WALKER

A lice Walker was born in 1944 in Eatonton, Georgia, the youngest of eight children; her parents were sharecroppers. She attended Spelman College and graduated from Sarah Lawrence College in 1965. She has been active in the civil rights movement; has written poetry, stories, and essays; has taught at several colleges, including Jackson State College in Mississippi, Wellesley College, and the University of Massachusetts; and has worked as an editor for *Ms.* magazine. Her novel *The Color Purple,* 1982, won the Pulitzer Prize and the American Book Award for fiction and was made into an award-winning film in 1985. Her other books include *Revolutionary Petunias and Other Poems,* 1973; *In Love and Trouble,* 1973; *Third Life of Grange Copeland,* 1970;

Meridian, 1976; *Living by the Word,* 1988; *Possessing the Secret of Joy,* 1992; *In Search of Our Mother's Gardens,* 1983; and *The Temple of My Familiar,* 1989.

Although she refuses to romanticize the hardships of southern black country life, Alice Walker celebrates the richness of the black writer's inheritance from rural life in the South: a love of the earth, a sense of a shared community, an abiding trust in humanity, and a love of justice.

1　My mother tells of an incident that happened to her in the thirties during the Depression. She and my father lived in a small Georgia town and had half a dozen children. They were sharecroppers, and food, especially flour, was almost impossible to obtain. To get flour, which was distributed by the Red Cross, one had to submit vouchers signed by a local official. On the day my mother was to go into town for flour she received a large box of clothes from one of my aunts who was living in the North. The clothes were in good condition, though well worn, and my mother needed a dress, so she immediately put on one of those from the box and wore it into town. When she reached the distribution center and presented her voucher she was confronted by a white woman who looked her up and down with marked anger and envy.

2　"What'd you come up here for?" the woman asked.

3　"For some flour," said my mother, presenting her voucher.

4　"Humph," said the woman, looking at her more closely and with unconcealed fury. "Anybody dressed up as good as you don't need to come here *begging* for food."

5　"I ain't begging," said my mother; "the government is giving away flour to those that need it, and I need it. I wouldn't be here if I didn't. And these clothes I'm wearing was given to me." But the woman had already turned to the next person in line, saying over her shoulder to the white man who was behind the counter with her, "The *gall* of niggers coming in here dressed better than me!" This thought seemed to make her angrier still, and my mother, pulling three of her small children behind her and crying from humiliation, walked sadly back into the street.

6　"What did you and Daddy do for flour that winter?" I asked my mother.

7　"Well," she said, "Aunt Mandy Aikens lived down the road from us and she got plenty of flour. We had a good stand of corn so we had plenty of meal. Aunt Mandy would swap me a bucket of flour for a bucket of meal. We got by all right."

8　Then she added thoughtfully, "And that old woman that turned me off so short got down so bad in the end that she was walking on *two* sticks." And I knew she was thinking, though she never said it: Here I am today, my eight children healthy and grown and three of them in college and me with hardly a sick day for years. Ain't Jesus wonderful?

In this small story is revealed the condition and strength of a people. 9 Outcasts to be used and humiliated by the larger society, the Southern black sharecropper and poor farmer clung to his own kind and to a religion that had been given to pacify him as a slave but which he soon transformed into an antidote against bitterness. Depending on one another, because they had nothing and no one else, the sharecroppers often managed to come through "all right." And when I listen to my mother tell and retell this story I find that the white woman's vindictiveness is less important than Aunt Mandy's resourceful generosity or my mother's ready stand of corn. For their lives were not about that pitiful example of Southern womanhood, but about themselves.

What the black Southern writer inherits as a natural right is a sense 10 of *community*. Something simple but surprisingly hard, especially these days, to come by. My mother, who is a walking history of our community, tells me that when each of her children was born the midwife accepted as payment such home-grown or homemade items as a pig, a quilt, jars of canned fruits and vegetables. But there was never any question that the midwife would come when she was needed, whatever the eventual payment for her services. I consider this each time I hear of a hospital that refuses to admit a woman in labor unless she can hand over a substantial sum of money, cash.

Nor am I nostalgic, as a French philosopher once wrote, for lost 11 poverty. I am nostalgic for the solidarity and sharing a modest existence can sometimes bring. We knew, I suppose, that we were poor. Somebody knew; perhaps the landowner who grudgingly paid my father three hundred dollars a year for twelve months' labor. But we never considered ourselves to be poor, unless, of course, we were deliberately humiliated. And because we never believed we were poor, and therefore worthless, we could depend on one another without shame. And always there were the Burial Societies, the Sick-and-Shut-in Societies, that sprang up out of spontaneous need. And no one seemed terribly upset that black sharecroppers were ignored by white insurance companies. It went without saying, in my mother's day, that birth and death required assistance from the community, and that the magnitude of these events was lost on outsiders.

As a college student I came to reject the Christianity of my parents, 12 and it took me years to realize that though they had been force-fed a white man's palliative, in the form of religion, they had made it into something at once simple and noble. True, even today, they can never successfully picture a God who is not white, and that is a major cruelty, but their lives testify to a greater comprehension of the teachings of

Jesus than the lives of people who sincerely believe a God *must* have a color and that there can be such a phenomenon as a "white" church.

13 The richness of the black writer's experience in the South can be remarkable, though some people might not think so. Once, while in college, I told a white middle-aged Northerner that I hoped to be a poet. In the nicest possible language, which still made me as mad as I've ever been, he suggested that a "farmer's daughter" might not be the stuff of which poets are made. On one level, of course, he had a point. A shack with only a dozen or so books is an unlikely place to discover a young Keats. But it is narrow thinking, indeed, to believe that a Keats is the only kind of poet one would want to grow up to be. One wants to write poetry that is understood by one's people, not by the Queen of England. Of course, should she be able to profit by it too, so much the better, but since that is not likely, catering to her tastes would be a waste of time.

14 For the black Southern writer, coming straight out of the country, as Wright* did—Natchez and Jackson are still not as citified as they like to think they are—there is the world of comparisons; between town and country, between the ugly crowding and griminess of the cities and the spacious cleanliness (which actually seems impossible to dirty) of the country. A country person finds the city confining, like a too tight dress. And always, in one's memory, there remain all the rituals of one's growing up: the warmth and vividness of Sunday worship (never mind that you never quite believed) in a little church hidden from the road, and houses set so far back into the woods that at night it is impossible for strangers to find them. The daily dramas that evolve in such a private world are pure gold. But this view of a strictly private and hidden existence, with its triumphs, failures, grotesqueries, is not nearly as valuable to the socially conscious black Southern writer as his double vision is. For not only is he in a position to see his own world, and its close community ("Homecomings" on First Sundays, barbecues to raise money to send to Africa—one of the smaller ironies—the simplicity and eerie calm of a black funeral, where the beloved one is buried way in the middle of a wood with nothing to mark the spot but perhaps a wooden cross already coming apart), but also he is capable of knowing, with remarkably silent accuracy, the people who make up the larger world that surrounds and suppresses his own.

15 It is a credit to a writer like Ernest J. Gaines, a black writer who writes mainly about the people he grew up with in rural Louisiana, that he can write about whites and blacks exactly as he sees them and *knows* them, instead of writing of one group as a vast malignant lump and of the other as a conglomerate of perfect virtues.

---

* Richard Wright (1908–1960) was an African American writer.

In large measure, black Southern writers owe their clarity of vision 16
to parents who refused to diminish themselves as human beings by succumbing to racism. Our parents seemed to know that an extreme negative emotion held against other human beings for reasons they do not
control can be blinding. Blindness about other human beings, especially
for a writer, is equivalent to death. Because of this blindness, which is,
above all, racial, the works of many Southern writers have died. Much
that we read today is fast expiring.

My own slight attachment to William Faulkner was rudely broken 17
by realizing, after reading statements he made in *Faulkner in the Univer-*
sity, that he believed whites superior morally to blacks; that whites had a
duty (which at their convenience they would assume) to "bring blacks
along" politically, since blacks, in Faulkner's opinion, were "not ready"
yet to function properly in a democratic society. He also thought that a
black man's intelligence is directly related to the amount of white blood
he has.

For the black person coming of age in the sixties, where Martin 18
Luther King stands against the murderers of Goodman, Chaney, and
Schwerner, there appears no basis for such assumptions. Nor was there
any in Garvey's day, or in Du Bois's or in Douglass's or in Nat Turner's.*
Nor at any other period in our history, from the very founding of the
country; for it was hardly incumbent upon slaves to be slaves and saints
too. Unlike Tolstoy, Faulkner was not prepared to struggle to change the
structure of the society he was born in. One might concede that in his fiction he did seek to examine the reasons for its decay, but unfortunately,
as I have learned while trying to teach Faulkner to black students, it is
not possible, from so short a range, to separate the man from his works.

One reads Faulkner knowing that his "colored" people had to come 19
through "Mr. William's" back door, and one feels uneasy, and finally enraged that Faulkner did not burn the whole house down. When the
provincial mind starts out *and continues* on a narrow and unprotesting
course, "genius" itself must run on a track.

Flannery O'Connor at least had the conviction that "reality" is at 20
best superficial and that the puzzle of humanity is less easy to solve than
that of race. But Miss O'Connor was not so much of Georgia, as in it. The
majority of Southern writers have been too confined by prevailing social

---

* Andrew Goodman and Michael Schwerner were white civil rights workers from New York City. James
Chaney was an African American civil rights worker from Mississippi; all three were murdered by Ku
Klux Klan members in Mississippi in 1964. Marcus Garvey (1887–1940), born in Jamaica, was an
African American proponent of black nationalism. W. E. Du Bois (1868–1963), an African American,
was one of the founders of the National Association for the Advancement of Colored People. Frederick
Douglass (1817–1895) was an African American abolitionist. Nat Turner (1800–1831) was an African
American slave and a revolutionary.

customs to probe deeply into mysteries that the Citizens Councils insist must never be revealed.

21   Perhaps my Northern brothers will not believe me when I say there is a great deal of positive material I can draw from my "underprivileged" background. But they have never lived, as I have, at the end of a long road in a house that was faced by the edge of the world on one side and nobody for miles on the other. They have never experienced the magnificent quiet of a summer day when the heat is intense and one is so very thirsty, as one moves across the dusty cotton fields, that one learns forever that water is the essence of all life. In the cities it cannot be so clear to one that he is a creature of the earth, feeling the soil between the toes, smelling the dust thrown up by the rain, loving the earth so much that one longs to taste it and sometimes does.

22   Nor do I intend to romanticize the Southern black country life. I can recall that I hated it, generally. The hard work in the fields, the shabby houses, the evil greedy men who worked my father to death and almost broke the courage of that strong woman, my mother. No, I am simply saying that Southern black writers, like most writers, have a heritage of love and hate, but that they also have enormous richness and beauty to draw from. And, having been placed, as Camus says, "halfway between misery and the sun," they, too, know that "though all is not well under the sun, history is not everything."

23   No one could wish for a more advantageous heritage than that bequeathed to the black writer in the South: a compassion for the earth, a trust in humanity beyond our knowledge of evil, and an abiding love of justice. We inherit a great responsibility as well, for we must give voice to centuries not only of silent bitterness and hate but also of neighborly kindness and sustaining love.

EXPLORING IDEAS

1. Walker says that the religion that was given to African Americans to pacify them as slaves was transformed into an antidote against bitterness. What is the difference between these two uses of religion? Don't both serve to make people content with an unjust situation?

2. Walker says that her mother is a "walking history" of her community. If you know someone like this—an oral historian of your family, your town, your neighborhood—interview that person, and write up the interview.

3. Walker says she is nostalgic for the "solidarity and sharing a modest existence can sometimes bring." Brainstorm this idea, and write a brief argument explaining why being poor is more likely to create a sense of solidarity and sharing than being rich.

4. Walker makes the following comparison between city and country: "between the ugly crowding and griminess of the cities and the spacious cleanliness (which actually seems impossible to dirty) of the country." Brainstorm differences between city and country and write an essay in which you agree or disagree with Walker.

5. Walker mentions the "little rituals" of one's growing up. What does the word "ritual" mean here? Brainstorm some rituals from your own growing up. Write a brief essay in which you identify your background with these rituals. Be sure to define clearly the word "ritual," and then stick to events that fit the definition.

6. Write an essay using the following thesis statement: "Blindness about other human beings, especially for a writer, is equivalent to death."

7. In your own words, explain Walker's complaint about William Faulkner. If you are familiar with Faulkner's works, agree or disagree with her. If you are not, focus on the more general issue of whether a writer should reflect his or her society or try to change it.

8. Write a brief essay in which you use the following thesis statement: "In the cities it cannot be so clear to one that he is a creature of the earth."

9. Walker says she does not intend to romanticize southern black country life. What does it mean to "romanticize" one's past? Write a two-part essay. Begin with a romantic description of some facet of your childhood life; then write a realistic account of the same facet.

EXPLORING RHETORIC

1. Alice Walker opens her essay with an incident or anecdote, a common technique that seems simple but should not be taken for granted. Narrative and dialogue is not as easy to write as it appears. Carefully study the details Walker uses here and how she integrates dialogue with narrative. Then write a brief narrative of your own, complete with dialogue, in which you introduce and illustrate a point. As Walker does with her sentence, "In this small story is revealed the condition and strength of a people," state the point of your story.

2. Why does Walker tell us that she rejected the Christianity of her parents when she was in college? What relevance to her main point does this information have?

3. How does Walker make a transition from her discussion of the religious background of African Americans to her focus on the heritage of black southern writers? What do the two have to do with each other?

4. What basic assumption is made about the nature of the poet by the suggestion that a farmer's daughter might not be the stuff of which poets are made? Why does Walker describe this anecdote?

5. Discuss the effectiveness of the metaphor in the following sentence: "A country person finds the city confining, like a too tight dress." How does the metaphor suit the subject and tone of Walker's essay?

6. Discuss the meaning of Walker's idea that the black southern writer has a "double vision."

7. What do Walker's references to famous African Americans such as Wright, Du Bois, Douglass, and Turner suggest about the expectations that she has of her audience?

8. How can Walker reconcile her statement that she hated southern black country life with the fact that she praises it that heritage? Are the two positions antithetical or complementary?

Anglo vs. Chicano: Why?

ARTHUR L. CAMPA

Arthur L. Campa was born in 1905 to American missionary parents in Mexico. He attended the University of New Mexico and Columbia University. He was a professor in the Department of Modern Languages at the University of Denver and a cultural attaché in several U.S. embassies. He died in 1978.

In a carefully structured academic essay, Arthur Campa describes several basic cultural differences between the value systems of Anglo-Americans and Hispanics, beginning with historical differences based on geography and moving to social differences implicit in the languages of the two cultures.

1 The cultural differences between Hispanic and Anglo-American people have been dwelt upon by so many writers that we should all be well informed about the values of both. But audiences are usually of the same persuasion as the speakers, and those who consult published works are for the most part specialists looking for affirmation of what they believe. So, let us consider the same subject, exploring briefly some of the basic cultural differences that cause conflict in the Southwest, where Hispanic and Anglo-American cultures meet.

2   Cultural differences are implicit in the conceptual content of the languages of these two civilizations, and their value systems stem from a long series of historical circumstances. Therefore, it may be well to consider some of the English and Spanish cultural configurations before these Europeans set foot on American soil. English culture was basically insular, geographically and ideologically; was more integrated on the whole, except for some strong theological differences; and was particularly zealous of its racial purity. Spanish culture was peninsular, a geographical circumstance that made it a catchall of Mediterranean, central

European and north African peoples. The composite nature of the population produced a marked regionalism that prevented close integration, except for religion, and led to a strong sense of individualism. These differences were reflected in the colonizing enterprise of the two cultures. The English isolated themselves from the Indians physically and culturally; the Spanish, who had strong notions about *pureza de sangre* [purity of blood] among the nobility, were not collectively averse to adding one more strain to their racial cocktail. Cortés led the way by siring the first *mestizo* in North America, and the rest of the conquistadores followed suit. The ultimate products of these two orientations meet today in the Southwest.

Anglo-American culture was absolutist at the onset; that is, all the dominant values were considered identical for all, regardless of time and place. Such values as justice, charity, honesty were considered the superior social order for all men and were later embodied in the American Constitution. The Spaniard brought with him a relativistic viewpoint and saw fewer moral implications in man's actions. Values were looked upon as the result of social and economic conditions. 3

The motives that brought Spaniards and Englishmen to America also differed. The former came on an enterprise of discovery, searching for a new route to India initially, and later for new lands to conquer, the fountain of youth, minerals, the Seven Cities of Cíbola and, in the case of the missionaries, new souls to win for the Kingdom of Heaven. The English came to escape religious persecution, and once having found a haven, they settled down to cultivate the soil and establish their homes. Since the Spaniards were not seeking a refuge or running away from anything, they continued their explorations and circled the globe 25 years after the discovery of the New World. 4

This peripatetic tendency of the Spaniard may be accounted for in part by the fact that he was the product of an equestrian culture. Men on foot do not venture far into the unknown. It was almost a century after the landing on Plymouth Rock that Governor Alexander Spotswood of Virginia crossed the Blue Ridge Mountains, and it was not until the nineteenth century that the Anglo-Americans began to move west of the Mississippi. 5

The Spaniard's equestrian role meant that he was not close to the soil, as was the Anglo-American pioneer, who tilled the land and built the greatest agricultural industry in history. The Spaniard cultivated the land only when he had Indians available to do it for him. The uses to which the horse was put also varied. The Spanish horse was essentially a mount, while the more robust English horse was used in cultivating the soil. It is therefore not surprising that the viewpoints of these two cultures should differ when we consider that the pioneer is looking at the 6 world at the level of his eyes while the *caballero* [horseman] is looking beyond and down at the rest of the world.

7   One of the most commonly quoted, and often misinterpreted, characteristics of Hispanic peoples is the deeply ingrained individualism in all walks of life. Hispanic individualism is a revolt against the incursion of collectivity, strongly asserted when it is felt that the ego is being fenced in. This attitude leads to a deficiency in those social qualities based on collective standards, an attitude that Hispanos do not consider negative because it manifests a measure of resistance to standardization in order to achieve a measure of individual freedom. Naturally, such an attitude has no *reglas fijas* [fixed rules].

8   Anglo-Americans who achieve a measure of success and security through institutional guidance not only do not mind a few fixed rules but demand them. The lack of a concerted plan of action, whether in business or in politics, appears unreasonable to Anglo-Americans. They have a sense of individualism, but they achieve it through action and self-determination. Spanish individualism is based on feeling, on something that is the result not of rules and collective standards but of a person's momentary, emotional reaction. And it is subject to change when the mood changes. In contrast to Spanish emotional individualism, the Anglo-American strives for objectivity when choosing a course of action or making a decision.

9   The Southwestern Hispanos voiced strong objections to the lack of courtesy of the Anglo-Americans when they first met them in the early days of the Santa Fe trade. The same accusation is leveled at the *Americanos* today in many quarters of the Hispanic world. Some of this results from their different conceptions of polite behavior. Here too one can say that the Spanish have no *reglas fijas* because for them courtesy is simply an expression of the way one person feels toward another. To some they extend the hand, to some they bow and for the more *íntimos* there is the well-known *abrazo*. The concepts of "good or bad" or "right and wrong" in polite behavior are moral considerations of an absolutist culture.

10   Another cultural contrast appears in the way both cultures share part of their material substance with others. The pragmatic Anglo-American contributes regularly to such institutions as the Red Cross, the United Fund and a myriad of associations. He also establishes foundations and quite often leaves millions to such institutions. The Hispano prefers to give his contribution directly to the recipient so he can see the person he is helping.

11   A century of association has inevitably acculturated both Hispanos and Anglo-Americans to some extent, but there still persist a number of culture traits that neither group has relinquished altogether. Nothing is more disquieting to an Anglo-American who believes that time is money

than the time perspective of Hispanos. They usually refer to this attitude as the "*mañana* psychology." Actually, it is more of a "today psychology," because Hispanos cultivate the present to the exclusion of the future; because the latter has not arrived yet, it is not a reality. They are reluctant to relinquish the present, so they hold on to it until it becomes the past. To an Hispano, nine is nine until it is ten, so when he arrives at nine-thirty, he jubilantly exclaims: "*¡Justo!*" [right on time]. This may be why the clock is slowed down to a walk in Spanish while in English it runs. In the United States, our future-oriented civilization plans our lives so far in advance that the present loses its meaning. January magazine issues are out in December; 1973 cars have been out since October; cemetery plots and even funeral arrangements are bought on the installment plan. To a person engrossed in living today the very idea of planning his funeral sounds like the tolling of the bells.

It is a natural corollary that a person who is present oriented should 12 be compensated by being good at improvising. An Anglo-American is told in advance to prepare for an "impromptu speech," but an Hispano usually can improvise a speech because "*Nosotros la improvisamos todo*" [we improvise everything].

Another source of cultural conflict arises from the difference be- 13 tween *being* and *doing*. Even when trying to be individualistic, the Anglo-American achieves it by what he does. Today's young generation decided to be themselves, to get away from standardization, so they let their hair grow, wore ragged clothes and even went barefoot in order to be different from the Establishment. As a result they all ended up doing the same things and created another stereotype. The freedom enjoyed by the individuality of *being* makes it unnecessary for Hispanos to strive to be different.

In 1963 a team of psychologists from the University of Guadalajara 14 in Mexico and the University of Michigan compared 74 upper-middle-class students from each university. Individualism and personalism were found to be central values for the Mexican students. This was explained by saying that a Mexican's value as a person lies in his *being* rather than, as is the case of the Anglo-Americans, in concrete accomplishments. Efficiency and accomplishments are derived characteristics that do not affect worthiness in the Mexican, whereas in the American it is equated with success, a value of highest priority in the American culture. Hispanic people disassociate themselves from material things or from actions that may impugn a person's sense of being, but the Anglo-American shows great concern for material things and assumes responsibility for his actions. This is expressed in the language of each culture. In Spanish one says, "*Se me cayó la taza*" [the cup fell away from me] instead of "I dropped the cup."

15   In English, one speaks of money, cash and all related transactions
with frankness because material things of this high order do not trouble
Anglo-Americans. In Spanish such materialistic concepts are circum-
vented by referring to cash as *efectivo* [effective] and when buying or
selling as something *al contado* [counted out], and when without it by
saying *No tengo fondos* [I have no funds]. This disassociation from material things is what produces *sobriedad* [sobriety] in the Spaniard according
to Miguel de Unamuno,* but in the Southwest the disassociation from
materialism leads to *dejadez* [lassitude] and *desprendimiento* [disinterest-
edness]. A man may lose his life defending his honor but is unconcerned
about the lack of material things. *Desprendimiento* causes a man to spend
his last cent on a friend, which when added to lack of concern for the future may mean that tomorrow he will eat beans as a result of today's
binge.

16   The implicit differences in words that appear to be identical in
meaning are astonishing. Versatile is a compliment in English and an insult in Spanish. An Hispano student who is told to apologize cannot do
it, because the word doesn't exist in Spanish. *Apología* means words in
praise of a person. The Anglo-American either apologizes, which is [a]
form of retraction abhorrent in Spanish, or compromises, another concept foreign to Hispanic culture. *Compromiso* means a date, not a compromise. In colonial Mexico City, two hidalgos once entered a narrow
street from opposite sides, and when they could not go around, they sat
in their coaches for three days until the viceroy ordered them to back
out. All this because they could not work out a compromise.

17   It was that way then and to some extent now. Many of today's conflicts in the Southwest have their roots in polarized cultural differences,
which need not be irreconcilable when approached with mutual respect
and understanding.

EXPLORING IDEAS

1. According to Campa, what is the difference between an "insular" culture like
the English and a "peninsular" culture like the Spanish? How have these geographic differences created cultural differences?

2. Write a brief essay in which you discuss the difference between the "absolutist" culture of Anglo-Americans and the "relativist" culture of the Hispanic.

3. What might be the basic differences between a people searching for something and a people trying to escape from something?

---

* Miguel de Unamuno (1864–1936) was a Spanish philosopher.

4. Discuss the implications of the difference in viewpoint between the pioneer who is looking at the world at the level of his eyes and the horseman who is looking beyond and down at the rest of the world. Use this as the basis of an essay about two different kinds of people or two individuals whom you know personally or you have read about.

5. Create examples of your own to clarify Campa's distinction between Anglo-American individualism and Hispanic individualism.

6. Discuss the pros and cons of courtesy in a relativist society such as Hispanic and an absolutist society such as Anglo-American. Brainstorm for an essay on the current American attitude toward courtesy.

7. Write a character sketch about two different people, in which you contrast the two different concepts of time that Campa describes.

8. Discuss the differences between the concept of being and the concept of doing that Campa describes. Then identify the pros and cons of each position.

9. Write a character sketch of someone who does not know the meaning of the word "apology" and for whom "compromise" is abhorrent. Write a character sketch of someone who apologizes often and always compromises.

EXPLORING RHETORIC

1. Explain in your own words why Campa wants to explore the cultural differences between Hispanic and Anglo-Americans even though he says such differences have been dwelled on by many other writers already. What kind of rhetorical tactic is this?

2. Write a brief stylistic analysis of paragraph 2 to define the level of formality of this essay. What word choices and sentence structures support your analysis?

3. Discuss the effectiveness of the metaphor "racial cocktail." What tone or attitude toward the Spanish does the metaphor suggest?

4. Analyze the comparison-contrast rhetorical tactics that Campa uses in paragraphs 3 through 6. Outline the basic points of the comparison and contrast.

5. Rewrite paragraph 7 in your own words, clarifying the basic points Campa makes.

6. Explain Campa's metaphor in the following statement: "The clock is slowed down to a walk in Spanish while in English it runs."

7. Identify the transition devices, words, and phrases Campa uses in paragraphs 8 through 13.

8. Why does Campa use a number of Spanish words in paragraph 15? What effect does this achieve? How would the paragraph have been different without the Spanish words?

9. Why does Campa tell the story of the two *hidalgos* in colonial Mexico City who would not back out of a narrow street? Is it likely that this event really happened, or is Campa exaggerating? How do you know?

America: The Multinational Society

ISHMAEL REED

I shmael Reed was born in 1938 in Buffalo, New York. He has taught at Harvard, Yale, Dartmouth, and the University of California at Berkeley. His books include two essay collections, *Shrovetide in Old New Orleans,* 1979, and *Writin' Is Fightin',* 1988; and the novels *The Free-Lance Pallbearers,* 1967, and *Mumbo Jumbo,* 1978.

Ishmael Reed argues that U.S. society is more properly characterized by a blending of cultural styles than it is by the racial conflict publicized by the media. Rather than owing its rich heritage only to European civilization and the work ethic of the early Puritans, the United States is a unique place where the cultures of the world crisscross.

> At the annual Lower East Side Jewish Festival yesterday, a Chinese woman ate a pizza slice in front of Ty Thuan Duc's Vietnamese grocery store. Beside her a Spanish-speaking family patronized a cart with two signs: "Italian Ices" and "Kosher by Rabbi Alper." And after the pastrami ran out, everybody ate knishes.
>
> *The New York Times,* 23 June 1983

1   On the day before Memorial Day, 1983, a poet called me to describe a city he had just visited. He said that one section included mosques, built by the Islamic people who dwelled there. Attending his reading, he said, were large numbers of Hispanic people, forty thousand of whom lived in the same city. He was not talking about a fabled city located in some mysterious region of the world. The city he'd visited was Detroit.

2   A few months before, as I was leaving Houston, Texas, I heard it announced on the radio that Texas's largest minority was Mexican-American, and though a foundation recently issued a report critical of bilingual education, the taped voice used to guide the passengers on the air trams connecting terminals in Dallas Airport is in both Spanish and English. If the trend continues, a day will come when it will be difficult to travel through some sections of the country without hearing commands in both English and Spanish: after all, for some western states, Spanish was the first written language and the Spanish style lives on in the western way of life.

3   Shortly after my Texas trip, I sat in an auditorium located on the campus of the University of Wisconsin at Milwaukee as a Yale professor—whose original work on the influence of African cultures upon

those of the Americas has led to his ostracism from some monocultural intellectual circles—walked up and down the aisle, like an old-time southern evangelist, dancing and drumming the top of the lectern, illustrating his points before some serious Afro-American intellectuals and artists who cheered and applauded his performance and his mastery of information. The professor was "white." After his lecture, he joined a group of Milwaukeeans in a conversation. All of the participants spoke Yoruban, though only the professor had ever traveled to Africa.

One of the artists told me that his paintings, which included African 4 and Afro-American mythological symbols and imagery, were hanging in the local McDonald's restaurant. The next day I went to McDonald's and snapped pictures of smiling youngsters eating hamburgers below paintings that could grace the walls of any of the country's leading museums. The manager of the local McDonald's said, "I don't know what you boys are doing, but I like it," as he commissioned the local painters to exhibit in his restaurant.

Such blurring of cultural styles occurs in everyday life in the United 5 States to a greater extent than anyone can imagine and is probably more prevalent than the sensational conflict between people of different backgrounds that is played up and often encouraged by the media. The result is that what the Yale professor, Robert Thompson, referred to as a cultural bouillabaisse, yet members of the nation's present educational and cultural Elect still cling to the notion that the United States belongs to some vaguely defined entity they refer to as "Western civilization," by which they mean, presumably, a civilization created by the people of Europe, as if Europe can be viewed in monolithic terms. Is Beethoven's Ninth Symphony, which includes Turkish marches, a part of Western civilization, or the late nineteenth- and twentieth-century French paintings, whose creators were influenced by Japanese art? And what of the cubists, through whom the influence of African art changed modern painting, or the surrealists, who were so impressed with the art of the Pacific Northwest Indians that, in their map of North America, Alaska dwarfs the lower forty-eight in size?

Are the Russians, who are often criticized for their adoption of 6 "Western" ways by Tsarist dissidents in exile, members of Western civilization? And what of the millions of Europeans who have black African and Asian ancestry, black Africans having occupied several countries for hundreds of years? Are these "Europeans" members of Western civilization, or the Hungarians, who originated across the Urals in a place called Greater Hungary, or the Irish, who came from the Iberian Peninsula?

Even the notion that North America is part of Western civilization 7 because our "system of government" is derived from Europe is being challenged by Native American historians who say that the founding fathers, Benjamin Franklin especially, were actually influenced by the system of government that had been adopted by the Iroquois hundreds of years prior to the arrival of large numbers of Europeans.

8   Western civilization, then, becomes another confusing category like Third World, or Judeo-Christian culture, as man attempts to impose his small-screen view of political and cultural reality upon a complex world. Our most publicized novelist recently said that Western civilization was the greatest achievement of mankind, an attitude that flourishes on the street level as scribbles in public restrooms: "White Power," "Niggers and Spics Suck," or "Hitler was a prophet," the latter being the most telling, for wasn't Adolph Hitler the archetypal monoculturalist who, in his pigheaded arrogance, believed that one way and one blood was so pure that it had to be protected from alien strains at all costs? Where did such an attitude, which has caused so much misery and depression in our national life, which has tainted even our noblest achievements, begin? An attitude that caused the incarceration of Japanese-American citizens during World War II, the persecution of Chicanos and Chinese-Americans, the near-extermination of the Indians, and the murder and lynchings of thousands of Afro-Americans.

9   Virtuous, hardworking, pious, even though they occasionally would wander off after some fancy clothes, or rendezvous in the woods with the town prostitute, the Puritans are idealized in our schoolbooks as "a hardy band" of no-nonsense patriarchs whose discipline razed the forest and brought order to the New World (a term that annoys Native American historians). Industrious, responsible, it was their "Yankee ingenuity" and practicality that created the work ethic. They were simple folk who produced a number of good poets, and they set the tone for the American writing style, of lean and spare lines, long before Hemingway. They worshiped in churches whose colors blended in with the New England snow, churches with simple structures and ornate lecterns.

10   The Puritans were a daring lot, but they had a mean streak. They hated the theater and banned Christmas. They punished people in a cruel and inhuman manner. They killed children who disobeyed their parents. When they came in contact with those whom they considered heathens or aliens, they behaved in such a bizarre and irrational manner that this chapter in the American history comes down to us as a late-movie horror film. They exterminated the Indians, who taught them how to survive in a world unknown to them, and their encounter with the calypso culture of Barbados resulted in what the tourist guide in Salem's Witches' House refers to as the Witchcraft Hysteria.

11   The Puritan legacy of hard work and meticulous accounting led to the establishment of a great industrial society; it is no wonder that the American industrial revolution began in Lowell, Massachusetts, but

there was the other side, the strange and paranoid attitudes toward those different from the Elect.

The cultural attitudes of that early Elect continue to be voiced in 12 everyday life in the United States: the president of a distinguished university, writing a letter to the *Times,* belittling the study of African civilizations; the television network that promoted its show on the Vatican art with the boast that this art represented "the finest achievements of the human spirit." A modern up-tempo state of complex rhythms that depends upon contacts with an international community can no longer behave as if it dwelled in a "Zion Wilderness" surrounded by beasts and pagans.

When I heard a schoolteacher warn the other night about the in- 13 vasion of the American educational system by foreign curriculums, I wanted to yell at the television set, "Lady, they're already here." It has already begun because the world is here. The world has been arriving at these shores for at least ten thousand years from Europe, Africa, and Asia. In the late nineteenth and early twentieth centuries, large numbers of Europeans arrived, adding their cultures to those of the European, African, and Asian settlers who were already here, and recently millions have been entering the country from South America and the Caribbean, making Yale Professor Bob Thompson's bouillabaisse richer and thicker.

One of our most visionary politicians said that he envisioned a time 14 when the United States could become the brain of the world, by which he meant the repository of all of the latest advanced information systems. I thought of that remark when an enterprising poet friend of mine called to say that he had just sold a poem to a computer magazine and that the editors were delighted to get it because they didn't carry fiction or poetry. Is that the kind of world we desire? A humdrum homogeneous world of all brains and no heart, no fiction, no poetry; a world of robots with human attendants bereft of imagination, of culture? Or does North America deserve a more exciting destiny? To become a place where the cultures of the world crisscross. This is possible because the United States is unique in the world: The world is here.

EXPLORING IDEAS

1. Discuss Reed's suggestion that there is more union of cultural styles in the United States than there is conflict between cultural styles. Do you think he is right? If so, what are the implications of this fact?

2. Do you agree with Reed that most of the cultural and educational Elect in the United States think of Western civilization as being primarily created by the people of Europe? Think of a teacher or commentator you have heard who has made this assumption.

3. Does Reed suggest that the ultimate implication of racism is the position taken by Adolf Hitler? Is racism always in danger of such extreme views? How does one draw the line between harmless racism and race-threatening racism?

4. Define the so-called Puritan work ethic, and discuss some of its implications. What are some of the pros and cons of this attitude?

5. Reed says the Puritans had a "mean streak." What were the underlying reasons for the "mean" things Reed says the Puritans did?

6. Does Reed think there is still an attitude traceable to the Puritan Elect in modern U.S. society? How does he identify this notion of the Elect with his previous statements about Western civilization's being primarily the product of Europe?

7. What kind of world does Reed envision for North America in his final paragraph? What does it have to do with art? Why is art so important to this vision?

EXPLORING RHETORIC

1. Discuss the purpose of the first four paragraphs of Reed's essay. Why does he provide four examples of his point before he even announces what his point is? Are there any differences between what the first two examples illustrate and what the last two illustrate?

2. Why does Reed primarily use examples of art to question the assumption that Western civilization is primarily European?

3. Why does Reed use the rhetorical technique of posing questions in paragraphs 5 and 6 instead of making assertions?

4. What does Reed mean by the phrase "small-screen view of political and cultural reality"?

5. How does Reed move to a discussion of the causes of racism and prejudice?

6. Discuss Reed's shift in the last paragraph to modern technology. Is this a justified shift or a deviation from his main topic?

PART FOUR

ANALYZING
AND ARGUING A CASE

From essays in which writers explore their own past, try to discover meaning in everyday activities, and examine human differences, we finally come to what some might say is the most basic human objective: trying to convince others that they should think the same way we do about something. An argument is more difficult to write than an essay based on personal experience or observation because, as Gilbert Highet says, a personal essay is like a conversation between oneself and an unseen friend, but an argument is like a quarrel between oneself and an unseen opponent.

In a written argument, you must assume that you are addressing people whose basic inclination is to disagree with you, for there is little point in arguing with those who think as you do. In fact, it is probably a good writing tactic always to assume that you are writing to an audience that will probably disagree with you, for it will remind you that you must make the strongest argument possible. The twelve essays in this section focus on four common cultural phenomena about which people may disagree.

Stephen King, the reigning king of horror fiction, makes an individual case based on his own personal experience as to why human beings are drawn to horror movies, whereas Robert

Brustein and Michael Ventura argue that horror movies have important cultural significance. Robert MacNeil and Marie Winn argue that television is both addictive and deceptive, whereas Tony Schwartz makes a case for the central importance of television in our increasingly technological society. William Buckley argues that Americans do not complain enough and tries to explain why, while Victoria Sackett maintains that Americans are so intolerant about trivial differences that they complain too much. Julianne Malveaux makes a personal case for the importance of anger in modern society. James Baldwin's argument in favor of black English, which is responded to directly by Rachel Jones, is a classic example of two writers who are diametrically opposed on the same issue, while Gloria Naylor argues that African Americans may transform racist language to suit their own purposes.

Writing a good argument is not a simple task; of all the forms of writing, it is the most heavily loaded with rhetorical devices and techniques calculated to convince and persuade. The prompts in the Exploring Ideas and Exploring Rhetoric sections at the end of each essay will encourage you to examine the nature of the arguments and the rhetorical techniques the writers use to make their case.

Why We Crave Horror Movies

STEPHEN KING

Stephen King was born in 1947 in Portland, Maine. He graduated from the University of Maine in 1970, with a degree in English. He found work as a janitor, laundry worker, and high school teacher before hitting it big with the novel *Carrie* in 1974. Since then, he has published numerous popular novels, including *Salem's Lot*, 1975; *The Shining*, 1977; *Tommyknockers*, 1988; and *The Dark Half*, 1989. Many of King's novels have been adapted to film, including the popular *Stand By Me*, 1986, based on the story "The Body" from his collection *Night Shift*, 1978.

King, who has made millions of dollars from our fascination with horror stories and movies, tries to describe the basis for that fascination. Like fairy tales, he claims, horror films encourage us to put away our need for analysis and be children again, fulfilling our nasty fantasies in a harmless way.

I think that we're all mentally ill; those of us outside the asylums 1
only hide it a little better—and maybe not all that much better, after all.
We've all known people who talk to themselves, people who sometimes
squinch their faces into horrible grimaces when they believe no one is
watching, people who have some hysterical fear—of snakes, the dark,
the tight place, the long drop . . . and, of course, those final worms and
grubs that are waiting so patiently underground.

When we pay our four or five bucks and seat ourselves at tenth-row 2
center in a theater showing a horror movie, we are daring the nightmare.

Why? Some of the reasons are simple and obvious. To show that we 3
can, that we are not afraid, that we can ride this roller coaster. Which is
not to say that a really good horror movie may not surprise a scream out
of us at some point, the way we may scream when the roller coaster
twists through a complete 360 or plows through a lake at the bottom of
the drop. And horror movies, like roller coasters, have always been the
special province of the young; by the time one turns 40 or 50, one's appetite for double twists or 360-degree loops may be considerably de-
pleted.

We also go to re-establish our feelings of essential normality; the 4
horror movie is innately conservative, even reactionary. Freda Jackson
as the horrible melting woman in *Die, Monster, Die!* confirms for us that
no matter how far we may be removed from the beauty of a Robert Red-
ford or a Diana Ross, we are still light-years from true ugliness.

And we go to have fun.   5

Ah, but this is where the ground starts to slope away, isn't it? Be- 6
cause this is a very peculiar sort of fun, indeed. The fun comes from

seeing others menaced—sometimes killed. One critic has suggested that if pro football has become the voyeur's version of combat, then the horror film has become the modern version of the public lynching.

7   It is true that the mythic, "fairy-tale" horror film intends to take away the shades of gray. . . . It urges us to put away our more civilized and adult penchant for analysis and to become children again, seeing things in pure blacks and whites. It may be that horror movies provide psychic relief on this level because this invitation to lapse into simplicity, irrationality and even outright madness is extended so rarely. We are told we may allow our emotions a free rein . . . or no rein at all.

8   If we are all insane, then sanity becomes a matter of degree. If your insanity leads you to carve up women like Jack the Ripper or the Cleveland Torso Murderer, we clap you away in the funny farm (but neither of those two amateur-night surgeons was ever caught, heh-heh-heh); if, on the other hand, your insanity leads you only to talk to yourself when you're under stress or to pick your nose on your morning bus, then you are left alone to go about your business . . . though it is doubtful that you will ever be invited to the best parties.

9   The potential lyncher is in almost all of us (excluding saints, past and present; but then, most saints have been crazy in their own ways), and every now and then, he has to be let loose to scream and roll around in the grass. Our emotions and our fears form their own body, and we recognize that it demands its own exercise to maintain proper muscle tone. Certain of these emotional muscles are accepted—even exalted—in civilized society; they are, of course, the emotions that tend to maintain the status quo of civilization itself. Love, friendship, loyalty, kindness—these are all the emotions that we applaud, emotions that have been immortalized in the couplets of Hallmark cards and in the verses (I don't dare call it poetry) of Leonard Nimoy.

10   When we exhibit these emotions, society showers us with positive reinforcement; we learn this even before we get out of diapers. When, as children, we hug our rotten little puke of a sister and give her a kiss, all the aunts and uncles smile and twit and cry, "Isn't he the sweetest little thing?" Such coveted treats as chocolate-covered graham crackers often follow. But if we deliberately slam the rotten little puke of a sister's fingers in the door, sanctions follow—angry remonstrance from parents, aunts and uncles; instead of a chocolate-covered graham cracker, a spanking.

11   But anticivilization emotions don't go away, and they demand periodic exercise. We have such "sick" jokes as, "What's the difference between a truckload of bowling balls and a truckload of dead babies?" (You can't unload a truckload of bowling balls with a pitchfork . . . a joke, by the way, that I heard originally from a ten-year-old). Such a joke may surprise a laugh or a grin out of us even as we recoil, a possibility

that confirms the thesis: If we share a brotherhood of man, then we also share an insanity of man. None of which is intended as a defense of either the sick joke or insanity but merely as an explanation of why the best horror films, like the best fairy tales, manage to be reactionary, anarchistic, and revolutionary all at the same time.

The mythic horror movie, like the sick joke, has a dirty job to do. It 12 deliberately appeals to all that is worst in us. It is morbidity unchained, our most base instincts let free, our nastiest fantasies realized . . . and it all happens, fittingly enough, in the dark. For those reasons, good liberals often shy away from horror films. For myself, I like to see the most aggressive of them—*Dawn of the Dead*, for instance—as lifting a trap door in the civilized forebrain and throwing a basket of raw meat to the hungry alligators swimming around in that subterranean river beneath.   13

Why bother? Because it keeps them from getting out, man. It keeps them down there and me up here. It was Lennon and McCartney who said that all you need is love, and I would agree with that.   14

As long as you keep the gators fed.

EXPLORING IDEAS

1. King begins by listing a number of activities that might suggest mental illness: talking to yourself, fearing snakes, fearing heights. Brainstorm some other common activities or fears that might be considered mental illness. Is everyone mentally ill in some way? If so, what does the term "mentally ill" really mean?

2. Brainstorm King's comparison between horror movies and roller coasters. What other activities do people engage in purposely to scare themselves? Reread the essay entitled "Cyclone" by Peter Schjeldahl in Part Two.

3. King says that such activities as roller coasters and horror movies are more for the young than for adults. Why is there this difference between young people and adults? What are some of the implications of this difference?

4. Although King says that horror movies are conservative, even reactionary, he does not support this opinion. Write an essay, using the following thesis statement: "The horror movie is innately conservative, even reactionary."

5. Write an essay using the following thesis sentence: "Pro football has become the voyeur's version of combat."

6. King says that the horror film intends to take away shades of gray. Brainstorm the pros and cons of seeing things in black and white terms as opposed to seeing things in shades of gray. Provide examples of activities that might be better seen as black and white, as well as examples of things that might be better seen in shades of gray.

7. King says that the horror film urges us to put away our penchant for analysis and become children again. Read the essay "Tucson Zoo" by Lewis Thomas elsewhere in this book for an example of the urge to put away analysis. Are there certain activities in human experience that should not be analyzed?

8. If horror films allow us a release from the potential lyncher in all of us, does pornography release us from the potential rapist in all of us? Is King right in saying that every now and then one has to "let loose"? How does society distinguish between ways in which one can be permitted to "let loose" and ways in which one cannot?

9. Write an essay on the most horrifying or disgusting horror film you have seen, agreeing or disagreeing with King's argument about the need for us to let our most basic instincts free.

EXPLORING RHETORIC

1. What tone does King establish in the first sentence of his essay? How does this sentence set up the reader to react to the essay that follows it?

2. What is the relationship between the first paragraph of King's essay and the next two paragraphs?

3. Explain the meaning of the image in the following sentence: "Ah, but this is where the ground starts to slope away."

4. Discuss King's attitude toward his subject, pointing out specific examples to support your position. Note, for example, King's "heh-heh-heh" at one point in the essay. Are there other examples of this kind of aside? Why does King do this?

5. Why does King use picking your nose as an instance of insanity for which the general public will let you alone? Is this a good example, or does King use it just to create a response? How do you know?

6. Why does King use the expression "our rotten little puke of a sister"? Compare this wording to Victoria Sackett's use of the phrase "fat little arm" in the essay "Discriminating Tastes" elsewhere in this section.

7. King says he is not defending the sick joke or insanity when he says, "If we share a brotherhood of man, then we also share an insanity of man." Then why does he use the sick joke and insanity as examples? Are not sick jokes and insanity possibly hurtful to a number of people?

8. Discuss the effectiveness of the metaphor in the following phrase: "lifting a trap door in the civilized forebrain and throwing a basket of raw meat to the hungry alligators swimming around in that subterranean river beneath."

9. How can King say that as a good liberal, he shies away from horror films when he has become a millionaire by writing horror novels and making horror films?

10. Comment on the effectiveness of King's conclusion. Does it maintain the tone established at the beginning of the essay?

Reflections on Horror Movies

ROBERT BRUSTEIN

Robert Brustein was born in 1927 in New York City. He attended Amherst College and received his Ph.D. from Columbia University. He has been director of the American Repertory Theater in Cambridge, Massachusetts, and has taught at Columbia, Cornell, and Vassar. His books include *The Theater of Revolt,* 1964; *Seasons of Discontent,* 1965; *The Third Theater,* 1969; *Revolution as Theater,* 1971; and *Making Scenes: A Personal History of the Turbulent Years at Yale, 1966–1979,* 1981.

The following essay combines an informal personal perspective with formal academic analysis and organization to explore the cultural implications—particularly American attitudes toward experimental science—of three types of horror movies: the Mad Doctor, the Atomic Beast, and the Interplanetary Monster.

Horror movies, perennial supporting features among Grade B and C 1 fare, have recently been enjoying a vogue, a fact in which I shamelessly rejoice. I have been hopelessly addicted to them since the age of eight when my mother, with great anxiety lest I be traumatized for life, accompanied me to see Frederic March in *Dr. Jekyll and Mr. Hyde.* Since then, I guess I have seen about two hundred horror films but, although my mother had a couple of bad nights, I have always remained impervious to the inviting promise of their advertising ("Will Give You Nightmares FOREVER"). My satisfactions are more simple. Horror films give me pleasure by their very faults: the woodenness of the acting, the inevitability of the plot, the obstinate refusal to make any but the most basic demand on my mind. I can suggest nothing more remedial after a night of agony at the theatre than a late horror show at a 42nd Street flea pit.

It may seem a little graceless of me, in view of the enjoyment I have 2 derived from these films, to analyze their "cultural significance" and run the risk of stifling any pleasure you (or I) might seek from them in future. But it has occurred to me over the years that, aside from modest shock motives, horror films always try to involve us in certain underground assumptions. They have been serving up a mess of cultural pottage whose seasoning gives science (and sometimes even all knowledge) a bad taste. Since I attended these films with childlike innocence, I consider these added motives an impudence, and I retaliate by pointing out to you what the hidden images are.

The horror movies I am mainly concerned with I have divided into 3 three major categories: Mad Doctor, Atomic Beast, and Interplanetary Monster. They do not exhaust all the types but they each contain two essential characters, the Scientist and the Monster, toward whom the attitudes of the movies are in a revealing state of change.

4   The Mad Doctor series is by far the most long lived of the three. It suffered a temporary decline in the forties when Frankenstein, Dracula, and the Wolf Man (along with their countless offspring) were first loaned out as straight men to Abbott and Costello and then set out to graze in the parched pastures of the cheap all-night movie houses, but it has recently demonstrated its durability in a group of English remakes and a Teenage Monster craze. These films find their roots in certain European folk myths. Dracula was inspired by an ancient Balkan superstition about vampires, the werewolf is a Middle European folk myth recorded, among other places, in the Breton *lais* of Marie de France, and even Frankenstein, though out of Mary Shelley by the Gothic tradition, has a medieval prototype in the Golem, a monster the Jews fashioned from clay and earth to free them from oppression. The spirit of these films is still medieval, combining a vulgar religiosity with folk superstitions. Superstition now, however, has been crudely transferred from magic and alchemy to creative science, itself a form of magic to the untutored mind. The devil of the vampire and werewolf myths, who turned human beings into baser animals, today has become a scientist, and the metamorphosis is given a technical name—it is a "regression" into an earlier state of evolution. The alchemist and devil-conjuring scholar Dr. Faustus gives way to Dr. Frankenstein the research physician, while the magic circle, the tetragrammaton, and the full moon are replaced by test tubes, complicated electrical apparati, and bunsen burners.

5   Frankenstein, like Faustus, defies God by exploring areas where humans are not meant to trespass. In Mary Shelley's book (it is subtitled "A Modern Prometheus"), Frankenstein is a latter-day Faustus, a superhuman creature whose aspiration embodies the expansiveness of his age. In the movies, however, Frankenstein loses his heroic quality and becomes a lunatic monomaniac, so obsessed with the value of his work that he no longer cares whether his discovery proves a boon or a curse to mankind. When the mad doctor, his eyes wild and inflamed, bends over his intricate equipment, pouring in a little of this and a little of that, the spectator is confronted with an immoral being whose mental superiority is only a measure of his madness. Like the popular image of the theoretical scientist engaged in basic research ("Basic research," says Charles Wilson, "is science's attempt to prove that grass is green"), he succeeds only in creating something badly which nature has already made well. The Frankenstein monster is a parody of man. Ghastly in appearance, clumsy in movement, criminal in behavior, imbecilic of mind, it is superior only in physical strength and resistance to destruction. The scientist has fashioned it in the face of divine disapproval (the heavens disgorge

at its birth)—not to mention the disapproval of friends and frightened townspeople—and it can lead only to trouble.

For Dr. Frankenstein, however, the monster symbolizes the triumph 6 of his intellect over the blind morality of his enemies and it confirms him in the ultimate soundness of his thought ("They thought I was mad, but this proves I am the superior being"). When it becomes clear that his countrymen are unimpressed by his achievement and regard him as a menace to society, the monster becomes the agent of his revenge. As it ravages the countryside and terrorizes the inhabitants, it embodies and expresses the scientist's own lust and violence. It is an extension of his own mad soul, come to life not in a weak and ineffectual body but in a body of formidable physical power. (In a movie like *Dr. Jekyll and Mr. Hyde,* the identity of monster and doctor is even clearer; Mr. Hyde, the monster, is the aggressive and libidinous element in the benevolent Dr. Jekyll's personality.) The rampage of the monster is the rampage of mad, unrestrained science which inevitably turns on the scientist, destroying him too. As the lava bubbles over the sinking head of the monster, the crude moral of the film frees itself from the horror and is asserted. Experimental science (and by extension knowledge itself) is superfluous, dangerous, and unlawful, for, in exploring the unknown, it leads man to usurp God's creative power. Each of these films is a victory for obscurantism, flattering the spectator into believing that his intellectual inferiority is a sign that he is loved by God.

The Teenage Monster films, a very recent phenomenon, amend the 7 assumptions of these horror movies in a startling manner. Their titles—*I Was a Teenage Werewolf, I Was a Teenage Frankenstein, Blood of Dracula,* and *Teenage Monster*—(some wit awaits one called *I Had a Teenage Monkey on My Back*)—suggest a Hollywood prank but they are deadly serious, mixing the conventions of early horror movies with the ingredients of adolescent culture. The doctor, significantly enough, is no longer a fringe character whose madness can be inferred from the rings around his eyes and his wild hair, but a respected member of society, a high school chemistry teacher (*Blood of Dracula*) or a psychoanalyst (*Teenage Werewolf*) or a visiting lecturer from Britain (*Teenage Frankenstein*). Although he gives the appearance of benevolence—he pretends to help teenagers with their problems—behind this facade he hides evil experimental designs. The monster, on the other hand, takes on a more fully developed personality. He is a victim who begins inauspiciously as an average, though emotionally troubled, adolescent and ends, through the influence of the doctor, as a voracious animal. The monster as teenager becomes the central character in the film and the teenage audience is expected to identify and sympathize with him.

In *I Was a Teenage Werewolf,* the hero is characterized as brilliant but 8 erratic in his studies and something of a delinquent. At the suggestion of his principal, he agrees to accept therapy from an analyst helping maladjusted students. The analyst gets the boy under his control and, after injecting him with a secret drug, turns him into a werewolf. Against his will he murders a number of his contemporaries. When the doctor refuses to free him from his curse, he kills him and is himself killed by the police. In death, his features relax into the harmless countenance of an adolescent.

9   The crimes of the adolescent are invariably committed against other youths (the doctor has it in for teenagers) and are always connected with those staples of juvenile culture, sex and violence. The advertising displays show the male monsters, dressed in leather jackets and blue jeans, bending ambiguously over the diaphanously draped body of a luscious young girl, while the female teenage vampire of *Blood of Dracula,* her nails long and her fangs dripping, is herself half dressed and lying on top of a struggling male (whether to rape or murder him it is not clear). The identification of sex and violence is further underlined by the promotion blurbs: "In her eyes DESIRE! In her veins—the blood of a MONSTER!" (*Blood of Dracula*); "A Teenage Titan on a Lustful Binge That Paralyzed a Town with Fear" (*Teenage Monster*). It is probable that these crimes are performed less reluctantly than is suggested and that the adolescent spectator is more thrilled than appalled by this "lustful binge" which captures the attention of the adult community. The acquisition of power and prestige through delinquent sexual and aggressive activity is a familiar juvenile fantasy (the same distributors exploit it more openly in films like *Reform School Girl* and *Drag-Strip Girl*), one which we can see frequently acted out by delinquents in our city schools. In the Teenage Monster films, however, the hero is absolved of his aggressive and libidinous impulses. Although he both feels and acts on them, he can attribute the responsibility to the mad scientist who controls his behavior. What these films seem to be saying, in their underground manner, is that behind the harmless face of the high school chemistry teacher and the intellectual countenance of the psychoanalyst lies the warped authority responsible for teenage violence. The adolescent feels victimized by society—turned into a monster by society—and if he behaves in a delinquent manner, society and not he is to blame. Thus, we can see one direction in which the hostility for experimental research, explicit in the Mad Doctor films, can go—it can be transmuted into hatred of adult authority itself.

10   Or it can go underground, as in the Atomic Beast movies. The Mad Doctor movies, in exploiting the supernatural, usually locate their action in Europe (often a remote Bavarian village), where wild fens, spectral castles, and ominous graveyards provide the proper eerie background. The Atomic Beast movies depend for their effect on the contemporary and familiar and there is a corresponding change in locale. The monster

(or *thing*, as it is more often called) appears now in a busy American city—usually Los Angeles to save the producer money—where average men walk about in business suits. The thing terrorizes not only the hero, the heroine, and a few anonymous (and expendable) characters in Tyrolean costumes, but the entire world. Furthermore, it has lost all resemblance to anything human. It appears as a giant ant (*Them!*), a prehistoric animal (*Beast from Twenty Thousand Fathoms*), an outsized grasshopper (*Beginning of the End*), or a monstrous spider (*Tarantula*). Although these films, in their deference to science fiction, seem to smile more benignly on scientific endeavor, they are unconsciously closer to the antitheoretical biases of the Mad Doctor series than would first appear.

All these films are similarly plotted, so the plot of *Beginning of the* 11 *End* will serve as an example of the whole genre. The scene opens on a pair of adolescents necking in their car off a desert road. Their attention is caught by a weird clicking sound, the boy looks up in horror, the girl screams, the music stings, and the scene fades. In the next scene, we learn that the car has been completely demolished and its occupants have disappeared. The police, totally baffled, are conducting fruitless investigations when word comes that a small town nearby has been destroyed in the same mysterious way. Enter the young scientist-hero. Examining the wreckage of the town, he discovers a strange fluid which when analyzed proves to have been manufactured by a giant grasshopper. The police ridicule his conclusions and are instantly attacked by a fleet of these grasshoppers, each fifteen feet high, which wipe out the entire local force and a few state troopers. Interrupting a perfunctory romance with the heroine, the scientist flies to Washington to alert the nation. He describes the potential danger to a group of bored politicians and yawning big brass but they remain skeptical until word comes that the things have reached Chicago and are crushing buildings and eating the occupants. The scientist is then put in charge of the army and air force. Although the military men want to evacuate the city and drop an atom bomb on it, the scientist devises a safer method of destroying the creatures and proceeds to do so through exemplary physical courage and superior knowledge of their behavior. The movie ends on a note of foreboding: Have the things been completely exterminated?

Externally, there seem to be very significant changes indeed, espe- 12 cially in the character of the scientist. No longer fang toothed, long haired, and subject to delirious ravings (Bela Lugosi, John Carradine, Basil Rathbone), the doctor is now a highly admired member of society, muscular, handsome, and heroic (John Agar). He is invariably wiser, more reasonable, and more humane than the boneheaded bureaucrats and trigger-happy brass who compose the members of his "team," and he even has sexual appeal, a quality which Hollywood's eggheads have never enjoyed before. The scientist-hero, however, is not a very convincing intellectual. Although he may use technical, polysyllabic language when discussing his findings, he always yields gracefully to the admonition to "tell us in our own words, Doc" and proves that he can speak as simply as you or I; in the crisis, in fact, he is almost monosyllabic. When the chips are down, he loses his glasses (a symbol of his intellectualism) and begins to look like everyone else. The hero's intellect is part of his costume and makeup, easily shed when heroic action is demanded. That he is always called upon not only to outwit the thing but to wrestle with it as well (in order to save the heroine) indicates that he is in constant danger of tripping over the thin boundary between specialist and average Joe.

13   The fact remains that there is a new separation between the scientist and the monster. Rather than being an extension of the doctor's evil will, the monster functions completely on its own, creating havoc through its predatory nature. We learn through charts, biological films, and the scientist's patient explanations that ants and grasshoppers are not the harmless little beasties they appear but actually voracious insects who need only the excuse of size to prey upon humanity. The doctor, rather than allying himself with the monster in its rampage against our cities, is in strong opposition to it, and reverses the pattern of the Mad Doctor films by destroying it.

14   And yet, if the individual scientist is absolved of all responsibility for the thing, science somehow is not. These films suggest an uneasiness about science which, though subtle and unpremeditated, reflects unconscious American attitudes. These attitudes are sharpened when we examine the genesis of the thing, for, though it seems to rise out of nowhere, it is invariably caused by a scientific blunder. The giant ants of *Them!*, for example, result from a nuclear explosion which caused a mutation in the species; another fission test has awakened, in *Beast from Twenty Thousand Fathoms*, a dinosaur encrusted in polar icecaps; the spider of *Tarantula* grows in size after having been injected with radioactive isotopes, and escapes during a fight in the lab between two scientists; the grasshoppers of *Beginning of the End* enlarge after crawling into some radioactive dust carelessly left about by a researcher. We are left with a puzzling substatement: science destroys the thing, but scientific experimentation has created it.

15   I think we can explain this equivocal attitude when we acknowledge that the thing "which is too horrible to name," which owes its birth to an atomic or nuclear explosion, which begins in a desert or frozen waste and moves from there to cities, and which promises ultimately to destroy the world, is probably a crude symbol for the bomb itself. The scientists we see represented in these films are unlike the Mad Doctors in another, more fundamental respect: they are never engaged in basic research. The scientist uses his knowledge in a purely defensive manner,

like a specialist working on rocket interception or a physician trying to cure a disease. The isolated theoretician who tinkers curiously in his lab (and who invented the atom bomb) is never shown, only the practical working scientist who strives to undo the harm. The thing's destructive rampage against cities, like the rampage of the Frankenstein monster, is the result of too much cleverness, and the consequences for all the world are only too apparent.

These consequences are driven home more powerfully in movies   16 like *The Incredible Shrinking Man* and *The Amazing Colossal Man,* where the audience gets the opportunity to identify closely with the victims of science's reckless experimentation. The hero of the first movie is an average man who, through contact with fallout while on his honeymoon, begins to shrink away to nothing. As he proceeds to grow smaller, he finds himself in much the same dilemma as the other heroes of the Atomic Beast series—he must do battle with (now) gigantic insects in order to survive. Scientists can do nothing to save him—after a while they can't even find him—so as he dwindles into an atomic particle he finally turns to God, for whom "there is no zero." The inevitable sequel, *The Amazing Colossal Man,* reverses the dilemma. The hero grows to enormous size through the premature explosion of a plutonium bomb. Size carries with it the luxury of power but the hero cannot enjoy his new stature. He feels like a freak and his body is proceeding to outgrow his brain and heart. Although the scientists labor to help him and even succeed in reducing an elephant to the size of a cat, it is too late; the hero has gone mad, demolished Las Vegas, and fallen over Boulder Dam. The victimization of man by theoretical science has become, in these two movies, less of a suggestion and more of a fact.

In the Interplanetary Monster movies, Hollywood handles the pub-   17 lic's ambivalence toward science in a more obvious way, by splitting the scientist in two. Most of these movies feature both a practical scientist who wishes to destroy the invader and a theoretical scientist who wants to communicate with it. In *The Thing,* for example, we find billeted among a group of more altruistic average-Joe colleagues with crew cuts an academic long-haired scientist of the Dr. Frankenstein type. When the evil thing (a highly evolved vegetable which, by multiplying itself, threatens to take over the world) descends in a flying saucer, this scientist tries to perpetuate its life in order "to find out what it knows." He is violently opposed in this by the others, who take the occasion to tell him that such amoral investigation produced the atom bomb. But he cannot be reasoned with and almost wrecks the entire party. After both he and the thing are destroyed, the others congratulate themselves on remaining safe, though in the dark. In *Forbidden Planet* (a sophisticated thriller inspired in part by Shakespeare's *Tempest*), the good and evil elements in science are represented, as in *Dr. Jekyll and Mr. Hyde,* by the split personality of the scientist. He is urbane and benevolent (Walter Pidgeon plays the role) and is trying to realize an ideal community on the far-off planet he has discovered. Although he has invented a robot (Ariel) who cheerfully performs man's baser tasks, we learn that he is also responsible, though unwittingly, for a terrible invisible force (Caliban) overwhelming in its destructiveness. While he sleeps, the aggressive forces in his libido activate a dynamo he has been tinkering with which gives enormous power to kill those the doctor unconsciously resents. Thus, Freudian psychology is evoked to endow the scientist with guilt. At the end, he accepts his guilt and sacrifices his life in order to combat the being he has created.

18   The Interplanetary Monster series sometimes reverses the central situation of most horror films. We often find the monster controlling the scientist and forcing him to do its evil will. In *It Conquered the World* (the first film to capitalize on Sputnik and Explorer), the projection of a space satellite proves to be a mistake, for it results in the invasion of America by a monster from Venus. It takes control of the scientist who, embittered by the indifference of the masses toward his ideas, mistakenly thinks the monster will free men from stupidity. This muddled egghead finally discovers the true intentions of the monster and destroys it, dying himself in the process. In *The Brain from Planet Arous,* a hideous brain inhabits the mind of a nuclear physicist with the intention of controlling the universe. As the physical incarnation of the monster, the scientist is at the mercy of its will until he can free himself of its influence. The monster's intellect, like the intellect of the Mad Doctor, is invariably superior, signified by its large head and small body (in the last film named it is nothing but brain). Like the Mad Doctor, its superior intelligence is always accompanied by moral depravity and an unconscionable lust for power. If the monster is to be destroyed at all, it will not be done by matching wits with it but by finding some chink in its armor. This chink quite often is a physical imperfection: in *War of the Worlds,* the invading Martians are stopped, at the height of their victory, by their vulnerability to the disease germs of earth. Before this Achilles heel is discovered, however, the scientist is controlled to do evil, and with the monster and the doctor in collaboration again, even in this qualified sense, the wheel has come full circle.

19   The terror of most of these films, then, stems from the matching of knowledge with power, always a source of fear for Americans—when Nietzsche's Superman enters comic-book culture he loses his intellectual and spiritual qualities and becomes a muscleman. The muscleman, even with X-ray vision, poses no threat to the will, but muscle in collaboration with mind is generally thought to have a profound effect on individual destinies. The tendency to attribute everything that happens in the heav-

ens, from flying saucers to Florida's cold wave, to science and the bomb ("Why don't they stop," said an old lady on the bus behind me the other day, "they don't know what they're doing") accounts for the extreme ways in which the scientist is regarded in our culture: either as a protective savior or as a destructive blunderer. It is little wonder that America exalts the physician (and the football player) and ignores the physicist. These issues, the issues of the great debate over scientific education and basic research, assert themselves crudely through the unwieldy monster and the Mad Doctor. The films suggest that the academic scientist, in exploring new areas, has laid the human race open to devastation by either human or interplanetary enemies—the doctor's madness, then, is merely a suitable way of expressing a conviction that the scientist's idle curiosity has shaken itself loose from prudency or principle. There is obviously a sensitive moral problem involved here, one which needs more articulate treatment than the covert and superstitious way it is handled in horror movies. That the problem is touched there at all is evidence of how profoundly it has stirred the American psyche.

EXPLORING IDEAS

1. Brustein says he likes horror movies because they make no demands on his mind. Brainstorm some other activities that people engage in precisely because they make no demands on the mind.

2. Brainstorm some film types other than horror movies that have "underground assumptions" or motives beyond their surface ones, for example, science fiction films, westerns, slasher films, or pornography.

3. Discuss Brustein's use of the following terms: "religion," "superstition," "science," and "magic." Brainstorm for an essay contrasting superstition with religion or science with magic.

4. What does Brustein mean that the Frankenstein monster is a parody of man? Try to develop a definition of the word "parody" by brainstorming the features of a well-known parody, such as Mel Brooks's films *Young Frankenstein* or *Space Balls*.

5. Compare Brustein's argument that the horror film is a victory for obscurantism with Stephen King's argument in the previous essay, "Why We Crave Horror Movies," that the horror film is conservative and reactionary.

6. Brainstorm some recent horror films to follow up on Brustein's observation that the horror films of the 1950s mixed conventions of early horror films with the ingredients of adolescent culture. What mixture of conventions makes up more recent films of this genre?

7. Write a humorous essay in which you compare "the monster as teenager" with an image of "the teenager as monster."

8. Is it true that sex and violence are the staples of juvenile culture? Why is sex often linked with violence? Brainstorm these topics, trying to understand both causes and effects.

9. Write an essay using the following topic sentence: "The acquisition of power and prestige through delinquent sexual and aggressive activity is a familiar juvenile fantasy."

10. Explain in your own words Brustein's argument that teenage monster films reflect hatred of adult authority.

11. Why is theoretical science singled out as the villain of these horror movies? Isn't theoretical science necessary? Could there be practical scientific discoveries without theoretical science? Why do people distrust theoretical science?

EXPLORING RHETORIC

1. Explain the metaphor in the following sentence: "They have been serving up a mess of cultural pottage whose seasoning gives science a bad taste." Is this metaphor particularly relevant to Brustein's topic, or does it tell us something about Brustein?

2. Brustein uses the rhetorical method of classification. Explain the purpose of this method and its basic technique. Outline Brustein's classification of films.

3. Discuss the effectiveness of the metaphor in the following phrase: "loaned out as straight men to Abbott and Costello and then set out to graze in the parched pastures of the cheap all-night movie houses." Abbott and Costello were a comedy team in the 1940s and 1950s.

4. Why is paragraph 4 so long? What kind of research did Brustein have to do to develop it?

5. Why does Brustein quote Charles Wilson (a former president of General Motors, who said, "What's good for General Motors is good for the country")?

6. Beginning writers are often criticized by instructors for merely writing a plot summary when asked to analyze a book or movie. Is much of Brustein's essay mere plot summary, or does he manage to integrate summary with analysis? What is the difference between analytical plot summary and mere plot summary?

7. Brustein writes a long plot summary of a film that he says will serve as an example of the whole genre. Write a plot summary of a film you have recently seen, preferably one that is representative of a certain type of film. Then compare your summary with Brustein's. What are some characteristics of an effective summary? How can you keep a summary from being boring?

8. After summarizing the film *Beginning of the End,* Brustein devotes several paragraphs to analyzing it. Read these paragraphs carefully, noting the methods Brustein uses to analyze the film as representative of its genre. Identify the language that signals analysis in these paragraphs.

9. Brustein says that the terror of interplanetary monster films stems from the matching of knowledge with power; he then uses the following reference:

"When Nietzsche's Superman enters comic-book culture he loses his intellectual and spiritual qualities and becomes a muscleman." Frederich Nietzsche, a German philosopher of the nineteenth century, developed an ideal of the Superman as a superior human, unbound by conventional notions of right and wrong. Why does Brustein compare Nietzsche's Superman with a muscleman? Why does he use this reference?

On Kids and Slasher Movies

MICHAEL VENTURA

Michael Ventura is a Los Angeles freelance writer. In the following essay, which appeared in the *L.A. Weekly* in 1989, Ventura argues that a tenyear-old boy's wearing the mask of a maniac killer from a slasher movie is symptomatic of the insanity of widespread violence in modern society. Whereas Stephen King (see "Why We Crave Horror Movies" elsewhere in this part) might see the boy's act as a harmless acting out of the insanity in all of us, Ventura says it is the worst thing he has ever seen—worse than the atomic bomb, worse even than the mass killing of innocent people in the Nazi concentration camp of Auschwitz.

It's a simple thing, really. I shouldn't take it so seriously, I realize that. 1 For it was only a child, a boy of about 10, buying a toy. For Halloween. This was the toy:

A sinister white mask and a quite convincing little rubber meat 2 cleaver. Packaged together in cellophane. It's the "costume" of a maniac killer from one of the slasher movies. The boy wants to play at being a faceless, unstoppable murderer of innocent people (mostly women). At this moment, in this Woolworth's, that's this boy's idea of fun.

Understand that I didn't stand there and decide intellectually that 3 this simple and small event is, when all is said and done, the worst thing I've seen. My body decided. My intestines, my knees, my chest. It was only later that I tried to think about it.

This boy's eagerness to "play" maniac killer is an event worse than 4 the Bomb, worse even than Auschwitz. Reduced to its simplest terms, the bomb is a fetish, an object of worship—like other objects of worship before it, it is used as an excuse for arranging the world in a certain fashion, allocating resources, assigning powers. It is insane, but in many ways it is an extension of familiar, even honored, insanities. As for the Nazi camps: The people being murdered knew, as they were being murdered, *that* they were being murdered; the murderers knew they were murdering; and, when the world finally knew, the camps became the measure of ultimate human evil. A crime to scar us all, and our descendants, forever.

5   There is nothing so clear in the Woolworth's scene. The boy is certainly not committing a crime. The toy's merchandisers are within their rights. To legislate against them would be to endanger most of our freedoms. The mother buying the toy is perhaps making a mistake, perhaps not. Without knowing the boy, and knowing him well, who's to be certain that it isn't better for him to engage in, rather than repress, such play? The mother did not put the desire for the toy in him. Three thousand years of Judeo-Christian culture did that. Nor has the mother the power to take that desire from him. Nobody has that power. If he can want the toy at all, then it almost doesn't matter whether the toy exists or not. Doesn't the boy's need for such play exist with or without the toy?

6   Nor would I be too quick to blame the boy's desire on television and slasher films. The Nazis who crewed the camps and the scientists who built the bomb did not need television and slasher films to school them in horror. In fact, the worst atrocities from the pharaohs to Vietnam were committed quite ably before the first slasher film was made. Keeping your child away from TV may make *you* feel better, but can any child be protected from the total weight of Western history?

7   In a world shorn of order, stripped of traditions, molting every decade, every year, a dancing, varicolored snake of a century—pointless violence is evident everywhere, on every level. Professional soldiers are statistically safer than urban women; senseless destruction is visited on trees and on the ozone and on every species of life. No one feels safe anywhere. This has become the very meaning of the 20th century.

8   So I am in a Woolworth's one day and I feel a sort of final horror as I watch a boy buy a psycho-killer toy so that he can pretend he's an unstoppable maniacal murderer. What is so horrible is that this boy is doing this instinctively, for his very survival. In order to live, in order not to go mad, this boy is acclimating himself to the idea of the killer-maniac, because killer-maniac energy is so present in his world. He's trying to inoculate himself through play, as all children have, everywhere, in every era. He thus lets a little bit of the energy into him—that's how inoculations work. Too little, and he is too afraid of the world—it's too terrifying to feel powerless amid the maniacal that's taken for granted around him; to feel any power at all he needs a bit of it inside him. But if he takes in too much, he could be swamped.

9   How horrible that he is forced to such a choice. You'd think it would be enough to stop the world in its tracks. And what can we do for him? Struggle for a different world, yes, but that won't change what's already

happened to him. What can we do for that boy except be on his side, stand by his choice, and pray for the play of his struggling soul?

EXPLORING IDEAS

1. What does Ventura mean that the bomb is a fetish, an object of worship used as an excuse for arranging the world in a certain fashion?

2. Explain Ventura's point about the Nazi death camp at Auschwitz. Why does he believe the camp is not as bad as the boy's buying the mask because the people involved knew what they were doing and what was happening to them?

3. What freedoms would be endangered if the sale of the mask were legislated against? How valuable are these freedoms compared with the danger of the mask?

4. Discuss the arguments about expressing emotions versus repressing them. Compare Ventura's perspective on this issue with Stephen King's perspective in his essay on horror movies elsewhere in this part.

5. Brainstorm for an essay on the value of play for children for expressing their feelings and acting out their fantasies or aggressions. How dangerous is such play? What kind of play do adults engage in to act out such forbidden fantasies?

6. Discuss some recent slasher films you have seen, and argue whether such films are dangerous or harmless. What basic fantasies do slasher films seem to objectify or embody? Brainstorm for an essay.

7. If Ventura is right that the Nazis or the bomb builders did not need television and slasher films to encourage or teach them such horrors, then why do so many people blame such films and television for so many antisocial acts?

8. Discuss Ventura's central point in paragraph 8. How is the boy protecting himself from going mad by buying the mask? Explain this concept in your own words.

EXPLORING RHETORIC

1. Discuss the tone Ventura uses in the first three paragraphs. Is he exaggerating when he says that his body decided that the boy's buying the mask was the worst thing he had ever seen?

2. Discuss the relevance of Ventura's comparison of the act he witnessed with the bomb and with Auschwitz. Why does he use these two examples?

3. Why does Ventura say it is three thousand years of Judeo-Christian culture that put the desire to buy the mask into the boy? Are other cultures also guilty of creating such desires?

4. Why does Ventura introduce the issue of keeping children away from television into his argument?

5. Is Ventura exaggerating in paragraph 7 when he says the fact that no one feels safe is the very meaning of the twentieth century? Are exaggeration and over-statement a central technique in this essay?

6. Discuss the effectiveness of Ventura's use of the metaphor of inoculation in paragraph 8.

7. What is the rhetorical effect of Ventura's final paragraph? Is he suggesting that we are helpless to do anything for the boy buying the mask? How is this so?

The Trouble with Television

ROBERT MACNEIL

Robert MacNeil, the well-known co-anchor of the Public Broadcasting Service's (PBS) news program, "MacNeil/Lehrer News Hour," was born in Montreal, Canada. He has published two books: *The People Machine: The Influence of Television on American Politics,* 1968, an analysis and criticism of news as entertainment; and *The Right Place at the Right Time,* 1982, a personal account of his own journalist experiences.

The following selection was first presented as a speech at the State University of New York at Purchase in 1984. It appeared in its present form in the *Reader's Digest* in 1985. MacNeil is not so much concerned with the escapist content of television as he is with its technique of presenting such small bits of information that it discourages concentration—an approach he sees to be infecting the attitude of the nation generally.

1   It is difficult to escape the influence of television. If you fit the statistical averages, by the age of 20 you will have been exposed to at least 20,000 hours of television. You can add 10,000 hours for each decade you have lived after the age of 20. The only things Americans do more than watch television are work and sleep.

2   Calculate for a moment what could be done with even a part of those hours. Five thousand hours, I am told, are what a typical college undergraduate spends working on a bachelor's degree. In 10,000 hours you could have learned enough to become an astronomer or engineer. You could have learned several languages fluently. If it appealed to you, you could be reading Homer in the original Greek or Dostoyevsky in Russian. If it didn't, you could have walked around the world and written a book about it.

3   The trouble with television is that it discourages concentration. Almost anything interesting and rewarding in life requires some construc-

tive, consistently applied effort. The dullest, the least gifted of us can achieve things that seem miraculous to those who never concentrate on anything. But television encourages us to apply no effort. It sells us instant gratification. It diverts us only to divert, to make the time pass without pain.

Television's variety becomes a narcotic, not a stimulus. Its serial, 4 kaleidoscopic exposures force us to follow its lead. The viewer is on a perpetual guided tour: 30 minutes at the museum, 30 at the cathedral, 30 for a drink, then back on the bus to the next attraction—except on television, typically, the spans allotted are on the order of minutes or seconds, and the chosen delights are more often car crashes and people killing one another. In short, a lot of television usurps one of the most precious of all human gifts, the ability to focus your attention yourself, rather than just passively surrender it.

Capturing your attention—and holding it—is the prime motive of 5 most television programming and enhances its role as a profitable advertising vehicle. Programmers live in constant fear of losing anyone's attention—anyone's. The surest way to avoid doing so is to keep everything brief, not to strain the attention of anyone but instead to provide constant stimulation through variety, novelty, action and movement. Quite simply, television operates on the appeal to the short attention span.

It is simply the easiest way out. But it has come to be regarded as a 6 given, as inherent in the medium itself; as an imperative, as though General Sarnoff, or one of the other august pioneers of video, had bequeathed to us tablets of stone commanding that nothing in television shall ever require more than a few moments' concentration.

In its place that is fine. Who can quarrel with a medium that so brilliantly packages escapist entertainment as a mass-marketing tool? But I 7 see its values now pervading this nation and its life. It has become fashionable to think that, like fast food, fast ideas are the way to get to a fast-moving, impatient public.

In the case of news, this practice, in my view, results in inefficient 8 communication. I question how much of television's nightly news effort is really absorbable and understandable. Much of it is what has been aptly described as "machine-gunning with scraps." I think the technique fights coherence. I think it tends to make things ultimately boring and dismissible (unless they are accompanied by horrifying pictures) because almost anything is boring and dismissible if you know almost nothing about it.

I believe that TV's appeal to the short attention span is not only inefficient communication but decivilizing as well. Consider the casual as- 9 sumptions that television tends to cultivate: that complexity must be avoided, that visual stimulation is a substitute for thought, that verbal precision is an anachronism. It may be old-fashioned, but I was taught that thought is words, arranged in grammatically precise ways.

10   There is a crisis of literacy in this country. One study estimates that some 30 million adult Americans are "functionally illiterate" and cannot read or write well enough to answer a want ad or understand the instructions on a medicine bottle.

11   Literacy may not be an inalienable human right, but it is one that the highly literate Founding Fathers might not have found unreasonable or even unattainable. We are not only not attaining it as a nation, statistically speaking, but we are falling further and further short of attaining it. And, while I would not be so simplistic as to suggest that television is the cause, I believe it contributes and is an influence.

12   Everything about this nation—the structure of the society, its forms of family organization, its economy, its place in the world—has become more complex, not less. Yet its dominating communications instrument, its principal form of national linkage, is one that sells neat resolutions to human problems that usually have no neat resolutions. It is all symbolized in my mind by the hugely successful art form that television has made central to the culture, the 30-second commercial: the tiny drama of the earnest housewife who finds happiness in choosing the right toothpaste.

13   When before in human history has so much humanity collectively surrendered so much of its leisure to one toy, one mass diversion? When before has virtually an entire nation surrendered itself wholesale to a medium for selling?

14   Some years ago Yale University law professor Charles L. Black, Jr., wrote: ". . . forced feeding on trivial fare is not itself a trivial matter." I think this society is being force-fed with trivial fare, and I fear that the effects on our habits of mind, our language, our tolerance for effort, and our appetite for complexity are only dimly perceived. If I am wrong, we will have done no harm to look at the issue skeptically and critically, to consider how we should be resisting it. I hope you will join me in doing so.

EXPLORING IDEAS

1. MacNeil says that it is difficult to escape the influence of television. Brainstorm some of the influences that you think television has on your own life.

2. MacNeil says: "Almost anything interesting and rewarding in life requires some constructive, consistently applied effort." Try to think of some exceptions to this rule.

3. Is it true that even dull and ungifted people can achieve amazing things with effort? Is this part of the principle behind the 1994 hit movie *Forrest Gump?* What makes this idea appealing?

4. Is it true that brief segments with a lot of variety are more likely to capture viewers' attention than long segments on the same subject? Does not the magazine in which MacNeil is writing—*Reader's Digest*—do the same thing? Are not MacNeil's arguments, which are brief and varied, more effective in getting the reader's attention than long paragraphs on one aspect of the problem?

5. What does MacNeil mean by "inefficient communication"? Explain what he means by saying that television news techniques fight "coherence." How do these techniques make news boring? Doesn't this seem to contradict his earlier statement that brief bits with a lot of variety are what get attention?

6. MacNeil says that almost anything is boring and dismissible if you don't know anything about it. Think of some examples from your own experience. Brainstorm for an essay on this topic.

7. MacNeil says that television assumes that visual stimulation is a substitute for thought. What about the old saying, "One picture is worth a thousand words"? Is this statement untrue?

8. Can television deal with the complexity that MacNeil says is characteristic of modern society, or is television, by its very nature, incapable of dealing with complexity?

9. MacNeil suggests that at no other time have people so surrendered themselves to one mass diversion. What about a time when people read books a great deal? What is the difference between those times when many people read books and the current time when many people watch a lot of television?

10. MacNeil asks people to join him in resisting the effects of television. How is it possible to resist these effects? What can be done to fight the effects of television?

EXPLORING RHETORIC

1. Discuss the effectiveness of the rhetorical tactic MacNeil uses in paragraphs 1 and 2.

2. MacNeil announces his central thesis in paragraph 3. Check to see if he continues to focus on this thesis in the rest of his essay.

3. Discuss the effectiveness of MacNeil's comparison of television to a guided tour. Are guided tours always so negative? Are there some values in guided tours that cast doubt on the effectiveness of MacNeil's comparison?

4. Discuss how MacNeil shifts his argument in paragraphs 7 and 8. Does he really prove that the values of television are pervading the life of the nation, or does he focus on only one aspect of the life of the nation?

5. How does MacNeil shift his focus again in paragraph 11? How is the issue of illiteracy related to the issues about television he has already raised?

6. Although MacNeil says he does not believe that television is the cause of illiteracy in this country, does he mention any other causes? What other causes might there be?

7. What is the structure of MacNeil's essay? Is there a logical reason for each shift of topic? Is his final argument more general or more specific than his initial one?

8. What is the tone of this essay? How important is the voice of the writer? How important is it to the reader to know that MacNeil is a well-known newscaster on the Public Broadcasting Service (PBS)?

Television Addiction

MARIE WINN

Marie Winn was born in Prague, Czechoslovakia, in 1936. She came to the United States in 1939 with her parents and attended school in New York City. She graduated from Radcliffe College and also attended Columbia University. She has been a frequent contributor to many periodicals, including the *New York Times Magazine, Parade,* and the *Village Voice,* and has written a number of books, mostly about children and the media, including *Children Without Childhood,* 1983; *The Plug-In Drug,* 1977; and *Unplugging the Plug-In Drug,* 1987.

Using an extended analogy to drug and alcohol addiction, Winn argues that all of the characteristics of the real addict are also applicable to people who seem helplessly addicted to television.

1   The word "addiction" is often used loosely and wryly in conversation. People will refer to themselves as "mystery book addicts" or "cookie addicts." E. B. White wrote of his annual surge of interest in gardening: "We are hooked and are making an attempt to kick the habit." Yet nobody really believes that reading mysteries or ordering seeds by catalogue is serious enough to be compared with addictions to heroin or alcohol. The word "addiction" is here used jokingly to denote a tendency to overindulge in some pleasurable activity.

2   People often refer to being "hooked on TV." Does this, too, fall into the lighthearted category of cookie eating and other pleasures that people pursue with unusual intensity, or is there a kind of television viewing that falls into the more serious category of destructive addiction?

3   When we think about addiction to drugs or alcohol we frequently focus on negative aspects, ignoring the pleasures that accompany drinking or drug-taking. And yet the essence of any serious addiction is a pur-

suit of pleasure, a search for a "high" that normal life does not supply. It is only the inability to function without the addictive substance that is dismaying, the dependence of the organism upon a certain experience and an increasing inability to function normally without it. Thus people will take two or three drinks at the end of the day not merely for the pleasure drinking provides, but also because they "don't feel normal" without them.

Real addicts do not merely pursue a pleasurable experience one time 4 in order to function normally. They need to *repeat* it again and again. Something about that particular experience makes life without it less than complete. Other potentially pleasurable experiences are no longer possible, for under the spell of the addictive experience, their lives are peculiarly distorted. The addict craves an experience and yet is never really satisfied. The organism may be temporarily sated, but soon it begins to crave again.

Finally, a serious addiction is distinguished from a harmless pursuit 5 of pleasure by its distinctly destructive elements. Heroin addicts, for instance, lead a damaged life: their increasing need for heroin in increasing doses prevents them from working, from maintaining relationships, from developing in human ways. Similarly alcoholics' lives are narrowed and dehumanized by their dependence on alcohol.

Let us consider television viewing in the light of the conditions that 6 define serious addictions.

Not unlike drugs or alcohol, the television experience allows the 7 participant to blot out the real world and enter into a pleasurable and passive mental state. The worries and anxieties of reality are as effectively deferred by becoming absorbed in a television program as by going on a "trip" induced by drugs or alcohol. And just as alcoholics are only vaguely aware of their addiction, feeling that they control their drinking more than they really do ("I can cut it out any time I want—I just like to have three or four drinks before dinner"), people similarly overestimate their control over television watching. Even as they put off other activities to spend hour after hour watching television, they feel they could easily resume living in a different, less passive style. But somehow or other, while the television set is present in their homes, the click doesn't sound. With television pleasures available, those other experiences seem less attractive, more difficult somehow.

A heavy viewer (a college English instructor) observes: 8

"I find television almost irresistible. When the set is on, I cannot ig- 9 nore it. I can't turn it off. I feel sapped, will-less, enervated. As I reach out to turn off the set, the strength goes out of my arms. So I sit there for hours and hours."

Self-confessed television addicts often feel they "ought" to do other 10 things—but the fact that they don't read and don't plant their garden or sew or crochet or play games or have conversations means that those activities are no longer as desirable as television viewing. In a way the lives of heavy viewers are as imbalanced by their television "habit" as a drug addict's or an alcoholic's. They are living in a holding pattern, as it were, passing up the activities that lead to growth or development or a sense of accomplishment. This is one reason people talk about their television viewing so ruefully, so apologetically. They are aware that it is an unproductive experience, that almost any other endeavor is more worthwhile by any human measure.

11   Finally it is the adverse effect of television viewing on the lives of so many people that defines it as a serious addiction. The television habit distorts the sense of time. It renders other experiences vague and curiously unreal while taking on a greater reality for itself. It weakens relationships by reducing and sometimes eliminating normal opportunities for talking, for communicating.

12   And yet television does not satisfy, else why would the viewer continue to watch hour after hour, day after day? "The measure of health," writes Lawrence Kubie, "is flexibility . . . and especially the freedom to cease when sated."* But heavy television viewers can never be sated with their television experiences—these do not provide the true nourishment that satiation requires—and thus they find that they cannot stop watching.

13   A former heavy watcher (filmmaker) describes such a syndrome:

14   "I remember when we first got the set I'd watch for hours and hours, whenever I could, and I remember that feeling of tiredness and anxiety that always followed those orgies, a sense of time terribly wasted. It was like eating cotton candy; television promised so much richness, I couldn't wait for it, and then it just evaporated into air. I remember feeling terribly drained after watching for a long time."

15   Similarly a nursery school teacher remembers her own childhood television experience:

16   "I remember bingeing on television when I was a child and having that vapid feeling after watching hours of TV. I'd look forward to watching whenever I could, but it just didn't give back a real feeling of pleasure. It was like no orgasm, no catharsis, very frustrating. Television just wasn't giving me the promised satisfaction, and yet I kept on watching. It filled some sort of need, or had to do with an inability to get something started."

17   The testimonies of ex-television addicts often have the evangelistic overtones of stories heard at Alcoholics Anonymous meetings.

---

* Lawrence Kubie, *Neurotic Distortion and the Creative Process* (Lawrence: University of Kansas Press, 1958).

A handbag repair shop owner says: 18

"I'd get on the subway home from work with the newspaper and 19 immediately turn to the TV page to plan out my evening's watching. I'd come home, wash, change my clothes, and tell my wife to start the machine so it would be warmed up. (We had an old-fashioned set that took a few seconds before an image appeared.) And then we'd watch TV for the rest of the evening. We'd eat our dinner in the living room while watching, and we'd only talk every once in a while, during the ads, if at all. I'd watch anything, good, bad, or indifferent.

"All the while we were watching I'd feel terribly angry at myself for 20 wasting all that time watching junk. I could never go to sleep until at least the eleven o'clock news, and then sometimes I'd still stay up for the late-night talk show. I had a feeling that I *had* to watch the news programs, that I *had* to know what was happening, even though most of the time nothing much was happening and I could easily find out what was by reading the paper the next morning. Usually my wife would fall asleep on the couch while I was watching. I'd get angry at her for doing that. Actually, I was angry at myself. I had a collection of three years of back issues of different magazines that I planned to read sometime, but I never got around to reading them. I never got around to sorting or labeling my collection of slides I had made when traveling. I only had time for television. We'd take the telephone off the hook while watching so we wouldn't be interrupted! We like classical music, but we never listened to any, never!

"Then one day the set broke. I said to my wife, 'Let's not fix it. Let's 21 just see what happens.' Well, that was the smartest thing we ever did. We haven't had a TV in the house since then.

"Now I look back and I can hardly believe we could have lived like 22 that. I feel that my mind was completely mummified for all those years. I was glued to that machine and couldn't get loose, somehow. It really frightens me to think of it. Yes, I'm frightened of TV now. I don't think I could control it if we had a set in the house again. I think it would take over no matter what I did."

A further sign of addiction is that "an exclusive craving for some- 23 thing is accompanied by a loss of discrimination towards the object which satisfies the craving . . . the alcoholic is not interested in the taste of liquor that is available; likewise the compulsive eater is not particular about what he eats when there is food around," write the authors of a book about the nature of addiction.* And just so, for many viewers the process of *watching* television is far more important than the actual contents of the programs being watched. The knowledge that the act of

---

* Stanton Peele and Archie Brodsky, *Love and Addiction* (New York: Taplinger, 1975).

watching is more important than *what* is being watched lies behind the practice of "roadblocking," invented by television advertisers and adopted by political candidates who purchase the same half-hour on all three channels in order to force-feed their message to the public. As one prominent candidate put it, "People will watch television no matter what is on, and if you allow them no other choice they will watch your show."*

EXPLORING IDEAS

1. Winn says the essence of a serious addiction is the pursuit of pleasure, the search for a "high" we don't get in normal life. Does she mean that all pleasures have the potential of being addictive? Brainstorm for an essay on this general topic or on the potential for addiction of a specific pleasure that we don't usually associate with addiction.

2. Use the following thesis statement for an essay: "Under the spell of the addictive experience, the addict's life is peculiarly distorted."

3. Winn says television allows us to blot out the real world. Brainstorm some other activities we pursue that allow us to blot out the real world and enter into a pleasurable and passive mental state. Discuss the values and dangers of such activities.

4. Is it really true that when you watch television, you become so passive that you just can't turn the television off? Why do you become so passive? Why is this more likely to happen with television than any other activity?

5. Television is often blamed for many societal ills—breaking up the family, causing poor reading skills, and so forth. What evidence is available to support these arguments? Did people do more interesting and valuable activities before television, or is this just a myth?

6. Is it true that only nourishment satisfies and that therefore one can never be satisfied or satiated by television? Why doesn't television provide nourishment? Why do some critics say that reading provides more nourishment than television?

7. Explore the comparison people sometimes make between watching television and eating. Is there some reason behind the fact that television guides often feature advertisements for weight-reducing plans?

8. Write an essay in which you describe what your life would be like without television.

9. Write an essay about how addiction to television is accompanied by a loss of discrimination toward the object of the craving. Is this true of other forms of addiction also?

10. What does "watching" have to do with the addictive effect of television? Why is it easier to turn off the radio than to turn off the television?

---

* Les Brown, "Democrats Reach Low TV Audience," *The New York Times,* July 20, 1975.

EXPLORING RHETORIC

1. Discuss the logic of Winn's first three paragraphs. Why does she begin with humorous references to addictions, move to questions about television as an addiction, and then shift to a general definition of addiction?

2. Discuss the rhetorical technique Winn uses to define "real addicts."

3. Discuss the rhetorical technique Winn uses to define television viewing as a serious addiction.

4. Why does Winn quote a famous psychoanalyst? Could she not have made the point herself that emotionally healthy people are flexible and know when to stop? What effect does the quotation have that her own statement would not?

5. Discuss the effectiveness of Winn's use of direct quotations from various television viewers. How would her argument have been different if she had just summarized the points made by the quotations?

6. Why does Winn add the detail about "roadblocking" in paragraph 23? Does this help support her argument, or is this just irrelevant information?

7. Would you classify Winn's argument as a formal academic argument, an informal argument, or a combination of the two? Justify your response by discussing characteristics of informal and formal arguments.

8. What kinds of information would you need to argue against Winn's points in this essay? Could you not argue against quotations from individual viewers about television's addictive effects by quoting viewers who claim that television is not addictive? How can you determine which quoted sources are more authoritative or decisive?

Communication in the Year 2000

TONY SCHWARTZ

Tony Schwartz has worked in television advertising, produced records, and hosted a weekly radio show. Now a professor of telecommunications at New York University, he is the author of *The Responsive Chord,* 1974, and *Media: The Second God,* 1983, from which the following selection is taken. Surveying the many new communication technologies that depend on television and hypothesizing on their social effects, Schwartz suggests that the medium may finally be able to fulfill its potential.

During these last two decades of the century, a broad range of communi-   1
cation technologies will develop and change how many of us work, learn, and use leisure time. We will send and receive electronic mail, talk back to our television sets and be heard by our program host, and participate in electronic business meetings with colleagues who are

scattered around the globe. The technological means are not science-fiction dreams; each exists today. However, it will take a number of years for them to be implemented on a large scale.

2   The new communication systems are fascinating hybrids which mix together technological developments in cable television, telephone-line transmission, computer science, and satellites. This creates a regulatory nightmare for government agencies which operate under laws designed to separate the computer, telephone, and television industries. These developments may be hindered if control of the new communication systems is in the hands of the moguls at the major networks and their counterparts in existing industries such as the telephone and data-processing companies. In the standard grabbing for money and monop-olistic control, such companies might want to use these developments for private ends and prevent them from reaching the public. The poten-tial of the new communication technology does not guarantee that these companies will make exciting new services generally available. For years, people were enjoined from using any but telephone company equipment on telephone company lines. Now that the law allows the use of other equipment, we have seen a proliferation of products designed for use with telephone lines: automatic dialing, answering machines, Teletext equipment, telephone amplifiers, wireless phones that can be used anyplace in the home or office, data-servicing equipment, and many more.

3   However, three characteristics of the new communication systems suggest that they may indeed arrive in our homes and offices. First, they have bucked the inflationary trend of the past decade and will probably continue bucking it through the mid-1980s. Thus, while the cost of roast beef and potatoes has risen and will continue to rise, the cost of large-scale integrated circuits and memory chips (the meat and potatoes of our new technology) has declined and will continue to decline for a few more years, following the pattern established by digital watches and pocket calculators, which began as very expensive items and then plum-meted in price as they became mass-produced. Digital watches that used to cost several hundred dollars are now available for eight or ten dollars. Computers costing ten or twelve thousand dollars do the work of earlier computers that cost several hundred thousand dollars. Second, the new communication systems do not require audiences in the millions to make them economically viable or socially appealing. They will find their audience through narrowcasting, rather than broadcasting, and they will serve special-interest groups. Third, most of the new communi-cation services are two-way. People can participate in these media, not merely receive them. In the past, a relatively small group of people cre-ated the movies, television programs, and other forms of mass entertain-ment for the public. With the new services, many more people (in a way, everyone) will create communications for others.

Perhaps the best way to think about these new communication ser- 4
vices is to begin with the telephone, that inexpensive, two-way, narrowcast medium which has been with us for so long. In audio, conferencing
microphones and speakers can replace telephones, so ten, twenty, or
more people in one room can talk freely to similar groups at other locations. A range of equipment exists which can transmit simple writing or
graphics over ordinary phone lines. The "electronic blackboard" is one
such device. With it, people at separate locations can talk to each other
and write information which everyone can see. Another technology,
called slow-scan television and facsimile transfer equipment, can send
still photographs, X rays, charts, etc., over telephone lines. These systems are currently operating in some business, medical, and educational
settings. A key element in their growth is the use of the telephone lines
for transmission. Equipment can be plugged in wherever a phone line
exists, and the cost of sending the information is the cost of a phone call.

Electronic mail also uses the telephone system. In this case, a central 5
computer with phone lines attached acts as a postal service. A person
with a modified electronic typewriter calls the central computer, then
types a message for another person, who also needs a modified electronic typewriter to receive it. He or she gets the message by going to the
electronic mailbox, i.e., calling the central computer. The computer then
prints out the message. Electronic mail is an adaptable and growing service in business. Some expect that when the cost of a first-class letter
reaches twenty-five cents, people will turn to electronic mail as an economically feasible alternative for private correspondence.

The growth of cable television is bringing about another new range 6
of services. First, cable television has the capacity for many channels.
Thus we have already witnessed the growth of several new channels of
special-interest programming: all movies (Home Box Office), all sports,
all news (Cable News Network). This trend will likely continue as additional narrowcast audiences are defined. Just as magazines are geared to
skiers, chess players, teenage women, and other groups, cable television
programming will probably pursue select non-mass audiences.

However, this is only the beginning of the changes ahead. A televi- 7
sion cable, like a telephone line, can be used for two-way communication. The home viewer can communicate back to the program or to other
viewers through the cable. The development of interactive cable television has already begun in a number of communities. The most widely
known of these is the Qube two-way cable system, which was first used
in Columbus, Ohio. The Qube system provides the viewer with a special
box that has several buttons. These buttons communicate back to the cable studio. Viewers can answer polling questions, express their views
about the program or performer they are watching, and direct how the
program should proceed. The ways in which viewers "vote" can be calculated instantly and displayed on the screen for all to see. Elsewhere

(Spartanburg, South Carolina), systems like Qube have been used to bring together and facilitate the work of people in educational and social services. In Rockford, Illinois, a similar system provides advanced training for teachers and firemen.

8   Even more exciting is a model interactive cable television system in Reading, Pennsylvania. Some twenty locations around Reading are wired as neighborhood communication centers. The interaction among the centers as the people talk to one another creates a new type of television involvement. People at home participate by calling in and speaking over a telephone connection that everyone can hear. Curiously, the interactive cable programming they create competes successfully with network programming.

9   A cable television channel may also be used to deliver specialized information to individual viewers. This makes use of a technology developed in Britain which allows many pages of print and graphic information to be multiplexed and combined electronically, then sent over the lines in a television signal. Using one cable television channel, it is possible to transmit eight hundred pages of print information in three seconds. Thus, a cable television channel can be used to transmit an electronic newspaper into the home, either printed on paper or projected onto a screen, or the cable channel can be connected to an electronic library and the user can go through an index and select information to be transmitted over the cable.

10   The problem with all of this new technology is not the equipment, which exists and works, but what to do with it now that we have it. What kinds of services, entertainment, and information do people want, and what will they buy, watch, and listen to? A few of the services and projects which have already succeeded may provide some clues about the future.

11   Alaska recently experimented with electronic town meetings. Via the combination of television and telephone, people were able to see the moderator and speakers, ask questions, and vote from their homes by telephone or electronic buttons. The success of the experiment may well be a sign of the future. More people watched the television town meetings than have participated in all town meetings since the founding of the state of Alaska. While voting in regular elections ran to 23 percent of the population, voting in the electronic town meetings ran to 66 percent of the population. Voters participated by voting yes or no on certain topics. Politicians who took part in the town meetings were reluctant to commit themselves early on any issue. This revealed their awareness of its political effects. Answers to research questions could be tabulated and exhibited before the next question was asked. Questionnaires could be adjusted and perfected in the course of asking the questions. Although the politicians were divided in their acceptance of this electronic

concept, the program had a 90-percent share of the television audience during the broadcast.

In Philadelphia, Pennsylvania, and Phoenix, Arizona, the police de- 12 partments have developed the use of two-way television to cut transportation costs and speed up the flow of communication. Some react instinctively against the use of advanced technology by a police department, but the results are impressive. In Phoenix, for example, public defenders meet with prisoner-clients over two-way picture telephones. (The prisoner-client must agree to use the system, and not all meetings are conducted over picture telephones.) This has resulted in more "meetings" between the public defenders and the prisoner-clients. At the same time, the system has reduced costs, because the public defenders can handle more clients.

In Philadelphia, witnesses to a crime can view color-slide mug shots 13 over a two-way cable television system. The slides are centralized, but the witness can view them from any precinct house. Similarly, using this two-way cable television system, detectives can retrieve centralized information (films, fingerprints, case records) from a data bank and view it at the local precinct. In addition, video conferences and prearraignment hearings are conducted over the cable. This highly sophisticated private cable television system has significantly reduced paper and transportation costs and freed police officers to spend more time on field work.

In southern Arizona, NASA [National Aeronautics and Space Ad- 14 ministration] and the Indian Health Service have set up a fascinating application of advanced space technology to provide health care. A central hospital which serves the Papago Indians is linked via two-way microwave to a specially equipped truck which travels throughout the reservation (hundreds of square miles). Paramedics in the truck can conduct sophisticated tests on patients. The results are communicated telemetrically to a doctor in the central hospital. In addition, the doctor and the patient many miles away can see and hear each other. Further, the paramedic and the doctor both have instant access to computerized medical histories which are stored one hundred miles away, in northern Arizona. The NASA system is quite expensive. However, it has paved the way for other, more cost-efficient medical services between a central hospital and remote health stations or clinics. We have already seen a form of medical telemetry between individuals at home and a doctor in the hospital, via telephone lines.

In Britain, two forms of electronic print services are well under way, 15 although neither can be classified as a success yet, because a number of gremlins need elimination. In one system, called Viewdata, a central computer contains many thousands of pages of information, from current sports results to recipes to airline schedules. Using a special decoder, a person calls the computer, and an ordinary television set displays the requested information that the computer transmits. Users can also obtain a computer printout of the information. In the other service, Broadcast Teletext, a computer at the television station contains a few hundred pages of information, e.g., television listings, movie schedules, weather, and news headlines. These pages are electronically "piggy-backed" on the regular television signal. A viewer who wants to read the pages must have a special decoder that can pull them out and display them on the television screen. It is also possible to obtain a hard copy of Broadcast Teletext pages.

16   Viewdata, which transmits printed matter, is particularly interesting to many business interests, since it can be used for electronic shopping. Viewdata transmits information over telephone lines and is, therefore, interactive. The person in the home can not only request information, e.g., airline schedules, but also purchase services. Viewdata can be used to make an airline reservation, do catalog shopping, and reserve a table at a restaurant.

17   If the new communication services (or a significant portion of them) make their way into the average home and office, the social effects may be quite far-reaching. First, television network programming will lose some of its control over the mass audience. People will still watch television, but they will have access to a wider range of programs. They will also use the television set as a display screen for some information and entertainment services other than programs. They will be able to receive weather reports, traffic reports, local sports, shopping news, and the like. They can have access to any section of their newspapers and magazines, or follow the activities of local and national government. They can also use television as a ticket-purchasing service. One need neither weep over nor applaud the demise of the television networks, as they are likely to be financially involved in the new communication services which prove successful.

18   A significant shift in work patterns may occur. The new communication services can substitute for a portion of the business travel which now occurs. Moreover, a greater number of people will work out of their homes, using the new technology to conduct business and link them to central offices. Before locating a corporate headquarters, industries will pay greater heed to available telephone network switching, cable systems, and satellite linkups.

19   The potential implications of the new communication services are dramatic. Technology will mediate more and more of the communication that now takes place between individuals. This technology and the services which it does or doesn't offer will affect the quality and character of our communication with others. It may develop as the telephone did, with content determined by users. Indeed, one hopes that the new

services will supplement, rather than supplant, interpersonal contact, creating new kinds of interactions among people. Developments could go either way.

The new technology could allow more sources of information to 20 reach the public. This may break up the common information environment which television has created. In the sixties and seventies, most people received most of their information from one source: television.

The new communication technologies provide a means for instanta- 21 neous feedback from the public. Each person in his home will be able to push a button to vote or express an opinion on public issues. This may lead to more participation in politics but also to even less voting in elections than exists today. If this occurs, the local response might be to incorporate the new communication process formally into government. People could vote directly on many laws and policy issues. In such circumstances, many elected officials might be replaced by administrators whose job would be to present issues for public voting. This might also lead to a speedup in government. Politics and laws could change more quickly. Cycles of recession and recovery might be reduced from many months to a few weeks. As information flow increases, so does social and political change.

Undoubtedly a number of problems will accompany the use of the 22 new communication technologies in governing a country. It might be valuable to consider them in much greater depth, because technology can lead to important social and political effects which are unforeseen but inevitable. These technologies can lead to a restructuring of government. The basic reason for having a representative government is that all the people cannot themselves be at the seat of government. Therefore we call on others to be there and to speak for us. But with the new technologies, for all practical purposes we *can* be there, and we may not need representatives, because we now represent ourselves.

No one chose to give the President twenty minutes to decide the fate 23 of the world. The design of missile technology chose it. And as we perfect our mastery of the second god, we must realize that we have given the god we created the power to change us and our ways.

EXPLORING IDEAS

1. Schwartz says that the new communication technology is real, not the stuff of science-fiction dreams. Brainstorm for an essay about how what was science fiction two or three decades ago is now science fact.

2. Schwartz warns against the new communication technology's falling under the control of commercial television. What dangers would this involve? Would government control be better or worse than control by private business?

3. When Schwartz's book was published in 1983, fax machines were in their infancy. How has their increased widespread use changed the way people do business today?

4. Schwartz believes that as postage costs go up, people increasingly will turn to electronic mail. Brainstorm on the increased use of e-mail since Schwartz wrote this essay.

5. Brainstorm how the widespread use of cable television has changed television viewing habits. What is the effect of "channel surfing" with a remote control?

6. Schwartz describes a technology that can transmit eight hundred pages of print information in three seconds over cable lines. Will this kind of technology make books obsolete? Brainstorm for an essay.

7. What are some of the possible implications of people's voting using interactive television instead of going to the polls and marking their choices on a ballot? Brainstorm the values and the possible dangers of such a voting method.

8. What are the possible effects of electronic shopping—on either cable shopping channels or computer networks such as Prodigy and America Online? Compare this kind of shopping with that described by Phyllis Rose in her essay, "Of Shopping," in Part Two.

9. More and more people are now doing their jobs at home, using fax machines, telephones, and computer networks. What are the advantages and disadvantages of this new telecommuting? Brainstorm for an essay on this topic.

10. Schwartz ends his essay by suggesting how the new technology may change the nature of representative government. Brainstorm some of the implications of the shift from representation to direct participation in the governing process by using interactive telecommunications.

EXPLORING RHETORIC

1. What is the purpose of paragraph 1 of Schwartz's essay? How well does it reflect the content of the rest of the essay?

2. Outline the structure of paragraph 3. How effective is this structure? How effective are the examples that Schwartz provides?

3. What methods does Schwartz use to move from one paragraph to another? Look for transition words and phrases in the first sentences of paragraphs 3 through 10.

4. What is the function of paragraph 12? How effectively does it signal a major transition in the essay?

5. Paragraphs 12 through 15 begin the same way. Is this technique an effective organizational strategy, or is it overly formal and artificial?

6. What major shift takes place in the essay in paragraph 17?

7. Note the technique Schwartz uses in paragraphs 19 through 21 of starting several sentences with the article "The" and then following with a sentence starting with the pronoun "This." What kind of rhetorical organizational pattern does this sentence structure reflect?

8. How would you characterize the basic tone and structure of this essay? Is this essay easy or difficult to outline? Is it easy or difficult to determine its central purpose?

Why Don't We Complain?

WILLIAM F. BUCKLEY, JR.

W illiam F. Buckley, Jr., born in 1925 in New York, graduated from Yale University. He has been editor-in-chief of *National Review* since 1955, a syndicated columnist since 1962, and host of public television's "Firing Line" since 1966. He has written *Saving the Queen,* 1976; *Stained Glass,* 1978; *Who's on First?* 1980; *Marco Polo If You Can,* 1982; *Overdrive: A Personal Documentary,* 1983; *The Story of Henri Tod,* 1984; *The Tall Ships,* 1986; *See You Later, Alligator,* 1985; *High Jinx,* 1986; *Racing Through Paradise: A Pacific Passage,* 1987; and *Mongoose R.I.P.,* 1988.

In his typical formal style, William Buckley uses himself as an example of his argument that Americans have become reluctant to complain about shoddy treatment and poor service. Arguing that such reluctance is a symptom of our increased dependence on technology and centralized government, Buckley claims that it is only a small step from failing to complain about an out-of-focus movie to being apathetic about government's running our lives.

It was the very last coach and the only empty seat on the entire train, so 1 there was no turning back. The problem was to breathe. Outside, the temperature was below freezing. Inside the railroad car the temperature must have been about 85 degrees. I took off my overcoat, and a few minutes later my jacket, and noticed that the car was flecked with the white shirts of the passengers. I soon found my hand moving to loosen my tie. From one end of the car to the other, as we rattled through Westchester County, we sweated; but we did not moan.

I watched the train conductor appear at the head of the car. "Tickets, 2 all tickets, please!" In a more virile age, I thought, the passengers would seize the conductor and strap him down on a seat over the radiator to share the fate of his patrons. He shuffled down the aisle, picking up tickets, punching commutation cards. *No one addressed a word to him.* He approached my seat, and I drew a deep breath of resolution. "Conductor," I began with a considerable edge to my voice. . . . Instantly the doleful eyes of my seatmate turned tiredly from his newspaper to fix me with a resentful stare: What question could be so important as to justify my sibilant intrusion into his stupor? I was shaken by those eyes. I am incapable of making a discreet fuss, so I mumbled a question about what time we were due in Stamford (I didn't even ask whether it would be before or after dehydration could be expected to set in), got my reply, and went back to my newspaper and to wiping my brow.

3   The conductor had nonchalantly walked down the gauntlet of eighty sweating American freemen, and not one of them had asked him to explain why the passengers in that car had been consigned to suffer. There is nothing to be done when the temperature *outdoors* is 85 degrees, and indoors the air conditioner has broken down; obviously when that happens there is nothing to do, except perhaps curse the day that one was born. But when the temperature outdoors is below freezing, it takes a positive act of will on somebody's part to set the temperature *indoors* at 85. Somewhere a valve was turned too far, a furnace overstocked, a thermostat maladjusted: something that could easily be remedied by turning off the heat and allowing the great outdoors to come indoors. All this is so obvious. What is not obvious is what has happened to the American people.

4   It isn't just the commuters, whom we have come to visualize as a supine breed who have got on to the trick of suspending their sensory faculties twice a day while they submit to the creeping dissolution of the railroad industry. It isn't just they who have given up trying to rectify irrational vexations. It is the American people everywhere.

5   A few weeks ago at a large movie theater I turned to my wife and said, "The picture is out of focus." "Be quiet," she answered. I obeyed. But a few minutes later I raised the point again, with mounting impatience. "It will be all right in a minute," she said apprehensively. (She would rather lose her eyesight than be around when I make one of my infrequent scenes.) I waited. It was *just* out of focus—not glaringly out, but out. My vision is 20-20, and I assume that is the vision, adjusted, of most people in the movie house. So, after hectoring my wife throughout the first reel, I finally prevailed upon her to admit that it *was* off, and very annoying. We then settled down, coming to rest on the presumption that: a) someone connected with the management of the theater must soon notice the blur and make the correction; or b) that someone seated near the rear of the house would make the complaint in behalf of those of us up front; or c) that—any minute now—the entire house would explode into catcalls and foot stamping, calling dramatic attention to the irksome distortion.

6   What happened was nothing. The movie ended, as it had begun *just* out of focus, and as we trooped out, we stretched our faces in a variety of contortions to accustom the eye to the shock of normal focus.

I think it is safe to say that everybody suffered on that occasion. And 7
I think it is safe to assume that everyone was expecting someone else to
take the initiative in going back to speak to the manager. And it is probably true even that if we had supposed the movie would run right
through the blurred image, someone surely would have summoned up
the purposive indignation to get up out of his seat and file his complaint.

But notice that no one did. And the reason no one did is because we 8
are all increasingly anxious in America to be unobtrusive, we are reluctant to make our voices heard, hesitant about claiming our rights; we are
afraid that our cause is unjust, or that if it is not unjust, that it is ambiguous; or if not even that, that it is too trivial to justify the horrors of a confrontation with Authority; we will sit in an oven or endure a racking
headache before undertaking a head-on, I'm-here-to-tell-you complaint.
That tendency to passive compliance, to a heedless endurance, is something to keep one's eyes on—in sharp focus.

I myself can occasionally summon the courage to complain, but I 9
cannot, as I have intimated, complain softly. My own instinct is so strong
to let the thing ride, to forget about it—to expect that someone will take
the matter up, when the grievance is collective, in my behalf—that it is
only when the provocation is at a very special key, whose vibrations
touch simultaneously a complexus of nerves, allergies, and passions,
that I catch fire and find the reserves of courage and assertiveness to
speak up. When that happens, I get quite carried away. My blood gets
hot, my brow wet, I become unbearably and unconscionably sarcastic
and bellicose; I am girded for a total showdown.

Why should that be? Why could not I (or anyone else) on that rail- 10
road coach have said simply to the conductor, "Sir"—I take that back:
that sounds sarcastic—"Conductor, would you be good enough to turn
down the heat? I am extremely hot. In fact, I tend to get hot every time
the temperature reaches 85 degr——." Strike that last sentence. Just end
it with the simple statement that you are extremely hot, and let the conductor infer the cause.

Every New Year's Eve I resolve to do something about the Milque- 11
toast in me and vow to speak up, calmly, for my rights, and for the bet-
terment of our society, on every appropriate occasion. Entering last New
Year's Eve I was fortified in my resolve because that morning at breakfast I had had to ask the waitress three times for a glass of milk. She finally brought it—after I had finished my eggs, which is when I don't
want it any more. I did not have the manliness to order her to take the
milk back, but settled instead for a cowardly sulk, and ostentatiously refused to drink the milk—though I later paid for it—rather than state
plainly to the hostess, as I should have, why I had not drunk it, and
would not pay for it.

12   So by the time the New Year ushered out the Old, riding in on my morning's indignation and stimulated by the gastric juices of resolution that flow so faithfully on New Year's Eve, I rendered my vow. Henceforward I would conquer my shyness, my despicable disposition to supineness. I would speak out like a man against the unnecessary annoyances of our time.

13   Forty-eight hours later, I was standing in line at the ski repair store in Pico Peak, Vermont. All I needed, to get on with my skiing, was the loan, for one minute, of a small screwdriver, to tighten a loose binding. Behind the counter in the workshop were two men. One was industriously engaged in servicing the complicated requirements of a young lady at the head of the line, and obviously he would be tied up for quite a while. The other—"Jiggs," his workmate called him—was a middle-aged man, who sat in a chair puffing a pipe, exchanging small talk with his working partner. My pulse began its telltale acceleration. The minutes ticked on. I stared at the idle shopkeeper, hoping to shame him into action, but he was impervious to my telepathic reproof and continued his small talk with his friend, brazenly insensitive to the nervous demands of six good men who were raring to ski.

14   Suddenly my New Year's Eve resolution struck me. It was now or never. I broke from my place in line and marched to the counter. I was going to control myself. I dug my nails into my palms. My effort was only partially successful.

15   "If you are not too busy," I said icily, "would you mind handing me a screwdriver?"

16   Work stopped and everyone turned his eyes on me, and I experienced that mortification I always feel when I am the center of centripetal shafts of curiosity, resentment, perplexity.

17   But the worst was yet to come. "I am sorry, sir," said Jiggs deferentially, moving the pipe from his mouth. "I am not supposed to move. I have just had a heart attack." That was the signal for a great whirring noise that descended from heaven. We looked, stricken, out the window, and it appeared as though a cyclone had suddenly focused on the snowy courtyard between the shop and the ski lift. Suddenly a gigantic army helicopter materialized, and hovered down to a landing. Two men jumped out of the plane carrying a stretcher, tore into the ski shop, and lifted the shopkeeper onto the stretcher. Jiggs bade his companion good-bye, was whisked out the door, into the plane, up to the heavens, down—we learned—to a nearby army hospital. I looked up manfully—into a score of man-eating eyes. I put the experience down as a reversal.

18   As I write this, on an airplane, I have run out of paper and need to reach into my briefcase under my legs for more. I cannot do this until my empty lunch tray is removed from my lap. I arrested the stewardess as

she passed empty-handed down the aisle on the way to the kitchen to fetch the lunch trays for the passengers up forward who haven't been served yet. "Would you please take my tray?" "Just a *moment*, sir!" she said, and marched on sternly. Shall I tell her that since she is headed for the kitchen *anyway*, it could not delay the feeding of the other passengers by more than two seconds necessary to stash away my empty tray? Or remind her that not fifteen minutes ago she spoke unctuously into the loudspeaker the words undoubtedly devised by the airline's highly paid public relations counselor: "If there is anything I or Miss French can do for you to make your trip more enjoyable, *please* let us ——" I have run out of paper.

I think the observable reluctance of the majority of Americans to as- 19 sert themselves in minor matters is related to our increased sense of helplessness in an age of technology and centralized political and economic power. For generations, Americans who were too hot, or too cold, got up and did something about it. Now we call the plumber, or the electrician, or the furnace man. The habit of looking after our own needs obviously had something to do with the assertiveness that characterized the American family familiar to readers of American literature. With the technification of life goes our direct responsibility for our material environment, and we are conditioned to adopt a position of helplessness not only as regards the broken air conditioner, but as regards the overheated train. It takes an expert to fix the former, but not the latter; yet these distinctions, as we withdraw into helplessness, tend to fade away.

Our notorious political apathy is a related phenomenon. Every year, 20 whether the Republican or the Democratic Party is in office, more and more power drains away from the individual to feed vast reservoirs in far-off places; and we have less and less say about the shape of events which shape our future. From this alienation of personal power comes the sense of resignation with which we accept the political dispensations of a powerful government whose hold upon us continues to increase.

An editor of a national weekly news magazine told me a few years 21 ago that as few as a dozen letters of protest against an editorial stance of his magazine was enough to convene a plenipotentiary meeting of the board of editors to review policy. "So few people complain, or make their voices heard," he explained to me, "that we assume a dozen letters represent the inarticulated views of thousands of readers." In the past ten years, he said, the volume of mail has noticeably decreased, even though the circulation of his magazine has risen.

When our voices are finally mute, when we have finally suppressed 22 the natural instinct to complain, whether the vexation is trivial or grave, we shall have become automatons, incapable of feeling. When Premier Khrushchev first came to this country late in 1959 he was primed, we are informed, to experience the bitter resentment of the American people against his tyranny, against his persecutions, against the movement which is responsible for the great number of American deaths in Korea, for billions in taxes every year, and for life everlasting on the brink of disaster; but Khrushchev was pleasantly surprised, and reported back to the Russian people that he had been met with overwhelming cordiality (read: apathy), except, to be sure, for "a few fascists who followed me around with their wretched posters, and should be horsewhipped."

23   I may be crazy, but I say there would have been lots more posters in a society where train temperatures in the dead of winter are not allowed to climb to 85 degrees without complaint.

EXPLORING IDEAS

1. Buckley opens with an anecdote to illustrate his central point. Write an anecdotal opening to an essay in which you disagree with Buckley's argument that American people do not complain.

2. Write an essay in which you describe your own confrontation with authority. Do not make it simply a narrative; illustrate the theme of the importance of the individual's standing up to authority.

3. Buckley states his thesis in paragraph 8. Is he justified in making such a broad generalization based on only a few experiences? What kind of information would you need to argue against his thesis?

4. Why does Buckley say he did not have the "manliness" to order the waitress to take the milk back? Note also the expression "speak out like a man." Find other places where Buckley uses similar language. What do these references suggest about Buckley's attitude toward male behavior?

5. Although Buckley seems to suggest that we should stand up and complain, some people say it is dangerous to assert yourself angrily in public. Brainstorm for an essay in which you argue that Buckley's urging us to be more assertive is foolish and irresponsible.

6. Brainstorm some reasons for Americans' refusal to complain other than the ones that Buckley suggests in paragraph 19.

7. Write an essay in which you support Buckley's suggestion that we are overly dependent on technology.

8. Buckley says that Americans' "notorious political apathy" is related to our reluctance to complain. Discuss the cause of political apathy on your campus or in your community.

9. Are Americans just too polite to complain? Discuss politeness, or the lack of politeness, in modern American society.

10. Buckley suggests that there is a relationship between complaining about a too-hot rail car and the tyranny of Nikita Khrushchev, premier of the Soviet

Union between 1958 and 1964. Is this a bit extreme, or does Buckley provide sufficient examples or evidence to support this relationship?

EXPLORING RHETORIC

1. Discuss the effectiveness of Buckley's opening two sentences. What tone do they create? How do they stimulate the reader's interest to read on?

2. Why does Buckley use the term "virile" to describe a previous era? Is this a sexist remark? What does it imply about male behavior?

3. Discuss the effect of the phrase "my sibilant intrusion into his stupor." How is this phrase like the phrase "supine breed"? What does this language suggest about Buckley?

4. Buckley says his wife would rather lose her eyesight than be around when he makes one of his scenes. This is, of course, exaggeration. Is this a favored technique Buckley uses in this essay? Try to find other examples.

5. Discuss the effect of Buckley's description of himself when he gets angry: "My blood gets hot, my brow wet, I become unbearably and unconscionably sarcastic and bellicose; I am girded for a total showdown." Does this essay exhibit some of these characteristics? Point out examples of sarcasm in the essay.

6. How are we to respond to the sentence that ends paragraph 17: "I put the experience down as a reversal"?

7. What is the relationship between Buckley's argument about the "technification" of modern life and his earlier reference to a more "virile" age?

8. Based on Buckley's comments about political apathy and the effect of powerful governments, what would you say his political affiliation is: Republican, Democrat, independent? Point out other places in his essay where his political affiliation is perhaps suggested.

9. Explain the relevance and discuss the effectiveness of Buckley's concluding paragraph. Is it consistent with the tone of the rest of his essay?

Discriminating Tastes:
The Prejudice of Personal Preferences

VICTORIA A. SACKETT

Victoria A. Sackett wrote the following essay as her regular column in the July–August 1987 issue of *Public Opinion* magazine, where she is deputy managing editor. As opposed to William F. Buckley, Jr., who says that we do not complain enough, Sackett argues that we complain too much. Using an extended analogy of a disease, she describes the plague of the prejudice

of personal preferences that is sweeping the nation and makes some suggestions about what has caused it.

1   The nation is suffering from a plague. It has nothing to do with our im-
mune systems or cicadas or controlled substances or insider trading. But
it is just as damaging to our individual well-being and our social fabric.
We've developed a persistent low-grade fever of intolerance that's sap-
ping our strength and making us all behave like cranky, spoiled brats.

2   This is not major-league prejudice, the kind we've seen in decades
past leveled at ethnic groups and scary new ideas. This is a common,
everyday strain of irritability whose target is Anyone who does Anything that we find vaguely Unpleasant.

3   The disease progresses in three distinct stages:

4   *Primary intolerance:* You begin to suspect that everyone else has the
symptoms. You will be dismayed and irked by other people's impatience. Suddenly the world will seem to be populated with fast-food
clerks who grow surly if a customer requests a napkin; cab drivers who
shower invective upon riders going anyplace but the airport; friends
who say, "Will you *please* get to the point?" instead of listening politely
to your too-long stories; and women who smite stopped trucks with
their umbrellas if the rear tires overlap a crosswalk.

5   *Secondary intolerance:* Behavior in others that never bothered you
in the past begins to give you all the symptoms of a neurological or
myocardial incident—muscles twitch, heart pounds, respiration rate
accelerates, vision tunnels, head throbs. In the presence of whatever
annoys you—gum-chewing, ice-crunching, high-pitched giggling, foot-
shuffling, finger-drumming, toe-tapping—you will be unable to hear,
see, smell, or think about anything but that which you would most like
to avoid. You will take indirect action: glaring, sighing heavily, twisting
in your seat, and glaring harder. You will begin to commit thought
crimes—adrenaline-fed dreams of slapping, yelling, and smiting with
your umbrella.

6   *Tertiary intolerance:* You give in to your fantasies and frustration and
take direct action to ease your discomfort. You speak to the offender.
"Would you mind not doing that? It bothers me," is the favored begin-
ner's phrase. It means quite simply, "Stop doing things the way you
want to and do them the way I want you to."

7   Once you've shushed your first talkative movie viewer, you know
that the virus has entered your bloodstream. All the antibodies built up
by your mother's fine teachings of patience have proven unequal to
their task. This can be life-threatening. One young man at a recent Lau-
rel, Maryland, showing of *The Untouchables,* for example, asked a noisy

neighbor to be quiet once too often and was beaten unconscious by the talker and nine companions.

The Pathology

The cruelty of this particular ailment is that efforts to alleviate the symp- 8 toms make it worse. The more vexations that you attempt to control, the more easily you will be vexed. Victory over one provocation just lowers your resistance to another; once you begin to suspect that you *can* get people to behave according to your specifications, chances are you will be unwilling to let them get away with much of anything. We've hardly noticed it happening, but this is what has turned small-time intolerance into a countrywide epidemic.

The irony is that, as the nation has grown more tolerant and wel- 9 coming of all kinds of ethnic and other diversity, individuals succumb- ing to their petty prejudices now comprise veritable lynch mobs. Their targets are the newly beleaguered minorities: cholesterol eaters (watch what happens at a family dinner when you ask for butter *and* sour cream *and* bacon bits for your potato. Someone will describe for you in clinical detail just what saturated fat does to your innards), perfume wearers (Ann Landers published the seat number of a subscription ticket holder at the Arena stage who wore a scent that bothered someone near her), and smokers of any variety (I have one friend of otherwise saintly pa- tience who can't *bear* the smell of fake logs burning. He was able to get his neighbors to stop).

Antismokers are the most contagious group. It begins in childhood. 10 Every three-year-old holds his or her nose, waves a fat little arm in the air, and says "That stinks" when an adult lights up. It's always been this way, even before the surgeon general frightened us. But in the olden days, mothers and fathers used this behavior as an opportunity to teach one of life's most valuable lessons: It's rude to boss people around, and you can't always have everything the way you want it.

Now these children are congratulated for their wisdom and adults 11 imitate *them*. It is true that both the small ones and the big ones have ar- guments in their favor. They can insist that it's their health and not their whim that is being indulged, but this is open to doubt. If smoking smelled good, chances are the investigations into its effects would have stopped with the damage it did to the smoker.

These days, smoke-haters are armed with a doctor's excuse for their 12 own intolerance. There's no such thing as being rude to a smoker. And 90 percent of the people who are snarling at the addict, driving him out of restaurants, workplaces, and entire communities, throwing pitchers of water at him, and teaching their children to say "That's disgusting" to him are less concerned about being infected by his cigars or cigarettes than they are concerned with manifesting the symptoms of their own disease—final-stage intolerance.

The Causes

13   Expanded to a global scale, tertiary intolerance could add up to something serious. Other than making each of us—the irritable as well as the irritating—less happy than we were when we could take things in stride, this plague of intolerance could threaten the fate of the world. What if our president, for instance, decided to take the advice of all the actresses and junior high school students who've been telling him that the Russians are just like us, so we should all lay down arms and be good friends? Then what if we found out that the Soviets were like us, but weren't what we liked—they smoke cigars, say, or shuffle their feet, or chew gum in movie theaters? Peace wouldn't have a chance.

14   Why have we become so testy? One explanation could well be the trend toward later marriage. People who live by themselves for prolonged periods tend to expect the world to be far more within their control than those who are constantly disrupted by the demands of spouses or offspring. Or, the other side of that, people who marry later tend to be those who enjoy the control they have over their own lives. Either way, there are more of them around, and they may be having their effect on the collective tolerance level.

15   The other culprit has to be assertiveness training. Since politeness came to be identified as meekness and repression, there have been no holds barred on expressing oneself. To avoid stating your wishes is to invite psychological damage, professional dead ends, and lack of respect from others. Few schools of thought have been swallowed so unquestioningly with such exasperating results.

16   Widespread irritability may just be one more irritation that we have to deal with in late twentieth-century America. Maybe human nature requires a certain irreducible minimum of intolerance, the way the human body requires minute quantities of "trace minerals" that keep everything from going haywire. If we chase prejudice out of one part of our souls, it pops up somewhere else. Legislation and enlightenment have accustomed us to large-scale diversity, so now we fuss about petty differences. This is still an exhausting and unpleasant state of mind, but it may be as close as we can come to conquering intolerance altogether. We can't, after all, always have everything the way we want it.

EXPLORING IDEAS

1. Is it fair to characterize people's intolerance of cigarette smokers and perfume wearers as equal in importance? Are both really a matter of telling others: "Stop doing things the way you want to and do them the way I want you to"?

2. Discuss Sackett's example of a man's being beaten up because he asked people to be quiet in a movie theater. Is this an extreme example, or are such incidents more and more likely to happen? Is it more dangerous to complain in public now than it once was? Discuss your answer.

3. Explain Sackett's argument that the more we try to alleviate the symptoms of this intolerance, the worse it gets. Have people become more willing to behave according to acceptable social expectations than they once were? Have others become more intolerant as a result? Brainstorm the causes of the intolerance Sackett describes.

4. Sackett says that Americans have become more tolerant of ethnic minorities while at the same time becoming less tolerant of cholesterol eaters, perfume wearers, and smokers. Is there any relationship between these two trends? Discuss your answer.

5. Sackett says that antismokers are the most contagious group. Why are so many people intolerant of smokers? Use the following thesis statement for an essay: "There's no such thing as being rude to a smoker." Is there no way to defend smokers?

6. Is Sackett serious in suggesting that intolerance is due to the trend toward later marriages? Brainstorm some reasons for this trend. What other effects might this trend have?

7. Compare Sackett's argument about the effect of assertiveness training with William Buckley's argument in the previous essay that we don't complain enough.

8. Agree or disagree with the following statement: "To avoid stating your wishes is to invite psychological damage, professional dead ends, and lack of respect from others." Is there an essay in this statement?

EXPLORING RHETORIC

1. Discuss the metaphors, such as "plague," "social fabric," "cranky, spoiled brats," "major league," and "target" that Sackett uses in the three introductory paragraphs. What is the primary metaphor Sackett uses? Do the other metaphors clash with it?

2. Discuss the effect of Sackett's use of the second-person "you" in her discussion of the "disease's" three distinct stages. How would the effect have been different if she had used the third-person "they" or the first-person "we"?

3. What tone is suggested by such language as "women who smite stopped trucks," "symptoms of neurological or myocardial incident," "thought crimes," and "This could be life-threatening"?

4. Discuss the effectiveness of the lists and the parallel phrases Sackett uses in paragraph 5.

5. Why does Sackett use the detail of a three-year-old's waving her "fat little arm"? What tone is suggested by this phrase?

6. What are the implication and the tone of Sackett's statement: "If smoking smelled good, chances are the investigations into its effects would have stopped with the damage it did to the smoker"?

7. Discuss the purpose of Sackett's example of "personal preferences" expanded to a global scale. Is the example of the president's listening to advice about Russia extreme and absurd, or does it support Sackett's central point?

8. Why does Sackett wait until the final three paragraphs to suggest the cause of the intolerance she describes? Would it not have been more effective to have examined the cause before she examined the effects? Discuss how she tries to make these causes convincing.

Angry

JULIANNE MALVEAUX

Julianne Malveaux was born in 1953 in San Francisco. She received her B.A. and M.A. from Boston College and her Ph.D. from MIT. She has been a research fellow for the Rockefeller Foundation and a professor of economics at the New School for Social Research in New York, San Francisco State University, and the University of California at Berkeley. She is a contributing editor of *Essence* magazine and the author of books on black women in the workplace and *Slipping Through the Cracks: The Status of Black Women,* 1986.

In this essay, Malveaux angrily justifies her own anger as part of the hell-raising tradition of black women in a racist society. But while she is proud of her social anger, she admits that she is learning to control her personal anger, picking her battles so that she does not wake up every morning ready to fight.

1   I don't mind raising hell. I thrive on it. I think of hell-raising as a useful endeavor. Of course, everybody doesn't have a stomach for raising hell. It requires you to get angry, to go out on a limb, to scream and shout, to shake trees and boggle minds, to move people from a comfort zone to a place where they are willing to consider change. In order to raise hell you've got to be an angry person. And that I am. Angry. Angry and proud. Upon hearing myself described by a white feminist as "one of those hostile Black women," I beamed with pleasure because she got ex-

actly what I was putting out: an anger and assertiveness that would not allow her simplest remark—on women, feminism or anything else—to go unchallenged. Her description gave me even more pleasure when I remembered that critics once described James Baldwin as an "angry Black man." If I can walk in company like that, I told myself, that's good company to keep.

Anger, writes author Carol Tavris, is a sign of something amiss, 2 something wrong. In her book *Anger: The Misunderstood Emotion,* Tavris writes of women and anger, of targeted anger and of anger used as a tool or weapon. She concludes that anger is okay, but urges women to look carefully at their anger and understand where it comes from and where it is focused.

Her book is one of a series of books that examines this intense emo- 3 tion. In the days of "do your own thing," people were encouraged to shout, scream and get angry to express their feelings. This kind of self-expression was said to be healthy, preferable to holding it in and letting feelings fester. Then other experts began studying anger and raising questions about its unharnessed use. Letting it all out, some said, hurt feelings, left residual resentments and created hostility.

I agree with Tavris: Anger is a sign of something gone wrong. Every 4 hell-raiser knows that. What alert Black woman living in this racist society doesn't have a right to be angry? Walk down any city street and see strong and healthy Black men out of work. Who doesn't feel a burst of anger? Flip through the pages of our federal budget and look at the tax dollars spent on MX missiles and B-1 bombers, not food or books. Isn't that cause for anger? Think about Michael Griffith chased to his death by white men in Howard Beach. Anger. The U.S. Supreme Court trying, again, to snatch our hard-won civil rights by challenging affirmative-action set-asides by asking for "proof" of discrimination in the recent *Richmond* vs. *Croson* ruling. Anger. Or what about the thousands of Black women who crave marriage and families and the forces that conspire to keep them from having them? Anger. And that Bill Moyers special "The Vanishing Family: Crisis in Black America," and the arrogance implicit in his wishful thinking? Anger. Or workfare programs, some of which look like a new kind of slavery, being implemented in city after city? Anger—a reaction to something very wrong.

But there are a lot of wrongs in this unjust world, and as I get older 5 and wiser I consider the advice of people who say "Pick your battles." I can't raise hell all the time; if I did, I'd be a raving, raging fool. So I step back from time to time and ask myself these questions: Why this anger? What does it mean? What do I want to do about it? Reflecting on my anger lets me fine-tune it, revise it, enjoy it, use it as a powerful, motivating tool.

6　　　My anger has fueled many a protest, been part of many a movement. My crisp letters, composed in the middle of the night, have caused many an institution to consider change. I got angry about San Francisco's investment in companies doing business in South Africa and wrote a successful initiative to remove pension funds from such businesses. I got angry that Robert H. Bork could be nominated to the Supreme Court, and so prepared dozens of letters for colleagues to send protesting that choice. Thousands of angry people like me, from all over the country, stopped that appointment. I was angry about the Feminization of Power campaign because it excluded the interests of women of color; I wrote an article that was printed in newspapers across the country. I got angry about a woman being denied her food stamps, so I helped her get them back.

7　　　Black women have a hell-raising tradition. Many of us share the social anger that I feel, and lots of us do things about it—organize for change, write letters to editors, make phone calls or march in protests. Often our anger is triggered by racism or sexism, but many of us choose to "take no stuff" in our personal lives as well: We speak up when things go wrong instead of swallowing our words to keep the peace. But "take no stuff" women often get labeled "bitches," "hostile" or "Sapphires," and people who are turned off by rage or raised voices parody our legitimate anger as extreme. Many women, not wanting to be "Sapphires," shy away from anger as something unfeminine.

8　　　But who defined anger as unfeminine? We can trace Black women's angry, hell-raising responses through the centuries. Angry Harriet Tubman responded to something wrong by leading hundreds of slaves through the Underground Railroad. Angry Sojourner Truth raised her voice and asked "And ain't I a woman?" Angry Ida B. Wells documented lynchings and agitated for change. Angry women from Delta Sigma Theta sorority marched down Pennsylvania Avenue in 1919 in support of women's suffrage. Angry Mary McLeod Bethune founded the National Council of Negro Women. Angry Rosa Parks said she wouldn't move to the back of the bus. Anger is not a dirty word; it is a justified and understandable response.

9　　　I'd be less than honest if I described my anger solely as the social kind. Sometimes my angry antennae settle on issues far less global than war and peace, race and rage, welfare and workfare. Yet my personal response to things gone wrong is often as strong as my political one: A friend fails to repay a loan as promised, and I respond with crushing and chilling anger. A man I am seeing fails to show up for a date, and I chew him up and spit him out with stinging words. A neighbor blocks my garage, preventing me from backing my car out; I call her everything but a child of God with wings. I am told that these displays of anger are inappropriate for the incidents that occur. Part of me agrees, but another part of me says I am just drawing lines around my personal rights the same way I do around my political and civil rights.

Perhaps I could learn to "lighten up" from time to time, but I re- 10 spond angrily to people who say they want social change but are unwilling to change the way they treat others. Often at the cost of harmony, I bristle vocally at contradictions. I find it infuriating that a man who works for a civil-rights organization will not pay his child support. That a woman working for an equal-rights-advocacy group will pay her household help less than minimum wage and claim it's economics. That a group of Black women will gather to talk about aging and dignity but not treat other sisters in their community with respect.

The minutiae, the little stuff that seems too petty to get angry about, 11 is often an indicator of something bigger. The man who always asks a woman to pour coffee at a meeting can be ignored or he can be called on it, even though he may say it was "unintentional" and do it again. (Of course, "unintentional" discrimination is the kind that has resulted in fewer than 3 percent of all middle managers having Black faces.) And then there are those liberal white people who say they are on "our side" with issues, but behave as if Jim Crow is alive and well. For example, an aide to a progressive congressman who clearly has her head in the right place on issues, but tells me she can't be bothered with the Black press (too small) and makes a point of confusing two Black women who write for the same paper (a mistake, or shades of a racist past?). Or that modern-day Miss Ann who goes to the head of a book line at a "peace and justice" rally because *she* is in a hurry.

There is not much one can do about minutiae except point them out 12 and risk being called disruptive, belligerent, hostile, difficult and angry. I'll admit a fourth of that, the angry part. I get angry that you have to go along to get along (if Black people always went along, we'd probably still be picking cotton). Angry enough to distance myself from friends who say I overreact, mind other people's business and take a "hard line" with "good people" who have just made one or two mistakes.

Sometimes I joke that I am so angry that I get up in the morning 13 fighting, but the ability to "pick my battles" is coming to me slowly. I'm learning to cover my trigger points so the gun doesn't always go off. The lesson hit home one Saturday when I sat in a restaurant with friends eating a long, leisurely lunch. Despite the fact that the place wasn't crowded, our waitress kept trying to hustle us out, plopping down the check just as we were asking for another pot of tea and walking by asking "Anything else?" every two minutes. I was shocked, then angered, when I heard her complain loudly that she wished "those Black women" would hurry up and leave. My first inclination was to ask for her supervisor. My second was to picket the place. But my friends sipped their tea with such serenity that I understood that we made our point as much by sitting there as by making an angry scene. I shrugged off my cloak of anger, slipped it around the back of my chair and turned inward, asking myself a series of questions.

14   Do we angry people have to carry our cloak everywhere? Does our anger prevent us from enjoying our lives? Are we people who must be watched askance because our friends and colleagues don't know what will set us off? When does our anger serve us and when does it do us wrong? When is it "acceptable" and when does it go too far? When should we let our anger go so we can keep our balance?

15   The way we women show our anger is as personal and unique as everything else about us. Some women wear anger like a special hat, later packing it back into tissue paper until another occasion arises. Others wear it like a stole, shrugging it off only occasionally when the weather makes it oppressive. Some feel anger, then hide it, like money under a mattress or a lace camisole beneath a severely tailored suit. Others exult in their anger like frisky ducks splashing the water for all it's worth. But we should understand that anger, neither bad nor unfeminine, is part of our legacy. It can be shouted or screamed, or even whispered or swallowed, but it is part of us. And when we stop feeling there is something wrong with our society, we will have divorced ourselves from our heritage.

16   The third cup of tea my friends and I sipped that Saturday was as delicious as the first; it blended with our kinship and my insights to make me feel content. I was glad that we sat at our table until we were ready to go, glad I didn't shatter our tranquility with a lecture to management. We departed in our own sweet time, leaving a small tip and a handwritten note that said, "The tip would have been larger if the service had been better." And we laughed on our way out, not so much at the incident as at the good time we had.

17   These reflections about anger don't have a resolution; anger never ends for a hell-raiser. As quickly as I learn to probe my anger, I learn to appreciate it. But as I read and think about my hell-raising ways and about the lives of other angry people I have begun to place my anger in some perspective—it doesn't define me, but it is a very essential part of who I am. And so when people ask me what I do, I tell them that I "write, talk and raise hell." In light of my history, I can't suppress the pleasure I feel when I'm described as a "strong and angry" Black woman.

EXPLORING IDEAS

1. Which experts do you agree with: those who say that angry self-expression is healthy or those who say that expressing anger causes hurt feelings and hostility? Explain why. Brainstorm for an essay on this subject.

2. What is the difference between anger and assertiveness? Can one be assertive without being angry? Are angry people always assertive? Discuss. Read Sackett's discussion of the effect of assertiveness in her essay elsewhere in this part.

3. Most of the things Malveaux is angry about concern injustices done to African Americans. Does this focus limit the scope and relevance of her reflections about anger, or are they universal?

4. Is it possible to be reflective about your anger, that is, to think about it and be reasonable about it? Or is anger most often irrational and an indication that one has not thought about things? Discuss the difference between rational and irrational anger.

5. What is the difference between productive anger and nonproductive anger? Are most social changes the result of anger or reason?

6. Often women in powerful positions in business and politics are called "bitches" by their enemies or opponents. Why? Is there an equivalent pejorative name for men in powerful positions?

7. Why is anger often called "unfeminine"? What assumptions and biases about women does this accusation suggest?

8. Malveaux says that small things that make her angry are signs of larger, more important things. Does she support this opinion, or does this sound like a justification for her own quick temper and impatience?

9. Brainstorm for an essay about getting angry or complaining about poor service in public places. See William Buckley's essay about why we don't complain and Victoria Sackett's essay about discriminating tastes elsewhere in this part.

10. Malveaux says that although anger does not define her, it is an essential part of who she is. Brainstorm for an essay about some basic or essential characteristic of who you are and reflect on it, as Malveaux has about anger.

EXPLORING RHETORIC

1. Discuss the two different tactics Malveaux uses to open her essay: personal statements about being angry and a reference to a book about anger. Which is more effective? How do the two tactics work together?

2. What rhetorical tactic does Malveaux use in paragraph 4 to indicate her agreement with the belief that anger means something has gone wrong?

3. Discuss Malveaux's rhetorical techniques in paragraph 6.

4. How does Malveaux connect biases about angry women and angry minorities in paragraphs 7 and 8?

5. Explain why Malveaux shifts the subject in paragraph 9, and how this shift either contributes to or detracts from her main argument.

6. Discuss the relationship between the subject of paragraph 9—in which Malveaux is talking about personal reasons for anger—and the subject of paragraph 10—in which she discusses social issues once again.

7. Discuss the rhetorical tactic that Malveaux uses to justify her anger in paragraph 12.

8. Discuss the device Malveaux uses in paragraphs 13 and 16. What is the difference between using several examples to make her point and using one long example?

9. Discuss the effectiveness of the metaphors that Malveaux uses in paragraph 15.

10. Examine the basic structure of Malveaux's essay. Divide it into its major parts; then examine the rhetorical devices she uses to make her point in each one of those parts.

If Black English Isn't a Language, Then Tell Me, What Is?

JAMES BALDWIN

James Baldwin was born in Harlem in New York City in 1924. In 1948, he left for Europe, where he lived for ten years and began his writing career. His books include *Go Tell It on the Mountain,* 1953; *Notes of a Native Son,* 1955; *The Fire Next Time,* 1963; and *No Name in the Street,* 1972. He died in 1987.

Baldwin argues that black English is not merely a dialect, that is, a socially distinct variation of English that identifies a certain ethnic or social group, but rather a language of its own. The underlying argument, one that Baldwin does not discuss specifically, is whether black English should therefore be accepted as the equal of what is called standard English.

1   The argument concerning the use, or the status, or the reality, of black English is rooted in American history and has absolutely nothing to do with the question the argument supposes itself to be posing. The argument has nothing to do with language itself but with the role of language. Language, incontestably, reveals the speaker. Language, also, far more dubiously, is meant to define the other—and, in this case, the other is refusing to be defined by a language that has never been able to recognize him.

2   People evolve a language in order to describe and thus control their circumstances or in order not to be submerged by a situation that they cannot articulate. (And if they cannot articulate it, they are submerged.) A Frenchman living in Paris speaks a subtly and crucially different language from that of the man living in Marseilles; neither sounds very much like a man living in Quebec; and they would all have great difficulty in apprehending what the man from Guadeloupe, or Martinique, is saying, to say nothing of the man from Senegal—although the "common" language of all these areas is French. But each has paid, and is pay-

ing, a different price for this "common" language, in which, as it turns out, they are not saying, and cannot be saying, the same things: They each have very different realities to articulate, or control.

What joins all languages, and all men, is the necessity to confront 3 life, in order, not inconceivably, to outwit death: The price for this is the acceptance, and achievement, of one's temporal identity. So that, for example, though it is not taught in the schools (and this has the potential of becoming a political issue) the south of France still clings to its ancient and musical Provençal, which resists being described as a "dialect." And much of the tension in the Basque countries, and in Wales, is due to the Basque and Welsh determination not to allow their languages to be destroyed. This determination also feeds the flames in Ireland for among the many indignities the Irish have been forced to undergo at English hands is the English contempt for their language.

It goes without saying, then, that language is also a political instru- 4 ment, means, and proof of power. It is the most vivid and crucial key to identity: It reveals the private identity, and connects one with, or divorces one from, the larger, public, or communal identity. There have been, and are, times and places, when to speak a certain language could be dangerous, even fatal. Or, one may speak the same language, but in such a way that one's antecedents are revealed, or (one hopes) hidden. This is true in France, and is absolutely true in England: The range (and reign) of accents on that damp little island make England coherent for the English and totally incomprehensible for everyone else. To open your mouth in England is (if I may use black English) to "put your business in the street." You have confessed your parents, your youth, your school, your salary, your self-esteem, and, alas, your future.

Now, I do not know what white Americans would sound like if there 5 had never been any black people in the United States, but they would not sound the way they sound. *Jazz*, for example, is a very specific sexual term, as in *jazz me, baby*, but white people purified it into the Jazz Age. *Sock it to me*, which means, roughly, the same thing, has been adopted by Nathaniel Hawthorne's descendants with no qualms or hesitations at all, along with *let it all hang out* and *right on! Beat to his socks*, which was once the black's most total and despairing image of poverty, was transformed into a thing called the Beat Generation, which phenomenon was, largely, composed of *uptight*, middle-class white people, imitating poverty, trying to *get down*, to get *with it*, doing their *thing*, doing their despairing best to be *funky*, which we, the blacks, never dreamed of doing—we were funky, baby, like *funk* was going out of style.

Now, no one can eat his cake, and have it, too, and it is late in the day 6 to attempt to penalize black people for having created a language that permits the nation its only glimpse of reality, a language without which the nation would be even more *whipped* than it is.

7   I say that the present skirmish is rooted in American history, and it
is. Black English is the creation of the black diaspora. Blacks came to the
United States chained to each other, but from different tribes. Neither
could speak the other's language. If two black people, at that bitter hour
of the world's history, had been able to speak to each other, the institution of chattel slavery could never have lasted as long as it did. Subse-
quently, the slave was given, under the eye, and the gun, of his master,
Congo Square, and the Bible—or, in other words, and under those conditions, the slave began the formation of the black church, and it is within
this unprecedented tabernacle that black English began to be formed.
This was not, merely, as in the European example, the adoption of a foreign tongue, but an alchemy that transformed ancient elements into a
new language: *A language comes into existence by means of brutal necessity,
and the rules of the language are dictated by what the language must convey.*

8   There was a moment, in time, and in this place, when my brother, or
my mother, or my father, or my sister, had to convey to me, for example,
the danger in which I was standing from the white man standing just behind me, and to convey this with a speed and in a language, that the
white man could not possibly understand, and that, indeed, he cannot
understand, until today. He cannot afford to understand it. This understanding would reveal to him too much about himself and smash that
mirror before which he has been frozen for so long.

9   Now, if this passion, this skill, this (to quote Toni Morrison) "sheer
intelligence," this incredible music, the mighty achievement of having
brought a people utterly unknown to, or despised by, "history"—to have
brought this people to their present, troubled, troubling, and unassailable and unanswerable place—if this absolutely unprecedented journey
does not indicate that black English is a language, I am curious to know
what definition of languages is to be trusted.

10   A people at the center of the western world, and in the midst of so
hostile a population, has not endured and transcended by means of
what is patronizingly called a "dialect." We, the blacks, are in trouble,
certainly, but we are not inarticulate because we are not compelled to defend a morality that we know to be a lie.

11   The brutal truth is that the bulk of the white people in America never
had any interest in educating black people, except as this could serve
white purposes. It is not the black child's language that is despised. It is
his experience. A child cannot be taught by anyone who despises him,
and a child cannot afford to be fooled. A child cannot be taught by anyone whose demand, essentially, is that the child repudiate his experience, and all that gives him sustenance, and enter a limbo in which he
will no longer be black, and in which he knows that he can never become
white. Black people have lost too many black children that way.

12   And, after all, finally, in a country with standards so untrustworthy,
a country that makes heroes of so many criminal mediocrities, a country

unable to face why so many of the nonwhite are in prison, or on the needle, or standing, futureless, in the streets—it may very well be that both the child, and his elder, have concluded that they have nothing whatever to learn from the people of a country that has managed to learn so little.

EXPLORING IDEAS

1. Baldwin says that language always reveals the speaker. Brainstorm for an essay in which you support this statement, citing specific examples to defend your point.

2. Baldwin says people develop a language to control their circumstances and to prevent being submerged. Support this statement by referring to a dialect or a special language common to an ethnic, occupational, or social group.

3. Some analysts argue that the reality of various cultures is conditioned by their language, pointing out, for example, that Eskimos experience snow differently from others because they have so many different words for types of snow. Other thinkers disagree. Can you agree with either side of this argument without doing special anthropological and linguistic research? How would you support your position?

4. If all variations of a single language constitute separate languages, as Baldwin seems to suggest, and if one of these variations is a key to one's identity, does Baldwin's argument run the risk of separating people even more than they already are?

5. If, as Baldwin seems to argue, black English evolved as a way for African Americans to survive white domination, does this mean that when African Americans are no longer discriminated against, they will no longer need black English?

6. What specific examples of black English that whites could not afford to understand does Baldwin provide? Can you think of examples of your own?

7. Why does Baldwin claim that white people never had any interest in educating black people, except as this could serve white purposes? Argue for or against this assertion.

8. Is Baldwin arguing in the last paragraph that only African Americans should educate African Americans? Discuss your answer.

9. Does Baldwin argue that black English is a language rather than a dialect or that African Americans should be allowed to keep their language? Or does one argument support the other? Explain your answer.

EXPLORING RHETORIC

1. How would you describe the style and tone of the first paragraph of Baldwin's essay? Is it formal, informal, serious, sarcastic? Point out the elements of the diction and the sentence style that support your analysis of the style and tone.

2. Why does Baldwin use examples from French, Basque, Welsh, and Irish languages to introduce his arguments about black English?

3. Why does Baldwin describe England as "that damp little island"? What tone does this wording suggest?

4. Why does Baldwin give examples of words and phrases from black English that have been adopted by the descendants of Nathaniel Hawthorne? Why does he make this reference to the nineteenth-century American writer?

5. Baldwin notes that the word "jazz" originally had a sexual meaning but that the sexual connotation has been lost and the term "purified." Brainstorm some other examples of sexual or vulgar terms for which the original meaning has been lost, such as calling someone a "brown-noser."

6. Why does Baldwin reverse the usual expression, "One cannot have his cake and eat it too"?

7. Discuss the effectiveness of the metaphors "Black English is the creation of the black diaspora," the black church as an "unprecedented tabernacle," and "alchemy that transformed ancient elements into a new language."

8. Analyze the sentence pattern of paragraph 9, in which Baldwin states his central thesis. Comment on its effectiveness.

9. Discuss the effectiveness of the parallel phrases that appear in the last paragraph of the essay. How is this paragraph an appropriate conclusion to Baldwin's argument?

What's Wrong with Black English

RACHEL L. JONES

Rachel L. Jones was born in 1961 in Cairo, Illinois. After receiving her education at Northwestern University and Southern Illinois University, she held internships on the *New York Times* and the *Washington Post* and has been a reporter for the *Chicago Reporter* and the *Miami Herald*.

Resenting the assumption that correct English is "white" and angry at being stripped of her own blackness by speaking standard English, Rachel Jones argues that black English is a dialect—not a language as James Baldwin claims—and that African Americans who use it are less likely to succeed than those who have a command of standard English.

1 William Labov, a noted linguist, once said about the use of black English, "It is the goal of most black Americans to acquire full control of the standard language without giving up their own culture." He also suggested that there are certain advantages to having two ways to express one's feelings. I wonder if the good doctor might also consider the goals of

those black Americans who have full control of standard English but who are every now and then troubled by that colorful, grammar-to-the-winds patois that is black English. Case in point—me.

I'm a 21-year-old black born to a family that would probably be con- 2 sidered lower-middle class—which in my mind is a polite way of describing a condition only slightly better than poverty. Let's just say we rarely if ever did the winter-vacation thing in the Caribbean. I've often had to defend my humble beginnings to a most unlikely group of people for an even less likely reason. Because of the way I talk, some of my black peers look at me sideways and ask, "Why do you talk like you're white?"

The first time it happened to me I was nine years old. Cornered in 3 the school bathroom by the class bully and her sidekick, I was offered the opportunity to swallow a few of my teeth unless I satisfactorily explained why I always got good grades, why I talked "proper" or "white." I had no ready answer for her, save the fact that my mother had from the time I was old enough to talk stressed the importance of reading and learning, or that L. Frank Baum and Ray Bradbury were my closest companions. I read all my older brothers' and sisters' literature textbooks more faithfully than they did, and even lightweights like the Bobbsey Twins and Trixie Belden were allowed into my bookish inner circle. I don't remember exactly what I told those girls, but I somehow talked my way out of a beating.

I was reminded once again of my "white pipes" problem while 4 apartment hunting in Evanston, Ill., last winter. I doggedly made out lists of available places and called all around. I would immediately be invited over—and immediately turned down. The thinly concealed looks of shock when the front door opened clued me in, along with the flustered instances of "just getting off the phone with the girl who was ahead of you and she wants the rooms." When I finally found a place to live, my roommate stirred up old memories when she remarked a few months later, "You know, I was surprised when I first saw you. You sounded white over the phone." Tell me another one, sister.

I should've asked her a question I've wanted an answer to for years: 5 how does one "talk white"? The silly side of me pictures a rabid white foam spewing forth when I speak. I don't use Valley Girl jargon, so that's not what's meant in my case. Actually, I've pretty much deduced what people mean when they say that to me, and the implications are really frightening.

It means that I'm articulate and well-versed. It means that I can talk 6 as freely about John Steinbeck as I can about Rick James. It means that "ain't" and "he be" are not staples of my vocabulary and are only used around family and friends. (It is almost Jekyll and Hyde-ish the way I can slip out of academic abstractions into a long, lean, double-negative-filled dialogue, but I've come to terms with that aspect of my personality.) As a child, I found it hard to believe that's what people meant by "talking proper"; that would've meant that good grades and standard English were equated with white skin, and that went against everything I'd ever been taught. Running into the same type of mentality as an adult has confirmed the depressing reality that for many blacks, standard English is not only unfamiliar, it is socially unacceptable.

7   James Baldwin once defended black English by saying it had added "vitality to the language," and even went so far as to label it a language in its own right, saying, "Language [i.e., black English] is a political instrument" and a "vivid and crucial key to identity." But did Malcolm X urge blacks to take power in this country "any way y'all can"? Did Martin Luther King Jr. say to blacks, "I has been to the mountaintop, and I done seed the Promised Land"? Toni Morrison, Alice Walker and James Baldwin did not achieve their eloquence, grace and stature by using only black English in their writing. Andrew Young, Tom Bradley and Barbara Jordan did not acquire political power by saying, "Y'all crazy if you ain't gon vote for me." They all have full command of standard English, and I don't think that knowledge takes away from their blackness or commitment to black people.

8   I know from experience that it's important for black people, stripped of culture and heritage, to have something they can point to and say, "This is ours, *we* can comprehend it, *we* alone can speak it with a soulful flourish." I'd be lying if I said that the rhythms of my people caught up in "some serious rap" don't sound natural and right to me sometimes. But how heart-warming is it for those same brothers when they hit the pavement searching for employment? Studies have proven that the use of ethnic dialects decreases power in the marketplace. "I be" is acceptable on the corner, but not with the boss.

9   Am I letting capitalistic, European-oriented thinking fog the issue? Am I selling out blacks to an ideal of assimilating, being as much like white as possible? I have not formed a personal political ideology, but I do know this: it hurts me to hear black children use black English, knowing that they will be at yet another disadvantage in an educational system already full of stumbling blocks. It hurts me to sit in lecture halls and hear fellow black students complain that the professor "be tripping dem out using big words dey can't understand." And what hurts most is to be stripped of my own blackness simply because I know my way around the English language.

10   I would have to disagree with Labov in one respect. My goal is not so much to acquire full control of both standard and black English, but to one day see more black people less dependent on a dialect that excludes them from full participation in the world we live in. I don't think I talk white, I think I talk right.

EXPLORING IDEAS

1. How does Jones's description of black English differ from the description given by James Baldwin in the previous essay?

2. How do you think James Baldwin would respond to Jones's argument that Malcolm X, Martin Luther King, Jr., and other prominent African Americans' use of standard English did not take away from their blackness or their commitment to black people?

3. Jones gives an example of being cornered by bullies when she was nine years old for not talking the way her black peers did. Have you ever been the victim of bullies because you were perceived as being different? Write an essay describing the incident and explaining what it meant.

4. Jones says that she read a great deal when she was a child. Does this mean she was a bookworm? How does Jones's "bookishness" affect the reader's response to her argument?

5. Jones says that studies indicate that the use of ethnic dialects decreases power in the marketplace. Is this true for other dialects besides black English? Or are some dialects acceptable while others are not?

6. Write an argumentative essay on the issue of people from different cultures being forced to accept the language of the culture in which they seek to live and work. Choose a specific example from Hispanic, Asian, or Native American cultures.

7. Is Jones arguing that African Americans must be more like whites? Is it possible that African Americans can adopt what Jones defines as "white language" and still maintain their own cultural identity?

8. Brainstorm some of the "stumbling blocks" for African Americans that Jones implies exist in the educational system.

9. Jones concludes by saying that she wants black people less dependent on a language that excludes them from full participation in "the world we live in." Is there something wrong with the world we live in that insists that a people must make their language conform to that of the majority?

EXPLORING RHETORIC

1. Why does Jones use "a noted linguist" to introduce her argument? Why does she refer to him as the "good doctor"?

2. Why does Jones describe her economic background? Why does she say she often has had to defend her humble beginnings?

3. Why does Jones use such language as, "I was offered the opportunity to swallow a few of my teeth"? What effect does this language have on the reader?

4. Note that Jones gives examples of books she read when a child. Why are no books by black writers on the list?

5. Why does Jones use the analogy of Jekyll and Hyde to refer to the way she can slip in and out of black English?

6. Discuss the effectiveness of Jones's examples of Malcolm X and Martin Luther King's using black English.

7. If Jones's main argument is that African Americans should conform to standard written English, then how can she say that she knows how important it is for them to have something they can point to and say, "This is ours, we can comprehend it, we alone can speak it with a soulful flourish"?

8. Discuss the effectiveness of Jones's conclusion. Why does she refer back to the linguist Labov?

"Mommy, What Does *Nigger* Mean?" A Question of Language

GLORIA NAYLOR

Gloria Naylor was born in 1950 in New York City. She worked as a missionary for Jehovah's Witness church for seven years before going to Brooklyn College of the City University of New York, where she received her B.A. in 1981. She earned her M.A. in Afro-American Studies at Yale University in 1983 and has written a number of articles for magazines such as *Ms.*, *Essence*, and *Life*. Her first book, *The Women of Brewster Place*, 1982, won the American Book Award for best first novel that year and was later adapted as a made-for-television movie of the same name. Her two other novels, *Linden Hills*, 1985, and *Mamma Day*, 1988, deal with the situation of African Americans both past and present.

The following essay, which was published in the *New York Times* in 1986, explores the difference between a white person's use of the word "nigger" to refer to African Americans and the use of the word by African Americans to refer to themselves.

1　Language is the subject. It is the written form with which I've managed to keep the wolf away from the door and, in diaries, to keep my sanity. In spite of this, I consider the written word inferior to the spoken, and much of the frustration experienced by novelists is the awareness that whatever we manage to capture in even the most transcendent passages falls far short of the richness of life. Dialogue achieves its power in the dynamics of a fleeting moment of sight, sound, smell, and touch.

2　　I'm not going to enter the debate here about whether it is language that shapes reality or vice versa. That battle is doomed to be waged whenever we seek intermittent reprieve from the chicken and egg dispute. I will simply take the position that the spoken word, like the written word, amounts to a nonsensical arrangement of sounds or letters without a consensus that assigns "meaning." And building from the meanings of what we hear, we order reality. Words themselves are innocuous; it is the consensus that gives them true power.

I remember the first time I heard the word *nigger*. In my third-grade 3 class, our math tests were being passed down the rows, and as I handed the papers to a little boy in back of me, I remarked that once again he had received a much lower mark than I did. He snatched his test from me and spit out that word. Had he called me a nymphomaniac or a necrophiliac, I couldn't have been more puzzled. I didn't know what a nigger was, but I knew that whatever it meant, it was something he shouldn't have called me. This was verified when I raised my hand, and in a loud voice repeated what he had said and watched the teacher scold him for using a "bad" word. I was later to go home and ask the inevitable question that every black parent must face—"Mommy, what does *nigger* mean?"

And what exactly did it mean? Thinking back, I realize that this 4 could not have been the first time the word was used in my presence. I was part of a large extended family that had migrated from the rural South after World War II and formed a close-knit network that gravitated around my maternal grandparents. Their ground-floor apartment in one of the buildings they owned in Harlem was a weekend mecca for my immediate family, along with countless aunts, uncles, and cousins who brought along assorted friends. It was a bustling and open house with assorted neighbors and tenants popping in and out to exchange bits of gossip, pick up an old quarrel, or referee the ongoing checkers game in which my grandmother cheated shamelessly. They were all there to let down their hair and put up their feet after a week of labor in the factories, laundries, and shipyards of New York.

Amid the clamor, which could reach deafening proportions—two or 5 three conversations going on simultaneously, punctuated by the sound of a baby's crying somewhere in the back rooms or out on the street—there was still a rigid set of rules about what was said and how. Older children were sent out of the living room when it was time to get into the juicy details about "you-know-who" up on the third floor who had gone and gotten herself "p-r-e-g-n-a-n-t!" But my parents, knowing that I could spell well beyond my years, always demanded that I follow the others out to play. Beyond sexual misconduct and death, everything else was considered harmless for our young ears. And so among the anecdotes of the triumphs and disappointments in the various workings of their lives, the word *nigger* was used in my presence, but it was set within contexts and inflections that caused it to register in my mind as something else.

6   In the singular, the word was always applied to a man who had distinguished himself in some situation that brought their approval for his strength, intelligence, or drive:

7   "Did Johnny *really* do that?"

8   "I'm telling you, that nigger pulled in $6,000 of overtime last year. Said he got enough for a down payment on a house."

9   When used with a possessive adjective by a woman—"my nigger"—it became a term of endearment for her husband or boyfriend. But it could be more than just a term applied to a man. In their mouths it became the pure essence of manhood—a disembodied force that channeled their past history of struggle and present survival against the odds into a victorious statement of being: "Yeah, that old foreman found out quick enough—you don't mess with a nigger."

10   In the plural, it became a description of some group within the community that had overstepped the bounds of decency as my family defined it. Parents who neglected their children, a drunken couple who fought in public, people who simply refused to look for work, those with excessively dirty mouths or unkempt households were all "trifling niggers." This particular circle could forgive hard times, unemployment, the occasional bout of depression—they had gone through all of that themselves—but the unforgivable sin was a lack of self-respect.

11   A woman could never be a "nigger" in the singular, with its connotation of confirming worth. The noun *girl* was its closest equivalent in that sense, but only when used in direct address and regardless of the gender doing the addressing. *Girl* was a token of respect for a woman. The one-syllable word was drawn out to sound like three in recognition of the extra ounce of wit, nerve, or daring that the woman had shown in the situation under discussion.

12   "G-i-r-l, stop. You mean you said that to his face?"

13   But if the word was used in a third-person reference or shortened so that it almost snapped out of the mouth, it always involved some element of communal disapproval. And age became an important factor in these exchanges. It was only between individuals of the same generation, or from any older person to a younger (but never the other way around), that *girl* would be considered a compliment.

14   I don't agree with the argument that use of the word *nigger* at this social stratum of the black community was an internalization of racism. The dynamics were the exact opposite: the people in my grandmother's living room took a word that whites used to signify worthlessness or degradation and rendered it impotent. Gathering there together, they transformed *nigger* to signify the varied and complex human beings they knew themselves to be. If the word was to disappear totally from the mouths of even the most liberal of white society, no one in that room was naive enough to believe it would disappear from white minds. Meeting

the word head-on, they proved it had absolutely nothing to do with the way they were determined to live their lives.

So there must have been dozens of times that *nigger* was spoken in front of me before I reached the third grade. But I didn't "hear" it until it was said by a small pair of lips that had already learned it could be a way to humiliate me. That was the word I went home and asked my mother about. And since she knew that I had to grow up in America, she took me in her lap and explained.

EXPLORING IDEAS

1. Discuss the difference between written language and spoken language that Naylor suggests in paragraph 1.

2. What does Naylor mean by "consensus" in paragraph 2?

3. What does Naylor mean in paragraph 5 when she says she has heard the word "nigger" in contexts that made it mean something other than what the little boy called her in school?

4. Why is it that Naylor's family can call some African Americans who they felt have overstepped the bounds of decency "niggers" but would not tolerate any white people's calling those same African Americans "niggers"?

5. Discuss some of the reasons that the third-person reference to a woman as "girl" is not acceptable to African Americans. The same might be true of calling a grown man "boy." Although it is not acceptable to call a grown white woman "girl," it seems quite acceptable to refer to a grown white man as "boy." Discuss why.

6. Compare Naylor's comments about "internalization of racism" to comments about the same subject by Gloria Yamato in her essay elsewhere in this book.

7. Discuss Naylor's point that her family and friends took a word that was used by whites to signify degradation and made it harmless. If this is true about this word, is it possibly true of other words that signify scorn? What if all overweight people called other overweight people "fatso"? Would that use deprive the word of its harmful nature? Brainstorm this as a possible topic.

EXPLORING RHETORIC

1. What is the function of the first two paragraphs of Naylor's essay? Could she have left them out altogether?

2. Why does Naylor use the words "nymphomaniac" and "necrophiliac" to compare with "nigger" in paragraph 3?

3. What is the function of Naylor's description of her family and home in paragraph 4?

4. Note the method by which Naylor cites her examples in paragraphs 6 through 10. Why did she not cite all of these in one long single paragraph?

5. Is Naylor's discussion of the use of the word "girl" to refer to African American women relevant to her overall discussion of the word "nigger," or is it a deviation from the main topic of the essay?

6. Discuss the effectiveness of Naylor's return to her opening anecdote in the final paragraph of the essay.

7. Outline Naylor's essay by determining its major sections and describing the purpose of each one.

PART FIVE

USING SOURCES

Argument is a challenging and difficult kind of writing not only because it is so filled with rhetorical devices, but also because it must be based on an informed knowledge of the phenomenon or issue being discussed. You cannot expect to convince an audience of your point unless you have some expertise in the subject, or have such a mastery of rhetorical devices that you can deceive your audience into thinking that you have such expertise. Obviously, it is safer and more ethical to develop the expertise than to depend on rhetorical tricks.

Presenting a convincing argument is not the only reason one might need to develop some expertise in a subject. All people who write must frequently do research: to find out what others have said about a subject, to discover the basic origins or to trace the historical development of a subject, to place a subject within a cultural perspective, to reexamine a subject from a new perspective, or to find the basis for contributing new information about a subject. Writing a paper that uses sources does not mean dipping into a variety of reference works for ideas and quotations and then pasting them together. People who write consult other sources on their subject in the service of making a point.

At the end of the sections on families and work, you will find a number of possible topics suggested by these ten essays, all of which require using sources. The essays in this section are possible sources for developing your own essays. You may also find information about families and work in other parts in this book. For example, several of the essays in Part One deal with relationships between parents and children, and several in Part Three deal with feminine and masculine stereotypes that have affected family life.

The problem of integrating the ideas of other writers in your own is not that these ideas are difficult to find but rather how to choose among the multitude of sources that are available to you. And because the nature of families and the world of work are topics that affect the lives of everyone, you are going to find much more information on these topics than you can possibly use. Therefore you must learn how to evaluate the information you find by determining if it is authoritative and adequately supported.

For example, Jane Howard's list of characteristics of "good" families derives from her own experience, from interviewing people, and from reading the works of others, while Arlene Skolnick's argument about how myths about the family differ from reality is based on her historical research on changing American attitudes toward the family. Knowing that Michael Novak is a resident scholar at the American Enterprise Institute for Public Policy Research, a well-known think-tank for conservative ideas, might lead you to expect that his discussion is more likely to be based on a philosophic attitude than the discussion by Jerrold Footlick, who, as senior editor of *Newsweek* magazine, you might expect to be more journalistically unbiased—unless, of course, you have some evidence that most of the news media today are liberal. Finally, knowing that George Gallup, Jr., is president of the Gallup poll might lead you to believe that his discussion is reliable because it is based on sociological research rather than a personal opinion—that is, unless you have some evidence that the polls and statistical evidence he has used are unreliable.

Because less formal research has been done on the world of work than on the nature of family, the essays in this section are more the result of individual thought and reflection than sociological research. Bertrand Russell, one of the most famous philosophers of the twentieth century, takes, as you might expect, a philosophical approach to the nature of work, discussing what he thinks it is good for and what makes it interesting. Erich Fromm, one of the twentieth century's best-known psychoanalysts, focuses on the history of work to support his argument that too often work has no dignity and purpose. However, Lance Morrow uses history for a different purpose: to question whether the work ethic has died or become weaker. Robert Coles uses the example of the French philosopher Simone Weil to develop his argument that industrial societies must pay more attention to the needs of workers if they are ever to receive the dignity that Erich Fromm says they have always lacked. And finally, Gloria Steinem focuses on the specific problem of women's right, not only to work, but to work for the same intrinsic purposes that Bertrand Russell describes.

You may have to go outside this book to consult some additional sources on these issues. If so, you will need to search library holdings for books on family life and work, of which there will be a large number, and you will also have to search social science indexes and guides to popular magazines, such as *The Reader's Guide to Periodical Literature*. If your library has CD-ROM databases, access to online databases such as Lexis/Nexis, or if you have access to such sources as Gopher or the World Wide Web on the Internet at your school, you may be able to do a great deal of your research at computer terminals. Check with your library for information on how to use these resources.

Some issues involving using sources are individual matters that I do not discuss here. For example, your instructor will tell you how research should be documented, including the bibliography and footnote format to use, if any. Your instructor will also discuss your campus's penalties for plagiarism (using someone else's ideas or words as your own), as well as his or her own policy on this often delicate and always serious matter.

FAMILIES

Families

JANE HOWARD

Jane Howard was born in Springfield, Illinois, in 1935. She has been a reporter, editor, writer, and university teacher. Her books include Please Touch: A Guided Tour of the Human Potential Movement, 1970; A Different Woman, 1973 (autobiography); Families, 1978; and Margaret Mead: A Life, 1984. In this selection from her book Families, Howard describes ten characteristics of what she calls "good families."

1 [In] Kurt Vonnegut, Jr.'s ... *Slapstick*, ... every newborn baby gets assigned a randomly chosen middle name, like Uranium or Daffodil or Raspberry. These middle names are connected with hyphens to numbers between one and twenty, and any two people who have the same middle name are automatically related. This is all to the good, the author thinks, because "human beings need all the relatives they can get—as possible donors or receivers not of love but of common decency." He envisions these extended families as "one of the four greatest inventions by Americans," the others being *Robert's Rules of Order,* the Bill of Rights, and the principles of Alcoholics Anonymous.

2   This charming notion might even work, if it weren't so arbitrary. Already each of us is born into one family not of our choosing. If we're going to go around devising new ones, we might as well have the luxury of picking their members ourselves. Clever picking might result in new families whose benefits would surpass or at least equal those of the old. The new ones by definition cannot spawn us—as soon as they do that, they stop being new—but there is plenty they can do. I have seen them work wonders. As a member in reasonable standing of six or seven tribes in addition to the one I was born to, I have been trying to figure which earmarks are common to both kinds of families:

3   (1) Good families have a chief, or a heroine, or a founder—someone around whom others cluster, whose achievements as the Yiddish word has it, let them *kvell,* and whose example spurs them on to like feats. Some blood dynasties produce such figures regularly; others languish for as many as five generations between demigods, wondering with each new pregnancy whether this, at last, might be the messianic baby who will redeem us. Look, is there not something gubernatorial about her footstep, or musical about the way he bangs with his spoon on his

cup? All clans, of all kinds, need such a figure now and then. Sometimes clans based on water rather than blood harbor several such personages at one time. The Bloomsbury Group in London six decades ago was not much hampered by its lack of a temporal history.

(2) Good families have a switchboard operator—someone like Lilia 4 Economou or my own mother who cannot help but keep track of what all the others are up to, who plays Houston Mission Control to everyone else's Apollo. This role, like the foregoing one, is assumed rather than assigned. Someone always volunteers for it. That person often also has the instincts of an archivist, and feels driven to keep scrapbooks and photograph albums up to date, so that the clan can see proof of its own continuity.

(3) Good families are much to all their members, but everything to 5 none. Good families are fortresses with many windows and doors to the outer world. The blood clans I feel most drawn to were founded by parents who are nearly as devoted to whatever it is they do outside as they are to each other and their children. Their curiosity and passion are contagious. Everybody, where they live, is busy. Paint is spattered on eyeglasses. Mud lurks under fingernails. Person-to-person calls come in the middle of the night from Tokyo and Brussels. Catchers' mitts, ballet slippers, overdue library books and other signs of extrafamilial concerns are everywhere.

(4) Good families are hospitable. Knowing that hosts need guests as 6 much as guests need hosts, they are generous with honorary memberships for friends, whom they urge to come early and often and to stay late. Such clans exude a vivid sense of surrounding rings of relatives, neighbors, teachers, students and godparents, any of whom at any time might break or slide into the inner circle. Inside that circle a wholesome, tacit emotional feudalism develops: you give me protection, I'll give you fealty. Such treaties begin with, but soon go far beyond, the jolly exchange of pie at Thanksgiving for cake on birthdays. It means you can ask me to supervise your children for the fortnight you will be in the hospital, and that however inconvenient this might be for me, I shall manage to. It means I can phone you on what for me is a dreary, wretched Sunday afternoon and for you is the eve of a deadline, knowing you will tell me to come right over, if only to watch you type. It means we need not dissemble. ("To yield to seeming," as Buber wrote, "is man's essential cowardice, to resist it is his essential courage . . . one must at times pay dearly for life lived from the being, but it is never too dear.")

(5) Good families deal squarely with direness. Pity the tribe that 7 doesn't have, and cherish, at least one flamboyant eccentric. Pity too the one that supposes it can avoid for long the woes to which all flesh is heir.

Lunacy, bankruptcy, suicide and other unthinkable fates sooner or later afflict the noblest of clans with an undertow of gloom. Family life is a set of givens, someone once told me, and it takes courage to see certain givens as blessings rather than as curses. Contradictions and inconsistencies are givens, too. So is the war against what the Oregon patriarch Kenneth Babbs calls malarkey. "There's always malarkey lurking, bubbles in the cesspool, fetid bubbles that pop and smell. But I don't put up with malarkey, between my step-kids and my natural ones or anywhere else in the family."

8 (6) Good families prize their rituals. Nothing welds a family more than these. Rituals are vital especially for clans without histories, because they evoke a past, imply a future, and hint at continuity. No line in the Seder service at Passover reassures more than the last: "Next year in Jerusalem!" A clan becomes more of a clan each time it gathers to observe a fixed ritual (Christmas, birthdays, Thanksgiving, and so on), grieve at a funeral (anyone may come to most funerals; those who do declare their tribalness), and devises a new rite of its own. Equinox breakfasts and all-white dinners can be at least as welding as Memorial Day parades. Several of us in the old *Life* magazine years used to meet for lunch every Pearl Harbor Day, preferably to eat some politically neutral fare like smorgasbord, to "forgive" our only ancestrally Japanese colleague Irene Kubota Neves. For that and other reasons we became, and remain, a sort of family.

9 "Rituals," a California friend of mine said, "aren't just externals and holidays. They are the performances of our lives. They are a kind of shorthand. They can't be decreed. My mother used to try to decree them. She'd make such a goddamn fuss over what we talked about at dinner, aiming at Topics of Common Interest, topics that celebrated our cohesion as a family. These performances were always hollow, because the phenomenology of the moment got sacrificed for the *idea* of the moment. Real rituals are discovered in retrospect. They emerge around constitutive moments, moments that only happen once, around whose memory meanings cluster. You don't choose those moments. They choose themselves." A lucky clan includes a born mythologizer, like my blood sister, who has the gift of apprehending such a moment when she sees it, and who cannot help but invent new rituals everywhere she goes.

10 (7) Good families are affectionate. This of course is a matter of style. I know clans whose members greet each other with gingerly handshakes or, in what pass for kisses, with hurried brushes of side jawbones, as if the object were to touch not the lips but the ears. I don't see how such people manage. "The tribe that does not hug," as someone who has been part of many *ad hoc* families recently wrote to me, "is no tribe at all. More and more I realize that everybody, regardless of age, needs to be hugged

and comforted in a brotherly or sisterly way now and then. Preferably now."

(8) Good families have a sense of place, which these days is not 11 achieved easily. As Susanne Langer wrote in 1957, "Most people have no home that is a symbol of their childhood, not even a definite memory of one place to serve that purpose . . . all the old symbols are gone." Once I asked a roomful of supper guests who, if anyone, felt any strong pull to any certain spot on the face of the earth. Everyone was silent, except for a visitor from Bavaria. The rest of us seemed to know all too well what Walker Percy means in *The Moviegoer* when he tells of the "genie-soul of the place which every place has or else is not a place [and which] wherever you go, you must meet and master or else be met and mastered." All that meeting and mastering saps plenty of strength. It also underscores our need for tribal bases of the sort which soaring real estate taxes and splintering families have made all but obsolete.

So what are we to do, those of us whose habit and pleasure and 12 doom is our tendency, as a Georgia lady put it, to "fly off at every other whipstitch?" Think in terms of movable feasts, for a start. Live here, wherever here may be, as if we were going to belong here for the rest of our lives. Learn to hallow whatever ground we happen to stand on or land on. Like medieval knights who took their tapestries along on Crusades, like modern Afghanis with their yurts, we must pack such totems and icons as we can to make short-term quarters feel like home. Pillows, small rugs, watercolors can dispel much of the chilling anonymity of a sublet apartment or motel room. When we can, we should live in rooms with stoves or fireplaces or anyway candlelight. The ancient saying still is true: Extinguished hearth, extinguished family. Round tables help, too, and as a friend of mine once put it, so do "too many comfortable chairs, with surfaces to put feet on, arranged so as to encourage a maximum of eye contact." Such rooms inspire good talk, of which good clans can never have enough.

(9) Good families, not just the blood kind, find some way to connect 13 with posterity. "To forge a link in the humble chain of being, encircling heirs to ancestors," as Michael Novak has written, "is to walk within a circle of magic as primitive as humans knew in caves." He is talking of course about babies, feeling them leap in wombs, giving them suck. Parenthood, however, is a state which some miss by chance and others by design, and a vocation to which not all are called. Some of us, like the novelist Richard P. Brickner, "look on as others name their children who in turn name their own lives, devising their own flags from their parents' cloth." What are we who lack children to do? Build houses? Plant trees? Write books or symphonies or laws? Perhaps, but even if we do these things, there still should be children on the sidelines,

if not at the center, of our lives. It is a sadly impoverished tribe that does not allow access to, and make much of, some children. Not too much, of course: it has truly been said that never in history have so many educated people devoted so much attention to so few children. Attention, in excess, can turn to fawning, which isn't much better than neglect. Still, if we don't regularly see and talk to and laugh with people who can expect to outlive us by twenty years or so, we had better get busy and find some.

14   (10) Good families also honor their elders. The wider the age range, the stronger the tribe. Jean-Paul Sartre and Margaret Mead, to name two spectacularly confident former children, have both remarked on the central importance of grandparents in their own early lives. Grandparents now are in much more abundant supply than they were a generation or two ago when old age was more rare. If actual grandparents are not at hand, no family should have too hard a time finding substitute ones to whom to give unfeigned homage. The Soviet Union's enchantment with day care centers, I have heard, stems at least in part from the state's eagerness to keep children away from their presumably subversive grandparents. Let that be a lesson to clans based on interest as well as to those based on genes.

The Family Out of Favor

MICHAEL NOVAK

Michael Novak was born in 1933 in Johnstown, Pennsylvania. He received his B.A. from Stonehill College and his M.A. degree from Harvard University. He has taught religion and philosophy at a number of universities and has been a resident scholar at the American Enterprise Institute for Public Policy Research in Washington, D.C. His books include Naked I Leave, 1970; The Rise of the Unmeltable Ethics, 1972; Confessions of a Catholic, 1983; Moral Clarity in a Nuclear Age, 1983; and Human Rights and the New Realism, 1986.

In this 1976 essay from Harper's, Novak provides a brief history of the importance of the family, describes what he considers to be the threats facing it, and argues that family life expresses our highest moral ideals.

1   Recently a friend of mine told me the following anecdote. At lunch in a restaurant, he had mentioned that he and his wife intended to have a second child soon. His listener registered the words, stood, and reached

out his hand with unmistakable fervor: "You are making a political statement. Congratulations!"

We live in lucky times. So many, so varied, and so aggressive are the antifamily sentiments in our society that brave souls may now have (for the first time in centuries) the pleasure of discovering for themselves the importance of the family. Choosing to have a family used to be uninteresting. It is, today, an act of intelligence and courage. To love family life, to see in family life the most potent moral, intellectual, and political cell in the body politic is to be marked today as a heretic.

Orthodoxy is usually enforced by an economic system. Our own system, postindustrial capitalism, plays am ambivalent role with respect to the family. On the one hand, capitalism demands hard work, competition, sacrifice, saving, and rational decision-making. On the other, it stresses liberty and encourages hedonism.

Now the great corporations (as well as the universities, the political professions, the foundations, the great newspapers and publishing empires, and the film industry) diminish the moral and economic importance of the family. They demand travel and frequent change of residence. Teasing the heart with glittering entertainment and gratifying the demands of ambition, they dissolve attachments and loyalties. Husbands and wives live in isolation from each other. Children of the upwardly mobile are almost as abandoned, emotionally, as the children of the ghetto. The lives of husbands, wives, and children do not mesh, are not engaged, seem merely thrown together. There is enough money. There is too much emotional space. It is easier to leave town than to pretend that one's lives truly matter to each other. (I remember the tenth anniversary party of a foreign office of a major newsmagazine; none of its members was married to his spouse of ten years before.) At an advanced stage capitalism imparts enormous centrifugal forces to the souls of those who have most internalized its values; and these forces shear marriages and families apart.

To insist, in the face of such forces, that marriage and family still express our highest moral ideals is to awaken hostility and opposition. For many, marriage has been a bitter disappointment. They long to be free of it and also of the guilt they feel, a residual guilt which they have put to sleep and do not want awakened. They loathe marriage. They celebrate its demise. Each sign of weakness in the institution exonerates them of personal failure.

Urban industrial life is not designed to assist families. Expressways divide neighborhoods and parishes. Small family bakeries, cheese shops, and candy stores are boarded up. Social engineers plan for sewers, power lines, access roads, but not for the cultural ecology which allows families of different histories and structures to flower and prosper.

The workplace is not designed with family needs in mind; neither are working hours.

7   Yet, clearly, the family is the seedbed of economic skills, money habits, attitudes toward work, and the arts of financial independence. The family is a stronger agency of educational success than the school. The family is a stronger teacher of the religious imagination than the church. Political and social planning in a wise social order begin with the axiom *What strengthens the family strengthens society*. Highly paid, mobile, and restless professionals may disdain the family (having been nurtured by its strengths), but those whom other agencies desert have only one institution in which to find essential nourishment.

8   The role of a father, a mother, and of children with respect to them, is the absolutely critical center of social force. Even when poverty and disorientation strike, as over the generations they so often do, it is family strength that most defends individuals against alienation, lassitude, or despair. The world around the family is fundamentally unjust. The state and its agents, and the economic system and its agencies, are never fully to be trusted. One could not trust them in Eastern Europe, in Sicily, or in Ireland—and one cannot trust them here. One unforgettable law has been learned painfully through all the oppressions, disasters, and injustices of the last thousand years: *If things go well with the family, life is worth living; when the family falters, life falls apart.*

9   These words, I know, go against the conventional grain. In America, we seem to look to the state for every form of social assistance. Immigrant Jews and Catholics have for fifty years supported progressive legislation in favor of federal social programs: for minimum wage, Social Security, Medicare, civil rights. Yet dignity, for most immigrant peoples, resides first of all in family strength. Along with Southern blacks, Appalachians, Latins, and Indians, most immigrants to America are family people. Indeed, virtually all Americans, outside our professional classes, are family people.

10   As for the media, outrageous myths blow breezily about. Everyone says that divorces are multiplying. They are. But the figures hide as much as they reveal. Some 66 percent of all husbands and wives stick together until death do them part. In addition, the death that "parts" a marriage comes far later now than it did in any previous era. Faithful spouses stay together for a longer span of years than ever. For centuries, the average age of death was, for a female, say, thirty-two, and, for a male, thirty-eight. That so many modern marriages carry a far longer span of years with a certain grace is an unprecedented tribute to the institution.

11   Finally, aggressive sentiments against marriage are usually expressed today in the name of "freedom," "openness," "play," or "serious commitment to a career." Marriage is pictured as a form of imprison-

ment, oppression, boredom, and chafing hindrance. Not all these accusations are wrong; but the superstition surrounding them is.

Before one can speak intelligently of marriage, one must discuss the 12 superstition that blocks our vision. We lack the courage nowadays to live by creeds, or to state our doctrines clearly (even to ourselves). Our highest moral principle is flexibility. Guided by sentiments we are embarrassed to put into words, we support them not by argument but by their trendiness.

The central idea of our foggy way of life, however, seems unambigu- 13 ous enough. It is that life is solitary and brief, and that its aim is self-fulfillment. Total mastery over one's surroundings, control over the disposition of one's time—these are necessary conditions for self-fulfillment. ("Stand not in my way.") Autonomy we understand to mean protection of our inner kingdom—protection around the self from intrusions of chance, irrationality, necessity, and other persons. ("My self, my castle.") In such a vision of the self, marriage is merely an alliance. It entails as minimal an abridgment of inner privacy as one partner or the other may allow. Children are not a welcome responsibility, for to have children is, plainly, to cease being a child oneself.

For the modern temper, great dreads here arise. Sanity, we think, 14 consists in centering upon the only self one has. Surrender self-control, surrender happiness. And so we keep the other out. We then maintain our belief in our unselfishness by laboring for "humanity"—for women, the oppressed, the Third World, or some other needy group. The solitary self needs distant collectivities to witness to its altruism. It has a passionate need to love humankind. It cannot give itself to a spouse or children. "Individual people" seek happiness through concentration upon themselves, although perhaps for the sake of service to others. Most television cops, detectives, cowboys, and doctors are of this tribe. The "family people" define themselves through belonging to others: spouse, children, parents, siblings, nieces, cousins, and the rest. For the family people, to be human is to be, so to speak, molecular. I am not solely I. I am husband, father, son, brother, uncle cousin; I am a family network.

There is, beyond the simplicities of half-hour television, a gritty real- 15 ism in family life. Outside the family, we choose our own friends, like-minded folk whose intellectual and cultural passions resemble ours. Inside the family, however, divergent passions, intellections, and frustrations slam and batter us. Families today bring together professions, occupations, social classes, and sometimes regional, ethnic, or religious differences. Family life may remain in the United States the last stronghold of genuine cosmopolitanism and harsh, truthful differences.

For a thousand years, the family was the one institution the peoples 16 of Eastern and Southern Europe, the Irish, and others could trust. The family constitutes their political, economic, and educational strength.

The public schools of the United States failing them, they reached into their families and created an astonishingly successful system of parochial schools. Hardly literate, poor, and diffident peoples, they achieved something of an educational miracle. Economically, the Jews, the Greeks, the Lebanese established one another in as many small businesses as they could open. The Italians, the Poles, the Slovaks, the Croatians gave each other economic help amounting to two or three thousands of dollars a year per family. Cousin Joe did the electrical work; Pete fixed cars; Emil helped paint the house; aunts and uncles and grandparents canned foods, minded the children; fathers in their spare time built playrooms, boats, and other luxuries in the basements of row houses.

17   The family network was also a political force in precinct, ward, or district. People of the upper classes could pass on to their children advantages of inheritance, admission to exclusive schools, and high-level contacts. Children of the immigrants also made their families the primary networks of economic and political strength. Kinship is a primary reality in many unions and in all urban political "machines." Mothers and fathers instructed their children simultaneously, "Don't trust anybody," and "The family will never let you down."

18   In contemporary conditions, of course, these old family methods and styles have atrophied. There is no way of going back to the past. (Not everything about the past, in any case, was attractive.) Education media help children to become sophisticated about everything but the essentials: love, fidelity, childbearing, mutual help, care for parents and the elderly. Almost everything about mobile, impersonal, distancing life in the United States—tax policies, real-estate policies, the demands of the corporations, and even the demands of modern political forms — makes it difficult for families that feel ancient moral obligations to care for their aged, their mentally disturbed, their retarded, their needy.

19   It is difficult to believe that the state is a better instrument for satisfying such human needs than the family. If parents do not keep after the children to do their schoolwork, can the large, consolidated school educate? Some have great faith in state services: in orphanages, child-care centers, schools, job-training programs, and nursing homes. Some want the state to become one large centralized family. Such faith taxes credulity. Much of the popular resistance to federal child care arises from distrust of social workers and childhood engineers who would be agents of state power. Families need help in child care, but many distrust the state and the social-work establishment.

20   An economic order that would make the family the basic unit of social policy would touch every citizen at the nerve center of daily life. The family is the primary teacher of moral development. In the struggles and conflicts of marital life, husbands and wives learn the realism and adult

practicalities of love. Through the love, stability, discipline, and laughter of parents and siblings, children learn that reality accepts them, welcomes them, invites their willingness to take risks. The family nourishes "basic trust." From this spring creativity, psychic energy, social dynamism. If infants are injured here, not all the institutions of society can put them back together.

Economic and educational disciplines are learned only in the home 21 and, if not there, hardly at all. Discipline in black families has been traditionally severe, very like that in white working-class families. Survival has depended on family discipline. Working-class people, white and black, cannot count on having their way; most of the time they have to be docile, agreeable, and efficient. Otherwise, they are fired. They cannot quit their jobs too often; otherwise their employment record shows instability. Blacks as well as whites survive by such rules, as long as authority in the home is strong. From here, some find the base for their mobility, up and out. Without a guiding hand, however, the temptations to work a little, quit, enjoy oneself, then work a little, are too much encouraged by one's peers on the street. *Either* the home, *or* the street: This is the moral choice. Liberals too seldom think about the economic values of strong family life; they neglect their own source of strength, and legislate for others what would never have worked for themselves.

What Happened to the Family?

JERROLD FOOTLICK, WITH ELIZABETH LEONARD

Jerrold Footlick is a senior editor of Newsweek magazine. In the following lead essay to a special issue of Newsweek in 1990, entitled "The 21st Century Family," Footlick, with journalist Elizabeth Leonard, charts the various changes in family life in the twentieth century and suggests what issues must be confronted in the twenty-first century.

The American family does not exist. Rather, we are creating many Amer- 1 ican families of diverse styles and shapes. In unprecedented numbers, our families are unalike: We have fathers working while mothers keep house; fathers and mothers both working away from home; single parents; second marriages bringing children together from unrelated backgrounds; childless couples; unmarried couples, with and without children; gay and lesbian parents. We are living through a period of historic change in American family life.

2   The upheaval is evident everywhere in our culture. Babies have babies, kids refuse to grow up and leave home, affluent Yuppies prize their BMWs more than children, rich and poor children alike blot their minds with drugs, people casually move in with each other and out again. The divorce rate has doubled since 1965, and demographers project that half of all first marriages made today will end in divorce. Six out of 10 second marriages will probably collapse. One third of all children born in the past decade will probably live in a stepfamily before they are 18. One out of every four children today is being raised by a single parent. About 22 percent of children today were born out of wedlock; of those, about a third were born to a teenage mother. One out of every five children lives in poverty; the rate is twice as high among blacks and Hispanics.

3   Most of us are still reeling from the shock of such turmoil. Americans—in their living rooms, in their boardrooms and in the halls of Congress—are struggling to understand what has gone wrong. We find family life worse than it was a decade ago, according to a *Newsweek* poll, and we are not sanguine about the next decade. For instance, two thirds of those polled think a family should be prepared to make "financial sacrifices so that one parent can stay home to raise the children." But that isn't likely to happen. An astonishing two thirds of all mothers are in the labor force, roughly double the rate in 1955, and more than half of all mothers of infants are in the work force.

4   Parents feel torn between work and family obligations. Marriage is a fragile institution—not something anyone can count on. Children seem to be paying the price for their elders' confusion. "There is an increasing understanding of the emotional cost of having children," says Larry L. Bumpass, a University of Wisconsin demographer. "People once thought parenting ended when their children were 18. Now they know it stretches into the 20s and beyond." Divorce has left a devastated generation in its wake, and for many youngsters, the pain is compounded by poverty and neglect. While politicians and psychologists debate cause and solution, everyone suffers. Even the most traditional of families feel an uneasy sense of emotional dislocation. Three decades ago the mother who kept the house spotless and cooked dinner for her husband and children each evening could be confident and secure in her role. Today, although her numbers are still strong—a third of mothers whose children are under 18 stay home—the woman who opts out of a paycheck may well feel defensive, undervalued, as though she were too incompetent to get "a real job." And yet the traditional family retains a profound hold on the American imagination.

5   The historical irony here is that the traditional family is something of an anomaly. From Colonial days to the mid-19th century, most fathers and mothers worked side by side, in or near their homes, farming or plying trades. Each contributed to family income, and—within carefully de-

lineated roles—they shared the responsibility of child rearing. Only with the advent of the Industrial Revolution did men go off to work in a distant place like a factory or an office. Men alone began producing the family income; by being away from home much of the time, however, they also surrendered much of their influence on their children. Mothers, who by social custom weren't supposed to work for pay outside the home, minded the hearth, nurtured the children and placed their economic well-being totally in the hands of their husbands.

Most scholars now consider the "bread-winner-homemaker" model 6 unusual, applicable in limited circumstances for a limited time. It was a distinctly white middle-class phenomenon, for example; it never applied widely among blacks or new immigrants, who could rarely afford to have only a single earner in the family. This model thrived roughly from 1860 to 1920, peaking, as far as demographers can measure, about 1890. Demographers and historians see no dramatic turning point just then, but rather a confluence of social and economic circumstances. Husbands' absolute control of family finances and their independent lives away from home shook the family structure. A long recession beginning in 1893 strained family finances. At the same time, new attention was being paid to women's education. Around this period, the Census Bureau captured a slow, steady, parallel climb in the rates of working women and divorce—a climb that has shown few signs of slowing down throughout this century.

The years immediately after World War II, however, seemed to mark 7 a reaffirmation of the traditional family. The return of the soldiers led directly to high fertility rates and the famous baby boom. The median age of first marriage, which had been climbing for decades, fell in 1956 to a historic low, 22.5 years for men and 20.1 for women. The divorce rate slumped slightly. Women, suddenly more likely to be married and to have children, were also satisfied to give up the paid jobs they had held in record numbers during the war. A general prosperity made it possible for men alone to support their families. Then, by the early '60s, all those developments, caused by aberrational postwar conditions, reverted to the patterns they had followed throughout the century. The fertility rate went down, and the age of first marriage went back up. Prosperity cycled to recession, and the divorce rate again rose and women plunged back heartily into the job market. In 1960, 19 percent of mothers with children under 6 were in the work force, along with 39 percent of those with children between 6 and 17. Thus, while the Cleaver family and Ozzie and Harriet were still planting the idealized family deeper into the national subconscious, it was struggling.

Now the tradition survives, in a way, precisely because of Ozzie and 8 Harriet. The television programs of the '50s and '60s validated a family style during a period in which today's leaders—congressmen, corporate executives, university professors, magazine editors—were growing up or beginning to establish their own families. (The impact of the idealized family was further magnified by the very size of the postwar generation.) "The traditional model reaches back as far as personal memory goes for most of those who [currently] teach and write and philosophize," says Yale University historian John Demos. "And in a time when parents seem to feel a great deal of change in family experience, that image is comfortably solid and secure, a counterpoint to what we think is threatening for the future."

9   We *do* feel uneasy about the future. We have just begun to admit that exchanging old-fashioned family values for independence and self-expression may exact a price. "This is an incendiary issue," says Arlie Hochschild, a sociologist at the University of California, Berkeley, and author of the controversial book "The Second Shift." "Husbands, wives, children are not getting enough family life. Nobody is. People are hurting." A mother may go to work because her family needs the money, or to afford luxuries, or because she is educated for a career or because she wants to; she will be more independent but she will probably see less of her children. And her husband, if she has a husband, is not likely to make up the difference with the children. We want it both ways. We're glad we live in a society that is more comfortable living with gay couples, working women, divorced men and stepparents and single mothers—people who are reaching in some fashion for self-fulfillment. But we also understand the value of a family life that will provide a stable and nurturing environment in which to raise children—in other words, an environment in which personal goals have to be sacrificed. How do we reconcile the two?

10   The answer lies in some hard thinking about what a family is for. What do we talk about when we talk about family? Many of us have an emotional reaction to that question. Thinking about family reminds us of the way we were, and the way we dreamed we might be. We remember trips in the car, eager to find out whose side of the road would have more cows and horses to count. We remember raking leaves and the sound of a marching band at the high-school football game. We remember doing homework and wondering what college might be like. It was not all fun and games, of course. There were angry words spoken, and parents and grandparents who somehow were no longer around, and for some of us not enough to eat or clothes not warm enough or nice enough. Then we grow up and marvel at what we can accomplish, and the human beings we can produce, and we sometimes doubt our ability to do the things we want to do—have to do—for our children. And live our own lives besides.

11   Practical considerations require us to pin down what the family is all about. Tax bills, welfare and insurance payments, adoption rights and

other real-life events can turn on what constitutes a family. Our expectations of what a family ought to be will also shape the kinds of social policies we want. Webster's offers 22 definitions. The Census Bureau has settled on "two or more persons related by birth, marriage or adoption who reside in the same household." New York state's highest court stretched the definition last summer: it held that the survivor of a gay couple retained the legal rights to an apartment they had long shared, just as a surviving husband or wife could. Looking to the "totality of the relationship," the court set four standards for a family: (1) the "exclusivity and longevity of a relationship"; (2) the "level of emotional and financial commitment"; (3) how the couple "conducted their everyday lives and held themselves out to society"; (4) the "reliance placed upon one another for daily services." That approach incenses social critic Midge Decter. "You can call homosexual households 'families,' and you can define 'family' any way you want to, but you can't fool Mother Nature," says Decter. "A family is a mommy and a daddy and their children."

A State of California task force on the future of the family came up 12 with still another conclusion. It decided a family could be measured by the things it should do for its members, which it called "functions": maintain the physical health and safety of its members; help shape a belief system of goals and values; teach social skills, and create a place for recuperation from external stresses. In a recent "family values" survey conducted for the Massachusetts Mutual Insurance Co., respondents were given several choices of family definitions; three quarters of them chose "a group who love and care for each other." Ultimately, to appropriate U.S. Supreme Court Justice Potter Stewart's memorable dictum, we may not be able to define a family, but we know one when we see it.

We enter the 21st century with a heightened sensitivity to family is- 13 sues. Helping parents and children is a bottom-line concern, no longer a matter of debate. Economists say the smaller labor force of the future means that every skilled employee will be an increasingly valuable asset; we won't be able to afford to waste human resources. Even now companies cannot ignore the needs of working parents. Support systems like day care are becoming a necessity. High rates of child poverty and child abuse are everybody's problem, as is declining school performance and anything else that threatens our global competitiveness. "By the end of the century," says Columbia University sociologist Shelia B. Kamerman, "it will be conventional wisdom to invest in our children."

Those are the familiar demographic forces. But there are other po- 14 tential tremors just below the surface. By 2020, one in three children will come from a minority group—Hispanic-Americans, African-Americans, Asian-Americans and others. Their parents will command unprecedented political clout. Minorities and women together will make up the majority of new entrants into the work force. Minority children are usually the neediest among us, and they will want government support, especially in the schools. At about the same time, many baby boomers will be retired, and they will want help from Washington as well. Billions of dollars are at stake, and the country's priorities in handing out those dollars are not yet clear. After all, children and the elderly are both part of our families. How should the government spend taxpayers' dollars —on long-term nursing care or better day care?

15   So far, the political debate on family issues has split largely along predictable ideological lines. Conservatives want to preserve the family of the '50s; they say there has been too much governmental intrusion already, with disastrous results. Their evidence: the underclass, a veritable caste of untouchables in the inner cities where the cycle of welfare dependency and teenage pregnancy thwarts attempts at reform. Liberals say government can and should help. We can measure which programs work, they say; we just don't put our money and support in the right places. Enrichment programs like Head Start, better prenatal care, quality day care—no one questions the effectiveness of these efforts. And liberals see even more to be done. "We have a rare opportunity to make changes now that could be meaningful into the next century," says Marian Wright Edelman, president of the Children's Defense Fund. But many elements that liberals would like to see on a children's agenda are certain to generate bitter political controversy. Among some of the things that could be included in a national family policy:

- Child and family allowances with payments scaled to the number of children in each family;
- Guarantees to mothers of full job protection, seniority and benefits upon their return to work after maternity leave;
- Pay equity for working women;
- Cash payments to mothers for wages lost during maternity leave;
- Full health-care programs for all children;
- National standards for day care.

16   Our legacy to the future must be a program of action that transcends ideology. And there are indications that we are watching the birth of a liberal/conservative coalition on family issues. "Family issues ring true for people across the political spectrum," says David Blenkenhorn, president of the Institute for American Values, a New York think tank on family policy issues. "The well-being of families is both politically and culturally resonant; it is something that touches people's everyday lives." The government is already responding to the challenge in some ways. For example, President George Bush agreed at the recent Educa-

tion Summit to support increased funding for Head Start, which is by common consent the most successful federal program for preschoolers, yet now reaches only 18 percent of the eligible children.

These issues will occupy us on a national level well into the next 17 century. Yet in our everyday lives, we have begun to find solutions. Some mothers, torn between a desire to stay home with their children and to move ahead in their careers, are adopting a style known as sequencing. After establishing themselves in their career or earning an advanced degree, they step off the career ladder for a few years to focus on children and home. When children reach school age, they return to full-time jobs. Others take a less drastic approach, temporarily switching to part-time work or lower-pressure jobs to carve out more time with their young children. But renewing careers that have been on hiatus is not easy, and women will always suffer vocationally if it is they who must take off to nurture children. There is, obviously, another way: fathers can accept more home and family responsibilities, even to the point of interrupting their own careers. "I expect a significant change by 2020," says sociologist Hochschild. "A majority of men married to working wives will share equally in the responsibilities of home." Perhaps tradition will keep us from ever truly equalizing either child rearing or ironing—in fact, surveys on chore sharing don't hold much promise for the harried working mother. But we have moved a long way since the 1950s. And just because we haven't tried family equality yet doesn't mean we won't ever try it.

That's the magic for American families in the 21st century: we can 18 try many things. As certainly as anything can be estimated, women are not going to turn their backs on education and careers, are not going to leave the work force for adult lives as full-time homemakers and mothers. And the nation's businesses will encourage their efforts, if only because they will need the skilled labor. Yet Americans will not turn their backs completely on the idealized family we remember fondly. Thus, we must create accommodations that are new, but reflect our heritage. Our families will continue to be different in the 21st century except in one way. They will give us sustenance and love as they always have.

The Faltering Family

GEORGE GALLUP, JR.

George Gallup, Jr., was born in 1930 in Evanston, Illinois, and received his education at Princeton University. He is president of the Gallup Poll, the well-known public opinion poll. His books include America's Search for

Faith (with David Poling), 1980; My Kid on Drugs? (with Art Linkletter), 1981; Adventures in Immortality (with William Proctor), 1982; and Forecast 2000 (with William Proctor), 1985. In the following selection from Forecast 2000, Gallup cites a number of opinion polls that suggest the major pressures being placed on the family in the United States today.

1 In a recent Sunday school class in a United Methodist Church in the Northeast, a group of eight- to ten-year-olds were in a deep discussion with their two teachers. When asked to choose which of ten stated possibilities they most feared happening, their response was unanimous. All the children most dreaded a divorce between their parents.

2 Later, as the teachers, a man and a woman in their late thirties, reflected on the lesson, they both agreed they'd been shocked at the response. When they were the same age as their students, they said, the possibility of their parents' being divorced never entered their heads. Yet in just one generation, children seemed to feel much less security in their family ties.

3 Nor is the experience of these two Sunday school teachers an isolated one. Psychiatrists revealed in one recent newspaper investigation that the fears of children definitely do change in different periods; and in recent times, divorce has become one of the most frequently mentioned anxieties. In one case, for example, a four-year-old insisted that his father rather than his mother walk him to nursery school each day. The reason? He said many of his friends had "no daddy living at home, and I'm scared that will happen to me" (New York Times, May 2, 1983).

4 In line with such reports, our opinion leaders expressed great concern about the present and future status of the American family. In the poll 33 percent of the responses listed decline in family structure, divorce, and other family-oriented concerns as one of the five major problems facing the nation today. And 26 percent of the responses included such family difficulties as one of the five major problems for the United States in the year 2000.

5 Historical and sociological trends add strong support to these expressions of concern. For example, today about one marriage in every two ends in divorce. Moreover, the situation seems to be getting worse, rather than better. In 1962, the number of divorces was 2.2 per 1,000 people, according to the National Center for Health Statistics. By 1982, the figure had jumped to 5.1 divorces per 1,000 people—a rate that had more than doubled in two decades.

6 One common concern expressed about the rise in divorces and decline in stability of the family is that the family unit has traditionally been a key factor in transmitting stable cultural and moral values from generation to generation. Various studies have shown that educational

and religious institutions often can have only a limited impact on children without strong family support.

Even grandparents are contributing to the divorce statistics. One recent study revealed that about 100,000 people over the age of fifty-five get divorced in the United States each year. These divorces are usually initiated by men who face retirement, and the relationships being ended are those that have endured for thirty years or more (*New York Times Magazine,* December 19, 1982). 7

What are the pressures that have emerged in the past twenty years that cause long-standing family bonds to be broken? 8

Many now agree that the sexual revolution of the 1960s worked a profound change on our society's family values and personal relationships. Certainly, the seeds of upheaval were present before that critical decade. But a major change that occurred in the mid-sixties was an explicit widespread rejection of the common values about sexual and family relationships that most Americans in the past had held up as an ideal. 9

We're just beginning to sort through all the changes in social standards that have occurred. Here are some of the major pressures that have contributed to those changes: 10

Pressure One: Alternative Lifestyles

Twenty years ago, the typical American family was depicted as a man and woman who were married to each other and who produced children (usually two) and lived happily ever after. This was the pattern that young people expected to follow in order to become "full" or "normal" members of society. Of course, some people have always chosen a different route—remaining single, taking many partners, or living with a member of their own sex. But they were always considered somewhat odd, and outside the social order of the traditional family. 11

In the last two decades, this picture has changed dramatically. In addition to the proliferation of single people through divorce, we also have these developments: 12

- Gay men and women have petitioned the courts for the right to marry each other and to adopt children. These demands are being given serious consideration, and there may even be a trend of sorts in this direction. For example, the National Association of Social Workers is increasingly supporting full adoption rights for gay people (*New York Times,* January 10, 1983).

- Many heterosexual single adults have been permitted to adopt children and set up single-parent families. So being unattached no longer excludes people from the joys of parenthood.

- Some women have deliberately chosen to bear children out of wedlock and raise them alone. In the past, many of these children would have been given up for adoption, but no longer.

    A most unusual case involved an unmarried psychologist, Dr. Afton Blake, who recently gave birth after being artificially inseminated with sperm from a sperm bank to which Nobel Prize winners had contributed (*New York Times,* September 6, 1983).

- In a recent Gallup Youth Poll, 64 percent of the teenagers questioned said that they hoped their lives would be different from those of their parents. This included having more money, pursuing a different kind of profession, living in a different area, having more free time—and staying single longer.

    Most surveys show increasing numbers of unmarried couples living together. Also, there are periodic reports of experiments in communal living, "open marriages," and other such arrangements. Although the more radical approaches to relationships tend to come and go and never seem to attract large numbers of people, the practice of living together without getting married seems to be something that's here to stay. The law is beginning to respond to these arrangements with awards for "palimony"—compensation for long-term unmarried partners in a relationship. But the legal and social status of unmarried people who live together is still quite uncertain—especially as far as any children of the union are concerned.

- Increasing numbers of married couples are choosing to remain childless. Planned Parenthood has even established workshops for couples to assist them in making this decision (*Los Angeles Herald-Examiner,* November 27, 1979).

13   So clearly, a situation has arisen during the last twenty years in which traditional values are no longer as important. Also, a wide variety of alternatives to the traditional family have arisen. Individuals may feel that old-fashioned marriage is just one of many options.

Pressure Two: Sexual Morality

14   Attitudes toward sexual morality have changed as dramatically in the last two decades as have the alternatives to traditional marriage. Hear what a widely used college textbook, published in 1953, said about premarital sex:

> The arguments against premarital coitus outweigh those in its favor. Except for the matter of temporary physical pleasure, all arguments about gains tend to be highly theoretical, while the risks and unpleasant consequences tend to be in equal degree highly practical. . . .

The promiscuity of young men is certainly poor preparation for marital fidelity and successful family life. For girls it is certainly no better and sometimes leads still further to the physical and psychological shock of abortion or the more prolonged suffering of bearing an illegitimate child and giving it up to others. From the viewpoint of ethical and religious leaders, the spread of disease through unrestrained sex activities is far more than a health problem. They see it as undermining the dependable standards of character and the spiritual values that raise life to the level of the "good society."

(This comes from *Marriage and the Family* by Professor Ray E. Baber of Pomona College, California, which was part of the McGraw-Hill Series in Sociology and Anthropology and required reading for some college courses.)

Clearly, attitudes have changed a great deal in just three decades. 15 Teenagers have accepted the idea of premarital sex as the norm. In one recent national poll, 52 percent of girls and 66 percent of boys favored having sexual relations in their teens. Ironically, however, 46 percent of the teenagers thought that virginity in their future marital partner was fairly important. Youngsters, in other words, display some confusion about what they want to do sexually, and what they expect from a future mate.

But of course, only part of the problem of defining sexual standards 16 lies with young people and premarital sex. The strong emphasis on achieving an active and rewarding sex life has probably played some role in encouraging many husbands and wives into rejecting monogamy. Here's some of the evidence that's been accumulating:

- Half of the men in a recent nationwide study admitted cheating on their wives (*Pensacola Journal*, May 30, 1978).

- Psychiatrists today say they see more patients who are thinking about having an extramarital affair and who wonder if it would harm their marriage (*New York Post*, November 18, 1976).

- A psychiatrist at the Albert Einstein College of Medicine says, "In my practice I have been particularly struck by how many women have been able to use an affair to raise their consciousness and their confidence."

So the desire for unrestrained sex now tends to take a place among 17 other more traditional priorities, and this can be expected to continue to exert strong pressure on marriage relationships.

Pressure Three: The Economy

The number of married women working outside the home has been in- 18 creasing steadily, and most of these women are working out of economic necessity. As a result, neither spouse may have time to concentrate on the nurturing of the children or of the marriage relationship.

19 One mother we interviewed in New Jersey told us about her feelings when she was forced to work full time in a library after her husband lost his job.

20 "It's the idea that I have no choice that really bothers me," she said. "I have to work, or we won't eat or have a roof over our heads. I didn't mind working part-time just to have extra money. I suppose that it's self-ish, but I hate having to work every day and then to come home, fix dinner, and have to start doing housework. Both my husband and I were raised in traditional families, where the father went to work and the mother stayed home and took care of the house and children [My husband] would never think of cooking or doing housework. I've raised my boys the same way, and now I'm paying for it. Sometimes, I almost hate my husband, even though I know it's not his fault."

21 Unfortunately, such pressures probably won't ease in the future. Even if the economy improves and the number of unemployed workers decreases, few women are likely to give up their jobs. Economists agree that working-class women who have become breadwinners during a recession can be expected to remain in the work force. One reason is that many unemployed men aren't going to get their old jobs back, even when the economy improves.

22 "To the extent that [the men] may have to take lower-paying service jobs, their families will need a second income," says Michelle Brandman, associate economist at Chase Econometrics. "The trend to two-paycheck families as a means of maintaining family income is going to continue" (*Wall Street Journal*, December 8, 1982).

23 In addition to the pressures of unemployment, the cost of having, rearing, and educating children is steadily going up. Researchers have found that middle-class families with two children *think* they're spending only about 15 percent of their income on their children. Usually, though, they *actually* spend about 40 percent of their money on them. To put the cost in dollars and cents, if you had a baby in 1977, the estimated cost of raising that child to the age of eighteen will be $85,000, and that figure has of course been on the rise for babies born since then (*New York Daily News*, July 24, 1977).

24 Another important factor that promises to keep both spouses working full time in the future is the attitude of today's teenagers toward these issues. They're not so much concerned about global issues like overpopulation as they are about the high cost of living. Both boys and girls place a lot of emphasis on having enough money so that they can go out and do things. Consequently, most teenage girls surveyed say they expect to pursue careers, even after they get married.

25 So it would seem that by the year 2000 we can expect to see more working mothers in the United States. The woman who doesn't hold down any sort of outside job but stays at home to care for her children

represents a small percentage of wives today. By the end of the century, with a few exceptions here and there, she may well have become a part of America's quaint past.

As women have joined the work force in response to economic 26 needs, one result has been increased emotional strains on the marriage and family relationships. But there's another set of pressures that has encouraged women to pursue careers. That's the power of feminist philosophy to permeate attitudes in grassroots America during the past couple of decades.

Pressure Four: Grassroots Feminist Philosophy

Many women may not agree with the most radical expressions of femi- 27 nist philosophy that have arisen in the past decade or so. But most younger women—and indeed, a majority of women in the United States—tend to agree with most of the objectives that even the radical feminist groups have been trying to achieve. The basic feminist philosophy has filtered down to the grass roots, and young boys and girls are growing up with feminist assumptions that may have been foreign to their parents and grandparents.

For example, child care and housework are no longer regraded 28 strictly as "women's work" by the young people we've polled. Also, according to the Gallup Youth Poll, most teenage girls want to go to college and pursue a career. Moreover, they expect to marry later in life and to continue working after they're married. Another poll, conducted by the *New York Times* and CBS News, revealed that only 2 percent of the youngest age group interviewed—that is, those eighteen to twenty-nine years old—preferred "traditional marriage." By this, they meant a marriage in which the husband is exclusively a provider and the wife is exclusively a homemaker and mother.

If these young people continue to hold views similar to these into 29 later life, it's likely that the changes that are occurring today in the traditional family structure will continue. For one thing, more day-care centers for children will have to be established. Consequently, the rearing of children will no longer be regarded as solely the responsibility of the family, but will become a community or institutional responsibility.

But while such developments may lessen the strain on mothers and 30 fathers, they may also weaken the bonds that hold families together. Among other things, it may become psychologically easier to get a divorce if a person is not getting along with a spouse, because the divorcing spouses will believe it's less likely that the lives of the children will be disrupted.

31   So the concept of broadening the rights of women vis-à-vis their
husbands and families has certainly encouraged women to enter the
working world in greater numbers. They're also more inclined to seek a
personal identity that isn't tied up so much in their homelife.

32   These grassroots feminist forces have brought greater benefits to
many, but at the same time they've often worked against traditional family ties, and we remain uncertain about what is going to replace them.
Feminists may argue that the traditional family caused its own
demise—or else why would supposedly content wives and daughters
have worked so hard to transform it? Whatever its theories, though,
feminism is still a factor that, in its present form, appears to exert a
destabilizing influence on many traditional familial relationships among
husbands, wives, and children.

33   As things stand now, our family lives are in a state of flux and will
probably continue to be out of balance until the year 2000. The pressures
we've discussed will continue to have an impact on our family lives in
future years. But at the same time, counterforces, which tend to drive
families back together again, are also at work.

34   One of these factors is a traditionalist strain in the large majority of
American women. The vast majority of women in this country—74 percent—continue to view marriage with children as the most interesting
and satisfying life for them personally, according to a Gallup Poll for the
White House Conference on Families released in June, 1980.

35   Another force supporting family life is the attitude of American
teenagers toward divorce. According to a recent Gallup Youth Poll, 55
percent feel that divorces are too easy to get today. Also, they're concerned about the high rate of divorce, and they want to have enduring
marriages themselves. But at the same time—in a response that reflects
the confusion of many adult Americans on this subject—67 percent of the
teens in this same poll say it's right to get a divorce if a couple doesn't get
along together. In other words, they place little importance on trying to
improve or salvage a relationship that has run into serious trouble.

36   There's a similar ambivalence in the experts we polled. As we've
seen, 33 percent of them consider family problems as a top concern today, and 26 percent think these problems will be a big difficulty in the
year 2000. But ironically, less than 3 percent suggest that strengthening
family relationships is an important consideration in planning for the future! It's obvious, then, that we're confused and ambivalent in our feelings about marriage and the family. Most people know instinctively,
without having to read a poll or a book, that happiness and satisfaction
in life are rooted largely in the quality of our personal relationships. Furthermore, the most important of those relationships usually begin at
home. So one of the greatest challenges we face before the year 2000,
both as a nation and as individuals, is how to make our all-important

family ties strong and healthy. It's only upon such a firm personal foundation that we can hope to venture forth and grapple effectively with more public problems.

The Paradox of Perfection

ARLENE SKOLNICK

Arlene Skolnick was born in 1933. A psychologist at the Institute for Human Development at the University of California at Berkeley, she has edited or coedited the following books: Family in Transition, 1983; The Intimate Environment, 1973; Rethinking Childhood, 1976; and The Psychology of Human Development, 1986. Skolnick provides a context of family history in this essay, focusing primarily on the difference between the myth of the ideal family and the realities of the changing family in the late twentieth century.

The American Family, as even readers of *Popular Mechanics* must know 1 by now, is in what Sean O'Casey would have called "a terrible state of chassis." Yet, there are certain ironies about the much-publicized crisis that give one pause.

True, the statistics seem alarming. The U.S. divorce rate, though it 2 has reached something of a plateau in recent years, remains the highest in American history. The number of births out-of-wedlock among all races and ethnic groups continues to climb. The plight of many elderly Americans subsisting on low fixed incomes is well known.

What puzzles me is an ambiguity, not in the facts, but in what we are 3 asked to make of them. A series of opinion polls conducted in 1978 by Yankelovich, Skelley, and White, for example, found that 38 percent of those surveyed had recently witnessed one or more "destructive activities" (e.g., a divorce, a separation, a custody battle) within their own families or those of their parents or siblings. At the same time, 92 percent of the respondents said the family was highly important to them as a "personal value."

Can the family be at once a cherished "value" and a troubled institu- 4 tion? I am inclined to think, in fact, that they go hand in hand. A recent "Talk of the Town" report in *The New Yorker* illustrates what I mean:

> A few months ago word was heard from Billy Gray, who used to play brother Bud in "Father Knows Best," the 1950s television show about the nice Anderson family who lived in the white frame house on a side street in some mythical Springfield—the house at which the father arrived each night swinging open the front door and singing out "Margaret, I'm home!"

Gray said he felt "ashamed" that he had ever had anything to do with the show. It was all "totally false," he said, and had caused many Americans to feel inadequate, because they thought that was the way life was supposed to be and that their own lives failed to measure up.

5   As Susan Sontag has noted in *On Photography*, mass-produced images have "extraordinary powers to determine our demands upon reality." The family is especially vulnerable to confusion between truth and illusion. What, after all, is "normal"? All of us have a backstairs view of our own families, but we know The Family, in the aggregate, only vicariously.

6   Like politics or athletics, the family has become a media event. Television offers nightly portrayals of lump-in-throat family "normalcy" (*The Waltons, Little House on the Prairie*) and even humorous "deviance" (*One Day at a Time, The Odd Couple*). Family advisers sally forth in syndicated newspaper columns to uphold standards, mend relationships, suggest counseling, and otherwise lead their readers back to the True Path. For commercial purposes, advertisers spend millions of dollars to create stirring vignettes of glamorous-but-ordinary families, the kind of family most 11-year-olds wish they had.

7   All Americans do not, of course, live in such a family, but most share an intuitive sense of what the "ideal" family should be—reflected in the precepts of religion, the conventions of etiquette, and the assumptions of law. And, characteristically, Americans tend to project the ideal back to the past, the time when virtues of all sorts are thought to have flourished.

8   We do not come off well by comparison with that golden age, nor could we, for it is as elusive and mythical as Brigadoon. If Billy Gray shames too easily, he has a valid point: While Americans view the family as the proper context for their own lives—9 out of 10 people live in one—they have no realistic context in which to view the family. Family history, until recently, was as neglected in academe as it still is in the press. [The summer 1980] White House Conference on Families is "policy-oriented," which means present-minded. The familiar, depressing charts of "leading family indicators"—marriage, divorce, illegitimacy—in newspapers and newsmagazines rarely survey the trends before World War II. The discussion, in short, lacks ballast.

9   Let us go back to before the American Revolution.

10   Perhaps what distinguishes the modern family most from its colonial counterpart is its newfound privacy. Throughout the 17th and 18th centuries, well over 90 percent of the American population lived in small rural communities. Unusual behavior rarely went unnoticed, and neighbors often intervened directly in a family's affairs, to help or to chastise.

11   The most dramatic example was the rural "charivari," prevalent in both Europe and the United States until the early 19th century. The pur-

pose of these noisy gatherings was to censure community members for familial transgressions—unusual sexual behavior, marriages between persons of grossly discrepant ages, or "household disorder," to name but a few. As historian Edward Shorter describes it in *The Making of the Modern Family:*

> Sometimes the demonstration would consist of masked individuals circling somebody's house at night, screaming, beating on pans, and blowing cow horns. . . . [O]n other occasions, the offender would be seized and marched through the streets, seated perhaps backwards on a donkey or forced to wear a placard describing his sins.

The state itself had no qualms about intruding into a family's affairs 12 by statute, if necessary. Consider 17th-century New England's "stubborn child" laws that, though never actually enforced, sanctioned the death penalty for chronic disobedience to one's parents.

If the boundaries between home and society seem blurred during 13 the colonial era, it is because they were. People were neither very emotional nor very self-conscious about family life, and, as historian John Demos points out, family and community were "joined in a relation of profound reciprocity." In his *Of Domestical Duties*, William Gouge, a 17th-century Puritan preacher, called the family "a little community." The home, like the larger community, was as much an economic as a social unit; all members of the family worked, be it on the farm, or in a shop, or in the home.

There was not much to idealize. Love was not considered the basis 14 for marriage but one possible result of it. According to historian Carl Degler, it was easier to obtain a divorce in colonial New England than anywhere else in the Western world, and the divorce rate climbed steadily throughout the 18th century, though it remained low by contemporary standards. Romantic images to the contrary, it was rare for more than two generations (parents and children) to share a household, for the simple reason that very few people lived beyond the age of 60. It is ironic that our nostalgia for the extended family—including grandparents and grandchildren—comes at a time when, thanks to improvements in health care, its existence is less threatened than ever before.

Infant mortality was high in colonial days, though not as high as we 15 are accustomed to believe, since food was plentiful and epidemics, owing to generally low population density, were few. In the mid-1700s, the average age of marriage was about 24 for men, 21 for women—not much different from what it is now. Households, on average, were larger, but not startlingly so: A typical household in 1790 included about 5.6 members, versus about 3.5 today. Illegitimacy was widespread. Premarital pregnancies reached a high in 18th-century America (10 percent of all first births) that was not equalled until the 1950s.

Form Follows Function

16 In simple demographic terms, then, the differences between the American family in colonial times and today are not all that stark; the similarities are sometimes striking.

17   The chief contrast is psychological. While Western societies have always idealized the family to some degree, the *most vivid* literary portrayals of family life before the 19th century were negative or, at best, ambivalent. In what might be called the "high tragic" tradition—including Sophocles, Shakespeare, and the Bible, as well as fairy tales and novels—the family was portrayed as a high-voltage emotional setting, laden with dark passion, sibling rivalries, and violence. There was also the "low comic" tradition—the world of henpecked husbands and tyrannical mothers-in-law.

18   It is unlikely that our 18th-century ancestors ever left the Book of Genesis or *Tom Jones* with the feeling that their own family lives were seriously flawed.

19   By the time of the Civil War, however, American attitudes toward the family had changed profoundly. The early decades of the 19th century marked the beginnings of America's gradual transformation into an urban, industrial society. In 1820, less than 8 percent of the U.S. population lived in cities; by 1860, the urban concentration approached 20 percent, and by 1900 that proportion had doubled.

20   Structurally, the American family did not immediately undergo a comparable transformation. Despite the large families of many immigrants and farmers, the size of the *average* family declined—slowly but steadily—as it had been doing since the 17th century. Infant mortality remained about the same and may even have increased somewhat, owing to poor sanitation in crowded cities. Legal divorces were easier to obtain than they had been in colonial times. Indeed, the rise in the divorce rate was a matter of some concern during the 19th century, though death, not divorce, was the prime cause of one-parent families, as it was up to 1965.

21   Functionally, however, America's industrial revolution had a lasting effect on the family. No longer was the household typically a group of interdependent workers. Now, men went to offices and factories and became breadwinners; wives stayed home to mind the hearth; children went off to the new public schools. The home was set apart from the dog-eat-dog arena of economic life; it came to be viewed as a utopian retreat or, in historian Christopher Lasch's phrase, a "haven in a heartless world." Marriage was now valued primarily for its emotional attractions. Above all, the family became something to worry about.

22   The earliest and most saccharine "sentimental model" of the family appeared in the new mass media that proliferated during the second quarter of the 19th century. Novels, tracts, newspaper articles, and

ladies' magazines—there were variations for each class of society—elaborated a "Cult of True Womanhood" in which piety, submissiveness, and domesticity dominated the pantheon of desirable feminine qualities. This quotation from *The Ladies Book* (1830) is typical:

> See, she sits, she walks, she speaks, she looks—unutterable things! Inspiration springs up in her very paths—it follows her footsteps. A halo of glory encircles her, and illuminates her whole orbit. With her, man not only feels safe, but actually renovated.

In the late 1800s, science came into the picture. The "professionalization" of the housewife took two different forms. One involved motherhood and childrearing, according to the latest scientific understanding of children's special physical and emotional needs. (It is no accident that the publishing of children's books became a major industry during this period.) The other was the domestic science movement—"home economics," basically—which focused on woman as full-time homemaker, applying "scientific" and "industrial" rationality to shopping, making meals, and housework.   23

The new ideal of the family prompted a cultural split that has endured, one that Tocqueville had glimpsed (and rather liked) in 1835. Society was divided more sharply into man's sphere and woman's sphere. Toughness, competition, and practicality were the masculine values that ruled the outside world. The softer values—affection, tranquility, piety—were worshipped in the home and the church. In contrast to the colonial view, the ideology of the "modern" family implied a critique of everything beyond the front door.   24

What is striking as one looks at the writings of the 19th-century " experts"—the physicians, clergymen, phrenologists, and "scribbling ladies"—is how little their essential message differs from that of the sociologists, psychiatrists, pediatricians, and women's magazine writers of the 20th century, particularly since World War II.   25

Instead of men's and women's spheres, of course, sociologists speak of "instrumental" and "expressive" roles. The notion of the family as a retreat from the harsh realities of the outside world crops up as "functional differentiation." And, like the 19th-century utopians who believed society could be regenerated through the perfection of family life, 20th-century social scientists have looked at the failed family as the source of most American social problems.   26

None of these who promoted the sentimental model of the family—neither the popular writers nor the academics—considered the paradox of perfectionism: the ironic possibility that it would lead to trouble. Yet it has. The image of the perfect, happy family makes ordinary families seem like failures. Small problems loom as big problems if the "normal" family is thought to be one where there are no real problems at all.   27

28   One sees this phenomenon at work on the generation of Americans born and reared during the late 19th century, the first generation reared on the mother's milk of sentimental imagery. Between 1900 and 1920, the U.S. divorce rate doubled, from four to eight divorces annually per 1,000 married couples. The jump—comparable to the 100 percent increase in the divorce rate between 1960 and 1980—is not attributable to changes in divorce laws, which were not greatly liberalized. Rather, it would appear that, as historian Thomas O'Neill believes, Americans were simply more willing to dissolve marriages that did not conform to their idea of domestic bliss—and perhaps try again.

A "Fun" Morality

29 If anything, family standards became even more demanding as the 20th century progressed. The new fields of psychology and sociology opened up whole new definitions of familial perfection. "Feelings"—fun, love, warmth, good orgasm—acquired heightened popular significance as the invisible glue of successful families.

30   Psychologist Martha Wolfenstein, in an analysis of several decades of government-sponsored infant care manuals, has documented the emergence of a "fun morality." In former days, being a good parent meant carrying out certain tasks with punctilio; if your child was clean and reasonably obedient, you had no cause to probe his psyche. Now, we are told, parents must commune with their own feelings and those of their children—an edict which has seeped into the ethos of education as well. The distinction is rather like that between religions of deed and religions of faith. It is one thing to make your child brush his teeth; it is quite another to transform the whole process into a joyous "learning experience."

31   The task of 20th-century parents has been further complicated by the advice offered them. The experts disagree with each other and often contradict themselves. The kindly Dr. Benjamin Spock, for example, is full of contradictions. In a detailed analysis of *Baby and Child Care,* historian Michael Zuckerman observes that Spock tells mothers to relax ("trust yourself") yet warns them that they have an "ominous power" to destroy their children's innocence and make them discontented "for years" or even "forever."

32   As we enter the 1980s, both family images and family realities are in a state of transition. After a century and a half, the web of attitudes and nostrums comprising the "sentimental model" is beginning to unravel. Since the mid-1960s, there has been a youth rebellion of sorts, a new "sexual revolution," a revival of feminism, and the emergence of the two-worker family. The huge postwar Baby-Boom generation is pairing off, accounting in part for the upsurge in the divorce rate (half

of all divorces occur within seven years of a first marriage). Media images of the family have become more "realistic," reflecting new patterns of family life that are emerging (and old patterns that are re-emerging).

Among social scientists, "realism" is becoming something of an 33 ideal in itself. For some of them, realism translates as pluralism: All forms of the family, by virtue of the fact that they happen to exist, are equally acceptable—from communes and cohabitation to one-parent households, homosexual marriages, and, come to think of it, the nuclear family. What was once labeled "deviant" is now merely "variant." In some college texts, "the family" has been replaced by "family systems." Yet, this new approach does not seem to have squelched perfectionist standards. Indeed, a palpable strain of perfectionism runs through the pop literature on "alternative" family lifestyles.

For the majority of scholars, realism means a more down-to-earth 34 view of the American household. Rather than seeing the family as a haven of peace and tranquility, they have begun to recognize that even "normal" families are less than ideal, that intimate relations of any sort inevitably involve antagonism as well as love. Conflict and change are inherent in social life. If the family is now in a state of flux, such is the nature of resilient institutions; if it is beset by problems, so is life. The family will survive.

TOPICS FOR EXPLORING SOURCES ON FAMILIES

1. Many of the writers in this section define family in broader terms than immediate relatives, using the term "extended family" to suggest a wide range of distant relatives and friends. Some have suggested that for various reasons, there are no more extended families. Do some research on this matter, and develop an argument about changes in the extended family in the past twenty-five years or so.

2. The word "family" has been used to designate a number of cultural groups. Jane Howard, for example, mentions the Bloomsbury Group in London, a group of artists and writers in the early part of the century. The Beats or Beat Generation writers of the fifties have also been considered a sort of artistic family. Do some research on other artistic or cultural "families" such as this. What artistic "families" are important in the nineties?

3. Researching family history is important to maintaining a sense of family. Such research involves more than mere genealogy—finding out who one's ancestors are; it also requires drawing on the rich resources of older members of the family who can remember events and tell stories. Many people today are interested in their roots. Do some research on the increased interest in genealogy and oral history in the past twenty-five years. What has caused this interest? What is the importance of oral history? Do some research on your own family and explain why such research is important.

4. In the American West, during the nineteenth century, the word "family" was used to refer to certain outlaw groups. The word "family" took on a much more sinister meaning in the 1960s when a group of followers of Charles Manson were named the "Manson Family" in newspapers and magazines. Since that time other charismatic figures, some of them religious figures, have influenced "family" groups of followers to engage in violent and destructive acts. Do some research on this use of the word "family," and try to develop an argument on the effect of charismatic leaders of such families.

5. Jane Howard discusses the importance of family rituals. Do some research on the nature and importance of rituals in various contexts—religious, social, cultural, and so forth—and then explain why rituals surrounding such life events as births, weddings, holidays, and funerals are important, or not important, for the maintaining of families. How important are rituals in your own family or culture?

6. The increasingly transient nature of people in the United States has affected families in the past several decades. People move for a variety of reasons, for example, business transfer, military reassignment, or a desire for a better life. Some say that Americans move more than people in other cultures. Find some data on how often people move from one area to another in the United States. Do some research on the reasons for and the effects of frequent moves.

7. Michael Novak points out that many people today have decided not to have children. Find some data to determine how prevalent this attitude is. Is it a new attitude? What has caused it? What effect might it have? Is a specific economic or cultural group making this decision? Can a couple without children be considered a "family"?

8. The so-called generation gap has always been a fact of human society; it perhaps creates its most profound impact within families in which parents do not understand children and children cannot identify with parents because of social changes that have taken place across generations. Is the generation gap more pronounced now than it was one or two generations ago? Find data to answer this question.

9. A relatively new phenomenon in U.S. society is how to care for aged parents and grandparents. In some cultures, there is no question that children have a personal responsibility to care for their parents, whereas in America, children must decide whether to care for aging parents or turn this task over to professional or social organizations. Do some research on this subject. Consider the needs of both parents and children.

10. Many social and economic factors have resulted in various forms of child abandonment in today's society. Michael Novak points out that the abandonment of children in varying degrees takes place not only in poor families but also in middle- and upper-class families as well. Parents, out of necessity or choice, focus less on their children than on their work or other activities. Define and clarify what you mean by child abandonment and do some research to determine whether abandonment takes place more in poor in in well-to-do families.

11. One of the strongest conventions of families is marriage. But marriage is an institution that many commentators say is crumbling in America and through-

out the rest of the world. Some research has indicated that whereas it is natural for humans to bond with each other, it is not natural for them to remain married to one person for life, or even to be faithful to one person for life. Is marriage doomed to failure?

12. Some have said that the breakup of the American family has contributed to declining school work by students. Do some research on this. What is the cause-and-effect relationship, if any, between the two phenomena?

13. Other causes of the breakup of the American family have been attributed to the feminist movement and the increase of so-called midlife crises in men. Do some research on these two phenomena. What are their causes and effects?

14. Do some research on the importance of family life for Native Americans, ghetto and rural southern African Americans, Latinos, and Appalachian mountain people. Have family attitudes changed in these groups? If so, what effect have these changes had?

15. What effect has the psychology of the so-called Me Generation had on family life? Do research on various pop psychology movements in the 1960s and 1970s. What are some of the tenets of these movements that may have affected family life?

16. Images of family life have changed radically on television from the 1950s up to the present. Do some research on such images of family life in the 1950s and 1960s as depicted in such shows as "Father Knows Best," "Ozzie and Harriet," "Leave It to Beaver," and "The Donna Reed Show." Compare them to family images in television shows today.

17. Many have suggested that the rise of urban youth gangs is directly related to the breakup of family. Do some research on the possible correlation between loss of family and the creation of a substitute family in gangs.

18. New kinds of family configurations have come into being in the last three decades, among them, single-parent families, gay families, and stepfamilies. Do some research on how the definition of family has changed over the past decades. What effects have these changes had on family life?

19. Do some research on single-parent families. What particular problems do such families encounter? What relationship is there, if any, between single-parent families and children who must care for themselves after school? What are the social effects of the increase in so-called latchkey children?

20. Discuss the benefits and problems of the increasing dependence on day care centers. Do some research on day care centers and their effect on child development and modern society.

21. In spite of attempts to reduce the differences between feminine and masculine expectations and responsibilities in modern society, what differences still exist within family structures between what women are expected to do and what men are expected to do?

22. Twenty-five years ago, there was little question that the mother would get custody of the children after divorce. Today more fathers are getting custody. What has caused this shift? Do some research on this subject. Find some data on how often fathers get custody and why they do.

23. Spouse abuse has received more attention in the past ten years than ever before. Is such abuse happening more now, or are more people willing to talk about it Are women more often the victims of such abuse than men? Why? Is spouse abuse something that children learn from their parents?

24. In cases of divorce, the father is more often seen as the one who deserts the family, the one who shirks his responsibility to support the family, the one who finds it easier to walk away from his role as parent. Is this assumption borne out by the facts? Are mothers becoming more willing to abandon their role as parent than before?

25. It may be that people are staying single longer now than they once did. Find out if this is indeed the case. Suggest some reasons for this. Discuss some of the implications for the family in particular and society in general.

WORK

Work

BERTRAND RUSSELL

Bertrand Russell was born in Trelleck, England, in 1872. He was educated at Trinity College, Cambridge. A famous philosopher, mathematician, and social activist, he won the Nobel Prize for Literature in 1950. His greatest works are The Principles of Mathematics, 1903, and Principia Mathematica, 1910–1913. Other important works include The Problems of Philosophy, 1912; Mysticism and Logic, 1918; Analysis of Mind, 1921; and History of Western Philosophy, 1945. He died in 1970.

In this essay, Russell argues that work is more desirable than idleness, for it prevents boredom and provides the opportunity for success. He also describes the two basic elements that make work interesting: the exercise of skill and the construction of something.

Whether work should be placed among the causes of happiness or 1 among the causes of unhappiness may perhaps be regarded as a doubtful question. There is certainly much work which is exceedingly irksome, and an excess of work is always very painful. I think, however, that, provided work is not excessive in amount, even the dullest work is to most people less painful than idleness. There are in work all grades, from mere relief to tedium up to the profoundest delights, according to the nature of the work and the abilities of the worker. Most of the work that most people have to do is not in itself interesting, but even such work has certain great advantages. To begin with, it fills a good many hours of the day without the need of deciding what one shall do. Most people, when they are left free to fill their own time according to their own choice, are at a loss to think of anything sufficiently pleasant to be worth doing. And whatever they decide on, they are troubled by the feeling that something else would have been pleasanter. To be able to fill leisure intelligently is the last product of civilization, and at present very few people have reached this level. Moreover the exercise of choice is in itself tiresome. Except to people with unusual initiative it is positively agreeable to be told what to do at each hour of the day, provided the orders are not too unpleasant. Most of the idle rich suffer unspeakable boredom as the price of their freedom from drudgery. At times they may find relief by hunting big game in Africa, or by flying round the world, but the number of such sensations is limited, especially after youth is past. Accordingly the more intelligent rich men work nearly as hard as if they were poor, while rich women for the most part keep themselves busy with innumerable trifles of whose earth-shaking importance they are firmly persuaded.

2   Work therefore is desirable, first and foremost, as a preventive of boredom, for the boredom that a man feels when he is doing necessary though uninteresting work is as nothing in comparison with the boredom that he feels when he has nothing to do with his days. With this advantage of work another is associated, namely that it makes holidays much more delicious when they come. Provided a man does not have to work so hard as to impair his vigor, he is likely to find far more zest in his free time than an idle man could possibly find.

3   The second advantage of most paid work and of some unpaid work is that it gives chances of success and opportunities for ambition. In most work success is measured by income, and while our capitalistic society continues, this is inevitable. It is only where the best work is concerned that this measure ceases to be the natural one to apply. The desire that men feel to increase their income is quite as much a desire for success as for the extra comforts that a higher income can procure. However dull work may be, it becomes bearable if it is a means of building up a reputation, whether in the world at large or only in one's own circle. Continuity of purpose is one of the most essential ingredients of happiness in the long run, and for most men this comes chiefly through their work. In this respect those women whose lives are occupied with housework are much less fortunate than men, or than women who work outside the home. The domesticated wife does not receive wages, has no means of bettering herself, is taken for granted by her husband (who sees practically nothing of what she does), and is valued by him not for her housework but for quite other qualities. Of course this does not apply to those women who are sufficiently well-to-do to make beautiful houses and beautiful gardens and become the envy of their neighbors; but such women are comparatively few, and for the great majority housework cannot bring as much satisfaction as work of other kinds brings to men and to professional women.

4   The satisfaction of killing time and of affording some outlet, however modest, for ambition, belongs to most work, and is sufficient to make even a man whose work is dull happier on the average than a man who has no work at all. But when work is interesting, it is capable of giving satisfaction of a far higher order than mere relief from tedium. The kinds of work in which there is some interest may be arranged in a hierarchy. I shall begin with those which are only mildly interesting and end with those that are worthy to absorb the whole energies of a great man.

5   Two chief elements make work interesting: first, the exercise of skill, and second, construction.

Every man who has acquired some unusual skill enjoys exercising it 6 until it has become a matter of course, or until he can no longer improve himself. This motive to activity begins in early childhood: a boy who can stand on his head becomes reluctant to stand on his feet. A great deal of work gives the same pleasure that is to be derived from games of skill. The work of a lawyer or a politician must contain in a more delectable form a great deal of the same pleasure that is to be derived from playing bridge. Here of course there is not only the exercise of skill but the out-witting of a skilled opponent. Even where this competitive element is absent, however, the performance of difficult feats is agreeable. A man who can do stunts in an aeroplane finds the pleasure so great that for the sake of it he is willing to risk his life. I imagine that an able surgeon, in spite of the painful circumstances in which his work is done, derives sat-isfaction from the exquisite precision of his operations. The same kind of pleasure, though in a less intense form, is to be derived from a great deal of work of a humbler kind. All skilled work can be pleasurable, pro-vided the skill required is either variable or capable of indefinite im-provement. If these conditions are absent, it will cease to be interesting when a man has acquired his maximum skill. A man who runs three-mile races will cease to find pleasure in this occupation when he passes the age at which he can beat his own previous record. Fortunately there is a very considerable amount of work in which new circumstances call for new skill and a man can go on improving, at any rate until he has reached middle age. In some kinds of skilled work, such as politics, for example, it seems that men are at their best between sixty and seventy, the reason being that in such occupations a wide experience of other men is essential. For this reason successful politicians are apt to be hap-pier at the age of seventy than any other men of equal age. Their only competitors in this respect are the men who are the heads of big busi-nesses.

There is, however, another element possessed by the best work, 7 which is even more important as a source of happiness than is the exer-cise of skill. This is the element of constructiveness. In some work, though by no means in most, something is built up which remains as a monument when the work is completed. We may distinguish construc-tion from destruction by the following criterion. In construction the ini-tial state of affairs is comparatively haphazard, while the final state of affairs embodies a purpose: in destruction the reverse is the case; the ini-tial state of affairs embodies a purpose, while the final state of affairs is haphazard, that is to say, all that is intended by the destroyer is to pro-duce a state of affairs which does not embody a certain purpose. This criterion applies in the most literal and obvious case, namely the con-struction and destruction of buildings. In constructing a building a previously made plan is carried out, whereas in destroying it no one decides exactly how the materials are to lie when the demolition is complete. Destruction is of course necessary very often as a preliminary to subsequent construction; in that case it is part of a whole which is constructive. But not infrequently a man will engage in activities of which the purpose is destructive without regard to any construction that may come after. Frequently he will conceal this from himself by the belief that he is only sweeping away in order to build afresh, but it is generally possible to unmask this pretense, when it is a pretense, by asking him what the subsequent construction is to be. On this subject it will be found that he will speak vaguely and without enthusiasm, whereas on the preliminary destruction he has spoken precisely and with zest. This applies to not a few revolutionaries and militarists and other apostles of violence. They are actuated, usually without their own knowledge, by hatred: the destruction of what they hate is their real purpose, and they are comparatively indifferent to the question what is to come after it. Now I cannot deny that in the work of destruction as in the work of construction there may be joy. It is a fiercer joy, perhaps at moments more intense, but it is less profoundly satisfying, since the result is one in which little satisfaction is to be found. You kill your enemy, and when he is dead your occupation is gone, and the satisfaction that you derive from victory quickly fades. The work of construction, on the other hand, when completed is delightful to contemplate, and moreover is never so fully completed that there is nothing further to do about it. The most satisfactory purposes are those that lead on indefinitely from one success to another without ever coming to a dead end; and in this respect it will be found that construction is a greater source of happiness than destruction. Perhaps it would be more correct to say that those who find satisfaction in construction find in it greater satisfaction than the lovers of destruction can find in destruction, for if once you have become filled with hate you will not easily derive from construction the pleasure which another man would derive from it.

8   At the same time few things are so likely to cure the habit of hatred as the opportunity to do constructive work of an important kind.

9   The satisfaction to be derived from success in a great constructive enterprise is one of the most massive that life has to offer, although unfortunately in its highest forms it is open only to men of exceptional ability. Nothing can rob a man of the happiness of successful achievement in an important piece of work, unless it be the proof that after all his work was bad. There are many forms of such satisfaction. The man who by a scheme of irrigation has caused the wilderness to blossom like the rose enjoys it in one of its most tangible forms. The creation of an organization may be a work of supreme importance. So is the work of those few

statesmen who have devoted their lives to producing order out of chaos, of whom Lenin is the supreme type in our day. The most obvious examples are artists and men of science. Shakespeare says of his verse: "So long as men can breathe, or eyes can see, so long lives this." And it cannot be doubted that the thought consoled him for misfortune. In his sonnets he maintains that the thought of his friend reconciled him to life, but I cannot help suspecting that the sonnets he wrote to his friend were even more effective for this purpose than the friend himself. Great artists and great men of science do work which is in itself delightful; while they are doing it, it secures them the respect of those whose respect is worth having, which gives them the most fundamental kind of power, namely, power over men's thoughts and feelings. They have also the most solid reasons for thinking well of themselves. This combination of fortunate circumstances ought, one would think, to be enough to make any man happy. Nevertheless it is not so. Michael Angelo, for example, was a profoundly unhappy man, and maintained (not, I am sure, with truth) that he would not have troubled to produce works of art if he had not had to pay the debts of his impecunious relations. The power to produce great art is very often, though by no means always, associated with a temperamental unhappiness, so great that but for the joy which the artist derives from his work, he would be driven to suicide. We cannot, therefore, maintain that even the greatest work must make a man happy; we can only maintain that it must make him less unhappy. Men of science, however, are far less often temperamentally unhappy than artists are, and in the main the men who do great work in science are happy men, whose happiness is derived primarily from their work.

One of the causes of unhappiness among intellectuals in the present 10 day is that so many of them, especially those whose skill is literary, find no opportunity for the independent exercise of their talents, but have to hire themselves out to rich corporations directed by Philistines, who insist upon their producing what they themselves regard as pernicious nonsense. If you were to inquire among journalists in either England or America whether they believed in the policy of the newspaper for which they worked, you would find, I believe, that only a small minority do so; the rest, for the sake of a livelihood, prostitute their skill to purposes which they believe to be harmful. Such work cannot bring any real satisfaction, and in the course of reconciling himself to the doing of it, a man has to make himself so cynical that he can no longer derive wholehearted satisfaction from anything whatever. I cannot condemn men who undertake work of this sort, since starvation is too serious an alternative, but I think that where it is possible to do work that is satisfactory to a man's constructive impulses without entirely starving, he will be well advised from the point of view of his own happiness if he chooses it in preference to work much more highly paid but not seeming to him worth doing on its own account. Without self-respect genuine happiness is scarcely possible. And the man who is ashamed of his work can hardly achieve self-respect.

11   The satisfaction of constructive work, though it may, as things are, be the privilege of a minority, can nevertheless be the privilege of a quite large minority. Any man who is his own master in his work can feel it; so can any man whose work appears to him useful and requires considerable skill. The production of satisfactory children is a difficult constructive work capable of affording profound satisfaction. Any woman who has achieved this can feel that as a result of her labor the world contains something of value which it would not otherwise contain.

12   Human beings differ profoundly in regard to the tendency to regard their lives as a whole. To some men it is natural to do so, and essential to happiness to be able to do so with some satisfaction. To others life is a series of detached incidents without directed movement and without unity. I think the former sort are more likely to achieve happiness than the latter, since they will gradually build up those circumstances from which they can derive contentment and self-respect, whereas the others will be blown about by the winds of circumstance now this way, now that, without ever arriving at any haven. The habit of viewing life as a whole is an essential part both of wisdom and of true morality, and is one of the things which ought to be encouraged in education. Consistent purpose is not enough to make life happy, but it is an almost indispensable condition of a happy life. And consistent purpose embodies itself mainly in work.

Work in an Alienated Society   ❦

ERICH FROMM

Erich Fromm was born in 1900 in Frankfurt, Germany, where he was educated and trained as a psychoanalyst. He fled the Nazis in 1940 and became a naturalized U.S. citizen. His books include Escape from Freedom, 1941; The Sane Society, 1955; The Art of Loving, 1956; and To Have or to Be, 1976. He died in 1980. In this selection from The Sane Society, Fromm focuses on the industrial worker who too often feels that work is merely an unnatural, disagreeable, and meaningless means of getting a paycheck, therefore devoid of dignity and purpose.

What becomes the meaning of *work* in an alienated society?   1

. . . Since this problem is of utmost importance, not only for the un- 2
derstanding of present-day society, but also for any attempt to create a
saner society, I want to deal with the nature of work separately and more
extensively in the following pages.

Unless man exploits others, he has to work in order to live. However 3
primitive and simple his method of work may be, by the very fact of production, he has risen above the animal kingdom; rightly has he been defined as "the animal that produces." But work is not only an inescapable
necessity for man. Work is also his liberator from nature, his creator as a
social and independent being. *In the process of work, that is, the molding
and changing of nature outside of himself, man molds and changes himself.* He
emerges from nature by mastering her; he develops his powers of cooperation, of reason, his sense of beauty. He separates himself from nature, from the original unity with her, but at the same time unites himself
with her again as her master and builder. The more his work develops,
the more his individuality develops. In molding nature and re-creating
her, he learns to make use of his powers, increasing his skill and cre-
ativeness. Whether we think of the beautiful paintings in the caves of
Southern France, the ornaments on weapons among primitive people,
the statues and temples of Greece, the cathedrals of the Middle Ages, the
chairs and tables made by skilled craftsmen, or the cultivation of flowers, trees or corn by peasants—all are expressions of the creative transformation of nature by man's reason and skill.

In Western history, craftsmanship, especially as it developed in the 4
thirteenth and fourteenth centuries, constitutes one of the peaks in the
evolution of creative work. Work was not only a useful activity, but one
which carried with it a profound satisfaction. The main features of
craftsmanship have been very lucidly expressed by C. W. Mills. "There is
no ulterior motive in work other than the product being made and the
processes of its creation. The details of daily work are meaningful because they are not detached in the worker's mind from the product of
the work. The worker is free to control his own working action. The
craftsman is thus able to learn from his work; and to use and develop his
capacities and skills in its prosecution. There is no split of work and play,
or work and culture. The craftsman's way of livelihood determines and
infuses his entire mode of living.*

With the collapse of the medieval structure, and the beginning of the 5
modern mode of production, the meaning and function of work changed

---

* C. W. Mills, White Collar, Oxford University Press, New York, 1951, p. 2201946, p. 179.

fundamentally, especially in the Protestant countries. Man, being afraid of his newly won freedom, was obsessed by the need to subdue his doubts and fears by developing a feverish activity. The outcome of this activity, success or failure, decided his salvation, indicating whether he was among the saved or the lost souls. *Work, instead of being an activity satisfying in itself and pleasurable, became a duty and an obsession.* The more it was possible to gain riches by work, the more it became a pure means to the aim of wealth and success. Work became, in Max Weber's terms, the chief factor in a system of "inner-worldly asceticism," an answer to man's sense of aloneness and isolation.

6   However, work in this sense existed only for the upper and middle classes, those who could amass some capital and employ the work of others. For the vast majority of those who had only their physical energy to sell, work became nothing but forced labor. The worker in the eighteenth or nineteenth century who had to work sixteen hours if he did not want to starve was not doing it because he served the Lord in this way, nor because his success would show that he was among the "chosen" ones, but because he was forced to sell his energy to those who had the means of exploiting it. The first centuries of the modern era find the meaning of work divided into that of *duty* among the middle class, and that of *forced labor* among those without property.

7   The religious attitude toward work as a duty, which was still so prevalent in the nineteenth century, has been changing considerably in the last decades. Modern man does not know what to do with himself, how to spend his lifetime meaningfully, and he is driven to work in order to avoid an unbearable boredom. But work has ceased to be a moral and religious obligation in the sense of the middle-class attitude of the eighteenth and nineteenth centuries. Something new has emerged. Ever-increasing production, the drive to make bigger and better things, have become aims in themselves, new ideals. Work has become alienated from the working person.

8   What happens to the industrial worker? He spends his best energy for seven or eight hours a day in producing "something." He needs his work in order to make a living, but his role is essentially a passive one. He fulfills a small isolated function in a complicated and highly organized process of production, and is never confronted with "his" product as a whole, at least not as a producer, but only as a consumer, provided he has the money to buy "his" product in a store. He is concerned neither with the whole product in its physical aspects nor with its wider economic and social aspects. He is put in a certain place, has to carry out a certain task, but does not participate in the organization or management of the work. He is not interested, nor does he know why one produces this, instead of another commodity—what relation it has to the

needs of society as a whole. The shoes, the cars, the electric bulbs, are produced by "the enterprise," using the machines. He is a part of the machine, rather than its master as an active agent. The machine, instead of being in his service to do work for him which once had to be performed by sheer physical energy, has become his master. Instead of the machine being the substitute for human energy, man has become a substitute for the machine. *His work can be defined as the performance of acts which cannot yet be performed by machines.*

Work is a means of getting money, not in itself a meaningful human   9 activity. P. Drucker, observing workers in the automobile industry, expresses this idea very succinctly: "For the great majority of automobile workers, the only meaning of the job is in the pay check, not in anything connected with the work or the product. Work appears as something unnatural, a disagreeable, meaningless, and stultifying condition of getting the pay check, devoid of dignity as well as of importance. No wonder that this puts a premium on slovenly work, on slowdowns, and on other tricks to get the same pay check with less work. No wonder that this results in an unhappy and discontented worker—because a pay check is not enough to base one's self-respect on."[†]

This relationship of the worker to his work is an outcome of the whole social   10 organization of which he is a part. Being "employed,"[‡] he is not an active agent, has no responsibility except the proper performance of the isolated piece of work he is doing, and has little interest except the one of bringing home enough money to support himself and his family. Nothing more is expected of him, or wanted from him. He is part of the equipment hired by capital, and his role and function are determined by this quality of being a piece of equipment. In recent decades, increasing attention has been paid to the psychology of the worker, and to his attitude toward his work, to the "human problem of industry"; but this very formulation is indicative of the underlying attitude; there is a human being spending most of his lifetime at work, and what should be discussed is the *"industrial problem of human beings,"* rather than *"the human problem of industry."*

Most investigations in the field of industrial psychology are con-   11 cerned with the question of how the productivity of the individual worker can be increased, and how he can be made to work with less friction; psychology has lent its services to "human engineering," an attempt to treat the worker and employee like a machine which runs better when it is well oiled. While Taylor was primarily concerned with a better organization of the technical use of the worker's physical powers,

---

[†] Peter F. Drucker, *Concept of the Corporation*, The John Day Company, New York, 1946, p. 179.
[‡] The English "employed" and the German *angestellt* are terms which refer to things rather than to human beings.

most industrial psychologists are mainly concerned with the manipulation of the worker's psyche. The underlying idea can be formulated like this: If he works better when he is happy, then let us make him happy, secure, satisfied, or anything else, provided it raises his output and diminishes friction. In the name of "human relations," the worker is treated with all devices which suit a completely alienated person; even happiness and human values are recommended in the interest of better relations with the public. Thus, for instance, according to *Time* magazine, one of the best-known American psychiatrists said to a group of fifteen hundred Supermarket executives: "It's going to be an increased satisfaction to our customers if we are happy. . . . It is going to pay off in cold dollars and cents to management, if we could put some of these general principles of values, human relationships, really into practice." One speaks of "human relations" and one means the most in-human relations, those between alienated automatons; one speaks of happiness and means the perfect routinization which has driven out the last doubt and all spontaneity.

12   The alienated and profoundly unsatisfactory character of work results in two reactions: one, the ideal of complete *laziness;* the other a deep-seated, though often unconscious *hostility* toward work and everything and everybody connected with it.

13   It is not difficult to recognize the widespread longing for the state of complete laziness and passivity. Our advertising appeals to it even more than to sex. There are, of course, many useful and labor saving gadgets. But this usefulness often serves only as a rationalization for the appeal to complete passivity and receptivity. A package of breakfast cereal is being advertised as *"new—easier to eat."* An electric toaster is advertised with these words: ". . . the most distinctly different toaster in the world! Everything is done *for* you with this new toaster. You need not even bother to lower the bread. Power-action, through a unique electric motor, *gently takes the bread right out of your fingers!"* How many courses in languages, or other subjects are announced with the slogan "effortless learning, no more of the old drudgery." Everybody knows the picture of the elderly couple in the advertisement of a life-insurance company, who have retired at the age of sixty, and spend their life in the complete bliss of having nothing to do except just travel.

14   Radio and television exhibit another element of this yearning for laziness: the idea of "push-button power"; by pushing a button, or turning a knob on my machine, I have the power to produce music, speeches, ball games, and on the television set, to command events of the world to appear before my eyes. The pleasure of driving cars certainly rests partly upon this same satisfaction of the wish for push-button power. By the effortless pushing of a button, a powerful machine is set in motion; little

skill or effort is needed to make the driver feel that he is the ruler of space.

But there is far more serious and deep-seated reaction to the mean- 15 inglessness and boredom of work. It is a hostility toward work which is much less conscious than our craving for laziness and inactivity. Many a businessman feels himself the prisoner of his business and the commodities he sells; he has a feeling of fraudulency about his product and a secret contempt for it. He hates his customers, who force him to put up a show in order to sell. He hates his competitors because they are a threat; his employees as well as his superiors, because he is in a constant competitive fight with them. Most important of all, he hates himself, because he sees his life passing by, without making any sense beyond the momentary intoxication of success. Of course, this hate and contempt for others and for oneself, and for the very things one produces, is mainly unconscious, and only occasionally comes up to awareness in a fleeting thought, which is sufficiently disturbing to be set aside as quickly as possible.

What Is the Point of Working?

LANCE MORROW

Lance Morrow was born in 1939 in Philadelphia, Pennsylvania. He received his education at Harvard University and has worked as a reporter for the Washington Star and as a contributing editor to Time magazine. He won the National Magazine Award in 1981 for his essays in Time. His books include The Chief: A Memoir of Fathers and Sons, 1985; America: A Rediscovery, 1987; and Fishing in the Tiber, 1989.

Morrow provides a brief history of attitudes toward work in American society and examines whether the work ethic has died or has become weaker because of changes in the psychology of work.

When God foreclosed on Eden, he condemned Adam and Eve to go to 1 work. Work has never recovered from that humiliation. From the beginning, the Lord's word said that work was something bad: a punishment, the great stone of mortality and toil laid upon a human spirit that might otherwise soar in the infinite, weightless playfulness of grace.

A perfectly understandable prejudice against work has prevailed 2 ever since. Most work in the life of the world has been hard, but since it was grindingly inevitable, it hardly seemed worth complaining about very much. Work was simply the business of life, as matter-of-fact as sex and breathing. In recent years, however, the ancient discontent has grown elaborately articulate. The worker's usual old bitching has gone to college. Grim tribes of sociologists have reported back from office and factory that most workers find their labor mechanical, boring, imprisoning, stultifying, repetitive, dreary, heartbreaking. In his 1972 book *Working*, Studs Terkel began "This book, being about work, is, by its very nature, about violence—to the spirit as well as to the body." The historical horrors of industrialization (child labor, Dickensian squalor, the dark satanic mills) translate into the 20th century's robotic busywork on the line, tightening the same damned screw on the Camaro's fire-wall assembly, going nuts to the banging, jangling Chaplin-esque whirr of modern materialism in labor, bringing forth issue, disgorging itself upon the market.

3   The lamentations about how awful work is prompt an answering wail from the management side of the chasm: nobody wants to work any more. As American productivity, once the exuberant engine of national wealth, has dipped to an embarrassingly uncompetitive low, Americans have shaken their heads: the country's old work ethic is dead. About the only good words for it now emanate from Ronald Reagan and certain beer commercials. Those ads are splendidly mythic playlets, romantic idealizations of men in groups who blast through mountains or pour plumingly molten steel in factories, the work all grit and grin. Then they retire to flip around iced cans of sacramental beer and debrief one another in a warm sundown glow of accomplishment. As for Reagan, in his presidential campaign he enshrined work in his rhetorical "community of values," along with family, neighborhood, peace and freedom. He won by a landslide.

4   Has the American work ethic really expired? Is some old native eagerness to level wilderness and dig and build and invent now collapsing toward a decadence of dope, narcissism, income transfers and aerobic self-actualization?

5   The idea of work—work as an ethic, an abstraction—arrived rather late in the history of toil. Whatever edifying and pietistic things may have been said about work over the centuries (Kahlil Gibran called work "love made visible," and the Benedictines say, "To work is to pray"), humankind has always tried to avoid it whenever possible. The philosophical swells of ancient Greece thought work was degrading; they kept an underclass to see to the laundry and other details of basic social maintenance. That prejudice against work persisted down the centuries in other aristocracies. It is supposed, however, to be inherently un-American. Edward Kennedy likes to tell the story of how, during his first campaign for the Senate, his opponent said scornfully in a debate: "This man has never worked a day in his life!" Kennedy says that the next morning

as he was shaking hands at a factory gate, one worker leaned toward him and confided, "You ain't missed a goddamned thing."

The Protestant work ethic, which sanctified work and turned it into 6 vocation, arrived only a few centuries ago in the formulations of Martin Luther and John Calvin. In that scheme, the worker collaborates with God to do the work of the universe, the great design. One scholar, Leland Ryken of Illinois' Wheaton College, has pointed out that American politicians and corporate leaders who preach about the work ethic do not understand the Puritans' original, crucial linkage between human labor and God's will.

During the 19th century industrialization of America, the idea of 7 work's inherent virtue may have seemed temporarily implausible to generations who labored in the mines and mills and sweatshops. The century's huge machinery of production punished and stunned those who ran it.

And yet for generations of immigrants, work *was* ultimately avail- 8 ing; the numb toil of an illiterate grandfather got the father a foothold and a high school education, and the son wound up in college or even law school. A woman who died in the Triangle Shirtwaist Co. fire [1911] in lower Manhattan had a niece who made it to the halcyon Bronx, and another generation on, the family went to Westchester County. So for millions of Americans, as they labored through the complexities of generations, work worked, and the immigrant work ethic came at last to merge with the Protestant work ethic.

The motive of work was all. To work for mere survival is desperate. 9 To work for a better life for one's children and grandchildren lends the labor a fierce dignity. That dignity, an unconquerably hopeful energy and aspiration—driving, persisting like a life force—is the American quality that many find missing now.

The work ethic is not dead, but it is weaker now. The psychology of 10 work is much changed in America. The acute, painful memory of the Great Depression used to enforce a disciplined and occasionally docile approach to work—in much the way that older citizens in the Soviet Union do not complain about scarce food and overpopulated apartments, because they remember how much more horrible everything was during the war. But the generation of the Depression is retiring and dying off, and today's younger workers, though sometimes laid off and kicked around by recessions and inflation, still do not keep in dark storage that residual apocalyptic memory of Hoovervilles and the Dust Bowl and banks capsizing.

Today elaborate financial cushions—unemployment insurance, union 11 benefits, welfare payments, food stamps and so on—have made it less catastrophic to be out of a job for a while. Work is still a profoundly respectable thing in America. Most Americans suffer a sense of loss, of diminution, even of worthlessness, if they are thrown out on the street. But the blow seldom carries the life-and-death implications it once had, the sense of personal ruin. Besides, the wild and notorious behavior of the economy takes a certain amount of personal shame out of jobless-ness; if Ford closes down a plant in New Jersey and throws 3,700 work-ers into the unemployment lines, the guilt falls less on individuals than on Japanese imports or American car design or an extortionate OPEC [Organization of Petroleum Exporting Countries].

12   Because today's workers are better educated than those in the past, their expectations are higher. Many younger Americans have rearranged their ideas about what they want to get out of life. While their fathers and grandfathers and great-grandfathers concentrated hard upon plow and drill press and pressure gauge and tort, some younger workers now ask previously unimaginable questions about the point of knocking themselves out. For the first time in the history of the world, masses of people in industrially advanced countries no longer have to focus their minds upon work as the central concern of their existence.

13   In the formulation of Psychologist Abraham Maslow, work func-tions in a hierarchy of needs: first, work provides food and shelter, basic human maintenance. After that, it can address the need for security and then for friendship and "belongingness." Next, the demands of the ego arise, the need for respect. Finally, men and woman assert a larger desire for "self-actualization." That seems a harmless and even worthy enter-prise but sometimes degenerates into self-infatuation, a vaporously self-ish discontent that dead-ends in isolation, the empty face that gazes back from the mirror.

14   Of course in patchwork, pluralistic America, different classes and ethnic groups are perched at different stages in the work hierarchy. The immigrants—legal and illegal—who still flock densely to America are fighting for the foothold that the jogging tribes of self-actualizers achieved three generations ago. The zealously ambitious Koreans who run New York City's best vegetable markets, or boat people try-ing to open a restaurant, or chicanos who struggle to start a small busi-ness in the *barrio* are still years away from est and the Sierra Club. Working women, to the extent that they are new at it, now form a powerful source of ambition and energy. Feminism—and financial need—have made them, in effect, a sophisticated-immigrant wave upon the economy.

15   Having to work to stay alive, to build a future, gives one's exertions a tough moral simplicity. The point of work in that case is so obvious that it need not be discussed. But apart from the sheer necessity of sus-taining life, is there some inherent worth in work? Carlyle believed that "all work, even cotton spinning, is noble; work is alone noble." Was he right?

It is seigneurial cant to romanticize work that is truly detestable and 16 destructive to workers. But misery and drudgery are always comparative. Despite the sometimes nostalgic haze around their images, the pre-industrial peasant and the 19th century American farmer did brutish work far harder than the assembly line. The untouchable who sweeps excrement in the streets of Bombay would react with blank incomprehension to the malaise of some $17-an-hour workers on a Chrysler assembly line. The Indian, after all, has passed from "alienation" into a degradation that is almost mystical. In Nicaragua, the average 19-year-old peasant has worked longer and harder than most Americans of middle age. Americans prone to restlessness about the spiritual disappointments of work should consult unemployed young men and women in their own ghettos: they know with painful clarity the importance of the personal dignity that a job brings.

Americans often fall into fallacies of misplaced sympathy. Psycholo- 17 gist Maslow, for example, once wrote that he found it difficult "to conceive of feeling proud of myself, self-loving and self-respecting, if I were working, for example, in some chewing-gum factory . . ." Well, two weeks ago, Warner-Lambert announced that it would close down its gum-manufacturing American Chicle factory in Long Island City, N.Y.; the workers who had spent years there making Dentyne and Chiclets were distraught. "It's a beautiful place to work," one feeder-catcher-packer of chewing gum said sadly. "It's just like home." There is a peculiar elitist arrogance in those who discourse on the brutalizations of work simply because they cannot imagine themselves performing the job. Certainly workers often feel abstracted out, reduced sometimes to dreary robotic functions. But almost everyone commands endlessly subtle systems of adaptation; people can make the work their own and even cherish it against all academic expectations. Such adaptations are often more important than the famous but theoretical alienation from the process and product of labor.

Work is still the complicated and crucial core of most lives, the occu- 18 pation melded inseparably to the identity; Freud said that the successful psyche is one capable of love and of work. Work is the most thorough and profound organizing principle in American life. If mobility has weakened old blood ties, our co-workers often form our new family, our tribe, our social world; we become almost citizens of our companies, living under the protection of salaries, pensions and health insurance. Sociologist Robert Schrank believes that people like jobs mainly because they need other people; they need to gossip with them, hang out with them, to schmooze. Says Schrank: "The workplace performs the function of community."

Unless it is dishonest or destructive—the labor of a pimp or a hit 19 man, say—all work is intrinsically honorable in ways that are rarely understood as they once were. Only the fortunate toil in ways that express them directly. There is a Renaissance splendor in Leonardo's effusion: "The works that the eye orders the hands to make are infinite." But most of us labor closer to the ground. Even there, all work expresses the laborer in a deeper sense: all life must be worked at, protected, planted, replanted, fashioned, cooked for, coaxed, diapered, formed, sustained. Work is the way that we tend the world, the way that people connect. It is the most vigorous, vivid sign of life—in individuals and in civilizations.

On the Meaning of Work

ROBERT COLES

Robert Coles was born in 1929. He received his medical degree from Columbia University and has been on several hospital staffs, including a position as research psychiatrist with Harvard University Health Services, where he is now professor of psychiatry and medical humanities. He is the author of over forty books, including Children of Crisis, 1968–1971, a three-volume work that won a Pulitzer Prize; Uprooted Children, 1970; The Wages of Neglect, 1972; The Moral Life of Children, 1987; The Political Life of Children, 1987; and The Call of Stories, 1990.

Drawing on the research and thought of French philosopher Simone Weil (1909–1943), who experienced and wrote about the plight of people who feel a sense of entrapment and meaninglessness at their work, Coles argues that modern industrial societies must pay more attention to the needs of working people for fellowship and dignity.

1 In early December of 1934 a serious and scholarly young French lady, about to turn twenty-six, took a job in a factory at the outskirts of Paris. Day after day she operated a drill, used a power press, and turned a crank handle. From doing so Simone Weil became tired and sad, but she persisted—and all the while kept a "factory journal." In time she moved to another factory, there to pack cartons under distinctly unfavorable circumstances. She felt cramped, pushed, and in general badly used, even as her co-workers did; eventually she was fired. Still undaunted, she found employment in the well-known Renault works, the pride of industrial France. She lived in a world of machines and shop stewards and intense heat and long working days. She saw men and women hurt and insulted, men and women grow weak and bitter and weary. She also saw men and women struggle hard to find what joy and humor they could

amid those long stretches of dangerous and exhausting work. Enraged, at a loss to know what she thought and believed to be true, she kept at her job. She also kept asking her co-workers to share their thoughts with her.

Simone Weil was a moral philosopher, a theologian, some would 2 say. She had no interest in studying factory life sociologically or analyzing the psychological "adjustment" of workers to their jobs. Nor was she trying to see how "the other half" lives for one or another reason. She had in mind no shocking news stories as she worked week after week, month after month. She was not out to prove that the modern worker is "exploited" or on the verge of joining some "revolution"—or alternatively, happy beyond anyone's comprehension but his own. Though her mind was capable of constructing its fair share of abstractions, she sensed the danger of doing so. An intellectual, she profoundly distrusted, even scorned, the dozens and dozens of writers and scholars and theorists who wrote with assurance about the workingman and his lot. Instead she wanted to place herself in the very midst of what interested her, there to learn from concrete experience—and only later would she stop and ask herself what she *believed*, what she had to *say*, about subjects like "the effect of work on the worker," subjects that she well knew a mind like hers was tempted to seize and probe and dissect without the slightest exposure to a Renault factory building, let alone those who work inside it.

Eventually she would carry her experiences to the countryside; she 3 learned to pick crops, plow the land, tend animals, and in general live the life of a peasant—to the point that she unnerved her hosts. She was no snob, no condescending "observer" bent on picking up a few facts, establishing a reputation of sorts, then hurrying off so as to cash in on the time spent "out there." The people with whom she stayed (at Bourges, about 100 miles due south of Paris) later remarked upon their guest's ability to cut through the barriers that naturally went to separate her from them—"and put herself at our level."

In fact Simone Weil wanted to do more than "understand" others, or 4 make them feel that she was stooping ever so gracefully. She saw factory workers and field hands as her brothers and sisters, out of a deep and certainly religious need to do so, a longing she described (for herself and for the rest of us) in *The Need for Roots*, written toward the end of her short yet intense life. (She died in 1943 at the age of thirty-three.) In the book she emphasizes that we need desperately—indeed die spiritually if we do not have—a community, one whose life, whose values and customs and traditions, whose *sanction*, a person doesn't so much think about as take for granted. If that is not very original and surprising, Miss Weil's notion of what a "community" is, or ought to be, goes much further; she sees us as always wanting to be in touch with others, not only our immediate families or more distant kin or our neighbors but those we work with, with whom we spend well over half our waking hours. For her, economists and political scientists (not to mention politicians), as well as psychologists and sociologists, all too often fail to grasp the true rhythms in life. True, they point out how much money we have or don't have, how much power one or another "class" has; or else they emphasize the lusts and rages we feel and try to express or subdue. Meanwhile, all over the world millions and millions of men and women (yes, and children) mark their lives by working, resting from work as best they can, and going back to work—until they die. And for Simone Weil it is with such day-to-day experiences that one who wants to comprehend man's nature and society's purposes ought to start.

5   Though she got on well with her fellow workers in several factories and on a farm, and though she held off at all times from extending cheap pity to those men and women, or condescension masked as moral outrage, or contempt dressed up as radical theory, she had to set down what she saw and heard. That is to say, she had to list the various kinds of suffering she saw among France's workers:

> We must change the system concerning concentration of attention during working hours, the types of stimulants which make for the overcoming of laziness or exhaustion—and which at present are merely fear and extra pay—the type of obedience necessary, the far too small amount of initiative, skill and thought demanded of workmen, their present exclusion from any imaginative share in the work of the enterprise as a whole, their sometimes total ignorance of the value, social utility, and destination of the things they manufacture, and the complete divorce between working life and family life. The list could well be extended.

6   She went on to do so; she extended her list and spelled out how life goes for millions of workmen in what she called "our industrial prisons"—where (she well knew) men are glad to be, rather than go hungry or be idle. But she was not primarily a social critic; perhaps more than anything else she was a visionary, hence easily written off as impractical—but uncannily able to say things starkly and prophetically and with apparent naïveté, which more cautious and "realistic" men only in time would come to see as indeed significant. So she noted how frightened and sullen her co-workers became, how drained they felt by the end of the day, how tempted they were to make minor mistakes, slow down, even at times cause considerable damage to the plant in which they worked or to the products they were turning out. Why is it so, she asked—why must men (in both America and Russia—that is, under capitalism and Communism alike) work in such huge, cold, impersonal places, and feel so fortunate (such is their vulnerability, their fear, their insecurity) for having even that kind of opportunity? The answer,

no doubt, is that efficiency demands it; in a modern industrial nation mass production has to take place in large factories. Yet, in the France of the 1930s, Miss Weil saw what we in America are now beginning to notice and worry about: the dangers which a cult of efficiency and productivity, unqualified by ethical if not spiritual considerations, can present us with. She saw how much her worker friends needed one another, how hard they tried to enjoy one another's company, notwithstanding all the factory rules and regulations. She saw how tempted they were to stay off the job, to feign illness or offer some other excuse that enabled them to take at least this day off. She saw how greedy and thoughtless an industrial empire can become: land, water, air, raw materials, the lives of people—everything is grist for those modern mills of ours, which in turn are defended as necessary for our "advanced civilization," while all the while we cough and hold our noses and our ears and see about us an increasingly bleak and contaminated land, and feel upset as well, at a loss, and more than a little angry. The words and phrases are familiar, indeed have become clichés: absenteeism, ecological disaster, alienation, dehumanization, the loss of a sense of community.

Simone Weil sensed in her intuitive way that something was wrong, 7 that a new order of attention must be given to the ordinary working man—whether he wears a blue collar or a white one—to his need for fellowship and dignity as well as money, to his struggle for meaning as well as possessions.

Working people with whom I have talked make quite clear the ways 8 they feel cornered, trapped, lonely, pushed around at work, and, as Simone Weil kept on emphasizing, confused by a sense of meaninglessness. These feelings, I have noticed, often take the form of questions—and I will take the liberty of paraphrasing some of them that I have heard: What am I doing that *really matters*? What is the point to it all—not life, as some philosophers say, but the specific, tangible things I do or make? What would I do if I had a real choice—something which I doubt I ever will have? Is there some other, some better way to work? Might we not break up these large factories and offices, work closer to our homes, closer to one another as workers—and work together on something that is not a fragment of this, a minor part of that, but is whole and significant and recognizable as important in our lives?

If those were "romantic" inquiries for a much-troubled and fussy 9 and brilliant French religious philosopher and political essayist in the 1930s, they may not be altogether impractical for us today. The workers I have heard may not speak as Simone Weil did; but like her they are able to be obsessed by the riddles and frustrations that life presents—and like her, they can spot trouble when it is in front of them, literally in the air, the dangerously contaminated air. As never before, our industrial societies are now being forced to look inward, so to speak, to become aware of the implications of our policies, among them those followed by the thousands of businesses which employ millions of workers. No doubt in the 1930s a skeptic could easily have made light of Simone Weil's concern that the French landscape outside various giant factories was in several ways being defaced. No doubt today what she (and over the decades many, many workers) wanted done inside those factories can still seem impractical. But that word "impractical" is one that history has taught us to think twice about. One generation's impracticality has a way of becoming another's urgent necessity.

The Importance of Work

GLORIA STEINEM

G loria Steinem was born in Toledo, Ohio, in 1934. She graduated from Smith College and did graduate work at the University of Calcutta and the University of Delhi in India. She helped found New York magazine and Ms. magazine, which she edited from 1972 to 1987. Her books include The Thousand Indias, 1957; The Beach Book, 1963; Outrageous Acts and Everyday Rebellions, 1983; Marilyn, 1987; and The Bedside Book of Self-Esteem, 1989.

Steinem argues that women should not have to defend working by claiming that they have to; rather, women have a basic human right to work for personal satisfaction and to make their own valuable contributions to society.

1   Toward the end of the 1970s, *The Wall Street Journal* devoted an eight-part, front-page series to "the working woman"—that is, the influx of women into the paid-labor force—as the greatest change in American life since the Industrial Revolution.

2   Many women readers greeted both the news and the definition with cynicism. After all, women have always worked. If all the productive work of human maintenance that women do in the home were valued at its replacement cost, the gross national product of the United States would go up by 26 percent. It's just that we are now more likely than ever before to leave our poorly rewarded, low-security, high-risk job of homemaking (though we're still trying to explain that it's a perfectly good one and that the problem is male society's refusal both to do it and to give it an economic value) for more secure, independent, and better-paid jobs outside the home.

3   Obviously, the real work revolution won't come until all productive work is rewarded—including child rearing and other jobs done in the home—and men are integrated into so-called women's work as well as vice versa. But the radical change being touted by the *Journal* and other

media is one part of that long integration process: the unprecedented flood of women into salaried jobs, that is, into the labor force as it has been male-defined and previously occupied by men. We are already more than 41 percent of it—the highest proportion in history. Given the fact that women also make up a whopping 69 percent of the "discouraged labor force" (that is, people who need jobs but don't get counted in the unemployment statistics because they've given up looking), plus an official female unemployment rate that is substantially higher than men's, it's clear that we could expand to become fully half of the national work force by 1990.

Faced with this determination of women to find a little indepen- 4 dence and to be paid and honored for our work, experts have rushed to ask: "Why?" It's a question rarely directed at male workers. Their basic motivations of survival and personal satisfaction are taken for granted. Indeed, men are regarded as "odd" and therefore subjects for sociological study and journalistic reports only when they *don't* have work, even if they are rich and don't need jobs or are poor and can't find them. Nonetheless, pollsters and sociologists have gone to great expense to prove that women work outside the home because of dire financial need, or if we persist despite the presence of a wage-earning male, out of some desire to buy "little extras" for our families, or even out of good old-fashioned penis envy.

Job interviewers and even our own families may still ask salaried 5 women the big "Why?" If we have small children at home or are in some job regarded as "men's work," the incidence of such questions increases. Condescending or accusatory versions of "What's a nice girl like you doing in a place like this?" have not disappeared from the workplace.

How do we answer these assumptions that we are "working" out of 6 some pressing or peculiar need? Do we feel okay about arguing that it's as natural for us to have salaried jobs as for our husbands—whether or not we have young children at home? Can we enjoy strong career ambitions without worrying about being thought "unfeminine"? When we confront men's growing resentment of women competing in the work force (often in the form of such guilt-producing accusations as "You're taking men's jobs away" or "You're damaging your children"), do we simply state that a decent job is a basic human right for everybody?

I'm afraid the answer is often no. As individuals and as a movement, 7 we tend to retreat into some version of a tactically questionable defense: "Womenworkbecausewehaveto." The phrase has become one word, one key on the typewriter—an economic form of the socially "feminine" stance of passivity and self-sacrifice. Under attack, we still tend to present ourselves as creatures of economic necessity and familial devotion. "Womenworkbecausewehaveto" has become the easiest thing to say.

Like most truisms, this one is easy to prove with statistics. Economic 8 need *is* the most consistent work motive—for women as well as men. In

1976, for instance, 43 percent of all women in the paid-labor force were single, widowed, separated, or divorced, and working to support themselves and their dependents. An additional 21 percent were married to men who had earned less than ten thousand dollars in the previous year, the minimum then required to support a family of four. In fact, if you take men's pensions, stocks, real estate, and various forms of accumulated wealth into account, a good statistical case can be made that there are more women who "have" to work (that is, who have neither the accumulated wealth, nor husbands whose work or wealth can support them for the rest of their lives) than there are men with the same need. If we were going to ask one group "Do you really need this job?", we should ask men.

9   But the first weakness of the whole "have to work" defense is its deceptiveness. Anyone who has ever experienced dehumanized life on welfare or any other confidence-shaking dependency knows that a paid job may be preferable to the dole, even when the handout is coming from a family member. Yet the will and self-confidence to work on one's own can diminish as dependency and fear increase. That may explain why—contrary to the "have to" rationale—wives of men who earn less than three thousand dollars a year are actually *less* likely to be employed than wives whose husbands make ten thousand dollars a year or more.

10   Furthermore, the greatest proportion of employed wives is found among families with a total household income of twenty-five to fifty thousand dollars a year. This is the statistical underpinning used by some sociologists to provide that women's work is mainly important for boosting families into the middle or upper middle class. Thus, women's incomes are largely used for buying "luxuries" and "little extras": a neat double-shammy that renders us secondary within our families, and makes our jobs expendable in hard times. We may even go along with this interpretation (at least, up to the point of getting fired so a male can have our job). It preserves a husbandly ego-need to be seen as the primary breadwinner, and still allows us a safe "feminine" excuse for working.

11   But there are often rewards that we're not confessing. As noted in *The Two-Career Couple,* by Francine and Douglas Hall: "Women who hold jobs by choice, even blue-collar routine jobs, are more satisfied with their lives than are the full-time housewives."

12   In addition to personal satisfaction, there is also society's need for all its members' talents. Suppose that jobs were given out on only a "have to work" basis to both women and men—one job per household. It would be unthinkable to lose the unique abilities of, for instance, Eleanor Holmes Norton, the distinguished chair of the Equal Employment Opportunity Commission. But would we then be forced to ques-

tion the important work of her husband, Edward Norton, who is also a distinguished lawyer? Since men earn more than twice as much as women on the average, the wife in most households would be more likely to give up her job. Does that mean the nation could do as well without millions of its nurses, teachers, and secretaries? Or that the rare man who earns less than his wife should give up his job?

It was this kind of waste of human talents on a society-wide scale 13 that traumatized millions of unemployed or underemployed Americans during the Depression. Then, a one-job-per-household rule seemed somewhat justified, yet the concept was used to displace women workers only, create intolerable dependencies, and waste female talent that the country needed. That Depression experience, plus the energy and example of women who were finally allowed to work during the manpower shortage created by World War II, led Congress to reinterpret the meaning of the country's full-employment goal in its Economic Act of 1946. Full employment was officially defined as "the employment of those who want to work, without regard to whether their employment is, by some definition, necessary. This goal applies equally to men and to women." Since bad economic times are again creating a resentment of employed women—as well as creating more need for women to be employed—we need such a goal more than ever. Women are again being caught in a tragic double bind: We are required to be strong and then punished for our strength.

Clearly, anything less than government and popular commitment to 14 this 1946 definition of full employment will leave the less powerful groups, whoever they may be, in danger. Almost as important as the financial penalty paid by the powerless is the suffering that comes from being shut out of paid and recognized work. Without it, we lose much of our self-respect and our ability to prove that we are alive by making some difference in the world. That's just as true for the suburban woman as it is for the unemployed steel worker.

But it won't be easy to give up the passive defense of "weworkbe- 15 causewehaveto."

When a woman who is struggling to support her children and 16 grandchildren on welfare sees her neighbor working as a waitress, even though that neighbor's husband has a job, she may feel resentful; and the waitress (of course, not the waitress's husband) may feel guilty. Yet unless we establish the obligation to provide a job for everyone who is willing and able to work, that welfare woman may herself be penalized by policies that give out only one public-service job per household. She and her daughter will have to make a painful and divisive decision about which of them gets that precious job, and the whole household will have to survive on only one salary.

17   A job as a human right is a principle that applies to men as well as women. But women have more cause to fight for it. The phenomenon of the "working woman" has been held responsible for everything from an increase in male impotence (which turned out, incidently, to be attributable to medication for high blood pressure) to the rising cost of steak (which was due to high energy costs and beef import restrictions, not women's refusal to prepare the cheaper, slower-cooking cuts). Unless we see a job as part of every citizen's right to autonomy and personal fulfillment, we will continue to be vulnerable to someone else's idea of what "need" is, and whose "need" counts the most.

18   In many ways, women who do not have to work for simple survival, but who choose to do so nonetheless, are on the frontier of asserting this right for all women. Those with well-to-do husbands are dangerously easy for us to resent and put down. It's easier still to resent women from families of inherited wealth, even though men generally control and benefit from that wealth. (There is no Rockefeller Sisters Fund, no J. P. Morgan & Daughters, and sons-in-law may be the ones who really sleep their way to power.) But to prevent a woman whose husband or father is wealthy from earning her own living, and from gaining the self-confidence that comes with that ability, is to keep her needful of that unearned power and less willing to disperse it. Moreover, it is to lose forever her unique talents.

19   Perhaps modern feminists have been guilty of a kind of reverse snobbism that keeps us from reaching out to the wives and daughters of wealthy men; yet it was exactly such women who refused the restrictions of class and financed the first wave of feminist revolution.

20   For most of us, however, "womenworkbecausewehaveto" is just true enough to be seductive as a personal defense.

21   If we use it without also staking out the larger human right to a job, however, we will never achieve that right. And we will always be subject to the false argument that independence for women is a luxury affordable only in good economic times. Alternatives to layoffs will not be explored, acceptable unemployment will always be used to frighten those with jobs into accepting low wages, and we will never remedy the real cost, both to families and to the country, of dependent women and a massive loss of talent.

22   Worst of all, we may never learn to find productive, honored work as a natural part of ourselves and as one of life's basic pleasures.

TOPICS FOR EXPLORING SOURCES ON WORK

1. Bertrand Russell says that even the dullest work, provided it is not excessive in amount, is preferable to idleness. Do some research on the human effects of working on an assembly line. What ways have businesses developed to lessen the boredom of such work?

2. Are computers, robots, and other electronic devices increasingly taking the place of humans in performing repetitive and routine work tasks? If so, is this a desirable change or an undesirable one? Discuss some of the possible implications of this change.

3. Bertrand Russell says: "To be able to fill leisure intelligently is the last product of civilization, and at present very few people have reached this level." Russell wrote these words in 1930. Have people's ability to fill leisure time changed drastically since then? Try to find out if leisure time has increased since 1930. Discuss some of the new ways that people now fill their leisure time.

4. Russell says that the "intelligent" rich work nearly as hard as if they were poor. Do some research on well-known rich people, such as Bill Gates of Microsoft Corporation, who continue to work hard when they do not have to for economic reasons. What motivates such people?

5. Traditionally, in American culture, women are not paid for the work they do at home, in spite of the fact that managing a home is a full-time job. Have attitudes toward the value of home management changed in the past two or three decades? Should women be compensated for the work they do at home? According to what formula?

6. Russell says that one of the chief elements that make work interesting is the exercise of a skill. Has the demand for skilled labor decreased over the past few decades? If so, what has caused this decrease? What effects does the decrease have on work and the products of work?

7. Providing rewards and incentives is often a management challenge in the workplace. If individuals are rewarded, others may feel jealousy and not be so willing to work with that person. If no one is rewarded, there may be little incentive to excel. One way that some companies have dealt with this issue is to reward groups rather than individuals, thus encouraging group effort. Do some research, and discuss the advantages and disadvantages of rewarding individuals and rewarding groups.

8. Erich Fromm says that human beings emerge from nature by mastering nature. Brainstorm some examples of this. Do some research on the results of such mastery. Examine both the positive and negative aspects of the human mastery of nature through work in a specific area.

9. Erich Fromm cites C. W. Mills, who argues that for the craftsman there is no split between work and play or work and culture. Do some research on the nature of play to determine its characteristics. Examine the implications of Mills's statement, and discuss what it is about the craftsman's work that makes it like play.

10. What is meant by P. Drucker's assertion, cited in Fromm's essay, that getting money is not in itself a meaningful human activity? Why is a paycheck not enough to base one's self-respect on? Is work the only way to gain self-respect? Is it true that the more money people make, the more they value their work? Do some research on the relationship between pay and satisfaction in the workplace.

11. Erich Fromm says that the alienated character of work results in a deep-seated hostility toward it. Consider the implications of this statement, and examine the opposite side of the argument: the workaholic, for whom work is everything, for whom work means more than family and friends. Which is more harmful: hostility to work or addiction to work?

12. Lance Morrow says that American management complains that no one wants to work anymore. How widespread is unemployment among those who do not wish to work? How widespread is the habit of calling in sick when there is nothing wrong? What other kinds of data can you find to support or argue against management's complaint that people no longer want to work?

13. How have attitudes toward work changed between your generation and that of your parents or guardians? In addition to doing some research in published reports, interview some people from both generations to find out first-hand what these differences in attitude are.

14. Many people today are choosing to work at home, using various electronic devices such as computers and modems, fax machines, and telephones to do their work. Discuss some of the advantages and disadvantages of this modern trend toward "telecommuting."

15. Robert Coles discusses the importance of community in the workplace. Do unions provide this sense of community where people work? What have companies done to try to provide a sense of community? Do some research on such areas as providing day care for children, social activities, and physical exercise facilities.

16. A great deal of research has been done on the differences between the Japanese attitude toward work and American attitudes. Do research on some of these differences, including those in management styles, the workplace, and cultural values.

17. A utopian society in which work is either nonexistent or else made meaningful has always been a human ideal. Do some research on fictional or real utopian schemes in the past. What is the importance of work for these schemes? Discuss some reasons for their success or failure.

18. Gloria Steinem says that wives of men who earn very little money are less likely to be employed than the wives of men who earn more money. What does this phenomenon mean? What are its causes?

19. Some politicians have argued that it is easier to avoid work today than in the past because of the many social services that are available. Do some research on this subject. Has support of the unemployed increased in the last generation? If so, what effect has this increase had?

20. In many families today, both partners work. Much has been written about the effect of this trend—on children, on the economy, on family structure. However, how different is this from the common situation in the nineteenth century when the wife was so burdened with household work that she had even less time for family than she does now?

21. Often people have been promised that the increase in technology would make it possible for people to have more leisure time than ever before. Has this promise been fulfilled? Why or why not? Do some research on the relationship between technology and leisure time.

22. Has the increase in technology made it necessary for people to hire experts to do work that they were once able to do themselves? For example, people used to be able to do minor repair on automobiles, replace tubes in their television sets, or repair a kitchen appliance. Is this becoming more and more impossible? What are the effects of this change?

ACKNOWLEDGMENTS

Robert Coles. "On the Meaning of Work," by Robert Coles first published in *The Atlantic Monthly,* October, 1971. Reprinted by permission of International Creative Management, Inc. Copyright © 1971 by Robert Coles.

Annie Dillard. All pages from "Untying the Knot," from *Pilgrim at Tinker Creek* by Annie Dillard. Copyright © 1974 by Annie Dillard. Reprinted by permission of HarperCollins Publishers, Inc.

Jerrold Footlick. "What Happened to the Family?" by Jerrold Footlick and Elizabeth Leonard from *Newsweek,* Winter/Spring Special Edition, 1990 on "The 21st Century Family". Copyright © 1990, Newsweek, Inc. All rights reserved. Reprinted by permission.

Erich Fromm. From *The Sane Society* by Erich Fromm. Copyright © 1955, 1983 by Erich Fromm. Reprinted by permission of Henry Holt & Co., Inc.

George Gallup. "The Faltering Family," from *Forecast 2000* by George Gallup. Copyright © 1984 by George Gallup. By permission of William Morrow & Company, Inc.

Kenneth Goings. "Memorabilia That Have Perpetuated Stereotypes About African-Americans," by Kenneth Goings from *Chronicles of Higher Education,* Feb. 14, 1990. Reprinted by permission of the author.

Amy Gross. "The Appeal of the Androgynous Man," by Amy Gross from *Mademoiselle,* May 1976. Reprinted by permission of the author.

Le Ly Hayslip. From *When Heaven and Earth Changed Places* by Le Ly Hayslip. Copyright © 1989 by Le Ly Hayslip and Charles Jay Wurtz. Used by permission of Doubleday, a division of Bantam, Doubleday, Dell Publishing Group, Inc.

Robert Heilbroner. "Don't Let Stereotypes Warp Your Judgment," by Robert Heilbroner from *Reader's Digest.* Reprinted by permission of the author.

Gilbert Highet. "How to Write an Essay," from *Explorations* by Gilbert Highet. Copyright © 1971 by Gilbert Highet. Reprinted by permission of Oxford University Press, Inc.

Robert Hoagland. "What I Think, What I Am" from *The Tugman's Passage,* published by Lyons & Burford. Copyright © 1976, 1982, 1995 by Edward Hoagland.

James D. Houston. "Manzanar, USA" from *Farewell to Manzanar* by James D. Houston and Jeanne Wakatsuki Houston. Copyright © 1973 by James D. Houston. Reprinted by permission of Houghton Mifflin Co. All rights reserved.

INDEX OF AUTHORS AND TITLES

Abbey, Edward, 99
America: The Multinational Society, 208
Androgynous Man, The, 155
Angelou, Maya, 60
Anglo vs. Chicano: Why?, 202
Angry, 260
Appeal of the Androgynous Man, The, 159
At War with My Skin, 53

Baldwin, James, 266
Being a Man, 169
Black Writer and the Southern Experience, The, 195
Brownmiller, Susan, 164
Brustein, Robert, 219
Buckley, William F., Jr., 249

Campa, Arthur L., 202
Carver, Raymond, 71
Cofer, Judith Ortiz, 179
Coles, Robert, 330
Come on In, 99
Communication in the Year 2000, 241
Complexion, 50
Conversational Ballgames, 128
Cyclone!, 110

Dillard, Annie, 91
Discriminating Tastes: The Prejudice of Personal Preferences, 255
Don't Let Stereotypes Warp Your Judgments, 145

End of Nature, The, 103

Faltering Family, The, 297
Families, 282
Family Out of Favor, The, 286
Femininity, 164
Finding a Voice, 25
Fitting In, 30
Footlick, Jerrold, 291
Fourth of July, The, 67
Friends, Good Friends—and Such Good Friends, 132
Fromm, Erich, 320

Gallup, George, Jr., 297
Getting a Job, 60
Going West, 40
Goings, Kenneth, 124
Gross, Amy, 159

Hayslip, Le Ly, 80
Heilbroner, Robert L., 145

Highet, Gilbert, 9
Hoagland, Edward, 6
Houston, James D., 44
Houston, Jeanne Wakatsuki, 44
How to Write an Essay, 9
Howard, Jane, 282

*If Black English Isn't a Language, Then
    Tell Me, What Is?,* 266
Importance of Work, The, 334

Jones, Rachel L., 270
Just Walk On By, 174

King, Stephen, 215
Kingston, Maxine Hong, 25
Kowinski, William Severini, 119

Learning to Listen, 19
Leonard, Elizabeth, 291
Lorde, Audre, 67

MacNeil, Robert, 232
Mallaise: How to Know If You Have It,
    119
Malveaux, Julianne, 260
Manzanar, 44
McKibben, Bill, 103,
Mead, Margaret, 137
*Memorabilia That Have Perpetuated
    Stereotypes About African Americans,*
    124
Metraux, Rhoda, 137
*"Mommy, What Does Nigger Mean?"
    A Question of Language,* 274
Morrow, Lance, 325
My Father's Death, 80
My Father's Life, 71
*Myth of the Latin Woman: I Just Met a
    Girl Named María, The,* 179

Naylor, Gloria, 274
Novak, Michael, 286

Of Shopping, 115
On Friendship, 137

On Kids and Slasher Movies, 229
On the Meaning of Work, 330

Paradox of Perfection, The, 305
Perrin, Noel, 155
Playing Catch, 34

Reed, Ishmael, 208
Reflections on Horror Movies, 219
Rodriguez, Richard, 50
Rose, Phyllis, 115
Russell, Bertrand, 315

Sackett, Victoria A., 255
Sakamoto, Nancy Masterson, 128
Schjedahl, Peter, 110
Schwartz, Tony, 241
Silko, Leslie Marmon, 186
Skolnick, Arlene, 305
*Something About the Subject Makes It
    Hard to Name,* 150
Staples, Brent, 174
Steinem, Gloria, 334

Talese, Gay, 34
Tarkov, John, 30
Television Addiction, 236
Theroux, Paul, 169
Thomas, Lewis, 95
Trouble with Television, The, 232
Tucson Zoo, The, 95

Untying the Knot, 91
Updike, John, 53

Ventura, Michael, 229
Viorst, Judith, 132

Walker, Alice, 195
Wanting an Orange, 106
Welty, Eudora, 19
What Happened to the Family?, 291
What I Think, What I Am, 6
What Is the Point of Working?, 325
What's Wrong with Black English,
    270

Why Don't We Complain?, 249
Why We Crave Horror Movies, 215
Winn, Marie, 236
Woiwode, Larry, 106
Wolff, Tobias, 40

Work, 315
Work in an Alienated Society, 320

Yamato, Gloria, 150
Yellow Woman and a Beauty of the Spirit, 186

Instructor's Guide
Interacting
with Essays

Charles E. May
California State University–Long Beach

D. C. Heath and Company
Lexington, Massachusetts   Toronto

Address editorial correspondence to:
D. C. Heath and Company
125 Spring Street
Lexington, MA 02173

Published simultaneously in Canada.

Printed in the United States of America.

International Standard Book Number: 0-669-41674-6

10 9 8 7 6 5 4 3 2 1

PREFACE

Since I wrote the suggestions for Exploring Ideas and Exploring Rhetoric that follow each of the fifty essays in the first four parts of *Interacting with Essays*, it is only fair that I share with users of the book some of the responses I had in mind. They certainly do not exhaust the richness of the essays included, but if nothing else, they will give you some ideas with which to disagree.

This Instructor's Guide also contains suggestions for using the software, **Interactive Essay**, available for this book, including printouts of the interactive exercises in the software for easy reference.

Charles E. May

Contents

SECTION I   ALTERNATE RHETORICAL CONTENTS   1

SECTION II   NOTES ON SELECTIONS AND SUGGESTED ANSWERS   7

PROLOGUE: ❧ Writing   9

EDWARD HOAGLAND, *What I Think, What I Am*   10

GILBERT HIGHET, *How to Write an Essay*   12

PART ONE ❧ **EXPLORING THE PERSONAL PAST**   15

EUDORA WELTY, *Learning to Listen*   16

MAXINE HONG KINGSTON, *Finding a Voice*   18

JOHN TARKOV, *Fitting In*   20

GAY TALESE, *Playing Catch*   22

TOBIAS WOLFF, *Going West*   24

JEANNE WAKATSUKI HOUSTON AND JAMES D. HOUSTON, *Manzanar*   26

RICHARD RODRIGUEZ, *Complexion*   28

JOHN UPDIKE, *At War with My Skin*   30

MAYA ANGELOU, *Getting a Job*   32

AUDRE LORDE, *The Fourth of July*   34

RAYMOND CARVER, *My Father's Life*   37

LE LY HAYSLIP, *MY FATHER'S DEATH*   39

PART TWO ✕ Exploring the Everyday World   43

ANNIE DILLARD, *Untying the Knot*   44

LEWIS THOMAS, *The Tucson Zoo*   46

EDWARD ABBEY, *Come On In*   48

BILL McKIBBEN, *The End of Nature*   50

LARRY WOIWODE, *Wanting an Orange*   52

PETER SCHJELDAHL, *Cyclone*   54

WILLIAM SEVERINI KOWINSKI, *Mallaise: How to Know If You Have It*   58

KENNETH GOINGS, *Memorabilia That Have Perpetuated Stereotypes About
          African Americans*   60

NANCY MASTERSON SAKAMOTO, *Conversational Ballgames*   62

JUDITH VIORST, FRIENDS, *Good Friends—and Such Good Friends*   64

MARGARET MEAD AND RHODA METRAUX, *On Friendship*   66

PART THREE ✕ Dealing with Differences   69

ROBERT L. HEILBRONER, *Don't Let Stereotypes Warp Your Judgments*   70

GLORIA YAMATO, *Something About the Subject Makes It Hard to Name*   72

NOEL PERRIN, *The Androgynous Man*   74

AMY GROSS, *The Appeal of the Androgynous Man*   76

SUSAN BROWNMILLER, *Femininity*   78

PAUL THEROUX, *Being a Man*   80

BRENT STAPLES, *Just Walk On By*   82

JUDITH ORTIZ COFER, *The Myth of the Latin Woman: I Just Met a Girl
          Named María*   84

LESLIE MARMON SILKO, *Yellow Woman and a Beauty of the Spirit*   86

ALICE WALKER, THE BLACK WRITER AND THE SOUTHERN EXPERIENCE   89

ARTHUR L. CAMPA, *Anglo vs. Chicano: Why?*   91

ISHMAEL REED, *America: The Multinational Society*   93

PART FOUR ❧ Analyzing and Arguing a Case   97

STEPHEN KING, *Why We Crave Horror Movies*   98

ROBERT BRUSTEIN, *Reflections on Horror Movies*   100

MICHAEL VENTURA, *On Kids and Slasher Movies*   102

ROBERT MACNEIL, *The Trouble with Television*   104

MARIE WINN, *Television Addiction*   106

TONY SCHWARTZ, *Communication in the Year 2000*   108

WILLIAM F. BUCKLEY, JR., *Why Don't We Complain?*   110

VICTORIA A. SACKETT, *Discriminating Tastes: The Prejudice of Personal Preference*   113

JULIANNE MALVEAUX, *Angry*   115

JAMES BALDWIN, *If Black English Isn't a Language, Then Tell Me, What Is?*   117

RACHEL L. JONES, *What's Wrong with Black English*   119

GLORIA NAYLOR, *"Mommy, What Does Nigger Mean?" A Question of Language*   121

SECTION III INTERACTIVE ESSAY 🖫   125

A READING/WRITING COMPUTER APPLICATION 127

INSTALLING INTERACTIVE ESSAY   139

USING INTERACTIVE ESSAY   143

TEXT OF INTERACT BUTTONS 153

JOHN TARKOV, *Fitting In*   154

GAY TALESE, *Playing Catch*   156

MAYA ANGELOU, *Getting a Job*   160

AUDRE LORDE, *The Fourth of July*   165

ANNIE DILLARD, *Untying the Knot*   168

LEWIS THOMAS, *The Tucson Zoo*   171

PHYLLIS ROSE, *Of Shopping*   173

WILLIAM SEVERINI KOWINSKI, *Mallaise: How to Know If You Have It*   176

NOEL PERRIN, *The Androgynous Man*   179

AMY GROSS, *The Appeal of the Androgynous Man*   182

SUSAN BROWNMILLER, *Femininity*   185

PAUL THEROUX, *Being a Man*   189

BRENT STAPLES, *Just Walk On By*   192

JUDITH ORTIZ COFER, *The Myth of the Latin Woman: I Just Met a Girl Named María*   196

STEPHEN KING, *Why We Crave Horror Movies*   201

MICHAEL VENTURA, *On Kids and Slasher Movies*   203

ROBERT MACNEIL, *The Trouble with Television*   205

MARIE WINN, *Television Addiction*   207

WILLIAM F. BUCKLEY, JR., *Why Don't We Complain?*   211

VICTORIA A. SACKETT, *Discriminating Tastes: The Prejudice of Personal Preference*   215

SECTION I

ALTERNATE
RHETORICAL
CONTENTS

ALTERNATE RHETORICAL CONTENTS[1]

Description

Gay Talese, "Playing Catch" 34
Tobias Wolff, "Going West" 40
Jeanne Wakatsuki Houston and James D. Houston, "Manzanar" 44
Maya Angelou, "Getting a Job" 60
Audre Lorde, "The Fourth of July" 67
Raymond Carver, "My Father's Life" 71
Le Ly Hayslip, "My Father's Death" 80
Annie Dillard, "Untying the Knot" 91
Larry Woiwode, "Wanting an Orange" 106
Peter Schjeldahl, "Cyclone" 110

Narration

Eudora Welty, "Learning to Listen" 19
Maxine Hong Kingston, "Finding a Voice" 25
Gay Talese, "Playing Catch" 34
Tobias Wolff, "Going West" 40
Jeanne Wakatsuki Houston and James D. Houston, "Manzanar" 44

---

[1] Page numbers refer to pages in the student edition.

Maya Angelou, "Getting a Job" 60

Audre Lorde, "The Fourth of July" 67

Raymond Carver, "My Father's Life" 71

Le Ly Hayslip, "My Father's Death" 80

Brent Staples, "Just Walk On By" 174

Judith Ortiz Cofer, "The Myth of the Latin Woman: I Just Met a Girl Named María" 179

Leslie Marmon Silko, "Yellow Woman and a Beauty of the Spirit" 186

Example

Richard Rodriguez, "Complexion" 50

John Updike, "At War with My Skin" 53

Bill McKibben, "The End of Nature" 103

Phyllis Rose, "Of Shopping" 115

Kenneth Goings, "Memorabilia That Have Perpetuated Stereotypes About African Americans" 124

Nancy Masterson Sakamoto, "Conversational Ballgames" 128

Robert L. Heilbroner, "Don't Let Stereotypes Warp Your Judgments" 145

Noel Perrin, "The Androgynous Man" 155

Amy Gross, "The Appeal of the Androgynous Man" 159

Susan Brownmiller, "Femininity" 164

Paul Theroux, "Being a Man" 169

Brent Staples, "Just Walk On By" 174

Judith Ortiz Cofer, "The Myth of the Latin Woman: I Just Met a Girl Named María" 179

Analysis

Gilbert Highet, "How to Write an Essay" 9

Annie Dillard, "Untying the Knot" 91

Lewis Thomas, "The Tucson Zoo" 95

Edward Abbey, "Come On In" 99

Phyllis Rose, "Of Shopping" 115

William Severini Kowinski, "Mallaise: How to Know If You Have It" 119

Kenneth Goings, "Memorabilia That Have Perpetuated Stereotypes About African Americans" 124

Nancy Masterson Sakamoto, "Conversational Ballgames" 128

Classification

Judith Viorst, "Friends, Good Friends—and Such Good Friends" 132

Margaret Mead and Rhoda Metraux, "On Friendship" 137

Gloria Yamato, "Something About the Subject Makes It Hard to Name" 150

Robert Brustein, "Reflections on Horror Movies" 219

Tony Schwartz, "Communication in the Year 2000" 241

Victoria A. Sackett, "Discriminating Tastes: The Prejudice of Personal Preference" 255

Process

Gilbert Highet, "How to Write an Essay" 9

Eudora Welty, "Learning to Listen" 19

Larry Woiwode, "Wanting an Orange" 106

Peter Schjeldahl, "Cyclone" 110

Comparison and Contrast

William Severini Kowinski, "Mallaise: How to Know If You Have It" 119

Nancy Masterson Sakamoto, "Conversational Ballgames" 128

Amy Gross, "The Appeal of the Androgynous Man" 159

Leslie Marmon Silko, "Yellow Woman and a Beauty of the Spirit" 186

Arthur L. Campa, "Anglo vs. Chicano: Why?" 202

Robert Brustein, "Reflections on Horror Movies" 219

James Baldwin, "If Black English Isn't a Language, Then Tell Me, What Is?" 266

Rachel L. Jones, "What's Wrong with Black English" 270

Analogy

John Tarkov, "Fitting In" 30

Gay Talese, "Playing Catch" 34

William Severini Kowinski, "Mallaise: How to Know If You Have It" 119

Nancy Masterson Sakamoto, "Conversational Ballgames" 128

Susan Brownmiller, "Femininity" 164

Marie Winn, "Television Addiction" 236

Victoria A. Sackett, "Discriminating Tastes: The Prejudice of Personal Preference" 255

Definition

Edward Hoagland, "What I Think, What I Am" 6

Robert L. Heilbroner, "Don't Let Stereotypes Warp Your Judgments" 145

Gloria Yamato, "Something About the Subject Makes It Hard to Name" 150

Noel Perrin, "The Androgynous Man" 155

Amy Gross, "The Appeal of the Androgynous Man" 159

Paul Theroux, "Being a Man" 169

Ishmael Reed, "America: The Multinational Society" 208

Julianne Malveaux, "Angry" 260

Gloria Naylor, "Mommy, What Does *Nigger* Mean? A Question of Language" 274

Argument and Persuasion

Phyllis Rose, "Of Shopping" 115

William Severini Kowinski, "Mallaise: How to Know If You Have It" 119

Kenneth Goings, "Memorabilia That Have Perpetuated Stereotypes About African Americans" 124

Margaret Mead and Rhoda Metraux, "On Friendship" 137

Gloria Yamato, "Something About the Subject Makes It Hard to Name" 150

Susan Brownmiller, "Femininity" 164

Paul Theroux, "Being a Man" 169

Alice Walker, "The Black Writer and the Southern Experience" 195

Ishmael Reed, "America: The Multinational Society" 208

Stephen King, "Why We Crave Horror Movies" 215

Robert Brustein, "Reflections on Horror Movies" 219

Michael Ventura, "On Kids and Slasher Movies" 229

Robert MacNeil, "The Trouble with Television" 232

Marie Winn, "Television Addiction" 236

Tony Schwartz, "Communication in the Year 2000" 241

William F. Buckley, Jr., "Why Don't We Complain?" 249

Victoria A. Sackett, "Discriminating Tastes: The Prejudice of Personal Preference" 255

Julianne Malveaux, "Angry" 260

James Baldwin, "If Black English Isn't a Language, Then Tell Me, What Is?" 266

Rachel L. Jones, "What's Wrong with Black English" 270

Gloria Naylor, "Mommy, What Does *Nigger* Mean? A Question of Language" 274

SECTION II

NOTES ON
SELECTIONS
AND SUGGESTED
ANSWERS

PROLOGUE

WRITING

What I Think, What I Am

EDWARD HOAGLAND

I n this informal little essay on the essay by a well-known specialist in the genre, Edward Hoagland reminds us that the personal essay owes as much the voice and personality of the writer ("What I Am") as it does to its subject matter ("What I Think"). Hoagland spends most of his efforts defining the essay by comparing it to the short story and, to a lesser extent, the nonfiction article.

EXPLORING IDEAS

1. Hoagland points out the personal voice of essayists by comparing them to newspaper columnists and movie reviewers. If your students are unfamiliar with newspaper columnists and movie reviewers, you might refer to talk-show hosts, who perhaps serve the same function. You might make your students aware of the importance of point of view in essays by having them compare the way in which the personalities of talk-show hosts—for example, Jay Leno and David Letterman late at night or Oprah Winfrey and Phil Donahue during the day—create a certain style.

2. I sometimes give students a survey in which I ask them questions about what they read when they were children, what their parents read to them, and what they read now. A frank discussion of why your students do or do not read very much might be a good consciousness-raising activity.

3. Hoagland is probably right in suggesting that stories existed before essays, for myths, story-structured explanatory models, existed before discursive explanatory models did. This is a good time to have your students talk about how anecdotes are used for illustration in essays. Most of the essays in the section "Exploring the Personal Past" are based on narrative or anecdote.

4. I don't know exactly what titles Hoagland has in mind when he refers to "spurious autobiography" or "spurious hallucination," but there are certainly enough superficial books written by, or ghost-written for, celebrities, and some of your students will have read these books. This may provide the opportunity to discuss the importance of honesty in personal writing and how in writing one always reveals one's character.

5. Hoagland's claim—that essays are like a human voice following the mind's flow yet must have a point—gets to the heart of the most difficult problem students have with organizing essays—focusing the mind's attention on a unified line of thought. Gilbert Highet discusses this idea in more detail in the following essay. Solicit your students' opinions as to why they have trouble organizing an essay when they just follow the mind's flow.

6. Hoagland's claim that an essay conveys the same point to each reader hangs on his contrast between stories and essays. Whereas stories can be ambiguous and open to multiple interpretations, essays, Hoagland claims, are more definite. You might lead students in a discussion here about how they have been puzzled by the various interpretations of stories and discuss why essays are not so ambiguous.

7. The universality of story suggested by Hoagland may have something to do with his idea that the story is a more basic, primitive, and accessible form than the essay. Essays may appear to be more elitist to students than stories, for, as Hoagland says, they are minds speaking to minds, particularly educated minds. There is an assumption of civility in essays not present in stories, an air of sophistication and shared point of view.

8. Hoagland's suggestion that essayists do not have to tell the full truth may be controversial. Students may have difficulty understanding that there is a kind of "artistic truth" that is higher than fidelity to factual reality. Convincing them that truth can be served by inventing, embellishing, or altering reality may be a delicate, even difficult matter.

EXPLORING RHETORIC

1. Since Hoagland says that the voice of the essayist is as important as the content of the essay, it might be good to discuss Hoagland's voice here, which is, by and large, a familiar and genial one that allows him to risk ironic phrases such as "if we ever find ourselves living in caves again." Hoagland's essay is a good example of his definition of essay, for it is directed to educated readers who share his general frame of reference.

2. Hoagland creates a kind of folksy tone with such words and phrases as "new-fangled," "hokey affair," and "greased pig."

3. The metaphor of the essay, hanging on a line between two poles, supports the folksy tone. By pointing out that the style of the essay writer has a "nap" to it, Hoagland means that essays are not as smoothly unified as stories are, for the personality of the writer keeps the content from falling together too neatly.

4. Hoagland's phrase "the artful I" provides the opportunity to discuss the creation of a persona when one writes an essay that may or may not be the same as the author of the essay. This concept, not an easy one, can be illustrated by discussing how authors write to convey a certain voice that is not the same as the voice of their everyday self.

5. Hoagland cites Twain to show how writers use narratives to illustrate a point in an essay that is as vivid as one in novels.

6. Although Hoagland mixes his metaphors here, both the "rough weather" metaphor and the evolutionary "hybridizing" metaphor suggest the ability of the essay to adapt to changing circumstances and survive.

How to Write an Essay

GILBERT HIGHET

Although relatively informal, Gilbert Highet's essay on essays is more academic than Hoagland's. The difference lies not so much in the language as in development and structure: Hoagland's essay is implicit and loose, Highet's explicit and tightly organized. (A companion pair of essays for discussing the difference between personal and academic analysis are the essays on horror movies by Stephen King and Robert Brustein in Part Four.)

EXPLORING IDEAS

1. Of the three reasons Highet cites for not learning how to write essays, the one he is most interested in is lack of definition and purpose—a lack he intends to make up for in his own essay. This may be a good opportunity to discuss the importance of essays' having both a point and a form—one of the more common problems students have when writing essays.

2. Highet's "be interested and you will be interesting" is good advice, of course, but students sometimes may act as if they are not interested in anything you want them to write about. Be sure they understand that the secret to becoming interested in any topic is to find an aspect of the topic they know something about (Highet's example of dealing with the topic of scenery by focusing on the gas works and the slag heaps), find an aspect that they can become interested in, or pretend they are interested in some aspect. (Pretense sometimes has a way of becoming real.)

3. A common definition tactic is to find out the origins of something; exploring the original motivation for something or how it was in its original state may provide valuable clues about its basic nature. I use the example of movies; because they began as silents, they developed a set of visual conventions or shorthand devices that still characterize the medium.

4. Even though the idea of an essay's being "thinking in print" that readers overhear is appealing, it is misleading if students think that essays may merely meander; rather, they must be focused thought. Allowing your mind to direct the structure of the essay works only when your mind is directed, disciplined, and focused on the subject.

5. Many people say that letter writing is a lost art, but with the rise of e-mail, letter writing may experience a resurgence, albeit with a difference. Using e-mail to send letters across the Internet is appealing because of the ease with which it can be done—no envelope to address, no paper to fold, no stamp to lick, no mailbox to find. Just write the letter, press a send key, and off it goes. If you use e-mail frequently, you might explore with your students some of the possible differences that result when using e-mail rather than regular mail.

6. Different writers discover the form of their essays at different points. Some work best by outlining in advance, then fleshing out the outline and making structural changes as they go; others brainstorm a draft and then look it over to discover some point that has emerged. A discussion of these alternatives might be worthwhile.

7. Students often feel that writing comes naturally to some people. They will say, "I never could write well," as if writing were an innate talent of some kind—either you have it or you don't. I like to confront this issue up front in my classes. Weaker writers need to know what stronger writers have done to become strong: read extensively, observe carefully, think analytically, and write frequently.

EXPLORING RHETORIC

1. Highet's opening paragraph uses a conventional essay tactic. He begins with a personal anecdote about his school experience, which is designed to make readers identify with him as a person who has had the same difficulties they have had.

2. Although Highet blames his teachers for not assigning strong topics, he seems to suggest that there are no weak topics, for a writer can make any topic vivid if he or she takes an interesting approach. It might be good to remind students about this when they complain that they don't know what to say about a topic.

3. How can an essay be merely "musings" or "thinking in print" if the subject of it has to be clear in your mind before you write? This problem is worth discussing, for students sometimes begin to write before the subject is clear in their minds, or else they ignore prewriting as a way of making something clear in their minds. Essays that give the illusion of being mere musings are, of course, the result of concentration.

4. "A thick coating of mud, chill and stifling" seems an extreme metaphor, but it certainly is tactile. You might ask your students to try to come up with their own metaphors for something that dampens their spirits. The slag heap–factory chimneys example illustrates how Highet took a topic he did not find interesting—scenery—and rescued it by making it his own.

5. Even if one cannot always draw the form of an essay, as Highet's newspaper friend suggests, the effort may be a good exercise, for it reminds students that essays are forms, structures, things in the world. Highet's essay might be thought of visually as strong blocks stacked on top of each other, each paragraph cemented to the next by a formal transition.

6. You might cite first sentences from some of the essays in this book as provocative openers—for example, "Complexion. My first conscious experience of sexual excitement concerns my complexion" (Rodriguez); "Yesterday I set out to catch the new season, and instead I found an old snakeskin" (Dillard); "My first victim was a woman—white, well-dressed, probably in her early twenties" (Staples). Discuss how snappy openings make entrance into an essay appealing.

7. Students who find writing essays hard work probably have little reading and writing experience. When they try to explain why they have difficulty, they may offer that they do not know what to say or know what to say but not how to say it. Either response provides an opportunity to discuss the importance of practice in both reading and writing if students are to develop relative ease in their own writing, although, as we all know, good writing never comes easily.

PART ONE

EXPLORING THE PERSONAL PAST

Learning to Listen

EUDORA WELTY

This is an excerpt from the first section of Welty's charming memoir of her childhood, *One Writer's Beginnings*. Developed from a set of three lectures delivered at Harvard in 1983, this modest little book was on the *New York Times* best-seller list for almost a year. Instead of presenting a simple chronology of her life, Welty focuses on what made her "think like a writer." This selection reveals how she learned to look at life not as a mere series of events, one thing after another, but rather as the stuff of story.

EXPLORING IDEAS

1. Psychologists tell us that when we recall the past, we recall not the flow of events but rather moments that stand out. Literary critic Northrop Frye has said this is how we spatialize time; James Joyce called such moments "epiphanies." Recollecting such moments may help students realize that writing about the past means recalling meaningful moments, or discovering the meaning of moments, not just reciting events.

2. Learning to love language: to savor the word, to delight in a phrase, to relish the syntax of a sentence—these things are familiar to writers but may seem alien to students who think of writing as merely a mechanical process. Helping students to think of words as sensuous and to see sentences as structures they can manipulate in many ways is essential in helping them to think like writers.

3. Students for whom television has been the primary storyteller may not be able to talk about the difference between being read to by a person and being told a story by technology. There is a loss of interactivity when children sit passively in front of a television set and are unable to comment or ask questions. However, with the advent of interactive computer programs, this may be changing; interactive games such as *Myst* and virtual reality experiences in which "readers" become participants in the story may make further changes in the way technology tells stories.

4. Writers are more likely to hear words when they read than see pictures, for they are aware of the physical presence of language. You might have your students read a paragraph from this essay and concentrate on hearing the words instead of seeing the pictures; it is a good habit for them to develop.

5. I often read a section from Welty's short story, "Why I Live at the P.O.," at this point to illustrate her ability to assume the voice of someone who reveals more of the self than she means to. Robert Browning's "My Last Duchess" is another good example. You might ask your students to think of people they know who are unaware of what they reveal about themselves when they talk. Ask them to try to simulate that person's voice in a monologue.

6. Francine Prose, the contemporary short story writer, wrote a little essay on gossip in the *New York Times* a few years ago in which she suggested that gossip is the way that most of us learn to tell stories: "Pacing, tone, clarity, and authenticity are as essential for the reportage of neighborhood news as they are for well-made stories," argues Prose.

7. Listening for the unspoken, or reading between the lines, is a skill we all learn, but it is particularly important for readers and writers, for it means being able to construct meaning out of simple talk or mere events by understanding what motivates or underlies the talk or the events. Welty's suggestion that storytellers can tell the truth by making up stories is related to Edward Hoagland's idea that writers are faithful to the "truthful point"—not necessarily the truthfulness of individual events.

EXPLORING RHETORIC

1. Although it may seem that Welty is self-indulgent in spending three paragraphs on the anecdote about the moon, the story is relevant to her central point about the relationship between language and truth to the physical world, for here she chides herself a bit for loving the sound of "moon" so much that she put it in the wrong part of the sky. Edward Abbey talks about the relationship between the scientist's way of looking at the world and the poet's way in his essay in Part Two.

2. By using the example of music, Welty suggests that listening stimulates movement or is translated into movement. This is related to her early example of the sound of "moon" taking on a physical presence. Your students will understand how music makes them want to move, for they know what it means to feel music as if it were tangible. If they can begin to feel that way about words, they can begin, as Welty did, to think like a writer.

3. The idea of the calling cards allows Welty to move from listening to words to listening to gossip, which for her becomes tangible "scenes"—not just events but "drama." The calling cards are means of socializing, and gossip is basically a social activity, a means of participating in a community.

4. Welty remembers a woman who kept her mother on the telephone just because she is "ready to talk," for she is someone who gets taken over by language, who becomes the language she uses, who is the sum of her talk. Moreover, her quality of belief, in which the little doodlebug nursery jingle becomes real so that Welty loves to call up her doodlebugs better than those in her own yard, makes Welty aware of that moment when the wish comes true and the story becomes real—a magical quality that all good stories have.

5. The image created of Fannie, the sewing woman with hands like claws and legs like stumps as she moves around Welty on her knees tacking her together, is more effective than a straightforward description, for Welty wants to create a mysterious image of her as gossiper, magic maker, author.

6. The image the essay creates of Welty as a child is that of a somewhat sheltered little girl surrounded by adults rather than other children, who spends her time reading, dreaming, and listening. The image we have of her as an adult is a wise woman who is self-consciously aware of the forces that have made her a writer of stature. A good Welty story to supplement this essay, one that Welty has said presents a portrait of her as a young author, is "A Memory."

Finding a Voice

MAXINE HONG KINGSTON

The subtitle of Maxine Hong Kingston's autobiography, *The Woman Warrior,* is *Memoirs of a Girlhood Among Ghosts.* Like Welty's memoirs, it focuses on Kingston's childhood rather than her entire life, but instead of exploring how she became a writer, as Welty does, Kingston examines her experiences as a cultural outsider living in America among "ghosts," the name her mother gives to all people who are not Chinese. Compare Welty's point of view, which suggests the wise elderly woman, to Kingston's, which retains something of the pained and puzzled child.

EXPLORING IDEAS

1. Kingston begins by counting on the reader to be aware of two related metaphors: being tongue-tied and cutting a knot to free up something. If your students are unfamiliar with knot-making as an art, you might suggest that clowns who tie balloons into animal forms are knot-makers of a sort. Kingston says she would have been an outlaw knot-maker in China, for she would like to create something that would be blinding in its complexity and beauty.

2. By asking students to discuss experiences they have had of speaking in public—making a speech or giving a report, for example—you might help them realize that they have been most uncomfortable when they have been least prepared. This experience can be related to their insecurity about writing. It may well be that the students who say they have trouble writing are the same ones who say that speaking in public makes them nervous.

3. Saying that she was only recently able to ask the postman for special-issue stamps suggests Kingston's continuing shyness, which may be both personal and cultural. Shyness is a curious quality, for while students may have no trouble recalling examples of their shyness, they may not be able to explain why they were (or are) shy. Use this opportunity to discuss how writing requires not only describing events but also suggesting the cause or meaning of them.

4. Discussing Kingston's anecdote of drinking out of a saucer is an opportunity to examine the similarities and differences between a simple social faux pas and a serious cultural error. Have your students brainstorm a list of such social "mistakes," and then rank them in order of their seriousness. Which are trivial and amusing and which serious and offensive?

5. Most of us have had the experience of being the victim of a bully. Some bullies are motivated by racial intolerance, perhaps like the Japanese who chased and hit Kingston, who is Chinese. Although there are many possible reasons that make bullies what they are, brainstorming a list of motives may reveal that all are based on the bully's feeling tougher, stronger, smarter, or otherwise better in some way than the victim.

6. Kingston spends several paragraphs of this selection describing the relative laxness of the Chinese school as compared to the demands made on her by the American school. Students in your class for whom English is a second language may be able to provide some valuable discussion here on the comfort of retreating back to a family or neighborhood where everyone speaks the same language and thus where they feel safe.

EXPLORING RHETORIC

1. "Cutting the Gordian knot" suggests solving by force what someone has created by craft or art. The knot is thus a metaphor for a particular kind of complexity (as Annie Dillard's use of the metaphor in her essay elsewhere in this book suggests), one that is hard to solve because its beginning or underlying structure is difficult to discern. Your students may think of other expressions to suggest something similar, such as "get to the bottom line," "cut the bull," "get to the heart of the matter."

2. When we recall an event, we may find that we do not see things from the perspective we had then, but rather from the viewpoint of our present self looking at ourself as we were then. Kingston knows this is particularly true when looking at the self as an infant, for there is no way to identify with that self; thus, it seems psychologically natural to refer to the infant she was in the third person.

3. The image of the mouth open like that of a baby bird emphasizes the sense of helplessness of the infant that Kingston imagines had her tongue cut. Describing the white line the frenum makes when you stick your tongue against the back of your upper front teeth emphasizes the keenness of the blade that she imagines sliced the frenum itself.

4. The fact that Kingston's mother treats the supposed cutting of the frenum so lightly, that none of the other children have it done, and that Kingston herself thinks it may be possible that her mother was lying suggest that the event did not really take place.

5. Kingston's mother uses the story of cutting the frenum as a metaphor for freeing the tongue and making Kingston less tongue-tied. Kingston's saying that the mother should have cut more creates a transition to her central point about having such difficulty talking.

6. Kingston's taking on the point of the view of herself as a child makes it possible for her to get away with such obvious exaggerations as saying that a telephone call makes her mouth bleed.

7. The phrases "I spoke to no one at school, did not ask before going to the lavatory, and flunked kindergarten" illustrate the rhetorical technique of setting up a series in which a certain expectation is created and then defeating that expectation in the last item in the series to make that item more emphatic.

8. Describing her voice as being like that of a crippled animal running on broken legs and saying that she could hear splinters in the voice and bones rubbing jagged against each other effectively reflect the pain that talking is for Kingston. The metaphor is consistent with other suggestions of pain in the essay, such as her throat bleeding when she talks on the telephone.

Fitting In

JOHN TARKOV

I have paired Tarkov's essay with a selection from Gay Talese's book *Unto the Sons* not only because both focus on the cultural gap between American-born sons and their European immigrant fathers, but because both use the typically American sport of baseball, although in quite different ways, as a metaphor to suggest this difference. Tarkov's essay is a memorial to his father and thus has some of the elegiac qualities common to such writing.

EXPLORING IDEAS

1. Tarkov begins in typical anecdotal fashion by identifying both the central metaphoric event around which the essay is built and the place where the recollection occurred to him, the church where his father's funeral service took place. In asking students to recall a place, suggest that they discover or invent some significance to attach to it so that the description is not merely spatial but also dynamic.

2. The issue that some sociologists and feminists raise about so-called male bonding is that such activities encourage stereotyped male activity of the kind that Amy Gross and Paul Theroux in their essays in Part Three find so repugnant. If you assign either of those two essays with this one, ask students about the implications of the disappearance of "masculine" behavior.

3. Tarkov returns to this image of the ball unmarked by human error at the end of his essay, for it introduces the theme of mild conflict as to who put the first scuff mark on the ball. Ask your students about the difference between the value of objects kept as if new, such as collectors' items, and objects that bear the traces of human use, such as family mementos.

4. It is, of course, a masculine stereotype that men do not talk about their feelings or show their emotions. However, Tarkov's refusal to tell how he felt about his father's death may reflect a typical writer's device of showing rather than telling. Ask your students to try to communicate a painful feeling by showing what they did rather than telling what they felt.

5. Defining sentimentality may help your students understand the problem of trying to communicate genuine sentiment without falling into sentimentality.

6. Maxine Hong Kingston, in the previous essay, describes how it feels to live in a culture not her own; Arthur L. Campa, in Part Three, explains some cultural differences between Anglos and Hispanics.

7. The issue here is whether generation gaps are inevitable and, if so, what causes them: the rapid nature of social change, or a basic difference between the way young people and older people look at the world.

8. Ishmael Reed discusses this controversial social issue in Part Three. Have your students consider whether it is possible both to blend into a cultural mix and to maintain cultural uniqueness at the same time.

9. Fathers have an idea of what they want their sons to be, and sons have an idea of what they wish their fathers were. Ask your students to consider what conflicts these expectations cause. Are fathers and sons more likely than mothers and daughters to have these hopes?

EXPLORING RHETORIC

1. Tarkov combines time and space in such a way that the thirty years seem compressed into a span little more than the two miles that separate the church and the parking lot. By connecting his recollection of the parking lot game of catch to the church where his father's funeral is taking place, Tarkov smoothly introduces his baseball metaphor.

2. Baseball seems a more appropriate symbol of America than football for many reasons. Have your students brainstorm some of the evidence: the song "Take Me Out to the Ball Game"; the well-known verse, "Casey at the Bat"; heroes such as Babe Ruth, Lou Gehrig, and Joe DiMaggio; and films such as *The Natural* and *Field of Dreams*. Neither football nor basketball has the same universal appeal as baseball. Consequently a boy playing catch in a parking lot with his father is a conventional image of male bonding in America.

3. There is a kind of tough kid or street kid suggestion made by "mouthed off"; "peevishness" seems more appropriate for a youngster than "cross," or "grouchy" or "cranky."

4. The image of the father's looking at the newspaper as if peering out the window on an unfamiliar landscape emphasizes the "stranger in a strange land" image Tarkov presents of his father.

5. The idea of the second generation's being absorbed over a flame so high that the first is left encrusted on the rim must have occurred to Tarkov when he considered some of the metaphoric implications of the melting pot. It suggests that whereas there is a powerful pressure in America to absorb the young into the mix, the older generation (and the notion of older being "crusty" is a conventional one) remains like a residue on the edge of things.

6. The notion of both Tarkov and his father as emissaries extends the metaphor of the father's being in one land looking out the window at another land that the son inhabits. The result is that although the two are not enemies or strangers, they have little to say to each other; their talk, as trivial as it is, becomes formalized, like that of official emissaries who deal in a certain protocol.

7. Part of the reason Tarkov never tells his father about his embarrassment is that the father can do nothing about what vaguely embarrasses Tarkov. Moreover, Tarkov wishes to convey the image of an indulgent son, who tolerates his father's Old World ways.

8. Tarkov uses baseball as a controlling metaphor in this essay. It is the male bonding image of the boy and father, a symbol of the minor conflict between them, and a symbol of the son's sense of superiority over the father, for the scuff mark on the ball is the result of the father's error. Sports in general ties the two men together as they drink beer and watch television.

9. The mixture of sadness and humor in this essay reflects the tone Tarkov creates of stereotyped masculine ways of showing feeling: the gentle cuff on the side of the face, the good-humored quarreling, the laugh about not sending the obituary notice to the *New York Times* that the father always complained about.

Playing Catch

GAY TALESE

This selection appears in Talese's epic personal history, *Unto the Sons,* which is less about his childhood than about the struggle of his immigrant ancestors, and, by extension, all other Italian immigrants who came to America in the early part of the twentieth century. In this anecdotal essay, Talese, who does not always stick to a chronological structure in the book, remembers being in the back seat of his parents' Buick in December 1943, recalling an event that took place in the summer of 1941.

EXPLORING IDEAS

1. Compare Talese's metaphor of being hooked on baseball to Marie Winn's metaphor of television watching as an addiction in Part Four. Students may be unaware that it is a fishing metaphor, which suggests a graphic image of being painfully caught.

2. Your students may not think that whistling a refrain from a song about Joe DiMaggio constitutes a strong rebellion, so point out that Talese says it is the first sign of rebellion. Ask them to try to recall their first hint of rebellion against a parent or guardian and discuss its significance.

3. Children can be very intolerant of adults until, becoming adults themselves, they often have a new insight. Ask your students to try to recall one such new insight they have had about their parents.

4. Parents no longer can use the line, "When I was your age, I walked five miles through the snow to go to school." But most adults have some such claim about how much harder life was when they were children. This can be a good topic for a humorous essay from the child's or the adult's point of view.

5. In an era in which half of all marriages end in divorce, some students may not want to talk about basic differences between their mother and father, for such differences resulted in pain. Others, however, may have suggestions about parental differences that were complementary rather than conflict ridden.

6. The wish to have been born into a different family has occurred to everyone at one time or another. Small group discussion of this issue can emphasize how many topics can be either comic or tragic, depending on one's perspective.

7. A child's awareness of adult secrets can be too delicate for students to deal with if it involves serious parental conflict. Adult secrets may make some children feel unfairly excluded, whereas others may want to have nothing to do with secrets. Graham Greene's short story "The Basement Room," made into an engaging film, named *The Fallen Idol,* deals with this issue.

8. Being caught playing when you were supposed to be working is not necessarily limited to children. Some employers say that employees' playing computer games on company time has become a serious problem.

9. The phrase "sorrowful moment" does not have to refer to a deep pain, but can refer to a minor event, such as the one Talese describes of his father's failure to catch the ball. Ask your students to recall what James Joyce described as moments of epiphany—seemingly minor but serious in their implications.

Exploring Rhetoric

1. Heroes and hero worship are implicit in Talese's essay, for his father, who knows nothing of baseball, fails to fulfill the role of hero for him. If your students know nothing about Jolting Joe, ask them to think about their own heroes, or lack of heroes, today.

2. The essay has two initial time frames: Talese as an adult remembering a childhood moment in December 1943 when he was planning to run away to the Yankee training camp, and the summer of 1941 when he became hooked on baseball and whistled the DiMaggio tune. These time frames may make the narrative a bit confusing, but they constitute a continuum from being hooked on baseball to planning to run away to baseball camp.

3. This sentence, a complex series of clauses and phrases, suggests by its language and syntax an adult recalling the way the child felt—not the same as the child describing how he felt.

4. The two paragraphs in which Talese talks about his uncles may not seem directly relevant to his disappointment in his father, but they do emphasize his later realization that the men of his father's generation did not have the leisure to play catch or follow baseball the way he does.

5. The phrase "emotional double agent" may not mean anything to students unfamiliar with novels and films of espionage, and Talese does not wish to suggest that his father was a spy. Rather, the image suggests the father's emotional dilemma of feeling torn between two different allegiances by having relatives in Italy who were fighting Americans.

6. Time shifts in the essay have already been referred to, but your students may find this one a bit jarring—not knowing whether to place the central anecdote at the same time as the ride in the Buick or the whistling of the DiMaggio tune. It probably takes place in the summer in between, thus emphasizing the continuum of events. Talese is less concerned with chronology than he is with a complex of events that seem to cluster together thematically. Eudora Welty discusses how children learn in separate moments rather than over time in her earlier essay in this part.

7. Time seems to slow down in the description of the father's missing the ball. Ask your students to think of it as being filmed in slow motion. Consider how each physical movement is described—for example, "I quickly took the ball in my right hand, cocked my arm, and threw it at him"; "He extended his arms upward and cupped his soft tailor's hands, and braced himself for the impact"; "I cringed as I saw the ball hit him solidly on the side of the neck, carom off a shoulder, rebound against the wall behind him, and come rolling slowly back to his feet, where it finally stopped. He squeezed it. He turned it around in his fingers."

8. This anecdote about how the father cannot play catch comfortably suggests remarkably well how a young American boy became aware of his father's discomfort with American customs. John Tarkov, in his essay earlier in this part, uses the example of the father's causing the first scuff on the new ball by awkwardly throwing it over his son's head.

Going West

TOBIAS WOLFF

This brief selection is from the beginning of Wolff's memoir, *This Boy's Life*, which deals primarily with his relationship with his mother and the man she lived with when they finally reach the end of the trip described here. Wolff, a fine short story writer, commands a narrative style that packs a lot of information in a few words. A close analysis of the style should convince students that good narrative results from a careful control of significant detail.

EXPLORING IDEAS

1. Central to Wolff's narrative is the character of the boy. The essay provides the opportunity to discuss how writers create images of themselves as they were at a past time. The man recounting these events is not the same as the boy experiencing them. The adult narrator, for example, knows that the runaway truck suggests life's vulnerability and that the mother feels protective of the boy after the accident, but the boy's only concern is how he can selfishly exploit that feeling to get the souvenirs that he knows his mother cannot afford.

2. The key sentence in the selection is at the end of paragraph 7: "I was caught up in my mother's freedom, her delight in her freedom, her dream of transformation." The boy's identification with the mother is central to the essay's effect, as the frequent repetition of the first-person-plural pronouns "we" and "us" suggests. Ask students to describe, from the point of view of their present understanding, a time when they had some intuition about a parent's feelings that they did not understand at the time.

3. The mother's account of her past indicates that she has been through transitions before. The details of her life prior to the 1929 crash of the stock market indicate a kind of romantic dream world, right out of F. Scott Fitzgerald's *The Great Gatsby*. The trip west is also a Gatsby-like dream that mother and son will strike it rich on uranium in Utah. The essay springs from the mother's romanticism and the boy's eager identification with it, for she is as childlike as the boy is.

4. The mother's determination to "make up for lost time" and the boy's determination to help her give the essay a sense of two people being of one mind. The anecdote of the mother's buying the boy the souvenirs after the truck accident suggests "making up" to the boy for something that the mother can no more control than the boy can control his selfish exploitation of her.

5. In writing a character sketch of the mother as she is revealed in this essay, students should analyze and synthesize her reaction to the boy after the truck accident, her stories about her past, her hope to find uranium, and her reaction to the news that they are too late for the uranium rush. Ask students to imagine themselves in the boy's situation and to describe how they would feel about such a mother.

EXPLORING RHETORIC

1. The opening sentence achieves a great deal in few words. It suggests that this is a cross-country trip (for why else would they cross the Continental Divide?), that they do not have much money, that it is only the two of them, and that the trip has not been easy. You can use this sentence to discuss the importance of dynamic opening sentences, reminding students that they can dramatically jump into the middle of something and then double back later to provide exposition.

2. Try having your students rewrite the first three paragraphs, replacing the metaphoric language with more neutral words such as "noise" for "bawling," "went past" for "shot past," "wobbling" for "shimmying wildly," "blew through the trees" for "sighed in the trees," "turned over" for "lay on its back," "small" for "pitifully small," and "blowing" for "feathering out." Ask them to discuss the difference in effect of these word choices.

3. Have students attempt a careful analysis of the language in paragraphs 6 and 7. They should note how Wolff creates an image of summer storms with "flickering skies that turned black and exploded and cleared just long enough to leave the air gauzy with steam." Discuss with them the image created of people with rotten teeth in the South who moved with "arthritic slowness and spoke in thick strangled tongues." Is this a stereotype or a convention of fiction? Have them try to describe the motel room scene using other language than "boggy rooms where headlight beams crawled up and down the walls and mosquitoes sang in our ears, incessant as the tires whining on the highway outside."

4. Wolff's tactic in paragraph 12 is to begin the narrative description in short sentences suggestive of the abruptness and immediacy of arriving in Utah and discovering that they are too late. He then moves to a longer sentence that implies the surprising state of affairs and ends with short sentences alluding to just how bad things really are. The paragraph provides a good opportunity to discuss how calculated syntax can be and how important sentence length and structure are for reflecting idea and emotion.

5. Whereas the personality of the mother is communicated by the details that the narrator uses to describe her, the personality of the boy is communicated less by content than by dialogue style. Have your students carefully examine the last paragraph of the essay. The sentence, "So we drove on through the desert," suggests the boy's confidence in the mother, though her hopes are naive and childlike. The boy's saying that he was "hooked" on the song "Mood Indigo" and that he croons "world-wearily" suggests a surface maturity that is actually quite childlike. This is a boy who wishes to be like an adult companion to his mother and is caught up in the excitement of her hopes and dreams. The final image of the two of them calling off the numbers on the Burma Shave signs at the top of their lungs completes this sense of the boy's being caught up in the romantic hope of the mother. The entire selection is as carefully controlled and thematically unified as a short story.

Manzanar

JEANNE WAKATSUKI HOUSTON AND JAMES D. HOUSTON

This chapter from *Farewell to Manzanar* focuses on life in an internment camp after about a year. It is notable for the way the authors unify the piece around the theme of shifting from outrage to a sense of normality. Practically every detail in the essay emphasizes this central theme; a careful analysis will help students realize the importance of choosing details for their relevance to a unifying impression or idea.

EXPLORING IDEAS

1. The fact that the wind in the trees reminds Houston of the surf in her old home in Ocean Park does not suggest homesickness but rather a comforting illusion that she is still home. Your students, however, might be more familiar with moving to a new place and contrasting it with an old familiar place. Ask them to try to create a sense of the excitement of exploring the new while simultaneously missing the old.

2. Ask your students to try to think of rituals or activities that characterize a group to which they belong—for a family group, perhaps periodic gatherings for holidays or certain special ways of doing things; for a club, a class, or a neighborhood, perhaps shared experiences or longtime relationships that create the cohesion of the group.

3. Part of the irony of the stay at Manzanar is that although the father is incarcerated, he has the time to take up hobbies that he enjoys. If students try to define the word "putter," suggest that they contrast it to more goal-directed work.

4. Although Houston suggests that natural forms are important to the Japanese in particular, all students will be able to recall a natural scene that imparted a spiritual feeling. Without necessarily getting into specific religious feelings, have them try to explain why a natural scene might make them experience spirit; see the essay by Edward Abbey in Part Two. Or you can ask them to describe a natural scene in such a way as to suggest its spiritual meaning—no simple task if you specify that they describe the scene rather than their feelings.

5. Since the overall theme of the essay is how Houston and her family make the best of a bad situation, a discussion of this theme can lead to a sharing of similar student experiences. This topic could be used for a timed writing, for it not only asks for narration-description but also analysis of what such an experience meant.

6. The yearbook pictures are an effective technique to complete the theme of normalizing an abnormal situation, for even as you see the normality of students walking with armloads of books, you notice they are walking by tarpaper shacks. The picture of the old woman walking down a path in which the wire of the camp is out of focus effectively communicates a sense of being at ease yet enclosed. Have your students describe a picture from their high school yearbook and explain how it represents a certain lifestyle or cultural value; then set up some small group activities in which they show the pictures and get some feedback on how successful their description or explanation has been.

EXPLORING RHETORIC

1. Although Houston says that the rows of pear and apple trees "stand for" the turning of life in the camp from the outrageous to the tolerable, she does not mean this in a literary, symbolic way, but rather that when she thinks of that shift—the central theme of the essay—the trees seem connected with it. Ask your students to recall a significant experience in their lives, a period of transition or transformation; then, ask them to think of a scene or object that seems connected with that experience and to describe the object in such a way as to suggest its relationship to the experience.

2. Although your students may be familiar with using hyperbole in everyday speech, they may not be so aware of the effectiveness of using exaggeration in writing. The idea of Houston's mother hurrying her own family into new living quarters before the previous residents had snapped their suitcases shut to leave depends on the absurd visual image it creates, for even as readers know it did not happen literally, the visual image humorously communicates the idea of the mother's haste. Have your students brainstorm some similar exaggerations.

3. Paragraph 11 focuses completely on the Japanese internees' growing gardens and thus domesticating the desert, creating a kind of oasis in which they seem to hang suspended. The picture at the end of the essay of the old woman who seems floating in the landscape repeats this image. Houston gives the impression of a netherworld that is neither quite real nor quite fantasy but somehow possessing the characteristics of both.

4. Because students are so familiar with film, you might ask them to visualize the montage technique of the paragraphs that describe what Houston's family is doing during this period of the Manzanar internment. Ask them to write a brief description of what this section would look like if it were filmed. Instead of focusing on the activities of the entire family, Houston emphasizes the example of her brother's dance band because it best suggests the curious blend of the normal and the strange of the internment. As Houston says in paragraph 12, the camp became a "world unto itself, with its own logic and familiar ways" as the people survived and controlled their rage and despair by re-creating "normality, some sense of continuing."

5. Just as Houston begins the essay with the image of the rows of trees that seem to signify for her the transition to normality in the camp, she ends it with the single picture from the yearbook of the old woman floating in the landscape. Note that the scene is in winter, but the old woman is wearing gardening clothes. The woman is on a path, but the path leads to the invisible wire fence that is out of focus. The picture suggests both the bleakness of winter and the hope of growth; moving toward a meaningful destination, though the way is blocked: the kind of illusion of freedom and normality that the Japanese created while in the camps to make their lives there bearable.

Complexion

RICHARD RODRIGUEZ

I have placed this selection from Rodriguez's autobiographical *Hunger of Memory* alongside that from Updike's memoir *Self-Consciousness* because both deal with male adolescent insecurity stemming from external appearance. It may be worth analyzing the two different approaches reflected by these essays: one primarily narrative, the other primarily analytical. Students may also wish to discuss differences between the reactions of the two boys to the sense of isolation that physical difference creates.

EXPLORING IDEAS

1. Rodriguez introduces the sexual theme that dominates the essay in the first full sentence, for it is his sense of "sexual inferiority" created by his different skin color that most torments him. He specifies this is his first "conscious" sexual excitement at age seven, for he wishes to emphasize the imaginative nature of the excitement; even infants experience sexual excitement as a result of physical stimulation.

2. A child's discovery that his parents have a secret life in the bedroom may be too sensitive for some of your students to discuss or even recall. Most psychologists suggest that children's discovery of parental sexuality has an important impact—positive or negative—on their own attitude toward sexuality when they grow older.

3. It is easy enough for adults to tell children that inner beauty is more important than surface appearance. However, adolescents know how important it is to have their appearance accepted. A little reminiscence and brainstorming about this idea should create some good discussion and essay ideas.

4. Adolescents may feel they are marked in many ways—too tall, too short; too fat, too skinny; too pale, too dark. Ask your students to describe the "perfect" appearance for both males and females against which they feel they are measured.

5. If it were not for attracting a sexual mate, would people still be so concerned about their physical appearance? Are men as concerned about their appearance around other men? Are women as concerned about their appearance around other women? A little brainstorming about these issues will raise others.

6. The metaphor of being divorced from one's body is worth exploring, for we are bombarded by the media about the importance of dieting, exercising, and looking good. If we do not think about our bodies, does that mean we are "divorced" from them? Are people who are always conscious about their bodies less divorced from them? How do we measure this idea?

7. Comparing physical sensations to imaginative experiences may get your students involved in discussing the difference between "thinking" about things and "doing" things. This could lead to a discussion of the stereotype of intellectuals as nerds who are physically unattractive and therefore cut themselves off from physical activities completely for the life of the mind.

8. Rodriguez's envy of the farm laborers is an envy of the simple physical life, as compared to his own self-conscious analytical life.

EXPLORING RHETORIC

1. The mother's smile is important to the opening of Rodriguez's essay, for it introduces his first awareness of the secret sexual life of his parents. The fact that the smile is both radiant and bashful suggests a contradiction of being both open and closed at once. The shyness suggests that this aspect of their life is secret and therefore is "astonishing" to Rodriguez. Students might explore the difference between Rodriguez's series of adjectives and such alternatives as "bright, shy, and surprising" or "happy, timid, and shocking."

2. There is nothing quite like the surprise we feel when, as Robert Burns has it in his poem "To a Louse," we see ourselves as others see us. One obvious place this happens is in dressing rooms with mirrors on all the walls when we see "sides" of ourselves that others see but we do not. It is this element of surprise and strangeness that Rodriguez evokes with detail. Ask your students to brainstorm a time when they saw themselves in a new way—a way in which others see them.

3. The scene in which Rodriguez tries to shave away his dark complexion is a poignant one—pathetic because it suggests such a feeling of desperation in a twelve year old, yet comic because it is naive and does not pose any real danger or cause damage. The image of pressing the blade to the skin makes the reader cringe, but the sentence, "All I succeeded in doing, however, was in shaving my arms bare of their hair," evokes a smile.

4. In paragraph 5, Rodriguez creates a montage-like list, introduced with the short fragments, "Thirteen years old. Fourteen," followed by a relatively long sentence and two balanced sentences: "With disgust then I would come face to face. . . . With disappointment I located myself." The series concludes with the short sentence, "Or I'd see my dark wrist against my long-sleeved shirt." Ask your students to imagine this series of sentences as a film montage. Do the sentence length and variety suggest how the visual images might be presented?

5. Rodriguez's description of his companions in high school physical education class suggests the stereotype of someone who becomes intellectual only because of his or her physical unattractiveness. Your students might want to consult the essay on stereotyping by Heilbroner in Part Three for a discussion of how and why we use stereotyping.

6. The adult Rodriguez knows that calling athletes "animals" when he was an adolescent is a reflection of the old sour grapes tendency to scorn that which one desires but cannot have. This might be a good time to remind students that essays recalling events in the past always have at least two points of view: that of the relatively unaware child and that of the relatively aware adult. John Updike's essay depends much more on the aware, analytical adult than Rodriguez's does. However, even Rodriguez's relatively straightforward recollection indicates the adult's awareness of the child's isolation.

At War with My Skin

JOHN UPDIKE

Unlike Richard Rodriguez, Updike does not describe his sexual unattractiveness but rather takes a more intellectual approach to his sense of divorce from his body. Although your students may be able to identify more easily with Rodriguez's straightforward recollection than with Updike's analytical meditation, Updike's essay is a good example of a writer who is trying to discover meaning in experience.

EXPLORING IDEAS

1. The idea of a foreign substance invading the body is a staple of horror films, from *Invasion of the Body Snatchers* to *Alien*. The result, suggests Updike, is the feeling of being an outcast. Ask students to brainstorm when they felt like an outcast because of some illness—perhaps because of a childhood disease such as chicken pox.

2. When you meet someone you have not seen in a long time, you may still hold that person in your mind as he or she was in the past. Such a meeting may bring back a memory you associate with the person, enabling you to reexperience it. Have students recall such an experience and analyze its significance.

3. Ask students to think of a connection with a parent, sibling, or friend based on some characteristic they share—perhaps a similar physical characteristic, such as hair or eye color; a similar background experience; or a similar set of likes and dislikes. Ask students to explain the nature of this kind of relationship or connection.

4. Some commentators have suggested that we have been living in a narcissistic age for some time—an age in which people are so concerned with physical appearance that they spend most of their time trying to look young, slim, and beautiful. Ask students to identify one person they know who qualifies as narcissistic, to identify and describe these characteristics, and to discuss the implications of such narcissistic behavior.

5. The brute world of childhood results both from adults' treating children as something less than human and from children's treating each other in a bullying sort of way. Ask your students to recall a time when they were treated in a brutish way, by either adults or other children. Ask them to consider whether such behavior is inevitable or preventable.

6. Updike notes a curious paradox about children: on the one hand, they attack each other openly, while on the other hand they feel sympathetic toward others who are being attacked, for they know what such attacks feel like. Ask your students to brainstorm some childhood activities they can recall that illustrate this paradox and to make some general comments about the nature of children that these activities reflect.

7. In Philip Roth's wonderful short story "Conversion of the Jews," the adolescent Ozzie Freedman rebels against his teacher by running to the roof of a school building. As he does so, he asks of himself, "Can this be me? Is it me? Is it me?" It is the question, Roth says, that the thief asks when he opens his first window or that the bridegroom asks before the altar. Ask your students to recall a similar experience in their own lives.

EXPLORING RHETORIC

1. The word "mottled" nicely characterizes Updike's spotty memory of his psoriasis, for it reflects the nature of the condition itself. The metaphor of "ripening into silvery scabs" suggests the mysterious invasion of a foreign substance more effectively than "developing white scabs" or "dry scabs" might.

2. The tone Updike establishes in the essay, using such language as "oleaginous," "bilious," and "palliations," suggests the sort of educated writer who might very well refer to the healing power of the sun as being that of a "living god."

3. Students should note that the paragraphs in this essay are much longer than those in Rodriguez's, for they are more analytical. The erudite tone Updike establishes prepares readers for paragraph 3, which provides a background medical explanation of psoriasis. At the end of this long paragraph, Updike returns to the healing power of the sun, pointing out the irony of modern medicine's using fluorescent tubes.

4. The syntactical balance of the two sentences—one referring to a present action and one to a past action—nicely parallels the similarity between the new fluorescent remedy and the old sun remedy.

5. Updike's use of alliteration in this sentence ("favors the fair" and "pallid progeny") is consistent with the tone he has already established of an educated man exploring the meaning and implications of a personal experience. Ask your students to consider how the following alternatives would change the tone: "The disease occurs most frequently among light-skinned people, the pale children of overcast countries such as Holland, Ireland, and Germany."

6. Students may have some trouble with the sentence: "Nature and the self, the great moieties of earthly existence, are each cloven in two by a fascinated ambivalence." Updike wants to explore the irony that whereas the whole world is divided into the two halves of nature and the self, the self is divided into a self-loathing and a narcissistic attention to the self, just as nature is divided also into that which caused the disease and that which can cure it.

7. To "candle" an egg is to hold it up to a light to examine it for freshness. It is a nice metaphoric literary device here to suggest the mother's sense of mild shame, for the rotten egg indicates something that is not the mother's fault. At the same time the comic nature of the metaphor assures the reader that the mother does not truly feel ashamed of her son.

8. "Picking a scab" suggests laying bare sores, refusing to let them heal over. Autobiographical scab pickers are those sensational writers who delight in revealing all the sordid and ugly aspects of their past. Updike, however, is not describing his psoriasis perversely to please himself or to titillate readers but rather to face squarely an unpleasant aspect of his past that has influenced him to be what he is.

Getting a Job

MAYA ANGELOU

This selection from Maya Angelou's autobiographical *I Know Why the Caged Bird Sings* is paired with a chapter from Audre Lorde's *Zami: A New Spelling of My Name* because both deal with the discovery of racial discrimination by African American adolescent females. Angelou's reminiscence describes several events and reactions; Lorde's, like a short story, centers on a single event and an immediate response.

EXPLORING IDEAS

1. In recalling their first jobs, students should try to remember not only the details of getting and maintaining the job but also their feelings about it and the significance of "having a job" for the first time. For suggestions on attitudes toward work, students can consult the essays on work in Part Five.

2. Students who have not yet chosen a major field of study may indeed be trying to discover work for which they feel suitable. Brainstorming for an essay about the job for which they feel most suited may lead to some analysis about aptitudes and favorite activities, as well as some projections about the future.

3. In exploring the topic of "becoming friends overnight," students should recall a time when they were thrown together with strangers—serving on jury duty, going on a retreat, attending a conference—and try to explain what made such an immediate sense of community possible.

4. Students might recall sayings that they always heard from their parents, grandparents, or other relatives and explore the "truth" of them. Or they might write a character sketch or analysis of someone they know who always uses such sayings.

5. Angelou's confrontation with the white conductor forces her to realize that the previous encounter with the receptionist was indicative of widespread racism. It is an important part of the essay, for it marks that point at which Angelou becomes determined to triumph over the racism and get the streetcar job.

6. Part of the realization that one is becoming an adult, Angelou discovers, comes from being treated like an adult by parents or guardians and, as a result, identifying with them. Ask students to brainstorm when this transition took place in their lives and to discuss the differences in these relationships it created.

7. Students may not agree that it is the effort rather than the achievement that constitutes the greatest pleasure in many activities. Ask them to consider the general truth of the statement by exploring one event in their lives in which they engaged to reach a goal and, having reached it, realized that it was process rather than product that stood out.

8. Angelou concludes her mostly narrative essay with some general analysis about moving from adolescence to adulthood and about the struggles of the African American female. Going from being ignorant of being ignorant to being aware of being aware is a significant transition in life. Instead of just generalizing about the concept, students should recall a specific experience when they made such a transition.

Exploring Rhetoric

1. The expression, "Life was cheap and death entirely free," is an example of the common rhetorical technique of reviving a cliché by extending its implications.

2. Angelou mixes her metaphors here somewhat; it is a bit jarring to think of a bulldog climbing a ladder. You might use this as an opportunity to remind students about the dangers of mixing metaphors.

3. Angelou's discovery that there is something a bit rundown and drab about the railway company offices reinforces the realization that the racism she experiences is also sleazy and without the imposing dignity of officialdom that she expected.

4. The drama metaphor is a central one, for which Angelou has prepared by referring to her mother's remarks as a "terse aside." She says about the encounter with the receptionist, described in a dialogue scene, that they are like actors who know the play by heart—more specifically, like Hamlet and Laertes bound by the play to duel to the death in the final scene.

5. The prune metaphor is obvious enough, although students may find the visual image too grotesque to accept. Being bounced back and forth like a shuttle-cock probably works better here than a tennis metaphor, both because of the relatively slow speed of the former as well as the cultural differences suggested between those who play badminton and those who play tennis. A honeycomb of determination with apertures for the days to go in and out is another extension of a clichéd metaphor ("a hive of activity").

6. Angelou, of course, does not have personal memories of these figures, but her reference to them suggests that as an African American she feels cut off from the previously familiar historical figures of San Francisco's past.

7. Angelou's essay is not just about discovering racism or about getting one's first job; it is also about how these encounters have led to a new sense of adult risk and responsibility. Ask students to outline the development of the essay from particular experiences to general realizations.

8. The last five paragraphs of the essay are the most general. Angelou meditates on the perilous paradox of adolescence—the joy of freedom and the anxiety of indecision. Students may find the statement, "Few, if any, survive their teens," puzzling. Angelou seems to be talking about the inevitable death of adolescence, for it is easier to buckle under the pressure to become an adult than to continue to battle the adult world.

9. The metaphor of rebelling against the descending sun also reflects the shift to adult responsibility, which is characterized not by a general sense of the future but by separate days. Once again Angelou extends a familiar concept: not only are one's "days numbered," they are also identified.

10. The last two paragraphs, in which Angelou comments on the struggle and success of the African American female, follows from her personal experience, for although she was caught in the crossfire of masculine prejudice, white hate, and black lack of power, she emerged a formidable woman deserving respect and acceptance.

The Fourth of July

AUDRE LORDE

Audre Lorde's discovery of the lack of democracy in the seat of U.S. democracy seems so ironically appropriate that it is more like fiction than reality. As a preface to discussing literary techniques in this essay, you might consider discussing the concept of irony. What makes an event ironic?

EXPLORING IDEAS

1. Ask students to brainstorm when one is "supposed" to stop being a child. Lorde suggests eighth-grade graduation as a convenient transition point; however, she says that she is not sure what her sister, who has just graduated from high school, is supposed to stop being. Are there different gradations of being a child? When does one "finally" become an adult?

2. Some places—such as Hollywood, the Grand Canyon, Las Vegas, New York City—conjure up images of expectation that may or may not be fulfilled when they are actually visited. Ask students to brainstorm visiting a place about which they had expectations. They may discover that being disappointed in an expectation makes a better essay than being fulfilled. Why is this probably so?

3. Ask students to consider the basic personality trait of ignoring something in hopes that it will go away. Obviously such an approach works in some cases but not in others. Ask students to brainstorm for an essay in which they classify those kinds of things that should be ignored and those that should not.

4. In trying to think of some vital information they were never told by their parents but were just supposed to know, many students may think of sexual information, since it is the kind of information that parents assume that children will learn in school or pick up from their friends. Lorde is interested in underlying reasons. Ask students to think of certain vital information they were supposed to know but were not told by parents or guardians.

5. Having a "flair for the dramatic," even the "quietly dramatic," as Lorde says her father has, is a talent for lifting experiences out of their ordinariness and making them special. Maya Angelou uses the metaphor of reality as drama in her description of her encounter with the receptionist in the previous essay, "Getting a Job." Ask students to brainstorm means by which reality is heightened by being stylized or dramatized, for example, during holidays or other special occasions.

6. Feeling that something is unjust while most of those around you pretend that nothing is wrong is a particularly frustrating and isolating experience with which many of your students may be able to identify. Not long ago, a minister of the church I attend preached a particularly virulent sermon against the supposed sins of homosexuality. I was horrified to see so many in the congregation nodding their heads in agreement. When I publicly complained, I was further astonished that no one else in the church seemed to agree with me. Ask your students to brainstorm such an experience, and write about how it made them feel and what they think it meant.

EXPLORING RHETORIC

1. Lorde's opening paragraph informs readers that this is her first trip to the "fabled and famous capital of our country," that it is meant to be a graduation gift to her and her sister, and that it marks the point at which she is "supposed" to stop being a child. These details prepare readers for a coming-of-age story related to American democratic ideals.

2. The detail about the Liberty Bell alerts readers to Lorde's patriotic sense of idealism as a child and therefore prepares them for the depth of her disappointment.

3. Lorde's list of food suggests the value of specific detail. A mayonnaise jar is more concrete than merely a jar, and the fact that the peaches have fuzz particularizes them. That the females like sweet pickles while the father likes dill pickles may be a stereotype, but it is a nice characterizing detail—more particular than just noting that the family brought pickles.

4. Paragraph 5 introduces the racism theme by suggesting that Lorde does not know why she cannot eat in the dining car of the train. Paragraph 6 adds information about her sister's high school senior class trip that she did not know about until later, which then prepares the reader for the long, generalized paragraph 7 in which Lorde, speaking as an adult, provides background information about the way her parents dealt with racism.

5. Lorde's refusal to capitalize the words "America" and the "United States" indicates a lack of respect for the special nature of those concepts. If you ask students to discuss such things as burning the flag or refusing to stand at the playing of the national anthem, be prepared for some radical differences of opinion about these shows of "disrespect."

6. Lorde does not mention that Marian Anderson was allowed to sing before 75,000 people at the Lincoln Memorial in Washington, D.C., because that detail does not contribute to her rhetorical purpose. Have your students discuss the ethical implications of omitting such information for rhetorical effect.

7. Lorde uses the detail about her sensitivity to light to emphasize the effect of whiteness in Washington; it prepares us for the repetition of the term in the final paragraph.

8. The mother has lighter skin than the father—a fact that Lorde emphasizes by describing the parade of the family lined up according to their varying shades of brown.

9. In analyzing the four paragraphs that describe the event in the soda parlor, students might focus on such details as the fact that the dim, cool soda fountain ironically seems to offer relief at first; that the girls are crisp and clean and thus amply suitable for the ice cream parlor, except, of course, for the bias against their color; the fact that the waitress is southern and that they, being from the North, cannot understand her accent at first; and that the family says nothing when they are refused service but all march out together in a dignified manner, "as if we had never been black before."

10. It seems appropriate that this essay, which seems so well focused to signify the cruel irony of the lack of democracy in the heart of a democratic government, should end with the literary device of repeating the motif of whiteness over and over again.

My Father's Life

RAYMOND CARVER

Carver's reminiscence, like John Tarkov's essay earlier in this part, is a tribute on the occasion of his father's death; it is paired with the next selection, from Le Ly Hayslip's book, which focuses on the aftermath of her father's death. Carver is a master of the subtle detail; while seeming to be merely a straightforward description, Carver's essay is actually an exploration of his ambiguous identification with his father.

EXPLORING IDEAS

1. Carver assumes that his father lacks the imagination that he himself possesses. As other essays in this part suggest, children only occasionally suspect that their parents have an inner, secret life; not until they grow older do they begin to identify with their parents. Ask your students to brainstorm moments when they felt that their parents had an inner life—or to explain why they never thought that they did.

2. Although Carver describes a number of details about his father, the recurring theme is his drinking. This is not a minor detail, for as Carver notes in the poem in which he tries to "connect up" with his father, he cannot hold his liquor either. Carver was an alcoholic, but after treatment he spent the last years of his life sober.

3. Although the focus is on the father throughout the essay, Carver describes getting married, having a child, and trying to raise his family. The technique emphasizes that his own struggles are parallel with those of his father, thus supporting the identification that is the essay's central theme.

4. The degeneration of Carver's father, primarily because of his drinking, gives the essay its chronological structure. Because the father is a blue-collar, nonreflective man, his loss of his good name and sexual virility suggest the loss of masculinity.

5. Have your students read the essay by Paul Theroux in Part Three for a discussion of how the stereotypes of masculinity encourage scorn for the career of becoming a writer. Although Carver wants to have his father's approval of his decision to be a writer, at the same time, he admires the kind of nonreflective masculine stereotypes his father seems to embody.

6. Interest in someone's dying minutes is not an easy topic to discuss, but many people feel an inevitable curiosity about someone's last moments, perhaps because of the abrupt interruption that death seems to impose—the marvel of someone being alive one moment and dead the next.

7. Paragraph 29 includes two "pictures" of Carver's father: one an actual photograph, the other a poem based on the photograph. This is a central paragraph in the essay, for in it Carver explicitly states the central focus: that in important ways he and his father are alike, particularly in their drinking.

8. Students should check Noel Perrin's and Paul Theroux's essays in Part Three for discussions of how Western society teaches males that they should not cry. In brainstorming this idea, students should consider the cultural distinctions between the behavior expected of males and that expected of females.

EXPLORING RHETORIC

1. Having learned his style from Chekhov and Hemingway, Carver is the master of the short, simple sentence and the seemingly realistic detail. The fact that Carver's name is the same as his father's, with the first and middle name reversed, is significant in this essay in which the central theme is Carver's identification with his father. The anecdote about his wife's thinking that he has died when his mother calls to tell of his father's death emphasizes this identification.

2. Creating dialogue for the mother rather than summarizing what she said brings the mother alive dramatically, for we can "hear" her voice. Students should be cautioned that writing good dialogue is not as easy as it appears, for it is usually stylized rather than merely a realistic transcription.

3. Carver describes his baby bonnet as about to become untied and wonders whether his father is going to work or returning to work to provide an illusion of dynamic reality of a static image. Urge your students to describe a photograph from their own past in such a way as to make it come alive.

4. Carver's use of this comparison to a razor suggests his father's sense of pride in keeping his saws sharp and cared for; it also suggests Carver's admiration for his father.

5. Carver's description of boyhood pranks with outdoor toilets makes his sense of shame for his family's social status more concrete, for it suggests that when his family has the only outdoor toilet in town, such toilets are no longer a source of mischief and fun but a cause for secrecy.

6. Carver compares the colander to a rolling pin because that is the conventional object with which wives hit their wayward husbands over the head. Imagining what it would feel like to be hit over the head with the colander is another example of the theme of Carver's identifying with his father.

7. Carver is a master of understated short sentences. The fact that he makes no comment about his father's appearance but uses short sentences—"He was skinny and pale and looked bewildered. His pants wouldn't stay up. He didn't look like my dad. My mother began to cry"—makes the poignancy of the scene even more powerful for the reader. Chekhov once said that it was better to say too little than too much, although he was not sure why this was the case.

8. The poem suggests the gap between the father's desire to strike a pose of bravery and boldness and Carver's awareness of his basic weakness; it also suggests Carver's admiration of his father and his own drinking problem.

9. Carver's use of October rather than June, the month when his father died, both for its multisyllabic sound and its atmosphere of death, is purely rhetorical. Remind students that writers often alter the specifics of literal truth for the sake of poetic truth.

10. The fact that Carver has the same name as his father lyrically introduces the theme of the essay and provides the concluding coda. This essay is so carefully organized around the theme of identification that students should have little difficulty outlining the major points of the central idea.

My Father's Death

Le Ly Hayslip

Carver's essay about his father shows more rhetorical control than this selection from Le Ly Hayslip's autobiographical book about coming of age in war-torn Vietnam. Not a professional writer, Hayslip provides a rather straightforward description of her efforts to give her father a traditional funeral and makes some general remarks about what her father's death taught her.

Exploring Ideas

1. If your students come from different cultures, you will get a variety of responses about the importance of having a man as head of the household. If you do not wish the issue to develop into an argument about male versus female abilities, shift the discussion to the issue of whether customs in some countries that violate Western ideas of female rights should be respected.

2. Mortality, perceived as the transition from living person to corpse, can seem unreal; this is what often makes people say, "I can't believe it," when someone they know dies. However, the experience of inaccessibility is a concrete felt loss. Ask students to brainstorm differences between death as an abstraction and death as a concrete experience.

3. Death seems so cataclysmic that the idea of doing practical things such as choosing a coffin seems strange and unreal. When an undertaker asks you what sort of coffin you want for someone you have loved, you may be struck with the absurdity of making such choices. Ask your students to write about taking care of ordinary matters in extraordinary circumstances.

4. Talking about religion in a class is often risky, especially if you suggest that one culture's superstitions are another culture's religious rituals. In small group sessions, have students brainstorm some funeral rituals of their culture or religion, and compare them with those of other students.

5. Funeral rituals comprise a combination of spiritual and practical activities. Have students brainstorm the underlying assumptions of some of the funeral rituals with which they are familiar, for example, sitting with the body during funeral wakes, dressing the body in the dead person's best clothes, and burying objects with the body.

6. Hayslip is careful to make sure that the rituals are followed in precise detail. Have your students brainstorm about the importance of rituals in which the activities must be followed precisely. What will happen if they are not? Is there some kind of magic involved in rituals? What is the purpose of formality and seriousness in such rituals as military ceremonies, religious rites, and holiday celebrations, for example?

7. Have students brainstorm about how people in their own culture are "supposed to act" after the death of a loved one. Why is this behavior expected? What happens when the expected behavior is not followed? If students write an essay about a time when they violated such social expectations, emphasize that the essay should not be merely a narrative account but a means to examine the meaning and significance of the behavior.

EXPLORING RHETORIC

1. There is no biological or logical reason that the morgue is so cold and forbidding that trees and grass refuse to grow outside; however, we accept this exaggeration because psychologically it seems right. Although it is realistically possible, it would seem poetically incongruous (unless intentionally ironic) if the place of death were surrounded by life. See Raymond Carver's decision to place his father's death in October rather than June because the fall seemed more appropriate than summer.

2. The image of the bodies' being covered with sheets and flies is a rhetorical device to shock readers by beginning with the ordinary and ending with the extraordinary. The phrase "hellish perfume" transforms what we usually expect to be pleasurable into its opposite, emphasizing its horror. Hayslip describes the experience in such graphic detail to emphasize how calmly and competently she handles it, one of the basic themes of the essay.

3. In paragraph 17, the parenthetical information about dying away from home could have been included in the main body of the sentence, but Hayslip wants to emphasize that it is something her father had told her. The second parenthetical comment could have been included in the body of the sentence, but the identity of the woman is not important. In paragraph 20, placing the information about the man's not knowing where the father is buried in parentheses makes it more emphatic than if it had been included in the sentence. There does not seem to be any reason that the phrase "using the medium's voice" is in parentheses.

4. Flipping coins to see if something is right or wrong treats a chance act as if it were predetermined. Ask students to brainstorm other such actions, for example, when they find themselves thinking that if a certain event happens, it will "mean" something.

5. Most of the language in this essay is rather straightforward, not characterized by metaphor or any particular stylized use of language such as Raymond Carver's essay uses. The sentence style reflects a matter-of-fact narrative of events and description of details. The resulting image we get of Hayslip is of a competent young woman determined to fulfill her duties to her dead father.

6. The final paragraph is the most analytical in the essay. Since this piece is mainly devoted to describing getting her father properly buried, once that has been achieved, Hayslip has the time to reflect on the meaning of her father's death and how she has handled it. The lesson she learns is, like the rest of the essay, straightforward: that her father's death has made her aware of the importance of life, especially the life of her own child. Hayslip's discovery of the importance of the lessons her father taught her in both life and death are conventional enough and expressed with relatively little sophistication. Thus, this essay may provide your students a more accessible example of the writer's technique of arriving at an analytical conclusion to a narrative-descriptive essay than those of many of the more polished, professional writers in this book.

PART TWO

EXPLORING THE EVERYDAY WORLD

Untying the Knot

ANNIE DILLARD

The essays by Annie Dillard and Lewis Thomas are classic examples of the process whereby writers explore a specific observation or experience until they derive a general meaning from it. Dillard's method of development and style is lyrical and elliptical; Thomas's essay is more logically organized and straightforwardly developed.

EXPLORING IDEAS

1. The human need to reconstruct an event based on circumstantial evidence involves the classic cause-and-effect process. Although such efforts allege to reveal the "truth," the "best" explanation is usually the one that accounts for the most evidence in the most convincing way. Archaeologists, historians, and lawyers are a few of the professionals who think in this way. Students may think of some personal experience with this method.

2. Several years ago, the British psychologist R. D. Laing wrote a book entitled *Knots,* in which he cryptically described emotional dilemmas. Untying a knot is a conventional metaphor for solving a complex puzzle for which one cannot find a point at which to begin. Have students recall a problem so complex that they felt they did not know where to start.

3. What is magic in one culture or historical milieu may be science in another, and vice versa. Moreover, some things that at first seem magical become quite ordinary once they are explained. Have your students brainstorm such an activity from nature, technology, or everyday life.

4. Dillard notes how in elementary schoolrooms the seasons are always marked by pictures and posters on the walls and windows. Have students recall some of these methods, or else discuss how in different areas of the country or different countries in the world the seasons are marked by natural changes, certain holidays, or recurring patterns of activity.

5. Dillard uses the metaphor "unseasonable weather" to suggest the underlying unpredictability in what is basically a predictable recurrence of seasons. Any time when something happens that disrupts the usual pattern of expected behavior might be called "unseasonable weather." Ask students to use this as a metaphor to suggest something that disrupted their usual routine for a time.

6. A Slinky, that fascinating springlike children's toy that walks down stairs, is a more original image of time than that of time as a river, for instead of endless flowing in a straight line, Dillard suggests, time is an endless loop that overlaps and folds back on itself. Ask students to consider what time is like for them and then to come up with a metaphor to represent it. For example, in a boring situation, time might gather in a thick puddle like cold molasses.

7. Instead of thinking of divine spirit as being like a man, someone whose hand you can shake, Dillard imagines it as like time—an endless loop with no beginning or end. Depending on their religious backgrounds, students may have many different cultural images of this spirit.

EXPLORING RHETORIC

1. Dillard is a meticulous writer. Her opening sentence is perfectly calculated to reflect the notion about time with which she begins but which changes with her new realization. Have students survey the opening sentences of several essays in this book and choose their favorite, explaining why they like it best. You might want to consult Dillard's wonderful little book, *The Writing Life,* in which she describes the importance of writing.

2. This is a good place at which to emphasize the importance of making a point in an essay. A mere description, no matter how interesting in itself, does not create an essay. As Hoagland and Highet point out in their discussions of essays in the Prologue, there must be a central focus—some motivating force or meaningful direction. Writers describe things in order to see what they mean.

3. Dillard uses the specific detail of the ice on the pond simultaneous with the blooming of the skunk cabbage to prepare readers for her later discussion about how there is a bit of every season in each season.

4. Dillard's description in paragraph 4 is an example of the kind of task in which technical writers must engage: describing a physical object or process in such a way that readers can visualize it. The fact that the snake skin is not a knot at all emphasizes Dillard's theme of appearance and reality.

5. This is part of Dillard's organizational method. Instead of moving through the essay in a continuous line, she, like the metaphor of the loop she creates, circles back on herself, unifying a number of related points lyrically.

6. The magic of divine power is a central theme in the essay. A fine line between ecstasy and madness is suggested by this Old Testament example of Nebuchadnezzar running around on all fours eating grass.

7. The fact that the snake skin is only an apparent knot emphasizes that it has no beginning or end; there is no place that one can get hold of it, untangle it, puzzle it out. At this point, Dillard refers back to her opening sentence in which she naively set out to "catch" spring. Her desire to stick a net into time reflects her wish to identify a discrete moment, to stop time momentarily so she can examine it. But once she realizes that time is an endless process, with no clear demarcations, she realizes that she cannot catch it.

8. The metaphor of the earth as a leviathan or huge sea monster is part of the pattern of Judeo-Christian allusions that Dillard creates in the essay. The idea that a sadist might have a calendar in which various sadistic acts would be depicted does not hold up very well, although initially, it seems appropriate to describe an October when a frost killed the leaves suddenly and made them hang like funereal drapings of crepe.

The Tucson Zoo

LEWIS THOMAS

Thomas begins with a generalization about the scientific method before moving to a concrete experience—just the opposite of Dillard's technique. Moreover, Thomas focuses his realization on some aspect of human behavior rather than on some aspect of the cosmic process, as does Dillard. Both, however, use concrete details to arrive at a general understanding.

EXPLORING IDEAS

1. Analysis—breaking some seemingly seamless activity into its separate parts in order to understand what it is or how it works—is not a natural activity with which many students are familiar. Analysis sometimes makes students cry out, "Why not just leave it alone and enjoy it?" which is, of course, what Thomas thinks at first when he sees the beavers and otters. Although the urge to analyze may not be natural, it is ultimately human, for it underlies the basic need to know what makes things tick.

2. "Play" is a complex phenomenon, about which there has been a great deal of research. You might want to consult the classic study *Homo Ludens* by Johan Huizinga for characteristics of play and the human motivation to engage in it. Ask your students to brainstorm some of the characteristics of different kinds of play and discuss how play differs from work.

3. Thomas uses the phrase "filled with life" to characterize the activity of the beavers and otters. Your students may know of someone "filled with life." A character sketch of such a person may lead to a new understanding of what the phrase means.

4. There are many human activities that people do not really need to have explained in order to enjoy them, for example, religion, art, and love. However, if your students brainstorm such an experience, have them explore it until they can reach a hypothesis about what an understanding of the phenomenon might add to their enjoyment of it.

5. Students are likely to think that someone who analyzes something really does not enjoy it. Have students consult Edward Abbey's essay (just after Thomas's) in which he makes a case for the importance of the combination of scientific analysis and poetic response for a full appreciation of beauty.

6. Although students may have trouble trying to determine whether one is most human when alone or with others (for that involves defining what it means to be human), they will probably be able to brainstorm for an essay in which they explain why they are most themselves when alone or with a group.

7. Thomas's basic conclusion is related to, but not identical with, the romantic notion of the noble savage: that humans in their natural state, without being contaminated by society, are good. William Golding's *Lord of the Flies* is a classic presentation of the opposite point of view.

8. Thomas argues that mutual cooperation between living things is necessary for survival, not the Darwinian law of the jungle, "Eat or be eaten." Ask students to focus on a social problem, such as gang violence, race prejudice, or the using up of natural resources, to explore this general topic in a specific way.

EXPLORING RHETORIC

1. Thomas's essay, which focuses more on discursive thought than description, appropriately begins with the style that characterizes the essay: general assertions rather than specific detail. The tag ending of paragraph 1—"So we say"—sets up the description of the event that challenges the previous generalization.

2. Using Thomas's opening description of the scientific method as reductionist, have students brainstorm the essential nature of such a method in a specific kind of inquiry, perhaps one with which they are familiar in their major field of study.

3. Thomas uses this exaggerated language to convey the sense of speechless elation he feels while observing the animals at play. Of course, the metaphors of "swept off your feet" and "floating" are exaggerations, but students should be able to recall such an experience. The problem is trying to convey in language an experience that seems to evade language's ability to capture it.

4. Thomas wants to communicate some kind of activity that is not rational or carefully thought out but rather instinctive—part of our genetic makeup. This is a crucial part of his argument.

5. Ants are the most conventional example of living creatures that bond together in a single organism of complete cooperation for the purpose of achieving a goal. The problem such an approach creates is that it does not allow for individuality, which Thomas says many think is the most human characteristic.

6. Thomas suggests that the belief that the most human characteristic is individualism is hard to maintain when you actually talk about it and follow out its implications. If you have to gather everyone together in a collective unit to tell them that they must be solitary, you become aware of the contradiction.

7. Although Thomas uses his experience at the zoo to question the scientific method, it is only a rhetorical ploy, for he immediately begins to use the scientific method to understand the meaning of his experience while watching the beavers and otters. It is this meaning—that altruism may be our most primitive attribute—that is at the heart of his essay.

8. Thomas might very well have ended with the penultimate paragraph, for it neatly affirms that which he initially challenged: the methods of science. However, he adds one coda-like paragraph about the nature of ants as a single organism to suggest a kind of synergy at work in which the whole exceeds the sum of the parts. His query when the ants merge into one creature that thinks, "What is the thought?" is a reminder of the basic human need to question and understand, which is at the center of the scientific method. The ability to feel awe and elation—to have one's hair stand on end—is a human ability that Thomas knows well. To want to know whether that happens to the individual ant is also a human characteristic.

Come On In

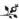

Edward Abbey

E dward Abbey and Bill McKibben both champion the natural world in their essays, but whereas Abbey has a point he wishes to make about the spiritual beauty of nature, McKibben has an argument to make about how humans have changed the idea or concept of nature forever. Abbey's essay is an invitation; McKibben's is a warning.

Exploring Ideas

1. Describing one's reaction to beauty is a challenge if one has the sense that beyond the physical appearance of the beautiful scene or object something spiritual infuses it. Ask your students to recall a moment when they saw a natural scene that inspired them with such a feeling and to try to describe it in such a way as to communicate that sense of spirit.

2. It is not easy to explain how the words that poets use are not the words of reason or that the colors painters use are not the colors of reality. Ask students to think of a landscape and then to consider a painting of that landscape. What exists in the painting that does not exist in the scene? Examine Raymond Carver's poem in his essay in Part One for an example of the "unreasonable words" the poet uses.

3. Students may have other experiences in mind besides seeing a natural landscape when brainstorming this topic. For example, they may have seen some human behavior that made them say, "I don't believe it," or some demonstration of skill that strained their credulity. What they should try to get at in this assignment is why they felt this way.

4. Abbey is talking about the same sense of mystery that Annie Dillard and Lewis Thomas describe in their essays: a synergistic sense that the total experience exceeds the mere sum of the parts and that even if you analyze every element of the phenomenon, something vital still evades you. Although Thomas and Abbey would not suggest that this means one should not analyze the natural world, they do believe that the sense of spirit created by the total experience is ultimately indescribable.

5. Many writers have tried to capture the "spirit of place." Ask students to recall some place they know or have visited that seems to have this sense of spirit and to describe the place in such a way that characterizes that spirit.

6. The difference between science and poetry Abbey assumes here is the difference between the truth of correspondence and the truth of coherence. The truth of science depends on empirical testing for verification: the truth of poetry depends more on its own complete unity and resulting beauty. However, Abbey suggests that scientific fact linked to other facts through a coherent theory and ultimately to an entire rational system has the coherence and internal beauty of poetry. The poet, like the scientist, must also be a careful observer of physical reality.

7. Looking at the ocean, a mountain, or a canyon may inspire fear, as Abbey suggests. Ask students to describe a landscape that has inspired fear in them. Suggest to them that the description of the landscape should convey the cause of the fear.

EXPLORING RHETORIC

1. Abbey's use of specific geologic terms suggests that if he is not a professional geologist, then he has some of the geologist's expertise.

2. Abbey compares the Colorado Plateau to a painting, a book, or a symphony because he wishes to show that there is something of art in the natural landscape, that the natural world has the same power to inspire as a great work of art has. He is preparing readers for his comparison of the scientist with the poet or painter.

3. Empirical truth does not always constitute the sole foundation of higher truth. If this were so, there would be no religion, nor would there be many of the works of the imagination that depict human desire rather than human reality. Moreover, although it is true that the earth is the ground of human physical life, it does not follow that it is the only ground of human imaginative life.

4. Abbey's use of the word "poetry" is more general perhaps than Keats's use of the term. We are more often likely to refer to a natural or human phenomenon as "pure poetry" when we simply mean "grace" rather than language that uses poetic technique. Abbey's use of the term "poetry" to refer to a chunk of quartzite means beauty of organization, not poems.

5. Dillard says, "The point I want to make." Thomas says, "I came away from the zoo with something, a piece of news about myself." Abbey uses the term "moral" to suggest the central point he wishes to make—in the general sense of "there's a moral to this story"—for it seems somehow appropriate for an essay in which he is trying to suggest that there is some spiritual sense that underlies the beauty of a natural scene.

6. Although Abbey is not making fun of those who are afraid of rugged natural landscapes, the language he uses suggests that he does not take their fears seriously, for he is obviously familiar and comfortable with such landscapes.

7. Abbey uses a balanced sentence style in paragraph 9 to create a sense of the importance of the point he is making about the natural world. Note, for example, the repetition of such phrases as "too valuable to be sacrificed . . . too rare to be withheld"; "not the source of fear but the greatest of its attractions"; "adventure not only in the physical sense, but also mental, spiritual, moral, aesthetic and intellectual adventure."

8. The long sentence that makes up paragraph 10, with its balanced infinitive phrases—"to breathe . . . to experiment . . . to gaze . . . to make"—takes the reader's breath away momentarily and thus prepares for the invitation in the

short sentence that makes up Abbey's title—"come on in"—the traditional invitation of one who is already in the water.

The End of Nature

BILL McKIBBEN

McKibben's essay is a warning that we have transformed the concept of nature into something "unnatural"; that is, nature can no longer be defined as some basically nonhuman force but only as a concept that has been contaminated by humans.

EXPLORING IDEAS

1. McKibben's argument is based on the assumption of some basic difference between nature and the human. Although it may be true that humans are as mysterious as nature, it is a different kind of mystery McKibben is interested in—one that has something to do with the sense of spirit that Dillard and Abbey talk about in their essays. The question students might consider here is whether this sense of nature's mystery exists within nature or is a function of human desire and projection.

2. There is something contaminating about humans, McKibben suggests. He does not object to the chain saw because of its noise or its fumes but because it is a human sound, not a "natural" one. McKibben suggests that there is something valuable and irreplaceable about the sense that a realm exists outside the human. This is not the same as the relaxing feeling of listening to the sound of wind in the trees or water over rocks but rather some sense of that which is untouched by humans.

3. McKibben's basic argument is an old one, of course: How far should humans be permitted to control or change natural processes? The idea of conquering the wilderness is a conventional one in human history, for it suggests triumphing over nature to create a certain quality of life. McKibben is not suggesting that we return to living in caves, but rather that we should realize the implications of destroying the concept of nature as an untouched nonhuman force.

4. McKibben suggests that nature is not so much a physical entity as a concept—an idea over which humans have no real control. When human activities change the way the sun shines or the wind blows, then the meaning of the wind and the sun will have changed, and thus the meaning of nature will have changed; for even though the wind blows, as McKibben says, it will not seem to blow from some inhuman place.

5. Ask your students to consider the difference between outdoor-type people and city folk as one way of arriving at some generalizations about the difference between nature and society.

6. The chain saw in the forest and the motorboat on the lake are McKibben's two basic examples of the human intrusion into the mysterious nonhuman realm he calls nature. The sound of the motorboat makes it impossible for him to forget everything except immediate physical experience. Ask students to brainstorm about the reasons people go camping, hiking, or exploring wilderness areas. McKibben seems to suggest that it is to forget that they are social creatures and to act as if they are mere physical beings in the world, responding not to other people but to their natural surroundings and their own physical being.

EXPLORING RHETORIC

1. To be swallowed up by the woods creates the sense McKibben wants to suggest of nature's being some other world, some giant nonhuman creature to which human beings should surrender and not try to conquer.

2. Whereas there may be something romantic and vulnerable about the sound of a lone axe rhythmically sounding in the forest, there is no such romance associated with the whine of a power saw. McKibben's fear is not that the power saw is destroying the forest or that the sound will drown out the songs of the birds, but rather that the noise of the power saw means that human beings who have the technology to create this saw have invaded the forest. It is this ability to change nature that the whine of the power saw suggests to McKibben.

3. Comparing recent environmental damage to stabbing a man with toothpicks suggests that nature cannot be killed by such activities, for environmental damage does not strike at the vital organs of nature. The real damage to nature is done by the production of carbon dioxide and other gases that can change basic atmospheric conditions.

4. By "ending nature," McKibben does not suggest the end of the world, when wind, rain, and sun will no longer exist but rather that the meaning of such things will change; for, like the sound of the chain saw in the forest or the motorboat on the lake, the meaning of nature will no longer be nonhuman.

5. McKibben does not make it clear why it is better to live under wind, sun, and rain unchanged by humans than it is to experience them as human-conditioned forces. For example, what difference might there be between living in an environment in which rain, sun, and wind are controlled by human forces and living with these as natural forces in the external world?

6. McKibben is not interested in making an argument here based on statistics and data; rather, his essay is like an introductory lyrical meditation on the effect of human interference on what we have always called nature. The final example of the motorboat on the lake is a variation of the example of the power saw in the forest that opens the meditation. The motorboat anecdote does not "prove" anything; it is merely one more personal example of how we cannot find a place where we are not forced to think of human society and people.

Wanting an Orange

LARRY WOIWODE

The essays by Larry Woiwode on eating an orange and Peter Schjeldahl on riding a roller coaster describe ordinary activities in such a way that they take on magic and special meaning. Woiwode's essay is a pure example of the description of an everyday activity that many of us think little about until a writer treats it as if it were a brand-new experience and makes it impossible for us to take it for granted ever again.

EXPLORING IDEAS

1. The key to writing an essay like this one is finding some activity that one knows well and savors, and then describing it in such detail as to make readers savor it also. What makes an essay more than mere description of such an activity is the expression of the writer's attitude toward it.

2. Russian formalist literary critics of the 1920s used the term "defamiliarization" to describe the means by which poets create an experience. The assumption is that if we engage in activities routinely out of habit, we do not really experience them at all; rather, we experience a kind of abstraction. Writers enable us to experience the concrete activity by breaking up the familiar generalized pattern we usually experience and enabling us to rediscover the particularity of the experience. Writers "make the stone stony," say the formalists.

3. Woiwode's essay is a tour de force of the "process" essay in which an activity is described in a detailed way. There is no significant idea content or theme in this essay, as there is in the essays by Dillard, Thomas, and Abbey—just the pure pleasure of recalling a pure pleasure and describing it in such a way as to infuse it with the magic of metaphor.

4. Just for the fun of it, you might have your students argue this point. Are oranges more complex than apples and bananas? What can you really do with a banana, for example, except smoothly peel back its outer layer and allow it to be mashed up in your mouth? However, you might try having your students write a short descriptive paragraph about a single fruit or vegetable. Have them read their paragraphs aloud, comparing the effectiveness either of the metaphoric potentiality of the object or the style of the writer.

5. Woiwode does everything he can to suggest the magical nature of the orange as an object from another world. To suggest that the orange is the forbidden fruit in the Garden of Eden story suggests the absolutely irresistible nature of the orange and the perfection of its spherical shape.

6. As many other essayists do, Woiwode concludes by referring back to his opening in which he describes how he and his brother used the ruse of a cold to get an orange. Woiwode suggests that there is something more than mere "want" that characterizes his feelings about an orange. And as his essay shows, mere "wanting" does not convey the fullness that the subject of oranges deserves. Finally, he suggests that each orange carries within itself the magic that has the ability to transform the world into which it comes.

EXPLORING RHETORIC

1. The fact that Woiwode and his brother fake a cold to get an orange in the middle of North Dakota winters of the 1940s establishes the nostalgic tone of the essay from the start.

2. Dialogue creates a sense of dramatic immediacy in the essay, especially in the little game that the boys play with their mother to get an orange.

3. Woiwode creates a sort of mock-serious tone in the essay. The phrase "depth of degradation" is, of course, an exaggeration, but it nicely suggests the mock seriousness of the endeavor, as does the old-fashioned "wended" rather than "traveled."

4. The phrase "as if" appears five times in paragraph 11 alone. Woiwode uses this classic construction that underlies all fiction to suggest the magical character of oranges, transforming them from the mundane to the extraordinary.

5. Visual imagery is the predominant sensory device in paragraphs 10 and 11, although the sense of smell is also important. Woiwode describes the crates at the depot that fill the musty place with a springtime acidity and the resinous smell of fresh wood when the crates are opened in the stores. The visual images are the purple tissue in which the oranges are wrapped, the paper labels at the end of the crate, and the pebbled orange color of the fruit itself with a blue-purple name stamped on it.

6. Woiwode describes a few oranges that have come loose from their wrappings to suggest that the oranges have a life of their own.

7. Much of paragraph 11 attempts to create the sense of a magical, supernatural world: the purple wrappings, the exotic "other world" of the label, the fruit looking like the sun, the foreign name stamped on the orange itself, and the fact that the orange always was at the extreme end of the Christmas stocking, as if in another world.

8. This imagery of "eruption" and "fireworks" is the most exotic in the essay. If it were filmed, it would probably be in slow motion to emphasize the idea of the eruption of fireworks from such a simple act as peeling the orange. The fact that the spray from the peel can actually be ignited adds to this image.

9. Biting off the green nib as if it were a detonator that can be disarmed so it can be eaten further emphasizes the fireworks metaphor already established; it also suggests the childlike delight that the orange creates.

10. Although peeling an orange is not a complex task, the fact that it may be done in a number of different ways emphasizes its exotic nature.

11. Although practically everyone knows the basic components of an orange, Woiwode takes such care to describe the elements of the orange that peeling and eating the fruit becomes concrete and specific rather than merely an abstract, routine experience.

12. It is as though Woiwode gets completely carried away with his description, pushing the details to such extremes that peeling and eating an orange becomes an almost religious experience. Perhaps any activity described so lovingly and in such detail can have this effect.

Cyclone

PETER SCHJELDAHL

I n this rhapsodic descriptive essay about a roller coaster at Coney Island, Peter Schjeldahl transforms an entertainment activity into a spiritual experience, complete with ritualized stages of the journey and advice to the unconverted about how to take the most "righteous ride."

EXPLORING IDEAS

1. Schjeldahl says that riding the Cyclone is an example of the "pure abstract heart of the human capacity for getting a kick out of anything." Brainstorming or discussing the value of activities engaged in just for fun's sake may not lead to a fruitful topic if students get stuck in generalities about the need to relax. Try focusing the discussion on how activities engaged in for fun often have other motivations, such as competition, socialization, or learning.

2. Some people talk to themselves when they are alone; others must have the television or stereo on. Have students discuss ways they prevent being alone from resulting in loneliness. Have them brainstorm ideas aimed toward writing a comparison-contrast essay on being alone versus loneliness.

3. There are obvious differences between harmless activities in which we engage to scare ourselves and activities with an element of real physical danger. It is one thing to go to a horror movie knowing that it is not real; it is another thing to plummet earthward held only by a bungee cord. What underlies these two different kinds of activities? What different kinds of motivation do they involve?

4. Have students focus on what Schjeldahl calls "happy wonderment." Whether it is seeing the beauty of a landscape, as Abbey describes it in his essay earlier in this part, or engaging in a heart-stopping activity, as Schjeldahl describes, have students try to explain what causes this sense of wonderment.

5. Have students focus on the implications of the metaphor of an activity's being like meeting an old friend and then describe a journey, a process, or a task they have engaged in that feels like an old friend.

6. This is similar to the activity suggested in number 3 above, except the focus here is on engaging in an activity that simulates or threatens actual physical death. If it is true that people do not want to die, why then would they want to feel as if they are going to die? If there really is no threat in such an experience,

do they have a true fear of death? What is involved in such experiences except the obvious feeling that one is cheating death?

7. Pain is hard to ignore when you experience it but hard to remember in any specific detail when it has passed. Have students brainstorm various aspects of the nature of pain. Ask them to describe an actual experience of pain in such a way as to make the reader identify with it and recognize it. Ask them to brainstorm about different tolerance levels for pain. Are there gender differences? Are women able to withstand pain more easily than men, or vice versa?

EXPLORING RHETORIC

1. Because the essay creates a tone of exultation, this opening hyperbole nicely introduces the sense that the experience of riding the Cyclone is one of those human activities whose ultimate pleasures it is hard to explain.

2. With its many exaggerations and heightened activities, there is a certain cartoon-like effect in this essay; thus, the image of plunging down so fast that, like a cartoon character, you leave your thought balloon behind seems appropriate. However, Schjeldahl also wants to suggest that (like Lewis Thomas's observation of animals playing in the Tucson Zoo) riding the Cyclone is not an activity that can be analyzed. Then, of course, like all other writers, he proceeds to analyze it.

3. Edward Abbey says in an earlier essay that there is poetry in a chunk of quartzite, whereas Schjeldahl says the Cyclone is like a poem about physics with separate stanzas. Why do these writers use poetry as the basis of comparison for these different kinds of activities? Ask students to brainstorm characteristics of poetry that make it a touchstone for beauty or perfection.

4. To call parts of the ride Kismet, Pasha, and Irene serves to characterize the different nature of separate sections: Kismet suggests destiny, Pasha is round and generous, and Irene suggests an ordinary-seeming girl whom you fall madly in love with. This is part of the sense of familiarity of each section.

5. Schjeldahl does not present himself as an expert on physiological and psychological responses here, for he says all he knows about endorphins he learned from the science section of the *New York Times*. His discussion of endorphins, however, does provide some causal explanation of the physiological effect of the Cyclone ride.

6. The metaphor of "ravishment" goes well with this essay, which focuses on being overwhelmed by a roller coaster ride. The analogy of the soul's being in some mystic state as a result of the Cyclone may sound a bit extreme, but the notion of the ride as being a truly spiritual experience is essential to the essay's effectiveness. Schjeldahl says this sense of having a lasting glimpse into the beyond that is not beyond is either something you know or you don't know, not something that can be explained.

7. Robert L. Heilbroner begins his essay on stereotypes in Part Three by asking: "Is a girl called Gloria apt to be better-looking than one called Bertha?" Schjeldahl says that Irene is the name of an ordinary-seeming girl whom a young man may idly pursue and then fall in love with. Ask students to consider where these stereotypes come from. Is a writer's reason for using stereotypes similar to Raymond Carver's reason for changing the date of his father's death from June to October because autumn seems more appropriate?

8. Compare Schjeldahl's description on how to ride the Cyclone with Woiwode's description on how to peel an orange. Do we need instructions for such activities? Is instruction really the purpose of the description? Have students brainstorm a trivial activity with which they are completely familiar and then write instructions telling someone else how to engage in it. Ask them what they learned from writing these instructions.

Of Shopping

PHYLLIS ROSE

Because it is so easy to make fun of shopping in a society in which shoppers have a multitude of choices, the essays by Phyllis Rose and William Severini Kowinski are light, humorous treatments. However, both have a point to make: Rose about the abstract nature of American shopping and Kowinski about the psychological effects of shopping malls.

EXPLORING IDEAS

1. To suggest that Eastern Europeans are materialistic about shopping while Americans are abstract may be only playing semantic games, for the distinction depends on whether one defines materialism as wanting to own objects or as knowing that one can own them if one wishes to. Rose's use of the word "abstract" suggests a sort of disinterestedness in the American shopper and a sense of possessiveness in the European shopper.

2. In paragraph 6 Rose lists several reasons why we shop: to cheer ourselves up, to practice decision making, to remind ourselves of how much is available to us, to assert our superiority over the objects that surround us. Some students will respond to this topic by saying that they shop only to buy what they need, but most will realize that they engage in shopping for more interesting reasons than just to obtain a specific object.

3. Human beings have the capacity to treat almost any activity as therapy. The trick is how one approaches it. Making baskets to sell to buy food is work, but making baskets for the sake of making baskets can be therapy.

4. Rose says that going to garage sales is the purest form of shopping, for one goes with no goal in mind. Not all your students have gone to garage sales, but those who have should be able to write a good set of instructions for how to approach them; all garage sales look the same after a while and thus embody a generalizable pattern that can be described.

5. Many writers in this part treat ordinary activities—riding a roller coaster, eating an orange, watching animals in the zoo—as spiritual ones. This is inevitable, given many writers' desire to seek and describe the meaning or motivation that underlies certain activities. The success of this topic may depend on the kind of shopping the student describes—recordings, computer software, sports equipment—but it is more likely to depend on the tone the writer creates.

6. Rose uses the comic situation of looking at herself in the mirror while trying on jeans to suggest the classic clash between reality and the ideal. Try to get your students to think of some similar minor experience of this realization, not some ego-threatening experience like those described by Richard Rodriguez and John Updike in their essays in Part One.

7. Although Rose begins with the concept of egalitarianism and ends with the notion of a communal experience, she does not make a direct connection between the two. However, the contrast between American shopping and Eastern European shopping (when Eastern Europe was largely communist) is an underlying theme of this essay.

Exploring Rhetoric

1. A list is a rhetorical device whose effectiveness depends on more than just enumerating items willy-nilly. Have your students look at the lists in paragraphs 1, 2, and 4, noting the balanced sentence structure and the combination of like and unlike items. Note the balance in this list—"four kinds of tahini, ten kinds of herb teas, raw shrimp in shells and cooked shelled shrimp"—and the shifts in this list—"tennis racquets, pantyhose, luggage, glassware, records, toothpaste. . . ."

2. Rose wants to suggest that shopping is more than merely acquiring items and that shopping in America has some of the same characteristics as democracy itself. Because she is only half-serious, the tone suggested by "elevated, graced, complimented" strikes just the right ironic combination of the serious and the comic.

3. The mock-elevated tone of "the world lies before us" and "triumph of civilization" is consistent with the satiric notion of a "wonderful egalitarianism" of American business, in which Rose ironically suggests that chain stores are examples of democracy in action.

4. Rose supplies a number of comic examples of the difference between American attitudes toward shopping and the attitudes of Eastern European immigrants. The image of the Soviet émigré's declaiming "fifty percent off all items today only" provides a nicely stylized representation of this difference.

5. Rose maintains a consistently satiric tone when she suggests that she can tell when the seasons change by the merchandise that department stores set out. No criticism of American materialism is suggested by the fact that we know spring is coming more readily by the appearance of outdoor grills and lawn furniture than by the appearance of the first crocus or robin. In her essay about seasonal

change, Annie Dillard says that the different posters and pictures that school children pin on the walls are signs of the changing of the seasons.

6. Rose's comparison of shopping with flirting seems consistent with the light tone of the essay. It does not bear too much exploration, however, for it suggests that marriage is by its very nature a distressing commitment, like buying a sweater that you are then stuck with forever, and that flirting is a desirable activity. Within the tone of the essay, however, such a comparison works on a surface level and does not invite any further exploration.

7. Given the central focus of the essay—that shopping is a spiritual activity, not a materialistic one—the final comparison of supermarkets and discount stores to cathedrals is perhaps inevitable. However, like many other comparisons in this essay, it does not invite being pushed to extremes. Rose does not want to elicit a sad "tsk-tsk" that Americans worship material things but rather a wry smile that Americans treat material things as if they were spiritual ones. Someone like Solzhenitsyn might very well write a serious and biting criticism of American's love of shopping, but Rose has a different rhetorical purpose in mind.

Mallaise: How to Know If You Have It

WILLIAM SEVERINI KOWINSKI

Kowinski is obviously having fun in this whimsical essay about shopping malls, coining such terms as "mallaise," "mal de mall," and "dismall-cumbobulation," but his tone is more sarcastic than the gentle humor of Phyllis Rose's essay on shopping, for there is something slightly insidious about the subliminal effects of shopping malls.

EXPLORING IDEAS

1. Regretting the loss of downtown as the place to shop may be sentimental nostalgia, or it may be that something important has been lost by the shift of shopping to malls. Students familiar with small town life should be able to help those who are not to understand the difference between shopping in local stores, where you know the owners and sales staff, and shopping in mall shops, where you know no one.

2. Enough research has been done on the subliminal effect of advertising that students interested in this topic should be able to find enough material to get them thinking about it. Suggest that students consult Marie Winn's essay on the addictive effect on television in Part Four for an activity that affects us in ways we are not aware of. Students might also want to consider the hidden purposes of such cultural phenomena as horror movies as described by Stephen King in Part Four.

3. Feeling disoriented or lost even though you know where you are is likely to occur in malls, Kowinski says, because one mall looks very much like another. Being in this sort of daze has a tendency to shut down the ability to make reasoned decisions.

4. Exaggeration is a common technique in this essay, for Kowinski basically tries to show that the very common activity of shopping in a mall can have unsuspected effects. To suggest that malls can make one feel apathetic and hopeless and even lose consciousness is part of this technique of exaggeration.

5. Bland food, bland clothing, bland television, bland novels, bland people, bland classes: all these are possible subjects for a description and analysis of the meaning of blandness.

6. Marie Winn's essay on television as an addictive habit in Part Four is much more serious than Kowinski's essay on malls. Have students read both and contrast their tone and purpose.

7. Kowinski uses the phrase, "overstimulation causes anxiety," to suggest one of the results of the mall's attempt to lull and stimulate the shopper, both at the same time. Ask students to focus on a particular activity that creates excitement, such as watching an exciting movie or attending a rock concert, and to describe the transition from excitement to anxiety and worry.

8. Phyllis Rose, in the previous essay, makes a point about the spiritual nature of shopping in America, whereas Kowinski describes the basic characteristics of shopping in malls. Both essays are humorous, but Kowinski's is more exaggerated, whimsical, and satiric.

9. Malls are part of the phenomenon of white flight to the suburbs and thus are part of middle-class America's efforts to shield itself from the surrounding world. Ask your students to brainstorm some of the implications of this phenomenon.

EXPLORING RHETORIC

1. The first three paragraphs feature parallel sentences: "Malls make some people . . . ," "Malls make people angry . . . ," "Malls affect people. . . ." The other sentences in the paragraphs amplify or elaborate on these three central points.

2. Experiencing such symptoms as feverishness, sudden fatigue, and high anxiety and feeling that one is about to swoon because of being in a mall are, of course, exaggerations, but they are consistent with the general tone of exaggeration in the essay.

3. Kowinski is probably very pleased with his invention of these terms, and they are clever and humorous, depending, as they do, on the relationship between the Latin prefix "mal," suggesting sickness, and the word "mall." They seem consistent with the overall tone and purpose of the essay.

4. Linking "disenchantment" with "divorce" is a rhetorical technique that depends not only on alliteration but also on abruptly shifting from a minor detail to a more serious one. It is highly doubtful that the inability to relate to each

other in malls leads to divorce, but such a suggestion is consistent with the exaggeration that marks the essay.

5. Kowinski uses the present tense to convey a sense of immediacy to the description by Lambert. The creation of the scene allows the reader both to see it and to identify with it.

6. The phrase "eye/hand-on-credit-card coordination" is an example of Kowinski's taking a common phrase and adapting it to his own humorous purposes.

7. Kowinski creates the sense of a kind of timeless, soundless, slow-motion world one floats through and in which figures glide by who seem familiar but are not. Kowinski describes the "gentle fuzz of soft lights and soft music," the gentle visual parade of clothes, fabric tags, and washing instructions, and surrealistic objects floating in and out of consciousness such as an ice cream cone and a cup of coffee. The details create a sense of real things being transformed into the strangely unfamiliar.

8. Kowinski is pushing his technique of exaggeration to ultimate extremes here, for if the mall is a sanctuary of safety in the midst of a threatening world, it only makes sense to extend the image to that of Nirvana, the Crystal City, a New Heaven on Earth. The exclamations suggest the extremity of this technique.

9. The phrase, "Have you been to the mall lately?" is an invitation to the disbelieving. It is similar to the invitation—although with a different, more sardonic effect—offered by Edward Abbey at the end of his earlier essay describing the wonders of nature in the Colorado Plateau. In both cases, the purpose of the invitation is to inform readers that the best way to know the phenomenon being described is to visit it and examine it themselves.

Memorabilia That Have Perpetuated Stereotypes About African Americans

KENNETH GOINGS

Whereas Kenneth Goings discusses the "effect" that memorabilia have had on African American stereotypes, Nancy Masterson Sakamoto, in the next essay, explains the "cause" of conversational conflicts between speakers of English and Japanese. Goings provides an impersonal historical survey; Sakamoto uses an extended metaphor to develop an argument based on her own observation.

EXPLORING IDEAS

1. A number of caricatures in film, television, and advertising have disappeared in the last few years. Some students may be familiar with the shuffling African American menial in old movies, the restaurant chain that once was called

Sambo's, the television commercial featuring the "Frito Bandito," the subservient image of the Native American "squaw" in movies and television, the radio/television characters Amos and Andy, and so forth.

2. Antiques from the Victorian era, for example, may reflect ornate elaboration in furniture style. Collectibles from the 1950s suggest the beginnings of widespread technological influence. Collectibles from the nineteenth-century American West may reflect the folklore of the cowboy.

3. When newspaper cartoonists create caricatures of famous movie stars or political figures, they usually overemphasize some physical characteristic, such as the size of the nose, the shape of the body, or the hair style. Since caricature, by its very nature, depends on such exaggerations, it is hard to think of caricatures that are not meant to evoke scorn or amusement.

4. Goings's argument is not only that such memorabilia are physical objectifications of racial prejudice but that they also reinforce such prejudice by being commonplace; they were so much a part of everyday life that no one questioned them. Numerous images have contributed to racial prejudice that are not strictly caricatures. Ask students to brainstorm some of these stereotypes and compare them with the caricatures they listed in Exercise 1.

5. The images of Angela Davis with her Afro haircut and the Black Panthers with their dark glasses and militant appearance may have been positive to African Americans, but they were the cause of anxiety and fear in many conservative white Americans. The baggy pants and oversize shirts that now characterize the dress of gang members may elicit different responses in different segments of society. Ask students to brainstorm some of the images of different cultural groups in recent years and discuss their positive and negative implications.

EXPLORING RHETORIC

1. Because Ralph Ellison's *Invisible Man* is one of the best-known twentieth-century accounts of the damage to African Americans caused by racial prejudice, Goings can count on the fact that most readers know the novel. The example he cites of the protagonist's futile attempt to rid himself of the broken pieces of the "jolly nigger bank" is Ellison's symbolic portrayal of how hard it is for African Americans to escape the stereotypes that have plagued them.

2. Goings says that African American collectibles that perpetuated harmful stereotypes began after the Civil War when, because slavery no longer was the determiner of African American status, new images of inferiority were created. The second period—the 1930s to the early 1960s—was characterized by a lessening of racial views, although many stereotypes remained; and the final period—the 1960s through the 1990s—has seen a shift to more positive images of African Americans as a result of the civil rights movement.

3. Goings is interested only in the derogatory stereotypes that have damaged African Americans, for those are primarily the ones that became collectibles. The images that developed in the militant 1960s—the Afro haircuts and African clothes—were created to suggest a positive identification with African heritage;

they are not likely to be immortalized into knickknacks that end up in an antique shop or a collector's cabinet.

4. A one-sentence paragraph outline might be similar to the following:

    I. Ralph Ellison's Invisible Man cannot rid himself of the pieces of the "jolly nigger bank."

    II. Black memorabilia have perpetuated racial stereotypes since the seventeenth century.

    III. Black memorabilia were used so frequently that they reinforced racial ideology.

    IV. The first period—from 1880 to 1930—was the worst time for blacks.

    V. During the second period—the 1930s to the early 1960s—racist views relaxed and memorabilia were less damaging.

    VI. The final period—the 1960s to the present—saw a change to more positive images of African Americans.

    VII. Positive stereotypes of blacks replaced negative ones.

    VIII. Images of black people were bought and sold just as slaves once were.

    IX. Unlike the Invisible Man, we may one day rid ourselves of these images forever.

5. Selling images of blacks after slavery was abolished is somewhat like selling blacks during the slave era, but the comparison cannot be pushed too far. The sale of people is more horrifying than the sale of an image of a person, and the industry of manufacturing and selling such items as salt and pepper shakers does not have the same powerful economic and moral implications that the sale of slaves did.

Conversational Ballgames

NANCY MASTERSON SAKAMOTO

Nancy Masterson Sakamoto's essay is a good example of how a writer uses personal observation to make a discovery about social interaction and then develops an extended metaphor to explore and present the resulting generalization in an expository essay.

EXPLORING IDEAS

1. Sakamoto says that Western-style conversations are like a game of tennis; as the conversational ball is swatted back and forth, the game becomes more exciting as each player tries to put a new spin or twist on the topic. But since the players/speakers are not trying to hit each other, the resultant excitement does not turn into anger. Have your students brainstorm ways that people use language to attack each other rather than the topic.

2. Is it possible for a conversation to be exciting if the participants are in agreement? Is it possible for a conversation to be exciting if the participants are not passionate about their positions? If the participants disagree and are passionate about their position, how can an exciting conversation not become an argument?

3. Ask your students to examine the metaphors of tennis and bowling for the two different kinds of conversation. Is there more a sense of direct one-to-one competition in a tennis match than in bowling? In the bowling metaphor, what conversational function do the pins represent? In bowling, is each player trying to get a high score each time he or she rolls the ball? Does that mean that a bowling-style conversation is like a virtuoso performance each time rather than a rapid give-and-take?

4. Ask African American, Hispanic, and Native American students in your class to brainstorm for metaphors to explain their own conversational styles. Extend this exercise to cultural regions. For example, people from the American South have different conversational styles than people in New England; people from the Southwest may have different conversational styles than people in the Midwest.

5. The cultural assumptions underlying the differences between the way Japanese and Americans carry on a conversation may lead to some true cultural differences, or they may lead only to stereotypes. Some students may suggest, for example, that the Japanese have more of a sense of formality and ceremony than Americans, who are perhaps more aggressive and free-style in their social interactions. Have students consult Arthur L. Campa's essay in Part Three for an academic study of some cultural differences between Hispanics and Anglos.

6. Have students consult the essay by Marie Winn on the addictive nature of television in Part Four for suggestions about how television so mesmerizes viewers that families spend less time conversing than they did in the past. As Winn points out, when people come to visit, they often find themselves in front of the television set. In his earlier essay on malls, William Kowinski suggests that while people are in malls, they do not engage in conversation.

Exploring Rhetoric

1. Sakamoto begins by grounding her argument in her own personal experience, describing how, even though she learned to speak Japanese, she still had trouble carrying on a conversation with Japanese people. Her transition from this difficulty to her understanding of what caused it provides a smooth introduction to her thesis statement in paragraph 3.

2. The sports metaphor seems a likely one, for in competitive sports there is always the sense of an exchange of some kind, as there is in conversation. However, conversation is surely not always competitive, as a tennis match, a volleyball game, or bowling is. Thus, if the competitive aspect of the sports metaphor rather than the exchange aspect were emphasized, the metaphor would begin to break down. Ask students to consider the conversational styles of certain individuals and to compare them to other human activities. For example, if one were to compare conversational styles of some people to different literary forms, are there some people whose style is like poetry and some whose style is like a didactic essay?

3. The idea in tennis, of course, is to hit the ball in such a way that the opponent will not be able to return it. If one did this in conversation, would there really be a conversation? Sakamoto's tennis metaphor may work only if the players are so evenly matched that they continue to hit the ball back and forth over an extended period—something that does not often happen in a tennis match. Ask your students to consider other ways that the metaphor begins to break down.

4. As is the case with most extended metaphors, it does not do to push the metaphor too far or take it too literally. The idea of trying to bowl with a tennis ball is ludicrous and works only if one does not visualize it too precisely. What Sakamoto means is that if people play tennis as if they were bowling, the game would fall apart.

5. Although we usually tell students not to shift from third person to second person in an essay, sometimes such a shift is an effective means of directly involving the reader in the action being described. When Sakamoto says, "When your turn comes, you step up to the starting line with your bowling ball and carefully bowl it," the reader is thrown into the action in a direct way.

6. This is a well-organized essay; thus, it is easy to see where Sakamoto shifts from her discussion of American tennis match conversations in paragraphs 4 through 8 to her discussion of Japanese-style conversations in paragraph 9; the first sentence in paragraph 9 marks the transition clearly. The shift back to her original concern about not being able to carry on a conversation with Japanese speakers is also marked clearly in paragraphs 12 and 13. The final transition takes place in paragraph 19 when she shifts to a discussion of how her theory explains the puzzle of dining conversation.

Friends, Good Friends—and Such Good Friends

JUDITH VIORST

Judith Viorst's essay on types of friends and Margaret Mead and Rhoda Metraux's essay on what constitutes friendship in different countries are both classification-definition essays; however, whereas Viorst's essay is informal and personal, Mead and Metraux's is formal and detached.

EXPLORING IDEAS

1. For Viorst, soul sisters bare their secrets to each other, whereas casual playmates usually do not. Ask students to think of a very close friend and a casual friend and explain the differences.

2. Those of your students who have children of their own will be able to write about this topic with relative ease, for parents' social life often depends on their children. Ask students who do not have children to recall how they may have been the source of their parents' social life.

3. This topic depends on students' contrasting the image they present to strangers—their public face—with the one they present to friends—their private face. Some students may feel that they never allow anyone to know who they really are, preferring to maintain various public faces to everyone.

4. Viorst describes special-interest friends as those that you may do things with but not necessarily those with whom you are intimate. "Being together" is more intimate for Viorst than "doing together."

5. Viorst describes cross-generational friendships as those in which an older woman plays the role of mother. A cross-generational friendship, as Viorst describes the term, requires not merely that one be older than the other but that the age difference be an important characteristic of the friendship.

6. If some of your students have been divorced or have divorced parents, they will be able to write about this seldom-mentioned result of divorce, perhaps with some pain and poignancy. Does this phenomenon mean that there are no true "couple friends," that friendships are always between individuals who align themselves with either the husband or the wife after a divorce?

7. Viorst says that a friendship between a man and a woman always has a sexual, flirty element. Does this mean that it is impossible for a man and woman to be friends without there being an underlying possibility of sexuality, and that it is therefore dangerous for a married person to be a friend with a member of the opposite sex?

8. The difference between harmless flirting and sexual harassment may be difficult to define when such flirting takes place in the workplace. Are we reaching a point when it is risky to engage in any flirting at work? Ask students to brainstorm flirting. Is it always related to sexuality? Is there such a thing as harmless flirting?

9. In one concise paragraph, Viorst distinguishes between medium friends, pretty good friends, and very good friends according to the level of intimacy accorded to each one. Ask your students to try to come up with a similar paragraph on their own.

EXPLORING RHETORIC

1. Viorst sets up a parallel definition of friends in the first two paragraphs with the phrase, "Women are friends, I once would have said." She then explains in the third paragraph how she has changed her mind about what constitutes friends.

2. Viorst presents herself as an educated and sophisticated urban woman who likes foreign films and French philosophers but not the bland music of Lawrence Welk or the gritty discomfort of camping. There is a certain amount of stereotyping involved in this image; ask your students to consult the essay by Robert L. Heilbroner in Part Three, a discussion of the necessity of some stereotyping.

3. The balanced phrases—"They'll lend us their cups and silverware ...,
They'll drive our kids to soccer ..., They'll take us to pick up our car ...,
They'll even take our cats when we go on vacation"—seem appropriate in a clas-
sification essay in which balanced descriptions are expected.

4. Viorst quotes dialogue from other women—Elaine, Suzanne, Joyce, Grace—
about friends. This is a typical newspaper technique of getting a quotation to
give the story a dynamic quality. Viorst uses dialogue to enliven her essay and
may very well have invented some of the dialogue, such as the aphoristic balance of Suzanne's statement, "What we're doing is *doing* together, not being together." Remind students of Gilbert Highet's suggestion in the Prologue that the
truth of the whole essay is more important than the truth of specific details.

5. Viorst is not above using a bit of self-mockery here, for in admitting that she
cares a lot about eye shadow and hemlines, she admits that she is not completely
liberated from traditional feminine roles.

6. Viorst defines historical friends by recalling a specific second-grade class, a
specific brother who got in a fight, and a specific sister who married an endodontist from Yonkers. We do not know if these are Viorst's personal experiences or if this is a rhetorical technique to define this kind of friend.

7. One reason for the short paragraphs is that the essay first appeared in a magazine in which the columns were narrow. However, the personal, chatty tone of
the essay also encourages the use of such short paragraphs.

8. Viorst says she includes a discussion of men friends because the women she
talked to urged her to do so. The difference between her discussion of women
friends and that of men friends is that she must justify the latter and explain elements not found in female friendships. She does not indicate the level of intimacy she has with men friends, and men friends are not included in her litany of
medium friends, pretty good friends, and very good friends.

9. Viorst's method of distinguishing different levels of intimacy by moving from
telling a medium friend about a fight with her husband to telling a very good
friend what caused the fight defines economically the differences between the
different levels of friendship. Most students will like this technique; some may
find it a bit too self-consciously clever.

On Friendship

MARGARET MEAD AND RHODA METRAUX

Although, as Lewis Thomas suggests in his essay earlier in this part, the
human need to bond with others may be universal, Mead and Metraux
claim that what humans expect of friendship is culturally determined. In
this formally organized essay, they define and classify friendships in France, Germany, England, and America.

EXPLORING IDEAS

1. In a highly mobile society, moving from one part of the country to another is commonplace. Many of your students will recall moving when they were children and losing good friends; others will describe recent moves and loss of friendships. Encourage them to explain why these losses were so difficult.

2. Summer love is the most conventional focus of this topic, although friendships made at camps and on vacations may also be explored, for they are made quickly and end soon.

3. Judith Viorst suggests in her essay that women have different concepts of friends than men do. Is this really true? If so, why? Mix students from different ethnic and cultural groups together in small groups, and have them compare attitudes toward friendships in their cultures.

4. Mead and Metraux suggest that friendships in France, Germany, and England are more particularized and more committed than in America. Thus, the friendliness of Americans suggests a lack of discrimination to Europeans.

5. The idea that the more you have to say about someone the less you really consider that person a friend might be applied to other areas of human experience also. Ask students to brainstorm a specific experience that exemplifies this characteristic.

6. Women's views of male friendships may very well differ from men's views of female friendships. Organize some small, mixed-gender discussion groups to compare views.

7. Do problems arise when men and women are friends because of the possibility of sexuality? Judith Viorst in her previous essay on friends does not think this is an issue; however, her attitude may be a function of the tone of her essay. Have students brainstorm a more serious approach to the issue.

8. This is a basic "definition" topic in which students are asked to differentiate pals from other kinds of friends. Have them look at Judith Viorst's essay earlier in this part for some suggestions.

9. If your students generally agree that women are more likely to maintain friendships from childhood than men are, then challenge them to explain, without falling into gender stereotypes, why this may be true.

10. Friends who become "part of the family" are a special category that students should try to differentiate from other types of friends who are not integrated into the family.

11. Fussing and fighting between brothers and sisters is such a common topic for television situation comedies that the challenge of writing about it is to find a fresh angle.

12. Whether students agree or disagree with the notion that Americans view friendships as tentative, they should be able to support their position by suggesting cultural, social causes.

EXPLORING RHETORIC

1. Since this essay is directed primarily to an American audience whose attitude toward friendships is tentative and shifting, Mead and Metraux begin by referring to one of the basic reasons for this attitude: the highly mobile nature of Americans.

2. The question at the end of paragraph 2—"Surely in every country people value friendship?"—is rhetorical, whereas the question that stands alone as paragraph 6 is a true question that Mead and Metraux try to answer.

3. The sentence—"The difficulty when strangers from two countries meet is not a lack of appreciation of friendship, but different expectations about what constitutes friendship and how it comes into being"—is not strictly a thesis statement. Mead and Metraux do not discuss cultural clashes; rather, they state the basic motivation for the essay: what the different expectations are.

4. The carefully organized formality of the essay is indicated by such paragraphs as 9 and 10 that begin with sentences that state the focus of the paragraphs.

5. The formality of the essay's structure is evident in such transition phrases as, "In Germany, in contrast with France." Paragraph 13 is filled with contrast markers: "much more," "not so much to," "But for Germans."

6. American ideas of friendship are referred to throughout the essay. For example, although the central focus of paragraph 13 is a contrast between German and French attitudes, at the end of the paragraph, Mead and Metraux refer to how Germans feel about friendships when they come to the United States.

7. Students will come up with very different sentences that characterize the contrast Mead and Metraux see between American views of friendship and those in Germany, France, and England. However, they should develop a sentence that suggests the difference between the rather formalized and categorized nature of friendships in Europe and the somewhat tentative and shifting nature of friendships in America because of the more mobile nature of American society.

8. The essay has six basic parts:
  Introduction: Americans are always moving and making new friends.
  Thesis: Cultures have different expectations about friendships:
    French friendships are primarily among men; they are compartmentalized and emphasize a one-to-one relationship.
    German friendships are sentimental and family oriented.
    English friendships depend on shared activities and are long-lasting.
  Conclusion: In spite of different styles in different countries, friendships also have several common elements.

PART THREE

DEALING WITH DIFFERENCES

Don't Let Stereotypes Warp Your Judgments

ROBERT L. HEILBRONER

Although both are definition essays on similar subjects, Robert Heilbroner's essay on stereotypes is a popular rendering of a formal academic analysis, whereas Gloria Yamato's essay on racism is a personal analysis combined with a passionate appeal.

EXPLORING IDEAS

1. Many stereotypes about names come from literary conventions whereby names are meant to suggest a character's personality or type. Charles Dickens, the master of this technique, spent many hours trying to come up with just the right name for a character, such as Pecksniff or Bumble. When D. W. Griffith modeled early film techniques after Dickens, he adapted this convention to movies.

2. Students should be able to come up with a number of such stereotypes. Ask them who is more intelligent: a man smoking a cigarette or a man smoking a pipe. Since Heilbroner says that the very function of stereotypes is to classify the variety of human beings into a handful of types, ask students to classify types on certain television shows, such as situation comedies, soap operas, or crime shows.

3. Have your students brainstorm a list of characteristics of gossip and another list of characteristics of stereotyping; then compare the lists to try to find similar attributes. Is gossip always harmful? Is it always motivated by curiosity and small-mindedness? Does it ever perform a valuable function?

4. What the study Heilbroner cites seems to suggest is that we actually "see" someone differently if we know that he or she belongs to a certain cultural group because we have prejudgments about the group that override any possible individual impression we may have of the person.

5. This is a risky topic, for there is no way to discuss it except to have students tell some racial or ethnic jokes. Have students analyze such jokes in writing as a way of laying bare the unjustified stereotypes on which they depend.

6. This is, of course, the "good news–bad news" about stereotyping. On the one hand, we have to stereotype to some extent, for if we did not put new experiences in established categories, we would never be able to understand them. However, if we forced all new experiences to fit these established categories, we would never learn anything new. What we must do is combine the forcing of the new experience into the old pattern with a continuing adjustment of the old pattern.

7. Heilbroner's assumption here is that grade B movies are more prone to stereotyping than higher-quality movies. Have students think of certain genres of grade B movies, for example, westerns, horror movies, and crime stories, and then consider what it would be like to live in such a movie.

8. As Gloria Yamato says about racism in the following essay, eliminating stereotypes is hard to do, for it requires people to realize that the images they hold are stereotypes rather than reality. Even if you point out examples that do not fall within the stereotypes, one might say they are "exceptions that prove the rule."

EXPLORING RHETORIC

1. Although one might very well expect that a girl named Gloria will be better looking than a girl named Bertha or that a person with glasses will be more intelligent than one without, by posing the questions in this direct way, Heilbroner makes the reader realize the absurdity of these stereotypes.

2. By pointing out that the only thing that distinguishes people with glasses is that they have bad eyes, Heilbroner mildly emphasizes the absurdity of the stereotypes with which he introduces the essay.

3. Heilbroner uses the second-person imperative in paragraphs 3 and 4—"Look into the favorite suspects . . . Delve into the main assets . . . Explore most prejudices"—to counteract the direct questions he poses in paragraph 1.

4. Heilbroner does not quote any of the stock jokes he refers to because if they made the reader laugh, he would be responsible for reinforcing them. Besides, he does not have to repeat them; every reader will know at least one such joke.

5. Heilbroner's suggestion that people who use stereotypes become stereotypes themselves is a rhetorical device of turning the tables. The logic of Heilbroner's argument is that if stereotyping is a process whereby we ignore particularities and generalize the world, then it follows that we lose the ability to be particular individuals who can see the world in our own unique way, and we become stereotypical in our responses.

6. Heilbroner defines stereotypes in paragraphs 1 through 5. Using the question "Why is it that we stereotype the world in such an irrational and harmful fashion?" he shifts to an explanation of why we stereotype in paragraphs 6 through 9. With the sentence, "Thus the trouble is that stereotypes make us mentally lazy," he shifts to a discussion of the effect of stereotyping on those who stereotype in paragraphs 10 through 12. With the sentence, "Impoverishing as they are, stereotypes are not easy to get rid of," he explains in paragraphs 13 and 14 why stereotypes are not easy to eliminate. Finally, with the question, "Can we speed the process along?" he concludes in paragraphs 14 through 18 with suggestions of what we can do to get rid of stereotypes.

7. In addition to the transition devices between the five major parts of the essay, Heilbroner uses such transition devices between paragraphs—for example, "The answer is," "Yet," "For it is," "We not only," "And finally," "Thus," "Hence," "Instead," "Nor," "First," "Second," "Third."

8. Heilbroner's essay is highly structured, as the five major parts and the paragraph transition devices noted in Exercises 6 and 7 suggest. Although students may not be aware of the structured nature of the essay at first, the final paragraphs, with their standard listing of "First," "Second," and "Third," should make it clear. Perhaps Heilbroner structures his essay so formally because he

wrote it to appear in *Reader's Digest,* a magazine featuring articles that can be skimmed rather hurriedly. Your own class's particular strengths and weaknesses will determine whether you wish to argue that essays suffer more from lack of organization than overorganization.

Something About the Subject Makes It Hard to Name

Gloria Yamato

As an African American woman who has no doubt felt the effects of prejudice, Gloria Yamato reflects her passionate involvement in this formally organized definition of the various types of racism by frequently using slang and dialect expressions. The result is an engaging combination of the formal and the personal.

Exploring Ideas

1. As Robert L. Heilbroner points out in the previous essay, a cruel stereotype lies at the heart of each prejudice. Yamato defines racism as the systematic mistreatment of one group of people by another based on race. Given these definitions, stereotyping (a mental act) causes racism (a social act).

2. Yamato argues that when people of color begin to believe the stereotypes held about them by others and to believe that they deserve racially motivated mistreatment, they have internalized racism.

3. For Yamato, "aware/blatant racism" is racism of the stereotyped southern conservative, whereas "aware/covert racism" is racism of the northern liberal who claims not to be racist yet refuses to rent an apartment to a person of color.

4. The phrase "nice someone to death" reflects the personal tone of the essay. Ask your students to describe a situation in which one is "nice" so much that it seems to be condescension. Is such "niceness" always "unaware/unintentional racism"?

5. Yamato says that the newest form of racism she is "hip" to is "unaware/self-righteous racism," which manifests itself by "good whites" who act as if they know what is best for people of color.

6. As a black woman, Yamato is most concerned with internalized racism, for she says it influences the way she sees herself and persuades her to accept the unfair treatment she receives as being deserved.

7. Yamato argues that "racism" is supported and reinforced by various other "isms." Some of the interrelationships are easier to understand than others. For example, while it is clear that class consciousness, or "classism," may lead to racism, it is not so clear what "classism" has to do with sexism. Yamato also suggests here that an "ism" cannot exist unless its internalized version also exists;

furthermore, when an "ism" increases, there is a proportionate increase in its internalized version.

8. Yamato argues that the melting pot ideology has made all of us "fast-food–gobbling generics" with no sense of our individual identity as part of a unique culture.

9. Yamato says it is lazy for well-meaning whites to expect people of color to teach them how not to be racist; whites should learn to do that on their own for themselves, not for people of color.

10. Yamato concludes by appealing to people of color not to give in to internalized racism. They should join together to combat racism, which, from her point of view, is only a white phenomenon. She does not consider Korean criticism of blacks or black distrust of Koreans, for example, examples of racism.

EXPLORING RHETORIC

1. Much of Yamato's essay is devoted to convincing both whites and people of color that there is no "quick fix" for the deep-seated and widely pervasive practice of racism. Her most severe criticism is leveled, in fact, against those who think that they have cured themselves of racism simply because they have taken a weekend workshop.

2. After referring to the naïveté of whites who think they are cured of racism, Yamato ends paragraph 1 by using such dialect expressions as "work on the sucker" and "Cuz" to emphasize by her own personal voice and tone that no one can get rid of racism in a weekend workshop.

3. For an extended analogy of a social phenomenon to an illness, have your students look at Victoria Sackett's essay in Part Four. William Kowinski also uses various analogies to illness in his discussion of shopping malls in Part Two. The illness metaphor is a conventional one for social phenomena that people claim are out of control and threatening to run rampant.

4. Yamato says that "unaware/unintentional racism" characterizes whites who mistakenly think that they have rid themselves of racism just because they say they are sorry and that they want to make it up to people of color. Although such people are well intentioned, their treatment of people of color is usually condescending, and therefore racist, even though they do not mean it to be so.

5. Some examples of Yamato's slang language in paragraph 8 are: "The owning class has enough power and privilege to not have to give a good whinney," "outright disenfranchised folk," "keeping the lid on," "the bottom of the heap," "that runs the show here," "the racism end of the stick," "hell to pay," "ice-cube's chance in hell." Such language suggests that these are matters that Yamato feels so strongly about that she no longer tries to restrain her language and stick to the formal tone of the overall essay.

6. In the first part of paragraph 8, Yamato discusses the issue of how some classes have such power that they are always going to be in a position of control, for the group that has the legal power to take away life the quickest is the strongest group. At this point, she provides the specific example that people of color would never have the power to pass laws to get whites sent to relocation camps for their own protection and the security of the nation as whites did to the Japanese Americans during World War II. (See the essay by Jeanne Wakatsuki Houston and James D. Houston in Part One.)

7. In the last three paragraphs, Yamato shifts from analysis and definition to recommendations to both whites and people of color about what they can do to rid themselves of racism. Her authority for making these recommendations is based on the analysis that precedes them, for the final paragraphs are primarily summary in nature.

The Androgynous Man

Noel Perrin

Although the primary result of the feminist movement is that women have been accorded social rights traditionally granted only to men, a much-publicized attitude change has been that men have assumed psychological attributes traditionally granted to women. Perrin, however, may belong so firmly to the "old school" attitudes toward masculine characteristics that his androgyny is more apparent than real.

Exploring Ideas

1. The inkblot test Perrin took is based on the assumption that it is masculine to think of man-made objects and weapons, whereas it is feminine to think of natural objects and innocent things. Ask your students to suggest some of these objects and to explain the source of these stereotypes. Can such differences be denied?

2. Perrin suggests that masculine stereotypes have been more harmful to men than to women because they have convinced men that they are permitted to play one role: that of the dominant male. Thus, they are not allowed to show emotion, admit that they know nothing about cars, or kiss their cat without fear of being thought less than what Perrin calls a "red-blooded American man."

3. Perrin's categories establish the 100 percent masculine man at the apex, the 75 percent masculine man as one who envies and tries to emulate the 100 percent masculine man, and the 50 percent masculine man as one who, although he has half the characteristics of women, still retains half of his all-man characteristics.

4. The issue of wife and child abuse is so well known today that students will have no trouble finding evidence to suggest its partial source in masculine stereotypes. What stereotypes are responsible for husband abuse?

5. Since Perrin sets up the all-man stereotype as the ultimate image of what it means to be male, he does not suggest that men would want to imitate any other male image. Ask your students about male images of intellect, poetic imagination, and sensitivity. Are these images stereotypically feminine? See Amy Gross's opinion in the following essay on androgyny.

6. The issue here is whether being "maternal" is tied to biology. If women can be maternal, though they have never had children, then is mothering biologically based? If not, then why cannot men be maternal? Perrin seems to suggest that being maternal is a passive, therefore feminine, attribute.

7. The stereotype that women are helpless with machines, whereas men are quite comfortable fixing things, can be dismissed humorously in an essay that exposes male helplessness and female competence about "what makes things tick."

8. I heard my daughter's softball coach tell her teammates the other day not to let the other team see them cry because they lost the game. Is that because in a traditionally "male" game players are not supposed to show weakness to the other team?

9. If an entire society were androgynous, as in some *Star Trek* alien race, what would male-female relationships be like? How would males and females relate to each other if there were no masculine-feminine stereotypes?

EXPLORING RHETORIC

1. Perrin opens his essay with the rhetorical convention of basing a generalization about society at large on a past personal experience. The fact that his discovery about masculine stereotypes takes place on a train trip to Colorado where he is going to be a horse wrangler for the summer emphasizes his anxiety about scoring high in feminine characteristics on the test.

2. Because Perrin admits here that he has certain feminine characteristics, he wants to make sure that no one will mistake him for being a sissy. Telling us that he had a good time in combat and that war is exciting certainly identifies him as belonging to a generation before Vietnam, when war lost its masculine glamour perhaps forever.

3. Because this test appeared in a magazine in 1943, when stereotypes about masculine and feminine attitudes and behavior were much more entrenched than they are today, many students may dismiss the test as irrelevant.

4. Because Perrin wrote this essay when he was in his late fifties, many students may feel that he is firmly entrenched in an older generation's attitudes toward masculine and feminine attributes. The issue students might consider is whether they feel Perrin is honest and self-aware about masculine and feminine attributes in himself.

5. Perrin bases his authority for writing an analysis of what it means for a man to be androgynous solely on his personal experience. A sociological analysis of the phenomenon of androgyny would probably be based on interviews with a number of men and women who represent a cross section of American society.

6. When students first read this essay, many may find themselves nodding their heads in agreement with Perrin but somehow feeling vaguely uneasy about his genuineness. Perrin's insistence on his own true masculinity—skinning horses, finding war to be fun, insisting that having feminine characteristics does not mean that he is gay, believing that nurturing means feeling good watching a child drink a glass of milk, buying a book called *Home Repairs Any Woman Can Do* because it seemed to be pitched toward his level of ability—may suggest a man who is determined to assert his masculinity in traditional ways and who oversimplifies what it means to be female.

7. Perrin is defensive about his masculinity and somewhat condescending toward what it means to be female. The implications and complications of genuinely being able to identify with the attitudes of the opposite sex are much more complex than Perrin's simplistic, old-fashioned approach might suggest.

8. Perrin's concluding paragraph ostensibly returns to the assumptions of the inkblot test, but he then shifts immediately to the clichéd and unrelated observation that God is neither masculine nor feminine and therefore—like a true androgyne—would score right in the middle on the test. The final sentence—"Fellow androgynes, it's a nice thought"—suggests that androgyny is close to godliness. It's a questionable conclusion.

The Appeal of the Androgynous Man

Amy Gross

The tone of Amy Gross's essay may be largely determined by the fact that it was originally published in *Mademoiselle*, a glossy magazine for women. Her purpose is to make a case for the superiority of the androgynous man as a companion and lover.

Exploring Ideas

1. Gross says that all the men she has liked and loved have had the characteristics of both male and female. However, when she lists the characteristics that she prefers in a man, she defines all of them as female characteristics. What male characteristics does Gross like? If there were such a thing as an androgynous woman, what male characteristics would she possess?

2. The image Gross paints of the all-man man is indeed a stereotype; nevertheless, she insists, many men fit the stereotype: They do not know how to shop except to buy a six-pack of beer and pretzels; they eat only steak and potatoes; they have no taste in books, art, or movies. How would we feel about a stereotype about people who ate fried chicken and watermelon?

3. Of all the activities in which human beings engage—work, play, love, sex, marriage, and so forth—how many have nothing to do with gender distinctions? Students may have a hard time coming up with activities that are completely gender-free.

4. If students accept the stereotype that the high school cheerleader always ends up with the football hero, then challenge them to explain why.

5. A discussion of whether masculine men do not really like women may lead to a discussion of the frequency with which masculine men abuse and rape women. Regardless of the stereotypes, this may not be borne out by sociological research. Sex offenders, for example, do not usually fit the masculine stereotype that Gross paints here.

6. Although Gross cites studies to confirm her bias that high masculinity and high femininity are correlated with low intelligence, the phrase "enlightened prejudice" may be a risky one. Her citation of the studies does not make clear how they define the terms "masculine," "feminine," or "intelligence."

7. Gross says that women (not women with traditionally feminine characteristics) have the desirable attributes of being open, intelligent, and creative, while only men who are like women have such characteristics. Are there *any* desirable male qualities?

8. You may or may not want to get into an open discussion about the qualities of a good male lover. However, if you ask men and women to brainstorm these characteristics separately, you may get widely varying opinions that males and females can then discuss together.

9. Gross assumes a male stereotype about women here: that "nice women" are not supposed to like sex and are willing to engage in it only to please men. Why might men want to believe this myth?

10. That point at which flirtation becomes attempted seduction may be hard to define. However, it is certainly an important issue in an era when people are sensitive to sexual harassment. Is there such a thing as harmless flirtation?

Exploring Rhetoric

1. Gross begins with a flippant tone, saying that when she was a child she thought she could talk to James Dean because he was anguished and she was twelve. Any current male movie star who manages to convey some sensitivity might be appealingly androgynous. However, this appeal usually depends on what female age group finds the star appealing. For example, Kevin Costner may be thought androgynous by mature women, whereas Brad Pitt might be thought androgynous by young women.

2. Gross makes use of a balanced series in the first few paragraphs. For example, note the series in the first paragraph beginning with "who doesn't play . . . who doesn't tell . . . who is not contemptuous" and the comparative series "more self amused, less inflated, more quirky, vulnerable and responsive," which is followed by the two balanced sentences, "He is more like me than the other sort. He is what social scientists and feminists. . . ."

3. The phrase "doing something endearingly feminine at the sink" strikes a note of sarcasm that Gross maintains throughout the essay—for example, in such phrases as "the little woman," "a wad of cake," "the brute," "the fragile beast," "ape-like way."

4. Gross is trying to be clever when she says she could never be involved with an Arab shepherd or a Bolivian sandalmaker, but the comparison suggests that she is more intelligent and therefore more worthwhile than either—something with which shepherds and sandalmakers might take issue. Extending this comparison, one might say that a rich person could never have anything in common with a poor one, an African American could never have anything in common with a white, and so forth.

5. Cleverness again overrides reason in Gross's list of her male preferences. For example, she says that in her experience "all-men men" read books that she would not want to see paragraphs of, that they do not care what women think, have no creativity, and are insensitive to the needs of others.

6. Paul Theroux also talks about the bias that all-men men have against creativity in the following essay. Does Gross suggest that there is some intrinsic reason that masculine men are dull and stupid? Is there no such thing, according to Gross, as a great athlete who is also creative and imaginative?

7. Gross defines the stereotype of the jock as one who competes in bed just as he does on the playing field. The basic metaphor she uses is that the jock treats sensuality as candy to be doled out, a ration that he cuts off as soon as he feels he has seduced a woman into going to bed with him.

8. Whereas in the previous essay Perrin communicates the basically conservative point of view of a man past middle age who oversimplifies what it means to be female, Gross conveys the image of a sophisticated urban woman who depends on simplistic stereotypes to convey her dislike of "all-men men." Although both advocate androgyny, I suspect that a dialogue between the two would lead to disagreement, for Perrin would think Gross is too extreme, and Gross would think that Perrin is deceiving himself that he is truly androgynous.

Femininity

SUSAN BROWNMILLER

While Susan Brownmiller's essay is a restrained critical analysis of what it means to be feminine, Paul Theroux's essay is a virulent attack on what it means to be masculine. Brownmiller defines femininity as an "aesthetic" that involves a central paradox: even as femininity gives women a competitive edge, it does so by exacting a terrible price.

EXPLORING IDEAS

1. The table-setting ritual Brownmiller describes, in which men are represented by knives and forks and women by spoons, is similar to the stereotypes suggested by the test Noel Perrin describes in his essay in this part. In trying to think of family rituals that are alive with meaning, many students will probably think of holidays and special family occasions, such as mealtimes, birthdays, vacations, or seasonal changes.

2. The joke that developed out of the popularization of Freud's method of interpreting dreams is that (in obvious replication of the male and female sexual organs) all cylindrical protruding objects are male and all circular cavities are female. When students begin to brainstorm male and female symbolic objects, they will quickly perceive the stereotyping involved.

3. Different generations will have different stories to tell about what influenced their image of masculine and feminine when they were growing up. For example, those who grew up in the fifties and sixties will recall such television shows as "Father Knows Best" and "The Donna Reed Show," which presented rigid images of what it meant to be a man or a woman.

4. Brownmiller calls femininity an "aesthetic" because she sees it as a human construct that sets up certain criteria for what it means to be "feminine," just as aesthetics sets up certain criteria of what it means to be "beautiful."

5. The irony of femininity is the center of Brownmiller's essay, for she argues that even as the world accords certain privileges to the feminine woman, it does so at a price, for to be feminine, a woman must limit her aspirations and refrain from taking an aggressively direct masculine approach to goals.

6. Brownmiller argues that men are given the distinction of being stronger and more competent in large part because women appear to be weaker and less competent. Thus, these male characteristics are not intrinsic but exist because women allow them to.

7. Have students hypothesize some reasons for Brownmiller's suggestion that more men are abandoning their sexual interest in women. It may be that more men are admitting their homosexuality now, which makes it appear as if fewer are sexually interested in women; it may be that as more men become androgynous (as Gross defines this in the preceding essay), they appear less interested in women sexually.

8. Brownmiller suggests two basic reasons for the renewed interest in femininity: Because men are losing interest in women sexually, women are becoming more feminine to compete for fewer men, and because we live in a harsh, competitive world, femininity offers the antidote of frivolity, sensitivity, and niceness.

EXPLORING RHETORIC

1. Brownmiller's essay is peppered with metaphors, perhaps overly so. Have students analyze paragraph 4, in which practically every sentence is built around a metaphor. In addition to the ones pointed out in Exercise 1 of Exploring Ideas, the paragraph contains metaphors of finance ("a bottom line"), sports ("the game had been called"), the Bible ("destroyed her birthright"), and law ("warning notices").

2. This is the central metaphor, and probably the most self-conscious one. It presents femininity as a modern woman hurrying toward some important meeting in high heels but tripping, because she is still hobbled by such images of femininity from the past as ruffled petticoats.

3. Brownmiller uses the metaphor of "rhapsodic symphony" because she has already introduced the idea of femininity as being an aesthetic. Thus, femininity is not like a natural sound but a human construct or composition that one must be able to follow. Someone tone-deaf to the composition may fail at being feminine.

4. Brownmiller's style, when it is not elaborately metaphoric, is primarily abstract. The sentences that appear in paragraph 7, for example, are long, complex, and balanced.

5. Brownmiller reasons that the characteristics that define masculinity are relative to those that define femininity. Men can act as if they are in control because women act as if they are not. Open shows of emotion are thought to be feminine only because such behavior does not lead to the masculine value of success. In other words, men can appear masculine precisely because women allow them to by appearing feminine.

6. Brownmiller does not provide any evidence that the competition of men and women for jobs is especially fierce now. However, students might brainstorm some reasons for this—for example, the higher cost of living has resulted in many more women working; the increase in divorce has forced more women to work; the feminist movement has pressured employers to hire more women.

7. Brownmiller's rhetorical tactic here is to suggest a cause-and-effect relationship between the renewed interest in femininity and the current competitive nature of society. Ironically, she suggests that as more women enter the work force and engage in previously masculine aggressive behavior, the more there is a need for women to be feminine to provide some relief from the harsh world that has resulted from this increased competition.

Being a Man

PAUL THEROUX

Paul Theroux's essay is likely to arouse some spirited discussion, for it makes an all-out attack on what American society means by "being a man"; his onslaught against athletes is particularly severe. The second half of the essay focuses on Theroux's personal complaint about the incompatibility of stereotyped "manliness" with the career of being a writer.

EXPLORING IDEAS

1. Theroux is not saying that all men are stupid and unfeeling but that the popular idea of what it means to "be a man" in America implies these characteristics. Certainly these are common stereotypes, but it is an oversimplification to say that they are the only characteristics of "manliness" in America.

2. Theroux uses extreme language to characterize the masculine stereotype, refusing to accept that there is anything good about being "manly." Not content to say that manliness is emotionally damaging, he also charges that it is "hideous" and "crippling."

3. Theroux suggests that because many men are convinced of the masculine ideal, they cannot allow themselves to have an equal, sharing relationship with women, which is why they do not understand them. The assumption that men can never understand women is a common stereotype; students will be able to brainstorm many examples from comic strips, television shows, and movies.

4. Judith Viorst discusses the problem of male-female friends in her essay in Part Two. In brainstorming this issue, students should consider culturally determined gender differences and whether such friendships always face the threat of sexuality.

5. Students may strongly disagree with Theroux's charge that there is something unnatural and prison-like about a boys' camp and with his implication that boys' camps lead to equally unnatural and prison-like men's social clubs, pool rooms, boxing matches, and the marines.

6. It may be difficult to argue with Theroux's suggestion that the rigid stereotypes of "manliness" always involve belittling women. However, students may want to argue for a new definition of "manliness" that accepts the equality of women.

7. Challenge your students to convince Theroux, who is more interested in the life of the mind than the life of the body, that sports are important.

8. Amy Gross is particularly harsh on the "manly ideal" in her essay on androgyny in this part. Is it true that the life of the body is incompatible with the life of the mind? Although your students may be able to come up with some examples of brilliant students who are also athletes, do these examples contradict Gross's and Theroux's general conclusions?

9. Raymond Carver, in his essay in Part One, fears that his father will not approve of his decision to be a writer. Is this part of the assumption that creativity is not masculine?

10. Have students argue, as Susan Brownmiller does in her essay, that, like the privileges of femininity, the privileges of masculinity exact severe penalties.

EXPLORING RHETORIC

1. Theroux's opening condemnation of shoe fetishism is itself an example of a stereotype. Both men and women become sexually aroused by a wide variety of such stimuli as certain clothes, smells, and objects. Nor is it clear what Theroux means when he writes, "It is an important thing to know about us," for fetishism seems to have nothing to do with the masculine stereotypes he complains about.

2. That the metaphor of masculinity is like wearing an ill-fitting coat nicely balances with the metaphor of femininity being like nakedness. Whereas the idea of masculinity just does not fit many men, femininity often suggests woman as a sexual object.

3. Theroux is obviously referring to the so-called danger of masturbation that supposedly results when young males are too imaginative and read too much.

The nineteenth-century view was that young men should get lots of exercise and fresh air to avoid the dangers of what was known as self-abuse.

4. Theroux makes some extreme statements in this essay. It is surely an exaggeration to say that a manly attitude toward sports creates "degenerates, sadists, latent rapists, and just plain louts." These are, of course, stereotypes; although practically everyone can think of examples to justify them, everyone can think of examples to contradict them also. Is there enough general truth to Theroux's claims to justify his making them?

5. Theroux's insistence that any objective study would verify his belief that the quest for manliness is "right-wing, puritanical, cowardly, neurotic, fueled largely by a fear of women" is a rhetorical ploy, for he cites no such study. He knows that the stereotype of the right wing as mindless and puritanical is held widely enough by liberals to ensure that his assertion will be accepted by many people.

6. Richard Rodriguez, in his essay in Part One, also talks about how he and his intellectual friends made fun of athletes. Amy Gross, in her essay in this part, argues that jocks make lousy lovers. Athletes, however, might very well retort that Rodriguez really envied the jocks he saw, that Gross is a social snob, and that Theroux is a sissy or a nerd. How does one mediate disagreement between these different perspectives?

7. Theroux says that many people think that journalism is the heartiest, manliest form of writing in America. Although that is an illusion, it is same kind of illusion or falsehood as the image of masculinity is in America.

8. Because the last half of the essay focuses on American authors, some students may feel that Theroux's essay is self-serving—that he is not concerned with the general issue of masculine images in America but rather that his professional choice to be a writer is not accepted as masculine work.

Just Walk On By

BRENT STAPLES

B rent Staples and Judith Ortiz Cofer use personal experiences to describe what it is like to be labeled as a stereotype rather than identified as an individual. Whereas Staples focuses on how being an African American male characterizes him as a suspect or a criminal, Cofer explains how being a Hispanic female reduces her to being a sex object or a menial.

EXPLORING IDEAS

1. Have your students consult Heilbroner's essay in this part about why and how we stereotype. Heilbroner suggests we are never justified in making a judgment about someone based on appearances; however, Staples admits that women are particularly vulnerable to street violence and that black males constitute a large number of the perpetrators of that violence. How can people avoid stereotyping and yet protect themselves from danger?

2. Staples knows that the woman feared him for no other reason than that he was a young black male; however, he also knows she had no way of knowing he was a "softy" out for a walk because of insomnia. The basic issue here is what kind of knowledge—factual or stereotypical—one must have in order to make decisions on how to act.

3. Football players, boxers, and soldiers are among those groups who try to convey the impression that they are to be feared. In some cases, law enforcement officers are also taught to become "fearsome entities."

4. Amy Gross, Susan Brownmiller, and Paul Theroux in other essays in this part discuss the masculine ideal of aggression and the romance of the power to intimidate. Ask your students to brainstorm some images of this power in television shows, films, and books in which this "romance" is perpetuated.

5. Encouraging them to ignore the tired old analogy of primitive man's need to assert his dominant role in the hierarchy of the pack and kill game for food, ask your students to brainstorm any reasons that men are supposed to be valiant in the face of hostile forces.

6. Have your students break into small groups and trade tales about experiences when they have been stereotyped or prejudged because of their race, culture, gender, external appearances, accent, behavior, or some other characteristic. Then have them choose one such experience, describe it, and try to explain its meaning for them in particular and for society in general.

7. Just as Judith Ortiz Cofer cites an example in the following essay in which a doctor is surprised at the big words an educated Hispanic friend of hers uses, Staples depends on the stereotypical assumption that a man who knows and appreciates classical music could not be a thief or a mugger. Part of this stereotype derives from the masculine idea that "all-men" men are not sensitive or creative that Amy Gross and Paul Theroux cite in their essays.

EXPLORING RHETORIC

1. Staples uses the word "victim" ironically in the first sentence, for it is a startlingly effective way to begin the essay. However, he soon makes it clear that the real victim of the stereotyping he describes is himself.

2. Staples's opening strategies are standard rhetorical tactics for an essay in which particular experiences are cited to illustrate a central point. Staples could have opened with any one of the other examples, but a woman's fear of a black male is probably the most pervasive instance of the stereotype he wishes to discuss. After describing the central example and providing a context for it, Staples cites additional examples.

3. An "unwieldy inheritance" suggests something over which Staples has no control and which cannot be handled easily. The "quarry" of a mugger suggests a small animal being stalked by a larger one. "Stalking sleep" is an ironic reference to the "quarry" metaphor. Muggers who "seeped into the area" suggests something that soils, such as oil or mud. The other metaphors of a physical "gulf," "hammering" down door locks, and a physical "screen" to filter out individuals are obvious.

4. The metaphor of "warrenlike" streets, suggesting a colony for small game animals, picks up the "quarry" and "stalking" metaphors already cited. However, the women's pulling their purse straps across their chests like bandoliers holding bullets seems to reverse the metaphor and make the women the hunters rather than the hunted.

5. Staples uses the analogy of the child's flailing aimlessly about until it randomly throws its bottle out of the crib and, seeing what effect that achieves, does it again. He says that, similarly, boyhood friends perceived that others saw them as tough guys (a myth) and then tested out what effect the pose would have. Seeing that it worked (the reality), they did it again and again, thus perpetuating the myth.

6. Staples begins several sentences in paragraph 13 with the first-person pronoun "I," moving from a past-tense statement of what he felt he had to do—"I began to take precautions to make myself less threatening"—to present-tense statements of what he did—"I move about with care . . . I give a wide berth." He then introduces a statement with a subordinate clause: "If I happen to be entering a building . . . I may walk by. . . ." Finally, he moves to a past-tense statement: "I have been calm and extremely congenial on those rare occasions when. . . ."

7. By citing the analogy of himself as a hiker wearing a cowbell to keep the bears away, Staples complicates the metaphor of himself as hunter and white people as hunted by suggesting that he is only passing through the area, not wanting to be a victim of the frightened animals within.

8. Generally, Staples's tone is consistent with the image he wishes to convey in the essay. He does not present an angry image, as Julianne Malveaux does in her essay in Part Four, nor does he present a resentful image, as Judith Ortiz Cofer does in the essay that follows. Rather, his tone suggests one who is at first amused at the unjustified fear he creates, then fearful of the threat this poses for him.

The Myth of the Latin Woman: I Just Met a Girl Named María

JUDITH ORTIZ COFER

Judith Ortiz Cofer does more than just complain about the stereotype of the "sizzling" Latin woman; she also suggests a cause of the stereotype by explaining how Puerto Rican cultural customs are misunderstood by Anglo men.

EXPLORING IDEAS

1. Complex cultural assumptions underlie the idea that a girl's virtue is related to family honor, not the least of which is the assumption that a female is the "property" of the father until a transfer to a husband can be arranged. In such a business deal, it is important that the property not be damaged.

2. Males sometimes complain that women should not dress provocatively if they do not wish to be stared at and pursued. Women retort that they should be free to dress as they wish without being treated as sex objects. Mixed-gender discussion groups can brainstorm this idea with a great deal of spirit.

3. Most students will remember an experience when they felt out of step. A good essay on this topic should describe the experience in such a way as to suggest its universality.

4. The fact that a female's "honor" is tied up with sexuality, whereas a male's honor is not is related to the issue raised in Exercise 1: that women are seen as property of men. When a woman engages in sexuality outside the property arrangement, she becomes tainted, damaged goods.

5. The easiest explanation for the metaphors connecting Hispanic women to heat, such as "sizzling" and "smoldering," is that it is related to the tropical climate of Latin American countries and to the famous spicy foods of those countries.

6. Every culture (and probably every era) has courting games in which young males and females are permitted to engage in tentative gestures of romantic or sexual pursuit. In North American societies, it may be meeting at a certain place or attending a certain kind of dance, for example.

7. Without statistical data to support the assertion that Latin women are more often victims of sexual harassment than others, students may have to fall back on personal experience and knowledge of the power of stereotypes from popular culture.

8. Being a character in a cartoon-populated universe is easier to conceive if students have seen the movie *Who Framed Roger Rabbit?* in which actual people interact with cartoon characters. Have students choose a particular cartoon universe, such as the universe of Mickey Mouse, Tom and Jerry, or Popeye, and brainstorm what that universe is like.

9. Other media-engendered stereotypes include the Frito Bandito commercials of some years ago, the shuffling African-American male in movies of the 1940s, the dumb blonde, and the happy-go-lucky, bumbling fat person.

10. The issue Cofer raises here is also raised by Robert Heilbroner in his essay about stereotypes in this part. Can one ever ignore such things as skin color, accent, and clothes, or are we always trapped into some measure of stereotyping?

EXPLORING RHETORIC

1. Students should realize that this is a purely rhetorical decision. Cofer very well could have begun with paragraph 6 and then related the incident in England; however, she has a better chance of snagging her audience's interest by opening with a dramatic incident than with general statements.

2. Rita Moreno is probably the best-known example of Hollywood's stereotyping of the Hispanic female by forcing her to talk in a funny accent, act seductively, and dance provocatively. The result has been that she has had difficulty finding any other kinds of roles. Movies have often stereotyped the Mexican male as either a lazy peasant or a vicious bandit.

3. It is ironic that the character of María in *West Side Story* was played by the Anglo actress Natalie Wood because the producers did not want to give the role to a relatively unknown Hispanic actress. Cofer does not resent being identified with the character in the movie, only with being seen as a fictional stereotype rather than as an individual human being.

4. Cofer introduces the metaphor when she says, "If you are a Latina . . . the Island travels with you." She then suggests that this very fact makes her an island—not a tropical island like Puerto Rico but an isolated and terrible place like Alcatraz Island in San Francisco Bay.

5. Although Cofer suggests cultural customs in Puerto Rico that support the stereotype of the Latin woman, she attempts to explain how the way women dress and behave in Puerto Rico is misinterpreted by Anglo men. She suggests that Anglo men need to understand that the cultural background of Latina dress and behavior is not meant to suggest sexual invitations.

6. The man who sang the obscene song to the tune of "La Bamba" was extremely rude, and the fact that he was intoxicated and trying to show off is no excuse for his behavior. Although your students may feel that they would never behave in such a crude fashion, you might ask them if they have ever told an ethnic joke or laughed when someone else told one. See Heilbroner's essay in this part for further discussion of ethnic jokes and Kenneth Goings's essay in Part Two for discussions of parodies of ethnic groups.

7. Cofer is gracious to suggest that the woman's mistaking her for a waitress was partially due to thinking that the sheaf of poems in her hand was the menu. However, does Cofer's resentment suggest that she thinks that she is better than a waitress because she is a poet? Why should one resent being taken for a waitress anyway? The issue here, of course, is not that Cofer scorns waitresses but that the woman assumed that because Cofer was Latina she had to be a waitress.

8. Cofer says she is one of the lucky ones, for she has an education that enables her to escape the stereotypes of the Latin woman as a menial. Have your students compare this suggestion to Brent Staples' whistling classical music to convince people that he is not to be feared, or to Rachel Jones's essay in Part Four in which she argues that African Americans should not resent learning standard English in order to be accepted into the mainstream culture.

Yellow Woman and a Beauty of the Spirit

Leslie Marmon Silko

Leslie Marmon Silko describes the communal world of the Laguna Pueblo tribe in the U.S. Southwest, while Alice Walker, in the next essay, describes the significance of African American community in the U.S. South. Silko discusses the importance of the old Pueblo stories that demonstrate the interrelatedness of all living things, particularly the stories of Yellow Woman, a mythic figure of courage and sexual power who defies traditional boundaries.

Exploring Ideas

1. Richard Rodriguez's essay about his complexion in Part One might be compared with the opening section of Silko's essay, for both writers deal with being different from other members of their culture because of external appearance. Whereas Rodriguez is darker than his companions, Silko is lighter.

2. Although Silko discusses a number of distinctions between the modern and the "old-time" view, she is primarily concerned with the modern discrimination between people because of differences and the old-time people's acceptance of all differences. Silko agrees with Ishmael Reed, who argues in his essay in this part that Puritans, with an absolutist view of right and wrong and a strong sense of the Elect, are responsible for modern racism.

3. Silko describes a time when tourists excluded her from their pictures of the Laguna Pueblo children because she did not look Indian. Have students compare this memory with Richard Rodriguez's anecdote in Part One of the first time he felt different.

4. In *Steps Toward an Ecology of Mind,* Gregory Bateson has argued that if we continue to think that the nonhuman world around us is mindless and therefore not entitled to ethical consideration, we will destroy the planet. Have students consult the essays by Bill McKibben and Edward Abbey in Part Two.

5. The assumption that it is bad to make comparisons between people has to do with human competition and progress. If people are not compared with each other, then what will stimulate one to excel? What is to prevent everyone from being content to stay at a static level of mediocrity? Have students read Kurt Vonnegut's story "Harrison Bergeron" (in *Welcome to the Monkey House*).

6. Although students may not be able to identify with people who take pride in having a facelift or liposuction, they may be able to identify with the social status gained by wearing certain brands of clothes in which the labels are openly displayed.

7. Have students discuss the difference between believing that being healthy is beautiful in itself and being healthy in order to be physically beautiful.

8. Have students examine the popular stereotypes common to film and television of the older man pursuing the younger woman for sexual reasons and the younger man pursuing the older woman for monetary reasons. Have them discuss the assumptions about masculine and feminine attitudes that underlie these stereotypes.

9. Have students compare the basic assumption that the values of the old-time Pueblo world are matriarchal with the basic assumptions underlying Amy Gross's essay earlier in this part that the most positive human values are female.

EXPLORING RHETORIC

1. Students often neglect the specific details that particularize an experience and are relevant to its general significance. In her brief narrative about visiting with her great-grandmother, Silko makes the experience unique and relevant to her point about becoming strong by noting seemingly minor details, such as freeing the garden hose stuck on a rock, being old enough to cross the road alone, and carrying the coal bucket and armloads of kindling.

2. The view of the "old-time people" is, like the Hispanic view Arthur Campa describes in his essay in this part, relativist rather than absolutist. If identity is always shifting rather than absolute, it is difficult to make distinctions between people, as modern people do, for everyone is potentially someone else, and there is a little of everyone in each of us.

3. It seems the old-time view can have it both ways. On the one hand, the Pueblos did not compare one person with another as a means of asserting the superiority of one over another. Yet if someone did deviate from the majority, that person was considered exceptional and valued rather than scorned and cast out.

4. The old Pueblo notion that sex with other people did not have to end with marriage is one more example of how the Pueblos did not emphasize rigid gender differences between the sexes, nor did they burden sex with the many rules and inhibitions that the Puritans brought with them.

5. Silko says she particularly likes Yellow Woman because she represents the strong woman who dares to cross traditional boundaries. It is the matriarchal nature of Pueblo cosmology that accounts for Yellow Woman's power being primarily sexual. Yellow Woman's sexual desire and attraction are sources of her power, not just her childbearing potential. Have students find and read Silko's short story "Yellow Woman," anthologized in many short-story textbooks, for Silko's modernizing of the Yellow Woman myth.

6. Although Silko does not make the comparison explicit, she relates her learning to shoot and hunt at an early age with the fact that Yellow Woman is also a hunter.

7. Many cultures use brief stories as a means of teaching and healing. The most obvious of these, the kind with which Anglo-American students will be most familiar, are parables, fables, and exemplary stories. Bruno Bettleheim, in his book *The Uses of Enchantment,* argues that fairy tales objectify childhood fears and help children cope with them.

8. The Yellow Woman figure may be a difficult one for modern feminists to accept, for her power lies in her sexuality, and many feminists have argued that the reduction of woman to her sexuality has caused women to be discriminated against in many ways. Yellow Woman, however, is not the passive object of male sexual desire but rather an aggressive pursuer. Have students read Susan Brownmiller's essay on femininity earlier in this part and then discuss the stereotypes of sex as a source of feminine power.

The Black Writer
and the Southern Experience

ALICE WALKER

While Alice Walker has no intention of romanticizing her childhood as a poor, rural, southern African American, she praises the sense of community, the compassion for the earth, and the love of justice she received as her heritage.

EXPLORING IDEAS

1. Some students may feel that the difference between religion as a pacifier against injustice and religion as an antidote against bitterness is more semantic than real. However, Walker suggests that religion did not reconcile southern African Americans to their plight, but rather that it enabled them to endure injustice and to create a community of people who generously helped each other.

2. Valuing and preserving oral history has become an important component of efforts to discover our roots. Students may turn to parents, grandparents, and other guardians for this exercise. Suggest that students use a tape recorder for the interview and then transcribe and edit the recording to focus on the most important elements of the account.

3. The easiest response to this suggestion is to argue that the poor are more in need of a sense of solidarity than the rich, for a rich person doesn't need others to support him or her. This may be related to the issue Walker raises about the importance of religion, for some students will suggest that religion is more likely to be depended on by the poor than the rich.

4. The dirtiness of the city and the cleanliness of the country may be a stereotype of popular culture images, or some students may agree with Walker that it is impossible to think of the country as being "dirty," since the very concept of dirtiness is human rather than natural.

5. By "rituals of growing up," Walker means the recurrent activities of one's childhood, such as meals and holidays, as well as certain events of childhood, which happen to everyone and thus seem somewhat ritualized and formalized.

6. Walker suggests that blindness to other human beings is equivalent to death, for it suggests a spiritual death. It means death for writers in particular, for one of the writer's most important tasks is to identify with others as unique individuals.

7. One does not have to be familiar with Faulkner's fiction to react to his statements in *Faulkner in the University* that whites are morally superior to blacks and that blacks are not ready to function in a democratic society. Have students discuss whether Faulkner, who, Walker admits, examines the reason for the decay of the South, also had a responsibility, as Walker suggests, to try to change the structure of southern society.

8. Some students may think that the statement, "In the city it cannot be so clear to one that he is a creature of the earth," is too obvious a truism to discuss. However, some students may argue that humans are not creatures of the earth but of society.

9. Have students brainstorm the difference between a romantic, sentimental description of some aspect of their past and a realistic description that just happens to be happy and loving.

Exploring Rhetoric

1. Many writers represented in this book begin their essays with narrative and descriptive anecdotes. Walker's opening is a classic example of this rhetorical technique, for it is a single incident that combines narrative with dialogue and is followed by an explicit statement of its meaning. Have students look at several other essays in this collection that begin with narrative anecdotes before trying an anecdotal opening of their own.

2. Walker does not stress the fact that she rejected the religion of her parents when she was in college, but she does say that she now realizes that her ancestors were able to transform what began as a white man's palliative into a noble understanding of the teachings of Jesus—primarily the love of one's neighbor.

3. Walker argues that the lives of poor southern African Americans testify to a greater understanding of the teachings of Jesus than the lives of those who believe that there is such a thing as a "white" church. She creates a parallel example to this bias in the anecdote of the white northerner who implied that a farmer's daughter could not be a poet.

4. The suggestion that a farmer's daughter might not be the stuff that poets are made of is based on a narrow definition from the English tradition of what it means to be a poet—primarily to be an aristocratic white male. Walker says this statement by a white middle-aged northerner made her as mad as she has ever been and argues that a poet should be able to write poems that are understood by his or her own people.

5. The metaphor that a country person finds the city too confining, like wearing a dress that is too tight, seems particularly appropriate here, for a country woman would suffer a too-tight dress only if she were "going to town."

6. The "double vision" of black southern writers refers to the fact that they have the ability to see their own world from within and to understand the world around them that has treated them so unfairly.

7. Walker expects that her audience should be at least as familiar with the name Nat Turner as with the name William Faulkner. By citing such spokespersons and defenders of African American life as Frederick W. Douglass and W. E. B. DuBois, Walker argues that William Faulkner's assertion that a black man's intelligence is directly related to the amount of white blood he has has never been true.

8. There is, of course, no contradiction between Walker's statement that she hated the poverty, the backbreaking work, the shabby houses, and the white man's greed that characterized her childhood and her statement that she loved the sense of community, generosity, and kindness that characterized her people. Have students brainstorm and describe a love-hate relationship with which they are familiar.

Anglo vs. Chicano: Why?

Arthur L. Campa

While Arthur L. Campa provides an academic explanation of the difference in cultural styles between Hispanics and Anglos and suggests some of the basic causes of these differences, Ishmael Reed argues in the following essay that the trend in American society is toward the blurring of cultural styles.

Exploring Ideas

1. Campa's argument based on geography is that since England is an island, its culture is also insular and self-contained, but because Spain is a peninsula extending into the Mediterranean, it is a composite culture combining Central European and North African peoples.

2. Campa says that Anglo-American culture has been absolutist from its beginnings, insisting that certain values were unchanging for all peoples and all times, while the Spanish brought to America a relativist viewpoint, holding that values were dependent on social and economic conditions.

3. Campa argues that the English, who came to America to escape persecution, saw the New World as a haven where they could put down roots, but the Spanish, who came to America as explorers, kept moving on restlessly.

4. The contrast between the English settlers looking at the world from eye level and the Spanish explorers looking at the world from atop a horse suggests that while the English were down-to-earth and focused on making the most of the moment, the Spanish were aristocratic and always looking toward the horizon.

5. Campa argues that Spanish individualism is based on momentary emotional reactions, while Anglo-American individualism is based on a plan of action and strives for objectivity. Ask students if they know individuals who exhibit these styles.

6. Campa says Hispanics have no fixed rules governing polite behavior or courtesy since courtesy is an expression of individual feelings toward the other; in an absolutist society such as that of the Anglo-American, there are social rules of right and wrong. Rules of polite behavior, such as saying "thank

you," "excuse me," and "please," may vary according to social class in Anglo-American society.

7. Because Hispanics treasure the present, says Campa, they do not plan for the future but rather improvise at the moment. Because time is money to Anglo-Americans, they are future oriented and always make plans.

8. Concrete accomplishments—what you do and what you produce—are important to Anglo-Americans, but Hispanic people do not associate what they do or produce with who they are.

9. Campa says there are no words in Spanish for "apology" or "compromise." Ask students to think of individuals for whom apology and compromise are so abhorrent that they seldom, if ever, do either. Then ask them to think of people who are quick to apologize and frequently compromise. Have them brainstorm both types and discuss the strengths and weaknesses of each.

EXPLORING RHETORIC

1. Campa begins by saying that although many writers have explained the differences between Hispanic and Anglo-American cultures, usually the audiences for these discussions have either been specialists looking for confirmation of their beliefs or readers who already agree with the points of view expressed. Because his essay is directed to a general audience, he considers the subject worth discussing further.

2. Word choice and sentence structure reflect a typically academic style, albeit one aimed at a general rather than a specialized audience. Some phrases students might note are: "implicit in the conceptual content," "particularly zealous of its racial purity," "differences were reflected in the colonizing enterprise," and "were not collectively adverse." Have students also note the complex and balanced sentence structure.

3. The "racial cocktail" metaphor does not seem particularly appropriate to the content, although, being a "mixed" drink, it does suggest the racial "mix" Campa is talking about. Perhaps the immediately preceding reference to the Spanish nobility prompted the "cocktail" metaphor.

4. Campa sticks to a rather formal comparison-contrast technique. Paragraphs 3 through 6 are equally divided into statements about Anglo-American and Hispanic attitudes and motives.

5. In paragraph 7, Campa discusses Hispanic individualism as a "revolt against the incursion of collectivity" and argues that such an attitude leads to a "deficiency in those social qualities based on collective standards," which Hispanics do not consider negative because "it manifests a measure of resistance to standardization in order to achieve a measure of individual freedom." A less abstract revision might be: "Spanish people think of themselves as individuals rather than members of a group. They think that individual freedom is worth the loss of effective standardized group action."

6. The metaphor of time walking versus time running is a relatively simple one. Writers often resort to metaphors when trying to describe time; see Annie

Dillard's essay in Part Two for an extended metaphor of time. Ask your students to try to come up with some time metaphors.

7. Campa creates a transition from paragraph 7 to 8 by repeating the words "fixed rules." The discussion of courtesy in paragraph 9 follows logically as a specific example of the general discussion of rules. Paragraph 10 begins with the transition phrase, "Another cultural contrast." There is no explicit transition device to paragraph 11, which discusses different attitudes toward time. Paragraphs 12 and 13 have clear transition markers in their opening sentences.

8. Campa introduces Spanish words in paragraph 15 to set the reader up for a discussion of implicit differences between Spanish and English words that seem identical in meaning.

9. Although the anecdote of the two stubborn *hildagos* is probably a myth or traditional story, it is not so fantastic that it could not have happened. Have your students brainstorm or invent a story to reflect an attitude of their own culture.

America: The Multinational Society

ISHMAEL REED

In the debate over America as a rainbow of cultural difference versus a melting pot of cultural blend, Ishmael Reed navigates a course in between, suggesting that the United States has always been a rich bouillabaisse mixture of cultures that retain their own distinctive flavor even as they combine.

EXPLORING IDEAS

1. Reed argues that in spite of the publicity over cultural clashes in American society, U.S. history and the current trend toward the blurring of cultural styles reveal more union than conflict. Students might read Lewis Thomas's essay in Part Two for a discussion of the human instinct toward union rather than conflict.

2. Reed argues that the term "Western civilization," meaning a civilization created by Europe, is more ambiguous than the cultural elect would like to believe, and he points out how such great monuments of European art and culture have been influenced by Asia and Africa. Defining Western civilization as solely European in origin has been an unquestioned assumption in history textbooks until only recently.

3. Reed cites Hitler as the ultimate monoculturalist. And indeed, racism pushed to ultimate extremes always runs the risk of the horror of attempted genocide. Students who think that ethnic jokes are examples of "harmless racism" might wish to consider whether racism is ever harmless.

4. The Puritan work ethic has multiple implications. Reed notes the following: religious piety and a sense of being the elect that led to intolerance; focus on work that allowed little time for frivolity and play; a simple approach to knowledge that distrusted the intellectual; an absolutist sense of rules of right and wrong that led to cruel punishments. Arthur Campa discusses some of these characteristics in the previous essay.

5. Reed suggests that the "mean streak" in the Puritans primarily stemmed from their sense of being the elect, for this attitude did not tolerate any differences or variations from the preestablished norm.

6. Reed suggests that Puritanism is the source of the racist attitude that caused the incarceration of Japanese Americans during World War II (see the essay by Jeanne Wakatsuki Houston and James D. Houston in Part One), the near extermination of Native Americans, and the murder of thousands of African Americans. He concludes his essay by arguing that this attitude of the early elect continues to be heard from U.S. educators.

7. An underlying assumption of Reed's essay is that art is the clearest indicator of cultural mix. His final vision is for a U.S. society in which all cultural styles join and exist side by side.

EXPLORING RHETORIC

1. This tactic of opening an essay with multiple examples of one's thesis before stating the point explicitly is a rhetorical decision that students will see in other essays. Have them look, for example, at the opening of Judith Ortiz Cofer's essay in this part for a similar approach. The first two examples—the poet describing the cultural mix of Detroit and the prediction that in some areas of the country both Spanish and English will be used—are more general than the specific examples of the white professor's lecturing on African American influence on American society and the African American paintings hanging in a McDonald's restaurant.

2. Reed tacitly assumes that art, rather than social organization or political structures, for example, is the clearest example of the influence of various cultures on Western civilization. He begins by referring to the influence of Islamic architectural style and a description of paintings with African and African American images and symbols hanging in a McDonald's restaurant. Many of his examples of the influence of Asia and America on Western civilization focus on music, painting, and poetry.

3. Reed uses questions about Beethoven's Ninth Symphony, cubist and surrealist painters, and Europeans with Asian and African ancestry as a rhetorical retort to those cultural elect who insist that Western civilization is solely European. Such rhetorical questions are often used to challenge commonly held points of view.

4. The "small-screen" metaphor refers, of course, to television, but it is more effective than if Reed had used the phrase "television view," for it suggests that Western civilization is much more complex than the simplistic popular media view often presented by television.

5. After citing examples of the cultural elect view of Western civilization in paragraphs 5 through 7—a view that inevitably ends with the monoculturalism of Adolph Hitler—Reed explicitly introduces the causal section of his essay in paragraph 8: "Where did such an attitude, which has caused so much misery and depression in our national life, which has tainted even our noblest achievements, begin?"

6. Reed's final example, in which he tells of a friend whose poem was accepted for publication by a computer magazine, is cited to illustrate the danger of an Orwellian future in which the United States is the brain of a world of information systems and in which magazines do not publish poetry or fiction. Reed seems to imply that the United States has the potential to be the heart of the world, where the arts from various cultures crisscross.

ANALYZING AND ARGUING A CASE

Why We Crave Horror Movies

STEPHEN KING

This essay by Stephen King, who has made a fortune on our fascination with horror stories, is a facile, personal point-of-view piece for a popular audience. The following essay by Robert Brustein, the well-known drama critic, is a classic example of an academic analysis of a popular culture phenomenon. Students will probably like the King piece better for its glib tone, although the Brustein piece is more thought-provoking, albeit more abstract.

EXPLORING IDEAS

1. As in most of this essay, King is only half serious in describing such phobias as fear of heights, snakes, and the dark as "mental illnesses." Have students brainstorm the pros and cons of the idea that "mental illness" is only a term to characterize deviations from what the majority consider normal.

2. Although King uses the metaphor of a roller coaster to describe one's experience in viewing a horror movie, are these experiences the same, or does riding a roller coaster pose a real physical danger that watching a horror movie does not?

3. If you have older adults in your class, create discussion groups of mixed ages to brainstorm King's idea that certain activities are only for the young. If this is so, have them explore why. If it is not so, then where did King get the idea?

4. By calling the horror movie "conservative," King does not suggest an explicit relationship to conservative politics but rather that horror movies present such extreme variants from the conventional that they make all of us feel quite normal.

5. Amy Gross and Paul Theroux, in their essays in Part Two, suggest that sports contests spring from the same impulse as that which inspires combat, for both exhibit and glorify male aggressiveness. King's statement suggests that those who cannot or will not fight can enjoy battle by watching professional football.

6. Horror films are not the only examples of popular culture media that create absolute images of good and evil. The Hollywood western is responsible for the common metaphor of men with white hats versus men with black hats to suggest this simple division. When students brainstorm this topic, they may discover that certain moral questions do not admit any shades of gray, while others are never simply black and white.

7. Lewis Thomas, in Part Two, describes an experience of wonder that he does not wish to analyze; Robert Brustein, in the following essay, apologizes for analyzing horror films. Students may feel that some experiences are too spiritual or beautiful to analyze and others too silly or unimportant.

8. The relationship between pornography and rape, about which much has been written, divides itself between those who think that pornography serves a cathartic purpose and those who think that it stimulates one to rape. The issue of how far society can allow its members to "let loose" and vicariously experience forbidden desires is a complex part of the debate.

9. Horror films since the 1970s have become more graphically violent than before. Have students read Michael Ventura's essay on slasher films in this part before working on this topic.

Exploring Rhetoric

1. King's glib tone seems suitable for his simplistic treatment of the psychological reasons that people like horror films. The reader's initial assumption that horror films do not have to be taken seriously is not likely to be changed by King's analysis.

2. King does not provide an explicit transition between his opening paragraph about mental illness and the next two paragraphs, which introduce the central subject of why we go to horror movies. Implicitly, the connection is that the fears we see objectified in horror films are the same as the phobias King lists in the first paragraph.

3. King's metaphor of the ground sloping away is part of the metaphoric complex of referring to something we are sure of as being on "solid" or "level ground," and referring to something we are not sure of as being on "shaky" or "uneven ground."

4. King's little asides, such as his demonic laugh when mentioning that Jack the Ripper and the Cleveland Torso Murderer were never caught and his parenthetical comment that he dare not call Leonard Nimoy's verse poetry, are part of his effort to create a personal and personable voice.

5. Talking to yourself when under stress is a predictable example of the kind of minor madness that King describes, but most students will think that picking your nose in public is just bad manners. King probably uses the example to make possible the comic line about not being invited to the best parties.

6. The reference to "rotten little puke of a sister" is a rhetorical tactic to suggest the kind of language that a child might use; it plays on a stereotype about the relationship between older brothers and younger sisters. Victoria Sackett uses a similar phrase for the same rhetorical purpose in her essay in this part.

7. Note that while Robert Heilbroner in his essay in Part Three does not provide an example of an ethnic joke when he mentions such jokes, King is not similarly restrained when he mentions sick jokes. Insanity and sick jokes are all part of the fun King is having with the topic, and his informal tone makes the joke about the truckload of dead babies tolerable, if barely. Students who are offended by the joke might legitimately point out that there is nothing funny about insanity or dead babies.

8. King's metaphor about the alligators swimming around in a subterranean river beneath our civilized mind refers to the Freudian distinction between the ego and the id, on which King bases his central premise. The metaphor suggests

that we all have these monsters in the unconscious and must deal with them in some way. You might have students compare King's basic premise here with the basic premise that underlies the essay by Lewis Thomas in Part Two. While King assumes a basic aggressive human nature, Thomas assumes a basic communal attitude.

9. King maintains his glib tone right down to the one-sentence final paragraph. Although good liberals might argue that all you need is love, King maintains his assumption that beneath the civilized exterior of all of us lies the monstrous urges of the id.

Reflections on Horror Movies

ROBERT BRUSTEIN

Robert Brustein's essay is a clear example of the rhetorical technique of classification and analysis. Separating horror movies into three categories, he analyzes each to show how they reflect changing social attitudes toward experimental science.

EXPLORING IDEAS

1. Students often cite television as an activity in which they engage because it makes no demands on the mind; they may say they watch television just to become a vegetable (couch potato). Be sure they read Marie Winn's essay on television in this part.

2. A number of sociological and psychological studies have been done on various Hollywood film genres, such as film noir, westerns, and romantic comedies. Have students choose a film type for which they can name several examples and then brainstorm some of the characteristics or conventions of the type.

3. The superstition and magic of one culture or era are the religion and science of another. Place students in small groups to compare religious beliefs with superstitious beliefs. Or have them discuss the fact that medical science has recently been receptive to folk remedies that once were considered magic.

4. The trick of defining "parody" is to explain how the parody is both like and unlike that which it parodies. Students might consider such related terms as "caricature," in which the characteristics of the original are maintained but exaggerated.

5. There may or may not be a relationship between obscurants (those who oppose intellectual development) and reactionaries (those who oppose liberalism and progress). Stephen King says horror films make us feel normal; Brustein says they flatter those who are intellectually inferior.

6. Slasher films (see Michael Ventura's essay, which follows) involve adolescent culture by making teenagers victims. The *Friday the 13th* series is the gory model for this trend.

7. Turning the tables and writing an essay on the "teenager as monster" rather than the "monster as teenager" might be fun. It might also suggest that horror films in which teenagers are victims constitute adult revenge against monstrous teenagers.

8. The relationship between sex and violence may be too delicate to discuss. It involves several issues, including the feminist position that rape is not a crime of sexual passion but a crime of violence against women.

9. Brustein's suggestion that teenagers fantasize getting power through sex and violence is an interesting one. Have students discuss the image of the female sexual temptress and the male sexual athlete in current films that appeal to teenagers.

10. Brustein argues that movies in which the teenager is a monster reflect the fact that adolescents feel victimized by authority and that if they act like delinquent monsters, it is society's fault.

11. Brustein suggests that the obscurant, fearing that there are some things human beings should not tamper with, distrusts theoretical science because it is guided by no moral principle or pragmatic purpose.

Exploring Rhetoric

1. Brustein probably uses the somewhat archaic term "pottage" rather than "stew" because it suggests some of the medieval flavor of horror films that he wishes to evoke.

2. Brustein announces his classification method quite explicitly in paragraph 3, and the divisions among the three categories "Mad Doctor," "Atomic Beast," and "Interplanetary Monster" are clearly delineated. The essay provides a good opportunity to discuss the classification method of analyzing a phenomenon into separate categories that have shared characteristics.

3. The metaphor is somewhat mixed, for a straight man has little to do with pastures, and besides, Abbott was Costello's straight man. However, the idea of the poor monster's grazing in parched pastures of old, rundown movie theaters creates an image that fits Brustein's playful tone.

4. When Brustein refers to the roots of the vampire, werewolf, and monster stories in European myths in this paragraph, he gives the legitimate impression, as academics often do, that he is an expert on these issues instead of having researched and found this general information in histories.

5. Brustein uses Wilson as the exemplar of a practical, tough-minded American businessman who, although he ultimately depends on theoretical research, publicly scorns it as trivial and a waste of time and money.

6. Mistaking mere plot summary for analysis is a common student problem. Since Brustein's classification analysis depends on generalized plot configurations, he must summarize the plots of some films to show their similarities. However, he summarizes only plot elements on which he comments to support his analysis.

7. Brustein summarizes the plot of the Atomic Beast film, *Beginning of the End,* because he says it is an example of the whole genre. Have students carefully examine the summary; Brustein does not describe every detail or action blow by blow, but rather briefly describes only scenes that reflect the generic characteristics of the film.

8. Brustein's technique in analyzing the film *Beginning of the End* is to indicate the differences between the Mad Doctor film and the Atomic Beast film. He first sets up a comparison-contrast between the character of the scientist in both film types; second, he shows how the relationship between the scientist and the monster is different in the two types; third, he explains that the victimization of people by theoretical science has moved from a mere suggestion to a fact in the Atomic Beast films.

9. If your students are anything like mine, many more of them will be familiar with the comic book hero Superman than with Nietzsche's concept. Brustein's general assumption here is that Americans are more fearful of intellectual superiority than physical superiority. The most frightening of all is the combination of intellectual knowledge with physical power. Brustein's conclusion is that horror films reflect the fear that the idle curiosity of the theoretical scientist, ungoverned by moral principles, makes us all vulnerable to danger.

On Kids and Slasher Movies

MICHAEL VENTURA

Ventura's essay is not a popular or academic analysis like King's or Brustein's; it is a polemic, typical of the personal think pieces that appear on op-ed pages and in Sunday opinion sections of the newspaper. Ventura bases his argument about the boy and the mask on the underlying assumptions about horror films that both King and Brustein lay bare.

EXPLORING IDEAS

1. Ventura's assertion that the boy's eagerness to "play" maniac killer is worse than the bomb is based on the assumption that the bomb is an abstraction, something not quite real or concretely dangerous, but rather, like a religious object, loaded with generalized meaning that makes possible some framework for seeing the world in a certain way.

2. Ventura says the boy's eagerness to "play" maniac killer is worse than Auschwitz because it is very clear how horrifying the mass murders in the camps were. However, there is nothing so clearly evil about the simple act of the boy's buying the mask.

3. To make the slasher masks illegal would be to limit freedom of expression, for if we assume that the masks (which are mere representations of murder) might stimulate one to engage in murderous behavior, then, by the same reasoning, we might assume that any symbolic representation in books or films might stimulate one to such behavior and should therefore be banned.

4. Catharsis versus motivation is the issue here. Does acting out in the imagination the kind of murderous behavior that Stephen King discusses in his essay earlier in this part release one from acting out such urges in real life? Or do representations of murderous behavior encourage one to engage in such behavior?

5. A great deal of research has been done on how children act out feelings through play. Have students brainstorm some kinds of adult play that serve the same purposes. For example, Amy Gross and Paul Theroux, in their essays on masculine behavior in Part Three, suggest that adult men watch professional football as a way of acting out aggression.

6. This topic involves a generic analysis of the slasher film, similar to the method of King or Brustein. Students should think of two or three such films they have seen and determine the salient characteristics of the films to decide the fantasies they embody.

7. Ventura says that many of the worst atrocities in history were carried out before the first slasher films were ever made. Thus, he argues, it is the whole of Western history that encourages murderous behavior or fantasies, not just horror films or television. Does this suggest that film and television are easy targets because the real cause of human evil leaves us helpless?

8. This is Ventura's most abstract point. Basically, he suggests that while the individual is not motivated by murderous urges, Western culture is. Thus, the boy buys the mask to role-play the maniac; if he does not, he will feel helpless at being surrounded by such madness.

EXPLORING RHETORIC

1. Ventura initially establishes a personal, conversational tone. Thus, the short, clipped sentences and fragments seem justified. By saying that his body "decided" that this was the worst thing he had ever seen, he suggests that he instinctively knows the horror of what the boy has done. He says that only later did he try to think about it; the essay is the result of that thought. By the end of the essay, Ventura justifies the extremity of his saying the mask on the child is the "worst" thing he ever saw, for he relates it to something basically horrifying about all of Western civilization.

2. Having already committed himself to saying that the boy's wearing the mask is the "worst" thing he ever saw, Ventura must justify that extreme statement by explaining how the mask on the boy is worse than two of the most obvious horrors of the twentieth century.

3. Ventura might very well have blamed the desire for the mask on other cultures besides the Judeo-Christian; however, since he is concerned only with Western civilization, he feels justified in centering his argument on the Judeo-Christian tradition. He does not blame the Greco-Roman tradition because, by implication, he suggests that the Judeo-Christian tradition is the primary framework for moral values in Western civilization.

4. Ventura anticipates that many people may blame social violence on television and movies; he wishes to deny this by arguing that the Nazis who built the camps and the scientists who built the bomb did so long before television and slasher movies. Ventura argues that we must lay the blame more broadly on Western culture, not on recent media.

5. Although his metaphor of this century as a varicolored snake is a bit melodramatic and extreme, Ventura feels confident enough to suggest that meaningless violence is the very meaning of the twentieth century, for he well knows that modern media make acts of violence immediately visible to everyone. The acts of gangs, terrorist groups, rapists, and mad people are displayed on television and in newspapers daily. Thus, such an extreme statement is likely to be accepted by a majority of readers.

6. Given the fact that inoculation involves injecting some of the virus that one wishes to defend against into the body, Ventura's metaphor seems apt. He extends it by suggesting the importance of the proper dosage of an inoculation, for if too little is injected, it will not work, and if too much is injected, it will overwhelm the body.

7. Ventura's conclusion is that the boy's wearing the mask is a horrifying but necessary condition of coping with the world. There is no way to make wearing the mask unnecessary for the boy, for he has already been infected by the horrors of Western civilization in the twentieth century. The only thing we can do is change the world itself.

The Trouble with Television

ROBERT MACNEIL

S o many critics and commentators have told us about "the trouble with television" that one begins to wonder whether anybody has anything good to say about it. While Robert MacNeil argues that television encourages the short attention span and Marie Winn claims that television is a harmful addiction, Tony Schwartz, with the true futurist's vision, declares that television is undergoing some socially beneficial changes.

EXPLORING IDEAS

1. Students can tackle this question by focusing on the effect of television viewing in general, as an activity that takes up much of one's time, or by focusing on some of the images created by television that have affected the way we perceive ourselves and the rest of the world.

2. Students may suggest that listening to music and looking at a painting are interesting and rewarding activities that do not require consistently applied effort. MacNeil, however, is not talking about passive pleasure but active understanding.

3. MacNeil says that dull and ungifted people can achieve things that seem miraculous to those who never concentrate on anything. The movie *Forrest Gump* perhaps appeals to the belief that even the least of us can have remarkable achievements if we try.

4. Although MacNeil's essay appeared in *Reader's Digest,* a magazine that specializes in brevity, he argues that brevity is bad. However, as short as MacNeil's paragraphs are, they require more concentration and thought than television commercials.

5. MacNeil tries to turn the tables here by arguing that instead of being efficient means of communication, the short segments we see on television are inefficient because they are fragmented and incoherent.

6. Ask students to list all the college courses or academic subjects they find boring. Then ask them to make a second list of courses and subjects they don't understand. Finally, ask them to determine any correlation between the two lists.

7. The old saw, "A picture is worth a thousand words," is seductive, especially in a visual age. Have students brainstorm differences between things that might best be communicated by pictures and things that might best be communicated by words. Can complex ideas be communicated by pictures?

8. Television seems to do best when focusing on the immediacy of events, not on the complexity of their meaning. The few times that television is praised are when it is used to cover social events as they occur. However, when television is used for analysis, it usually resorts to "talking heads" using language.

9. In the nineteenth century, many people were fascinated with the events in popular novels. However, novels were read by a select segment of the educated public, while television is accessible to all segments of the public.

10. MacNeil does not have any concrete suggestions for combating the ill effects of television. He simply concludes by suggesting that we should be concerned about these effects and begin to think of ways to fight them.

Exploring Rhetoric

1. MacNeil opens with the rhetorical tactic of using statistical figures and hypothetical cases. It is a bit shocking to think that in the time we spend sitting in front of the television in a single decade we might have become an astronomer or have learned several languages.

2. This is a short, tight essay. After MacNeil announces his thesis in paragraph 3—that the trouble with television is that it discourages concentration—he sticks with it throughout, moving from suggestions about how television achieves this to arguments about why such simplicity is harmful: claiming that television's approach is inefficient communication and decivilizing as well, since everything about our society is becoming more complex.

3. The comparison to a guided tour seems apt, for on such a tour one gets only a brief glimpse of something that may be quite complex. However, the comparison breaks down when one considers that the purpose of a guided tour is to provide expert direction to those who are unfamiliar with new territory.

4. In paragraphs 7 and 8, MacNeil shifts from television as an entertainment medium to his own specialty, television as a news medium. And it is as a news medium that he feels the values of television are pervading the nation as a whole, for television caters to the public's need for getting information in the quickest, most efficient way. However, MacNeil denies that television does present information in an efficient way, suggesting that it is fragmentary and incoherent.

5. MacNeil suggests that television contributes to illiteracy because, by depending on visual images and appealing to a short attention span, it does not encourage reading skills or critical thinking skills.

6. MacNeil defends himself against the charge of posing simplistic causes for complex effects by stating that he does not believe that television is the cause of illiteracy in this country, although it is clear from his argument that he believes that it is one of the major contributors. Have students brainstorm other reasons that 30 million adult Americans cannot read or write well enough to answer a want ad. They may suggest, for example, increased population, changes in educational approaches, a weak economy, or political attitudes toward funding education.

7. MacNeil moves from describing the basic trouble with television—that it discourages concentration—to the more specific problem that this technique causes when it involves news, and finally to how this generally contributes to illiteracy. He shifts from one part of the argument to another quite emphatically. His final argument—that although everything about the United States is becoming more complex, its principal communication medium depends on fragments of information and simplistic solutions—is the one that dominates his essay.

8. It is obvious that MacNeil thinks the trouble with television is a serious issue for the nation at large. Because he is respected as an analyst of the news on public television, not merely a handsome face that reads the news on commercial television, his argument has some authority.

Television Addiction

MARIE WINN

B y claiming that television watching is an addiction, Marie Winn is not merely using a metaphor, as Victoria Sackett does with disease as a metaphor for discriminations in her essay later in this part. Winn argues that by all definitions of the term, television watching is a real, harmful addiction.

EXPLORING IDEAS

1. Robert Brustein, in his essay earlier in this part, says he has been "hopelessly addicted" to horror movies since he was eight. Some people say they are addicted to chocolate, to rock music, to just about anything else that they wish to repeat continually because it gives them pleasure. Ask your students to brainstorm some everyday activities and things to which they feel addicted.

2. Students might focus on the fact that while they are engaged in an addictive experience, their attention is unnaturally focused on it and therefore they are relatively unaware of all else, much as what occurs when one is obsessed with something.

3. In addition to the obvious addictions to alcohol and drugs that allow one to blot out the real world, other activities that blot out the real world might be listening to music, daydreaming, or reading a book. If the real world is extremely stressful, it may be desirable to blot it out occasionally to reduce stress.

4. Many students will be able to identify with the phenomenon of "vegging out" in front of the television and not being able to overcome inertia to get up and turn the set off. Have them consider whether this is a result of the medium itself or a result of the particular nature of television programming.

5. Brainstorming this topic may require some direct or indirect research. What interesting and rewarding family activities were possible before television? Were there other reasons that families were closer before television, such as lack of transportation or tighter parental control?

6. Winn uses the term "nourishment" to suggest something that fulfills a need, not merely something that temporarily satisfies a desire. Winn says that because television does not fill a need, one can never be satisfied with it. Critics suggest that reading fulfills complex needs, not simplistic desires.

7. The practice of eating snacks while watching visual media existed in movie houses long before television, and this may have carried over to television. The creation of TV dinners and TV trays furthered the connection.

8. If students do not wish to give up television for a week or two, ask them to imagine what they might do for a week or two without it.

9. Winn suggests that addicts lose all sense of discrimination; for example, for someone addicted to chocolate, any kind of chocolate, regardless of quality, would be enough. Some students may claim that, based on this criterion, many activities they engage in are not addictions.

10. The visual nature of television may make us more fixated on it than on radio, for we feel that if we look away, we will miss something; thus, we focus intensely on the screen.

EXPLORING RHETORIC

1. Winn's opening rhetorical tactic is to make clear that her use of the term "addiction" to apply to television is not loose and merely metaphoric, such as being "addicted" to cookies or mystery novels, but that she is concerned with addiction's basis in pleasurable activities that one wishes to repeat yet that may have negative results.

2. Winn argues that real addicts do not merely pursue a pleasurable activity; they have a compelling need to repeat the activity again and again because they feel less than complete without it. Moreover, a real addiction is not merely a harmless pursuit of pleasure, Winn claims; a real addiction is destructive.

3. After setting up the criteria of the need to repeat the experience, the sense of incompleteness without it, and its destructive aspects, Winn spends the remainder of her essay showing that television shares these characteristics of serious addiction.

4. Winn does not present herself as an expert on addiction but as an analyst of television viewing; by quoting an expert on addiction she gives her argument a sense of authority it would not have otherwise.

5. Winn's use of direct quotations is a journalism technique to stimulate interest and ensure authenticity. Whereas writers might be suspected of taking liberties with paraphrases, we assume that they quote accurately. Quotations also convey a sense of a real person's speaking rather than an abstraction.

6. One of Winn's central points about the addictive nature of television is that it is accompanied by a loss of discrimination, for people addicted to television will watch anything. The practice of "roadblocking"—making sure that all three networks carry the same commercial or information at the same time—seems to support this point, as does the quotation from a political candidate who says that people watch anything that is on if they are given no choice.

7. Winn's use of experts to verify her definition of addiction and factual information about such practices as roadblocking suggests the techniques of an academic analyst. Her liberal use of quotations from actual television viewers is a combination of a popular journalism technique and anecdotal sociological research. Her overall analysis of the effects of television is largely based on individual responses rather than statistical analysis of a cross-section of representative viewers. All of these techniques suggest a popular rather than an academic argument.

8. Since Winn's arguments and analyses derive from individual viewers and since we have no way of knowing whether these are representative viewers, it would be a relatively simple matter to cite one's own respondents to argue against her points, one by one. However, weighing heavily in her favor is the verifiable fact, cited by Robert MacNeil in his earlier essay, that so many people watch so much television. Also in her favor is the fact that many people would agree that they have experienced many of the symptoms of addiction that she describes.

Communication in the Year 2000

TONY SCHWARTZ

 hile MacNeil criticizes television programming and Winn argues that the medium itself is addictive, Schwartz argues for the importance of television—when it is combined with computer technology—for facilitating communication. Many of Schwartz's predictions, made in 1981, have already become reality.

EXPLORING IDEAS

1. This topic should be an easy one for students to brainstorm, for home computers, fax machines, and interactive televideo conferencing did not exist three decades ago.

2. Schwartz argues that if commercial interests control the new technology, then much of it may be denied to the general public. He also notes, however, that government control is a nightmare because current laws separate the various communication industries. An example of such problems is the Internet, an unregulated network of computers that may face commercial or government control because of its increasing popularity.

3. Schwartz mentions facsimile (fax) machines as a new technology in 1981. Now, as the prices of such machines have gone down, many people have them; however, they have not replaced the U.S. Postal Service for delivering text material.

4. The cost of postage has gone up since Schwartz wrote this essay, and e-mail has dramatically increased, especially in commercial services such as America OnLine. Ask your students how much they use e-mail and how it has changed the way they communicate.

5. As cable access has increased, the viewing audience of the three major networks has declined. In the past, many viewers had only three channels to choose from; now they have dozens, and they "surf" cable by clicking a remote. Some students may not know what television was like before cable and the remote control device.

6. Computer gurus have been predicting the paperless office and the electronic library for some time now, but for portability and ease of reading any time and any place, books have yet to be replaced by computers.

7. Some students may suggest that electronic voting will be easier to manipulate, given the history of hackers' successfully breaking into top-secret computer files.

8. Now that several cable channels are devoted to twenty-four-hour television shopping and people can buy products by ordering them through computer services such as Prodigy, some critics suggest that we are getting ever further away from shopping as a communal activity in small-town shops.

9. Telecommuting has increased dramatically since Schwartz wrote this essay; however, some argue that telecommuting cuts down on collaborative work, isolates workers in their homes, reduces productivity, and encourages a less than professional attitude.

10. Schwartz's most extreme prediction is that since representative government is based on the impossibility of receiving input from every citizen, interactive technology that makes it possible for every citizen to be heard may change government so that it is determined by all the people.

EXPLORING RHETORIC

1. Schwartz's first paragraph is a good example of the rhetorical technique of beginning an essay with a condensed statement of the contents of the entire piece.

2. Schwartz's second paragraph is carefully structured, moving from one step to another logically and causally, with clear transition markers. After stating that the new technology is a hybrid form, he posits a significant result of this combination: problems for government regulation. Because of the difficulty of governmental control, Schwartz claims, big business may control the new technology and keep it out of the hands of consumers; an example of this is how breaking up the telephone company led to the development of many new technologies.

3. Schwartz uses very obvious transition markers such as "however," "these," "also," "another," "however," and "more," "also," and "this"—all part of the formal outline structure of the essay.

4. Paragraph 10 is almost solely a transition paragraph, signaling the shift from a discussion of examples of the new equipment to a discussion of the practical uses that can be made of the equipment and some of the projects that have already proven successful.

5. Schwartz sets up a formal structure for these paragraphs, beginning each one with "In Philadelphia," "In southern Arizona," "In Britain," to signal a discussion of a new and successful use of the new technology in each of these areas. The technique signals the outline structure of the essay.

6. Once again, Schwartz clearly signals a shift by announcing it in the first sentence. At this point, he moves from a discussion of several successful implementations of the new technology to a discussion of the possible social effects of the new communication services.

7. As in paragraphs 12 through 15, Schwartz begins several paragraphs in the same grammatical way with, "The potential implications," "The new technology," "The new communications technologies." These grammatical parallels push Schwartz's essay very close to an outline form.

8. This essay is easy to outline because the form is so obvious and clear. Such a form lends itself to the efficient communication of information with very little personal voice or stylistic variation.

Why Don't We Complain?

WILLIAM F. BUCKLEY, JR.

William Buckley says we don't complain enough about authority; Victoria Sackett suggests we complain too much about minor matters; and Julianne Malveaux justifies both social and personal anger. Buckley's essay is a clear example of an author's developing an argument about a social issue from personal experience.

Exploring Ideas

1. Have students look at the essays by Noel Perrin, Brent Staples, and Alice Walker in Part Three for other examples of the technique of beginning a conceptual essay with an anecdote. Have them recall or make up an anecdote to begin an essay about why people complain too much.

2. Buckley focuses primarily on our failure to complain to people who control our lives in some way—whether on a commuter train or in a movie theater—because he wants to conclude with an argument about political apathy.

3. In paragraph 8, Buckley states that we do not complain because "we are becoming increasingly anxious in America to be unobtrusive, we are reluctant to make our voices heard, hesitant about claiming our rights." To argue against Buckley, one need only cite examples in which people do complain against authority, as Julianne Malveaux does in her essay later in this part.

4. Compare this idea of the importance of "manliness" with a similar assumption in Noel Perrin's essay and with Amy Gross's and Paul Theroux's condemnation of such assumptions in Part Three.

5. With publicity about drive-by shootings, freeway shootings, vengeful bombings, and other violent responses to real and imagined grievances, police warn people not to provoke others by cursing, shaking a fist, or yelling.

6. Buckley blames our refusal to complain on an increased sense of helplessness in an age of technology and centralized political and economic power. Your students may suggest such causes as fear of reprisal, increased violence, increased fear of authority, and a new tolerance for minor annoyances.

7. As technology becomes more complex, we become more dependent on experts. For example, at one time, many people felt confident they could make minor repairs on their cars; now that many cars are largely dependent on computers, such repairs need experts.

8. Political apathy is a reality on many college campuses, especially large urban campuses where many students attend classes only part time and do not feel any real connection to campus governance. Students should be able to brainstorm this topic.

9. Americans have seldom been accused of being too polite. As Nancy Masterson Sakamoto suggests in her essay in Part Two and Arthur Campa suggests in his essay in Part Three, Japanese and Hispanic cultures feel that Americans are not courteous enough.

10. Buckley's leap of logic from an overheated rail car to the tyranny of Nikita Khrushchev is made possible by his equating politeness with apathy. He suggests that if we refuse to complain about trivial things, we will not rebel against tyranny either.

Exploring Rhetoric

1. Buckley creates a typically sarcastic tone in the first two sentences, a tone that he sustains throughout the essay. The sentence, "The problem was to breathe," is an exaggeration that—like Brent Staples's opening sentence about his first "victim" in his essay in Part Three—snags the readers' attention.

2. Buckley simply assumes that everyone knows what he means by a "virile" age. However, such sexist assumptions may not be so commonplace as they once were. Buckley associates virility with aggressive retaliation against a real or imagined slight. See the essays by Amy Gross and Paul Theroux in Part Three for further discussion of such assumptions.

3. "Sibilant intrusion" and "supine breed" are examples of typical Buckley alliterative use of fancy language. We tolerate them because they create the stiff and formal tone of the curmudgeon, a role that Buckley has parlayed into a well-known national voice of conservatism.

4. Part of Buckley's charm as a writer is his mixture of stiff formality with sarcasm and exaggeration; a number of examples can be found in this essay, the most obvious being the silliness about anticipating a helicopter to arrive and take the man in the ski shop to a nearby hospital.

5. Buckley makes it clear in describing himself as "bellicose" and "girding his loins" that he is self-consciously sarcastic. He emphasizes his struggle with sarcasm in paragraph 10 when he considers how he should approach the conductor and ironically regrets it when he "icily" says to the man in the ski shop, "If you are not too busy, would you mind handing me a screwdriver?"

6. The sentence, "I put the experience down as a reversal," is an ironic understatement, for Buckley's complaint against the man in the ski shop is in response to his New Year's resolution that he would "speak out like a man against the unnecessary annoyances of our times."

7. Buckley implies that a "virile" age was an age in which men were men and did not depend on technology to get their work done. The idea derives from a tacit assumption that there is something "manly" about an age like that of the American West in the nineteenth century, when men took care of everything without technology. Noel Perrin seems to be of the same generation and attitude as Buckley in his essay about androgyny in Part Three.

8. Many of your students may not know that William Buckley, Jr., is one of the reigning intellectual leaders of American Republican conservatism. In fact, some may not know that conservatism is characterized by a distrust of centralized government. Some analysis and brainstorming, however, should reveal Buckley's political affiliation.

9. It is ironic that Buckley, a political spokesman who has had little patience with protests of the liberal left, would here argue that the conservative right should put up posters announcing a political protest. Ending the essay by returning once again to his complaint against the overheated train car may not be an effective rhetorical tactic, for, in comparison to complaining against such a tyrant as Khrushchev, it seems petty and trivial.

Discriminating Tastes: The Prejudice of Personal Preferences

VICTORIA A. SACKETT

Compare Victoria Sackett's essay with the essay on malls by William Kowinski in Part Two; each is based on an extended metaphor. Sackett's essay may also be compared with Gloria Yamato's discussion of a more serious prejudice in Part Three.

EXPLORING IDEAS

1. Since 1987, when Sackett's essay was published, intolerance of cigarette smokers has become more severe because of new research about the dangers of second-hand smoke. Surely, smoking is a more serious offense against society than wearing perfume.

2. In the previous essay, William Buckley urges us to complain more. Some critics have suggested that in our increasingly violent society, it is better to keep our complaints against offensive behavior to ourselves for fear of violent reprisal.

3. Sackett suggests that the more we act on our desire to complain, the more things we will find to complain about, for once we see how easy it is to succeed, we will not let anyone get away with anything.

4. Sackett does not argue for a cause-effect relationship between our increasing tolerance of ethnic minorities and our increasing intolerance of people who smoke and wear perfume. However, in the last paragraph of her essay, she does suggest that perhaps everyone needs a certain minimum of intolerance; as we reduce intolerance for minorities, we must find something else to be intolerant about. Have students brainstorm this idea.

5. Very few people today, other than representatives of tobacco companies, defend smokers, except when they are using the general argument of preserving individual freedom of choice. Students could easily write an essay on the thesis, "There's no such thing as being rude to a smoker"; however, it might be more of a challenge to write an essay on why we should *not* be rude to smokers.

6. Sackett provides no real evidence that the increase in intolerance is related to the trend toward later marriages, except for the commonsense argument that people who live alone for many years become so used to having things their own way that they are intolerant of others. Does this also mean that all unmarried people are intolerant and that all married people are tolerant, by definition?

7. Assertiveness training, popular in the 1960s and 1970s, especially with women's groups, was devised to give people, especially women, permission to express their feelings directly. Some critics argued that it succeeded only in teaching people how to be selfish and rude. The relationship between assertiveness and rudeness underlies William Buckley's argument in the previous essay.

8. The idea that if you do not state your wishes you will be psychologically damaged is one of the tenets of assertiveness training. Have students brainstorm this in small groups; there should be a fairly equal division between those who agree and those who do not.

EXPLORING RHETORIC

1. Although Sackett's central and controlling metaphor is that of a plague or a disease, she also uses more casual metaphors such as the cliché about the "social fabric," "major league" for something serious, and "brats" to refer to adults who act like children.

2. Sackett's rhetorical tactic of using second person to refer to the symptoms of the disease is meant to involve readers directly in the action she describes. The reader would not have felt as implicated if she had used the third-person "they."

3. Like William Buckley in the previous essay, Sackett uses sarcasm and exaggeration extensively. The sarcastic tone seems appropriate for an essay in which the author is ridiculing some behavior that she finds silly.

4. Sackett's list of "gum-chewing, ice-crunching, high-pitched giggling, foot-shuffling, finger-drumming, toe-tapping" is almost as irritating as the actions themselves, so that the list of responses—"glaring, sighing heavily, twisting in your chair, and glaring harder"—seems appropriately severe. This balance is emphasized by the repetition of the second-person phrase "You will."

5. The phrase "fat little arm" is part of the sarcastic tone that Sackett has already established in the essay, for it is clear that she has no patience with a child who says to a cigarette smoker, "That stinks." Stephen King, in his essay on horror movies earlier in this part, uses a similar tactic of referring to a child in a sarcastic way.

6. Sackett argues that the second-hand smoke issue is just a smoke screen. In effect, she complains that it is not the danger of second-hand smoke that bothers nonsmokers but the smell of the smoke that they simply do not like. Sackett's argument here, however, may be merely a red herring, for it is not the smell that bothers nonsmokers but the fact that smoke in the air interferes with their breathing.

7. Have your students compare William Buckley's leap in logic from complaining about an overheated train car to complaining against political tyranny with Sackett's leap from intolerance about cigarette smoking to the president of the United States taking advice from junior high school students. The relevance of the Russian allusion here is not clear, for there is no relationship between Russians' being "just like us" and intolerance against such practices as cigarette smoking.

8. Sackett's essay suggests that she is really less interested in causes than in symptoms, and her sarcastic, flippant tone suggests that she is more interested in making a clever, facile case than she is in seriously investigating the reasons for the prejudice of personal preferences.

Angry

JULIANNE MALVEAUX

I n the argument over whether it is better to express feelings and complain or to repress feelings and avoid hurt feelings and hostility, Julianne Malveaux comes down solidly on the side of the former. The tone of her essay perfectly reflects its content, for it is unabashed, forthright, and angry.

EXPLORING IDEAS

1. This is the central issue around which the essays by Buckley, Sackett, and Malveaux revolve. Have students read all three and then write an essay in which they take a side, and argue it vigorously, as to whether it is better to express or repress.

2. Whether assertiveness reflects selfishness and bad manners or is an honest expression of one's convictions is another aspect of the argument of the Buckley, Sackett, and Malveaux essays. Does assertiveness always become anger? Is the anger Malveaux describes self-righteous or self-indulgent?

3. Malveaux identifies herself immediately as an African American woman and begins her essay with reasons that African Americans have a right to be angry. However, she expands her defense of anger to include a reaction to any social injustice.

4. One issue about anger that Malveaux raises is whether one can decide to be angry or whether anger just happens. Michael Ventura, in his essay earlier in this part, says that his reaction was instinctive and that only later did he think about it. Is this the way anger against social injustice manifests itself?

5. Some students may suggest that irrational anger against social injustice is counterproductive because it may solidify the position of the opposition. Others may argue that there is no such thing as controlled anger, that the only effective defense against social injustice is unrestrained self-righteous anger.

6. Just after the Republican party took control of the U.S. House of Representatives in 1994, the Speaker of the House, Newt Gingrich, was reported to have called President Clinton's wife, Hillary, a "bitch," a term often reserved for independent women of power. Calling a man a "son of a bitch" is not the same, for that term sometimes carries with it a grudging sense of respect.

7. To suggest that anger is "unfeminine" is to fall into the stereotypes of masculine behavior as being aggressive and feminine behavior as being passive. Have students consult the essays by Susan Brownmiller and Paul Theroux in Part Three for discussions of these stereotypes.

8. Malveaux does not support her claim that she gets angry at small things because they are signs of larger things; later in the essay, she admits that she is not always justified at getting angry at small things and is learning to target her anger.

9. Getting angry at others because they do not behave as we want them to or because we do not get the kind of service we want, as Sackett and Buckley discuss in their essays, is not the same as the anger against social injustice that Malveaux describes.

10. Malveaux's essay is an example of an author's explaining a defining quality of the self. Suggest to your students jealousy, generosity, impatience, or something else as defining characteristics.

Exploring Rhetoric

1. Malveaux believes it is more effective to open a personal essay with statements about one's own anger than to cite an expert on the nature of anger. Malveaux's tactic in introducing the statement of the expert in the second paragraph is to set up the two different points of view that experts have expressed so that she can agree with the one she quotes.

2. Malveaux's tactic in paragraph 4 is to use Tavris's statement that anger is a sign of something gone wrong as a way to lead into her discussion of her anger at social injustice done to African Americans. She accomplishes this task powerfully by citing several specific such injustices in recent history.

3. In paragraph 6, Malveaux uses the orator's rhetorical tactic of repeating a powerful first-person phrase, "I got angry about . . . I got angry that . . . I was angry about . . ."

4. Malveaux begins by stating that black women have a tradition of hell-raising, not only against those who discriminate against them because of race but also against those who discriminate against them because of gender. After noting that many women shy away from anger as unfeminine, she then cites several famous black women, such as Harriet Tubman, Sojourner Truth, and Rosa Parks, who did not hold back their anger at injustice.

5. Malveaux shifts from anger at social injustice to her own personal anger in paragraph 9. However, her anger at someone for standing her up for a date or blocking her garage pales in significance when compared to her anger at a black man's being killed by whites. The fact that she is justified in cursing someone out for a serious social offense does not necessarily entitle her to do the same because of a personal one.

6. Malveaux shifts from her anger at personal affronts, such as being stood up for a date in paragraph 9, to anger against people who say one thing and do another, in paragraph 10.

7. Malveaux argues in paragraph 12 that if black people had just gone along and not gotten angry, they would still be picking cotton. However, this suggests that the freeing of black slaves was a direct result of African Americans' rebelling against their masters, which is not completely true.

8. After describing several examples of things that make her angry, Malveaux uses one extended example in paragraphs 13 through 16 to describe how she is learning to temper and target her anger. By using several examples at first,

Malveaux convinces her reader by the sheer act of strident accumulation. When she reaches that point of her essay at which she claims she is learning to be a bit more restrained, a more leisurely single example seems appropriate.

9. Although Malveaux argues against feminine stereotypes in this essay, when she wants a metaphor for anger, she uses typically feminine allusions, such as wearing a special hat for special occasions or donning a stole that one can shrug off easily.

10. Malveaux begins by asserting her belief in the value of anger, moves to a discussion of anger at social injustice against African Americans, shifts to a justification for her own personal anger, and then explains how she is learning to target her anger.

If Black English Isn't a Language, Then Tell Me, What Is?

JAMES BALDWIN

James Baldwin argues that African Americans are right to refuse to be defined by a language that does not recognize them; Rachel Jones, in the following essay, says that African Americans cannot afford to reject standard English if they wish to succeed. Baldwin argues for the political importance of black English; Jones debates the social and economic importance of standard English.

EXPLORING IDEAS

1. Have students explain how the language of such writers as Tobias Wolff, Richard Rodriguez, Audre Lorde, and Maya Angelou in Part One reveal the personality of the speakers.

2. Ask students to consider how certain social or professional groups, such as fraternities, sororities, computer wizards, or athletes, use their own special language to define themselves and to prevent themselves from being submerged.

3. The anthropological issue about whether language determines perception has been widely debated by experts in recent years; thus, it is doubtful that students can contribute anything meaningful to this discussion without doing some research into the issues. However, ask students to consider how people who are experienced in certain fields and have a language to define their experience see things differently from those who have little knowledge of the field. For example, a surfer may indeed experience the ocean differently than a non-surfer does.

4. For example, one of the differences that separate those who live in the Republic of Ireland and those who live in Northern Ireland is the fact that southerners have tried to hold on to Gaelic, whereas those in the North affirm English as their language.

5. Baldwin argues that holding on to black English is a way of rebelling against those who speak a language that rejects them. He suggests that African Americans may never reach a point at which they are no longer discriminated against. However, it may be true that African Americans who use standard English are less discriminated against than those who use black English.

6. Although it would seem to be easy for Baldwin to provide an example of black English that white people could not understand, he does not. And lacking an example, it is not clear how white people cannot afford to understand it because it would reveal too much about them.

7. Again, Baldwin does not provide any examples of whites' refusal to educate black children. Your students may be able to point to the obvious fact that schools in many black urban centers receive less funding than schools in white suburbs.

8. Baldwin argues that black children should not be taught by anyone who would force them to give up their heritage, including making them "talk white," since that would force children into a limbo where they are neither white nor black.

9. Baldwin must assert that black English is not a dialect but rather a language of its own in order to give weight to his argument that black English defines the black experience and that to take it away is to ask blacks to deny that experience.

Exploring Rhetoric

1. Baldwin begins with a serious, formal style of balanced sentences, making his two central points clear at the very opening of his essay: that the issue of black English is a social, not a linguistic, issue, and that African Americans' affirmation of black English is a rejection of a language that refuses to recognize them.

2. Baldwin wishes to place the issue of black English within a context of other peoples who have insisted on holding onto their own language as a way of preserving their identity.

3. Baldwin's sympathies are obviously with the underdog Ireland, for he could very well have called Ireland a "damp little island" but does not.

4. Although Hawthorne was not a Puritan, many of his stories are about Puritans, and he certainly represents one of the most respected early American users of standard English; thus, he seems an appropriate forefather of users of standard English.

5. Sexually suggestive terms or vulgar terms become assimilated into the language when their original, usually metaphoric, meaning has been forgotten. One becomes a brown-noser from the servile act of kissing another on the behind, but few people have this image in mind when they use the phrase.

6. By saying, "No one can eat his cake and have it, too," rather than using the more familiar order, Baldwin momentarily defamiliarizes the term and makes it sound original.

7. The word "Diaspora" refers to all those Jews who were dispersed to live among Gentiles after the Babylonian captivity; with a lowercase "d" it refers to the dispersion of any originally homogeneous group of people. By using the term here, Baldwin gives the selling of Africans into slavery a grand biblical aura, further suggested by using the term "unprecedented tabernacle" to describe the creation of the black Christian church in America. The metaphor of alchemy suggests the transforming of ancient disparate elements into a new, unified treasure such as gold.

8. Baldwin uses the rhetorical tactic of accumulative balanced sentences in paragraph 9, repeating such phrases as "this passion, this skill, this 'sheer intelligence,' this incredible music." Then, after interrupting this balanced series with another series—"present, troubled, troubling, and unassailable and unanswerable place"—he concludes with his final "if" clause: "If this absolutely unprecedented journey does not indicate that black English is a language, I am curious to know what definition of language is to be trusted."

9. Baldwin uses balanced phrases to emphasize his conclusion, repeating "a country with . . . a country that . . . a country unable"— concluding with a final repetition of the word "country": "They have nothing whatsoever to learn from the people of a country that has managed to learn so little."

What's Wrong with Black English

RACHEL L. JONES

Rachel Jones takes on James Baldwin in this essay in which she argues that what is wrong with black English is that it prevents African Americans from achieving economic and social success because it suggests illiteracy. It may be that she and Baldwin are discussing two different aspects of black English.

EXPLORING IDEAS

1. Whereas Baldwin primarily focuses on individual words that black English has contributed to the language, Jones focuses on nonstandard grammatical structures characteristic of black English. Baldwin argues that black English gives African Americans their identity; Jones suggests that it labels them as uneducated.

2. I do not know how Baldwin would have responded to Jones's argument that Martin Luther King, Jr., did not have to say, "I has been to the mountaintop, and I done seed the Promised Land." Perhaps he would say that this construction is not really what he means by black English; perhaps he would cite passages in which King used words that Baldwin attributes to black English.

3. Almost everyone has been the victim of a bully at one time or another, and many people retain strong feelings about the experience because of the sense of unfairness and helplessness it causes. Many students will be able to write on this topic.

4. Once writers identify themselves as authors or bookish, they immediately place themselves in a stereotype. Have students read Richard Rodriguez's and Raymond Carver's essays in Part One.

5. Many dialects besides ethnic ones may unfairly stereotype people. For example, people from the American South may be unfairly stereotyped when they talk to people in the North. People from the Appalachian Mountains of Kentucky and West Virginia are assumed to be ignorant hillbillies when they speak.

6. Students who come from homes in which one language is spoken and must attend school where a different language is expected will be aware of the bilingual issues that this question raises. The more general issue that all students should be able to respond to is whether it is legitimate to expect people to learn the language of the area where they will live and work.

7. Jones is arguing only that African Americans should learn correct standard English—not that they need to give up the many special terms they have created, not that they need to accept white values, and not that they need to forget their heritage.

8. Jones would probably agree with Baldwin that whites have often failed horribly in educating African Americans; however, she would not agree with Baldwin that black English should be taught or even accepted in American schools.

9. Whereas Baldwin says standard English excludes African Americans, Jones says that black English will exclude them even more. The disagreement is based on how the two writers define "the world we live in." Baldwin would argue that blacks have a right to maintain their own world and language; Jones would argue that the reality is that the world we live in is the world dominated by correct English.

Exploring Rhetoric

1. Note that while Julianne Malveaux, in her essay on anger earlier in this part, begins with personal statements and then quotes an expert, Jones leads off with a quotation from an expert and then moves to personal experiences. It may be that Jones knows, given the sensitivity of the issue she discusses and the respect with which her opponent James Baldwin is held, she needs to begin with some authority, not merely her own experience.

2. Jones wants to make clear right away that she is black and that she was poor; she is not one of the privileged middle-class blacks whom many African Americans have called Uncle Toms or "oreos" (black on the outside, white in the center). She wants to be identified with those African Americans who most often use black English.

3. Jones tries to gain the sympathy of readers not only by telling about the experience when she was bullied as a child but also by using such an expression as, "I was offered the opportunity to swallow a few of my teeth," which sounds mock formal. She does not want to appear to take herself so seriously.

4. We do not know whether Jones read black authors, but the effect of her mentioning such writers as Frank L. Baum and Ray Bradbury and such series as the Bobbsey Twins and Trixie Belden is to make her sound like a typical bookish young girl whose race is not important.

5. The Jekyll-Hyde allusion is only marginally literary, since Robert Louis Stevenson's famous parable of a character with a split personality is well known.

6. James Baldwin might have difficulty explaining why he uses correct English in his own writing rather than the black English he makes such a strong case for. And Jones is surely right to remind Baldwin that Barbara Jordan did not gain political power by saying, "Ya'll crazy if you ain't gon' vote for me." If political figures and writers use black English only when talking to blacks, does this suggest some condescension on their part?

7. Jones never makes this part of her argument explicit or clear. However, she seems to suggest that African Americans may have to maintain a dual language: the language of black English when they are home or with other blacks and standard English when they wish to succeed in the workplace.

8. Jones's return to the statement by Labov with which she began is a common rhetorical device to give a sense of completion and wholeness to her essay.

Mommy, What Does *Nigger* Mean? A Question of Language

GLORIA NAYLOR

While James Baldwin and Rachel Jones argue about whether African Americans should or should not give up black English, Gloria Naylor points out that the meaning of ethnically sensitive words depends on the social context in which they are used.

EXPLORING IDEAS

1. Identifying herself as a professional writer who depends on the written word for livelihood, Naylor claims that writing is only second-hand and that spoken language truly reflects the richness of human life.

2. Naylor points out that words have only an arbitrary relationship to the concept to which they are assigned. The meaning of a word is dependent on what the majority of the users of a language decide it means.

3. This sentence introduces the main part of Naylor's argument about the context of language use, for one of her major points is that within certain contexts African Americans may call each other "niggers," and with some pride.

4. Naylor emphasizes that African Americans would call others "niggers" only in a derogatory way if those being so labeled have no self-respect.

5. Naylor says that a black female would never be called a "nigger" as a sign of self-worth the way males might be, for the term is reserved as a sign of the essence of manhood. Moreover, although it is a sign of respect to address a black female as "girl," it is a sign of disapproval to refer to a black female as a "girl" in the third person.

6. Gloria Yamato, in her essay on racism in Part Three, reserves her most severe criticism for blacks who have internalized racism and begin to believe that they deserve the scorn and hatred that have been heaped on them. Naylor does not believe that African Americans' use of the word "nigger" to refer to each other is a sign of such internalization of racism but rather a transformation of an appellation of scorn into a sign of self-worth.

7. Naylor seems to suggest that a suppressed minority can transform a word that signifies scorn into its opposite. Ask students to come up with other such terms and brainstorm whether such a transformation is always possible. If not, why not?

EXPLORING RHETORIC

1. The first two paragraphs are like a formal prologue to an informal essay. Although the point Naylor makes about the difference between written and spoken language and the point she makes about words' assuming meaning as a result of a consensus of the users of the language do not have a direct bearing on her central argument, they do serve as the conceptual basis for the point she wants to make about the use of the word "nigger."

2. In addition to the fact that such words as "nymphomaniac" or "necrophiliac" would probably not be familiar to a third grader, they also have the rhetorical advantage of being alliterative with the word "nigger."

3. Since Naylor has already argued that the meaning of words is determined by the community of users of a language, she wishes to establish a sense of a tightly knit community in which words could be used with a high level of consensus on what they mean.

4. Naylor organizes her examples into separate paragraphs not only because this follows the convention of devoting a separate paragraph to each separate speaker but also because this technique makes the quotations sound more emphatic.

5. Because Naylor has pointed out that the word "nigger" is used within the African American community as a sign of the "pure essence of manhood," she feels somewhat bound to provide balance with a brief discussion of an honorific term of respect for women.

6. Naylor's return to the incident in the third grade when she was called a "nigger" is rhetorically effective, for it allows her to return to the anecdote where she left off when she began the expository part of her essay—that point at which she asks her mother what *nigger* means.

7. Although relatively informal, Naylor's essay breaks down into clearly definable parts. After her two-paragraph prologue in which she establishes the conceptual base of her central point, she describes the anecdote of being called a "nigger" when she was in the third grade. The question she asks her mother—"What does 'nigger' mean?"—she can then answer herself by noting that its meaning depends on the context within which it is used. The center of the essay describes those contexts when the word is permissible, followed by a brief discussion of when the corollary word "girl" is permissible. She concludes with a general statement of how African Americans have transformed the hateful word "nigger" into a word signifying their self-worth.

SECTION III

INTERACTIVE ESSAY

A Reading/ Writing Computer Application

Designed and Developed by Charles E. May to Accompany the Textbook Interacting with Essays

Word processing programs have been the most useful computer application in the college writing classroom because they objectify and make manageable a procedure that was previously impossible—the creation of a "tacit text" positioned between the undeveloped and disconnected ideas in the writer's mind and the fixed and rigid inscriptions on the page—a text solid enough to be visualized as an object, yet flexible enough to be modified effortlessly and repeatedly. However, the ease with which word processing enabled students to do brainstorming and revision did not automatically cause an improvement in their writing. As writers and teachers have always known, writing is a hard-earned skill developed largely from emulating those who have mastered it. The problem for the teacher is how to encourage students to read in such a way that they learn writing skills from other writers and how to stimulate them to practice those skills.

Description of Interactive Essay

Interactive Essay, a software program I developed to accompany the textbook anthology *Interacting with Essays,* uses several features unique to computers to teach students how to interact with texts in order to engage in the ideas of the essay, develop their own ideas, and learn from the techniques of the writer. I have used these features successfully with several hundred students over the past few years and have reached some tentative conclusions, based on reading research and my own experience, about the reasons for their success.

As much as writing teachers may dislike the idea, students are more accustomed to getting information from video screens than from printed pages. By providing the full text of twenty essays on the screen, complete with heuristic hypertext prompts, **Interactive Essay** takes advantage of student familiarity with video screens for providing information, as well as the irresistibility of interactive "hot spots" or buttons on a screen, with which many students are familiar from playing video games.

Moreover, research indicates that reading text on a computer screen is less "efficient" than reading text in a book; that is, one cannot read as fast. As a result, readers are not allowed to skim hurriedly to the end of the text. Heuristic prompts and queries embedded in the text further contribute to this slowdown. Consequently, students put themselves in a more analytical state of mind when they read from a computer screen than when they read from a book. They perceive the text as a complex mechanism with which they can interact, not as a simple container to which they are passively subjected.

Students feel more "captive" to text on the computer screen and less apt to drift off to other matters than they are when reading a book. One student in my class wrote, "Being on the computer made me focus more on what I was reading. Once I got started, I felt compelled to finish it." Moreover, students respond more fully to heuristic prompts embedded on the screen within the text than they do on paper to questions clustered at the end of the text. One student said, "Responding to the questions on a sheet of paper just makes you want to answer the questions and get it over with. Prompts in **Interactive Essay** don't. I don't know why." The fact that students don't just try to "get it over with" on the computer the way they do when responding on paper to heuristic prompts in a book is a curious phenomenon. Part of the reason for it may be that questions embedded within the text rather than tagged on at the end of the text help students focus on key points in the essay at those points rather than in retrospect. Moreover, the ability to respond to what one is reading at the time one is reading creates a seamless link between the two processes. One student suggested, "The computer makes responding easier for some reason, maybe because you're typing and reading as you go along."

Although I am sure this idea will fly in the face of some of our most cherished beliefs about a bound book, students are likely to feel a closer sense of interaction with the computer than with a book. As one student said, "Because I was involved with the computer I felt a closer relationship to what I was reading. When asked to consider an idea, I was, by the nature of the interactive relationship with my computer, more involved."

Interactive Essay creates the illusion that it is the text, not the teacher, that provides the prompts and asks the questions. If questioned directly, students admit that they know someone had to create the queries and prompts and embed them in the essay; however, when they begin reading the essay and responding to it, they forget that fact. This is a common phenomenon; computer users often refer to computer applications as if they had some innate consciousness, and indeed some computer-assisted instruction programs encourage this misapprehension. The effect of this illusion in **Interactive Essay** is that students do not think that a teacher is leading them along to a preconceived conclusion but think that the text itself is trying to help them understand. As one student wrote to me, "Without **Interactive Essay,** I would not have developed my own analytical skills; I would have learned only how you saw the essay. This way, without your guidance, I came to my own conclusions." Several students said that after reading a number of essays in the program, they began to predict the kinds of prompts and queries before clicking on a button to reveal them. Thus, the final effect of using **Interactive Essay** throughout the semester is to make the student no longer need it.

Application

The way the application is set up on the screen is quite simple.

Screen 1 (page 130) shows what a typical page of **Interactive Essay** looks like. The text of the essay—in this case, page 13 of Maya Angelou's essay, "Getting a Job"—appears in the square window on the left. The four small rectangles at the top right of the screen, named **Explore Grammar, Explore Context, Explore Idea,** and **Explore Rhetoric,** are buttons. When students click the mouse on one of the buttons, a window will "pop up" in the title and author area below these buttons. The **Grammar, Context, Idea,** and **Rhetoric** buttons at the bottom left are navigation buttons that take readers to areas where they may "collect" their writing throughout the essay and do further editing. The **Notes** button takes readers to a "scratch pad" area where they may take miscellaneous notes on their reading. The **Draft** button takes readers to an area where they may compose the draft of an essay and copy and paste material from the other work areas. The **Contents** button takes readers to the table of contents. The **Quit** button simply exits the program.

Screen 2 (page 131, top) shows what happens when students click on the **Explore Grammar** button at the top right. A window pops up below, drawing their attention to a grammar principle illustrated in this section of the text. The **Explore Grammar** button is replaced by an **Interact Grammar** button.

Screen 3 (page 131, foot) shows what happens when students click on the **Interact Grammar** button. A grammar exercise, illustrating the principle that has been noted in the **Explore Grammar** window, appears in the area of the essay text. Students can respond to the exercise in the

Maya Angelou, "Getting a Job" page 13	**Explore Grammar**

When the spring classes began, I resumed my commitment with formal education.

I was so much wiser and older, so much more independent, with a bank account and clothes that I had bought for myself, that I was sure I had learned and earned the magic formula which would make me a part of the life my contemporaries led.

Not a bit of it. Within weeks, I realized that my schoolmates and I were on paths moving away from each other. They concentrated great interest on who was worthy of being student body president, and when the metal bands would be removed from their teeth, while I remembered conducting a streetcar in the uneven hours of the morning.

Without willing it, I had gone from being ignorant of being ignorant to being aware of being aware. And the worst part of my awareness was

Explore Context
Explore Idea
Explore Rhetoric

Getting a Job

by

Maya Angelou

Grammar | Context | Idea | Rhetoric | ← | → | Notes | Draft | Contents | Quit | ? |

SCREEN 1. See page 129.

Maya Angelou, "Getting a Job" page 13

Interact Grammar

Explore Context
Explore Idea
Explore Rhetoric

When the spring classes began, I resumed my commitment with formal education.

I was so much wiser and older, so much more independent, with a bank account and clothes that I had bought for myself, that I was sure I had learned and earned the magic formula which would make me a part of the life my contemporaries led.

Not a bit of it. Within weeks, I realized that my schoolmates and I were on paths moving away from each other. They concentrated great interest on who was worthy of being student body president, and when the metal bands would be removed from their teeth, while I remembered conducting a streetcar in the uneven hours of the morning.

Without willing it, I had gone from being ignorant of being ignorant to being aware of being aware. And the worst part of my awareness was

The clause "which would make me a part of the life my contemporaries led" is not separated from the the phrase "magic formula" by a comma because it is a restrictive clause; the sentence would not be clear without it. Usually the pronoun "that" introduces a restrictive clause, although "which" may be used for emphasis.

Grammar | Context | Idea | Rhetoric | ◀ ▶ | Notes | Draft | Contents | Quit | ? | ↵

SCREEN 2. See page 130.

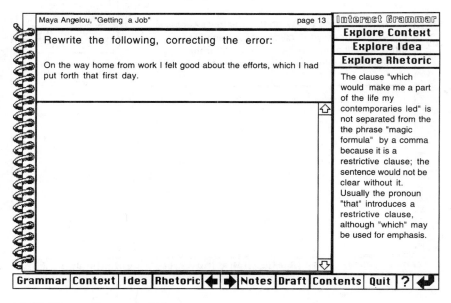

Maya Angelou, "Getting a Job" page 13

Interact Grammar

Explore Context
Explore Idea
Explore Rhetoric

Rewrite the following, correcting the error:

On the way home from work I felt good about the efforts, which I had put forth that first day.

The clause "which would make me a part of the life my contemporaries led" is not separated from the the phrase "magic formula" by a comma because it is a restrictive clause; the sentence would not be clear without it. Usually the pronoun "that" introduces a restrictive clause, although "which" may be used for emphasis.

Grammar | Context | Idea | Rhetoric | ◀ ▶ | Notes | Draft | Contents | Quit | ? | ↵

SCREEN 3. See page 130.

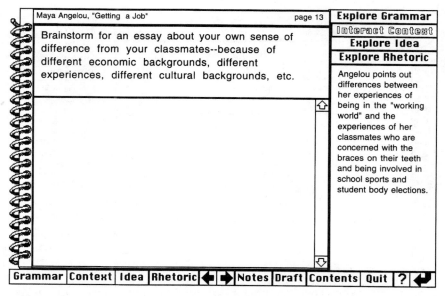

SCREEN 4.   See page 134.

Maya Angelou, "Getting a Job"   page 13   **Explore Grammar**

Interact Context
Explore Idea
Explore Rhetoric

When the spring classes began, I resumed my commitment with formal education.

I was so much wiser and older, so much more independent, with a bank account and clothes that I had bought for myself, that I was sure I had learned and earned the magic formula which would make me a part of the life my contemporaries led.

Not a bit of it. Within weeks, I realized that my schoolmates and I were on paths moving away from each other. They concentrated great interest on who was worthy of being student body president, and when the metal bands would be removed from their teeth, while I remembered conducting a streetcar in the uneven hours of the morning.

Without willing it, I had gone from being ignorant of being ignorant to being aware of being aware. And the worst part of my awareness was

Angelou points out differences between her experiences of being in the "working world" and the experiences of her classmates who are concerned with the braces on their teeth and being involved in school sports and student body elections.

Grammar | Context | Idea | Rhetoric | ← | → | Notes | Draft | Contents | Quit | ? | ↵

SCREEN 5.   See page 134.

Maya Angelou, "Getting a Job"   page 13   **Explore Grammar**

Interact Context
Explore Idea
Explore Rhetoric

Brainstorm for an essay about your own sense of difference from your classmates--because of different economic backgrounds, different experiences, different cultural backgrounds, etc.

Angelou points out differences between her experiences of being in the "working world" and the experiences of her classmates who are concerned with the braces on their teeth and being involved in school sports and student body elections.

Grammar | Context | Idea | Rhetoric | ← | → | Notes | Draft | Contents | Quit | ? | ↵

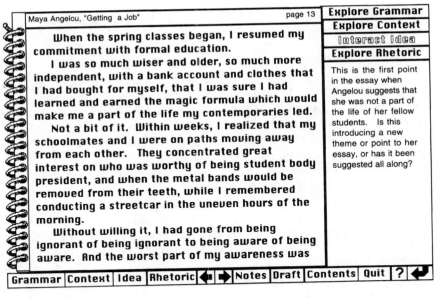

SCREEN 6.   See page 134.

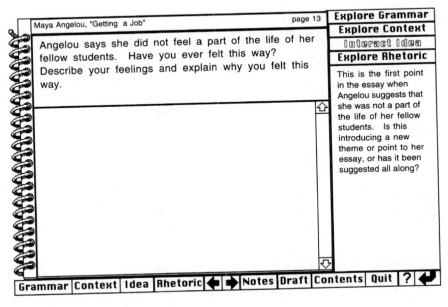

SCREEN 7.   See page 134.

rectangle window just below the exercise. The **Interact Grammar** button is changed to inverse video to reflect the fact that it is the interaction currently being worked on. Students can make the pop-up windows go away by simply clicking anywhere within them.

Screen 4 (page 132, top) shows that when students click on the **Explore Context** button, a window pops up below the buttons that calls their attention to a social or cultural context for the discussion. *Screen 5* (page 132, foot) shows that a student has clicked on the **Interact Context** button to reveal a brainstorming idea related to the context noted in the **Explore Context** window. The student may respond in the window just below. The response windows are scrolling windows; thus, students can write as much as they wish there.

Screen 6 (page 133, top) and *Screen 7* (page 133, foot) indicate that a student has first clicked on the **Explore Idea** button to note an aspect of Angelou's development of her ideas and then clicked on the **Interact Idea** button to respond to an essay or brainstorming suggestion related to Angelou's idea.

Screen 8 (this page) and *Screen 9* (page 135, top) indicate that a student has first clicked on the **Explore Rhetoric** button to pop up a suggestion or question about a rhetorical technique in the essay and then clicked on the **Interact Rhetoric** button to respond to or analyze the technique.

SCREEN 8. See above.

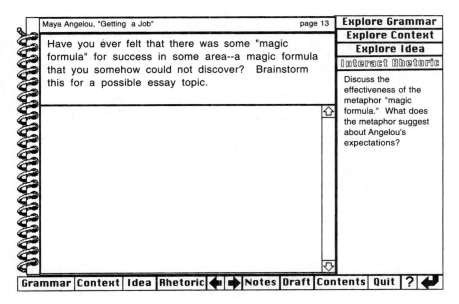

| Maya Angelou, "Getting a Job" | page 13 | **Explore Grammar** |

Have you ever felt that there was some "magic formula" for success in some area--a magic formula that you somehow could not discover? Brainstorm this for a possible essay topic.

Explore Context
Explore Idea
Interact Rhetoric

Discuss the effectiveness of the metaphor "magic formula." What does the metaphor suggest about Angelou's expectations?

Grammar | Context | Idea | Rhetoric | ← → | Notes | Draft | Contents | Quit | ?

SCREEN 9. See page 134.

Collect | Return | Delete | **Grammar Exercises** | Essay | Export | Print

Ralph Lewis
Angelou--Grammar Exercises
Dr. Jones
6/15/95

1. When I went for my first job interview, I was very nervous, so I sat and listened to some quiet music before I left the house.

2. Walking into the personnel office quite confidently, I was not afraid of the interviewer.

3. By the end of his first day on the new job, he realized that he had underestimated how much work was expected of him.

Grammar | Context | Idea | Rhetoric | ← → | Notes | Draft | Contents | Quit | ?

SCREEN 10.   See page 136.

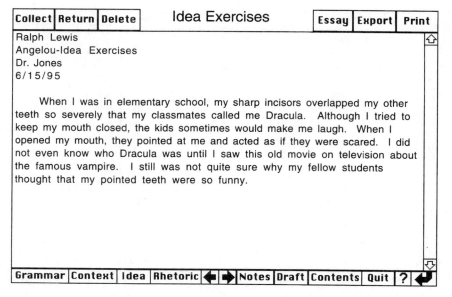

| Collect | Return | Delete | Idea Exercises | | Essay | Export | Print |

Ralph Lewis
Angelou-Idea Exercises
Dr. Jones
6/15/95

When I was in elementary school, my sharp incisors overlapped my other teeth so severely that my classmates called me Dracula. Although I tried to keep my mouth closed, the kids sometimes would make me laugh. When I opened my mouth, they pointed at me and acted as if they were scared. I did not even know who Dracula was until I saw this old movie on television about the famous vampire. I still was not quite sure why my fellow students thought that my pointed teeth were so funny.

| Grammar | Context | Idea | Rhetoric | ← | → | Notes | Draft | Contents | Quit | ? | ↵ |

SCREEN 11. See below.

Screen 10 (page 135, foot) indicates that a student has navigated to the **Grammar** work area and clicked on the button at the top left named **Collect** to collect all the grammar exercises worked on throughout the essay. At this point students may click on the **Print** button and print out the grammar exercises to hand in to the instructor.

Screen 11 (this page) indicates that a student has navigated to the **Idea** work area and has clicked on the button named **Collect** to collect a brainstorming idea from an **Interact Idea** window within the essay. At this point students may revise and edit the brainstorming idea, may print it out, or may click on the **Export** button and export it out of **Interactive Essay** to a plain text file that can be retrieved in any word processing program for further revision, editing, and printing.

Uses for Interactive Essay

Interactive Essay is designed to be used in a variety of ways, depending on the individual student's needs. Students weak in the conventions of grammar may be assigned **Explore Grammar** prompts and **Interact Grammar** exercises in an essay. Students for whom English is a second language may wish to consult the **Explore Context** and **Interact Context**

windows for definitions of unfamiliar words and idioms and explanations of cultural references in an essay. Students seeking writing topics may examine the **Explore Idea** and **Interact Idea** windows, trying a number of brainstorming suggestions until they find one with which they feel comfortable. Students can also examine prompts and exercises in the **Explore Rhetoric** and **Interact Rhetoric** sections on each page to become more sensitive to rhetorical strategies and conventions used by writers. The Study Guide to the software contains all the **Interact Grammar, Interact Context, Interact Idea,** and **Interact Rhetoric** exercises for the essays to enable instructors to tailor assignments to fit individual student needs.

Interactive Essay may be used in an on-campus computer classroom, with the instructor making individual or group assignments and serving as a guide while students work on them. It may also be used by students at home or in drop-in computer labs on campus for homework assignments. **Interactive Essay** combines many of the features of an essay anthology, a rhetorical text, and a grammar handbook in one application. It makes the dual processes of reading and writing a single, student-centered activity in which the skills that students learn from reading essays by professional writers can be immediately and directly applied.

INSTALLING
INTERACTIVE ESSAY

Interactive Essay is available for both the Macintosh computer running System 6.0.5 or later and IBM-compatible computers running Windows 3.1 or later.

Macintosh

Installing the Macintosh Version
of Interactive Essay on Your Hard Drive

Interactive Essay for the Macintosh requires HyperCard 2.1 or later, or HyperCard Player 2.1 or later. Your **Interactive Essay** disks contain one file named **Contents** and four folders named **Personal, Difference, Everyday,** and **Argument.**

You should already have HyperCard 2.1 or later or HyperCard Player 2.1 or later and a stack named "Home" installed on the hard drive of your Macintosh. Since HyperCard or HyperCard Player has been distributed free with the Macintosh since HyperCard was created, either HyperCard or HyperCard Player is installed on most Macintosh computers. Create a new folder inside your HyperCard or HyperCard Player folder; name the new folder **Interactive Essay.** Insert your disks in your Macintosh one at a time and double-click the disk icon to open it. Double-click your new **Interactive Essay** folder to open it. Drag the

Contents icon and the four folders named **Personal, Difference, Everyday,** and **Argument** into the new folder you created on the hard drive.

Your **Interactive Essay** software is now installed on your Macintosh hard drive and ready to use.

Double-click the **Contents** icon to open the table of contents. Click on the title of the essay you wish to read. *Please Note:* The first time you click on an essay title, a HyperCard window will pop up and ask you where the essay is located. Click on the **Folder** button at the top of the window (or the **Desktop** button at the right of the window) until you find the folder and the essay you are looking for. Double-click the title to go to it. When you click on the **Contents** button at the bottom right of the essay, you will be asked where the **Contents** stack is. Once again, click on the **Folder** button at the top of the window (or the **Desktop** button at the right of the window) until you find **Contents.** Double-click **Contents** to go to the table of contents. You will have to do this only the first time you use **Interactive Essay.** After that, the location of your files will be recorded on the **Home** stack of HyperCard or HyperCard Player on your hard drive.

Using Interactive Essay on 3.5 Disks

If you wish to use the **Interactive Essay** files on 3.5 disks (for example, in a campus computer lab that does not allow files to be copied to the hard drive), be sure that the computer you are using has HyperCard 2.1 or later or HyperCard Player 2.1 or later installed on it. Since HyperCard or HyperCard Player has been distributed free with the Macintosh since HyperCard was created, either HyperCard or HyperCard Player is installed on most Macintosh computers.

If you wish to do so, you may also use **Interactive Essay** on your own 3.5 disks on a computer on which **Interactive Essay** has been installed on the hard drive. However, if you use **Interactive Essay** on your 3.5 disks, do not use the **Contents** stack to select essays. Instead, when you insert your disk, double-click the folder you wish to use; then double-click the stack icon for the essay you wish to read.

IBM-Compatible with Windows

Installing Interactive Essay on IBM-Compatible Computers Running Windows 3.1 or Windows 95

Interactive Essay for Windows was created with Asymetryx ToolBook 1.5. It requires the following Runtime files (included with **Interactive Essay**) to be installed on your hard drive:

TBKBASE.DLL
TBKCOMP.DLL
TBKUTIL.DLL
TBOOK.EXE

These files require approximately 1 megabyte of hard disk space.

To install **Interactive Essay** on your hard drive in Windows 3.1, complete with a Program Group folder and a Program Item icon, do the following:

- Open Windows 3.1. Choose **Run** from the File Menu.
- Insert **Interactive Essay** Disk 1 in either your A or B floppy disk drive.
- At the Run prompt, type a:\setup or b:\setup, depending on the letter of the drive that contains **Interactive Essay** Disk 1.
- Click OK and follow the screen prompts. The Setup program will install all ToolBook Runtime files and all **Interactive Essay** files in a subdirectory named **I-Essay** on your hard drive.

A new program group folder named **I-Essay** will be created on your Windows screen, with a single ToolBook icon named **Interactive Essay** inside as the program item. To open **Interactive Essay,** double-click the **I-Essay** folder icon to open it and then double-click the **Interactive Essay** icon.

To install **Interactive Essay** in Windows 95, do the following:

- Start your computer and wait for Windows 95 to finish booting and for the Windows 95 desktop to appear.
- Insert Disk 1 of **Interactive Essay** into your floppy disk drive.
- Press the Start button on the Windows 95 taskbar. The taskbar's default location is at the bottom of your computer screen in Windows 95. The Start button default is in the lower left-hand corner.
- From the Start button, choose Settings; then select Control Panel from the hierarchical menu.
- When your Control Panel window appears, double-click on the Add/Remove Programs icon.
- With the Install/Uninstall tab selected, press the Install button on the right.
- Press the Next> button at the bottom of the screen, wait for Windows 95 to find the **Interactive Essay** setup program on Disk 1, and then follow the instructions that appear on the screen.

A new program group folder named **I-Essay** will be created for you, with a ToolBook icon named **Interactive Essay** inside. To open **Interactive**

Essay, press the Start button again, choose programs, and then select **I-Essay** from the hierarchical menu.

Your **Interactive Essay** software is now installed on your IBM-compatible computer hard drive and ready to use. Double-click the **Interactive Essay** book icon to go to the table of contents.

Note: **Interactive Essay** cannot be installed and used on a network file server.

USING INTERACTIVE ESSAY

Using Interactive Essay with Macintosh

Navigating Interactive Essay

To read through an essay, you may "turn pages" by clicking on the right or left arrow at the bottom center of the screen. You may also use the right and left arrow keys on your Macintosh keyboard to navigate forward or backward through screens or pages. The crooked arrow at the extreme bottom right of the screen will take you back to the last screen or page you were using.

Using the Menu Bar

Interactive Essay was designed with HyperCard 2.1 to fit the standard Macintosh screen of the Macintosh Plus, the Macintosh SE, and the Macintosh Classic. Because **Interactive Essay** may be used on the standard old-style Macintosh screen, the menu bar at the top of the screen is hidden, for it may obscure part of the display. However, if you wish to use the commands on the menu bar to navigate **Interactive Essay** or to change the fonts of text you type into **Interactive Essay**, press the space bar and the command key at either side of the space bar simultaneously to make the menu bar appear. Press the space bar and the command key simultaneously again to make the menu bar disappear.

FILE MENU

- **Open Stack**—Although you may open an essay by clicking on **Open Stack,** you will usually open essays by choosing a title from the **Contents** stack or by double-clicking the essay stack icon of your choice.

- **Compact Stack**—**Interactive Essay** is designed to compact your essay stacks automatically when you close them or quit.

- **Print Card**—Do not use the **Print Card** command to print your work; use the **Print** button within **Interactive Essay** instead.

- **Quit**—You may quit **Interactive Essay** by clicking on the Quit button at the bottom right of each screen or from the **Quit** command of the File menu.

EDIT MENU

- **Undo**—The undo command will undo your last text editing command.

- **Cut, Copy, Paste**—To cut or copy text, click at the beginning of the text and, while holding down the mouse button, drag across the entire text you wish to cut or copy. While the text is in inverse video, click on the **Edit** menu and click on **Cut** or **Copy**. Whatever text you have selected will be placed in the Macintosh clipboard. *Remember:* The **Cut** command cuts the text from its original location; the **Copy** command makes a copy of the text. To paste the text you have selected, go to the place where you wish to insert it and click once to establish the vertical cursor insertion point. Then go to the **Edit** menu and choose **Paste**.

- You cannot delete cards from **Interactive Essay**, for they are protected from deletion.

GO MENU

- **Back**—Go back to the last screen you were using.
- **Home**—Go to the **Home** stack.
- **Help**—Use the **Help** button, indicated by a ?, at the bottom right of the screen for help with **Interactive Essay**.
- **Recent**—Review up to the last 42 screens you looked at; click on one of the screen icons to go to it immediately.
- **First**—Go to the first screen or page in the essay.

- **Prev**—Go to the previous screen or page in the essay.
- **Next**—Go to the next screen or page in the essay.
- **Last**—Go to the last screen or page in the essay.
- **Find**—Search for specific text. Choose **Find** and then type in the word or words for which you wish to search and press Return.

FONT AND STYLE MENUS

When you insert text by typing, collecting, or cutting and pasting in the prompt response boxes, the **Notes** page, the **Draft** page, or the **Collect** pages, you may change the font or the style and size of the font by dragging across the text you wish to change and making a choice from the Font and Style menus.

Suggestions for Exploring and Interacting with the Essays

When you click on an **Explore** button at the top right of each essay page, a reading prompt will appear that will assist you in exploring grammar principles, contextual backgrounds, thematic ideas, or rhetorical techniques on that page.

When you click on an **Explore** button to make a reading prompt appear, that button becomes an **Interact** button.

When you click on an **Interact** button, the essay page is replaced with a window that contains a writing prompt that will assist you in interacting with grammar principles, contextual backgrounds, thematic ideas, or rhetorical techniques on that page. Click once at the top left corner of the response window below the writing prompt and begin typing your response.

To make any **Explore** reading prompt or **Interact** writing prompt go away, simply click anywhere inside the prompt window.

When you have completed a series of **Interact** writing prompts, click on the appropriate navigation button at the bottom left of the screen to navigate to a collection point where all your work will be gathered in one place for editing, printing, or exporting. For example, if your instructor assigns a group of **Interact Grammar** exercises, work through them by first using the **Explore Grammar** buttons to discover the grammar principle involved and to see the principle illustrated in the essay. Second, click on the **Interact Grammar** buttons one at a time and edit the grammar exercises that appear. Finally, click on the **Grammar** navigation button at the bottom left of the screen to go to a Grammar collection page where all your grammar exercises can be collected in one place for editing, printing, or exporting.

Suggestions for Responding to Prompts and Saving Your Responses

TYPING IN THE PROMPT WINDOWS, THE **NOTES** PAGE, THE **DRAFT** PAGE, OR THE **COLLECT** PAGE

Do not use the Tab key to indent a paragraph. The Tab key has a special function in HyperCard.

Do not use the arrow keys to move the cursor through text you have typed, for the arrow keys have special functions in HyperCard. To edit something you have typed, use your mouse to position the cursor and click once to establish an insertion point.

Interactive Essay automatically saves all work that you type in the prompt response windows, the **Collect** pages, and the **Notes** and **Draft** pages. The **Count** button at the top left of the **Notes** and **Draft** pages will give you a word count for those pages.

USING THE **INTERACT GRAMMAR, INTERACT CONTEXT, INTERACT IDEA,** AND **INTERACT RHETORIC COLLECT** SCREENS

The purpose of the **Collect** screens is to give you a convenient place to collect all the work you have done throughout the essay in the **Interact** prompts and exercises. For example, if you have been reading an essay and responding to several of the brainstorming suggestions in the **Interact Idea** sections, you will probably wish to pull your thoughts together in one place so that you can further develop some of them, edit them, print them out for a hard-copy reference, or export them to a word processing program for spell checking and further revision.

Remember: When you click on the **Collect** button, whatever text is in the **Collect** Window will be replaced by whatever text is in the prompt response windows throughout the essay. Thus, make sure you enter in all the information in the prompt response windows throughout the essay before you press the **Collect** button. If you choose to type directly on the **Collect** page, do not press the **Collect** button again.

EXPORTING YOUR WORK

The purpose of the **Export** button on the **Collect** pages, the **Notes** pages, and the **Draft** pages is to allow you to export your work out of **Interactive Essay** into a word processing program of your choice. Once you have exported your work, you may delete your work in **Interactive Essay**, exit the program, and load your exported files into your word processing application, where you can use your spell-checker, thesaurus, and other revision tools to further edit your work.

When you click on **Export** from the **Collect** page, the **Notes** page, or the **Draft** page, you will be asked the name of the text you wish to export. Click on the **Folder** button or the **Desktop** button and choose where you wish to save your work. The default will be the folder in which **Interactive Essay** is stored. If you are using a computer in a campus lab that many students use, you may wish to click on **Desktop** and choose the name of your inserted disk on which to save your work.

Get in the habit of exporting your files by the last name of the author of the article, plus an extension to indicate the type of **Interact** file that it is. For example, when exporting **Interact** files from the Annie Dillard essay, use the following method:

File Name	Type of File
Dillard.grammar	interact grammar
Dillard.context	interact context
Dillard.idea	interact idea
Dillard.rhetoric	interact rhetoric

Quitting Interactive Essay

When you quit **Interactive Essay** by clicking on the **Quit** button or choosing **Quit HyperCard** from the File Menu, you will be asked if you wish to delete your work. If you click **Yes; Delete** all the work you have typed in, cut and pasted, or collected in all the prompt response windows, the **Collect** pages, the **Notes** screen, and the **Draft** screen will be deleted. *CAUTION:* MAKE SURE THAT YOU HAVE EXPORTED ALL THE WORK YOU WISH TO SAVE BY CLICKING ON THE EXPORT BUTTON ON THE FOUR **COLLECT** SCREENS, THE **NOTES** PAGE, OR THE **DRAFT** PAGE TO EXPORT THE TEXT TO A WORD PROCESSOR.

You will usually wish to delete all your work when you finish a work session if you are using **Interactive Essay** installed on a hard drive in a campus lab used by many students. This will ensure that your work will not be seen by a student who uses the computer after you. You may not wish to delete all your work if you are using **Interactive Essay** on your own computer at home.

Using Interactive Essay with Windows

Navigating Interactive Essay

To read through an essay, click on the right or left arrow in the center bottom of the screen. You may also navigate by holding down the control and pressing the right or left arrow keys. The crooked arrow at the bottom right corner takes you back to the screen you were looking at immediately before.

Using the Menu Bar

FILE MENU

- **Open**—Usually you will open essays by clicking on their titles on the table of contents page. However, you may open an essay file by choosing the **Open** command under the file menu and selecting the disk drive and the file name of the essay you wish to open.

- **Print Pages**—Do not print your work from this **Print Pages** command. Instead, use the **Print** command from within **Interactive Essay**.

- **Exit**—Although you will usually quit **Interactive Essay** by clicking on the **Quit** button at the bottom right of the essay page, you may also click on **Exit** to quit.

EDIT MENU

- **Undo**—The undo command will undo the last command you gave, either from the keyboard or the mouse.

- **Cut, Copy, Paste**—The Cut, Copy, and Paste commands will allow you to cut, copy, and paste text from within **Interactive Essay** to your Windows word processing program. Click at the beginning of the text you wish to cut or copy and, while holding the mouse button down, drag across the text until it is highlighted. Release the mouse button and choose either **Cut** or **Copy** from the **Edit** menu. *Remember:* The **Cut** command cuts the text from its original location; the **Copy** command makes a copy of the text. Go to the place where you wish to paste the text and click an insertion point with your mouse. Then choose **Paste** from the **Edit** menu.

TEXT MENU

To change the font, size, or style of the text you type into the prompt response boxes, the **Collect** pages, the **Notes** page, or the **Draft** page, click at the beginning of the text you wish to change and drag across it while holding down the mouse button. Then go to the **Text** menu and choose **Character**. When the **Character** box appears, click on the arrow to the right of the **Font** line and choose the font you wish. Click on the arrow to the right of the **Point Size** box and choose the size you want. You may also choose bold, italic, underline, and strikeout as the style you wish. Click on **OK**.

PAGE MENU

The page menu may be used for navigating through **Interactive Essay**. The commands are as follows:

- **Next**—Go to next page.

- **Previous**—Go to previous page.

- **First**—Go to first page in the essay.

- **Last**—Go to last page in the essay (the Draft page).

- **Back**—Go to last page you were looking at.

- **History**—This gives you a list of the names or page numbers of the last 100 pages you visited in **Interactive Essay**. To go to a page, double-click its name or number in the list box.

- **Search**—To use the Search command, click on the word **Search** and then type in the word or words you wish to search for. Then click the **Find** button.

Suggestions for Exploring and Interacting with the Essays

When you click on an **Explore** button at the top right of each essay page, a reading prompt will appear that will assist you in exploring grammar principles, contextual backgrounds, thematic ideas, or rhetorical techniques on that page.

When you click on an **Explore** button to make a reading prompt appear, that button becomes an **Interact** button.

When you click on an **Interact** button, the essay page is replaced with a window that contains a writing prompt that will assist you in interacting with grammar principles, contextual backgrounds, thematic ideas, or rhetorical techniques on that page. Click once at the top left corner of the response window below the writing prompt and begin typing your response.

To make any **Explore** reading prompt or **Interact** writing prompt go away, simply click anywhere inside the prompt window.

When you have completed a series of **Interact** writing prompts, click on the appropriate navigation button at the bottom left of the screen to navigate to a collection point where all your work will be gathered in one place for editing, printing, or exporting. For example, if your instructor assigns a group of **Interact Grammar** exercises, work through them by first using the **Explore Grammar** buttons to discover the grammar principle involved and to see the principle illustrated in the essay. Second, click on the **Interact Grammar** buttons one at a time and edit the grammar exercises that appear. Finally, click on the **Grammar** navigation button at the bottom left of the screen to go to a **Grammar** collection page where all your grammar exercises can be collected in one place for editing, printing, or exporting.

Suggestions for Responding to Prompts and Saving Your Responses

TYPING IN THE PROMPT WINDOWS, THE NOTES PAGE, THE DRAFT PAGE, OR THE COLLECT PAGE

Do not use the Tab key to indent a paragraph. The Tab key has a special function in Toolbook.

Interactive Essay will save all work you type in the prompt response windows, the **Collect** pages, and the **Notes** and **Draft** pages when you Quit or go back to Contents. *Remember:* When asked "save current changes?" click the **Yes** button. The **Count** button at the top left of the **Notes** and **Draft** pages will give you a word count for those pages.

USING THE INTERACT GRAMMAR, INTERACT CONTEXT, INTERACT IDEA, AND INTERACT RHETORIC COLLECT SCREENS

The purpose of the **Collect** screens is to give you a convenient place to collect all the work you have done throughout the essay in the **Interact** prompts and exercises. For example, if you have been reading an essay and responding to several of the brainstorming suggestions in the **Interact Idea** sections, you will probably wish to pull those ideas together in one place so that you can further develop some of them, edit them, print them out for a hard-copy reference, or export them to a word processing program for spell-checking and further revision.

Remember: When you click on the **Collect** button, whatever text is in the **Collect** Window will be replaced by whatever text is in the prompt response windows throughout the essay. Thus, make sure you enter in all the information in the prompt response windows throughout the essay before you press the **Collect** button. If you choose to type directly on the **Collect** page, do not press the **Collect** button again.

EXPORTING YOUR WORK

The purpose of the **Export** button on the **Collect** pages, the **Notes** pages, and the **Draft** pages is to allow you to export your work out of **Interac-**

tive **Essay** into a word processing program of your choice. Once you have exported your work, you may delete your work in **Interactive Essay**, exit the program, and load your exported files into your word processing application, where you can use your spell-checker, thesaurus, and other revision tools to further edit your work.

When you click on **Export** from the **Collect** page, the **Notes** page, or the **Draft** page, you will be asked the name of the text you wish to export as well as the location where you wish to store it. Type in the disk drive, the directory (if any), and the name of the file. For example, to save your Interact Rhetoric work for the essay by Maya Angelou on the A drive, type **a:angelou.ir**. To save your Interact Idea work for the essay by Annie Dillard in a subdirectory named *work* on your C drive, type **c:\work\dillard.ii**. Use the following as extensions for the four different Interact assignments: **ig** for interact grammar, **ic** for interact context, **ii** for interact idea, and **ir** for interact rhetoric.

Quitting **Interactive Essay**

When you quit **Interactive Essay** by clicking on the **Quit** button or choosing **Exit** from the File Menu, you will be asked if you wish to delete your work. If you click **Yes; Delete** all the work you have typed in, cut and pasted, or collected in all the prompt response windows, the **Collect** pages, the **Notes** screen, and the **Draft** screen will be deleted.

CAUTION: MAKE SURE THAT YOU HAVE EXPORTED ALL THE WORK YOU WISH TO SAVE BY CLICKING ON THE EXPORT BUTTON ON THE FOUR **COLLECT** SCREENS, THE **NOTES** PAGE, OR THE **DRAFT** PAGE TO EXPORT THE TEXT TO A WORD PROCESSOR.

You will usually wish to delete all your work when you finish a work session if you are using **Interactive Essay** installed on a hard drive in a campus lab used by many students. This will ensure that your work will not be seen by a student who uses the computer after you. You may not wish to delete all your work if you are using **Interactive Essay** on your own computer at home.

TEXT
OF INTERACT
BUTTONS

Included here are the writing activities for the Interact Context, Interact Grammar, Interact Idea, and Interact Rhetoric buttons in each essay in **Interactive Essay**. In effect, this section shows you what is behind each Interact button in the software so that you can select particular essays or Interact writing activities within a selected essay to assign to your class or to individual students. The number assigned to each Interact activity corresponds to the page number on which that button appears in **Interactive Essay.** For example, if you want your class to respond to Interact Context activity 1 for John Tarkov's essay "Fitting In," you would instruct them to click on the Interact Context button on the first page of that essay in **Interactive Essay** and to respond accordingly.

John Tarkov, "Fitting In"

Interact Context

1. Write a paragraph or two on the pros and cons of the practice of immigrants setting up their own cultural communities within a foreign country. Be sure to focus on both the good and the bad implications of this practice.

2. Write a paragraph or two on why you think baseball is the most typical American sport. Why should it be more "American" than football, basketball, or any other sport?

3. Write a paragraph or two about the kind of behavior that American males often use to show affection for each other. Suggest some reasons for this behavior. What effect does this behavior have on American men?

4. People who leave one country for another or even one part of the U.S. for another part often find it difficult to cut themselves off from what they consider "home." Try to explain this phenomenon.

5. In our culture there is a stereotype of men gathered together around a television on Saturday watching a ball game. Describe such a gathering, making the stereotypes as typical, yet as interesting, as you can.

6. Why do fathers and sons often have very little of substance to say to each other? Is there a barrier between the two generations? Or is this typical male behavior? Do mothers and daughters have the same problem?

7. Write one or two paragraphs contrasting soccer with American football. Why do you think American men prefer football to soccer?

8. Many sports have rules that penalize players if they don't follow the rules, e.g., the penalty box in hockey, yardage penalties in football, and foul shots in basketball. Why must there be such rules in sports?

Interact Grammar

1. Retype the following sentence, punctuating properly:
When I was a child growing up in a small town in the Midwest my father was often out of town on business but I enjoyed the weekends when he did come home for he always took me fishing in the summer and sledding in the winter.

2. Revise the following sentence by correcting the verb tenses:
It is difficult to remember when I am a small child, for my memory will be weaker now than it is ten years ago when I am younger.

3. Edit the following sentence, punctuating properly:
When I was a child my father's primary concern was for one thing his work he did however spend as much time as he could with us kids.

4. Edit the following sentence, punctuating properly:

Boys and men refer to their fathers by many different names "dad" "the old man" "pop" "poppa" "pappy" however fathers do not have many names for their sons.

5. Edit the following sentence, punctuating properly:

It once seemed perfectly natural for my father and me to play a little baseball together on Saturday but now when I "hit a few" to my son it is called "male bonding" a phrase that suggests something forced and artificial.

6. Combine the following into two balanced sentences:

My grandfather is eighty years old. He is very strong. He works in the fields all day. I am forty; I am weak; I work in an office.

7. Combine the following into a single sentence with subordinate clauses:

My father died. I was twenty years old. I became a father a year later.

8. Tighten up the following sentence by rewriting it:

In the early 1940s I grew up in a small town in the Midwest and I was very happy and I had few worries and adult responsibilities were far away from me in the future.

Interact Idea

1. Write a paragraph or two in which you describe a place you remember from your childhood. As you write the description, try to discover and explain why this place popped into your mind before any other place.

2. Keeping things "just as they were when new" is an obsession with some people. Write a paragraph or two about someone like this; explain why you think they are this way and what effect you think this has on their life.

3. Have you ever had an experience that was too painful to talk about or that left you speechless? Describe that experience and try to explain why you were not able to talk about it then.

4. Describe an experience in which you tried to learn the customs of another country, another culture, another generation, or another value system. What kinds of activities are best for doing this? Why?

5. In one paragraph, discuss some positive aspects of immigrants, and minorities, being absorbed into American culture. In a second paragraph discuss the positive aspects of holding on to one's cultural identity.

6. Brainstorm a list of visions you think your father had for you. Then brainstorm a second list of visions you had for your father. Try to discover an essay topic in these two lists. Write a thesis statement for that essay.

7. In many cultures there is a short period of mourning between the time of someone's death and the burial. Sometimes this period is like a party, with food, laughter, and music. Write a paragraph or two explaining this.

8. Think of a sport or game that you could use as a metaphor for some aspect of life. Write a paragraph or two developing and explaining the metaphor.

Interact Rhetoric

1. What thematic significance is suggested by a father's playing baseball with his son in a parking lot? Why is a parking lot more effective than a field? Why is baseball more effective than football?

2. Discuss Tarkov's reluctance to describe how he felt when he heard of his father's death. How do we know how he felt, even though he does not say so? How can one communicate feelings without describing them?

3. Discuss what his father's failure to "get the hang" of America means to Tarkov.

4. Brainstorm some typical kinds of relationships between fathers and sons. Find a topic for an essay on one or more of them.

5. Write a paragraph or two in which you explain how Tarkov is using the metaphor of himself and his father as emissaries. In what way are they emissaries to each other? How do they follow the rules of emissary behavior?

6. Tarkov tells us he has been embarrassed by his father, but he never tells his father. Why doesn't he? What effect does confiding in strangers what he would not tell his father have on the tone and purpose of the essay?

7. Make a rough outline of the structure of Tarkov's essay. List only those major sections of the essay where, as in a movie, he shifts from one scene or emphasis to another.

8. Write a brief analysis of Tarkov's use of the baseball metaphor in this essay. Explain how the metaphor works and comment on its effectiveness.

Gay Talese, "Playing Catch"

Interact Context

1. Brainstorm for an essay on why baseball players are more apt to be heroes to men and young boys than basketball players or football players. Or argue against this point of view if you disagree with it.

2. It is sometimes suggested that fathers are identified not by who they are but by what they do. A common childhood question is "What does your father do?" Brainstorm for an essay about this topic.

3. Brainstorm about a time when you had to face certain restrictions on where you could go or what you could buy because of social unrest, war, economic limitations, etc. How did this experience affect you?

4. Brainstorm for an essay about your own experience working as a child—mowing lawns, delivering newspapers, babysitting, etc. Did you ever feel you were being treated unfairly just because you were a child?

5. Many things that once were thought to be harmless (or that were tolerated) have now been found to be dangerous and have been restricted by laws. Try to find an essay in this topic by brainstorming.

6. What is the relationship between a double agent and being double-crossed? Define "double-cross." Have you ever been double-crossed by someone? Describe the betrayal and discuss how it affected you.

7. Based on movies you have seen, brainstorm for an essay on the difference between the way World War II was fought in Europe, the Pacific, and Africa. What are the differences in the film images of the three different war zones?

8. Brainstorm some everyday superstitions in which you, or those you know, engage. Do people really believe in these superstitions, or do they engage in them for some other reason?

9. Volunteer civic, religious, and educational organizations are important, but do some people spend too much of their time in such volunteer efforts? Brainstorm for an essay on this topic.

10. Did you ever work for your parents when you were a child? If so, did you get paid for your work or was the work considered part of your responsibilities? Should children receive pay for their work for parents or guardians?

11. Can you tell what a person does by his or her appearance? Brainstorm for a humorous essay on the relationship between what people do and what they look like.

12. The game of pool was once associated with juvenile delinquency. Brainstorm reasons for this. Is this image of playing pool true now? Why or why not?

13. Brainstorm some nonverbal gestures common to your cultural background. What do the gestures mean? Why do people use such gestures instead of using language?

Interact Grammar

1. Retype the following, punctuating correctly:
In the 1950s when I was an adolescent my heroes were such rock and roll singers as Little Richard and Fats Domino.

2. Rewrite the following, punctuating properly:
During the 1950s when rock and roll was beginning many parents worrying that the music would lead to immoral behavior tried but without much success to have it banned.

3. Invent a sentence using the following pattern:
After reading this, I marked the passage of each day, anticipating spring when I would travel across the marshlands to the stadium where the Yankees would play.

4. Retype the following, punctuating correctly:

Parents are always reminding their children about how tough life was when they were young, today's children however don't usually listen.

5. Retype the following, punctuating properly:

Searching for information about your ancestors a tedious but exciting task can become an obsessive habit.

6. Retype the following, punctuating properly:

If you intend to do a thorough search for records of your ancestors you must plan to spend a great deal of time.

7. Correct the verb tenses in the following:

If I spent more time reading when I was a child, my writing would be better when I was in college.

8. Retype the following, punctuating properly:

When my father was in high school he enjoyed sports but he did not read many books or spend much time writing.

9. Rewrite the following sentence, balancing it:

He wanted to learn how to repair things like his father and being a good cook like his mother.

10. Retype the following, punctuating correctly:

When I was a teenager facing the need to make some money for myself I got a job caddying at the local golf course.

11. Rewrite the following, punctuating correctly:

Baseball is America's favorite sport, every summer thousands go out to the games.

12. Rewrite the following in parallel form:

When I was young, my parents and I did many things together: we played ball, taking walks, and go to movies.

13. Retype the following, punctuating properly:

As I watched my father turn red in the face with embarrassment I felt very sorry for him.

Interact Idea

1. Try to recall one of your own heroes or heroines when you were a child. Brainstorm for an essay in which you try to explain why the person was a hero.

2. Brainstorm for an essay about a generation gap you have experienced. It can be a humorous essay, for instance, about how your parents hate the music you like and vice versa, or it can be a serious essay about an important difference.

3. Brainstorm for an essay about a time you made a discovery about a parent or guardian that explained behavior that you had not understood before.

4. Write a humorous essay about how parents are always telling their children how tough life was when they were children. Or write an essay about what you tell, or will tell, your own children about how tough you have had it.

5. When you were a child, did you ever have to assume the responsibilities of an adult? If so, what effect do you think this has had on you?

6. Discuss a time when you were able to understand and sympathize with something you knew that a parent or guardian was feeling. What are the implications of this identification?

7. Brainstorm some differences between the personality of your mother and that of your father. What effects did these differences have on your childhood?

8. What is the difference between superstitious beliefs and religious beliefs? Try to examine this question objectively rather than taking a strong religious stand on it.

9. If this is not too painful to write about, brainstorm about some time when you wished that you belonged to a family other than your own.

10. Discuss the significance of a father and a son's playing ball together. Read "Fitting In" by John Tarkov elsewhere in this section for another description of playing catch.

11. Recall a time when you were caught doing something you were not supposed to by a parent or guardian. Describe how you felt, what happened, and what the event meant.

12. Write about a confrontation you had with a parent, guardian, teacher, or someone else in authority. It may be a major confrontation or a minor, symbolic confrontation.

13. Recall a time when you witnessed a parent's or a guardian's being embarrassed. What caused the embarrassment? How did it affect your opinion of the parent or guardian?

Interact Rhetoric

1. As you read this essay, make some notes about the words, sentences, and references that indicate whether the point of view is that of a young boy or a grown man.

2. Make a list of words Talese uses that seem fancier than they need to be, such as "albeit" instead of "although." Write a paragraph or two in which you explain why he uses these fancy words instead of simpler ones.

3. As you read through this essay, note all the places where Talese shifts the time perspective. How many different points of his life does he comment on in this essay?

4. The level of language writers use should suit the subject about which they are writing and the tone they wish to create. How is Talese's language suited to his subject and desired tone?

5. Discuss Talese's conflict between the fact that he is American and that he has relatives fighting Americans in Italy. What does this have to do with his central point in this essay?

6. Discuss Talese's rhetorical tactic of moving from rebellion against his father to a sympathetic understanding of him. How does he suggest his growing identification with his father?

7. Many writing teachers recommend that students use simple words instead of fancy words. Why do they recommend this? Don't fancier words sound more impressive and intelligent than simpler ones?

8. Why do many writing teachers recommend that students place their thesis statement or a statement of their central point somewhere near the beginning of their essay?

9. Like stories, personal experience essays usually have a theme that runs through them, some central point that the writer keeps coming back to. Why is a theme important for personal experience essays?

10. Write a description of a real physical event, such as Talese's description of the boy, walking through the cloud of steam to the cool breeze outside, that also has symbolic significance.

11. Write a paragraph describing a parent or guardian. Try to use details that characterize the person.

12. Write a description of a situation when you were in suspense about what was going to happen. Try to re-create how you felt by describing what happened.

13. Describe an encounter between yourself and a parent or guardian when there was nothing to say, when silence was the only response possible. Explain why.

Maya Angelou, "Getting a Job"

Interact Context

1. Some historians suggest that womens' rights improved significantly when a large number of women entered the workforce during World War II. Brainstorm some reasons for this.

2. Why does Angelou wish to wear a uniform? What is it about a uniform that is often so appealing to people? Brainstorm for an essay.

3. Familiar old sayings are not always the best advice. Think of one—such as "If at first you don't succeed, try, try again"—and show how it is bad advice.

4. If you have ever had the experience of looking for a job by answering ads in the classified section of the newspaper, describe that experience and discuss what you learned from it.

5. Brainstorm for an essay in which you discuss the importance of role-playing or playacting in everyday life.

6. Brainstorm an incident in which you felt you were the victim of someone's dreaming up or concocting a story. How were you trapped by the concocted story? How did you deal with it?

7. Why is it dehumanizing to make jokes at the expense of African Americans but often acceptable to make fun of Southern whites?

8. Have you ever had to seek help from a social, political, or religious organization? Do you know someone who has? Describe the experience. What are the pros and cons of such organizations?

9. Make a list of aphorisms that have become clichés. Suggest ways to make them seem new again.

10. We often say to someone, "It's not what you say but the way you say it." Describe an experience you have had when the way a person said something was more important than what the person said.

11. Have you ever lived in an area set apart from the rest of the city or town because of economic, social, or class distinctions? Try to explain to someone who has not lived in such a situation how you feel about that.

12. To go "honky-tonking" is to make the rounds of bars or saloons. Have you ever gone "honky-tonking"? Describe the experience. Why did you do it? What is the point of such an experience?

13. Brainstorm for an essay about your own sense of difference from your classmates—because of different economic background, different experiences, different cultural background, etc.

14. Describe a time when you were "truant" from school or work. Is being truant basically a playful, childlike activity or a serious neglect of responsibility? Brainstorm this.

15. Brainstorm for an essay on the pressures adults place on teenagers to grow up.

16. Do females face more difficult and demanding changes during adolescence than males do? Brainstorm for an essay.

Interact Grammar

1. Retype the following, punctuating correctly:
When I went for my first job interview I was very nervous so I sat and listened to some quiet music before I left the house.

2. Rewrite the following, correcting the error:
Walking into the personnel office quite confidently, the interviewer did not frighten me.

3. Retype the following, punctuating correctly:

John said, Martin Luther King's speech was most powerful when he shouted free at last, free at last.

4. Retype the following, correcting verb tense:

By the end of his first day on the new job, he realized that he underestimates how much work was expected of him.

5. Write a short dialogue in which you identify the speakers and the tone they use. Rewrite the same dialogue, and this time try to suggest who the speakers are and what the tone is without explicitly identifying either.

6. Rewrite the following, correcting the error:

When the receptionist called he and I to the front desk, we timidly walked over to where she sat.

7. Rewrite the following, correcting the error:

Not really sure when the interview was over. I began to feel uncomfortable with the long silence.

8. Rewrite the following, correcting the error:

Whom was the person hired for the job, and to who was sent the letter beginning "We are sorry to inform you."

9. Rewrite the following sentence, making it parallel:

It is not easy to be a good son or daughter, but a respected friend to your parents is even harder.

10. Rewrite the following, punctuating correctly:

On Monday morning which was cold and rainy I arrived at my new job thirty minutes early.

11. Rewrite the following, punctuating correctly:

On my first day of work I met the staff spoke briefly to the boss and found out where the restrooms were.

12. Rewrite the following, correcting the error:

Getting ready to go to lunch on my first day at work, worries about the best place to go bothered me.

13. Rewrite the following, correcting the error:

On the way home from work I felt good about the efforts, which I had put forth that first day.

14. Rewrite the following, punctuating correctly:

I wondered if I had done my work well if I had been approved of by the boss and if I had been liked by my coworkers.

15. Combine the following two sentences into a compound sentence, punctuating properly:

I came home very tired from a hard day's work. I did not feel like doing anything but watching television.

16. Rewrite the following, punctuating correctly:

I went to bed that night confident that I had spent a first day at work, which was impressive and pleasurable.

Interact Idea

1. Have you ever had a job that you felt was beneath your intellectual level? Explain how you handled such a job.

2. The incidents described by Angelou took place in the early 1940s. Are African American adolescents more furious about race prejudice now than they were then? Why or why not?

3. Write a character sketch about someone you know or know about who always uses old sayings to give advice. Use either a serious or a humorous tone in writing the essay.

4. Describe an experience in which your first look at a place did not match your expectations. For example, some people are disappointed when they first see Hollywood, California, for it is not as glamorous as most imagine it to be.

5. Have you ever had an experience that felt as if the script had already been written for it? Re-create or describe the experience and explain what it meant.

6. A sudden realization is sometimes called an "epiphany." Describe an epiphany you have had. What did the experience mean?

7. Recall a time when you deceived yourself or lied to yourself about something. Why did you do this? What effect did it have on you?

8. Describe a place that felt cold, unfriendly, or even malicious to you. Do not focus on the people in the place, but on the place itself. Describe it in such a way that your feelings about it are communicated.

9. Brainstorm for an essay about the point at which you and a parent or guardian began to develop a mutual admiration for each other. Focus on the word "admiration."

10. Since Angelou does not suggest how she finally got the job, invent your own explanation.

11. Recall a time when you felt justified in lying or breaking certain rules. Explain your justification.

12. Have you ever been treated maliciously by your boss or supervisor? Was it purposeful, or do you just suspect that it was? How did you handle the situation?

13. Angelou says she did not feel a part of the life of her fellow students. Have you ever felt like this? Describe your feelings and explain why you felt this way.

14. Describe a time when you felt more mature than those around you. What does the word "maturity" mean in this context?

15. Angelou says, "Few, if any, survive their teens." How did you survive your teens? Or did you? Explain.

16. Compare Judith Ortiz Cofer's discussion of the particular difficulties of growing up a Latin woman (Part Three) with Angelou's suggestions about growing up an African American woman.

Interact Rhetoric

1. Write a paragraph describing the personality of Angelou based on your reading of the opening of her essay. Support your analysis with details from the first paragraph.

2. Which is the most difficult to write—a passage in which you quote people directly or a passage in which you report what people say indirectly? Explain.

3. Do you know someone who speaks in such a way that you have difficulty understanding him or her? Describe what problems this creates. What, if anything, can be done about the problems?

4. Create a conversation, using direct quotations, in which you are being interviewed for a job.

5. Rewrite the following sentences, supplying specific details to make the scene more real:

I was very nervous during the interview. The room was warm. The interviewer seemed bored.

6. Have you ever been in a situation in which you had to "act" as if you were enthusiastic, sad, excited, joyful, etc., when you were not? Explain how you achieved this and how it made you feel.

7. Have you ever had an experience in which you wanted to shout something but could not? Describe the experience. Why could you not shout it out?

8. Look back over the essay and point out the different stages of feelings that Angelou has had about her efforts to get a job.

9. At this point in the essay you should be able to discuss your feelings about Angelou when she was a teenager. Do you like or dislike her? Could you be friends with her? Why or why not?

10. Brainstorm for an essay on the necessity for lying. Is lying never justified, or are there times when it is the only course of action to take?

11. Angelou uses "shimmied" and "scooted" to suggest the way the streetcars moved up and down the hills of San Francisco. Write a sentence in which you use other metaphors to suggest that movement.

12. Describe how a family, a neighborhood, or a group can be a protective shield. Have you ever felt protected by such a group? What are the pros and cons of such protection?

13. Have you ever felt that there was some "magic formula" for success in some area—a magic formula that you somehow could not discover? Brainstorm this for a possible essay topic.

14. Describe a time when you changed from "being ignorant of being ignorant" to "being aware of being aware."

15. Write a paragraph in which you describe "youthful unknowing" by using a different metaphor than the "tightrope" metaphor Angelou uses.

16. Write an analysis of the basic structure of Angelou's essay. What are its major sections and how do they relate to each other?

Audre Lorde, "The Fourth of July"

Interact Context

1. Most countries have a day on which they celebrate an act of independence, such as a declaration or a battle. Recall one memorable time when you took part in such a celebration. Describe it and explain what it meant.

2. The Liberty Bell is a symbol of American freedom and independence. Brainstorm some other symbols of either the U.S. or another country and explain why these symbols are important.

3. Did you take a class trip when you were a senior in high school? If so, what was it like? If not, what do you think of such a convention? What value might such a trip have?

4. Have you ever stayed in a hotel, motel, or campground that was dirty, run-down, or uncomfortable? What was the experience like? Why did you stay there? What do you feel about the stay?

5. Do you know of mixed racial heritage in your own background? What are the advantages and disadvantages of coming from a mixed racial background?

6. Brainstorm about some other social, religious, historical, or patriotic society or organization with which you are familiar. Brainstorm some ways in which their actions are not always true to their stated ideas.

7. Have you ever seen or read about an event that could be called a "travesty"? If so, describe it and explain why it was a grotesque imitation of something, such as a "travesty of justice."

8. Did you have a favorite place to gather or "hang out" with friends and classmates when you were an adolescent? Describe it and explain why it was important.

9. Have you ever had to communicate with someone whose dialect was different from yours? Describe the experience and discuss the difficulty.

10. Patriotic feelings were much higher during World War II than they were during the war in Vietnam. Although the reasons for this are complex, discuss at least one reason for this difference.

Interact Grammar

1. Create a compound sentence out of the following:
I took a vacation trip with my family last year. I did not enjoy it.

2. Rewrite the following, correcting the error:
We decided to drive the car on our vacation instead of flying, that was a big mistake.

3. Rewrite the following, punctuating correctly:

We had started the trip with great expectations of family fun but by the time we reached the state line we were quarreling with each other.

4. Explain the reason for each comma:

Phyllis's high school senior trip had been to Washington, but the nuns had given her back her deposit in private, explaining to her that the class, all of whom were white, except Phyllis, would be staying in a hotel where she would not be happy.

5. Retype the following, punctuating correctly:

When Mother could not calm down the kids in the backseat, she turned the job over to Dad who pulled over to the side of the road and turned around with a frown.

6. Rewrite the following, punctuating correctly:

When I think of all the vacations, that my family and I endured together, I do not know how we survived them.

7. Rewrite the following, making it parallel:

We wandered around the store looking at the souvenirs and to try to find something we liked.

8. Rewrite the following, correcting the pronoun case:

My brother and me, we decided to hide from our parents in the store, but they found we boys behind the toy counter.

9. Rewrite the following, punctuating correctly:

Very carefully one at a time we sneaked through the door around the corner and into the candy store as if we were spies on a secret mission.

10. Rewrite the following, punctuating correctly:

By the time our vacation was over I was sick of the car sick of motels sick of greasy restaurant food and sick of my family too.

Interact Idea

1. Describe a point in your life when you were told that you had to stop being a child or that you were supposed to stop being a child. Explain what this meant to you.

2. Recall a time when you felt a particularly strong spirit of patriotism for the U.S. or another country. Describe the feeling and what it meant. If you have never felt this way, explain why.

3. Note that the father likes dill pickles while the mother and daughters like sweet pickles. Brainstorm for a humorous essay on foods as more or less gender-specific. For example, not many women like liver, and "real men don't eat quiche."

4. Were there certain subjects that your parents or guardians simply did not talk about when you were a child? What were they? Why didn't they talk about them? What did this silence mean?

5. Recall a time when your parents or guardians tried to protect you from some reality by just not telling you about it. What effect did this have on you?

6. Brainstorm at least one thing for which you are patriotically proud of your country and at least one thing for which you are ashamed. Explore each thoroughly. Which one do you consider more typical of your country?

7. Have you ever experienced a physical condition, such as allergies, a skin disorder, hay fever, etc., that affected your life when you were a child? If so, describe it and explain its effect on you.

8. Do you know someone who has a "flair for the dramatic"? Write a brief character sketch of the person.

9. Recall a time when you suddenly realized that people saw you in a quite different way than you saw yourself. Describe the experience and explain what it meant.

10. Brainstorm for an essay entitled "The Time I Left Childhood."

Interact Rhetoric

1. Write a brief description of the personality of the writer of this essay based on the first paragraph. What is she like? How do you know?

2. Describing food in such a way that it makes the reader hungry is not easy. But try to describe your favorite food in such a way that it makes someone hungry to eat it.

3. Recall a time in your childhood when neatness and cleanliness were emphasized. Who emphasized them? Why? What does such an emphasis mean? What effect did it have? Is there an essay in this topic?

4. Many people in the U.S. show respect for symbols of American democracy, such as the flag, the national anthem, the U.S. capital, etc. Are you familiar with any examples of disrespect to the U.S.? What is your opinion?

5. Who is telling this narrative: Lorde as an adolescent or Lorde as an adult? If it is Lorde as an adolescent, how does she suggest the adult? If it is Lorde as an adult, how does she suggest the adolescent?

6. People often use exaggerations in everyday speech, especially in arguments. Brainstorm your own experience with someone who exaggerates to try to win arguments. How do you deal with such tactics?

7. How much does the effect of this essay depend on the fact that it takes place in Washington, D.C.?

8. Write a description of the image of your own family—out to dinner, on a trip, going to a show, etc. How does your family appear to others in public?

9. Have you ever had to leave a place indignantly? Have you ever had to "make an exit" dramatically? Describe the experience and explain what it meant.

10. Write an analysis of Lorde's essay in which you focus on the rhetorical tactics she uses to make her point and affect the reader.

Annie Dillard, "Untying the Knot"

Interact Context

1. Describe a situation when you mistakenly inferred or suspected that something had happened based only on circumstantial evidence. Describe the evidence, how you reached your conclusion, and why you were wrong.

2. Brainstorm how little or much you know about creatures in the natural world. Is such knowledge valuable or worthless? Explain why or why not.

3. Brainstorm for an essay about the stereotype that boys are more likely to play with snakes than girls are. Is the idea that boys are made of snakes and snails and girls are made of sugar and spice changing now?

4. Sometimes we wish we had freedom to act in ways that most people would think mad. Write a description of a time when you wished for this kind of freedom; explain what you did about it, and why.

5. Brainstorm for an essay on your experience of the regular recurrence of things, such as seasons, holidays, daily activities. Have you ever experienced a disruption in your routine of the recurrence of things? What was it like? Do you need such routine?

6. Brainstorm some reasons why it is important for people to know Biblical stories, Greek and Roman myths, Native American myths, African folklore, Asian myths, Mexican folklore.

7. Annie Dillard lived alone in the woods for a period of time and observed the natural life around her. Brainstorm some of the benefits and dangers of living alone in a deserted area.

8. Although sadism is usually associated with inflicting physical pain, causing emotional pain to others may sometimes be considered sadistic. Brainstorm for an essay on an example of emotional sadism with which you are familiar.

9. Children's toys once were simpler than they are in this age of computer games and electronic gadgets. Brainstorm for an essay on simpler, older toys, explaining why they were better or worse than modern toys.

10. Talking about spiritual matters is difficult, for such matters are based on feelings and faith rather than fact and reason. Brainstorm for an essay about your own experience with the difficulty of explaining spiritual matters or having them explained to you.

Interact Grammar

1. Retype the following, providing the correct punctuation:
I like to walk in the woods on a fall day, the leaves are so colorful and the air is so crisp.

2. Retype the following, correcting the errors:

I live in the city so I seldom have an opportunity to walk in the forest and enjoy it's beauty.

3. Retype the following, punctuating correctly:

I wish that I had more time to spend in the natural world and that I could get out more often but my job makes it very difficult to get away.

4. Retype, inserting hyphens or dashes where appropriate:

I walked down the well traveled path a route I had taken many times when I was a child with a feeling of well being.

5. Retype, punctuating properly:

When my father was a child he had never heard of the word "ecology" but he did know the word "conservation" he joined a group dedicated to preserving our natural resources.

6. Retype, punctuating correctly:

That beautiful shell that sits on my mantle which I found on one of my many walks along the beach near my home is one of my favorite possessions.

7. Identify the noun clauses in the following sentence by typing them in the box below:

I know that I should get out of the city more often, but what I would like to do is not always what I am able to do.

8. Retype, punctuating properly:

An occasional walk in the woods will make you more appreciative of the natural world more aware of your dependence on other creatures and more determined to preserve our natural resources.

9. Retype the following, punctuating correctly:

If we don't start protecting our natural resources the result will be disastrous we will simply run out of all that makes life possible.

10. Retype the following sentence, punctuating correctly:

The ecology movement beginning in the sixties has made us more careful about what we use what we throw away and how we treat the world around us.

Interact Idea

1. Describe a walk in some area of the natural world with which you are familiar—the beach, the desert, the woods. Be precise about those details which indicate both your knowledge of and your feelings about the natural world.

2. What point could you make about something you found in the natural world, such as a broken bird's egg, an empty turtle shell, the tracks of a deer, a beached fish, or the skeleton of a small animal?

3. Some problems are so complicated that we are apt to say, "I don't know where to begin." Brainstorm for an essay on a problem that made you think this.

4. Some people who live in warm climates often say they miss the changing of the seasons. Brainstorm for an essay on why changing seasons are, or are not, important to you.

5. Describe an experience you have had that you thought "would never end"—an experience in which time seemed to slow down or drag on forever. What gave the experience this sense of time?

6. How would you explain to someone the most significant differences between humans and other animals?

7. Describe the effect of "unseasonable weather"—cold weather during the summer or a hot day in December, for example—on your state of mind and the state of mind of those around you.

8. Write a description of your favorite season, making clear why it is your favorite without actually saying so.

9. Look back over Dillard's essay and outline the steps by which she moves from specific ideas about the snakeskin to these very general ideas about time and divine spirit.

10. Edward Abbey, in his essay in this section, says that any good poet must begin with a scientific view of the world and any scientist must be something of a poet. How does Dillard illustrate characteristics both of the scientist and the poet?

Interact Rhetoric

1. How do you think Dillard feels about nature? Support your answer by referring to specific language in this first paragraph.

2. Write the first paragraph for a planned essay on the inevitability of death by describing something you have observed in the natural world.

3. Discuss what impressions you have of Annie Dillard at this point in the essay, before she states explicitly what the point of her essay is.

4. Writing a detailed description of a physical object is not always easy. Think of some object with which you are familiar and write a detailed description of it without naming it. Then ask someone to try to identify the object.

5. What does Dillard's meditation about the first man on earth and the notion of recurrence tell us about her? Does she sound like a naturalist, a philosopher, a poet, a teacher, or a scientist?

6. Brainstorm recollections of when you were in elementary school and regularly made seasonal decorations to place on the walls. Describe them and explain what they meant to you as a child.

7. Some people love to travel, while others prefer to stay at home. Brainstorm some basic differences between these two types of people. Which are you? Explain your preference.

8. Write a description of a natural scene—woods, desert, beach, mountains, etc.—in which you suggest that the scene is alive or like something alive.

9. If the fall season is like a funeral, with the leaves looking like crepe, what is the spring season like? Describe a spring scene using a specific metaphor to suggest the usual spring sense of rebirth.

10. Dillard has said that she is not a scientist but a "wanderer with a background in theology and a penchant for quirky facts." Explain how this essay is more reflective of religion than science.

Lewis Thomas, "The Tucson Zoo"

Interact Context

1. Describe a feeling of "apprehension"—when you anxiously anticipated something happening.

2. Describe an experience of being "transfixed," "elated," "swept off your feet." What did the experience feel like? What caused it?

3. The left side of the brain is said to control analytical and rational thinking, while the right side of the brain is said to control artistic and integrative thinking. Are you predominantly right-brain or left-brain dominant in your thinking? Support your answer.

4. Some people say they have acted "instinctively" when they mean they acted instantly without thinking. Describe an experience when you acted "instinctively," that is, without thinking. What do you think about the experience now?

5. Write a paragraph in which you describe craving some particular kind of food. How do you handle such cravings? Is it better to resist them or give in to them?

6. If the seventies were called the "me" generation years, what should we call the nineties? Brainstorm for an essay on this topic.

7. Sometimes people say that they are "genetically programmed" to do certain things. What behavioral characteristics do you feel you have inherited? Brainstorm for an essay on this topic.

8. Recent studies have shown that people work better if the group to which they belong gets rewarded for work well done rather than the individual. Discuss some of the implications of this finding.

Interact Grammar

1. Retype the following, correcting the subject-verb agreement errors:
The antics of my dog makes me laugh, but the growls that come out of his small body frightens me.

2. Rewrite the following, correcting the errors in tense:

When I was a teenager, I own a dog, but now that I am an adult, I did not have time to spend with animals.

3. Retype the following, correcting the error:

Most people want a puppy when they buy a dog, I don't want a puppy because they are too much trouble to train.

4. Retype the following, correcting the errors:

I have discovered three important things about puppies they are noisy full of mischief and hard to resist.

5. What is the rule for each comma in the following:

When we got our first puppy, we were delighted, but we did not know it was going to be so much trouble, so much work, and so much fun.

6. Retype the following, correcting punctuation:

When your dog has learned some basic commands coming to you when you call sitting and staying when you order her to you can then move on to more complex commands.

7. Rewrite the following sentence, using a relative clause and an infinitive phrase:

Puppies are very hard especially the training and I do not think I will buy one.

8. Rewrite the following, using an introductory dependent clause to create one complex sentence:

You have to teach puppies that you are the "leader of the pack." You must do this at the beginning of their training.

Interact Idea

1. Brainstorm for an essay on various activities that people destroy by analyzing them too much. Choose one of them for an essay.

2. Sometimes we have experiences that seem to leave us speechless. Describe such an experience that you have had; then try to describe what caused the experience.

3. Think of an experience you have had that you just did not want to "know" anything about. Describe the experience. Explain why you felt this way.

4. Describe some experience or phenomenon that used to overwhelm you with a sense of wonder—until you analyzed it and lost that sense of wonder. What was lost and what was gained by this new knowledge?

5. Agree or disagree with Thomas's idea that a sense of affection for other living things and the need for friendship are basic, even instinctive, human characteristics. Use specific examples to support your response.

6. Is it necessarily true that individualistic people are selfish? Does one have to give up one's individuality to be altruistic or to love another? Brainstorm for an essay in which you agree or disagree with Thomas's argument on this point.

7. Brainstorm for an essay in which you agree or disagree with Thomas's argument on this page. Support your case that either altruism or aggression is the basic human trait that ensures the survival of the human race.

8. Brainstorm some positive and some negative aspects of working in a group in which the group as a whole is more important than each individual member of the group.

Interact Rhetoric

1. Can you tell from the first two paragraphs of this essay whether it is going to be a personal experience essay or an essay about a thesis or concept? How do you know?

2. Write a brief description of your living room in such a way that someone reading it could draw a diagram of the room.

3. How would you characterize the style of Thomas's essay? Is it primarily scientific, poetic, or personal? Support your answer with some specific details.

4. Write a brief analysis of Thomas's sentence style on this page. Discuss length, structure, variety, and balance. Explain what tone this style creates.

5. Thomas does not provide a transition from the discussion of friends to the example of the ants. Rewrite the first sentence of the paragraph about the ants, providing an effective transition.

6. Discuss the effectiveness of Thomas's technique of seeming to accept the argument that he is arguing against. Does this not risk confusing a reader who is not reading closely? What value does this technique have?

7. Outline Thomas's essay, making clear its argumentative structure.

8. Discuss the effectiveness of Thomas's conclusion. If the group of ants cannot "think" as a group, is it good or bad that they act as a group? If the group can think, but no single ant can actually feel excited about the thought, is this good or bad?

Phyllis Rose, "Of Shopping"

Interact Context

1. Computers are being used more and more to replace tasks once performed by people. For example, you can now buy gas or go to the bank without ever having to deal with a person. Brainstorm for an essay on the pros and cons of this development.

2. Andy Warhol once said that in the future everyone would be famous for fifteen minutes. What do you think Warhol meant by this statement? Brainstorm some ordinary people who have been "famous for fifteen minutes."

3. Technology advances so rapidly that some things, like 8-track tapes and phonograph records, are displaced completely in a single generation. Brainstorm some other examples of this displacement and comment on its effect.

4. If you have ever visited a foreign country or an area of your own city characteristic of another culture, describe your reaction to some basic differences you observed there. What do you think these differences mean?

5. Just about any activity, if performed in the right way, can be "therapy." Brainstorm for an essay in which you agree or disagree with this statement. Or, if you agree with it, brainstorm for an essay on an activity in which you engage for therapy.

6. Most people feel that they are connoisseurs of something. Brainstorm for an essay in which you define yourself or someone you know as a connoisseur.

7. Brainstorm for an essay on some disparity you see in yourself between what you are and your ideal of what you would like to be.

8. Brainstorm for an essay on some political or social issue currently being debated that no longer seems relevant to the times.

9. Brainstorm for an essay on other misunderstandings about American society and values that you think are held by people from other cultures.

Interact Grammar

1. Retype the following, correcting the error:
When I go shopping for food, I like to visit a small store near home, that is run by an elderly couple.

2. Retype the following, punctuating correctly:
I do not like the wide variety of supermarkets eight kinds of soap ten types of toothpaste six brands of toilet paper and a whole shelf of laundry detergent.

3. Retype the following, punctuating correctly:
When you only want to buy one or two items it is a lot of trouble to go to a large supermarket and stand in line.

4. Retype the following, punctuating correctly:
The little old couple, who operate the store where I buy my milk and bread, have known me for years.

5. Rewrite the following sentence, changing the dependent clause to an infinitive phrase:
I do business at small markets because shopping there supports the store owners who live in my neighborhood.

6. Retype, punctuating properly:
Shopping at a neighborhood store something we should all think about doing is good for the economy of local areas.

7. Revise the following to eliminate the sentence fragment:

I try to think of the opposite, a kind of shopping in which the object is all-important, the pleasure of shopping at a minimum. For example, the purchase of blue jeans.

8. Retype the following, punctuating properly:

I only shop at stores, where I can count on a friendly face.

9. Retype, punctuating properly:

I always meet my neighbors most of whom are very friendly at the grocery store, where I do my shopping.

Interact Idea

1. Describe a time when you felt "elevated, graced, complimented" by a structure, such as a sports arena, a shopping center, an entertainment center, in your area. Explain what the structure means to you and your community.

2. Brainstorm for an essay in which you agree or disagree with Rose's statement that chain stores suggest egalitarianism in business.

3. Describe someplace that you like to go for sociability, to be with people for company and conversation. If you do not go to such a place, speculate on the value of such a practice. Is it worthwhile or a waste of time?

4. Brainstorm for an essay in which you argue that supermarkets and discount department stores either are or are not the best examples of what is characteristic of American society.

5. Brainstorm for an essay in which you discuss some of the reasons why you shop. If you feel that you only shop to buy specific items, describe someone you know who shops for other reasons.

6. Brainstorm for an essay in which you argue either for or against the statement "Money is power."

7. Brainstorm for some other activities that might be called "spiritual," such as exercise, running, listening to music, etc. Explain what makes the activities spiritual.

8. Brainstorm for an essay on how clothes create distinctions between people. Brainstorm some of the reasons for which some schools require students to wear uniforms.

9. Argue against Rose's main point that shopping for most Americans is not materialistic.

Interact Rhetoric

1. Describe someplace you have visited that displayed a wide variety of objects. Write a paragraph that contains a list describing the wide variety of the objects.

2. Write a paragraph about shopping in which you pose a rhetorical question.

3. Point out those places in this essay where the author is not being completely serious, but is using an exaggeration for rhetorical effect. What is the overall effect of this technique?

4. Are we becoming more and more cut off from our natural environment, for example in malls, entertainment centers, and sports arenas that create their own environment? Brainstorm for a humorous essay about increasingly living in an artificial world.

5. Rewrite the following, creating a parallel structure:
I like to shop at small stores because I like friendly service, they do not overwhelm me with merchandise, and people I know are always there.

6. Point out the comparisons Rose makes between shopping and other activities. Show how they break down when pushed too far.

7. Discuss the personality of Rose as it is reflected in this essay. How important is Rose's personality to the central point she makes?

8. Outline the structure of Rose's essay. Explain the relationship between the different parts of the essay.

9. Extend Rose's comparison of shopping centers, supermarkets, and discount stores to cathedrals as far as you can. At what point does the comparison break down or no longer work?

William Severini Kowinski, "Mallaise: How to Know If You Have It"

Interact Context

1. Brainstorm for an essay about a place that you have strong feelings about, either positive or negative. Describe it in such a way that you explain what causes these feelings.

2. Describe an experience of "malaise" you have had—a time when you just felt vaguely uneasy, but you were not sure why.

3. Describe a feeling of "apathy" you have experienced or that you have witnessed in an individual or a group. What are the characteristics of this experience? What are its effects?

4. Brainstorm some other aspect of society, besides malls or television, that you think is "bland" or "plastic."

5. Describe a sense of "torpor" you have experienced or witnessed in another, a "zombie-like" feeling of walking about in a daze or a dream.

6. Brainstorm for a humorous essay about the widespread use of Muzak and its effect on people. Describe the kind of music played by Muzak and where you are most apt to hear it.

7. Describe a "psychological structure" with which you are familiar—either a natural environment, such as a forest or beach, or a human construct—such as a theme park or a rock concert.

8. Kowinski suggests that commercials are sometimes more memorable than regular television programming. Try to think of one or two commercials that are memorable to you. Explain what makes them so memorable.

9. Brainstorm a definition of "anxiety" by thinking of experiences when you have been anxious; explain how these experiences felt and what caused them.

10. Brainstorm for an essay describing a time when your civic duty conflicted with what you considered to be your moral duty, that is, your sense of what is right and what is wrong.

11. Nirvana is the Buddhist state of absolute bliss. Describe an experience of your own that was "blissful." What caused it? How did it feel?

12. Describe a social situation that you have experienced in which you felt estranged or cut off from those around you.

Interact Grammar

1. Retype the following, punctuating correctly:
I like shopping in small towns the people are friendly the stores are small and the air is not conditioned.

2. Retype the following, punctuating properly:
Going into a mall is like entering another world and I always feel that if I am not very careful I will get lost in it and never find my way out.

3. Retype the following, punctuating correctly:
I go to a mall for three reasons to see a movie to grab a bite and to buy a specific item.

4. Retype the following, punctuating correctly:
"I get so sick of school" a friend of mine said "that I just want to walk off campus and never come back" and she might just do that too.

5. Retype the following, punctuating properly:
The most serious effect of school sickness which I heard one day from a friend of mine is the feeling that you always have an assignment to do.

6. Retype the following, punctuating correctly:
The primary effects of school sickness are a sense of overload a feeling of confusion and an awareness that you do not know as much as you thought you did.

7. Rewrite the following, correcting the shift in person:
When you feel you have a bad case of school sickness, one should reexamine just why you are going to school in the first place.

8. Retype the following, correcting the modifier:
Listening to a lecture for an hour, the professor droned on and on it seemed to me.

9. Retype the following, correcting the agreement error:

The warmth of the lecture hall and the drone of the teacher's voice makes many students fall asleep.

10. Retype the following, punctuating properly:

My own experiences of school sickness have occurred in several places grade school, high school, and college. There is only one thing to do for this ailment Just buckle down and bear it.

11. Retype the following, punctuating properly:

I believe that school sickness which has never been studied thoroughly is a widespread illness among students of all ages.

12. Retype the following, punctuating properly:

I would love to be able to cure myself of school sickness but I am just not sure what the best cure would be.

Interact Idea

1. Brainstorm for an essay on a mall with which you are familiar in which you try to explain how that mall makes you feel when you are in it.

2. Hallucination means experiencing something as real that does not really exist in the external world. Brainstorm for an essay on the difference between daydreams and hallucinations.

3. Brainstorm for an essay on a fast-food chain with which you are familiar. Explain what its characteristic features are and why you like it or don't like it.

4. Many people say that the art of conversation is dead. However, what about the popularity of talk radio or daytime talk shows? Are these examples of the art of conversation? Why or why not?

5. Brainstorm some other experience you have had that involved contradictory feelings such as excitement and relaxation. Does television create this combination of feelings? What about amusement parks, going to the beach, etc.?

6. Brainstorm for an essay in which you discuss how certain kinds of activities make you experience time in different ways.

7. Describe an experience in which you felt yourself at the mercy of your surroundings, and in which you felt you were being unconsciously manipulated.

8. Brainstorm for an essay about how shopping and advertising do not encourage buyers to make careful choices, but rather to buy impulsively.

9. Describe an experience when you felt you were being unconsciously affected by your environment and found a way to rebel against it. What made the method of rebellion work?

10. Brainstorm for an essay on some other complex ailment that has a very simple cure, such as just saying "no." Explain why such a simple cure is not so simple after all.

11. Brainstorm for an essay in which you argue that malls are one more example of "white flight" from the inner city to the suburbs.

12. Brainstorm for an essay in which you give someone practical advice for shopping in a mall without falling victim to mallaise.

Interact Rhetoric

1. Develop an extreme opening sentence, similar to Kowinski's, for a proposed essay on the effects of holiday shopping or shopping for someone's birthday.

2. Try to invent some special terms to designate school sickness, that is, having negative reactions to a campus, a classroom, teachers, etc.

3. Write a paragraph in which you suggest a humorous cure for the symptoms of school sickness. If being at school makes you sick, what might you do to deal with those feelings?

4. Interview one or two of your classmates about how they feel about school sickness. Write a paragraph in which you quote their responses.

5. By comparing mall shoppers to zombies, Kowinski suggests there is something frightening about the effect of malls. Brainstorm for an essay on another social experience in which people seem transformed, for example, at a sale or at a rock concert.

6. Write a paragraph in which you describe a supermarket by using the technique of making a list.

7. Look for other examples of clever language usage in Kowinski's essay. Write a brief analysis of Kowinski's playing with language.

8. Argue with Kowinski's comparison of mall shopping to television watching by suggesting all the ways you can think of in which the two activities are different.

9. Write a sentence using alliteration to describe how you feel while shopping in a supermarket.

10. How would you characterize the overall tone of this essay? Is it sarcastic, serious, frivolous? Support your answer with examples and analysis.

11. Discuss the basic technique of exaggeration that Kowinski uses in this essay. Write a brief analysis in which you explain why it works or why it does not.

12. Write a brief analysis of the central tone of Kowinski's essay. How important is this tone to the effectiveness of the essay?

Noel Perrin, "The Androgynous Man"

Interact Context

1. Brainstorm differences between traveling by train and traveling by plane.

2. Brainstorm images of the American cowboy from movies, advertising, and television. Write a definition of this stereotyped image.

3. Write an imaginative essay about a past or future society in which everyone is androgynous. How would such a society differ from the kind of society with which we are familiar today?

4. Brainstorm some other characteristics associated with the qualities of one's blood, such as "blue blood," "hot blood," "cold blood," etc. Is there enough material for an essay on this topic?

5. Brainstorm the image of the "women's liberationist" or "feminist" that has developed since the 1960s. Can these be classified? Which ones are stereotypes and which are genuine types? What's the difference?

6. Write a brief narrative that illustrates one or more of the unique qualities of cats. Draw from your own experience or make it up. But make sure that the details suggest your own attitude toward cats.

7. Many clothing manufacturers prominently display their brand name on their products. What does this trend mean? Are some brands distinctively male and some female, or are they androgynous? Find an essay here.

8. There once was a time when people were able to "fix" just about anything that went wrong. Brainstorm for an essay about how machines are becoming too sophisticated for that now. What are the implications of this change?

9. Brainstorm some ideas about the feminist argument that God should not always be referred to as "He." Consider arguments for this change, as well as difficulties the change might create for Judeo-Christian believers.

Interact Grammar

1. Retype the following, punctuating correctly:
I sometimes have doubts about my gender identity but since I have discovered that many people have such doubts I no longer worry about it.

2. Rewrite the following, correcting the error:
After having determined that the real definition of "masculinity" has nothing to do with traditional stereotypes, there should be no anxiety about male image.

3. Use a noun clause beginning with "The fact that" to combine the following sentences:
His doubts about his masculinity lasted only a short time. His wife was very happy about that.

4. Retype the following sentence, punctuating properly:
Modern men are not so trapped in stereotyped images as men of our father's generation, today, men have more freedom.

5. Rewrite the following with corrections:
Never having been to a seminar on sexism, fear of the unknown made him nervous.

6. Rewrite the following, correcting the error:
Many men have gone to sensitivity training sessions, but it does not seem to help.

7. Rewrite the following, correcting the errors:

He was not able to except the advise of his women friends because he did not believe they're ideas. "Its just not true," he insisted.

8. Rewrite the following, correcting the errors:

She was afraid that a reaction, that was developing among conservative groups, would destroy many of the rights, that women had fought so hard to achieve.

9. Rewrite the following, correcting the error:

A decline in male sexist attitudes seem to be taking place.

Interact Idea

1. Brainstorm the nature of shyness. What do you know about it? What causes it? What effects does it have? What are shy people like? Can you discover an essay in this topic?

2. It is a common notion that women are more repulsed by blood, flesh, and physical violence than men are. Do you agree or disagree? What do you think is the source of this notion?

3. Brainstorm a list of feminine characteristics that men are "permitted" to have. Brainstorm another list of feminine characteristics that men are not "permitted" to have because they suggest homosexuality.

4. Are men more apt to imitate "all-males" than any other type of men? Brainstorm some "he-man" characteristics that other men imitate. Why don't men want to imitate other types?

5. Brainstorm both positive and negative impacts that the liberation of women has had on men. Try to discover your own position on this issue. Can you find a personal essay or a comparison/contrast essay in this material?

6. Brainstorm the differences between cat-lovers and dog-lovers. Write a comparison/contrast essay on this. Try for a comic tone.

7. Brainstorm some other activities that men of Perrin's generation would think are more appropriate for women than for men. Does the current generation still hold on to any of these distinctions?

8. Brainstorm some ideas for an essay about your own sense of helplessness or facility in repairing things around the house. What kinds of things make you feel either helpless or confident?

9. Brainstorm for an essay on different interpretations of the word "he-man." Are there different kinds of "he-men"? How did such a doubled phrase develop?

Interact Rhetoric

1. Write a one-paragraph anecdotal opening to a possible essay about a trip you once took. Narrate and describe it in such a way that the reader gets some idea of what you are like.

2. Write a brief analysis of Perrin's unstated attitude toward masculine/feminine stereotypes. Discuss specific examples of his language that indicate this attitude.

3. Write an analysis of this essay in which you show that Perrin is still caught in the masculine/feminine distinctions he claims to be free of.

4. Why should we listen to Perrin's opinions about masculinity and femininity? What methods does he use to make us trust his authority, or at least to take his ideas seriously?

5. Write a brief personal anecdote describing your discovery of the difference between "masculine" and "feminine." Then write a general statement explaining that difference within the social context of your discovery.

6. How would the effect of this paragraph be different if Perrin made the cat female, smaller, less adventurous, more "sentimental," etc.?

7. Write a comic version of Perrin's description of his reaction to small children from the point of view of someone who does not find children so endearing.

8. Write an informal essay in which you describe feeling "dumb" because you had to deal with an "expert" on some subject, e.g., a repairman, a computer expert, etc. What does the experience reflect about you, about society, etc.?

9. Try to recall an experience when you were told to "act like a man" or "act like a woman." Does such an expression mean the same as "act like a grown-up"? What kinds of experiences make adults say this to children?

Amy Gross, "The Appeal of the Androgynous Man"

Interact Context

1. Define the word "quirky" by describing someone you know who is "quirky." What are the characteristics of being "quirky"?

2. Brainstorm for a humorous essay on the many slang terms that people use to refer to husbands, wives, parents, and children. What do the various terms suggest?

3. Write a definition of "uncouth" by describing its basic characteristics and providing examples of uncouth behavior.

4. Brainstorm for an essay on "male chauvinism." Is there such a thing as "female chauvinism"? What are its characteristics as contrasted with male chauvinism?

5. The Arab shepherd and Bolivian sandalmaker reference is meant to be funny. But it raises the issue of differences that stand in the way of involvement: which is more important—cultural difference or economic difference?

6. A female writer once said that her ideal of the perfect man would be a truck driver who writes poetry. What kinds of assumptions about female expectations of males does this ideal imply?

7. Brainstorm for an essay about the stereotypes of male versus female dependability that Gross uses in the expressions "true-blue in the trenches" and "milk comfort."

8. Brainstorm for an essay on the stereotypes of the relationship between homosexuality and effeminate appearance and behavior. Why is such a connection thought to be a negative one in American culture?

9. People often accuse others of being "neurotic" without using that term clinically to suggest a mental disorder. If they do not mean a mental disorder, then what do such people mean by the term "neurotic"?

10. Describe a time when you made a "gut response" to something or when something had a "gut appeal." How well can such an appeal be trusted? Are there certain kinds of things for which people have a gut response?

11. Is the ability to identify with another more apt to be a feminine characteristic than a masculine one? If so, why? If not, explain.

Interact Grammar

1. Retype the following, punctuating correctly:
Young boys are usually taught the following masculine rules don't cry don't show your emotions and always be tough.

2. Retype the following, punctuating properly:
The times are changing and gender demands on boys are less than before but most young boys still feel the pressure of being masculine.

3. Retype the following, choosing the correct form of "it's" and "its":
Its/It's not fair that boys are held to the rule that they must not cry; they remember its/it's effect for the rest of their lives.

4. Create a compound sentence out of the following sentences, punctuating properly:
Boys are taught that they must not cry. Girls are taught that crying is all right.

5. Rewrite the following, combining the two sentences with a restrictive dependent clause:
My daughter is on a girl's softball team. Her coach teaches masculine stereotypes such as "do not let the opponents know that you are hurt."

6. Rewrite the following, clarifying the pronoun reference:
Harder demands are made on boys than on girls because their fathers insist that they act grown-up more quickly.

7. Retype the following, punctuating correctly:
If men are polite to women they may be accused of being sexist but if they are not polite they may be accused of being ill-bred. This is the way that many men feel today.

8. Rewrite the following, changing from passive to active voice:

Passive behavior is taught to females by their mothers from an early age because mothers have been taught to be passive by their own parents.

9. Rewrite the following sentence, correcting the misplaced modifier:

Having been trained to be strong and silent since childhood, it is difficult to change when an adult.

10. Rewrite the following sentence, correcting the pronoun reference:

Nursery rhymes and fairy tales have always taught the child that they must act according to rules of feminine and masculine behavior.

11. Rewrite, correcting the pronoun referent:

Feminine women are often attracted to masculine men because she is as convinced of the truth of gender stereotypes as he is.

Interact Idea

1. Write a description of the stereotypical American male who sits around watching football on television with his friends.

2. Brainstorm for an essay on some of the things that men are expected to know how to do and some of the things that women are expected to know how to do.

3. Brainstorm for an essay on "manners" as a gender-specific quality. Do women usually have better manners than men? If so, why? If not, explain.

4. To Gross, it seems more reasonable that men be like women than women be like men. Why?

5. Write a definition of falling in love for three hours. Is love not love unless it is forever? How long must it last to be called love? Is there a time requirement for love?

6. If the all-man man does not like women and the androgynous man likes women as much or as little as he likes anyone else, what does this imply about sexual desire?

7. What is "enlightened prejudice"? If a psychological or sociological study correlated low intelligence with a certain race or skin color, would such a study go unchallenged? How could you determine its validity or truth?

8. Brainstorm a list of other qualities we usually think of as feminine. Are there no negative qualities that are feminine? Would you be accused of sexism if you pointed out negative female qualities?

9. Brainstorm for an essay on the stereotypes of the difference between the kind of help and concern that men show as opposed to the kind of help and concern that women show. Else, argue that there are no differences.

10. Brainstorm for an essay in which you discuss some of Western culture's stereotypes for the most desirable male sexual partner. What are the origins of these stereotypes? How valid are they?

11. Is Gross's assumption that "nice women" are not supposed to have a sexual appetite an outdated assumption that is no longer true, or is this still part of Western cultural assumptions?

Interact Rhetoric

1. Write a brief description of the tone established in the first paragraph of this essay. What assumptions can you make about Gross based on this paragraph?

2. Point out those places in this essay where Gross uses the language of the kind of man she is criticizing. Why does she do this? What effect does the technique have?

3. Write an analysis of the stereotyped language that Gross uses in this essay to define the kind of man she criticizes.

4. What is the difference between girls being called "tom-boys" and boys being called "sissies"?

5. Write a brief description of what you think Amy Gross is like. Cite evidence from her essay to support your analysis of her personality.

6. Write a brief analysis of Gross's tactic of exaggeration in this essay, commenting on examples to support your analysis. Is the tactic rhetorically effective, or is it too extreme?

7. Note other places in this essay where Gross states that all-men men are less intelligent, less sensitive, and less artistic than less "masculine" men without citing any evidence that can be examined or challenged.

8. What is the ratio in this essay between Gross's dependence on authorities and her dependence on her own experience? Which is more convincing?

9. How would you characterize the overall tone of Gross's essay? Discuss specific examples to support your analysis of tone.

10. Point out those places in this essay in which Gross not only stereotypes men, but women as well. What kind of stance does she take toward other women—that they are her intellectual equals, that she is superior to them, that they need instruction, or what?

11. Write a couple of paragraphs in which you discuss how convincing Gross's argument about the superiority of androgynous men is. Be sure to discuss the rhetorical strategies she uses to make her argument.

Susan Brownmiller, "Femininity"

Interact Context

1. Brainstorm some superstitions of your own culture about the meaning of common, everyday events. Discuss what these superstitions mean and how they are unique to your culture.

2. Try to recall a type of clothing you wore as a child and explain how it characterized your culture, your gender, or your age.

3. If you have ever watched soap operas, or know someone who does, brainstorm for an essay on why soap operas are so appealing, even addictive.

4. Describe a time when you felt you were in limbo, that is, in an uncertain state in which you felt you could not move forward or backward.

5. Brainstorm for an essay about the "good old days when men were men and women were women." Then, ask yourself if you really wish for a return to those days. If so, why? If not, why?

6. Brainstorm for an essay on the characteristics you think you have inherited from your parents and the characteristics you think you have developed yourself.

7. Brainstorm for an essay on what characteristics of the opposite sex that you think you possess.

8. Brainstorm for an extended definition of "irony," citing examples of ironic events you have experienced, people you know who are ironic, and examples of irony from literature you have studied.

9. How would you characterize the "ethos" of the current generation, which has sometimes been called "generation X"?

10. Brainstorm for an extended definition of the word "romantic." Consider, for example, romance novels, romantic movies, a romantic person, the Romantic period of English literature, romance of adventure and heroism.

11. Brainstorm for an essay in which you explore some of the reasons for the "economic disparity" between men and women.

12. Write a character sketch of someone you know who is "unabashed" in his or her behavior. What are some of the pros and cons of such behavior?

13. Recall when someone gave you a "mandate." How did you respond to it? How do you generally respond to mandates? What is it about mandates that makes you respond this way?

Interact Grammar

1. Retype the following, punctuating correctly:
When I was a child in the 1940s I was taught that boys were to be aggressive and girls who supposedly were weaker than boys were to be passive.

2. Retype the following, correcting the punctuation:
I did not understand the reasons for making distinctions between boys and girls but I accepted them for I felt I had no alternative.

3. Retype the following, punctuating correctly:
Very early I learned all the things boys were supposed to do go fishing make slingshots play baseball talk tough and be strong.

4. Rewrite the following, correcting the error:
When I was a child I read many books, that emphasized gender differences.

5. Retype the following, punctuating correctly:
I always felt nervous about doing anything that might make people call me a sissy, as a result I often pretended to be more masculine than I really felt.

6. Retype the following, punctuating correctly:

Young children should not be forced to obey strict rules for gender differences they should not be expected to follow the gender stereotypes adults hold they should be free to ignore so-called male and female differences.

7. Rewrite the following, correcting the error:

To blindly follow the dictates of gender differences means to never know your true personality.

8. Rewrite, punctuating correctly:

My father was disappointed when I did not want to play football in high school he was counting on me to carry on the tradition he started.

9. Retype the following, using correct punctuation:

I often felt lonely as a child for I was not sure about my own gender identity and I had no one to talk to about my confusion.

10. Retype the following, punctuating correctly:

Boys are taught to be tough, because many think it is sissy not to be tough.

11. Rewrite the following, correcting the error:

Because of my anxiety about being thought a "sissy," I began acting in ways, which made me appear tough.

12. Rewrite the following, punctuating correctly:

To quote the nursery rhyme, it is easier for girls to be like boys snakes and snails and puppy dog tails than it is for boys to be like girls sugar and spice and everything nice.

13. Retype the following, punctuating correctly:

When I finally passed through this state of gender doubt and had affirmed my so-called masculinity I sometimes wondered if I had given up some important part of my personality.

Interact Idea

1. Brainstorm for some of the rules for gender identification in your parents' generation that no longer apply today.

2. Brainstorm for an essay in which you argue that boys are more often forgiven for not doing what is expected of them than girls because people say "boys will be boys." Why don't people say "girls will be girls"?

3. Brainstorm for an essay in which you argue either for or against the proposition that girls and boys have no real freedom to choose their gender roles.

4. Brainstorm for an essay in which you discuss some of the implications of young girls acting like boys or young boys acting like girls.

5. Brainstorm for an essay in which you discuss basic differences between the way women felt about themselves before and after the women's movement.

6. Are little girls today more apt to play feminine roles than grown women? Or are little girls more apt to be unaware of feminine roles? Brainstorm for an essay on this topic.

7. Brainstorm for an essay in which you argue that feminine women are either most concerned about being attractive to men or most concerned about caring about their appearance.

8. Brainstorm for an essay in which you argue that the advantages of femininity are outweighed by the disadvantages, or else argue that the disadvantages are compensated for by the advantages.

9. Some people have argued that men and women are so different that they seem to have come from different planets. Brainstorm some of the most radical differences between men and women.

10. Brainstorm for an essay in which you argue either that men try harder to please women than women try to please men, or vice versa.

11. Brainstorm for an essay in which you explain why women are no longer limited by biology. Were there times in the past in which they were limited by biology, or was that also a myth?

12. Brainstorm for an essay in which you argue that men are not losing their sexual interest in women. What kind of evidence do you need to "prove" this statement?

13. Brainstorm for an essay on the topic of femininity's being governed by a code of "niceness."

Interact Rhetoric

1. Brainstorm some more everyday objects that are identified with males and females because of their shape or use. What assumptions about males and females are these identifications based on?

2. Rewrite the following sentence, making it informal:
"Being good at what was expected of me was one of my earliest projects, for not only was I rewarded, as most children are, for doing things right, but excellence gave pride and stability to my childhood existence."

3. Why does Brownmiller use such language as "pored" instead of "read," "decipher" instead of "understand," and "exasperation" instead of "bother"?

4. Discuss the effectiveness of the metaphors Brownmiller uses on this page. Are they helpful in making clear the situation of women, or are they distracting?

5. Brownmiller uses a clothing metaphor to characterize the transition of women from the era gone by. Is it possible to create a similar metaphor based on the clothing of men? Why or why not?

6. What effect does Brownmiller's frequent use of balanced, parallel phrases and clauses have? What kind of tone does this create in the essay?

7. Point out those metaphors in Brownmiller's essay that seem natural and effective and those that seem strained and forced. How can you tell the difference?

8. Point out some places in Brownmiller's essay in which you think she makes statements for rhetorical effect rather than to supply necessary content.

9. Write a brief analysis of the structure of Brownmiller's argument at this point in the essay. Why does she move from a statement about the no-win situation of women to a discussion of the basic differences between masculine and feminine?

10. Brownmiller says that a large portion of male gender distinction is due to women and thus unearned. Does she also suggest that a large portion of female gender distinction is due to men and thus unearned? Or does she avoid this for rhetorical purposes?

11. Write a paragraph explaining the logic of Brownmiller's statement that such things as whimsy, unpredictability, and emotion are only thought to be feminine because they do not lead to success.

12. Discuss Brownmiller's tone in her parenthetical statement, "call it love, if you wish" and her language choice in the comment, "sensing opportunity, choose to demonstrate their interest through variety and a change in partners."

13. Does Brownmiller suggest at the conclusion of her essay that it is all right for women to be feminine? Explain briefly how she arrived at this conclusion after beginning by denouncing femininity.

Paul Theroux, "Being a Man"

Interact Context

1. Although "obsessions" can be a serious psychological disorder, many people say they are obsessed with things with which they are fascinated or which they desire strongly, such as chocolate, cats, certain kinds of music, etc. Discuss one of your obsessions.

2. Write a character sketch of a coquette, or flirt, and discuss how attitudes toward flirting may be changing. What are the dangers of flirting?

3. Describe an experience when someone belittled you or when you belittled someone. Try to explain what motivated such behavior and what effect it had.

4. What is a "latent rapist"? Brainstorm other common uses of the term "latent," such as "latent homosexual." How can anyone be "potentially" anything?

5. Describe someone you know who is a "philistine." What is the underlying cause or motivation of philistinism?

6. Discuss the trend toward "rugged outdoor activities," such as hiking, camping, rock climbing, etc., in the past decade. What has caused such a trend?

7. Describe someone you know who is "pugnacious," always quarrelsome, and ready for a fight. What motivates such behavior?

8. Describe an experience when you became "dispirited" about something for which you were formerly enthusiastic. What caused this change? How do you feel about it now?

9. If you have read any of the works of Jack Kerouac, Norman Mailer, John Irving, Eric Segal, Joyce Carol Oates, or Joan Didion, write a brief account of your knowledge of them. If you have not, explain why you have not read any of them.

10. What is your basic reaction to the subject "women's liberation"? What is the first thing that comes to your mind when you hear the term? Why?

Interact Grammar

1. Rewrite the following, correcting the error:
I am tired of having all the evils of civilization blamed on men, it is time that men defended themselves against such charges.

2. Rewrite the following, correcting the errors:
Being masculine does not mean being stupid, it means not only being strong in the face of adversity; but it also means being dependable in a crisis.

3. Rewrite, correcting the errors:
Men are often compared to animals wolves, apes, or bears to suggest that they are predatory and unthinking hardly human at all.

4. Retype the following, correcting the error:
I know that men are often taught to be tough and I realize that such an attitude leads to insensitivity but I do not think that all men should be accused of insensitivity.

5. Rewrite the following, correcting the errors:
Men, who insist on being masculine, are not necessarily stupid; I don't know how the social movement, that is known as "feminism," made so many women think this is true.

6. Rewrite the following, correcting the errors:
It is hard being a man, when so many accusations are aimed at men. However, I like being a man because I still believe that men have many good qualities.

7. Rewrite the following, correcting the error:
I only have one problem with being a man today I cannot tolerate being blamed for all the problems of the world.

8. Retype the following, correcting the errors:
Men should not be blamed for being the cause of all the evil of the world as some feminists argue nor should they be blamed for being the cause of all female unhappiness as many women seem to believe.

9. Rewrite the following, correcting the error:
When enough men grow tired of having their masculinity blamed for all of society's ills perhaps they will make a case for the good things that men have achieved.

10. Retype the following, correcting the error:
I realize that many women may disagree with my opinions about being a man, however, I am willing to stand by them.

Interact Idea

1. If being a man means being stupid and unfeeling, then does this mean that men who are sensitive and intelligent are not being manly? What are they being instead? Brainstorm for an essay on this topic.

2. Brainstorm for an essay in which you explain what it is about women that men do not understand, or in which you suggest that men's alleged failure to understand women is a myth.

3. Theroux says it is hard to imagine any concept of manliness that does not belittle women. Try imagining such a concept of manliness that does not belittle women; write a brief description of this concept.

4. Whether you agree with Theroux or not about the effect of sports, write a few paragraphs in which you try to explain why he thinks sports is responsible for creating "bad marriages, social misfits, moral degenerates, sadists, latent rapists, and just plain louts."

5. Brainstorm for an essay in which you disagree with Theroux that group activities are somehow damaging, while solitary activities are creative.

6. Brainstorm for an essay on some other professions that are not considered "manly." Explain why they are not considered manly.

7. Brainstorm some of the basic assumptions underlying the idea that the life of the mind is not compatible with being masculine.

8. Explain why fiction writing might be equated with a kind of "dispirited failure" except when it produces wealth. Why is fiction writing less manly than nonfiction writing?

9. Brainstorm for an essay in which you discuss the relationship between an author's works and the facts of that author's life.

10. Brainstorm for an essay in which you agree with Theroux's statement that women's lib has done much more for men than for women.

Interact Rhetoric

1. Write a brief comparison/contrast between masculinity and femininity using Theroux's metaphors of masculinity being like wearing an ill-fitting coat and femininity being like nakedness.

2. Briefly analyze the tone of Theroux's essay here, focusing particularly on the use of such language as "terrible ambition," "hideous and crippling lie," "destructive," "emotionally damaging and socially harmful."

3. Based on Theroux's essay up to this point, write a brief analysis of what you think his personality is like. Support your analysis with details from the first three pages of the essay.

4. If, according to Theroux, the "manly" attitude toward sports is so damaging, is there any attitude toward sports that he would approve of? Describe such an attitude and its effects.

5. Point out all those places in the essay in which Theroux suggests his political affiliation. Discuss what effect this has on his overall argument.

6. Point out all the places in the essay that suggest that Theroux's essay is his personal defense of or revenge against his own experiences as a child and a young man.

7. Discuss the popular image of the journalist presented in movies and television. Is Theroux's argument based on this fictional image of journalism or on the actual profession of journalism? If it is based on this fictional image, how does this affect his argument?

8. Discuss the relationship between the characteristics of "masculine" writers that Theroux discusses here: drinking, hunting, carrying a weapon, wearing a lumberjack shirt.

9. Point out all those places in Theroux's essay in which he exaggerates or uses irony for rhetorical effect.

10. Discuss the effectiveness of Theroux's conclusion. Explain what he means by the statement "And this is also why men often object to feminism but are afraid to explain why."

Brent Staples, "Just Walk On By"

Interact Context

1. Describe a time when you were prejudged because of the way you dressed or wore your hair. Or else, describe a time when you prejudged someone else for these reasons. Discuss the results of this prejudgment.

2. What do you know about ghettos? Have you lived in a ghetto? Do you know someone who lives in a ghetto? Have you visited a ghetto? Have you only read about ghettos or seen one on television? Compare your response with that of others in your class.

3. Describe a time when you were in a "dicey" situation. Why were you in such a risky situation? How did you handle it? What did you learn from it?

4. Do you have a hobby, a pastime that you pursue "avidly"? Is there a rock group or a movie star of whom you are an "avid" fan? Explain the nature of your enthusiasm for this hobby, pastime, or entertainment personality.

5. Discuss your attitude toward panhandlers. Do you sympathize with them, resent them, fear them? Try to explain the reasons for this attitude. How do you handle panhandlers when you see them on the street?

6. Describe a time when you felt "alienated" from your family, your friends, your classmates, your neighbors, or any other group with which you were associated. What caused this state of alienation? How did you deal with it?

7. Discuss the male romance of intimidation, the male desire for control and power. Describe a personal experience you have had with such behavior and try to explain its cause.

8. Illustrate the difference between "bravado" and "timidity" by comparing two people you know personally or publicly. What are the good points and bad points of both kinds of behavior?

9. Describe an experience that you might define as "labyrinthine" because it was so twisted and complicated. It could be a place you visited or a complex emotional experience in which you felt lost and unable to find your way out.

10. Discuss a time when you, or someone you know, felt "paranoid" about someone or something. How did you or the person you know deal with the situation?

11. Describe a time when you were "skittish" about someone and gave them a "wide berth." Why did you feel this way? How did you handle the situation?

12. Describe a situation in which you were in a strange area and felt you had to act in a certain way to protect yourself, to communicate to others, or to reassure yourself, such as walking in a certain way, whistling, etc.

Interact Grammar

1. Retype the following, punctuating correctly:
When I entered the new school for the first time I felt nervous and lonely.

2. Rewrite the following, correcting the error:
Nervously entering the classroom, all the students turned to look at me.

3. Retype the following, punctuating properly:
The large crowded classroom seemed filled with hostile frowning faces.

4. Retype the following, punctuating properly:
Only one student in the room made me feel welcome, she smiled at me and pointed to an empty seat near her.

5. Retype the following, punctuating properly:
I quickly walked over to the area, where the friendly girl was sitting, and sat down in the chair, that she had pointed out to me.

6. Retype the following, punctuating properly:
She obviously knew that I was nervous on my first day and I was grateful that she made me feel welcome.

7. Retype the following, punctuating properly:
I felt more relaxed once I had sat down, the other students turned around to face the front, the teacher resumed his lecture.

8. Retype the following, using dashes properly:
Being the new kid in school lonely, friendless, and frightened I felt set apart from everyone as if I were from another planet.

9. Combine the following two simple sentences from Staples's essay into one complex sentence:

I entered a jewelry store on the city's affluent Near North Side. The proprietor excused herself and returned with an enormous red Doberman pinscher straining at the end of a leash.

10. Rewrite the following sentence, correcting the error:

Sitting through that first long class period, the clock seemed to slow down and almost stop.

11. Retype the following, punctuating properly:

I usually deal with nervousness and fear in one of two ways I keep quiet and try to be invisible or I act brave and tough.

12. Retype the following, punctuating properly:

Although it happened long ago in the past, I will never forget the day, that I first went to my new school and felt isolated and alone.

Interact Idea

1. Brainstorm for an essay about a time when you were afraid of someone because of how the person looked, or when you felt someone was afraid of you because of your appearance. Try to explain the cause of this fear and whether it was justified or not.

2. The central issue Staples wishes to emphasize is that he has not been treated as an individual but rather as a member of a stereotyped group. Brainstorm for an essay about a time when you were characterized as a member of a group rather than as an individual.

3. Write a brief statement from the point of view of the young woman who is frightened of Staples in the first paragraph, explaining why she was afraid and justifying her behavior.

4. Refer to the essay by Robert Heilbroner in *Interacting with Essays* and brainstorm for an essay explaining why a certain amount of prejudice or stereotyping is necessary.

5. Some cities have cracked down on panhandling on the streets, putting beggars in jail. Has this been done because people need protection or because merchants fear loss of business? Argue the pros and cons of this crackdown.

6. Brainstorm for an essay about why women may be the victims of assault more often than men. Is it because such assaults are often sexual, because women are perceived as weaker, because women have been conditioned to be passive victims, or what?

7. Brainstorm for an essay about how you created an image of yourself when you were an adolescent. Discuss how you wanted others to see you and how you achieved your goal by the way you dressed, acted, talked, related to others, etc.

8. Brainstorm for an essay in which you argue that such male characteristics as being brave and valiant and seizing the "fighter's edge" are not nonsense, but rather desirable and necessary.

9. Staples tells of an incident in which he had no way of proving who he was. Describe an incident in which you had no way of proving who you were. What problems did this cause? How were the problems resolved?

10. Staples suggests a no-win situation here. Although white fear of him makes him angry, he must smother his anger so that he will not cause fear. Describe a situation when you felt you were "damned if you did and damned if you didn't." How did you resolve it?

11. Describe a time when you felt you had to be careful about how you acted and what you said—for example, being pulled over by a policeman, meeting your future in-laws, being bawled out by your boss, etc. How did you feel? How did you handle the situation?

12. Describe a time when you wanted to convince people who did not know you that you were educated, cultured, and a person of good taste. How did you handle the situation? What were the results?

Interact Rhetoric

1. Discuss the tone of Staples's opening paragraph, focusing on such language as "first victim," "came upon her," "swung onto the avenue," "Not so," "She cast back," "hands shoved into the pockets," "running in earnest."

2. Analyze the extended implied metaphor of the hunter and the hunted in the second paragraph, pointing out the language that suggests it and discussing its effectiveness.

3. Characterize the general level of the language in this essay. Is it formal, informal, casual, academic? Cite specific examples to support your judgment.

4. Compare the percentage of space Staples devotes to reasons why whites should not be afraid of him with reasons why they are afraid of him.

5. To what extent does Staples rely on metaphors in this essay? Pick out several metaphors in the essay and discuss whether overall they are effective or distracting.

6. Write an analysis of the structure of the following sentence: "Yet these truths are no solace against the kind of alienation that comes of being ever the suspect, against being set apart, a fearsome entity with whom pedestrians avoid making eye contact."

7. Discuss what Staples means by the "male romance with the power to intimidate." Is this phrase clear or vague? Does it suggest that the male need to intimidate is in error or foolishly romantic? What does the word "romance" mean in this context?

8. Write a paragraph outline of Staples's essay in which you create one sentence to summarize or describe the purpose of each paragraph in the essay. How well organized is the essay overall?

9. A central issue Staples's essay raises is whether people are justified in fearing black male strangers. If you believe from his essay that he is not to be feared, do you also believe that no black male stranger is to be feared?

10. The only external references Staples makes is to Podhoretz and Hoagland. He could have referred to statistical information or sociological background about black males charged with or found guilty of mugging. Why doesn't he cite such information?

11. What is the tone of Staples's essay? Is it angry and resentful, defeated and reconciled, ironic and sarcastic? Support your analysis with details.

12. Comment on Staples's basic approach in this essay. Is it primarily written for white people to read? Does Staples attempt to placate and reassure white people? Why is he not more angry than he is?

Judith Ortiz Cofer, "The Myth of the Latin Woman: I Just Met a Girl Named María"

Interact Context

1. Brainstorm some of the basic conventions of the type of film known as a "musical." What relationship does a musical have to the real world? What makes musicals popular?

2. Brainstorm for an essay on how minority actors and actresses have often had to play stereotyped roles in movies and television.

3. Write an essay about a time when you attended an event for which you were not properly dressed. Explore some of the reasons behind the requirement that one must be properly dressed.

4. Describe a time when you engaged in a "marathon" event. If you have never engaged in such an event, try to brainstorm some of the reasons for such events.

5. Try to define the term "vulgar" by making a list of people and events that you consider vulgar. Is "vulgar" a term that only people of high social class use, or are there some things that everyone defines as vulgar?

6. How can you tell the difference between innocent flirting and a "come-on"? Is there such a thing as "innocent" flirting? Are all "come-ons" sexist and discriminatory to women?

7. Although "provocative" simply means that which arouses interest, when it is used to describe a person, it usually means something more than that. What do we mean when we call a person "provocative"?

8. Describe an extended family with which you are familiar. What are the values of an extended family? Are extended families as common now as they once were? Explain why or why not.

9. Why is the word "obscenity"—which means something that should be kept "behind the scene"—usually associated with sexuality? Why has the presentation of "obscene" images and acts in books and film been banned in the past?

10. What is the difference between a "colleague" and a "fellow worker"? Do only professionals, such as doctors and lawyers, have colleagues? What is the difference between the relationship between professionals and the relationship between laborers?

11. Brainstorm for an essay about the kind of music that was popular during the 1950s in the U.S. What was the music like? How did it represent the youth of that time?

12. Since the origin of the word "jerk" (used to refer to an annoyingly dull or stupid person) is obscure or unknown, try inventing an explanation for the origin of this term.

13. Write an essay about a time in your life when you had to do menial work. Describe the work, explain why you had to do it, and discuss how you felt about such work. What is wrong with "menial" work anyway?

14. Write an essay about an experience you have had, or have witnessed, when you, or someone else, was mistakenly placed in the wrong social or economic category. What did this experience mean?

15. Cofer says that in "retrospect" she realizes that the experience she had was not as bad as she thought at the time. Write about an experience in which you felt one way at the time it happened and differently in "retrospect."

16. Write about a time when you committed a "faux pas." Was it serious or trivial? What effect did it have? How do you feel about it now?

17. Write about an experience in which you were given an "entrée" to some activity or place that you had not been allowed to enter previously. What did this new "power to enter" mean?

18. Should children who do not speak English be educated in their own language in the U.S., or should they be compelled to learn English? This issue of "bilingualism" is being debated in many places today. Brainstorm the pros and cons of the issue.

Interact Grammar

1. Retype the following, correcting the error:
People who come from the mountains of Appalachia are discriminated against, they are called hillbillies and thought to be ignorant.

2. Rewrite the following, correcting the errors:
In the hills of Eastern Kentucky where I spent most of my childhood I seldom met people, who thought I was ignorant just because I lived in the mountains.

3. Rewrite the following, correcting the error:

I was not aware that I would be discriminated against outside of Appalachia. Since I had lived there all my life.

4. Rewrite the following, correcting the errors:

Only once when I was a child did I come in contact with prejudice against Appalachian people. Before we went on vacation to northern Ohio I have no idea that we will be laughed at for the way we talked.

5. Retype the following, correcting the errors:

I left my home in the mountains for a northern college when I was eighteen, I did not expect the ridicule I would receive and I still do not quite understand why I was treated as if I had never worn shoes.

6. Retype the following, correcting the error:

The day that I arrived on the college campus where I would spend the next four years stay in my memory.

7. Rewrite, correcting the errors:

It is a cruel stereotype for people to believe that us Appalachians are ignorant and thus to look down on my family and I.

8. Retype the following, correcting the error:

People will no longer tolerate songs and jokes that make fun of Hispanics and African Americans, however, they will laugh their heads off at songs and jokes about ignorant rednecks.

9. Retype the following, correcting the error:

When I asked a question in the college classes I attended I heard some students laugh at my Eastern Kentucky accent.

10. Rewrite the following, correcting the error:

While finishing the question, the students who laughed at me began whispering to each other.

11. Retype the following, correcting the errors:

I decided that I would not allow anyone to make fun of or to laugh at my Appalachian background again but I was not really sure what I could do to prevent it.

12. Retype the following, correcting the errors:

When I began my first teaching job in California it was during the so-called liberated sixties I continued to confront prejudice against people from the Appalachian mountains.

13. Rewrite, correcting the faulty parallelism:

The basic characteristics of people from Appalachia are the way they talk, having a strong sense of independence, and to be hard working.

14. Rewrite the following, correcting the error:

Although I have not lived in Eastern Kentucky for thirty years I still have some of the accent I developed as a child.

15. Rewrite the following, correcting the error:

Remembering the solid values of my Appalachian background, the bigots who think all people from the hills are ignorant no longer bother me.

16. Rewrite the following, correcting the error:
I am from Eastern Kentucky and I am proud of it and I would never do anything to try to deny that cultural origin.

17. Rewrite the following, correcting the faulty parallelism:
I recently read that a city in Ohio made discrimination against Appalachian people illegal, for many of them come there to find work, looking for a place to live, and better living conditions.

18. Retype the following, correcting the error:
Since the term comes from working hard in the fields and getting sunburned on the back of the neck, I think people from Appalachia should be proud to be called "rednecks."

Interact Idea

1. Describe an experience in which you were angry but had to pretend that you were not. Why did you have to pretend? How do you feel about the experience now?

2. Describe a time when you had to make a special effort to "belong" to a group.

3. Brainstorm for an essay in which you discuss why sexual virtue is more important for females than for males in some cultures.

4. Brainstorm for an essay in which you describe an experience in which you misunderstood what was expected of you and were consequently embarrassed. How did this misunderstanding happen? How did it make you feel? How did you handle it?

5. Brainstorm for an essay in which you describe an experience that you thought to be vulgar. If this has never happened to you, describe an experience in which you witnessed something you defined as vulgar. Explain the basis of the "vulgarity."

6. Describe a time when you were involved in "mixed cultural signals." What caused this error? How did you handle it? How was the problem resolved?

7. Brainstorm for an essay in which you discuss why women are often accused of dressing provocatively, while men are seldom accused of dressing provocatively.

8. Brainstorm for an essay on why it has often been thought that women need to be protected from sexuality, while men do not need such protection.

9. Brainstorm for an essay in which you explain why achieving maturity is often associated with sexuality. Is this a myth, or is there some basis for this association?

10. Have you ever been "put in your place" by someone, or have you ever put someone else in his or her place? Describe the situation, explaining why it happened and what the results were.

11. Brainstorm the names of some songs with which you are familiar that have stereotyped various cultural groups. Discuss how these have contributed to stereotypes about these groups.

12. Brainstorm for an essay on some of the basic assumptions that underlie distinctions between uneducated laborers and educated professionals, especially concerning the attitudes of these groups toward minorities.

13. Brainstorm for an essay in which you point out the most predominant stereotypes of African Americans, Native Americans, Hispanics, and Asians in Hollywood movies.

14. Brainstorm for an essay in which you explain how images of cultural and ethnic minorities in the media affect economic opportunities for members of those minorities.

15. Brainstorm for an essay in which you argue that people are more willing to forgive someone of their own sex for an insult than a member of the opposite sex. Or argue that people are more apt to forgive members of the opposite sex.

16. Brainstorm for an essay in which you explain how your education will make life different for you than for someone who has no education.

17. Brainstorm for an essay in which you explain why women who are thought to be sexually exciting or excitable are also often thought to be whores.

18. Brainstorm for an essay in which you agree or disagree with some feminists' arguments that God should be considered female.

Interact Rhetoric

1. Based on this opening anecdote, describe Cofer's personality. On what do you base this judgment?

2. Create a metaphor in which you compare your own place of origin with something that reflects its basic nature.

3. Discuss Cofer's purpose in introducing information about how she was taught to dress and act in her native Puerto Rico.

4. Brainstorm for an essay in which you list television shows that focus on cultural minorities. What cultures are most represented? What ones are least represented? How do you account for differences between cultures represented?

5. What effect does this anecdote about the Career Day error have on the reader? How does it make you feel about Cofer?

6. Based on her essay, write a description of what you think Cofer looks like. Discuss whether your description is a result of what she says or how you stereotype her.

7. Discuss why Cofer does not extend her discussion to argue that women should be allowed to dress any way they please—regardless of which culture they come from—and be free from sexual harassment.

8. Brainstorm for an essay on various kinds of tributes or gifts traditionally given to women and not to men, e.g., flowers, songs, poems, candy, etc.

9. Discuss those aspects of Cofer's argument that focus on Latinas being thought of metaphorically. How do these metaphors affect the way Latinas are perceived?

10. Discuss to what extent Cofer's argument depends on the fact that she is an educated professional.

11. Describe an experience in which you felt that your culture, race, or religion was insulted. What was the nature of the insult? How did you react to it?

12. Point out those places in the essay in which Cofer seems to suggest that people with an education are somehow better than people without an education. Is this a justifiable prejudice or not?

13. Write a brief analysis of Cofer's essay in which you make a case of which stereotype—the sexual or the menial—she is most concerned about. Explain why you think she is more concerned about one than the other.

14. Has your initial image or opinion of Cofer changed at this point in the essay? Explain.

15. Write a brief analysis in which you argue that Cofer is, or is not, sympathetic to feminism. Point out her statements that support your argument.

16. What aspects of Cofer's essay suggest that she is a poet?

17. Write a brief analysis about how important the personal element is in Cofer's essay. Is it more or less important than her description of general cultural stereotypes?

18. Write a brief analysis in which you point out the strongest and the weakest of Cofer's arguments.

Stephen King, "Why We Crave Horror Movies"

Interact Context

1. Brainstorm for a personal essay on a fear or phobia that you have. Try to explain the reasons for the fear and argue that it is a common one that many people have. Be sure to distinguish between a normal fear and an abnormal fear.

2. Explain why King says that horror movies are basically conservative. What are some of the conservative elements of horror movies you have seen?

3. Brainstorm for an essay on the similarities or differences between fairy tales and horror films. Use one or more specific fairy tales and films as your examples.

4. A number of movies have been made in the 1990s that feature mass murderers; some critics have suggested that these mass murderers have been made heroic or appealing. Brainstorm about some of these films and comment on the image they create of the murderer.

5. Are you a person who values maintaining the status quo? Or do you usually prefer change? Brainstorm for an essay about some things you wish to remain the same and some things you wish to change. Focus on personal things or social things.

6. Brainstorm for an essay defining "sick jokes," explaining why they are popular, with whom they are popular, and what function they serve.

7. Brainstorm for an essay in which you explain why you like a particular horror movie. Try to account for its appeal to basic human emotions.

Interact Grammar

1. Retype the following, punctuating correctly:
I have never liked horror movies, they frighten me; especially when they are violent.

2. Retype the following, punctuating correctly:
The old-fashioned horror movies left a lot to the imagination, the newer ones are more explicitly violent.

3. Rewrite the following, correcting the errors:
I don't think that horror movies make my friends and I do anything that we have been taught not to do.

4. Retype the following, punctuating correctly:
If you go to horror movies often you will become insensitive to violence some people say, others say that horror movies are a healthy release from violent feelings.

5. Retype the following, punctuating properly:
When I was a little kid I watched one horror movie that frightened me terribly, I had nightmares for weeks afterwards.

6. Retype the following, punctuating properly:
The old horror movies that I saw as a child were based on a very simple assumption let the audience imagine the violence.

7. Retype the following, punctuating properly:
I like horror movies science fiction movies adventure movies and thrillers to name just a few.

Interact Idea

1. Brainstorm for an essay about common, everyday behavior that some people might call "crazy" or "insane" but that would not be cause for someone to be treated or institutionalized.

2. Brainstorm for an essay on other cultural phenomena that seem more for the young than the old, such as rock concerts, computer games, etc. Why are such things of less interest to adults than to youth?

3. Argue against King's point about the beneficial effect of horror movies. How are horror movies harmful? See the essay by Michael Ventura on slasher movies elsewhere in *Interacting with Essays*.

4. Do you agree or disagree with King that there is a potential lyncher in all of us? Brainstorm this idea, suggesting examples to support your position; explain why this may or may not be true.

5. Do horror movies encourage such behavior as slamming someone's fingers in the door? Do violent movies create or encourage violent behavior? How can you prove this or convince someone else of this connection?

6. Read Lewis Thomas's essay "The Tucson Zoo" and compare his argument that humans are basically altruistic with King's argument that people are basically anticivilized.

7. Although the issue is too complex to argue without consulting other sources, brainstorm for an essay in which you present your own feelings about whether explicit sex and violence in movies cause antisocial behavior or provide a safe and healthy release.

Interact Rhetoric

1. Write an argument about why people are willing to pay money to scare themselves, such as riding roller coasters, watching horror movies, or bungee jumping.

2. Brainstorm for an essay in which you compare fears based on fiction or fantasy, such as horror movies, with fears based on physical reality, such as roller coasters.

3. Brainstorm for an argument about why human beings need pro football in place of combat and horror movies in place of lynching. In what ways do football and horror films substitute for these acts?

4. Write a brief analysis of the kind of image of himself that Stephen King creates in this essay. What language or rhetorical tactics in the essay communicate this image?

5. What is the basic tone of King's essay? What kind of audience do you think it is directed to? Is he being serious about the purpose of horror movies, or is he just kidding? How do you know?

6. How convincing is King's basic argument about the nature of human behavior and the purpose of horror movies? Point out weaknesses in his evidence and his logic.

7. Discuss the effectiveness of King's concluding metaphor of horror movies being like lifting a trapdoor in the brain and throwing raw meat to the alligators swimming around in underground rivers.

Michael Ventura, "On Kids and Slasher Movies"

Interact Context

1. Discuss briefly a slasher movie you have seen. If you have never seen one, explain why. Why do you think these movies are popular?

2. During the 1950s many Americans were so afraid of the Bomb that they built bomb shelters in which to hide in case of a nuclear war. What attitude do you think the present generation has toward the Bomb? What are the causes of this attitude?

3. The issue of "expression versus repression" is an important one in Ventura's essay. Brainstorm for an essay in which you argue for one or the other based on your own experience.

4. Ventura uses the metaphor "molting" to suggest a complete change that takes place regularly in U.S. society. Brainstorm some complete social changes that have taken place during your own life.

5. Describe a time when you had to "acclimate" yourself to a new experience. Was the process difficult? How did you achieve it? What have been the results?

6. Rewrite Ventura's conclusion, making his vague, metaphoric suggestions more specific and detailed.

Interact Grammar

1. Rewrite the following, correcting the sentence errors:
Horror movies once were not so violent. Creating fear by suggestion. Not by showing blood and gore.

2. Rewrite the following, correcting the error:
Trusting the audience to imagine the horrors that took place out of camera range, theaters in the 1940s featured films that were more subtle than they are today.

3. Retype the following, punctuating correctly:
If horror movies today were as mild as they were in the 1940s would people pay to see them?

4. Retype the following, correcting the punctuation:
Sitting tensely keeping my hands over my eyes and holding my breath I waited for the movie monster to pounce however in the old movies I never saw the monster rip someone's head off.

5. Rewrite the following, correcting the errors:
The old movies never showed graphic violence. Because they were more controlled by censorship codes than movies are now.

6. Retype the following, punctuating correctly:
I think I prefer the older horror movies to the new ones for their subtlety for their suggestiveness and for their respect for my own imagination.

Interact Idea

1. Brainstorm for an essay on some kind of play that you engaged in as a child that conditioned you in some way and made you what you are today. Or else explain why you think that childhood play had no effect on your present personality.

2. What do you know about the Holocaust—the killing of six million Jews by the Nazis during World War II? From what sources did you receive this information? What kind of personal reaction do you make to this information?

3. Ventura seems to be arguing that if there were laws against slasher movies and slasher masks, it would make no difference. Do you agree or disagree? Explain your position.

4. Ventura says that the reason that no one feels safe in the 20th century is that society has been stripped of order and tradition. What kind of order is he talking about here—so-called "law and order"? What kinds of traditions is he referring to? Brainstorm a response.

5. Brainstorm some other examples of how play prepares children for the world.

6. Brainstorm for an essay in which you make clear what the basic conflict is in the fact that a young boy buys a slasher mask. If the boy does not face a struggle, then what is the conflict for his parents or for society in general?

Interact Rhetoric

1. Discuss whether you think Ventura is justified in drawing such extreme conclusions from one single example.

2. Discuss what argumentative methods Ventura uses in this essay. Are they primarily specific examples, comparison/contrast, logic? Do they primarily depend on shock or reason? Support your analysis with details.

3. Write a brief paragraph outline of Ventura's essay in which you make clear the structure of his argument.

4. Point out those sections of Ventura's argument in which he makes broad, unsupported generalizations for rhetorical effect.

5. Analyze Ventura's "inoculation" metaphor in this essay. Does the metaphor suggest that in order to tolerate the violence in our world, we need to be hardened to it by seeing it enacted in pretense? Does this justify violence in movies and television?

6. What is the basic purpose or point of Ventura's essay? What did he hope to accomplish by writing it?

Robert MacNeil, "The Trouble with Television"

Interact Context

1. Define the word "average" by describing someone who is ordinary.

2. Describe something that "diverts" and "gratifies" you. Explain why you enjoy this "diversion" and how it gratifies you.

3. Write a brief analysis of a specific segment of television programming, e.g., daytime programming, late-night programming, prime-time programming, supporting MacNeil's assertion that it appeals to a short attention span.

4. Describe an object or a characteristic that has been "bequeathed" or handed down to you by a previous generation. How does it reflect the previous generation? What is its value?

5. Describe an "anachronism" with which you are familiar. For example, the 1995 movie *The Brady Bunch* presents a family that is an anachronism because they still live in the 1960s.

6. Brainstorm how different communication and the reception of information would be without television.

7. Describe some beliefs or behaviors accepted by a large number of people about which you are "skeptical." Explain why you have doubts about these beliefs or behaviors.

Interact Grammar

1. Rewrite the following, using the correct tense:
If I unplug my television now, in five years I will save enough time to get my bachelor's degree.

2. Rewrite the following, correcting the errors:
If I suggest pulling the plug on the television, my children say its not fair that I blame it's influence for their values and behavior.

3. Rewrite the following, correcting faulty parallelism:
The best way to protect your children from the harmful effects of television is to limit their viewing time, controlling what they watch, and a good example.

4. Retype the following, using correct punctuation:
In my opinion, there is so much junk on television that it is quite rightly called the "boob tube".

5. Retype the following, punctuating correctly:
My children watch television for all the wrong reasons to avoid doing their work to avoid thinking about anything to turn off the world around them.

6. Rewrite the following, punctuating correctly:
Basically, television is a device, which encourages people not to think; it is not like a book, which usually requires some thoughtful interaction.

7. Rewrite the following, correcting the error in subject-verb agreement:
Violence shown on many television programs nowadays give me reason enough to restrict my children's viewing.

Interact Idea

1. Brainstorm a list of kinds of programs you can watch on television that are educational and valuable. Try to convince MacNeil that not all time spent watching television is wasted.

2. Brainstorm for an essay about those interesting and rewarding activities in life that do not require constructive, consistently applied effort.

3. Brainstorm for an essay in which you suggest several other activities besides television that appeal to a short attention span.

4. Brainstorm for an essay in which you argue that there is no way for television to present news in depth the way newspapers and magazines can, or else in which you suggest some ways that television can present news in depth.

5. Brainstorm for an essay in which you argue that education is the basic criterion for being "civilized," or else in which you argue that there are other criteria equally as valuable.

6. Brainstorm for an essay in which you argue that the 30-minute situation comedy on television provides "neat resolutions to human problems that usually have no neat resolutions." Choose one such sitcom as your example.

7. Brainstorm for an essay in which you protest against all the claims in this essay that have been made about the dangers of television.

Interact Rhetoric

1. Discuss the basic assumptions underlying MacNeil's comparing the time the average person watches television with the time it takes to get a college degree, read Dostoevsky, and learn a language.

2. Point out places in MacNeil's essay where he uses exaggeration or unsupported generalizations to make a point.

3. Why does MacNeil not mention specific programming on television, such as soap operas, situation comedies, MTV, etc.? Why does he focus only on the issue of attention span? Discuss his rhetorical reason for this decision.

4. Write a brief statement in which you indicate what MacNeil would do to make television better, more acceptable.

5. Write a brief analysis of MacNeil's essay in which you argue that his argument is based on elitist assumptions.

6. Discuss the relationship between selling "neat solutions to human problems" and the 30-second commercial suggested by MacNeil. Does MacNeil suggest that television exists primarily for the sake of programming or for the sake of commercials?

7. How serious does MacNeil think the dangers of television are? How would he compare these dangers to those resulting from poverty, prejudice, and violence?

Marie Winn, "Television Addiction"

Interact Context

1. Using a "wry" tone, write a one-paragraph description of a harmless addiction of your own, such as chocolate, science-fiction novels, a hobby, etc.

2. Describe an experience that gives you a "high." How would you describe the feeling of euphoria, intoxication, or elevation the experience gives you? Is this high addictive? Is it dangerous? Explain.

3. Describe an experience when you felt "under a spell" or bewitched. What caused this feeling? How did you deal with it?

4. Brainstorm for an essay in which you define the word "trip," pointing out how the meaning of the word has changed and describing the various uses of the term.

5. Brainstorm for an essay in which you distinguish between different kinds of activities that leave one "sapped" or "enervated." Are all such activities harmful, or are some of them beneficial?

6. Brainstorm for an essay about an activity for which you feel "rueful." Argue that you are justified in this feeling or that you are wrong to feel this way.

7. The word "syndrome" has been used to refer to many other groups of symptoms besides medical disorders. Brainstorm for an essay on as many other uses of this term as you can think of.

8. Brainstorm for a definition of the word "catharsis" in which you describe various means of achieving such a cleansing.

9. One commentator has suggested that diet aids and exercise equipment are often advertised in printed television guides since people who watch television a great deal tend to be overweight. Brainstorm for an essay on this connection.

10. Describe a period when you felt "mummified," or frozen in inactivity. What caused this experience? How did you escape it?

11. Brainstorm for an essay in which you distinguish between desirable discrimination and undesirable discrimination.

12. Now that cable and satellite television has made many channels available, is Winn's claim that television watching is addictive more or less serious?

Interact Grammar

1. Retype the following, correcting the error:
Television has a powerful influence on the way we view reality for it is the chief source of our information of the world and it is more immediate and dramatic than newspapers and books.

2. Retype the following, correcting the error:
Television is a phenomenon, that touches every aspect of our daily lives.

3. Retype the following, correcting the error:
It is increasingly hard for people to imagine life without television, it has been in our homes for so long it is like a member of the family.

4. Retype the following, correcting the error:
When television was in its infancy during the 1950s it was a novelty that fascinated millions of people.

5. Rewrite the following, correcting the error:

Current opinion on television, reflecting the thoughts of many educated people, suggest that the medium encourages easy solutions to difficult problems.

6. Rewrite the following, correcting the error:
The fact that people spend so many hours watching television programs mean that they are not spending those hours doing anything productive.

7. Rewrite the following, correcting the error:
Television does not exist primarily to entertain viewers, its main purpose is to sell products.

8. Retype the following, correcting the error:
Many people don't like to admit they watch television so they often say that they only watch educational television.

9. Retype the following, supplying the appropriate punctuation:
The most famous example of television's deceiving viewers It has been dramatized in a 1990s movie is the quiz show scandal of the 1950s.

10. Retype the following, correcting the error:
The television quiz show, that created such a scandal in the 1950s, gave the correct answers to the contestants.

11. Retype the following, correcting the error:
Most viewers felt they had been cheated by the fact that the contestants were given the answers on the quiz show, however, the producers of the show claimed it was all done for entertainment.

12. Retype the following, correcting the punctuation:
The television quiz show scandal ended what many commentators called television's "age of innocence".

Interact Idea

1. Brainstorm for an essay on the difference between an "addiction" and a "habit." For example, some people say that a smoker is addicted to nicotine, while lighting up a cigarette at certain times is a habit.

2. Brainstorm for an essay on Winn's suggestion that addicts do not feel "normal" when they do not satisfy their addiction. What does "normal" mean in this context?

3. Brainstorm other experiences besides addictions that can make one's life seem "distorted."

4. Brainstorm for an essay on other activities which people deceive themselves about.

5. Do we engage in many activities that make us feel we "ought" to do something else? Does this mean they are harmful? Should people engage only in those things they feel they "ought" to do?

6. If television often presents activities that are unreal, how can it make other experiences seem unreal, "while taking on a greater reality for itself"? Brainstorm for an essay on how television succeeds in doing this.

7. Brainstorm for an essay in which you distinguish between being satisfied with something and simply having had enough of it.

8. Brainstorm for an essay in which you argue that there are some programs on television that do provide nourishment and satisfaction.

9. Describe your own pattern of television watching. Defend it by explaining its purpose and value.

10. Brainstorm a list of activities you would engage in if you had no television in your home. If you have no television, brainstorm a list of activities that such an absence makes possible.

11. Brainstorm for an essay in which you explain why the process of watching television seems more important to many people than what they are watching.

12. Brainstorm for an essay in which you make suggestions about how television programmers can be forced to put more meaningful shows on television. Or is there something about television or our society that makes that unlikely?

Interact Rhetoric

1. If Winn's central focus is on television as a serious addiction, why does she begin with a brief introduction about innocent addictions? Discuss this rhetorical tactic.

2. Some people say they cannot "function" without their morning cup of coffee or the morning newspaper. What is the difference between such everyday rituals and addictions?

3. Point out those places in Winn's argument where she exaggerates for rhetorical effect.

4. Brainstorm some specific examples for Winn's argument that people can ignore the real world by watching television.

5. Brainstorm for an essay on the topic of "Television Viewers Anonymous" in which you compare self-confessed television addicts with alcoholics in Alcoholics Anonymous.

6. If television is as harmful as Winn says that it is, why is it not regulated by the government? Hasn't the government tried to regulate things "bad for us" in the past, such as gambling, drinking alcohol, smoking?

7. Discuss Winn's tactic of quoting heavy television viewers in her essay. How do we know if these are representative viewers? How could someone arguing against Winn's point combat these quotations?

8. Discuss why Winn does not use any statistics or information about television's effect on children in her essay.

9. Discuss the representativeness of the people that Winn quotes in her essay. How typical are they in terms of television watching? How representative are they of different social and economic levels?

10. Brainstorm some other suggestions (besides getting rid of the television) that Winn might have suggested to people addicted to television.

11. Write a brief outline of Winn's essay, making clear the development of her argument.

12. Write a one-paragraph conclusion to Winn's essay.

William F. Buckley, "Why Don't We Complain?"

Interact Context

1. Brainstorm for an essay on the problems of commuting to and from work on mass transit. Discuss the advantages and disadvantages of this kind of travel to and from work.

2. Describe an experience when you had to walk through something that was like a gauntlet. For example, walking down the aisle at a wedding, walking up an aisle to make a speech, walking between two lines of players at a sports event.

3. Buckley accuses American people of being too sleepy (stupor) or too lazy (supine) to complain. Brainstorm for an essay in which you argue that people are not as energetic as they once were.

4. The word "harass," which means to torment or pester someone, has taken on a serious legal meaning in the last few years. Brainstorm a definition of "harassment" in this legal sense.

5. Describe an experience when you participated in, or witnessed, an event when a group of people expressed their disapproval of a speaker, a show, or an action. Discuss the pros and cons of such behavior.

6. Write a paragraph in which you describe a time when you were "anxious" about something. Then write another paragraph in which you describe a time when you were "eager."

7. What is the difference between being angry and being ready to fight?

8. The Christian New Testament states that the meek shall inherit the earth. Argue either for or against this statement.

9. Write a character sketch of someone that you know who sulks or who is ostentatious.

10. Is it possible that people can communicate with others mentally? Consider people who have known each other for a long time. What about people who finish other people's sentences?

11. Write a brief description of a time when you were "mortified." Indicate by your tone whether this was a serious or a trivial humiliation.

12. Buckley describes a minor experience when he is at the mercy of those who are paid to serve him. Describe an experience when you have been at the mercy of others and explain what the experience meant.

13. Define the term "unctuously" by writing a character sketch of someone who acts in this way or by writing a description of an action that would exemplify this kind of behavior.

14. College students are often accused of being indifferent to campus politics, seldom voting in campus elections or participating in campus policy-making. Write a cause-effect essay explaining why.

15. Write a political statement of your own beliefs about how much government should be involved in the lives of the people. Use examples to clarify your position.

16. The Communist party of the Soviet Union was once the obvious villain in Hollywood espionage movies. What group has become the new villain now that the Communist party no longer dominates Russia?

Interact Grammar

1. Retype the following, punctuating properly:
Many people are lazy and rude now so I have started to fight back by complaining.

2. Retype the following, using a colon appropriately:
My mother taught me the meaning of rudeness unrefined and uncouth behavior.

3. Retype the following, correcting the punctuation error:
I was raised to be polite to my elders, however, it seems that children today have no respect for anyone.

4. Retype the following, correcting the pronoun error:
It makes you wonder whom is responsible for the rudeness of children today: the parents or the children themselves.

5. Retype the following, punctuating properly:
I think that children should be taught old-fashioned virtues they should respect their elders they should mostly be seen and not heard they should be grateful for all their parents do for them.

6. Combine the following sentences into one balanced sentence:
Children think they are smarter than adults. Children think they do not have to listen to adults. Children are spoiled. They are used to getting their own way.

7. Combine the following into one balanced sentence:
I go into a store. I expect good service. I expect a cheerful reception. I am spending my money. The clerks should try to please me. Their job depends on it.

8. Rewrite the following, correcting the misplaced modifier:
Being a good consumer who spends a lot of money, store clerks should give me their very best service.

9. Rewrite the following, correcting the subject-verb agreement error:
When I shop in a store with high prices that cater to a small group of customers, I expect the very best service.

10. Rewrite the following, punctuating properly:

Many high fashion stores which used to be in the center of town are now to be found in malls in the suburbs.

11. Rewrite the following, punctuating properly:
I like to shop in malls because they offer a wide variety and they are convenient but compared to shopping in small stores downtown they are so impersonal.

12. Rewrite the following, correcting the errors in punctuation:
I miss shopping in small-town stores, with a friendly atmosphere, and people that knew your name, and asked about your family.

13. Rewrite the following, correcting the error in pronoun case:
When my mother took me shopping when I was a child, the shopkeepers knew her and always welcomed her and I.

14. Rewrite the following, correcting the punctuation error:
However, those days of small-town shopping are over for me, now I must fight crowds and deal with surly clerks in big department stores.

15. Rewrite the following, correcting the subject-verb agreement error:
I can't help believing that an important part of American values have been lost with the loss of small-town shops.

16. Rewrite the following, punctuating properly:
When I drag myself out of the house to go shopping now I brace myself for the traffic jams and try to convince myself that I have to make the trip, shopping is not a pleasure anymore but rather something that has to be done.

Interact Idea

1. Brainstorm for an essay in which you argue that "virility" is synonymous with "barbarism." If this is true, what is synonymous with "civilization"?

2. Describe a time when you "made a scene" in public about something. Or else describe why you wanted to make a scene but did not. Explain why you acted as you did.

3. Brainstorm for an essay in which you argue that we are often dependent on incompetent people for our daily needs. Suggest some reasons for this.

4. Brainstorm for an essay about the pros and cons of making a scene in public. Is making a scene ever justified?

5. Describe an event when you waited for someone else to protest something or when you took things into your own hands and initiated a protest when no one else would. Explain why you acted the way you did.

6. Brainstorm for an essay about a cause which you think is worth standing up for. Explain why it is not unjust, ambiguous, or trivial.

7. Brainstorm for an essay on the pros and cons of anger. Is it good to get angry and lose your temper or bad, or both good and bad?

8. Brainstorm for an essay in which you argue that many times when people say they are fighting for a just cause they are really acting out of personal reasons.

9. Define "cowardliness." Why is cowardliness considered such a negative quality? Why is it associated with being "unmanly"?

10. Some people think that clerks and salespeople nowadays are mostly incompetent and rude. Argue for or against this idea by citing examples. How can you "prove" this is true or false?

11. Describe an experience when you became the center of unwanted attention because of something you said or did.

12. Whatever happened to the rule "The customer is always right"? Does it still hold true, or has it disappeared in American society? Support your answer and discuss the cause of this rule or its disappearance.

13. Suggest other reasons for people's failure to complain besides the one that Buckley suggests.

14. Buckley suggests that our failure to complain is related to our increasing dependence on technology. How would you respond to this argument? What would Buckley have us do—return to the horse and buggy, use candles instead of electricity?

15. Brainstorm for an essay on "complaining as a natural instinct." This will require that you define "instinct." Brutality may be a natural instinct also, but does that make it desirable? Do we have to suppress some natural instincts?

16. Buckley seems to suggest that Americans have a right to hate Khrushchev and to express that hatred. Are there some people or actions that we have a responsibility to complain about? Brainstorm this as a possible paper topic.

Interact Rhetoric

1. Discuss the effect of the word "flecked" to describe the white shirts in the car. Why does Buckley say that he "found his hand moving" rather than simply saying that he loosened his tie?

2. Rewrite the following in less "fancy" language:
"Instantly the doleful eyes of my seatmate turned tiredly from his newspaper to fix me with a resentful stare: What question could be so important as to justify my sibilant intrusion into his stupor?"

3. What is the general effect of a writer's using such formal language as Buckley does? Does it suggest intelligence or showing off?

4. Brainstorm two more examples from your own experience to support Buckley's point about people not complaining anymore. Explain how they support his point.

5. Discuss the tone of voice Buckley uses in this essay. In what ways is the tone more characteristic of writing than of talking?

6. Suggest some other explanation for the actions of the people in the train and the movie theater besides the one that Buckley presents. Show how your explanation is better than Buckley's.

7. What effect does Buckley's description of his own anger have at this point in the essay? What kind of image of the man do we get from this description?

8. Write a definition of sarcasm in which you provide examples of sarcastic language. Is sarcasm a form of mental cruelty? Or is sarcasm an effective way to deal with people or things you do not like?

9. Write a brief analysis of Buckley's tone in the middle paragraph on this page. Describe what kind of impression we get of Buckley from his language and style.

10. Rewrite the following in your own words:
"He was impervious to my telepathic reproof and continued his small talk with his friend, brazenly insensitive to the nervous demands of six good men who were raring to ski."

11. Buckley's description of the helicopter is obviously an exaggeration. Discuss the rhetorical effectiveness of exaggeration. Give examples from everyday speech of such rhetorical exaggeration.

12. At this point in the essay, you are probably aware that Buckley never uses an ordinary word when he can come up with a fancy one. Discuss the effect of this use of fancy language.

13. Discuss how much of Buckley's argument is based on exaggeration or over-dramatization of the events he describes.

14. Discuss either the similarity or the difference between the complexity of government and the complexity of technology. What do people mean when they refer to government as a giant machine?

15. Write two versions of a letter of complaint to some group, company, or agency that has done something to make you angry recently. Make one of them polite and one of them sarcastic.

16. Brainstorm the pros and cons of public protest. What are the virtues of such behavior? What are the dangers?

Victoria A. Sackett, "Discriminating Tastes"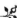

Interact Context

1. Why does Sackett use "insider trading" as one of her examples of kinds of plagues that society suffers?

2. What is the difference between being "irked" and being angry? What is the difference between being "surly" and being rude?

3. Some say that if you commit a crime in your thoughts it is the same as doing it. Others might say that it is the act, not the thought, that constitutes a crime. Brainstorm this issue.

4. A number of movies have been made about crime during the Prohibition period in Chicago in the 1920s. What makes this period so fascinating to modern audiences?

5. Discuss some of the effects of the recent emphasis on the dangers of cholesterol and a high-fat diet. How has it changed product marketing and eating habits?

6. Brainstorm for an essay on how natural products have been replaced by fake products in modern society.

7. Brainstorm some of the results of the controversy about second-hand smoke, e.g., no-smoking sections of restaurants, smoke-free buildings, new city ordinances on smoking.

8. Is it a contradiction that in a democracy people are expected to let politicians know what they think, but that when they do they are ridiculed because they don't know about the complicated world of politics?

9. Write a comparison/contrast essay on the difference between "assertiveness" and "belligerence."

10. Although the body needs fat to survive, many foods now are advertised as "low fat" or "light." Discuss this trend toward "lightness" in foods and how it is manipulated by advertisers.

Interact Grammar

1. Retype the following, correcting the punctuation error:
Many people feel they must protect themselves against second-hand smoke, that is endangering their health.

2. Retype the following, supplying the correct punctuation:
I dislike strong perfume because I am allergic to it smoke for it makes my eyes water automobile exhaust which is polluting our air and the noise of the city which makes life stressful.

3. Retype the following, uses dashes appropriately:
I realize that my objections to modern pollution most of which make me sound like a petty complainer are not taken seriously by everyone.

4. Rewrite the following, correcting the subject-verb agreement error:
Many people feel that a complaint about the effects of pollution are not very effective anymore.

5. Retype the following, using colons and commas appropriately:
The following foods contain excess fat or cholesterol that may be harmful whole milk cheese eggs and all meats.

6. Retype the following, correcting the punctuation errors:
People, who complain about smoke and perfume, are not very popular, but they feel they must make a statement about what offends or harms them.

7. Retype the following, punctuating properly:

I cannot tolerate people, who smoke too much eat animal flesh and drive big gas-guzzling cars.

8. Retype the following, correcting the misplaced modifier error:

Driving back to the city after a day in the mountains, the traffic congestion is nerve-wracking.

9. Retype the following, punctuating properly:

When I first come to the freeway at the bottom of the mountain road I am almost afraid to enter into all that traffic.

10. Retype the following, punctuating properly:

I reluctantly drove home on the freeway that monstrous six-lane strip of asphalt that I have learned to hate.

Interact Idea

1. What is the difference between a major prejudice and a minor one that underlies Sackett's argument? Are all prejudices damaging or are there some that are desirable?

2. An old saying goes: "Patience is a virtue; possess it if you can—always in a woman, never in a man." Are men more impatient than women? Brainstorm for a humorous essay on this topic.

3. Discuss the fourth stage of the disease—the one Sackett does not mention—drivers who shoot at people who cut them off, looters who are fed up with being cheated, vandals who are angry at authority.

4. Using Sackett's metaphor of disease, if reducing the symptoms does not work, how can one either inoculate oneself against the disease or cure oneself completely?

5. Do you agree that Americans have become more tolerant of ethnic and racial differences in recent years? If so, what has caused this? If you do not agree, explain why you disagree.

6. Are children more rude than they used to be? Do they show less respect for their elders? Are they more spoiled? Brainstorm for an essay on this topic.

7. Analyze Sackett's argument that the issue of second-hand smoke would not have come up if smoking didn't smell bad. Is this an effective argument? Discuss why or why not.

8. Write an essay in which you try to mediate between William Buckley's suggestion that we don't complain enough and Sackett's suggestion that we complain too much.

9. Brainstorm for an essay on why people marry later today than they once did.

10. Brainstorm for an essay in which you argue either for or against Sackett's implication that we can never completely rid ourselves of intolerance.

Interact Rhetoric

1. Point out the flaws in Sackett's comparison between the prejudice of personal preference and a plague or a disease. Where does the metaphor break down?

2. What does the subject of Sackett's essay have to do with the tone she uses? Does the subject demand this tone, or is it her attitude toward the subject that creates the tone?

3. The second-person point of view is often used in a process essay, in which you explain how to do something. Use the second person to describe how to use the software program you are using right now.

4. How is the disease metaphor related to the "life-threatening" example Sackett describes here? Is it the disease that is life-threatening or the people toward whom one directs the disease, that is, the intolerance and impatience?

5. Is it an insult to African Americans to compare their suffering from prejudice to such petty prejudices as Sackett describes? Brainstorm for an essay on this topic.

6. Discuss those places in the essay in which Sackett's tone seems sarcastic. Is sarcasm an effective rhetorical device in this essay? Explain why or why not.

7. Discuss Sackett's use of loaded words in this essay, words that suggest that those "infected" with intolerance are not justified in their complaints.

8. Point out examples of exaggeration in Sackett's essay. What is the purpose of these exaggerations as a rhetorical device? How well do they work in Sackett's essay?

9. Write an essay in which you describe someone who is "assertive." Discuss the pros and cons of such assertiveness.

10. Write an analysis of Sackett's argument. Does it depend on evidence, reason, or rhetoric? Support your analysis by citing details from the essay.